# WILLS, TRUSTS, AND ESTATES

### Peter Wendel

**Professor of Law, Pepperdine University**

W9-CNU-683

## The *Emanuel Law Outlines* Series

**PUBLISHERS**

1185 Avenue of the Americas, New York, NY 10036
www.aspenpublishers.com

© 2004 Aspen Publishers, Inc.
A Wolters Kluwer Company
*www.aspenpublishers.com*

Permissions
Aspen Publishers
1185 Avenue of the Americas
New York, NY 10036

Printed in the United States of America

1 2 3 4 5 6 7 8 9 0

ISBN 0-7355-4545-6

This book is intended as a general review of a legal subject. It is not intended as a source of advice for the solution of legal matters or problems. For advice on legal matters, the reader should consult an attorney.

To my students,
from whom I've learned so much


and


To my children, Carolyn, Paul, John, and Kristin, the
joys of my life

# Summary of Contents

# Table of Contents

CHAPTER 1

# INTRODUCTION TO WILLS, TRUSTS, AND ESTATES

CHAPTER 2

# INTESTACY: THE DEFAULT DISTRIBUTION SCHEME

CHAPTER 3

# LIMITATIONS ON THE TESTAMENTARY POWER TO TRANSFER

CHAPTER 4

# TESTAMENTARY CAPACITY

CHAPTER 5

# WILLS EXECUTION, REVOCATION, AND SCOPE

CHAPTER 6

# CONSTRUING WILLS

CHAPTER 7

# NONPROBATE TRANSFERS: WILL SUBSTITUTES

CHAPTER 8

# TRUSTS: CREATION, LIFE, AND TERMINATION

CHAPTER 9

# CHARITABLE TRUSTS

CHAPTER 10

# POWERS OF APPOINTMENT: DISCRETIONARY FLEXIBILITY

CHAPTER 11

# CONSTRUING TRUSTS: FUTURE INTERESTS AND CLASS GIFTS

CHAPTER 12

# THE RULE AGAINST PERPETUITIES

CHAPTER 13

# TRUST ADMINISTRATION AND THE TRUSTEE'S DUTIES

CHAPTER 14

# ESTATE AND GIFT TAXES

# Preface

Thank you for buying this book—and my children who are attending college thank you as well!

Wills, Trusts, and Estates is an intrinsically interesting class because it is all about who gets your property when you die. As law students, many of you will have a hard time associating with that issue because (1) mentally you still think that you are going to live forever, and (2) at this stage in your life, your debts probably exceed your assets so the issue in the course is moot as applied to you. To help bring the course and subject matter alive, envision your larger family situation and apply the issues in the course to different family members as appropriate. Sooner or later someone close to you will lose a loved one and you will want to be able to help that person through a very difficult time in his or her life. Even if you do not practice in this area, being able to explain the basics of a will, trust, or the probate process to the person will help the person, at least from a property perspective, through this critical period.

If you have lost a loved one recently, or if a family member is seriously ill, some of the issues in this course may be painful for you. If you are in that situation, I would advise you to let your professor know in advance so that both of you can avoid a potentially difficult classroom situation.

As you move through the material, you will see that most of the rules, viewed and analyzed individually, are fairly straightforward and easy to understand. The degree of difficulty in the course is the overwhelming volume of rules. To keep all the rules clear, I strongly recommend that you keep the macro approach to the course in mind. Even if your professor does not cover the first chapter of the book, you should read at least the Capsule Summary for Chapter 1. The flowchart in the Capsule Summary for Chapter 1 sets out the roadmap for the whole course.

The best way to use this book depends on the student and the professor. Ideally, each of you should read the casebook, analyze the material, go to class and take good notes, and then create your own outline. As you create your own outline, if you find that you are having difficulty in wording certain rules or in understanding certain doctrines, you can refer to the appropriate sections of this outline (see the **Casebook Correlation Chart**) for well-written rule statements and rule explanations and elaborations. If, however, you find yourself struggling with the material (either because of the nature of the material or because of the way that your professor is presenting the material), I would recommend that you read the appropriate sections of the outline before you read the casebook and go to class. That should give you a better understanding of what it is you are supposed to be extracting from the casebook and class discussions. In addition, some students need to see the "big picture" before they can fully understand the significance of the particular case or statute they are reading and analyzing. If you are that type of student, I recommend that you read the **Capsule Summary** of that topic before you begin reading the material in the book for that chapter. The Capsule Summary for that chapter will help to give you the big picture for the chapter so that you can absorb and understand the detailed information in the chapter as you read it the first time.

Learning psychologists emphasize that repeatedly covering material is the best way to move it from short-term memory to long-term memory. The **Quiz Yourself** section of each chapter is designed both to test your knowledge and understanding of the material, and to help transfer that knowledge from your short-term memory to your long-term memory. Because there are so many rules in this course, I strongly recommend that you answer the questions at the end of each chapter as you complete that chapter. Waiting until the end of the semester will not leave enough time for your long-term memory to properly absorb all the rules. Moreover, writing out your answers to the Quiz Yourself questions will give you some practice in exam-writing techniques. When you compose your essays, remember to write the rule before you apply it.

As the end of the semester approaches, you can review the Capsule Summary to refresh your recollection of the material and to spot those areas of the course where you are still weak. Use the outline to supplement your own outline and to fill in any gaps in your understanding. Moreover, you should read the **Exam Tips** to become sensitized to fact patterns, issues, and overlapping scenarios that commonly arise on a typical Wills, Trusts, and Estates exam.

Many people have contributed to this project. I would like to thank the multitude of students I have taught at Pepperdine, UCLA, and Loyola–Los Angeles for keeping the material fresh and challenging, and who have given me so many different insights into, and perspectives on, the material. I want to thank Barbara Roth at Aspen for her patience, support, and suggestions. I want to thank Mei Wang and Lisa Wehrle at Aspen for their editorial assistance with the Dukeminier version of the outline. I want to thank my research assistant, Alyson Leichtner, for her help. And lastly, I want to thank my good friend and colleague Robert Popovich for his invaluable assistance with Chapter 14.

I wish you the best with your Wills, Trust, and Estates course. I think you will find it interesting, challenging, and enjoyable.

*Peter Wendel*
*Professor of Law*
September 2004                                      *Pepperdine University School of Law*

# Casebook Correlation Chart

Note: general sections of the outline are omitted for this chart.

| Wills, Trusts, and Estates Emanuel Outline (by chapter heading) | Clark, Lusky, Murphy, Ascher, & McCouch, *Cases and Materials Gratuitous Transfers* (4th ed. 1999) | Dobris, Sterk, & Leslie, *Estates and Trusts* (2nd ed. 2003) | Scoles, Holbach, Link, & Roberts, *Problems and Materials on Decedents' Estates and Trusts* (6th ed. 2000) | Waggoner, Alexander, Fellows, & Gallanis, *Family Property Law* (3d ed. 2002) |
|---|---|---|---|---|
| **CHAPTER 1**<br>**INTRODUCTION TO WILLS, TRUSTS, AND ESTATES** | | | | |
| I. The Power to Transfer Property at Death | 1-10 | 8-16 | 4-10 | 7-10 |
| II. The Right to Transfer Property at Death | 17-32 | 8-16 | 10-19 | 11-13 |
| III. Course Overview | | 1 | | 16-21 |
| IV. The Probate Process: An Overview | 10-17; 614-658 | 45-46; 986-1033 | 1-4; 24-30 291-294; 749-843 | 14-15; 21-26 1300-1305 |
| V. "Dead Hand" Control | 32-43 | 1-8 | 369-382 | |
| VI. Estate Planning | 43-48 | 28 | 19-24; 294-297 | 1-7 |
| VII. Professional Responsibility | | 28-44 | 30-31; 314-335 | 743-750 |
| **CHAPTER 2**<br>**INTESTACY: THE DEFAULT DISTRIBUTION SCHEME** | | | | |
| I. The Intestate Distribution Scheme | 49-56 | 62-72 | 32-36 | 33-38 |
| II. Surviving Spouse: Who Qualifies | 58-59 | 72-80 | 39 | 80-118 |
| III. Surviving Spouse: Calculating Share | 56-58 | 72 | 36-39 | 40-46 |
| IV. Descendants/Issue: Calculating Shares | 61-67; 106-108 | 80-85; 264 | 39-42; 69-72 | 46-54 |
| V. Shares of Ancestors and Remote Collaterals | 67-73 | 85-93 | 42-46 | 56-65 |
| VI. Issue: Who Qualifies | 73-92; 108 | 93-137; 155-157 | 46-64; 73-74 | 74-76; 118-143 |
| VII. Survival Requirement | 59-61 | 137-144 | 46 | 38-39 |
| VIII. Bars to Succession | 92-106; 109-113 | 16-28; 144-155 | 64-69; 75 | 66-73; 507-515 |
| **CHAPTER 3**<br>**LIMITATIONS ON THE TESTAMENTARY POWER TO TRANSFER** | | | | |
| I. Spousal Protection Schemes: An Overview | 114-117 | 158-161 | | 581-586 |
| II. Surviving Spouse's Right to Support | 117-123 | 190-193 | 106-107 | 607-609; 639-641 |

# Casebook Correlation Chart (Cont.)

| Wills, Trusts, and Estates Emanuel Outline (by chapter heading) | Clark, Lusky, Murphy, Ascher, & McCouch, *Cases and Materials Gratuitous Transfers* (4th ed. 1999) | Dobris, Sterk, & Leslie, *Estates and Trusts* (2d ed. 2003) | Scoles, Holbach, Link, & Roberts, *Problems and Materials on Decedents' Estates and Trusts* (6th ed. 2000) | Waggoner, Alexander, Fellows, & Gallanis, *Family Property Law* (3d ed. 2002) |
|---|---|---|---|---|
| III. Surviving Spouse's Right to a Share of the Marital Property | | 158-161 | 107-109; 124-125 | |
| IV. The Elective Share Doctrine | 123-151 | 161-190 | 109-123; 573-586 | 592-607; 609-636 |
| V. Community Property | 151-159 | 195-196 | 108-109 | 586-589 |
| VI. The Omitted/Pretermitted Spouse | 171-172 | 193-194 | 130-133 | 648-649 |
| VII. The Omitted/Pretermitted Child | 159-71 | 196-208 | 125-130 | 641-648 |
| VIII. Limitations on Charitable Gifts | 172-174 | | 133-134 | |
| **CHAPTER 4** **TESTAMENTARY CAPACITY** | | | | |
| I. General Testamentary Capacity | 178-190 | 380-394; 398-402; | 76-80; 801-804 | 211-230 |
| II. Insane Delusion | 190-199 | 394-398 | 80-88 | 230-232 |
| III. Undue Influence | 199-239 | 403-428; 435-457; | 92-106; 805-814 | 238-266 |
| IV. Fraud | 239-251 | 428-435 | 88-92 | 266-270 |
| **CHAPTER 5** **WILLS EXECUTION, REVOCATION, AND SCOPE** | | | | |
| I. Executing a Valid Will | 252-258 | 209-212 | 158-163 | 165-169 |
| II. Common Law Approach to Attested Wills | 258-279 | 212-223 | 163-175 | 170-181; 185-201 |
| III. Modern Trend Approach to Attested Wills | 279-297 | 223-233 | 180-185 | 182-184 |
| IV. Holographic Wills | 301-316 | 233-241 | 176-179 | 204-211 |
| V. Scope of a Will | 317-330 | 242-264 | 186-198 | 275-284 |
| VI. Revocation | 330-337; 344-361 | 337-359 | 224-244 | 295-347 |
| VII. Contracts Concerning Wills | 337-344 | 359-375 | 245-263 | 651-675 |
| **CHAPTER 6** **CONSTRUING WILLS** | | | | |
| I. Admissibility of Extrinsic Evidence: General Rule | 371-382 | 302-336 | 198-223 | 677-709; 718-741 |
| II. Scrivener's Error | | 336 | | 709-717 349-374 |
| III. Changes in Testator's Property | 383-393 | 264-285 | 436-453 | 497-500 374-387 |
| IV. Changes in the Beneficiary | 393-401 | 286-302 | 453-454; 457-472 | 485-497 |

# Casebook Correlation Chart (Cont.)

| Wills, Trusts, and Estates Emanuel Outline (by chapter heading) | Clark, Lusky, Murphy, Ascher, & McCouch, *Cases and Materials Gratuitous Transfers* (4th ed. 1999) | Dobris, Sterk, & Leslie, *Estates and Trusts* (2d ed. 2003) | Scoles, Holbach, Link, & Roberts, *Problems and Materials on Decedents' Estates and Trusts* (6th ed. 2000) | Waggoner, Alexander, Fellows, & Gallanis, *Family Property Law* (3d ed. 2002) |
|---|---|---|---|---|
| **CHAPTER 7**<br>**NONPROBATE TRANSFERS: WILL SUBSTITUTES** | | | | |
| I. Inter Vivos Gifts | 402-435 | 46-51 | 284-285 | |
| II. Overview of Nonprobate Transfers | | 58-61 | 264-266 | 17-21 |
| III. Contracts with Payable-on-Death Clauses | 435-437 | 509-511; 968-985 | 266-270; 278-283 | 452-454; 460-469 |
| IV. Multiple Party Bank Accounts | 439; 488-493 | 52-58; 504-511 | 270-275; 562-566 | 454-458 |
| V. Joint Tenancies | 437-439 | 51-52 | 276-277 | |
| VI. Revocable Deeds | 440-444 | | 287-291 | 458-460 |
| VII. Inter Vivos Trusts | 444-453 | 503-504; 511-549 | 553-562; 566-572 | 446-452 |
| VIII. Pour-over Wills and Inter Vivos Trusts | 361-371 | 519-532 | 593-601 | 469-485; 500-503 |
| IX. Planning for the Possibility of Incapacity | 297-301 | 594-596; 902-967 | 141-157 | 542-560 |
| **CHAPTER 8**<br>**TRUSTS: CREATION, LIFE, AND TERMINATION** | | | | |
| I. Introduction: Conceptual Overview | 454-467; 563-573 | 473-475 | 336-352 | 751-766 |
| II. Requirements to Create a Valid Trust | 467-488; 493-498 573-577; 612-613 | 475-503 | 352-369; 525-553 | 767-825 |
| III. Life of Trust: Extent of Beneficiaries' Interests | 518-522; 658-665 | 549-565 | 605-618 | 845-856 |
| IV. Life of Trust: Creditors' Rights/Spendthrift Clauses | 498-518; 523-537 | 565-609 | 590-593; 618-625 634-663 | 534-542; 827-845 856-883 |
| V. Trust Modification and Termination | 537-563 | 628-653; 1087-1092 | 664-708; 779-785 | 883-913 |
| **CHAPTER 9**<br>**CHARITABLE TRUSTS** | | | | |
| I. Charitable Purpose | 573-586 | 653-663 | 710-730 | 915-940 |
| II. Cy Pres | 586-611 | 663-685 | 731-740 | 940-973 |
| III. Enforcing the Terms of a Charitable Trust | | | 740-745 | 973-977 |

# Casebook Correlation Chart (Cont.)

| Wills, Trusts, and Estates Emanuel Outline (by chapter heading) | Clark, Lusky, Murphy, Ascher, & McCouch, *Cases and Materials Gratuitous Transfers* (4th ed. 1999) | Dobris, Sterk, & Leslie, *Estates and Trusts* (2d ed. 2003) | Scoles, Holbach, Link, & Roberts, *Problems and Materials on Decedents' Estates and Trusts* (6th ed. 2000) | Waggoner, Alexander, Fellows, & Gallanis, *Family Property Law* (3d ed. 2002) |
|---|---|---|---|---|
| **CHAPTER 10**<br>**POWERS OF APPOINTMENT: DISCRETIONARY FLEXIBILITY** | | | | |
| I. Introduction | 811-813; 838-840 | 686-690; 717-721 | 423-426; 431-434 | 981-984 |
| II. Creating a Power of Appointment | 823-824 | | | 986-988 |
| III. Releasing a Power of Appointment | 828-830 | 708-717 | 427-431 | 1022-1024 |
| IV. Exercising a Power of Appointment | 824-828 | 690-706 | 505-514 | 999-1010 |
| V. Attempted Appointment that Fails | 831-837 | 706-708 | 426-427; 521-524 | 1011-1020 |
| VI. Failure to Exercise a Power of Appointment | 837-838; 840-841 | 699-700 | 514-521 | 1020-1022 |
| **CHAPTER 11**<br>**CONSTRUING TRUSTS: FUTURE INTERESTS AND CLASS GIFTS** | | | | |
| I. Future Interests | 737-746 | 744-757 | 383-397 | 1026-1048 |
| II. Preference for Vested Remainders | | 757-780 | 403-408; 473-477 481-495 | 1053-1061 1065-1152 |
| III. Class Gifts | 780-785 | 781-818 | 454-457; 477-481 495-500 | 1253-1262 |
| **CHAPTER 12**<br>**THE RULE AGAINST PERPETUITIES** | | | | |
| I. Introduction | 746-752; 772-780 | 819-839 | 408-423; 1072-1084 | 1171-1206 |
| II. Classic Rule against Perpetuities Scenarios | 753-772 | 839-851 | 1099-1100 | 1206-1218 |
| III. Class Gifts and the Rule against Perpetuities | 785-797 | 851-862 | 1101-1108 | |
| IV. Power of Appointment and the Rule against Perpetuities | 813-823 | 862-877 | 1108-1119 | 1262-1274 |
| V. The Rule against Perpetuities Saving Clause | 797-802 | 877-884 | | 1218-1227 |
| VI. Reforming the Rule against Perpetuities | 803-811 | 884-902 | 1119-1140 | 1227-1253 |

# Casebook Correlation Chart (Cont.)

| Wills, Trusts, and Estates Emanuel Outline (by chapter heading) | Clark, Lusky, Murphy, Ascher, & McCouch, *Cases and Materials Gratuitous Transfers* (4th ed. 1999) | Dobris, Sterk, & Leslie, *Estates and Trusts* (2d ed. 2003) | Scoles, Holbach, Link, & Roberts, *Problems and Materials on Decedents' Estates and Trusts* (6th ed. 2000) | Waggoner, Alexander, Fellows, & Gallanis, *Family Property Law* (3d ed. 2002) |
|---|---|---|---|---|
| **CHAPTER 13**<br>**TRUST ADMINISTRATION AND THE TRUSTEE'S DUTIES**<br>    I. Trustee's Fiduciary Duties | 665-684; 707-722 735-736 | 1033-1080; 1102-1106 | 845-901; 929-935 1033-1041 | 1308-1334 1355-1360 |
|    II. Trustee's Powers | | 1080-1086 | 921-929 | |
|    III. Trust Investments | 684-707; 722-735 | 1092-1102 | 935-1055 | 1334-1355 |
|    IV. Trustee's Liability to Third Parties | | | 909-913 | 1364-1366 |
| **CHAPTER 14**<br>**ESTATE AND GIFT TAXES**<br>    I. Overview | 842-848 | 458-460 | 297-314 | 391-397 |
|    II. The Federal Gift Tax Scheme | 849-866 | 464-468; 609-615 721-743 | | 397-407 |
|    III. The Federal Estate Tax: An Overview | 894-897 | 460-464 | | 408 |
|    IV. Calculating the Decedent's Gross Estate | 866-894 | | | 408-417 |
|    V. The Marital Deduction | 897-908 | 468-472; 615-626 | | 417-422 |
|    VI. The Generation-Skipping Transfer Tax | 908-914 | 626-628 | | 422-427 |
|    VII. State Death Taxes | | | | |

# Capsule Summary

This Capsule Summary can be used to provide an overview of the material in the course and/or for review at the end of the course. Reading the Capsule Summary, however, is not a substitute for mastering the material in the main outline. Numbers in brackets refer to the pages in the main outline where the topic is discussed.

## CHAPTER 1
## INTRODUCTION TO WILLS, TRUSTS, AND ESTATES

### I. THE POWER TO TRANSFER PROPERTY AT DEATH

**A. Introduction:** The macro issue raised by the course is "who gets your property when you die?" To the extent the answer is "whomever you intend," that answer assumes that a decedent has the power to transfer property at death. Whether a decedent should have such power raises a number of theoretical and public policy issues. [1, 4]

**B. Public policy debate:** Some argue the power to transfer wealth at death is natural and good in that it encourages one to save and promotes family values, while others argue the power to transfer wealth at death perpetuates economic disparity and unfairly rewards those lucky enough to have been born to rich parents. [2-3]

### II. THE RIGHT TO TRANSFER PROPERTY AT DEATH

**A. Power to transfer:** A decedent has the right to dispose of his or her property at death. Although the states have broad authority to regulate the process, the states cannot completely abrogate the right. [3-4]

### III. COURSE OVERVIEW

**A. Overview:** Who takes a decedent's property depends first on whether the property is nonprobate or probate property. Nonprobate property is limited to (1) property held in joint tenancy, (2) life insurance contracts (modern trend expands this exception to include all contracts with a payable-on-death clause), (3) legal life estates and remainders, and (4) inter vivos trusts. Nonprobate property passes pursuant to the terms of the nonprobate instrument. Probate property passes pursuant to the terms of the decedent's will, otherwise through intestacy. [4-6]

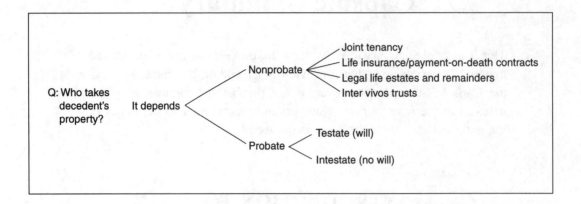

## IV.  THE PROBATE PROCESS: AN OVERVIEW

**A. Probate is the default:**  The decedent must take affirmative steps (execute a valid will or create a valid nonprobate instrument) to avoid having the property pass through probate. [6]

**B. Probate administration:**  The probate court appoints a personal representative. He or she has the job of collecting the decedent's probate assets, paying off creditors' claims, and distributing the property to those who are entitled to receive the property. [6-9]

**C. Notice to creditors:**  Most states have "nonclaim statutes" that impose a shortened statute of limitations on claims against a decedent's estate. Historically, nonclaim statutes required only constructive notice by publication to creditors to bring their claims or be forever barred. Recently, however, the Supreme Court ruled that where a creditor is known or reasonably ascertainable, the Due Process Clause requires actual notice. [9-11]

**D. Costs and delays of probate:**  Probating a typical estate is a costly process that can take any-where from one to two years for even simple estates and ties up the decedent's probate assets during the process. [12-13]

## V.  "DEAD HAND" CONTROL

**A. "Dead hand" control:**  A decedent may condition a beneficiary's gift on the beneficiary behaving in a certain manner as long as (1) the condition does not violate public policy, or (2) judicial enforcement would not constitute state action violating a constitutionally protected fundamental right. [13]

**B. Validity:**  Dead hand control is generally upheld unless the condition constitutes a complete restraint on marriage, requires a beneficiary to practice a certain religion, encourages divorce or family strife, or directs the destruction of property. [13-15]

## VI.  ESTATE PLANNING: AN INTRODUCTION

**A. Key objectives:**  In advising a party about his or her estate plan, the key objectives that an estate planning attorney should keep in mind are (1) the party's intent, (2) avoiding estate taxes, and (3) avoiding probate. [15]

# VII. PROFESSIONAL RESPONSIBILITY

**A. Common law:** Under the common law approach, the attorney owes no duty of care to, and is not in privity of contract with, intended beneficiaries. Accordingly, intended beneficiaries have no standing to sue for malpractice. [15-16]

**B. Modern trend:** Under the modern trend, an attorney owes a duty of care to intended beneficiaries, and intended beneficiaries are third-party beneficiaries with respect to the contract between the attorney and testator. Intended beneficiaries have standing to sue for malpractice. [16-17]

CHAPTER 2

# INTESTACY: THE DEFAULT DISTRIBUTION SCHEME

# I. THE INTESTATE DISTRIBUTION SCHEME

**A. Introduction:** The default distribution scheme is intestacy. If a decedent fails to dispose of all of his or her property through nonprobate instruments or a valid will, the decedent's property will pass pursuant to the state's descent and distribution statute to the decedent's heirs. [22-23]

**B. A typical intestate distribution scheme:** Although the details vary from state to state, the basic order of who takes is fairly similar: (1) surviving spouse; (2) issue; (3) parents; (4) issue of parents; (5) grandparents/issue of grandparents; (6) next of kin; (7) escheats to the state. How much each takes is where the differences typically arise state to state. [23-25]

# II. SURVIVING SPOUSE: WHO QUALIFIES

**A. Marriage requirement:** The term *spouse* assumes that the couple has gone through a valid marriage ceremony (most states include "putative spouses"—where the couple goes through what at least one spouse believes is a valid marriage ceremony, but the marriage is either void or voidable). Cohabitants do not qualify unless the jurisdiction recognizes common law marriage and the couple meets the requirements for common law marriage. Once married, even if a couple legally separates, for inheritance purposes they continue qualify as spouses until a court enters its final order of dissolution. [25-26]

# III. SURVIVING SPOUSE: CALCULATING SHARES

**A. Typical state statute:** Under a typical state descent and distribution statute, the surviving spouse takes 100 percent of the decedent's intestate property if the decedent has no surviving issue, parents, or issue of parents; 50 percent if the decedent has one child (alive or dead but survived by issue) or no surviving issue but surviving parent(s) or issue of parents; and 33 percent if the decedent has more than one child (alive or dead but survived by issue). [26-27]

**B. Uniform Probate Code (UPC):** Under the UPC, the surviving spouse takes 100 percent of the decedent's intestate property if no issue or parents—or 100 percent if all of the decedent's issue are also issue of the surviving spouse and the latter has no other issue; $200,000 plus 75 percent of the rest if the decedent has no surviving issue but surviving parent(s); $150,000 plus 50 percent of the rest if all of the decedent's surviving issue are also issue of the surviving spouse but the latter has other issue; or $100,000 plus 50 percent of the rest if one or more of the decedent's surviving issue are not issue of the surviving spouse. [27-28]

# IV. DESCENDANTS/ISSUE: CALCULATING SHARES

A. **Calculating shares:** The term *descendant/issue* includes not only one's children, but also all of one's blood descendants. The jurisdictions are split over what it means to divide the decedent's property equally among the decedent's issue when the issue are not equally related to the decedent. Depending on the jurisdiction, the property is divided per stirpes, per capita, or per capita at each generation (if the decedent dies testate or with nonprobate property, the written instrument can expressly provide for which approach applies). [28-31]

B. **Per stirpes:** Under the per stirpes approach, the first division of decedent's property always occurs at the first generation of issue (whether anyone is alive at that generation or not); the property is divided into one share for each party who is alive at that generation and one share for each party who is dead at that generation but who is survived by issue; and the shares for those who are dead but survived by issue drop by bloodline to their respective issue. [31-32]

C. **Per capita with representation/modern per stirpes:** Under the per capita approach, the first division of decedent's property always occurs at the first generation of issue in which there is a live taker; the property is divided into one share for each party who is alive at that generation and one share for each party who is dead at that generation but who is survived by issue; and the shares for those who are dead but survived by issue drop by bloodline to their respective issue. [32-33]

D. **Per capita at each generation:** Under the per capita at each generation approach, the first division of decedent's property always occurs at the first generation of issue in which there is a live taker; the property is divided into one share for each party who is alive at that generation and one share for each party who is dead at that generation but who is survived by issue; and the shares for those who are dead but survived by issue drop by the pooling approach (the shares are added together and then distributed equally among the issue of the deceased parties at the prior generation). [33-35]

# V. SHARES OF ANCESTORS AND REMOTE COLLATERALS

A. **Collateral relatives:** The decedent, the decedent's spouse, and the decedent's issue are the decedent's immediate family. All the decedent's other relatives are called his or her *collateral relatives*. If the decedent has no spouse or issue, how the decedent's property is distributed to his or her collateral heirs varies by jurisdiction. There are three possible approaches: the parentelic approach, the degree of relationship approach, and the degree of relationship with a parentelic tiebreaker approach. [35-38]

# VI. ISSUE: WHO QUALIFIES

A. **Qualifying as an issue:** Establishing a parent-child relationship means each can inherit from and through the other. Such a relationship can be established naturally, whether the parents are married or not; by adoption, which severs the relationship with the natural parents as a general rule; or through equitable adoption. [38-45]

1. **Parents married:** Where the natural parents are married, the general rule is that both parties (the natural parents and the child) can inherit from and through each other.

2. **Adoption:** Adoption establishes a parent-child relationship between the adopted child and the adoptive parents. As a general rule, adoption severs the relationship between the adopted child and his or her natural parent of the same gender as the adopting parent. In many jurisdictions, however, if the adoption is by a stepparent, following the adoption the child can still inherit from and through the natural parent of the same gender as the adopting stepparent, but the natural parent cannot inherit from or through the child.

3. **Equitable adoption:** Equitable adoption arises where (1) the natural parents and adoptive parents agree on the adoption, (2) the natural parents perform by giving up custody of the child, (3) the child performs by moving in with the adoptive parents, (4) the adoptive parents partially perform by taking the child in but failing to complete the adoption, and (5) the adoptive parent dies intestate. The child is entitled to a claim against the adoptive parent's estate equal to his or her intestate share.

4. **Child born out of wedlock:** Where the parents are unmarried, the general rule is the child can inherit from and through the natural parents (assuming paternity can be established), but for the natural parents or relatives of the natural parents to inherit from or through the child, the natural parents or relatives must acknowledge and support the child (the UPC requires this even where the parents are married).

B. **Advancements:** At common law, inter vivos gifts to a child were irrebuttably presumed to count against the child's share of the decedent's intestate estate. Under the modern trend, inter vivos gifts do not count against an heir's share of the decedent's intestate estate unless there is a writing by the donor contemporaneous with the inter vivos gift expressing such an intent or a writing by the donee acknowledging such an intent. [45-48]

**Hotchpot:** Where there is an advancement, the amount of the advancement is added back into the decedent's intestate estate, and then each heir's share of the hotchpot is determined. In distributing the decedent's intestate property, an heir who received an advancement has the value of the advancement credited against his or her share (of the hotchpot amount). [45-47]

# VII. SURVIVAL REQUIREMENT

A. **Survival requirement:** At common law, to qualify as an heir one had to prove by a preponderance of the evidence that he or she survived the decedent by a millisecond. Under the modern trend, some jurisdictions require the heir to prove by clear and convincing evidence that he or she survived the decedent by a millisecond, while other jurisdictions require the taker to prove by clear and convincing evidence that he or she survived the decedent by 120 hours (5 days). [48-51]

**Scope:** The survival requirement applies to all parties who claim a right to take some of the decedent's property—whether the property is nonprobate, probate testate, or intestate property. In some jurisdictions, the survival requirement is the same for all three types of property, while in other jurisdictions the survival requirement varies depending on the type of property. [48]

## VIII. BARS TO SUCCESSION

**A. Introduction:** Even where an individual is otherwise entitled to take from a decedent (be it nonprobate or probate property, testate or intestate property), the taker will be barred from taking under the homicide doctrine or if he or she disclaims. [52]

**B. Homicide doctrine:** If the taker killed the decedent, and the killing was felonious and intentional, the killer is treated as if he or she predeceased the decedent for purposes of distributing the decedent's property. The doctrine applies to all types of property—nonprobate, probate testate, and intestate property (where the property is joint tenancy, by operation of law it is converted into tenancy in common). This is a civil issue subject to the preponderance of the evidence burden of proof. The jurisdictions are split as to whether the issue of the killer should be barred from taking the share that would otherwise go to the killer. [52-54]

**C. Disclaimer:** If a party properly executes a disclaimer, declining to accept a testamentary gift the taker otherwise would have received, treat the party who disclaimed as if he or she predeceased the decedent for purposes of distributing the decedent's property. [54-56]

CHAPTER 3

# LIMITATIONS ON THE TESTAMENTARY POWER TO TRANSFER

## I. SPOUSAL PROTECTION SCHEMES: AN OVERVIEW

**A. Introduction:** Every jurisdiction has several doctrines that protect surviving spouses (and, to some degree, children/issue) that have the effect of limiting one's power to transfer one's property at death. A surviving spouse has a right (1) to support, and (2) to a share of the couple's marital property. [65-67]

## II. SURVIVING SPOUSE'S RIGHT TO SUPPORT

**A. Spousal support:** In virtually every state, a surviving spouse has a right for support (typically for life) under (1) the social security system; (2) private pension plans pursuant to ERISA (Employee Retirement Income Security Act of 1974); (3) the homestead exemption; (4) the personal property set-aside; and (5) the family allowance. [67-68]

## III. SURVIVING SPOUSE'S RIGHT TO A SHARE OF THE MARITAL PROPERTY

**A. Separate property vs. community property:** The scope of a surviving spouse's right to a *share* of the deceased spouse's property depends on whether the jurisdiction follows the separate property approach (in which case the right is called the elective or forced share) or the community property approach (in which case the right is part of the community property doctrine). [68-69]

# IV. THE ELECTIVE SHARE DOCTRINE

**A. The elective (or forced) share:** Under the separate property system, although each spouse owns his or her earnings acquired during marriage as his or her separate property, upon death the elective share doctrine provides that the surviving spouse is entitled to a share of the deceased spouse's property regardless of the terms of the deceased spouse's will. How much property the surviving spouse is entitled to (typically one-third of the estate subject to the elective share), and what property is subject to the elective share, varies from jurisdiction to jurisdiction. [69-70]

**B. Traditional approach:** At common law and in a number of states, the elective share entitles the surviving spouse to a share of the deceased spouse's probate estate, regardless of the terms of the deceased spouse's will. A spouse can avoid the elective share, however, by putting his or her assets into nonprobate arrangements. [70]

**C. Modern trend:** The modern trend is to expand the reach of the elective share to limit the deceased spouse's ability to avoid the doctrine by using nonprobate arrangements. The jurisdictions are split, however, over how best to identify when the elective share doctrine should be expanded to cover nonprobate transfers. [70-74]

    **1. Illusory transfer test:** Under the illusory transfer approach, the courts analyze whether the nonprobate arrangement really constituted an inter vivos transfer or whether the decedent retained such an interest (life estate, right to revoke, right to appoint) in the property that the transfer is more testamentary than inter vivos (and thus the property in question is subject to the elective share).

    **2. Present donative intent test:** Under the present donative intent test, the courts focus on whether the deceased spouse had a real and present donative intent at the time he or she created the nonprobate transfer. The courts focus on the circumstances surrounding the transfer, especially how much of an interest the party gave away.

    **3. Intent to defraud test:** Under the intent to defraud test, the issue is whether the decedent intended to defraud the surviving spouse of his or her elective share rights in the property. The jurisdictions that follow the intent to defraud approach are split over which approach should be taken—a subjective approach (did the decedent actually intend to defraud the surviving spouse of his or her elective share rights in the property in question) or an objective approach (focusing on a variety of factors).

    **4. 1969 UPC "augmented estate" approach:** The surviving spouse is entitled to receive one-third of the deceased spouse's augmented estate. The augmented estate includes not only the decedent's probate estate, but also certain nonprobate and gratuitous inter vivos transfers made during the marriage: (1) any transfers in which the deceased spouse retained the right to possession or income from the property; (2) any transfers in which the deceased spouse retained the power to revoke or the power to use or appoint (dispose of) the principal for his or her own benefit; (3) any joint tenancies with anyone other than the surviving spouse; (4) gifts to third parties within two years of the deceased spouse's death in excess of $3,000 per donee per year; and (5) property given to the surviving spouse either inter vivos or via nonprobate transfers (including life estate interests in trusts). Life insurance proceeds to someone other than the surviving spouse are expressly excluded.

5. **1990 UPC marital property approach:** The surviving spouse starts out entitled to only 3 percent of the deceased spouse's augmented estate and the percentage increases 2 to 3 percentage points a year, reaching 50 percent after 15 years of marriage. The augmented estate includes both spouses' property, including property the deceased spouse transferred before marriage if he or she retained substantial control over the property, and life insurance proceeds paid to parties other than the surviving spouse.

D. **Funding with a life estate:** Where a surviving spouse claims an elective share, the general rule is that the property given to the surviving spouse under the will counts first against the elective share (so as to minimize the disruptive effect the elective share has on the deceased spouse's estate plan). Where, however, the deceased spouse left the surviving spouse only a life estate interest (which arguably constitutes only "support" for life and not an outright "share"), most states will not count the life estate interest against the elective share. [74]

E. **Exercising the elective share:** The elective share is a personal right that only the surviving spouse can claim—not his or her estate, heirs, or creditors. If the surviving spouse is incompetent, the spouse's guardian can, in the "best interests" of the spouse and with the probate court's approval, claim the elective share for the spouse. [74-75]

F. **Waiver:** Although spouses can waive the elective share inter vivos, the waiver must be in writing, signed, and executed after a fair disclosure of the other party's financial situation. A waiver is not enforceable if it was not made voluntarily, or if it was unconscionable when executed. [75-76]

# V. COMMUNITY PROPERTY

A. **Basics:** Under the community property system, property acquired before marriage, and property acquired by gift, descent, or devise during the marriage, is each spouse's separate property. Property otherwise acquired by either spouse during the course of the marriage (typically earnings) is community property. Each spouse has an undivided one-half interest in each community property asset. Upon the death of a spouse, the surviving spouse owns his or her one-half of each community property asset outright, and the deceased spouse's half of each community property asset goes into his or her probate estate, from which he or she can devise it to anyone. [76-78]

B. **Migrating couples:** Migrating couples pose special problems because (1) property is characterized as separate property or community property at the time it is acquired according to the laws of the jurisdiction where the parties are domiciled at the time of acquisition, (2) changing domicile does not change the characterization of property, and (3) the applicable time of death spousal protection approach depends on the couple's domicile at time of death. [78-79]

1. **Migrating from separate to community property:** Where a couple migrates from a separate property state to a community property state, the risk is that the surviving spouse will be underprotected. The spousal protection doctrine at time of death will be the community property approach, but if the couple spent most of their marriage in the separate property jurisdiction the risk is that the couple's assets will be primarily, if not exclusively, separate property. Quasi-community property attempts to deal with this

problem by providing that upon the spouse's death, his or her separate property that would have been characterized as community property if the couple had been domiciled in a community property jurisdiction when the property was acquired is characterized as quasi-community property and is treated like community property for distribution purposes—but not all of the community property jurisdictions recognize quasi-community property.

2. **Migrating from community to separate property:** Where a couple migrates from a community property state to a separate property state, the risk is that the surviving spouse will be overprotected. The spousal protection doctrine at time of death will be the elective share approach. The risk is that the surviving spouse will "double dip" in the spousal protection schemes. Upon the death of the first spouse, the surviving spouse will get his or her half of the community property outright, and the deceased spouse's half will go into probate, from which the surviving spouse can claim an elective share in the deceased spouse's probate property. The Uniform Disposition of Community Property Rights at Death Act provides that a deceased spouse's share of the community property is not subject to the elective share doctrine—but not all separate property jurisdictions have adopted it.

# VI. OMITTED/PRETERMITTED SPOUSE

A. **Omitted/pretermitted spouse doctrine:** Where an individual executes a valid will, thereafter marries, and thereafter dies without revoking or revising the will, a presumption arises that the testator did not intend to disinherit his or her new spouse. The presumption, however, is rebuttable, if (1) the will expresses the intent to disinherit *that* spouse; (2) the testator provided for that spouse outside of the will and intended for the transfer to be in lieu of the spouse taking under the will; or (3) the spouse waived his or her right to claim a share of the deceased spouse's estate. If the presumption is not rebutted, the omitted spouse generally receives his or her intestate share of the testator's probate estate. [80-81]

B. **Scope:** The courts generally hold that (1) a general disinheritance clause is not sufficient to constitute an intent to disinherit *that* spouse, and (2) a gift in a will to a party who ends up being the decedent's spouse generally does not bar the omitted spouse doctrine unless the testator made the gift in contemplation of the beneficiary being his or her spouse. [80]

C. **UPC:** The UPC broadens the evidence that can be used to prove that the spouse's omission from the will was intentional to include evidence (1) from the will, (2) other evidence that the will was made in contemplation of the testator's marriage to the surviving spouse, or (3) a general provision in the will that it is effective notwithstanding any subsequent marriage. The UPC also limits funding of the omitted spouse's share to property not devised to the decedent's issue (1) who were born before the testator married the surviving spouse, and (2) who are also not issue of the surviving spouse. [81-82]

D. **Revocable trusts:** In some states, the omitted spouse doctrine has been extended to cover both probate property and property in a revocable inter vivos trust created by the deceased spouse. [82]

# VII. OMITTED/PRETERMITTED CHILD

**A. Omitted/pretermitted child doctrine:** Where an individual executes a valid will and thereafter has a child, and thereafter dies without revoking or revising his or her will, a presumption arises that the testator did not intend to disinherit the child. The presumption, however, is rebuttable if (1) the will expresses the intent to disinherit that child; (2) the testator provided for the child outside of the will and intended for that transfer to be in lieu of the child taking under the will; or (3) the testator had one or more children when the will was executed and devised substantially all of his or her estate to the other parent of the omitted child. As a general rule, the omitted child receives his or her intestate share. [82-83]

**B. Children alive when will executed:** Some states expand the scope of the classic omitted child doctrine to include children alive when the will was executed but not named in the will. Some states even cover omitted issue of a child who died before the testator. [82]

**C. Evidence of intent to disinherit:** Under the "Missouri" type statute, the intent to disinherit the omitted child must come exclusively from the terms of the will. Under the "Massachusetts" type statute, extrinsic evidence is admissible to help determine if the disinheritance was intentional. [83]

**D. Accidentally overlooked child:** Some states provide that if a testator fails to provide for a child in a will because the testator mistakenly believes that the child is dead, the child receives the share he or she would under the omitted child doctrine. Some states also cover a child not provided for in a will because the testator did not know about the child. [83]

**E. UPC:** The UPC omitted statute applies only to children born or adopted after execution of the will. Evidence of the intent to disinherit is limited to the express terms of the will. If the testator had no children when he or she executed the will, the child is entitled to his or her intestate share unless the testator left substantially all of his or her property to the surviving spouse and the omitted child is a child of the surviving spouse, in which case the omitted child is not entitled to a share. If the testator had one or more children living when the will was executed and the testator devised property to one or more of the children, the omitted child's share comes out of the gift to the other children and the child's share is determined by calculating what the children would have taken if each child received an equal share of the gifts to the children. The UPC covers children omitted because the testator thought the child dead, but not children omitted because the testator did not know about them. [84]

**F. Revocable trusts:** In some states, the omitted child doctrine has been extended to cover both probate property and property in a revocable inter vivos trust created by the deceased parent. [85]

# VIII. LIMITATIONS ON CHARITABLE GIFTS

**A. Mortmain statutes:** Almost all states used to have mortmain statutes—statutes that limited testamentary gifts to charitable recipients. Some limited the amount one could give to charitable recipients, others voided gifts within a prescribed time period before death. The modern trend embraced by virtually every jurisdiction has been to either repeal such statutes or to have the courts hold them invalid under the Equal Protection Clause. [85]

## CHAPTER 4

# TESTAMENTARY CAPACITY

## I. GENERAL TESTAMENTARY CAPACITY

**A. Overview:** The traditional method of opting out of intestacy is to execute a will. The first requirement for creating a valid will is testamentary capacity. The testator must have testamentary capacity at the time he or she executes or revokes a will. [93-94]

**B. Testamentary capacity:** Testamentary capacity is the ability of the testator to know (1) the nature and extent of his or her property; (2) the natural objects of his or her bounty; (3) the nature of the testamentary act he or she is performing; and (4) how all of these relate to constitute an orderly plan of disposing of his or her property. Absent evidence to the contrary, there is a strong presumption of testamentary capacity. (Testamentary capacity is higher than marriage capacity but lower than contractual capacity, so the appointment of a conservator does not, in and of itself, mean the testator lacks testamentary capacity.) [94-96]

**C. Defects in capacity:** Even if the testator has testamentary capacity generally, if the will or any part thereof is caused by a defect in capacity (insane delusion, undue influence, or fraud), the court will strike as much of the will as was affected by the defect. [96]

## II. INSANE DELUSION

**A. Defined:** An insane delusion is a false perception of reality that the testator adheres to against all reason and evidence to the contrary. The jurisdictions are split over *the test* for what constitutes an insane delusion. [96-100]

1. **Majority approach:** If a rational person could not reach the same conclusion under the circumstances, the belief is an insane delusion.

2. **Minority approach:** If there is any factual basis to support the belief, the belief is not an insane delusion. (Note that this approach is more protective of testator's intent.)

**B. Causation:** Even where the testator has an insane delusion, the delusion must cause the testator to dispose of his or her property in a way that he or she would not have done otherwise. Some jurisdictions apply a "might have affected" approach to causation, while others apply a "but for" approach. (Note that the "but for" approach is more protective of testator's intent.) [98-99]

## III. UNDUE INFLUENCE

**A. Defined:** Undue influence occurs where another substitutes his or her intent for the testator's intent; and where there is coercion (typically mental or emotional, not physical). [100]

**B. Traditional rule statement:** The plaintiff bears the burden of proving that (1) the testator was susceptible; (2) the defendant had the opportunity; (3) the defendant had a motive; and (4) causation. [100-101]

**C. Presumption doctrine:** Because undue influence is difficult to prove and the alleged undue influencer is in the best position to produce the relevant evidence, most jurisdictions have a "burden shifting" approach to undue influence the burden will shift to the alleged undue influencer to show *no* undue influence if the plaintiff meets the requirements of the presumption doctrine. The details of the presumption approach vary from jurisdiction to jurisdiction, but in many jurisdictions if the plaintiff can prove (1) the defendant and the testator were in a confidential relationship, (2) the testator was of weakened intellect, and (3) the defendant takes the bulk of the testator's estate, then a presumption of undue influence will arise and the burden of proof will shift to the defendant to rebut the presumption. [101-103]

**D. No contest clauses:** If a testator suspects that someone may challenge his or her will, the testator may include a clause that provides that if the beneficiary challenges the will (or any provision in the will), the beneficiary is barred from taking under the will. No contest clauses are generally valid, but narrowly construed. Even if a beneficiary challenges a will (or clause) and loses, some jurisdictions will not enforce the clause if there is *probable cause* to support the challenge (whatever its basis), while other jurisdictions will not enforce the clause if (1) there is *reasonable cause* to support the claim, *and* (2) the challenge is based on a claim of forgery, revocation, or misconduct by a witness or the drafter. [103-104]

**E. Gifts to drafting attorney:** The general rule is that any time an attorney who drafts an instrument receives a substantial gift under it, a presumption of undue influence arises unless the attorney is related to or married to the client. Most jurisdictions require clear and convincing evidence that the gift was truly the testator's intent to overcome the presumption; some jurisdictions create an irrebuttable presumption of undue influence. (Some jurisdictions apply the presumption regardless of the size of the gift; others apply the presumption to any gift to the testator's attorney, even if the attorney did not draft the instrument; and some jurisdictions require an independent attorney to counsel the testator and to determine that the gift is the testator's true intent, to overcome the presumption.) [104-105]

# IV. FRAUD

**A. Rule statement:** Fraud occurs where there is an intentional misrepresentation, made knowingly and purposely to influence the testator's testamentary scheme, that causes the testator to dispose of his or her property in a way in which he or she would not have done otherwise. There are two types of fraud. [105-107]

1. **Fraud in the execution:** A person intentionally misrepresents the nature of the document (either completely or in part) that the testator is signing.

2. **Fraud in the inducement:** A person intentionally misrepresents a fact to the testator to induce the testator to execute a will (or amend a provision in a will or to revoke a will) in reliance upon the misrepresentation.

**B. Tortious interference with an expectancy:** Tortious interference with an expectancy is a tort action. The plaintiff still has to prove either fraud or undue influence. Nevertheless, bringing the claim as one of tortious interference with an expectancy has several advantages: (1) it is not a will contest for purposes of a no contest clause; (2) punitive damages may be available; and (3) the action is subject to the standard statute of limitations, not the shortened probate statute of limitations. [107-108]

CHAPTER 5

# WILLS EXECUTION, REVOCATION, AND SCOPE

## I. EXECUTING A VALID WILL

**A. Overview:** Assuming an individual has testamentary capacity, the next requirement for a valid will is that it be properly executed. Determining whether a will has been properly executed is a function of two variables: the jurisdiction's Wills Act formalities and how strictly the courts require the testator to comply with those formalities. [114-116]

## II. COMMON LAW APPROACH TO ATTESTED WILLS

**A. Attested wills:** The three basic requirements for an attested will are a writing that is signed and witnessed. Each jurisdiction, however, adds a variety of other, ancillary requirements. Great care must be paid to each jurisdiction's Wills Act statute to ascertain all the necessary execution formalities in each jurisdiction. [116]

**B. Judicial approach:** Historically, the courts have required strict compliance by the testator with the statutory requirements. Strict compliance requires 100 percent absolute compliance. Even the slightest deficiency or error in the execution ceremony will invalidate the will, regardless of how clear the testator's intent is. [116-117]

**C. Typical statutory requirements:** Although the statutory requirements vary from jurisdiction to jurisdiction, a number are common to most states. These requirements have given rise to a number of ancillary rules. [117-120]

   **1. Signature:** Anything the testator intends to be his or her signature will constitute his or her signature. (If the testator is interrupted while in the act of signing, and the testator does not complete his or her signature, the assumption is that the testator intended to write his or her whole signature and the partial signature was not intended to constitute a valid signature.) Most states permit another to sign for the testator as long as the signature is made in the testator's presence and at the testator's direction.

   **2. Witnesses:** Most jurisdictions require the testator to sign or acknowledge his or her signature in the presence of two witnesses present at the same time. The witnesses must sign the will (and, in most jurisdictions, must know they are signing a will).

   **3. Presence:** A requirement in virtually every Wills Act statute is that one party must perform in the "presence" of another party (i.e., the testator has to sign in the presence of the witnesses, and/or the witnesses have to sign in the presence of the testator). Under the traditional line of sight approach, the party in whose presence the act has to be performed must be capable of seeing the act being performed if he or she looks at the moment it is being performed. Under the modern trend conscious presence approach, the party in whose presence the act has to be performed has to understand, from the totality of the circumstances, that the act is being performed.

   **4. Order of signing:** Many courts hold that there is an implicit order of signing requirement in that the testator must perform (sign or acknowledge) before *either* of the witnesses can sign the will. The modern trend holds that it does not matter who signs first as long as the testator and witnesses all sign as part of one transaction (as long as no one leaves the room before all parties have signed the will).

5. **Writing below signatures:** Where there is writing (typed or handwritten) below the testator and/or witnesses' signatures, the validity of the writing depends on (1) whether the state requires the testator and/or witnesses to subscribe the will (sign at the will at the end) (in which case the gift is invalid), and (2) if the will need not be signed at the end, the validity of the writing depends on *when* the gift was added to the will (if before it was signed—valid; if after it was signed—invalid).

6. **Delayed attestation:** At common law, the witnesses had to sign the will immediately after the testator signed or acknowledged the will. Under the modern trend, delayed attestation is permitted as long as the witnesses sign within a reasonable time of the testator signing or acknowledging.

D. **Interested witness:** If one of the two witnesses to a will takes under the will, the witness has a conflict of interest. At early common law, the whole will was void. Today the jurisdictions vary in their approach to the interested witness doctrine. Some void the entire gift to the witness, others purge the interested witness of the "excess" interest that he or she would take if this will were valid, while others say the interested witness scenario creates only a rebuttable presumption of wrongdoing on the part of the interested witness (and apply the purging approach if the witness cannot rebut the presumption). [120-121]

E. **Swapped wills:** Where two testators with the same testamentary scheme (typically husband and wife) accidentally sign each other's will, the traditional common law approach was that the wills were invalid. Some courts will try to save the wills under the misdescription doctrine, under which all incorrect references in the will are struck and then the will is read to see if the court can construe and give effect to what is left. Under the modern trend, the will *may* be probated under scrivener's error. [121-122]

# III. MODERN TREND APPROACH TO ATTESTED WILLS

A. **Overview:** The modern trend tries to facilitate the execution of attested wills by reducing the number of statutory requirements and/or by reducing the degree of compliance the courts require with respect to the execution requirements. [122]

B. **UPC execution requirements:** The UPC has simplified the execution process by (1) reducing the number of execution requirements, and (2) by easing several of the requirements that remain. [123]

1. **Acknowledgment:** At common law, if the testator used the acknowledgment method of executing the will, the testator had to acknowledge his or her signature. Under the UPC, if the testator uses the acknowledgment method of execution, the testator can acknowledge either the signature or *the will* in front of the witnesses.

2. **Witnesses present at the same time:** At common law, the testator had to sign or acknowledge in the presence of two witnesses *present at the same time*. Under the UPC,

the witnesses need not be present at the same time—the testator can sign or acknowledge in front of the witnesses separately.

3. **Conscious presence:** The UPC expressly provides that where another signs for the testator, the conscious presence approach applies to the requirement that the party sign in the testator's *presence* and at his or her direction.

4. **Writing below signature:** The UPC does not require the testator or the witnesses to subscribe the will (sign at the bottom or end).

5. **Delayed attestation:** The UPC provides that the witnesses may sign the will within a reasonable time after witnessing the testator sign or acknowledge (this also implicitly rejects the requirement that the witnesses have to sign in the testator's presence).

C. **UPC judicial approach:** The UPC repudiates strict compliance. At first it advocated substantial compliance, but the most recent version of the UPC advocates the harmless error/dispensing power approach. [123-125]

1. **Substantial compliance:** Substantial compliance holds that a will was properly executed as long as (1) there is clear and convincing evidence that the testator intended the document to be his or her will; and (2) there is clear and convincing evidence that the testator substantially complied with the Wills Act formalities.

2. **Harmless error/dispensing power:** Harmless error/dispensing power holds that the will was properly executed as long as there is clear and convincing evidence that the testator intended the document to be his or her will.

D. **Interested witnesses:** The UPC has abolished the interested witness doctrine completely. [121]

# IV. HOLOGRAPHIC WILLS

A. **Rule statement:** Holographic wills need not be witnessed, however, (1) there must be a writing; (2) the writing has to be in the testator's handwriting (either completely or at least the material provisions—the jurisdictions are split); (3) the writing must be signed by the testator; and (4) the writing must express testamentary intent (the intent that the document be the decedent's will). (Some jurisdictions also require (5) that the writing be dated.) The jurisdictions are split over whether the testamentary intent must be expressed in the testator's handwriting or whether it can be expressed in printed material on the document. [125-128]

# V. SCOPE OF A WILL

A. **Introduction:** There are a handful of doctrines that define the scope of a will and permit intent not expressed in a will to be given effect. [128]

B. **Integration:** Those pieces of paper physically present when the will is executed and that the testator intends to be part of the will constitute the pages of the will. [128]

C. **Republication by codicil:** A codicil has the effect of reexecuting, republishing, and thus redating the underlying will—but if redating the underlying will appears inconsistent with the testator's intent, the courts do not have to redate the will. [128-129]

**D. Incorporation by reference:** A document not executed with Wills Act formalities may be incorporated by reference and given effect along with the will if (1) the will expresses the intent to incorporate the document, (2) the will describes the document with reasonable certainty, and (3) the document was in existence at the time the will was executed (the courts apply this last requirement strictly). [129-130]

**E. Facts of independent significance:** A will may refer to a fact or event that is to occur outside of the will, and that fact or event may control either *who* takes under the will or *how much* a beneficiary takes, as long as the referenced fact has its own significance independent of its effect upon the will. [130-132]

# VI. REVOCATION

**A. Introduction:** A validly executed will (attested or holographic) can be revoked by act; by writing (if the writing qualifies as a will); by presumption; or by operation of law. [132]

**B. Revocation by act:** A testator can revoke a will by act if (1) the act is destructive in nature (tearing, burning, obliterating, scratching, etc.), and (2) the testator has the intent to revoke when the act is performed. Someone other than the testator can perform the act as long as it is performed in the testator's presence and at his or her direction. At common law, the act had to affect at least some of the words of the will. Under the modern trend, the act need not affect the words of the will as long as the act affects some part of the will. (The act of writing can be a destructive act for revocation purposes.) Some jurisdictions do not permit partial revocation by act. [132-133]

**C. Revocation by writing:** A testator can revoke a will by writing if the writing qualifies as a will—either attested or holographic. A subsequent will can revoke a prior will either expressly or implicitly (through inconsistency), and either in whole or in part—in which case it will be a codicil. A codicil is a will that merely amends and/or supplements an existing will, and that does not completely replace an existing will. [133-134]

**D. Revocation by presumption:** Where a will was last in the testator's possession and cannot be found after the testator's death, a presumption arises that the testator revoked the will (by act). The presumption can be rebutted if the proponents prove by a preponderance of the evidence that a more plausible explanation exists for why the will cannot be found. If the presumption is rebutted, the will is not revoked, and under the lost will doctrine, the will can be probated if its terms can be established by clear and convincing evidence. [134-136]

**Partial revocation by act:** The jurisdictions are split over whether to permit partial revocation by act because of its potential for fraud and because a partial revocation is intrinsically a new gift.

**E. Revival:** If a testator executes will #1, and thereafter executes will #2 (a will or codicil), and thereafter revokes will #2, the jurisdictions are split over what is necessary to revive will #1. Under the English approach, will #2 never revoked will #1, so when will #2 is revoked, will #1 is "uncovered" and can be probated. The majority American approach, however, is that will #2 revokes will #1 the moment will #2 is executed. The jurisdictions that follow the American approach are split over what is necessary to revive will #1 when will #2 is revoked. Some jurisdictions require that will #1 be reexecuted. Other jurisdictions provide that all that is necessary to revive will #1 is that the testator intended to revive will #1. Under this latter approach, however, the key is *how* was will #2 revoked. Where will #2 is revoked by act, the general rule is that the courts will take virtually any evidence of the testator's intent to revive will #1. Where will #2 is revoked by writing (will #3), the intent to revive will #1 must be expressed in will #3. (Under the UPC, if will #2 is a codicil, revocation of the codicil automatically revives the provisions of the underlying will that the codicil had revoked.) [136-137]

**F. Dependent relative revocation:** Even where a will has been properly revoked, if (1) the testator revoked the will, in whole or in part, (2) based upon a mistake, and (3) the testator would not have revoked but for the mistake, the revocation will not be given effect under dependent relative revocation. The courts appear to also require that either (4)(a) the mistake must be set forth in the revoking instrument and be beyond the testator's knowledge, or (4)(b) there must be a failed alternative scheme (typically an attempt at a new will that failed). [137-139]

**G. Revocation by operation of law:** Where the testator divorces, all the provisions of the will in favor of the ex-spouse are automatically revoked by operation of law. (In some jurisdictions, the doctrine applies not only to the ex-spouse, but also to the ex-spouse's family members; and in some jurisdictions the doctrine applies not only to wills, but also to nonprobate instruments.) [139-140]

# VII. CONTRACTS CONCERNING WILLS

**A. Contracts relating to wills:** A person may contract to execute a particular will, to make a particular devise, or not to revoke a particular will or devise. If the contract is valid under contract law, it will be enforced against the testator's estate before the decedent's estate is distributed. At common law, the alleged contract could be oral. Under the modern trend/UPC approach, there must be a writing signed by the decedent evidencing the contract. [140-141]

**B. Joint will/mutual wills:** A joint will is a will executed by two different people that each intends to constitute his or her will. Mutual wills are separate wills that have the same basic dispositive scheme. While older cases were more willing to imply a contract not to revoke when there was a joint will or mutual wills, the modern trend general rule is that the execution of a joint will or mutual wills does not give rise to even a presumption of a contract not to revoke. The intent to form a contract not to revoke must be express. Where there is a contract not to revoke, it typically applies to all property acquired by either spouse, the surviving party has a life estate with a right to reasonable consumption, and the courts are split over whether the contract beneficiaries must survive to the time of possession. [141-143]

**C. Contract rights vs. spousal protection rights:** Where a surviving spouse remarries and then dies, and the surviving spouse's spouse claims his or her spousal protection rights, if such rights constitute a breach of the contract not to revoke, the jurisdictions are split over whether the contract beneficiaries under the contract not to revoke come first (typically the children of the first marriage) or whether the spousal protection rights of the surviving spouse come first. [143-144]

CHAPTER 6

# CONSTRUING WILLS

## I. ADMISSIBILITY OF EXTRINSIC EVIDENCE: GENERAL RULE

**A. Overview:** Assuming a properly executed will, upon the testator's death it has to be probated. Probating a will means construing and giving effect to its provisions. [158]

**B. Admissibility of extrinsic evidence:** The starting assumption is that the written will is the best evidence of the testator's intent and extrinsic evidence should not be admissible to vary its meaning. Consistent with this assumption, the general rule is that extrinsic evidence is admissible only if there is an ambiguity in the will. [159-164]

   **1. Common law:** Under the plain meaning rule, in determining whether there is an ambiguity in the will, the words of the will are given their usual plain meaning, and extrinsic evidence that the testator intended a different meaning is not admissible. If the will contains an ambiguity, under the common law approach extrinsic evidence is admissible to help construe the ambiguity only if it is a latent ambiguity (not apparent on the face of the will); extrinsic evidence is not admissible if the ambiguity is a patent ambiguity. Doctrines that evolved to permit the admissibility of extrinsic evidence to help resolve latent ambiguities were the misdescription doctrine, the equivocation doctrine, and the personal usage exception doctrine.

   **2. Modern trend:** Under the modern trend, the courts have repudiated the plain meaning rule and will take evidence of the circumstances surrounding the testator at the time he or she executed the will to help determine if there is an ambiguity in the will. In addition, the modern trend has abolished the distinction between latent and patent ambiguities and admits extrinsic evidence anytime there is an ambiguity in the will. An ambiguity is language in the will that is reasonably susceptible to two or more interpretations. Only extrinsic evidence that is consistent with one of the reasonable interpretations is admissible to help construe the ambiguity, and historically the courts favored extrinsic evidence of "the circumstances surrounding the testator at time of execution" (hard to fabricate) as opposed to alleged oral declarations made by the testator (easy to fabricate).

## II. SCRIVENER'S ERROR

**A. Rule statement:** Under the modern trend, if there is clear and convincing evidence of a scrivener's error, and clear and convincing evidence of its effect upon testator's intent, extrinsic evidence is admissible to establish and to correct the error. (Scrivener's error is a new doctrine, and the full scope of the doctrine has yet to be established.) [164-165]

## III. CHANGES IN TESTATOR'S PROPERTY

**A. Types of gifts:** There are three different types of gifts that one can make in a will. A specific gift is where the testator intends to give a specific item (typically that the testator owns at time of execution). A general gift is a gift of a general pecuniary value, where any item or items matching the gift will satisfy the gift. A demonstrative gift is a general gift from a specific source—demonstrative gifts are a subset of general gifts and are treated the same as other general gifts. A residuary gift is a gift of all the testator's property that he or she has not given away specifically or generally. [165-166]

**B.  Ademption:** Under the common law approach, if the testator makes a specific gift and the item that is the subject of the specific gift is not in the testator's estate at time of death, under the identity approach an irrebuttable presumption arises that the gift was revoked and the beneficiary takes nothing. Under the UPC, a presumption against revocation arises, and the beneficiary is entitled to any replacement property the testator owns at time of death or, if none, the monetary equivalent of the gift. [166-169]

**1.  Avoidance doctrines:** Because ademption is such a harsh doctrine, a number of avoidance doctrines have arisen: (1) classify the gift as general, not specific, so the ademption doctrine does not apply; (2) if the item is still in the testator's estate but it has changed, argue that the change is merely one in form, not substance, in which case the beneficiary would still be entitled to the item; or (3) construe the will at time of death, not execution, and give the beneficiary the matching item in the testator's estate at death even if that is not the item to which the testator was referring when the will was executed.

**2.  Softening doctrines:** A couple of doctrines that soften the impact of ademption have also arisen: (1) if, as a result of the transfer of the item that was the subject of the specific gift, the testator is owed an outstanding balance, the outstanding balance goes to the beneficiary; and (2) if the specific gift was transferred while a conservator or durable power of attorney agent was acting for the testator, the beneficiary is entitled to the monetary equivalent of the net sale price.

**3.  UPC:** The latest version of the UPC presumes that where a specific gift is no longer in the testator's estate, the gift should not be adeemed. If the testator has acquired property to replace the original specific gift, the beneficiary gets the replacement property. If the testator has not acquired replacement property, the beneficiary is entitled to the monetary equivalent of the specific gift unless that is inconsistent with the testator's intent.

**C.  Stocks:** At common law, the beneficiary got the benefit of any change in the stock between time of execution and time of death if the gift of stock was a specific gift. The modern trend presumes the testator's intent was to give a percentage interest in the company and in the event of a stock split or dividend, the only way to satisfy the testator's intent is to give the beneficiary the benefit of the change in stock, even if the gift is a general gift. The UPC gives the beneficiary the benefit of any change in the stock initiated by a corporate entity as long as at the time of execution the testator owned stock that matched the description of the gift of stock given in the will. [169-170]

**D.  Satisfaction:** At common law, if a beneficiary under a will receives an inter vivos gift from the testator of the same type of property as the gift in the will, and the beneficiary is the testator's child, a rebuttable presumption arises that the inter vivos gift counts against the child's testamentary gift. Under the modern trend/UPC approach, if the testator makes an inter vivos gift to any beneficiary under his or her will, the gift does not count against the beneficiary's testamentary gift unless there is a writing evidencing such an intent. If the donor creates the writing, it must be contemporaneous with the gift; if the donee creates the writing, it can be created anytime. [170-171]

**E. Abatement:** If at time of death the testator has made more gifts than he or she has assets, the doctrine of abatement states that residuary gifts should be reduced first, general gifts second, and specific gifts last. Some states permit the court to vary from this order if abating the residuary first appears inconsistent with the testator's overall testamentary scheme (the testator intended the residuary taker to take the bulk of his or her probate property and abating the residuary clause would be inconsistent with this intent). [171]

**F. Exoneration of liens:** At common law, if a specific gift is burdened with debt (i.e., a mortgage or lien), absent contrary intent expressed in the will, it is presumed that the beneficiary of the specific gift is entitled to have the debt completely paid off (out of the residuary typically) so that the beneficiary takes the gift free and clear of any debt. Under the modern trend, the beneficiary takes subject to the debt absent an express clause directing that the debt is to be satisfied before the gift is made. [172]

# IV. CHANGES IN THE BENEFICIARY

**A. Lapse:** Where a beneficiary predeceases the testator, the gift is said to lapse and will fail. [172]

**B. Failed gifts:** Failed specific gifts and failed general gifts fall to the residuary clause, if there is one, otherwise to intestacy; failed residuary gifts fall to intestacy. If part of the residuary fails, under the common law that part fell to intestacy, while under the modern trend that part goes to the other residuary takers. [172-173]

**C. Anti-lapse:** Anti-lapse may save a gift that otherwise would lapse and fail. Anti-lapse provides that where there is a lapsed gift, if (1) the predeceased beneficiary meets the requisite degree of relationship to the testator (varies by jurisdiction), and (2) the predeceased beneficiary has issue who survive the testator, then (3) the gift to the predeceased beneficiary will go to the issue of the predeceased beneficiary (4) as long as the will does not express an intent that anti-lapse should not be applied (low threshold—historically, an express survival requirement or an express gift over to an alternative taker constituted an express contrary intent). [173-176]

**Spouses excluded:** As a general rule, the anti-lapse doctrine does not apply to gifts to spouses where the spouse predeceases the testator because a spouse does not meet the requisite degree of relationship requirement.

**D. Class gifts:** The class gift doctrine may also save a gift that would otherwise fail. A class gift has a built-in right of survivorship so that if one member of the class predeceases the testator, his or her share is redistributed among the surviving members of the class. Whether a gift to a group is a class gift is a question of testator's intent. Where it is not clear whether a gift to multiple individuals is a class gift, courts focus on four factors: (1) how the beneficiaries are described, (2) how the gift is described, (3) whether all the individuals share a common characteristic, and (4) the testator's overall testamentary scheme. The more factors favoring a class gift, the more likely a court is to find the gift to be a class gift. [176-178]

**Anti-lapse and class gifts:** Where a member receiving a class gift dies survived by issue, the jurisdictions are split over which doctrine should be applied first to try to save the otherwise failed gift—anti-lapse or the class gift doctrine. The modern trend is to apply anti-lapse first (which would save the gift by giving it to the issue of the predeceased beneficiary) before applying the class gift doctrine (which would save the gift by giving it to the other members of the class).

CHAPTER 7

# NONPROBATE TRANSFERS: WILL SUBSTITUTES

## I. INTER VIVOS GIFTS

**A. Inter vivos gifts:** Where one gifts his or her property to another while alive, the donor typically retains no interest that will pass into the donor's probate estate upon death. A valid inter vivos gift requires intent to presently relinquish dominion and control over the item and delivery. As a general rule, delivery must be actual delivery if possible, but if actual delivery is impossible or impractical, the delivery may be constructive or symbolic. If the property is real property, ideally there should be a writing that complies with the statute of frauds, but if there is no writing, the gift may still be enforceable under partial performance. [184-187]

**B. Gifts causa mortis:** Gifts causa mortis are inter vivos gifts made in contemplation of an impending death. Such gifts are intrinsically conditional in that the donor intends that the gift is automatically revoked if the donor does not die as expected; the gift is revocable while the donor is still alive; the donee must survive the donor; and creditors may reach the property if the donor's estate is insufficient to satisfy their claims. [187-188]

## II. OVERVIEW TO NONPROBATE TRANSFERS

**A. Introduction:** One can opt out of intestacy either (1) by executing a valid will, or (2) by creating a valid nonprobate instrument. Historically, there were only four ways a decedent could pass property at time of death by using nonprobate arrangements, though the modern trend has been to expand the scope of the nonprobate arrangements. [188-189]

## III. CONTRACTS WITH PAYABLE-ON-DEATH CLAUSES

**A. Common law:** At common law, the only type of contract with a payable-on-death clause that qualified as a valid nonprobate transfer was a life insurance contract (even though the effect of the contract is to pass the insurance proceeds upon the insured's death immediately to the beneficiary identified in the contract). [189-190]

**B. Modern trend:** The modern trend/UPC expands the life insurance nonprobate exception to include all third-party beneficiary contracts with a payable-on-death clause. [190-191]

## IV. MULTIPLE PARTY BANK ACCOUNTS

**A. Multiple party bank accounts:** Historically, banks forced parties interested in creating multiple party bank accounts to use the joint tenancy account, even if that was not what the parties intended. There are three possible intents the parties may have had when they created the account: (1) a true joint tenancy, (2) an agency account, or (3) a payable-on-death account. Upon the death of one of the parties, the courts take extrinsic evidence of the parties' true intent and treat the property accordingly if there is clear and convincing evidence of an intent other than a true joint tenancy (although at common law, the payable-on-death intent was invalid so the property would pass into the depositor's probate estate). Under the modern trend, the presumption is that inter vivos the parties own in proportion to their contributions, and at death there is a right of survivorship. The presumption, however, can be rebutted if there is clear and convincing evidence of a different intent—and that intent will control the disposition of the funds in the account. [191-193]

**B. Totten trusts:** Totten trust saving accounts were the precursors to the payable-on-death account. Totten trusts arose where a depositor took title to the account in trust for the benefit of another. In most jurisdictions, totten trusts are revocable (so withdrawals by the depositor are permitted), the beneficiary has to survive the depositor, and the depositor can devise the property subject to the totten trust. [194]

# V. JOINT TENANCIES

**A. Joint tenancies:** The right of survivorship means that upon the death of one joint tenant, his or her share is extinguished and the shares of the remaining joint tenants are recalculated. No property is passed at death, so nothing passes through probate. [195]

# VI. REVOCABLE DEEDS

**A. Revocable deeds:** A revocable deed functions very much like a will. Because of that, at common law they were generally held to be invalid attempts at avoiding the Wills Act formalities, while the modern trend generally upholds them as valid will substitutes. [195-196]

# VII. INTER VIVOS TRUSTS

**A. Introduction:** The trustee holds legal title. The beneficiaries hold equitable title. Even if the trust is revocable and the settlor is the life beneficiary, there is no need to transfer legal title upon the death of the settlor. The property placed in the trust inter vivos passes pursuant to the terms of the trust and is nonprobate property. [196-198]

# VIII. POUR-OVER WILLS AND INTER VIVOS TRUSTS

**A. Introduction:** A pour-over will and trust combination is the most common estate planning combination today—though the property being poured over to the trust under the terms of the will does not avoid probate. Where a will has a pour-over clause giving probate property to the trustee of the testator's separate trust, the pour-over clause must be validated under either incorporation by reference, facts of independent significance, or the Uniform Testamentary Additions to Trusts Act (UTATA). [198-199]

**B. Facts of independent significance:** Under facts of independent significance, the trust must have its own significance independent of its effect upon the decedent's probate property—i.e., the trust must be funded inter vivos and have property in it when the testator dies. Subsequent amendments to the trust can be given effect regardless of when they are created, but many jurisdictions subjected the trust to probate court supervision (at least as to the probate property being poured into the trust). [199-200]

**C. Incorporation by reference:** Under incorporation by reference, the trust instrument is being incorporated by reference into the will. The critical requirement is that the trust instrument must be in existence when the will is executed. The trust need not be funded inter vivos, but the trust that is created is a testamentary trust subject to probate court supervision for the duration of its life, and subsequent amendments to the trust are not valid absent a subsequent codicil to the will. [200]

**D. UTATA:** Under the most widely adopted version of UTATA, the pour-over clause is valid as long as (1) the will refers to the trust; (2) the trust terms are set forth in a separate writing other than the will; and (3) the settlor signed the trust instrument prior to or concurrently with the execution of the will (under the most recent version of UTATA, the trust instrument need only be signed before the settlor/testator dies, not before or concurrently with the will). The trust need not be funded inter vivos, yet it will not be subject to probate court supervision after it is created; and amendments to the trust can be given effect regardless of when they are created. [201-203]

**E. Revocable trusts:** From an estate planning perspective, there are many inter vivos and testamentary benefits associated with revocable trusts (but there are also some increased costs and administrative hassles associated with them). [203-204]

## IX. PLANNING FOR THE POSSIBILITY OF INCAPACITY

**A. Overview:** Good estate planning includes planning for the possibility that the person may become incapacitated before he or she dies. With respect to property issues, the most common tool to deal with that possibility is the durable power of attorney. With respect to personal decisions about one's health care, the tools are either a living will or a durable power of attorney for health care decisions. [204-205]

CHAPTER 8

# TRUSTS: CREATION, LIFE, AND TERMINATION

# I. INTRODUCTION: CONCEPTUAL OVERVIEW

**A. Bifurcated gift:** A trust is a bifurcated gift. One party (the settlor) gives property to a second party (the trustee) to hold and manage for the benefit of a third party (the beneficiary). The trustee holds legal title to the trust property and manages the trust property. The beneficiaries hold equitable title. The trustee owes a fiduciary duty to the beneficiaries to manage the trust property in their best interests. The same party can be settlor, trustee, and beneficiary as long as there is another co-trustee or beneficiary. A trust is created the moment it is funded. As a general rule, a trust will not fail for want of a trustee—the court will appoint a trustee if necessary. The trust is an ongoing gift, often lasting for decades. This means that the trust property is bifurcated between the income and principal, and the equitable interest typically is bifurcated between a beneficiary who holds the possessory estate (typically a life estate) and the beneficiaries who hold the future interest(s) (typically a remainder). [212-217]

# II. REQUIREMENTS TO CREATE A VALID EXPRESS TRUST

**A. Trust requirements:** To have a valid trust: (1) the settlor must have the intent to create a trust; (2) the trust must be funded; (3) the trust must have ascertainable beneficiaries; and (4) the terms of the trust *may* have to be in writing. [217-218]

**Remedial trusts:** Constructive trusts and resulting trusts are remedial trusts that arise by operation of law as a matter of equity, and they are not subject to the traditional trust requirements. Constructive trusts typically arise and are imposed by courts to prevent unjust enrichment. The court will order the party currently holding title to the property to transfer the property to the party that the court concludes, as a matter of equity, is entitled to the property. Resulting trusts arise whenever a trust fails in whole or in part. The court will order the property transferred back to the settlor (or the settlor's estate if the settlor is dead).

**B. Intent:** The intent to create a trust arises anytime one party transfers property to a second party for the benefit of a third party. Use of any pertinent term of art (i.e., "trustee" or "trust" or "in trust") generally will be deemed to have expressed the intent. [218-219]

    **1. Precatory trust:** In a precatory trust, a donor makes a gift to a donee with the "wish" or "hope" that the donee will use the property for the benefit of another. *A precatory trust is not a trust*—there is no legal obligation to use the property for the benefit of the other party, only a moral obligation.

    **2. Gifts that fail for want of delivery:** Where a party makes a gratuitous promise to make a gift in the future, but then dies before properly transferring the property, as a general rule the failed gift (for want of delivery) cannot be saved by converting the intent to make a gift in the future into a present declaration of an intent to create a trust with the declarant as trustee.

**C. Funding:** A trust is funded when property is transferred to the trust/trustee. Virtually any property interest will qualify as an adequate property interest—except for future profits and expectancies. [219-222]

**D. Ascertainable beneficiaries:** Beneficiaries are ascertainable if they are identified by name or if there is an objective method of identifying the beneficiaries. The only exception to the requirement that the beneficiaries must be ascertainable is where a trust is created for unborn children—the courts will monitor the trustee's actions. [222-224]

**Honorary trusts:** Where a private trust would otherwise fail for want of ascertainable beneficiaries, but the purpose of the trust is such that it is impossible to have ascertainable beneficiaries (i.e., care of a pet or gravesite) and the purpose is specific and honorable, and not capricious or illegal, under the honorary trust doctrine the courts will permit the trust to continue as long as the "trustee" agrees to honor the terms of the trust. (Technically, such trusts are subject to the Rule against Perpetuities and that may cause the trust to fail, but under the modern trend to the Rule against Perpetuities, courts usually find a way around the Rule against Perpetuities problem—as least for 21 years.)

**E. Writing:** The terms of the trust must be in writing if (1) the trust is an inter vivos trust that includes real property, or (2) the trust is a testamentary trust. [224-227]

    **1. Remedy—failed inter vivos trust:** Where a settlor executes a deed transferring real property to a trustee, and the settlor and trustee *orally* agree on the terms of the inter vivos trust but the deed is silent as to the trust, the trust fails for want of writing. At common law, the "trustee" was permitted to keep the real property as his or her own because strict application of the Statute of Frauds barred evidence of the oral trust agreement to vary the terms of the deed. Under the modern trend, a constructive trust is imposed on the trustee to prevent unjust enrichment (particularly where the trustee procured the transfer as a result of fraud or undue influence or if the trustee stood in a confidential relationship with the donor), and the trustee will be ordered to transfer the property to the intended beneficiaries.

2. **Remedy—failed testamentary trust:** Where a beneficiary under a will agrees to hold the property in question as a trustee for the benefit of others, but the terms of the testamentary trust are not in the will (or incorporated by reference), the testamentary trust fails for want of writing. Under the common law approach, the key is whether the failed testamentary trust is a secret or semi-secret trust. A secret trust is one in which the face of the will makes no reference to the testator's intent that the beneficiary identified in the will was to take in a fiduciary capacity as a trustee and not as an ordinary beneficiary. Where the failed testamentary trust is a secret trust, a constructive trust is imposed and the property is ordered distributed to the intended beneficiaries. A semi-secret trust is one in which the will hints at or expresses the testator's intent that the beneficiary is to take for the benefit of others, but the identity of the trust beneficiaries and/or the terms of the trust are not set forth in a writing that can be given effect. Under the traditional common law approach, where a semi-secret trust failed, a resulting trust is imposed on the trustee and the property is ordered returned to the testator's probate estate. Under the modern trend, a constructive trust is typically imposed on both a secret and a semi-secret trust.

# III. LIFE OF TRUST: EXTENT OF BENEFICIARIES' INTERESTS

A. **Trust life:** Once a trust is validly created, the primary issue during the life of the trust is the extent of the beneficiaries' interest in the trust. Each beneficiary's interest can be either mandatory or discretionary, and each beneficiary's interest can be in the income and/or the principal. [227]

B. **Mandatory trust:** If the trustee *must* distribute all the income to a beneficiary on a regular basis, the trust is a mandatory trust. [227]

C. **Discretionary trust:** If the trustee has discretion over when to distribute the income and/or principal, the trust is a discretionary trust. Because of the trustee's fiduciary duty to the beneficiaries, however, under a discretionary trust, the trustee still has a duty to inquire and a duty to act reasonably and in good faith in exercising his or her discretion. Courts generally hold that attempts at giving a trustee absolute or sole discretion are invalid (for that would no longer be a trust), but such language usually is construed as removing the duty that the trustee act reasonably—the trustee need only act in good faith. In exercising his or her discretion, the trustee should also take into consideration the settlor's intent as to the purpose of the trust or the purpose of the beneficiary's interest. (For example, a discretionary trust for a beneficiary's "comfortable support and maintenance" has become a term of art meaning that the beneficiary is to be kept at the standard of living he or she had upon becoming a beneficiary.) [227-230]

D. **Spray/sprinkle trust:** When the trustee *must* distribute all the income among a group of beneficiaries, and the trustee has discretion as to how much each beneficiary is to take, the trust is known as a spray or sprinkle trust. [230]

## IV. LIFE OF TRUST: CREDITORS' RIGHTS/SPENDTHRIFT CLAUSES

**A. Creditors' rights:** A creditor's rights depend first on whether the creditor is a creditor of (1) a beneficiary *other than the settlor* or (2) a beneficiary who is also the settlor. [231]

**B. Creditors of beneficiary (who is not the settlor):** A creditor of a beneficiary steps into the beneficiary's shoes and acquires the exact same rights the beneficiary had, no more and no less. If the beneficiary's interest was mandatory, the creditors have the same right to receive the property. If the beneficiary's interest was discretionary, the creditors cannot force the trustee to exercise his or her discretion. [231-232]

**C. Spendthrift trust:** If the settlor includes a spendthrift clause (a clause that prohibits beneficiaries from transferring their interest) in the trust, the general rule is that the beneficiary's creditors cannot step into the beneficiary's shoes—they cannot reach the beneficiary's interest in the trust. [232-234]

    **1. Exceptions:** Not all creditors are subject to spendthrift clauses. As a general rule, children entitled to child support, ex-spouses entitled to alimony, creditors who provide basic necessities, and the government entitled to taxes, are creditors who are not subject to a spendthrift clause but rather step into the beneficiary's shoes. These creditors can still reach the beneficiary's interest to the extent it was mandatory, but they cannot force a trustee to exercise his or her discretion in favor of them.

    **2. Support trusts:** A support trust is a trust that requires the trustee to pay as much income (and, if expressly provided in the trust, principal as well) as necessary for the beneficiary's support and education. The key is that the trustee can distribute *only as much as necessary* for support, not the use of the word *support*. The benefit to qualifying as a support trust is that even in the absence of an express spendthrift clause, the beneficiary cannot transfer his or her interest and only creditors who provide basic necessities are entitled to reach the beneficiary's interest in the trust.

**D. Creditors of beneficiary (who is also the settlor):** It is against public policy to permit one to shield one's assets from creditors. Accordingly, creditors of a beneficiary who is also the settlor can reach the beneficiary's interest in the trust to the full extent that the trustee *could* use the trust property for the benefit of the beneficiary/settlor (i.e., the creditors can reach the property whether the beneficiary/settlor's interest is mandatory or discretionary). Moreover, spendthrift clauses in favor of a beneficiary who is also the settlor are null and void. [235-237]

## V. TRUST MODIFICATION AND TERMINATION

**A. Introduction:** A trust ends naturally when all the trust principal is disbursed pursuant to the terms of the trust. Under special circumstances, however, the terms of the trust may be modified or the trust may be terminated prematurely. (The discussion implicitly assumes an irrevocable trust—if the trust were revocable, all that would be necessary to modify or teminate the trust is for the settlor to revoke the trust.) [237]

**B. Revocability:** If a trust is silent as to its revocability, in all but two states it is irrevocable. If the trust is revocable, and it expressly provides for a particular method of revocation, only that method will suffice. If the trust is revocable, and it does not provide for a particular method of revocation, any method that adequately demonstrates the settlor's intent to revoke should suffice (including the revocation methods that apply to wills). [238-239]

**C. Settlor and beneficiaries consent:** If the settlor and all the beneficiaries consent, the trust can be modified or terminated, regardless of the trustee's objections. [239-241]

**Securing consent of all beneficiaries:** Where some of the beneficiaries are minors or are unborn, one way to attempt to secure their consent is to petition the court to appoint a guardian ad litem to represent the interests of the minor or unborn beneficiaries. An alternative way to attempt to secure the consent of minor or unborn beneficiaries is under the doctrine of virtual representation. If the interests of the minor or unborn beneficiaries are virtually identical to those of living adult beneficiaries, a court may permit the latter to represent the interests of the former.

**D. Trustee and beneficiaries consent:** If the trustee and all the beneficiaries consent, the trust can be modified or terminated, regardless of the settlor's objections. [241]

**E. Beneficiaries consent but trustee objects:** Where all the beneficiaries consent but the trustee objects, the common law courts developed doctrines that permit the beneficiaries to overcome the trustee's objections under limited circumstances. [241-245]

1. **Termination—Claflin doctrine:** At common law, under the Claflin doctrine, the courts would order a trust to be terminated prematurely, even if the trustee objected, if (1) all the beneficiaries consented, and (2) there was no unfulfilled material purpose. What constitutes an "unfulfilled material purpose" is fact sensitive and turns on the wording and purpose of each trust, but there are a handful of trust purposes that almost all courts have held to constitute an unfulfilled material purpose: (1) discretionary trusts, (2) spendthrift trusts, (3) support trusts, and (4) trusts in which the property is not to be distributed to the beneficiary until he or she reaches a specific age.

2. **Modification:** At common law, the courts would order the terms of a trust to be modified if (1) all the beneficiaries consented, and (2) there was an unforeseen change in circumstances that materially frustrated settlor's intent. The trust would be modified to promote the settlor's presumed intent under the circumstances. At common law, the courts construed what constitutes an "unforeseen" change and what constitutes "materially frustrating" very narrowly to protect settlor's intent. The modern trend construes those terms broadly to give the beneficiaries greater control over the trust property. The mere fact that a proposed modification would be more advantageous to one or more beneficiaries, however, is not enough to warrant modifying a trust even if all the beneficiaries consent.

CHAPTER 9

# CHARITABLE TRUSTS

## I. CHARITABLE PURPOSE

**A. Charitable trusts:** A charitable trust is one that has a charitable purpose. A purpose is charitable if it is for: (1) the relief of poverty; (2) the advancement of education; (3) the advancement of religion; (4) the promotion of health; (5) governmental or municipal purposes; or (6) any other purposes the accomplishment of which is beneficial to the community at large. Benevolent trusts (trusts that perform kind acts) are not charitable trusts unless they accomplish one of the specific charitable purposes. [255-256]

**B. Benefits:** There are two principal advantages, from a trust law perspective, of classifying a trust as a charitable trust. [257]

    **1. Not subject to the Rule against Perpetuities:** Because charitable trusts serve charitable purposes for the community at large, charitable trusts are not subject to the Rule against Perpetuities.

    **2. No ascertainable beneficiaries requirement:** Because charitable trusts have to serve the community at large, or at least a good segment of the community at large, there is no requirement that the trust have ascertainable beneficiaries. In fact, the trust cannot have ascertainable beneficiaries because that is inconsistent with the idea of the trust benefiting the community at large, or a subset of the community at large.

## II. CY PRES

**A. Rule statement:** Where a trust with a general charitable purpose expresses a particular charitable purpose, and it becomes impossible, impractical, or illegal to carry out that particular charitable purpose, rather than imposing a resulting trust, modify the particular trust purpose to another particular charitable purpose within the trust's general charitable purpose. [257-259]

**B. Administrative deviation:** If accomplishing the trust purpose becomes impossible or impractical for administrative reasons, the courts are empowered to order, and should apply, administrative deviation to remove the obstacle before modifying the settlor's intent under cy pres. [259-260]

## III. ENFORCING THE TERMS OF A CHARITABLE TRUST

**A. Enforcing charitable trust terms:** The state attorney general of each state has the duty of supervising the administration of each charitable trust. Because most state attorney general's offices are overwhelmed, many courts have granted standing to members of the community who have a special interest in the trust to bring suit against the charitable trustee for breach of trust. [260]

CHAPTER 10

# POWERS OF APPOINTMENT: DISCRETIONARY FLEXIBILITY

## I. INTRODUCTION

**A. Power of appointment:** An important tool that estate planners can use to add flexibility to the administration of a trust is a power of appointment. A power of appointment is similar to a power to revoke in the hands of a beneficiary other than the settlor. A power of appointment gives the donee the power to override the distributive terms of the trust and to direct the trustee to distribute some or all of the trust res outright to the appointees. A power is discretionary and imposes no fiduciary duty on the party who holds as a general rule. The power adds flexibility in that if circumstances change, the party holding the power of appointment has the discretionary power to change the distributive provisions of the trust by overriding the original terms (but the party also has the power to override the original distributive provisions even if circumstances do not change). [263-265]

**B. General power:** A power is a general power of appointment if the group of appointees in whose favor the power can be exercised (i.e., the property can be appointed to) *includes* either the donee, the donee's estate, the donee's creditors, or creditors of the donee's estate. [265-266]

**C. Special power:** A power is a special power of appointment if the group of appointees in whose favor the power can be exercised *excludes* the donee, the donee's estate, the donee's creditors, *and* creditors of the donee's estate. [266]

**D. Inter vivos vs. testamentary:** In creating a power, the donor can also specify when the power may be exercised—only inter vivos, only upon the donee's death (testamentary), or either. [266]

**E. Creditors' rights:** If the power of appointment is a special power, the donee is treated like an agent and creditors of the donee have no right to reach the property subject to the power. If the power of appointment is a general power, the donor's creation of the power is treated like an offer to make a gift to the donee. If the donee exercises the power, the donee is treated as having accepted the gift and creditors of the donee can reach the appointed property regardless of to whom the property was appointed. If, however, the donee does not exercise the general power of appointment, as a general rule creditors of the donee cannot reach the property subject to the power. (In a few states, creditors of a donee holding a general power of appointment can reach the property subject to the power even if the power is not exercised.) [266-267]

## II. CREATING A POWER OF APPOINTMENT

**A. Intent to create:** If one party intends to give another party a discretionary power to appoint property, the first party has created a power of appointment. No technical words are necessary to create a power. [267-268]

**B. Power to consume:** If a beneficiary is given a life estate and a power to consume, the power to consume will be deemed a general power of appointment unless it is limited to an ascertainable standard relating to health, education, support, or maintenance of the holder of the power to consume. [268]

## III. RELEASING A POWER OF APPOINTMENT

**A. Release:** A donee may release a power of appointment, in whole or in part (either in whose favor the property may be appointed or when the power may be exercised). [268]

**B. Inter vivos exercise of testamentary power vs. release:** A testamentary power of appointment is one that can be exercised only upon the donee's death. An inter vivos attempt at exercising the power is invalid, as is an inter vivos contract as to how the donee will exercise the power at death. Where, however, the effect of the inter vivos contract is substantially the same as the effect of a release of the power, many courts will enforce the agreement not as a contract but as an inter vivos release of the testamentary power. [268-269]

## IV. EXERCISING OF POWER OF APPOINTMENT

**A. Exercise:** A power of appointment is exercised anytime the donee intends to exercise the power. The instrument creating the power may stipulate how express the donee must be to exercise the power. [269]

B. **Testamentary powers and residuary clauses:** Where a testator holds a testamentary power of appointment and his or her residuary clause makes no express reference to a power of appointment (standard residuary clause), the jurisdictions are split as to whether the residuary clause exercises the power. [269-271]

1. **Majority rule:** The majority rule is that a standard residuary clause does not exercise either a general or special testamentary power of appointment, though some jurisdictions hold that where the testator held a testamentary power of appointment there is sufficient ambiguity to admit extrinsic evidence to help determine whether the testator intended the residuary clause to exercise the power.

2. **Minority rule:** In a minority of states, a standard residuary clause adequately expresses the testator's intent to exercise a general power of appointment that the testator held, but not a special power of appointment.

3. **UPC approach:** A standard residuary clause expresses the intent to exercise a power of appointment the testator held only if (1) the power is a general power of appointment and the creating instrument does not contain an express gift over in the event the power is not exercised, or (2) the testator's will manifests an intention to include the property subject to the power.

4. **Blended residuary clause:** Many residuary clauses include a generic reference to any power of appointment the testator may hold ("I hereby give all my property, *including any property over which I hold a power of appointment,* to . . ."). Where the instrument creating the power does not require a specific reference to the power, the jurisdictions are split over whether such a generic reference is sufficient to exercise the power. The UPC requires the reference to be specific—such a blended residuary clause would not be enough in and of itself.

5. **Lapse and anti-lapse:** Where the testamentary power is properly exercised, but the appointee predeceases the donee, application of anti-lapse turns on the type of power. As a general rule, where the power is a general power of appointment, the courts apply anti-lapse—if the appointee meets the degree of relationship with the donee. Where the power is a special power of appointment, the traditional approach has been not to apply anti-lapse if the issue of the predeceased appointee are not eligible members under the instrument creating the power, but the modern trend applies anti-lapse even if the issue of the predeceased appointee are not express members of the original class of eligible objects of appointment.

C. **Limitations:** Although general powers of appointment can be exercised as the donee sees fit (outright, in trust, or even subject to a new power of appointment), the general rule is that absent authority in the instrument creating the power to do otherwise, the holder of a special power of appointment must appoint the property outright. The modern trend, however, permits the holder of a special power to appoint either in trust or subject to a new power as long as both the donee and the objects of the new power were included in the original class of possible appointees. [271-273]

# V. ATTEMPTED APPOINTMENT THAT FAILS

A. **Ineffective appointment:** Where the donee expresses the intent to exercise the power of appointment, but the expression is ineffective for one reason or another, the appointive property in question will be treated as if the power were not exercised unless it is saved by either allocation or capture. [273]

**B. Allocation:** Where the holder of a special power creates an instrument (typically a will) that purports to blend the appointive property with his or her own property (typically a blended residuary clause) and then gives all the combined property to a group of beneficiaries, the allocation doctrine (1) "unblends" the property, and (2) allocates the appointive property first and only to eligible appointees and then allocates the rest of the holder's property as necessary to try to carry out the distribution scheme expressed in the instrument. This ensures that only eligible appointees take the appointive property while trying to give effect to the holder's distributive intent. Any appointive property that is not distributed to eligible takers under this doctrine passes as if the power had not been exercised. [273]

**C. Capture:** Where the holder of a general power creates an instrument (typically a will) that purports to blend the appointive property with his or her own property (typically a blended residuary clause) and then gives all the combined property to a group of beneficiaries, if one or more of the gifts fail, the holder of the appointive property is deemed to have appointed the failed gift to him- or herself (or probate estate if the instrument is a will), and the appointive property will be distributed accordingly. [273]

# VI. FAILURE TO EXERCISE A POWER OF APPOINTMENT

**A. Failure to exercise:** If the donee fails to exercise the power of appointment, the appointive property will be distributed pursuant to the donor's instructions in the event the power was not exercised. Where the donor has not made express provision for such an event, the property will be returned to the donor (or the donor's estate), unless the power was a special power of appointment to an ascertainable limited group, in which case the property may be distributed equally among the possible appointees if the court finds that was the donor's implied intent. [274]

CHAPTER 11

# CONSTRUING TRUSTS: FUTURE INTERESTS AND CLASS GIFTS

# I. FUTURE INTERESTS

**A. Overview:** Almost invariably, the equitable interests in a trust are some combination of a possessory estate and future interest(s). A possessory estate is the right to possess the property right now; a future interest is the present right to possess and enjoy the property in the future. There are a number of construction issues that can arise in creating possessory estates and future interests. [279-280]

**B. Future interest in settlor:** If the settlor holds the future interest, the interest must be a reversion, a possibility of reverter, or a right of entry. The most common is the reversion—it follows a life estate, a fee tail, or a term of years in which the future interest is expressly or implicitly retained by the grantor. [280-281]

**C. Future interests in beneficiary:** If a beneficiary holds the future interest, the interest must be a vested remainder, a contingent remainder, or an executory interest. The most common is the remainder—it follows a life estate, a fee tail, or a term of years in which the future interest is given expressly to a party other than the grantor. A remainder is contingent unless it is vested; it is vested if (1) the holder is ascertainable, and (2) there is no express condition precedent (expressed in the same clause creating the remainder or the preceding clause) that the holder must satisfy *before* he or she has the right to take possession. [281-284]

# II. PREFERENCE FOR VESTED REMAINDERS

**A. Introduction:** The common law courts favored construing an ambiguous remainder as vested as opposed to contingent. Vested remainders have a number of benefits over contingent remainders. [284]

**B. Destructibility:** At common law, if a contingent remainder did not vest before or at the moment the preceding finite estate ended, the contingent remainder was destroyed. (The modern trend abolishes the destructibility of contingent remainders doctrine.) Vested remainders were never subject to the doctrine. [284]

**C. Accelerating into possession:** Vested remainders are entitled to immediate possession regardless of how or when the preceding estate ends. At common law, a contingent remainder could not become possessory until all the express condition precedents were satisfied, and if the contingent remainder did not vest in time, it would be destroyed under the destructibility of contingent remainders doctrine. [284-285]

**Disclaimers:** If a life tenant disclaimed, under the common law approach, whether a remainder accelerated into possession turned on whether the remainder was contingent or vested. Under the modern trend, some courts have held that it depends on the testator/settlor's probable intent if he or she had known that the life tenant would disclaim. To reduce the high costs of administration associated with this rule, some disclaimer statutes expressly provide that the disclaiming party is treated as if he or she predeceased the decedent, and whether a remainder accelerates into possession depends on the effect of treating the disclaimant so.

**D. Transferability:** At common law, vested remainders were transferable but contingent remainders were not. Under the modern trend, both vested and contingent remainders are transferable. [285-286]

**Transmissibility:** If a party holding a remainder dies before the end of the preceding estate, the remainder passes to the remainderman's probate estate where he or she can devise it or it will pass to his or her heirs. (This rule, however, presumes that the remainder was not destroyed under the destructibility of contingent remainders when the remainderman died.)

**E. Preference for early vesting:** Where the language in an instrument is ambiguous as to whether the remainder is to vest upon the death of the transferor or the death of the life tenant, the preference is to construe the language so that the remainder vests upon the death of the life tenant. [286-290]

1. **Remainderman predeceases life tenant:** If the remainderman predeceased the life tenant, at common law the remainder interest passed into the remainderman's probate estate where it was devisible and inheritable. Under the modern trend, lapse and anti-lapse applies where the remainderman predeceases the life tenant.

2. **Express survival requirement:** Where a grantor includes an express survival requirement, and the language is ambiguous as to whether the remainderman must survive the grantor, the life tenant, or one or more remaindermen, it is a question of grantor's intent. More often than

not, however, the courts construe the language as requiring the party in question to survive to the moment he or she is entitled to possession.

3. **"Die without issue" divesting condition:** Where a remainderman's interest is expressly divested if he or she "dies without issue," but the instrument is ambiguous as to whether it applies only if the remainderman dies before the life tenant or whenever the remainderman dies, absent evidence of the grantor's preference the courts tend to construe the divesting condition as applying only if the remainderman dies before the life tenant.

4. **Rules in Clobberie's case:** Clobberie's case established three rules of construction concerning gifts with ambiguous language delaying delivery: (1) where the gift is "all the income to [the beneficiary's name], with principal to be paid when he or she reaches a specific age or upon marriage, . . ." if the beneficiary dies before marrying or reaching the specified age, his or her interest is transmissible; (2) where the gift is "to [the beneficiary's name] *at* [a specific age]," if the beneficiary dies before reaching that age the gift fails; and (3) where the gift is "to [the beneficiary's name], to be paid when the beneficiary reaches [a specific age]," if the beneficiary dies before reaching that age, his or her interest is transmissible.

5. **UPC approach:** The UPC has advocated applying a lapse/anti-lapse approach to *all* future interests in trusts (revocable or irrevocable), unless the instrument expressly provides otherwise. (This proposal has been widely criticized and has not been widely adopted.)

# III. CLASS GIFTS

A. **Class gifts:** Where a gift is given to a class, a variety of construction issues can arise. [290]

B. **Class closing:** At some point, the class must close. It can close naturally when no one else can enter the class, or it can close under the rule of convenience, automatically, by operation of law, as soon as one member of the class is entitled to possession of his or her interest. No one else can enter the class, even if he or she otherwise appears to be eligible to join the class. [290-292]

1. **Direct, outright gifts:** Where an instrument (typically a will) provides for outright gifts to a class of beneficiaries, the class closes upon the transferor's death.

2. **Gifts of specific amounts:** Where an instrument (typically a will) provides for an outright gift of a specific amount to each class member, the class closes at the time of distribution (typically at the death of the transferor).

3. **Gifts of future interests:** Where an instrument creates a future interest in a class, and the gift is a periodic payment of income, the class closes upon each periodic date for distribution of the income and reopens with the beginning of the next period for the duration of the period. Where the gift is a one-time distribution of principal, the earliest the class will close is upon the end of the preceding estate.

C. **Implied survival requirement:** Courts tend to imply a survival requirement where a gift is to the grantor's heirs, issue, descendants, or similar "multigeneration" gifts, but not where the gift is a "single-generation" gift (i.e., children or siblings). [292-293]

**D. Express survival requirement—gifts to "surviving" children:** If a child dies before taking possession, and the instrument fails to provide for what is to happen to the child's interest, the general rule is the issue of the surviving child do not take. [293]

**E. Adopted children:** The transferor's intent will control whether adopted children qualify as issue under a written instrument, but if the instrument is silent, while the common law tended to exclude adopted children, the modern trend is to include them. [293-294]

**F. Gifts to "heirs":** Remainders to a designated party's "heirs" create problems concerning who is included (as a general rule a surviving spouse is included) and when should the class of heirs be determined (when the designated individual dies or when the remainder becomes possessory). The common law preference for vested remainders favored determining the designated party's heirs when the party dies, regardless of when distribution is to occur. The modern trend/UPC determines who qualifies as an heir when the property is to be distributed to the heirs. [294-295]

1. **Doctrine of worthier title:** If a document purports to create a remainder in the settlor's heirs, the remainder is converted into a reversion in the grantor.

2. **Rule in Shelley's case:** If a document purports to create a remainder in real property in the heirs of a life tenant, the remainder is given to the life tenant.

**G. Per capita vs. per stirpes vs. per capita at each generation:** Gifts to "issue" are intrinsically ambiguous where the instrument fails to indicate whether the property should be distributed per stirpes, per capita by representation, or per capita at each generation. The majority approach is to apply the jurisdiction's default approach. The Restatement (Second) of Property applies the per capita by representation approach. The UPC applies the jurisdiction's default approach, even if the express language is to the "issue by representation." [296]

**H. Income to class, single member dies:** A rebuttable presumption arises that the gift to the class is in joint tenancy with right of survivorship such that the income is to be redistributed among the surviving members of the class. The presumption is rebutted if the instrument expresses a contrary intent, either expressly or implicitly. [296-297]

CHAPTER 12

# THE RULE AGAINST PERPETUITIES

## I. INTRODUCTION

**A. The Rule against Perpetuities:** A future interest must vest, if at all, within the lives in being at the time of its creation plus 21 years, or the interest is void. [303-304]

**B. Traditional approach:** The rule is applied in the abstract the moment the interest is created, it does not wait to see whether the interest vests within the perpetuities period, and it is not concerned with probable scenarios. If there is but one scenario, no matter how implausible, in which the interest would vest, but not until after the perpetuities period, the interest is void from the moment of its attempted creation. The party must show logically that the interest must vest, if at all, within the lives in being when the interest was created plus 21 years (the perpetuities period). [304-308]

**C. Scope:** The rule applies to contingent remainders, vested remainders subject to open, executory interests, and powers of appointment. [305]

**D. Creation:** The future interest must vest within the lives in being when the interest is *created* plus 21 years. Interests are created under a deed when it is delivered, under a will when the testator dies, under an irrevocable trust when it is funded, under a revocable trust when it becomes irrevocable, and special rules covered below apply to interests created under powers of appointment. [307-308]

## II.  CLASSIC RULE AGAINST PERPETUITIES SCENARIOS

**A. Introduction:** There are a handful of Rule against Perpetuities scenarios that are both well known and that demonstrate the abstract nature of the doctrine. [308]

**B. The fertile octogenarian:** In applying the Rule against Perpetuities, the common law courts assumed conclusively that a person was fertile until death, regardless of her age. For example, assume a settlor creates an irrevocable trust for the benefit of a woman, *W,* who is 80 years old. The trust provides "to *W* for life, then to her children for life, then to her first grandchild." The woman has two children, and when the interest is created, neither of them has any children. The interest in the first grandchild violates the Rule against Perpetuities because the woman could have another child, *C* (who would not be a life in being at the time the interest was created), and more than 21 years later *C* could have a child who could be the first grandchild—thereby vesting the interest but not until after the perpetuities period. [308-309]

**C. The unborn widow:** A person's widow cannot be identified until the designated person dies, so any future interest following a future interest to a widow needs to be analyzed carefully to see if it violates the Rule against Perpetuities. For example, "to *H* for life, then to *H*'s widow for life, then to *H*'s children then surviving." If you assume *H*'s widow is living, the interest in *H*'s children then surviving would be valid, but because *H*'s widow could be unborn at the time the interest is created, the interest in H's children surviving when the unborn widow dies violates the Rule against Perpetuities. [309]

**D. The slothful executor:** The potential for delayed and/or prolonged administration of a decedent's estate means that gifts to be made to *unnamed* generic takers upon distribution of the decedent's estate usually violate the Rule against Perpetuities. For example, if *T*'s will provides that she leaves her estate "to my heirs who are alive when the court orders distribution of my estate," that interest would violate the Rule against Perpetuities because all the lives in being plus 21 years may pass before the court orders distribution of T's probate estate. [309-310]

## III.  CLASS GIFTS AND THE RULE AGAINST PERPETUITIES

**A. Class gifts:** If a gift to a class violates the Rule against Perpetuities as to one member of the class, it violates the rule as to all members of the class. The class must close *and* vest (conceivably different events) completely or the gift to the class is invalid. The courts, however, have recognized a couple of exceptions to this rule. [310-311]

**B. Gifts to subclasses:** If the future interest in question can be characterized as a gift to subclasses as opposed to a single class, although the gift may be invalid as to some subclasses, it may be valid as to other subclasses. [311-312]

**C. Gifts of specific amounts:** If the future interest is to a class, but each class member's share is a specific sum not indeterminate upon the final number of class members, the courts have held that even though the gift to some members of the class may violate the rule, the gift is valid as to those members whose share is definitively ascertainable within the perpetuities period. [312]

# IV. POWERS OF APPOINTMENT AND THE RULE AGAINST PERPETUITIES

**A. Powers of appointment:** As long as a general inter vivos power of appointment becomes exercisable or fails within the perpetuities time period, the power is valid even if it is not exercised until after the perpetuities period. General testamentary powers of appointment and *special* powers of appointment are valid as long as there is no scenario under which the donee can exercise the power *after* the perpetuities period. With respect to any interests created by the exercise of a valid general inter vivos power of appointment, the perpetuities periods starts with the exercise of the power. With respect to interests created by the valid exercise of a general testamentary power or special power, the interests created are analyzed as if they were created by the instrument that created the power. [312-315]

# V. THE RULE AGAINST PERPETUITIES SAVING CLAUSE

**A. Saving clause:** Because of the difficulty in understanding the Rule against Perpetuities, the courts will enforce an express "saving clause" that provides that despite the express terms of the trust, the trust will terminate at the latest upon the running of the perpetuities period. [315-316]

# VI. REFORMING THE RULE AGAINST PERPETUITIES

**A. Modern trend:** Because of the harshness of the Rule against Perpetuities, particularly because it is applied in the abstract regardless of real life probabilities, the modern trend is to modify the rule. There are several different approaches to such modification. [316-317]

**B. Cy pres:** Under the cy pres doctrine, where a future interest in a trust violates the Rule against Perpetuities, the court is empowered to modify the trust so that it will not violate the rule. [317]

**C. Wait-and-see:** Instead of applying the Rule against Perpetuities in the abstract to see if there is one possible scenario in which the future interest vests but not until after the running of the perpetuities period, the courts wait and see if the future interest in question actually does not vest until after the perpetuities period. Under the Uniform Statutory Rule Against Perpetuities, the analysis is simplified even further in that the perpetuities period is a set 90 years (as opposed to the traditional "life in being plus 21 years" perpetuities period). [317-318]

**D. Abolishing the Rule against Perpetuities:** Some states have abolished the Rule against Perpetuities, permitting trusts to last forever. [318]

CHAPTER 13

# TRUST ADMINISTRATION AND THE TRUSTEE'S DUTIES

## I. TRUSTEE'S FIDUCIARY DUTIES

**A. Duty of loyalty:** The trustee owes a duty of absolute loyalty to the beneficiaries. Everything the trustee does must be done in the best interests of the beneficiaries. The duty of loyalty means that the trustee must act reasonably and in good faith. [324-328]

    **1. Duty against self-dealing:** Self-dealing arises where the trustee (or members of the trustee's family) transact with the trust. The trustee has an inherent conflict of interest where there is self-dealing. Where a trustee engages in self-dealing, an irrebuttable presumption of breach of the duty of loyalty arises. Under the "no further inquiry" rule, the reasonableness of the transaction and/or the trustee's good faith are irrelevant. Where, however, (1) the trust authorizes self-dealing, or (2) all the beneficiaries consent after full disclosure, self-dealing is permitted if the transaction is reasonable and the trustee is acting in good faith.

    **2. Duty to avoid conflicts of interest:** A conflict of interest arises where the trust deals with another party with whom the trustee has an interest that may affect the trustee's assessment of the proposed transaction. The no further inquiry rule does not apply, but the transaction must be reasonable and the trustee must act in good faith.

**B. Duty to care for the property:** The trustee must take proper care of the trust property. The trustee has (1) a duty to take secure possession of the trust property in a timely manner; (2) a duty to care for and maintain the trust property; (3) a duty to segregate the trust property from other property (particularly the trustee's own property); and (4) a duty to earmark—clearly identify the trust property as trust property. (At common law, if the trustee breached the duty to segregate and earmark, the trustee was strictly liable. Under the modern trend, the breach must cause damage before the trustee is liable.) [328-329]

**C. Duty not to delegate:** A trustee cannot delegate those activities and responsibilities that he or she can reasonably be expected to perform. Trustees may delegate ministerial activities—those that do not require the exercise of discretion. [329-330]

    **1. Modern trend duty to delegate:** The modern trend recognizes that some trustees are unqualified to undertake certain responsibilities inherent in holding and managing trust property—in particular, the duty to invest trust property properly. The Uniform Prudent Investor Act and the Restatement (Third) of Trusts provide that the trustee must act in the best interests of the beneficiaries in deciding whether to delegate discretionary responsibilities, including investment-making responsibilities, and to whom to delegate them.

    **2. Duty to supervise:** Where the trustee does delegate either ministerial or discretionary responsibilities, the trustee still has an ongoing duty to monitor and supervise the actions of the agents to whom the responsibilities have been delegated.

**D. Duty of impartiality:** A trustee has a duty of loyalty to all the beneficiaries. The trustee must balance the competing interests of the different beneficiaries. The trustee has a duty to produce a reasonable income for the life beneficiaries while preserving the principal for the remaindermen. [330-332]

**Duty to sell:** Even where the trust expressly authorizes the trustee to retain the trust property (particularly the "inception" assets), where the trust property is either underperforming (principal appreciating significantly but producing little income) or overperforming (producing substantial income stream but principal depreciating), the trustee has a duty to sell the trust property within a reasonable time period. If the trustee does not dispose of the underperforming or overperforming asset in a timely manner, the trustee has duty to re-allocate the sale proceeds so that the beneficiaries who were adversely affected by the delayed sale are compensated.

E. **Duty to inform:** The trustee has a duty to provide beneficiaries with complete and accurate information when requested. Even where the settlor expressly authorizes withholding information, at a minimum, the beneficiary is entitled to information about his or her interest in the trust. Where the trustee proposes selling a significant portion of the trust assets, the trustee must notify the beneficiaries in advance unless the value of the assets are readily ascertainable or disclosure would be seriously detrimental to the beneficiaries' interests. [332-333]

F. **Duty to account:** The trustee has a duty to account on a regular basis so that the trustee's performance can be assessed. If the trust is a testamentary trust, the trustee has a duty to account to the probate court. If the trust is an inter vivos trust, the trust may authorize the trustee to account directly to the beneficiaries. As a general rule, proper accounting starts the statute of limitations on any claim against the trustee for actions taken by the trustee that are disclosed in the accounting. If the trustee files a fraudulent accounting, and the beneficiaries later discover the fraud, the beneficiaries will not be barred from reopening the accounting. Under the doctrine of constructive fraud, where an accounting makes factual representations that turn out to be false, if the trustee made the representations honestly and in good faith but failed to undertake reasonable efforts to ascertain the accuracy of the factual representations, such false factual representations in the accounting will constitute a "constructive" or "technical" fraud and will provide grounds for reopening an otherwise properly allowed accounting. [333-334]

## II. TRUSTEE'S POWERS

A. **Common law:** At common law, the office of trustee had no inherent powers, only those that were either expressly granted to the trustee by the deed or declaration of trust or those implicitly provided in light of the express trust powers and purpose. [334]

B. **Modern trend:** At first, to simplify the granting of trust powers, states adopted long lists of statutory powers that the settlor could incorporate by reference to the statutory provision. More recently, the trustee has been granted automatically all the powers a prudent person would need to manage the trust in light of its purpose. [334]

## III. TRUST INVESTMENTS

A. **Traditional "statutory list" approach:** Traditionally, the presumed purpose of a trust was to *preserve* the trust property. Historically, the legislature would identify categories of investments that were presumed appropriate, but even then an investment in a particular entity or activity on the list had to be otherwise reasonable and proper. Moreover, each investment decision was analyzed in isolation. The risk level of other investments and the profits generated by other investments were irrelevant in assessing the propriety of a particular investment. [334-335]

**B. Model Prudent Man Investment Act:** The Act, first adopted in 1940, abolished statutory lists and authorized any investment that a prudent person would make, barring only "speculative" investments. The most common statement of the prudent person standard is that the trustee should invest with the same care as a prudent person would with respect to his or her own property, taking into consideration the dual goals of preserving the principal while generating a reasonable stream of income. [335]

**C. Modern trend:** The modern trend is that a trust is a vehicle for holding and managing assets, and, as reflected in the Restatement (Third) of Trusts and the Uniform Prudent Investor Act, the modern trend adopts the prudent investor approach. The prudent investor approach requires the trustee to spread the risk of loss by diversifying the trust investments. The prudent investor approach abolishes the duty to segregate and permits pooling of trust funds to reduce transaction costs and to achieve economies of scale. The prudent investor approach adopts the portfolio approach to assessing trust investments. The performance of the trust's investments is assessed on a portfolio basis, not on individual investments—the key is an acceptable level of risk at an aggregate level, not an investment-by-investment assessment of the level of risk. The focus is on total rate of return, not individual investments, investment decisions, or the return on a particular investment. [336-338]

**Duty to delegate:** The prudent investor rule also modifies the duty not to delegate, providing that an unsophisticated trustee has a duty to delegate investment decisions to professionals who are in a better position to make the necessary investment analysis and decisions.

**D. Principal and income:** Settlor's intent controls what constitutes income and what constitutes principal. To the extent the settlor does not express an intent on the issue, historically income was that money generated by the principal. The initial property transferred to the trust, and any property received as a result of a conveyance of that property, constituted principal. The modern trend (as reflected in the 1997 Principal and Income Act) also modifies the traditional rules concerning allocating income and principal. Because the focus is on total return, and not on income vs. principal, the trustee is authorized to reassign some of the return, if necessary, to make sure that both types of beneficiaries are treated fairly. [338-340]

**Unitrust:** Under a unitrust, the life beneficiaries are entitled to a specified percentage of the value of the trust principal each year, so there is no need to distinguish income from principal. All property generated is assigned to principal, and, at the appropriate intervals, the specified percentage of the trust principal is distributed to the appropriate beneficiaries.

# IV. TRUSTEE'S LIABILITY TO THIRD PARTIES

**A. Trustee's liability to third parties:** At common law, the trustee was personally liable, both in contract and in tort, for contracts entered into by the trust or for torts committed within the course of managing the trust. The trustee was entitled to reimbursement if the actions were authorized, but if the trust assets were inadequate, the trustee was personally liable. The modern trend limits the trustee's personal liability by limiting claims against the trustee to claims in his or her representative capacity as a general rule. [340]

## CHAPTER 14
# ESTATE AND GIFT TAXES

## I. OVERVIEW

    **A. Introduction:** Gratuitous transfers of property, both inter vivos and testamentary, may trigger tax consequences under the gift and estate tax system. [346-348]

## II. THE FEDERAL GIFT TAX SCHEME

    **A. Federal gift tax:** Inter vivos gifts that exceed the annual gift tax exclusion constitute a taxable gift during that year. Depending on the amount of cumulative taxable gifts, a donor may owe federal gift taxes. [349]

    **B. Gift:** For gift tax purposes, the key is *not* the transferor's intent, but whether the transferor has received adequate consideration and whether the transferor has abandoned sufficient dominion and control over the property to put it beyond recall or the right to demand the beneficial enjoyment of the property. Where the transferor has retained the power to revoke, appoint, or change the owner, the transferor has not abandoned sufficient dominion and control. [349-353]

## III. THE FEDERAL ESTATE TAX: AN OVERVIEW

    **A. Federal estate tax:** Depending on the value of a decedent's net property holdings at death, and the amount of his or her inter vivos gifts, a decedent may owe a federal estate tax at death. There are several steps in determining whether a decedent owes a federal estate tax: (1) calculate the decedent's gross estate; (2) calculate the decedent's taxable estate; (3) calculate the estate tax; and (4) apply credits to determine estate tax liability. [353]

## IV. CALCULATING THE DECEDENT'S GROSS ESTATE

    **A. Decedent's gross estate:** The decedent's gross estate consists of the value of virtually all property the decedent owned and transferred at time of death via probate or nonprobate means. The nonprobate property includes property transferred by right of survivorship, transfers where the decedent retained a life estate or control of the beneficial rights, revocable transfers, transfers where the decedent retained a reversionary interest, selected transfers within three years of death, and property over which the decedent held a general power of appointment. [353-359]

## V. THE MARITAL DEDUCTION

    **A. The marital deduction:** One spouse can transfer an unlimited amount of property to the other spouse without any gift or estate tax consequences as long as the transfer meets the requirements for the marital deduction—the key requirement being that the interest must be something other than a life estate or other terminable interest. [359-361]

# VI. GENERATION-SKIPPING TRANSFER TAX

**A. Generation-skipping transfer tax:** Where a transferor attempts to transfer property to a transferee who is more than one generation below the transferor, a federal generation-skipping transfer tax is imposed. The tax imposed is the highest possible federal estate tax rate, but various exemptions and exclusions apply. [361]

# VII. STATE DEATH TAXES

**A. State death tax:** All states except Nevada have a pick-up death tax, an inheritance tax, or some other form of state death tax. [361-362]

## CHAPTER 1

# INTRODUCTION TO WILLS, TRUSTS, AND ESTATES

## *ChapterScope*

This chapter focuses on the macro issue raised by the course: **"Who gets your property when you die?"** To the extent the answer is "whomever you intend," this chapter examines the theoretical and public policy issues inherent in that answer. In particular, the chapter examines:

- **Public policy considerations:** Is the power to transfer wealth at death *natural and good*, or does it *perpetuate economic disparity* and unfairly reward those lucky enough to have been born to wealthy parents?

- **The scope of the power:** Although a decedent has the right to dispose of his or her property at death, the *states have broad authority to regulate the process*.

- **Course overview:** The whole course can be reduced to a single issue: *Who takes a decedent's property at his or her death?* The answer depends first on whether the property is *nonprobate* or *probate* property. *Nonprobate* property passes pursuant to the terms of the nonprobate instrument, be it joint tenancy, life insurance/payment on death contracts, legal life estate and remainders, or inter vivos trusts. *Probate property* passes pursuant to the terms of the *decedent's will, otherwise through intestacy*.

- **The probate process:** A personal representative is appointed, and he or she has the job of collecting the decedent's probate assets, paying off creditors' claims, and distributing the property to those who are entitled to receive it.

- **"Dead hand" control:** A decedent may condition a beneficiary's gift on the beneficiary behaving in a certain manner as long as the condition does not violate public policy. Such "dead hand" control is *generally upheld unless* the condition constitutes a *complete restraint on marriage, requires* a beneficiary to *practice a certain religion, encourages divorce or family strife*, or directs the *destruction of property*.

- **Professional responsibility:** Under the *common law* approach, the attorney owes *no duty* of care to, and is *not in privity of contract* with, intended beneficiaries. They have no standing to sue for malpractice. Under the *modern trend*, an attorney owes a *duty of care* to intended beneficiaries, and intended beneficiaries are *third-party beneficiaries* with respect to the contract between the attorney and testator. Intended beneficiaries have standing to sue for malpractice.

## I. THE POWER TO TRANSFER PROPERTY AT DEATH

### A. Introduction

1. **Historical perspective:** The power to transfer one's property by passing it to one's heirs (spouse, children, and family members) was recognized well before the power to transfer

one's property by will. The scope of one's power to transfer at death is generally considered to be a matter of civil law as opposed to natural right.

**2. Cultural differences:** The scope of one's power to transfer property at death varies greatly from society to society. In many countries, one's children cannot be disinherited. They are entitled to a share of the deceased's property, regardless of the deceased's attempts to dispose of his or her property otherwise. In some societies, one cannot will away his or her property; it can pass only to one's heirs.

## B. Public policy debate

**1. Pro:** A person should have the power to transfer his or her property at death because it is consistent with a system of private property; it encourages and rewards a life of hard work; it is consistent with and promotes family ties; it encourages individuals to accumulate wealth for old age and to give to family; and it encourages family members to love, serve, and protect their elders.

**2. Con:** A person should *not* have the power to transfer his or her property at death because it perpetuates economic disparity and discrimination; it constitutes an unearned windfall to those who happen to have wealthy relatives; unearned wealth creates power and privilege that is undeserved; and unearned wealth denies equal opportunities to all children.

**3. Rebuttal:** Inter vivos investments in "human capital"—health, education, culture, and connections—arguably account more for disparity in opportunities and wealth than inherited wealth.

**4. Academic vs. public opinion:** Academics tend to favor stiffer inheritance taxes, arguing that such taxes are inherently fairer than other forms of taxation. The public in general, however, tends to oppose inheritance taxes. Whether this is because people believe (unrealistically) that they will end up with great wealth, which they want to be able to transfer at their death, or whether this reflects some larger notion of the role of property rights and governmental rights, is unclear.

**5. Historical compromise—permit but tax:** Historically, the United States has tried to balance these competing public policy arguments by permitting wealth to be transferred upon death, but imposing an estate and gift tax at significantly higher rates than those applied to earned income.

**6. Modern trend—phased-in elimination of estate tax:** The anti-estate tax proponents currently hold the upper hand, as reflected by the most recent amendments to the federal estate and gift tax laws that increase the tax exemption over the next several years, and the proposal to abolish the estate tax. The debate over the balance between maximizing a person's ability to dispose of his or her property at death and using the estate and gift tax system to redistribute wealth and equality is far from over.

## C. Shifting patterns

**1. Demographics:** Most state inheritance schemes are built around the notion of a family. To the extent the traditional American family is undergoing change, pressure is growing to recognize nontraditional families and relationships within a state's inheritance scheme (who qualifies as a spouse? who qualifies as a child?). You should keep an eye on these issues as you cover the material.

2. **Property transfers:** Professor John H. Langbein has postulated that the field of wills and trusts is itself a dying field. Rather than parents spending their lives accumulating wealth to transfer to their children at their death, Professor Langbein argues that the principal means of transferring wealth from one generation to the next will be by parents funding their children's education.

# II. THE RIGHT TO TRANSFER PROPERTY AT DEATH

## A. Right vs. privilege

1. **Governmental power to regulate:** It was generally presumed that the power to pass one's property at death was not a constitutionally protected right. In *Irving Trust Co. v. Day,* 314 U.S. 556, 562 (1942), the United States Supreme Court said as much: "Nothing in the Federal Constitution forbids the legislature of a state to limit, condition, or even abolish the power of testamentary disposition over property within its jurisdiction."

2. **Government cannot abrogate completely:** In *Hodel v. Irving,* 481 U.S. 704 (1987), however, the Supreme Court reversed itself and held that the "escheat" provision of the Indian Land Consolidation Act of 1983 constituted an unconstitutional "taking" of decedent's property without just compensation. The Act completely deprived Indian landowners, without compensation, of the right to dispose of their fractional interests in Indian land by intestacy or devise, but not through nonprobate means, if the decedent's interest represented 2 percent or less of the total acreage in the tract and earned less than $100 during the preceding year. The decedent's fractional interest would escheat to the tribe. The Court found the statute overly broad and unconstitutional. Apparently, the Court was bothered that the statute virtually abrogated an important right (the power to transfer at death) and that the statute was not well drafted to achieve its stated goals. The statute applied even in cases where permitting the property to pass to one's heirs would have resulted in increased consolidation of the property, the goal of the statute.

3. **Right to transfer vs. right to receive:** To the extent constitutional protections apply to property transfers at death, the protections arguably apply only to the decedent's power to dispose of his or her property at death, not necessarily to a particular heir's or beneficiary's right to receive property from a decedent.

## B. State variations: While all states recognize the right to transfer one's property at death, the details of what constitutes a valid will, and to whom the property will pass if there is no valid will, vary greatly from state to state.

# III. COURSE OVERVIEW

## A. Macro issue: The course can be boiled down to a single issue: Who gets the decedent's property when he or she dies?

## B. Macro answer: First and foremost, the answer turns on what type of property is involved: nonprobate or probate.

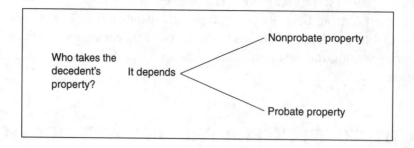

**C. Probate vs. nonprobate property:** A will disposes of the decedent's probate property only. There are a number of ways to dispose of property without the property having to pass through probate. These property arrangements are collectively referred to as nonprobate property. Probate is the default.

**D. Nonprobate property:** The decedent has to take affirmative steps for the property to qualify as nonprobate property. Historically, there were four types of property arrangements that qualified as nonprobate.

1. **Joint tenancy:** Joint tenants hold the property in question concurrently. They own it in whole and in fractional shares. The key characteristic of joint tenancy is its ***right of survivorship.*** Upon the death of one joint tenant, his or her fractional share is extinguished, and the shares of the surviving joint tenants are recalculated. Technically, no property interest "passes" upon the death of a joint tenant.

2. **Life insurance:** Life insurance is an agreement between the insured and the insurance company that upon the insured's death, benefits will be paid to the beneficiary or beneficiaries selected by the insured. Life insurance proceeds are not probate property and can be distributed directly to the beneficiaries without being subject to the probate process. At common law, life insurance contracts were the only type of contract with a payment-on-death clause that qualified as a valid will substitute.

   **Modern trend—payment-on-death contracts:** A life insurance policy is a contract with a payment-on-death (P.O.D.) clause. The modern trend recognizes *all* contracts with P.O.D. clauses as valid nonprobate transfers exempt from the probate process.

3. **Legal life estates and remainders:** When the party who holds a legal life estate dies, although the right to possession passes to the party holding the remainder, that transfer is the result of the original grantor's division of the property between the life estate and remainder, not the result of the deceased life tenant passing a property interest. Properly created legal life estates and remainders avoid probate.

4. **Inter vivos trusts:** A trust is an artificial legal entity that holds and manages the property placed in the trust. There are several different types of trusts: inter vivos trusts, testamentary trusts, and UTATA trusts (Uniform Testamentary Additions to Trusts Act). Of the three, only property properly transferred to an inter vivos trust during the life of the party avoids passing through probate.

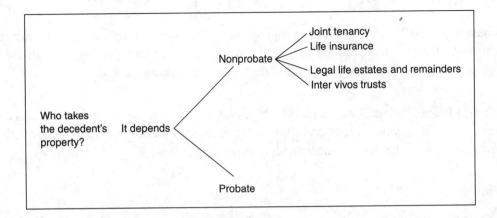

**E. Nonprobate property takers:** The decedent's nonprobate property goes to the transferees identified in the written instrument properly creating the nonprobate property arrangement. The property does not pass through probate.

**F. Probate property:** If the property in question does not qualify as nonprobate property, the property automatically falls to probate—the default system.

1. **Will vs. intestacy:** Who takes the decedent's probate property depends on whether the decedent had a valid last will and testament. A properly executed will constitutes an expression of a person's intent as to who should take his or her property when he or she dies. If a decedent does not have a will, or if the will does not dispose of all the decedent's property, the property passes via intestacy to the decedent's heirs.

2. **Intestacy is the default:** If a decedent takes no steps to opt out of intestacy, all his or her property will pass through intestacy.

3. **Opting out of intestacy:** One can opt out of intestacy by properly executing a will or by properly executing a will substitute—one of the recognized nonprobate methods of transferring property. If one properly executes a will substitute, the property in question totally avoids probate. If, however, one opts out of intestacy by executing a will, the property still passes through probate.

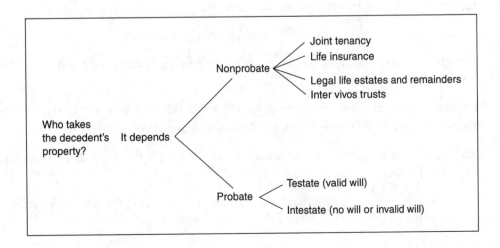

# IV. THE PROBATE PROCESS: AN OVERVIEW

**A. Probate is the default:** Nonprobate property passes pursuant to the terms of the instrument in question to the transferees identified in the instrument—without passing through the probate system. Probate property must pass through the probate system.

**B. Probate administration:** Probate is a very complex process. At many law schools, it is a separate course. While it is impossible to do justice to the probate process here, some sense of the process and terminology is helpful to understanding some of the issues in wills and trusts.

**C. Terminology**

- **Testate:** If the decedent dies with a valid last will and testament, the decedent is said to have died *testate* and his or her property will be distributed pursuant to the terms of the last will and testament.

- **Intestate:** If the decedent dies without a valid last will and testament, the decedent is said to have died *intestate* and his or her property will be distributed pursuant to the state statute on descent and distribution.

- While at first blush the terms *testate* and *intestate* appear mutually exclusive, such is not the case. If a decedent dies with a will that disposes of some, but not all the decedent's property, one could say that the decedent died both testate and intestate.

- **Testator:** A male who executes a valid will.

- **Testatrix:** A female who executes a valid will.

  Increasingly today the term *testator* is gender neutral, referring to both males and females who die with a valid will.

- **Devise:** A gift of real property under a will. Can also be used in its verb form: to devise; devises.

- **Devisee:** A beneficiary receiving real property under a will.

- **Bequest:** A gift of personal property under a will. Can also be used in its verb form: to bequeath, bequeaths.

- **Legacy:** A gift of personal property under a will.

- **Legatee:** A beneficiary receiving personal property under a will.

  Increasingly today the term *devise* is used to describe testamentary gifts of either real or personal property.

- **Personal representative:** The person appointed by the probate court to oversee the administrative process of wrapping up and probating the decedent's affairs.

- **Executor:** What the personal representative is called if the decedent died testate and the will names the personal representative.

- **Administrator:** What the personal representative is called if the decedent died intestate or testate but the will fails to name a personal representative.

Increasingly today the more generic *personal representative* term is used without bothering to note if the person is an executor or administrator.

- **Probate court:** The state court with special jurisdiction over determining who is entitled to receive the decedent's probate property.

- **Statute of descent and distribution:** If a decedent dies intestate as to some or all of his or her property, such property will be distributed to those individuals identified to receive such property under the state's statute of descent and distribution.

- **Heirs:** Under a statute of descent and distribution, the decedent's *real* property "descends" to the decedent's heirs.

- **Next-of-kin:** Under a statute of descent and distribution, the decedent's *personal* property is "distributed" to the decedent's next-of-kin.

Increasingly today the term *heir* is used to describe anyone receiving property (real or personal) under a state's intestate scheme.

**D. The probate process:** Probating a decedent's estate is important because it (1) provides for an orderly transfer of title for the decedent's property; (2) ensures that creditors receive notice, an opportunity to present their claims, and payment; (3) extinguishes claims of creditors who do not present their claims to the probate court; and (4) ensures that the decedent's property is properly distributed to those who are entitled to receive it.

1. **Opening probate:** The probate court in the county where the decedent was domiciled at time of death has primary (or domiciliary) jurisdiction over the decedent's probate estate. The court has jurisdiction over the decedent's personal property and the decedent's real property located within that jurisdiction.

   Probate is opened by presenting the decedent's death certificate. Depending on the situation, the probate court issues "letters testamentary" appointing an executor or "letters of administration" appointing an administrator. A majority of the jurisdictions require notice to interested parties before selection and appointment of the executor or administrator.

   **Ancillary jurisdiction:** Ancillary jurisdiction may be necessary if the decedent owned real property located in a different jurisdiction from his or her domicile. Ancillary jurisdiction ensures (1) that local creditors in the jurisdiction where the real property is located receive notice and an opportunity to present their claims, and (2) that there is compliance with that jurisdiction's recording system.

2. **Real property:** Although title to the decedent's personal property passes to the decedent's personal representative upon the decedent's death by operation of law, title to the decedent's real property passes to the decedent's devisees or heirs upon the decedent's death by operation of law. Probate of the will, however, is necessary to perfect that title.

   **Example:** In *Eckland v. Jankowski,* 95 N.E.2d 342 (Ill. 1950), Thorwald Hegstad died January 23, 1945. Probate was opened, no will was offered for probate, his estate was administered, and the administrator was discharged on August 14, 1946. On November 30, 1946, his heirs conveyed a certain parcel of real estate previously owned by Thorwald to the Berlands for $12,000. On February 8, 1947, the Berlands conveyed the property to the appellees for $13,000. Six months later Eckland found Thorwald's will that purported to transfer a one-half interest in the real property to Eckland. On December 10, 1947, the will was admitted to probate. A purchaser of land is charged with constructive notice of whatever is in the recorder of deeds office and whatever is in the records of the circuit, probate, and country courts in the county where the land is situated. At the time the appellees purchased the land, there was nothing in the records that would have given them notice of the will. Therefore the appellees, as subsequent bona fide purchasers, prevailed over the devisee.

3. **Will contests:** If a party wishes to file a claim challenging the validity of a will offered for probate, most jurisdictions have a statute requiring that the contest be brought in a timely manner after probate is opened, or the claim is barred.

4. **Probate administration:** Once the court issues its letters, the personal representative is authorized to begin his or her responsibilities.

**E. Personal representative's powers:** The jurisdictions are split as to the personal representative's powers to administer the estate. Some jurisdictions require probate court supervision and authorization at almost every step of the way, thereby incurring greater expense for the estate. Other states permit unsupervised administration under most circumstances, with one final accounting being filed with the probate court at the end.

**F. Personal representative's duties:** The personal representative has several duties.

1. **Inventory decedent's assets:** First, the personal representative has a duty to ascertain and take control of the decedent's probate property, which he or she inventories to the probate court.

2. **Give notice to and pay creditors:** Second, the personal representative gives notice of the opening of probate and that creditors of the decedent are required to file any and all claims within a set statutory period or their claims will be forever barred. The personal representative must pay those creditors who present valid claims within the prescribed time period. In addition to paying creditors, the personal representative must file federal and state estate tax returns and, if necessary, pay any taxes due.

3. **Distribute decedent's probate property:** Whatever property is left over after paying creditors' claims is then distributed to those who are entitled to receive under the decedent's last will and testament an/or to those entitled to receive under the state's statute of descent and distribution, depending on whether the decedent died testate or intestate (or both).

4. **Finality of probate:** Probate can be reopened for a variety of reasons, and wills probated late, but the courts typically protect debtors who paid the original personal representative in good faith and/or third parties who qualify as bona fide purchasers who dealt with the original personal representative, devisees, or heirs. Once a probate decree has been entered and the time for appeal has run, the general rule is that the decree can be upset if there is a showing of fraud, accident, or mistake.

**Example:** In ***Allen v. Dundas,*** 100 Eng. Rep. 490 (K.B. 1789), the defendant, the Treasurer of the Navy, was indebted to the decedent. Robert Brown offered for probate a will that appointed him sole executor. The court admitted the will to probate and appointed Brown executor. The defendant paid the debt to Brown. Thereafter it was proved that the will was forged and that the decedent died intestate. The court held that the defendant could not be required to pay a second time.

**G. Creditors' claims:** In the interest of wrapping up a decedent's affairs and transferring the decedent's property to his or her devisees or heirs in a timely manner free of any claims, most jurisdictions have "nonclaim statutes" imposing shortened statutes of limitations on claims against a decedent's estate. As a general rule, creditors must bring their claims in a timely manner or their claims are forever barred.

1. **Nonclaim statutes:** Nonclaim statutes typically come in two basic forms. One requires creditors to bring their claims within a very short period of time of probate being opened (two to six months typically) or the creditor's claim is barred. The other form calls for a longer period of time (one to five years typically) from the time of the decedent's death.

2. **Publication notice:** Traditionally, nonclaim statutes required only constructive notice by publication to creditors to bring their claims or be forever barred.

3. **Actual notice:** In *Tulsa Professional Collection Services, Inc. v. Pope,* 485 U.S. 478 (1988), the Supreme Court ruled that where the identity of a creditor is known or reasonably ascertainable, the Due Process Clause requires that the creditor receive actual notice before a creditor's claims could be barred.

    **Example:** In *U.S. Trust Company of Fla. Sav. Bank v. Haig,* 694 So. 2d 769 (Fla. Dist. Ct. App. 1997), decedent sold a house to appellees, took back a purchase money mortgage, and executed a five-year guaranty that the house would be free of cracks and leaks due to structural defects (damages for which could be offset against the mortgage). When the decedent died, appellant was appointed personal representative, notice of administration was published, and the claims period closed pursuant to state statute 90 days later—on February 8, 1995. Appellees wanted to extend the time to file a claim against the estate because they were unaware of decedent's death until eight days after the claims period closed. The statute authorized the court to extend the period only upon a showing of fraud, estoppel, or insufficient notice of the claims period. Appellees claimed insufficient notice because they were ascertainable creditors entitled to actual notice. The court held that they were at best contingent creditors, dependent upon a finding of cracks or leaks caused by a structural defect. As such they were not entitled to actual notice and grounds for extending the claims period did not exist. (The court expressly noted, however, that its ruling did not address the issue of appellees' right to offset their claims against the mortgage.)

**H. Creditors' claims arising post-death:** Creditors whose claims arise after the death of the decedent pose unique procedural and substantive issues.

1. **Common law:** Under the traditional common law approach, a fiduciary can be held personally liable, under either contract law or tort law, for the actions of the estate. If the fiduciary was acting within the scope of his or her appointment when the liability arose, or if the fiduciary is personally without fault for the tort, the fiduciary is entitled to reimbursement from the estate. If, however, the fiduciary was acting outside the scope of his or her appointment, if the fiduciary is personally at fault, or if there are insufficient funds to cover the liability, the fiduciary remains personally liable for the contract or tort.

    **Example:** In *Onanian v. Leggat,* 317 N.E.2d 823 (Mass. App. 1974), defendant was appointed executor with a power to sell certain real property devised under the decedent's will. Defendant received at least two offers, and entered into an agreement to sell the property to the plaintiff for $32,500 subject to a license to sell from the probate court. The probate court granted the executor a license to sell at private sale or for a larger sum at public auction, if the executor thought it best to do so. The defendant notified the plaintiff that the sale would be by auction. The plaintiff purchased the land at auction for $35,155, and then sued the defendant in his personal capacity for breach of contract. The court found the defendant liable. The court noted that while the executor is entitled to reimbursement for expenses reasonably and necessarily incurred for the benefit of the estate, whether he was entitled to reimbursement for these damages was a matter for the probate court.

   **a. Contract terms:** The courts generally uphold contract terms expressly providing that the fiduciary is not personally liable if the estate breaches the contract.

   **b. Insurance:** The fiduciary can minimize the financial exposure by taking out insurance to cover any tort liability committed during the estate administration.

   **c. Procedural note:** The general rule is that the contract or tort claimant had to sue the fiduciary in his or her personal capacity first, recover from his or her assets, and if insufficient, then sue to enforce the fiduciary's right to reimbursement.

2. **Modern trend:** The modern trend is to limit suits against a fiduciary to suits in his or her representative capacity. As applied to contract claims, the limitation arises as long as the fiduciary gives notice that he or she is acting in a representative capacity (as fiduciary for the estate), and in the tort setting, the limitation arises as long as the fiduciary was not personally at fault for the tort.

   **a. Procedural note:** Under the modern trend, creditors can sue the fiduciary in his or her representative capacity and the estate directly.

   **b. Example:** In *Vance v. Estate of Myers,* 494 P.2d 816 (Alaska 1972), Holbert was appointed administrator of the estate of Charles Myers. The probate court authorized Holbert to continue operating decedent's business, Chuck's Corner Bar. The appellant, suing as guardian ad litem for her husband, brought suit against several parties, including Holbert, claiming that Holbert served alcoholic beverages to the appellant's husband even though he was clearly intoxicated, and that, as a result of their actions, appellant's husband was injured in an altercation at the bar. Holbert was served with the complaint shortly before the close of administration, and the probate court was aware of the complaint when it ordered the discharge of Holbert. Appellant claimed that probate should not have been closed and the administrator discharged while the tort action was pending. The court adopted the modern trend, based on the modern theory that an economic enterprise should bear the burden of the losses caused by it, and held that the administrator may be sued in his or her representative capacity and collection may be from the estate if it is determined that the liability arose out of a common incident of the kind of business activity in which the administrator was properly engaged on behalf of the estate.

   **c. Uniform laws:** The core principles of the modern trend have been adopted by both the Uniform Probate Code, §7-306, and the Uniform Trust Code, §1108.

**I. Costs and delays of probate:** Probating a typical estate is a costly process that ties up the decedent's probate assets during the process. The process is costly due to probate court fees, personal representative's fees, attorney's fees, and miscellaneous other fees that may be applicable. On average, probate of even a fairly simple, uncontested estate can take anywhere from one to two years.

1. **Fiduciary fees:** The fee structure varies from state to state, but in most states it is set statutorily. Some states have a set fee schedule depending on the amount of assets over which the fiduciary has control, while other states simply require that the fees be "reasonable." In addition, individuals are always free to negotiate their own fees with the fiduciary. Fees for lawyers tend to vary as well, with some lawyers charging fees that parallel the fiduciary fees and others charging by the hour.

2. **Example:** In *Matter of Warhol,* 629 N.Y.S.2d 621 (Surrogate's Ct. 1995), the issue was whether the retainer agreement between the Andy Warhol's executor and the attorneys of the estate was enforceable. The initial agreement was for 2½ percent of the estate. When it became apparent that the estate was larger, the fee was reduced to 2 percent, and then later the parties agreed the fee would be equal to an executor's commission. In assessing the reasonableness of the fee, the court stated that the attorney bore the burden of establishing that the terms were fully and fairly presented to and understood by the client and that under the circumstances they are fair and reasonable. The court noted that what constitutes a reasonable fee depends on (a) the nature of the services rendered; (b) the size of the estate; (c) the responsibility undertaken; (d) the difficulty of the legal issues; (e) the ability of the attorney; and (f) the amount of time spent. The court awarded the total fee at $7.2 million. On appeal, the court reduced the fee to $3.5 million. *See In re Estate of Warhol,* 637 N.Y.S.2d 708 (App. Div. 1996). The court noted in particular that services performed by the attorney that are executorial in nature may not properly be considered in determining the legal fees. In addition, the court decreased the value of the attorney's fees on the grounds that the attorney was not a specialist in the field.

**J. Probate and "titled" property:** As a practical matter, probate is necessary to transfer title to those assets, real or personal, that were titled in the decedent's name. Where the probate asset has a written form of title in the decedent's name, a probate court order is needed to transfer title properly.

**K. Avoiding probate:** Due to the costs and hassles inherent in probate, more and more people are trying to avoid probate. In theory, a person can avoid probate by putting all his or her property in nonprobate property arrangements. In practice, however, it is very difficult to put all one's property in nonprobate arrangements.

1. **Nontitled probate assets:** As a practical matter, probate can be avoided if all the decedent's property is "nontitled" personal property. But if the takers opt not to open probate, those who take the decedent's property may take subject to creditor's claims.

2. **"Small estate" probate statutes:** All states have a "small estate" probate procedure that may be employed if the size and nature of the decedent's probate property permits. Such procedures basically permit expedited probate with minimal court supervision or involvement, thereby minimizing the attendant costs and delays.

# V. "DEAD HAND" CONTROL

**A. Definition:** Money is, to some degree, power. "Dead hand" control arises where a decedent continues to exercise power over his or her property, and by exercising power over the property exercises control over a beneficiary, by *conditioning a gift to a beneficiary upon a beneficiary behaving in a certain way.*

1. **Arguments in support:** It is the decedent's property. Given that a decedent could have conditioned an inter vivos gift on a donee acting in a certain manner, the decedent should have the right to condition a testamentary gift on a beneficiary acting in a certain manner. A beneficiary has no right to receive the property. Given that a decedent can completely disinherit a beneficiary, the decedent should be able to condition or restrict an intended beneficiary's inheritance.

2. **Arguments against:** Circumstances change, and because the donor is deceased, he or she no longer has the capacity or flexibility to take ever-changing circumstances into consideration in structuring his or her gifts. In addition, some conditions can be so contrary to fundamental rights or generally accepted public policy they should be considered invalid conditions.

B. **Valid conditions:** Testamentary conditional gifts ("dead hand" control) are valid unless they violate public policy, or judicial enforcement of the condition would constitute state action violating constitutionally protected fundamental rights. The courts have been reluctant to find that upholding the conditional terms of the gift constitutes sufficient state action to offend the Constitution, and the courts have been very reluctant to hold conditional gifts as contrary to public policy.

C. **Invalid conditions:** There are a handful of conditions that generally have been held to be invalid as against public policy.

1. *Absolute* **restraints on marriage:** Gifts conditioned on the beneficiary not marrying anyone—at least as to first marriages—are generally considered to violate the fundamental right to marry and are *void*.

   a. **Exception—partial restraints:** Partial restraints on marriage that impose only reasonable restrictions generally are not contrary to public policy and are *valid*. What constitutes a "reasonable" restriction is very fact sensitive. The courts pay particular attention to the age of the intended beneficiary and the time frame of the intended restriction/condition.

   b. **Exception—temporal/religion requirement:** Gifts requiring a beneficiary to marry within a reasonable time period, even to someone of a particular religious background, have been held *valid*. Such gifts arguably do not restrict an individual's right to marry; they merely encourage them to marry within a certain timeframe and within a particular religion.

      **Example:** In *United States Nat'l Bank of Portland v. Snodgrass*, 275 P.2d 860 (Or. 1954), a father's testamentary gift to his daughter required that she not marry a Catholic before she was 32 years old. The daughter married a Catholic before turning 32. The daughter challenged the condition, claiming it: (1) violated her fundamental right to marry, a right protected by the First and Fourteenth Amendments to the Constitution, and (2) violated public policy generally. The court ruled the condition was valid because (1) enforcing the condition did not constitute sufficient state action as to offend the Constitution, and (2) *partial* restraints on marriage are upheld if they do not unreasonably restrict the freedom of the beneficiary's choice, and the condition here was merely a partial (only against Catholics—not against marriage generally) and temporary (only 11 years from the legal age at which she could marry without parental consent) restriction.

2. **Requiring beneficiary to practice a particular religion:** Gifts that require a beneficiary to remain faithful to a particular religion are generally held to violate public policy concerning religious freedom and are *invalid.*

3. **Gifts that *encourage* separation and/or divorce:** Gifts that require a beneficiary to separate or divorce before receiving the gift are generally deemed against public policy and are void; but gifts that provide for a beneficiary only in the event of separation and/or divorce are not necessarily deemed to encourage divorce. The controlling factor appears to be the decedent's dominant intent: to encourage the separation/divorce, or merely to provide support in the event of separation/divorce.

4. **Gifts that *promote* family strife:** Gifts conditioned upon family members ostracizing and/or not communicating with other family members generally have been held to violate public policy and are *void.*

5. **Gifts with directive that property be destroyed:** Although individuals generally are free to destroy property while they are alive, they generally are not free to destroy property upon their death and such directives are *invalid.* Destruction of property inter vivos carries with it an economic cost that deters owners. Destruction of property at death carries with it no meaningful economic cost for the decedent and deprives society of the opportunity to determine the best use of the property.

D. **Remedy:** Where there is a conditional gift that violates public policy, the critical variable is whether there is a "gift over" clause: a clause in the instrument that provides where the gift is to go if the condition or restriction is not satisfied.

1. **"Gift over" clause:** Where there is a gift over clause, and the conditional gift violates public policy, more often than not the courts will strike the condition as void as against public policy, but the courts will not give the property to the beneficiary subject to the condition. Instead, the property will be distributed to the beneficiary under the express gift over clause.

2. **No "gift over" clause:** Where there is no express gift over clause, if there is a conditional gift that violates public policy, more often than not the courts will simply strike the void condition/restriction and permit the beneficiary subject to the condition to take the property free and clear of any conditions.

# VI. ESTATE PLANNING: AN INTRODUCTION

A. **Estate planning objectives:** Estate planning can be a very complicated process, depending on a person's personal and financial situation, and his or her intent. In advising a party about his or her estate plan, there are several key objectives, discussed below, that should be kept in mind.

1. **Decedent's intent:** The principal purpose of estate planning is to ensure that the person's intent with respect to who gets what, and when, is honored.

2. **Avoid estate taxes:** One of the primary purposes of estate planning is to avoid or minimize federal and/or state estate/inheritance taxes.

3. **Avoid probate:** Probate can be very costly and cumbersome, tying up the decedent's probate property for years. Estate planning to avoid probate is rather simple, at least as to the decedent's larger assets and/or those assets that the decedent does not use often. If those assets are

held in a valid nonprobate arrangement (joint tenancy, an inter vivos trust, or a payment-on-death contractual arrangement), the remaining probate assets may qualify for small estate probate treatment.

# VII. PROFESSIONAL RESPONSIBILITY

**A. Standing to sue:** The scope of an attorney's professional responsibility is critical to determining who has standing to sue the attorney for malpractice.

   **1. Tort theory:** To sue an attorney for malpractice based on a tort theory, one has to prove negligence. To prove negligence, one has to prove a duty of care existed between the defendant attorney and the plaintiff.

   **2. Contract theory:** To sue an attorney for malpractice based on a contract theory, one has to show privity of contract.

**B. Common law approach:** Under the common law approach, the attorney-client relationship is construed very narrowly to protect attorneys from claims of malpractice from frustrated individuals who thought they were going to take under the decedent's estate planning instruments but did not.

   **1. Tort—no duty:** Under the common law approach, the attorney owes a duty of reasonable care to only the client, the testator, but not to any intended beneficiaries. Only the testator, while alive, or the personal representative, after the testator's death, has standing to sue the drafting attorney for negligence.

   **2. Contract—no privity:** Under the common law approach, the attorney is in privity of contract only with the other party to the contract. Third-party beneficiary contracts were not recognized. An estate planning attorney is in privity of contract with the testator only, not with any intended beneficiaries. Only the testator, while alive, or the personal representative, after the testator's death, has standing to sue the drafting attorney for breach of contract.

   **3. Pro:** The common law approach protects attorneys from baseless and/or fraudulent claims from frustrated individuals who thought they were going to take under the decedent's estate planning documents but did not.

   **4. Con:** The common law approach bars valid claims from intended beneficiaries where the attorney has erred.

**C. Modern trend—majority approach:** Under the majority modern trend approach, the attorney-client relationship is construed broadly such that intended beneficiaries have standing to sue the testator's attorney for malpractice.

   **1. Tort—duty:** Under the modern trend approach, a majority of courts that have considered the issue have extended the attorney's duty to intended beneficiaries based on the reasonable foreseeability of injury to the intended beneficiaries if the attorney fails to exercise due care.

   **2. Contract—privity:** Under the modern trend approach, a majority of courts that have considered the issue have held that a nonparty to a contract can sue for breach of contract if the nonparty qualifies as a third-party beneficiary. Once the client identifies to the estate planning attorney to whom the client wishes his or her property to go, the intended beneficiary achieves third-party beneficiary status and is in privity of contract with the attorney. The intended beneficiary has standing to bring a malpractice action if the attorney errs.

3. **Pro:** The modern trend approach permits valid claims from intended beneficiaries where the attorney has erred.

4. **Con:** The modern trend approach fails to protect attorneys from baseless and/or fraudulent claims from frustrated individuals who thought they were going to take under the decedent's estate planning documents but did not. Such claims drive up malpractice insurance premiums for attorneys who practice estate planning, making the cost of obtaining a will more expensive for everyone.

D. **Modern trend—compromise approach:** A handful of jurisdictions, concerned that adopting the modern trend would subject attorneys who practice estate planning to too many baseless claims from frustrated beneficiaries, have adopted the modern trend approach of extending duty and privity beyond the client to include intended beneficiaries—but only those intended beneficiaries identified in the testator's estate planning instruments (typically a will or trust).

1. **Pro:** The modern trend compromise approach permits some valid claims from intended beneficiaries who are identified in the will where the attorney has erred.

2. **Con:** The compromise approach fails to provide a remedy for intended beneficiaries, no matter how clear the evidence, who fail to get mentioned in the will. The intended beneficiary becomes caught in a legal "catch-22" where he or she has no standing unless mentioned in the will, yet it is the failure to include the intended beneficiary in the will that is the basis for the professional malpractice claim.

---

## *Quiz Yourself* on
## *INTRODUCTION TO WILLS, TRUSTS, AND ESTATES*

1. Chelsea marries Ken, Jr. Chelsea's mother, Hillary, is outraged. Decades later, Hillary writes a will that provides as follows: "I leave all my property to my daughter, Chelsea, if she is not married when I die; but if she is married, I leave all my property as follows: one-quarter to my sister, Ann; one-quarter to my brother, Bob, and the rest to the National Democratic Party." Both Ann and Bob were married when Hillary executed the will. Hillary never told Chelsea about the provision in the will. Years later, when Hillary dies, Chelsea challenges the provision in the will conditioning the gift to her. What are Chelsea's strongest claims, and is the conditional gift valid? _____

2. Brad and Jennifer are happily married and live in a noncommunity property state. They purchase Nirvanacres as true joint tenants. Brad has a car, in his name alone, that he purchased before he married Jennifer. He has an insurance policy in the amount of $50,000 that he purchased before his marriage that designates his mother as the beneficiary. He has a checking account with $100,000 in it from a commercial he made during the marriage. Jennifer has a boat that she purchased before she married Brad. She has $500,000 in a checking account from a sitcom she made during the marriage. Tragically, Brad drowns while surfing when some of the locals, protecting their turf, bump him off his board. Brad dies with a valid will giving his car to his friend from Missouri, Sheryl. The will has no other

provisions. What is the extent of Brad's property (what is nonprobate, what is probate testate, and what is probate intestate)? _____

  **a.** (If your course covers community property, what would your answer be if they lived in a community property jurisdiction?  _____ )

3. Bozo the attorney drafted a will and trust for the Smiths. Bozo set up a "by-pass" trust in the trust to minimize the estate taxes upon the death of the couple. He forgot, however, to include a clause directing that the by-pass trust be funded so as to take advantage of the available tax benefits. As a result of his alleged failure, the estate was subject to estate and gift taxes, costing the estate $1,000,000. The beneficiaries sue, alleging malpractice. Do the beneficiaries have standing to sue?  _____

---

## Answers

1. The conditional gift is valid. Chelsea can claim that the clause is against public policy because (a) it constitutes a complete restraint on marriage; and (b) it encourages divorce. Unfortunately for Chelsea, both claims will fail. Hillary apparently put the condition in the will because she did not like Chelsea's husband, not because she was against marriage in general. Both Ann and Bob were married at the time she executed the will making gifts to them, yet she did not condition her gifts to them on their being unmarried at the time of her death. The clause does not constitute a complete restraint on marriage, it merely reflects her misgivings about Chelsea's marriage to Ken, Jr. Nor is the clause invalid because it encourages divorce. There is no evidence that Hillary ever told Chelsea. Chelsea did not find out about the provision until Hillary died, when it was too late to change her marriage status to take advantage of the gift. Thus there was no attempt to induce Chelsea to divorce. The conditional gift is valid.

2. The first task is to check for any valid nonprobate assets. Brad and Jennifer owned Nirvanacres as joint tenants, one of the recognized nonprobate means of transferring property. Upon Brad's death, his interest is extinguished and Jennifer now owns Nirvanacres as her separate property. Life insurance is another recognized nonprobate means of transferring property. Upon Brad's death, the $50,000 insurance proceeds will be distributed immediately to his mother. Brad's car and his checking account are his probate property. Brad's will validly devises his car to Sheryl. The rest of Brad's property (the money in his checking account) will fall to intestacy where it will be distributed pursuant to the state's descent and distribution statute to his heirs.

  **a.** Assuming Brad and Jennifer live in a community property jurisdiction, their nonprobate assets would be the same as above (the insurance policy was purchased with earnings acquired premarriage so it is Brad's separate property; and the facts say they took the house as true joint tenants). Brad's car is still his separate property because it was acquired premarriage. He can devise it to Sheryl. But his earnings during marriage, and Jennifer's earnings during marriage, are community property assets. Upon his death, he has a half interest in his earnings during the marriage (half of $50,000 equals $25,000) that goes into his probate estate, and he has a half interest in Jennifer's earnings during marriage (half of $500,000 equals $250,000) that goes into his probate estate. His will does not cover these assets, so they will fall to intestacy where they will be distributed pursuant to the state's descent and distribution statute.

**3.** Under the traditional common law approach, Bozo would not be liable to the beneficiaries. Under the common law approach, an attorney owed no duty to the intended beneficiaries, only to the client. The beneficiaries have no standing to sue for malpractice. Under the modern trend approach, an attorney owes a duty of care to the intended beneficiaries as third-party beneficiaries of the attorney-client relationship. The beneficiaries have standing to sue Bozo for both negligence and breach of contract. Under the compromise modern trend approach, it would depend on whether the beneficiaries were named in the estate planning instruments. If so, they would have standing. If not, they would not have standing.

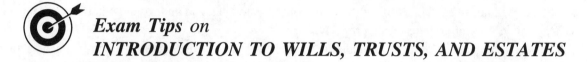

# Exam Tips on
# INTRODUCTION TO WILLS, TRUSTS, AND ESTATES

The first chapter is primarily an overview that gives you some background and context, introduces a number of themes that will be repeated throughout the book, and throws in a couple of traditional rules that do not really fit anywhere else in the book.

## Study suggestion: keep the big picture in mind at all times

As you move through the course, rule by rule, you will quickly realize that for the most part the rules are fairly straightforward and logical. The problem is that there is a rule for virtually every conceivable scenario. The degree of difficulty in the course is not with any given rule, but rather with the volume of rules and plethora of overlaps that can arise. The key to keeping the material straight is to keep the big picture in mind.

☞ Some rules apply to all types of property (nonprobate, probate testate, and probate intestate), while other rules apply only to one or two types of property. As you learn each rule, think about the scope of its application.

## Analytical key: the material is presented in reverse analytical order

The material starts with the default and works its way up the distribution scheme. The material starts with intestacy, then examines wills (the traditional method of opting out of intestacy), and then examines nonprobate transfers (the modern preferred method of opting out of intestacy). Analytically, one should reverse the process.

☞ First, check for nonprobate property: If there is any nonprobate property, it will pass to the transferees properly identified in the nonprobate instrument.

☞ Whatever fails to qualify as nonprobate property is probate property. Who takes the decedent's probate property depends on whether the decedent died with a valid will. If the decedent died with a valid will that properly disposes of all his or her property, the decedent died testate. The decedent's property will pass to the beneficiaries identified in the will.

☞ If the decedent died without a will (intestate), or with a will that does not properly dispose of all the decedent's property, the property will be distributed pursuant to the jurisdiction's statute of descent and distribution to the decedent's heirs.

### The power to transfer one's property at death

The power to transfer property at death is rarely tested. If tested, it would either be a pure theory question or you would need to see a statute that abrogates an individual's ability to transfer his or her property at death. Raise and address both the public policy considerations and the constitutional considerations.

### The probate process: an overview

The material on probate administration is intended just to give you a sense of the process, some background, and to help you understand the context in which some of these issues arise. If your professor is a stickler for terminology, you need to study the nuances of the different terms. Most professors will not sweat the details of the terminology as long as you understand what is going on and use the modern trend generic terms properly.

The key issues under probate administration typically are (1) the modern requirement of actual notice to ascertainable creditors (but not contingent or conjectural creditors), and (2) the modern trend approach limiting post-death creditors to suing the fiduciary in his or her representative capacity.

### "Dead hand" control

Of the material in the first chapter, this is one of the more tested areas. It can be overlapped with either a devise in a will or a gift in trust—though probably more often it will be attached to a gift in trust.

☞ If you see a conditional gift, remember the general rule—conditional gifts are valid, unless the condition falls within one of the well-recognized exceptions. If the conditional gift does not fall squarely within one of the exceptions, argue by analogy to the closest exception. Focus on the nature of the beneficiary's affected right and the degree of unreasonableness caused by the requirements of the condition.

### Estate planning

The material on estate planning is just to give you some appreciation for what an estate planning attorney should take into consideration when meeting with a client and advising him or her. The material in this section is rarely tested directly.

### Professional responsibility

The professional responsibility material presented in this section is critical. It is often a latent issue on a traditional fact pattern type exam. As you will see repeatedly throughout the book, if an attorney fails to comply with a wills and/or trusts rule (an issue that will be raised directly by the fact pattern), the latent follow-up issue is whether the party adversely affected by the attorney's conduct can sue the attorney for malpractice. You want to keep that issue in the back of your mind as you move through the facts on an exam. If you conclude that a will has not been properly executed, that it was not properly revoked, or that a will or trust was not drafted properly, consider whether the party adversely affected by the outcome can sue the attorney for malpractice.

☞ If a malpractice claim can be brought, the key is which approach the jurisdiction follows. If the fact pattern does not tell you, analyze in the alternative. State and apply the common law first, then the modern trend.

CHAPTER 2

# INTESTACY: THE DEFAULT DISTRIBUTION SCHEME

## *ChapterScope*

This chapter examines the default distribution scheme—intestacy. If a decedent fails to dispose of all his or her property through nonprobate instruments or a will, the decedent's property will pass pursuant to the state's descent and distribution statute to the decedent's heirs. In particular, the chapter examines:

- **A typical intestate distribution scheme:** Although the details vary from state to state, the basic order of *who takes* is fairly similar: (1) surviving spouse; (2) issue; (3) parents; (4) issue of parents; (5) grandparents/issue of grandparents; (6) next-of-kin; (7) escheats to the state. *How much* each takes is where the differences typically arise from state to state.

- **Surviving spouse:** To qualify as a surviving spouse, the couple must have gone through a valid marriage ceremony (or at least what one of them believes is a valid ceremony).

- **Surviving spouse's share:** The surviving spouse's share varies greatly from jurisdiction to jurisdiction and depends in part on whether the decedent was survived by other family members (focusing primarily on the decedent's issue, parents, and issue of parents).

- **Calculating shares to issue:** The jurisdictions are split over what it means to divide the decedent's property equally among the decedent's issue when the issue are not equally related to the decedent. Depending on the jurisdiction, the property can be divided *per capita, per stirpes*, or *per capita at each generation*.

- **Qualifying as an issue:** Establishing a parent-child relationship means each can inherit from and through the other. Such a relationship can be established (1) *naturally*, whether the parents are married or not; (2) *by adoption*, which severs the relationship with the natural parents as a general rule; or (3) through *equitable adoption*, where the adoptive parent agrees to adopt, but fails to complete the adoption, yet the child has a claim against the adoptive parent's estate equal to his or her intestate share.

- **Advancements:** At common law, inter vivos gifts to a child were irrebuttably presumed to count against the child's share of the parent's estate. Under the modern trend, inter vivos gifts do not count against an heir's share of the decedent's estate absent a contemporaneous writing by the donor expressing such intent or a writing by the donee acknowledging such intent.

- **Survival requirement:** At common law, to qualify as a taker one had to prove by a preponderance of the evidence that he or she survived the decedent. Under the modern trend, some jurisdictions require the taker to prove by clear and convincing evidence that he or she survived the decedent, while other jurisdictions require the taker to prove by clear and convincing evidence that he or she survived the decedent by 120 hours.

- **Bars to taking:** Even where an individual is otherwise entitled to take from the decedent (nonprobate or probate, testate or intestate property), the taker will be barred from taking under (1) the homicide doctrine (if the taker killed the decedent, and the killing was felonious and

ntentional, the killer is treated as if he or she predeceased the decedent), or (2) if the taker
lisclaims his or her interest (treat the party who disclaimed as if he or she predeceased the
decedent).

# I. THE INTESTATE DISTRIBUTION SCHEME

## A. Introduction

    **1. Intestacy the norm:** Despite the benefits of nonprobate transfers and wills, the majority of
people die intestate. Any property not disposed of by nonprobate means falls to probate, and
any probate property not disposed of by will falls to intestacy.

    **2. Descent and distribution statute:** Under intestacy, a decedent's personal property is dis-
tributed according to the descent and distribution statute of the state where the decedent was
domiciled at the time of death. The decedent's real property is distributed according to the
descent and distribution statute of the state where the real property is located.

## B. A typical intestate distribution scheme: 
The basic structure of most descent and distribution
statutes is the same in that it is *family centered*. The statute will provide a list, in order, of *who
takes* in the event an individual dies intestate, and *how much* each individual is entitled to take.
A typical intestate distribution scheme is as follows:

| <u>Who takes?</u> | <u>How much?</u> |
|---|---|
| 1. Surviving spouse | 100% if no surviving issue, parents, or issue of parents; or |
| | 50% if 1 child, or issue of one deceased child, or no child |
| |     but parents or issue of parents; or |
| | 33% if >1 child (alive or deceased with issue). |

Any property not passing to a surviving spouse passes as follows:

| | |
|---|---|
| 2. Issue | Equally |
| 3. Parents | Equally |
| 4. Issue of parents | Equally |
| 5. Grandparents | Equally |
| 6. Issue of grandparents | Equally |
| 7. Next-of-kin | By degree of relationship |
| 8. Escheat to the state | 100% |

    **1. Tiered approach:** The categories of possible takers are listed in order, in tiers. Any property
not passing to the surviving spouse falls to the first tier where there is a live taker. Once that
tier is determined, all the property that the surviving spouse did not take is distributed at that
tier. No property falls to a lower tier.

        **a. Example:** Pete dies intestate survived by his wife, Gerri, his four children, and his mom.
Under the typical intestate distribution scheme, his wife Gerri would take 33 percent of his
property, and the rest would be distributed equally among his four children. His mom
would not receive any property.

**b. Example:** Ann dies intestate survived by her children and her grandmother. Under the typical intestate distribution scheme, her property would be distributed among her children. Her grandmother would not receive any property.

2. **State variations:** While the basic "order of takers" is the same in most states, even at the macro level some states differ. For example, California permits the issue of a predeceased spouse to take before grandparents. Moreover, at the micro level, there are a plethora of minute details upon which different jurisdictions disagree.

3. **Community property:** The intestate distribution scheme above presumes that the jurisdiction does not recognize community property. (Community property jurisdictions presume that all property acquired during marriage is community property, but property acquired before marriage and gifts, inheritance, and devises acquired during marriage by either spouse are that spouse's separate property. See Ch. 3, V.) Under community property, upon the first spouse's death the community property is immediately divided 50 percent to the surviving spouse outright, and 50 percent to the deceased spouse. The deceased spouse's 50 percent goes into probate where he or she may devise it as he or she wishes. If, however, the deceased spouse dies intestate, typically all of the deceased spouse's half of the community property goes to the surviving spouse. The deceased spouse's separate property is distributed pursuant to an intestate scheme similar to that set forth above.

4. **Coverage note:** Because individual treatment of each state's intestate scheme is beyond the scope of this outline, the material will focus on the key components of the typical scheme and of the Uniform Probate Code. Students need to pay close attention to whether their professor requires them to be responsible only for the Uniform Probate Code, the probate code of the state where the law school is located, or some combination thereof.

C. **The UPC approach:** The Uniform Probate Code intestate distribution scheme, UPC §§2-102 through 2-105, has fewer tiers of takers and a different method of calculating their respective shares:

| Who takes? | How much? |
|---|---|
| 1. Surviving spouse | 100% if no issue or parents; or |
| | 100% if all decedent's issue are also issue of surviving spouse and surviving spouse has no other issue; or |
| | $200,000 + 75% of rest if no issue but surviving parent; or |
| | $150,000 + 50% of rest if all issue are also issue of surviving spouse and surviving spouse has other issue; or |
| | $100,000 + 50% of rest if one or more issue is not issue of surviving spouse. |

Any property not passing to a surviving spouse passes as follows:

| | |
|---|---|
| 2. Issue | Equally |
| 3. Parents | Equally |
| 4. Issue of parents | Equally |
| 5. Grandparents/issue | 50% to paternal grandparents or survivor; otherwise to their issue equally; |

                50% to maternal grandparents or survivor; otherwise to their
                  issue equally;
                If no surviving grandparents or issue on one side, all to the
                  other side.

6. Escheat to the state    100%

1. **UPC favors surviving spouse:** Compared to most state intestate schemes, the UPC gives the surviving spouse a larger share of the deceased spouse's intestate estate.

2. **UPC favors state:** Note the different philosophies about the propriety of the decedent's property going to the state. Under the UPC, the decedent's property escheats to the state much sooner than it would under most state statutes.

## II. SURVIVING SPOUSE: WHO QUALIFIES

**A. Marriage requirement:** The term *spouse* as used in descent and distribution statutes assumes that the couple has gone through a valid marriage ceremony.

**B. Cohabitants:** Nonmarried couples that live together generally do not qualify as spouses and have no inheritance rights upon the death of one.

    **1. Common law marriage:** Common law marriage doctrines generally provide that if a couple lives together for the requisite period of time and holds themselves out as a married couple, the couple will be treated as a married couple even though they fail to go through a valid marriage ceremony. If cohabitants meet the requirements for common law marriage, they will have the inheritance rights of a married couple. Not all jurisdictions recognize common law marriages.

    **2. Same-sex couples:** In a few states, same-sex couples may register with the state as "reciprocal beneficiaries" or "domestic partners" and then receive inheritance and elective share rights similar to those of a spouse. Where permitted, such rights vary greatly from state to state.

**C. Putative spouses:** Putative spouses generally do qualify as spouses. Putative spouses exist where the couple goes through what at least one of them believes is a valid marriage ceremony, but for some reason the marriage is either void or voidable (e.g., one spouse is already married and not divorced; the marriage ceremony is not valid; the marriage violates the state's degree of relationship requirements). As long as one of the parties reasonably believes in good faith that the marriage is valid, the spouses qualify as putative spouses and will be treated as spouses for purposes of most intestate schemes.

**D. Married but separated:** Spouses who are legally separated generally still qualify as spouses for purposes of the intestate distribution scheme. Even if the parties have filed for divorce, the parties remain legally married until the court enters the final judgment or decree of dissolution of marriage.

**Example:** In *Estate of Goick*, 909 P.2d 1165 (Mont. 1996), Michael and Barbara Goick filed for divorce. At the April 25, 1991, hearing in the proceedings, the parties agreed to all issues except the division of household goods, which the parties were to settle within two weeks. The parties then presented sufficient evidence to support a decree of divorce. After the hearing, the judge told the parties they were divorced. The parties, however, failed to reach an agreement on the dissolution of the household goods. No further proceedings occurred and no final decree or order was issued. On November 30, 1992, Michael died, and two days later Barbara moved to dismiss the divorce proceedings, which the court granted the next day. Because no final divorce decree or order was issued, Barbara qualified as Michael's surviving spouse for intestate succession purposes.

**E. Spousal abandonment:** In some states, if one spouse abandons the other, the abandoning spouse may be disqualified from inheriting from the other spouse.

# III. SURVIVING SPOUSE: CALCULATING SHARE

**A. Policy concerns:** How much the surviving spouse takes turns on the details of each state's descent and distribution scheme. The key policy issue is how much the surviving spouse *should* take. In particular, (1) should the surviving spouse take *all* of the deceased spouse's intestate property if there are surviving issue; and (2) should the surviving spouse take *all* of the deceased spouse's intestate property if there are surviving parents or issue of parents (siblings and their issue)?

**B. Traditional intestate distribution scheme:** Under the traditional intestate distribution scheme, a surviving spouse took 100 percent of the deceased spouse's intestate property only if there were no surviving issue, parent, or issue of parents.

**If surviving issue:** If the predeceased spouse had surviving issue, the surviving spouse's share often depended on how many surviving "children" (alive or dead but survived by issue) survived the decedent.

1. **If one surviving child:** If the deceased spouse is survived by one child (alive or dead but survived by issue), typically the surviving spouse takes 50 percent of the predeceased spouse's intestate property.

2. **If more than one surviving child:** If the deceased spouse is survived by more than one child (alive or dead but survived by issue), typically the surviving spouse takes 33 percent of the predeceased spouse's intestate property.

3. **If surviving parent(s) or issue of parent(s):** If the predeceased spouse has no surviving issue, but has surviving parent(s) or issue of parent(s), typically the surviving spouse takes 50 percent of the deceased spouse's intestate property.

4. **Small estates:** Some states give the surviving spouse the first $50,000 or $100,000 of the deceased spouse's intestate estate and then the appropriate fraction of the rest of the deceased spouse's probate intestate estate. The effect is to give the surviving spouse all of the deceased spouse's intestate estate where the estate is small enough.

**C. UPC approach:** A surviving spouse is better off under the UPC than under the typical intestate distribution scheme. UPC §2-102.

**If surviving issue:** Unlike most state statutes, the Uniform Probate Code gives the surviving spouse 100 percent of the decedent's property, even if the decedent has surviving issue, if (1) the surviving spouse is also the parent of the surviving issue, and (2) the surviving spouse has no other issue. UPC §2-102(1)(ii).

1. **Rationale:** The assumption is that most spouses trust the surviving spouse to determine how best to use the property for the benefit of the surviving issue, as opposed to giving the surviving issue their own share outright (and incurring the administrative hassles and expenses if any of them are minors).

2. **Whose surviving issue:** The surviving spouse will take less than 100 percent of the deceased spouse's intestate property if the deceased spouse has surviving issue and either (1) not all of them are also issue of the surviving spouse, or (2) all are issue of the surviving spouse, but the surviving spouse also has issue of his or her own who were not issue of the predeceased spouse.

   a. **Not all issue are issue of surviving spouse:** Where the deceased spouse has surviving issue, but not all of them are also issue of the surviving spouse, the surviving spouse takes the first $100,000 + 50 percent of the rest of the predeceased spouse's intestate property. The remaining 50 percent is distributed equally among the deceased spouse's issue. UPC §2-102(4).

   b. **Surviving spouse has own issue:** Where the deceased spouse has surviving issue, and all of them are issue of the surviving spouse, but the surviving spouse has issue of his or her own who were not issue of the predeceased spouse, the surviving spouse takes the first $150,000 + 50 percent of the rest of the predeceased spouse's intestate property. The remaining 50 percent is distributed among the deceased spouse's issue. UPC §2-104(3).

   c. **Stepparent syndrome:** The UPC is more concerned about the surviving spouse properly taking care of the deceased spouse's issue where not all of the deceased spouse's issue are issue of the surviving spouse. In that case, the surviving spouse takes less and the issue take more. The potential for the dreaded "Cinderella/evil stepparent" syndrome arguably is present where not all of the predeceased spouse's issue are issue of the surviving spouse.

3. **No issue but surviving parent(s):** Where the deceased spouse has no issue but is survived by one or more parents, the UPC gives the surviving spouse the first $200,000 + 75 percent of the rest of the deceased spouse's property. UPC §2-102(2). Surviving parents are worse off under the UPC than under a typical state statute.

4. **No surviving issue or parent(s), but surviving issue of parents:** Most states give the surviving spouse 100 percent of the deceased spouse's property only if there are no surviving issue, parents, *or issue of parents.* The UPC gives the surviving spouse 100 percent of the deceased spouse's property if there are no surviving issue or parents. The UPC does not consider issue of parents when determining the surviving spouse's share. UPC §2-102(1)(i).

5. **Tiered approach to takers:** Just like with the typical intestate distribution scheme, any property not passing to a surviving spouse falls to the first tier where there is a live taker, and all the falling property is distributed at that tier.

D. **State's spousal share:** Each state's intestate distribution statute must be read with great care to determine (1) the different possible *fractional shares* of the surviving spouse, and (2) *what determines* which fractional share the surviving spouse receives.

# IV. DESCENDANTS/ISSUE: CALCULATING SHARES

**A. Property to descendants/issue:** If there is no surviving spouse, or there is a surviving spouse but he or she does not take all the decedent's property, both the typical intestate scheme and the UPC give the property to the decedent's descendants/issue equally.

**Descendants/Issue vs. children:** The terms *descendants* and *issue* are synonymous, and the terms are broader than the term *children*. One's ***descendants/issue*** are *all* of one's offspring—one's children, and their children, and their children, and so on. One's ***children*** are only the first generation of one's issue. Different intestate distribution statutes use either the term *descendants* or *issue*. We will use the term *issue* in this material. You should use the term used in the probate code you are studying and/or the term used by your professor.

**B. Calculating shares—analytical steps:** If a decedent's issue take under intestacy, they take equally. But this statement is overly simplistic and masks a number of subtle issues.

1. **Taking equally:** Where all of the decedent's children survive the decedent, what constitutes taking "equally" is rather straightforward. For example, suppose the decedent dies survived by three children, *A*, *B*, and *C*:

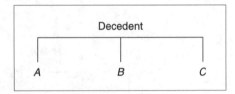

The decedent's property should be divided equally among his or her three children, one-third each. The question becomes more complicated if one or more of the children have issue of their own:

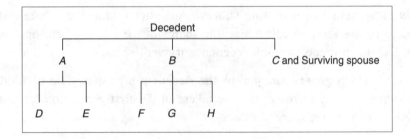

2. **Determining which issue take:** There are three fundamental principles that need to be kept in mind when distributing property to a decedent's issue.

   ■ **Issue of predeceased children take in their place:** If the decedent had a child who predeceased the decedent but is survived by issue, the issue will share in the distribution of the decedent's property. It is often said that the surviving issue of the predeceased child take "by representation"—they step up and represent the predeceased relative. In the example above, if *A* predeceased the decedent, *A*'s issue who survive the decedent would take *A*'s share by representation. *A*'s one-third would be split equally by *A*'s issue.

- **If a person takes, his or her issue do not:** In the example above, if *B* survives the decedent, *B* would receive a share but *B*'s issue (*F*, *G*, and *H*) would not receive a share of the decedent's estate.

- **Absent adoption, only blood relatives qualify as heirs.** If *C* predeceases the decedent, survived by his wife and *her* children from a prior marriage, neither *C*'s surviving wife nor her issue from the prior relationship are entitled to share in the distribution of the decedent's ***intestate*** property. As a general rule, sons-in-law, daughters-in-law, and stepchildren do not qualify as eligible takers under the intestate distribution scheme.

3. **Taking equally where issue of unequal degree:** It is easy to calculate equal shares when all the surviving issue are of equal degree of relationship to the decedent. It is more difficult to determine what constitutes "equal shares" when the issue are of unequal degree. There are three different approaches to how to calculate the shares when the surviving issue are of unequal degree. To understand the three approaches, it is necessary to understand the sub-issues inherent in the problem. For example:

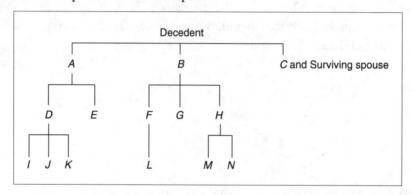

Assume *A*, *B*, *C*, *D*, *F*, and *G* predecease the decedent (you might want to draw a line through those who predeceased the decedent), who dies intestate. Assuming no surviving spouse, the issue is who takes the decedent's property.

4. **Analytical steps in calculating shares:** Analytically, there are three distinct subissues that need to be answered in calculating the shares of the takers where one or more of the decedent's children predecease the decedent survived by issue.

**First, at which generation should the decedent's property be divided first:** At the first generation, even if there are no live takers in the first generation, or at the first generation where there is a live taker?

**Second, at whichever generation the estate is divided first, how many shares should the estate be divided into?** The answer to this step is always the same: one share for each descendant who is alive at that generation, and one share for each descendant at that generation who is dead but survived by issue.

**Third, how are the "dropping" shares distributed?** The "dropping shares" are the shares for the descendants who are dead but survived by issue. Should the dropping shares drop by bloodline to the issue of that party, or should the dropping shares be "pooled" and distributed equally among the eligible takers at the next generation?

Although the answer to the second step is always the same, there are different possible answers to the first and third steps. Three different doctrines have developed that correspond to three of the different possible combinations of possible answers to the different steps: the *per stirpes* approach; the *per capita with representation* approach; and the *per capita at each generation* approach.

5. **Distributions to issue of collaterals:** Where a decedent's property is distributed to the issue of collateral relatives (see section IV below), the per stirpes, per capita, and per capita at each generation doctrines apply as well in calculating the shares.

C. **Per stirpes:** Under the per stirpes approach (also known as the "strict" per stirpes approach and/ or the old English approach), *always* make the first division of the decedent's property at the first generation of descendants, whether there are any live takers or not, and the dropping shares drop by bloodline.

**Mechanics of the per stirpes approach:**

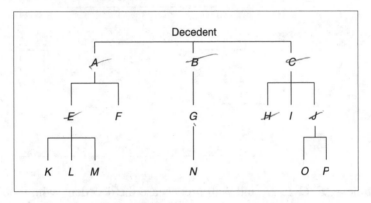

**Assume *A*, *B*, *C*, *E*, *H*, and *J* all predecease the decedent, who then dies intestate. Who takes the decedent's property assuming no surviving spouse?**

- Step 1: Under per stirpes, always divide the decedent's property at the first generation (among decedent's children), even if everyone at that generation is dead.

- Step 2: One share for each party who is alive, one share for each party who is dead but survived by issue. Here, although *A*, *B*, and *C* are all dead, *A*, *B*, and *C* are all survived by issue, so each receives a one-third share.

- Step 3: Under per stirpes, the shares for each party who is dead but survived by issue drop by bloodline. Each share drops only to the issue of the predeceased party. *A*'s one-third will drop to his or her issue; *B*'s one-third will drop to his or her issue; and *C*'s one-third will drop to his or her issue.

When distributing *A*'s one-third, drop to the next generation of *A*'s descendants and divide it one share for each party who is alive at that level, and one share for each party who is dead but survived by issue. *A*'s one-third will be divided equally between *E* and *F*, one-sixth each, and *E*'s one-sixth will drop by bloodline to *E*'s issue, *K*, *L*, and *M*, to be shared equally, one-eighteenth each.

*B*'s one-third will drop by bloodline to *B*'s issue, *G*. Because *G* is alive and takes, *N* takes nothing.

*C*'s one-third will drop by bloodline to *C*'s descendants. Dividing up *C*'s share at the next generation, the formula is one share for each party who is alive, one share for each party who is dead but survived by issue. *H* predeceased *C* and is not survived by issue, so *H* does not take a share. *I* is alive, so *I* takes a share. *J* is dead but survived by issue, so *J* takes a share. *C*'s one-third will be split one-sixth to *I*, one-sixth to *J*. *J*'s one-sixth will drop by bloodline to *O* and *P*, one-twelth each.

**D. Per capita with representation/modern per stirpes:** Under the per capita with representation approach (also known as the per capita approach, or the modern per stirpes approach—though the latter name is more confusing), make the first division of the decedent's property at the first generation where there is a live taker, and the dropping shares drop by bloodline.

**1. Mechanics of the per capita with representation/modern per stirpes approach:**

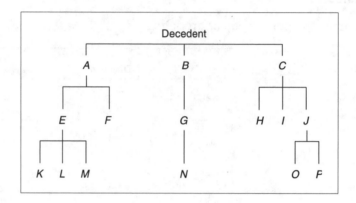

Assume *A, B, C, E, H,* and *J* all predecease the decedent, who then dies intestate. Who takes the decedent's property assuming no surviving spouse?

- Step 1: At which generation should the decedent's property be divided first? Under per capita with representation, always divide at the first generation where there is a live taker. Here, divide at the second generation, *E*'s generation.

- Step 2: How many shares should the property be divided into? One share for each party who is alive, one share for each party who is dead but survived by issue. Here, *F*, *G*, and *I* are alive (three shares), and *E* and *J* are dead but survived by issue (two shares), so one-fifth each (no share for *H*).

- Step 3: How are the dropping shares (the shares for the dead parties survived by issue) distributed? Under per capita with representation, they drop by bloodline.

  *E*'s one-fifth will drop by bloodline to *E*'s issue, *K, L,* and *M*, to be shared equally, one-fifteenth each. *J*'s one-fifth will drop by bloodline to *O* and *P*, one-tenth each.

**2. Criticism:** Under both per stirpes and per capita with representation, there is the potential for descendants of equal degree to the decedent to take unequally.

Here, under the per stirpes approach, although *K, L, M, O,* and *P* are all the decedent's grandchildren, and thus equally related to the decedent, they take unequally. *K, L,* and *M* took one-eighteenth, and *O* and *P* took one-twelfth each. Under the per capita with representation approach, although *K, L, M, O,* and *P* are all greatgrandchildren of the decedent, and thus related to the decedent by the third degree, they take unequally. *K, L,* and *M* took one-fifteenth each, while *O* and *P* took one-tenth each.

**3. Benefit of per capita at each generation:** The per capita at each generation approach (next) ensures that all descendants who are equally related to the decedent take equally. Per capita at each generation pools the dropping shares (the shares for descendants who are dead but survived by issue). The pooling terminology is just an artificial way of saying that the dropping shares are added together and then divided equally among all the eligible takers at the next generation.

**E. Per capita at each generation approach:** Under the per capita at each generation approach, always make the first division of the decedent's property at the first generation where there is a live taker, and the dropping shares drop by pooling—combine them and distribute them equally among the eligible takers at the next generation.

**Mechanics of the per capita at each generation approach:**

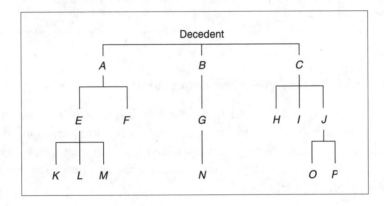

**Assume *A*, *B*, *C*, *E*, *H*, and *J* all predecease the decedent, who then dies intestate. Who takes the decedent's property assuming no surviving spouse?**

- Step 1: At which generation should the decedent's property be divided first? Under per capita at each generation, always divide at the first generation where there is a live taker. Here, divide at the second generation, *E*'s generation.

- Step 2: How many shares should the property be divided into? One share for each party who is alive, one share for each party who is dead but survived by issue. Here, *F*, *G*, and *I* are alive (three shares), and *E* and *J* are dead but survived by issue (two shares), so one-fifth each (no share for *H*).

- Step 3: How are the dropping shares (the shares for the dead parties survived by issue) distributed? Under per capita at each generation, pool the dropping shares. There are two dropping shares. Add them together (*E*'s one-fifth + *J*'s one-fifth = two-fifths) and divide the total equally among the eligible takers at the next generation. *K*, *L*, *M*, *O*, and *P* are the eligible takers at the next generation (N is not eligible because her parent took already).

- Dividing the pool (two-fifths) among the eligible takers (two-fifths divided by 5) results in *K*, *L*, *M*, *O*, and *P* each taking two-twenty-fifths. Under the per capita at each generation approach, all descendants at a generation who take will take equally.

## Summary of Distribution to Issue

| | **Per Stirpes** | **Per Capita with Representation** | **Per Capita at Each Generation** |
|---|---|---|---|
| **Where is the estate divided first?** | First generation always | First generation live taker | First generation live taker |
| **How many shares is the estate divided into at that generation?** | One share each party alive; one share each party dead but survived by issue | One share each party alive; one share each party dead but survived by issue | One share each party alive; one share each party dead but survived by issue |
| **How to treat dropping shares?** | Drop by bloodline | Drop by bloodline | Drop by pooling |

### F. Miscellaneous rules concerning shares to issue

1. **Power to opt out:** Each jurisdiction has a default approach as to how to distribute a decedent's property among his or her issue. The default approach will always apply to intestate distributions. But an individual can opt out of a jurisdiction's default approach by executing a valid will or nonprobate instrument that expressly provides for an alternative method of distributing the decedent's estate.

2. **UPC approach:** The original version of the UPC (the 1969 version) adopted the per capita with representation approach. The revised version of the UPC has adopted the per capita at each generation approach. UPC §2-106. Most jurisdictions, however, are split between the per stirpes and the per capita with representation approaches.

3. **Disinheriting one's heirs:** Assuming one does not want a particular heir to take any of his or her intestate property, what must one do to disinherit that particular heir?

   a. **Common law:** The only way a decedent could disinherit an heir was to execute a valid will that disposed of all the decedent's property so that nothing passed through intestacy (thereby depriving the heir of any chance of taking). If the decedent's will expresses an intent to disinherit the heir, but some or all the decedent's property is distributed through intestacy and the heir in question qualifies to receive a share, the heir would take despite the decedent's clear intent.

   b. **Modern trend/UPC:** Under the modern trend/UPC approach, a decedent can disinherit an heir by properly executing a will that expresses such an intent, even if some or all the decedent's property passes through intestacy and the heir otherwise would have qualified to take some of the property. The heir is treated as if he or she predeceased the decedent. (If the disinherited heir is survived by issue, the issue will take by representation unless the will expressly disinherits them as well.) UPC §2-101(b).

# V. SHARES OF ANCESTORS AND REMOTE COLLATERALS

**A. Introduction:** Each person sits in the middle of a family tree. An individual may have his or her own family (spouse, issue), while at the same time be part of a number of other families (child of parents, grandchild of grandparents, etc.). When a decedent dies intestate, his or her property is distributed first to his or her immediate family. If, however, there is no surviving spouse or issue, the property will flow "up" to the decedent's ancestors and collateral relatives. There are three different major approaches to how the decedent's property should be distributed when it flows up to ancestors and remote collaterals: (1) the parentelic approach; (2) the degree of relationship approach; and (3) the degree of relationship with a parentelic tiebreaker approach.

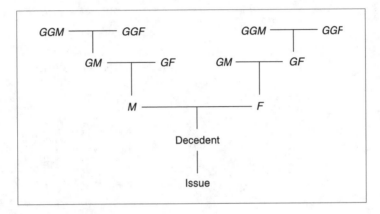

**Collateral relatives:** The decedent, the decedent's spouse, and the decedent's issue are the decedent's immediate family. The decedent's other relatives are called his "collateral relatives." The decedent's parents (M for mother and F for father) and their other issue are called first-line collaterals, because their line is the first line removed from the decedent's immediate family. The decedent's grandparents (GM and GF) and their issue (other than the decedent's parents) are called second-line collaterals. Great-grandparents (GGM and GGF) and their issue (other than the decedent's grandparents) are called third-line collaterals, and so on. (Technically, the head of each parentelic line constitute the "ancestors," and the other relatives in the collateral line are "collateral relatives" of the decedent.)

**B. Parentelic approach:** Every intestate scheme starts with the decedent's immediate family and then moves out along collateral lines, starting with the closer lines and moving to the more remote. This is known as the parentelic approach. This approach keeps going out by collateral lines until the probate court finds a line in which there is a live taker. The property is then distributed to the decedent's relatives in that parentelic line. In distributing the property, the per stirpes, per capita, or per capita at each generation doctrines will apply, depending on the default approach in the state.

**C. Degree of relationship approach:** The degree of relationship approach focuses on the degree of relationship between the decedent and claiming relative, regardless of which parentelic line the taker is in. Under the degree of relationship approach, one simply counts the degrees of relationship between the decedent and the relative, and those relatives of the closest degree (lower degree) take to the exclusion of those of a more remote degree (higher degree). Some jurisdictions start with the parentelic approach but at some point (either after the first collateral line or the second collateral line) switch to the degree of relationship approach.

1. **Determining degree:** To determine a person's degree of relationship, count from the decedent up to the closest common ancestor (the head of a parentelic line—a grandparent or great-grandparent, or so on), and then down to the live relative.

2. **Example:** Assume the decedent dies intestate survived by only A, B, C, and D.

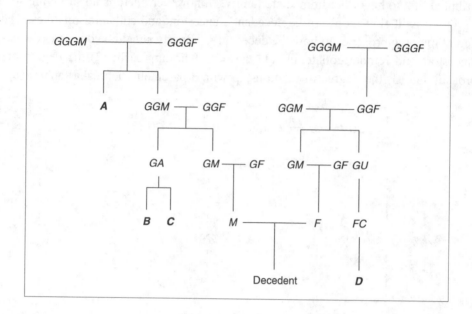

To calculate the degree of relationship between A, B, C, and D to the decedent, the key is to identify the closest common ancestor (the closest grandparent) that both parties share. Count the steps up from the decedent to that common ancestor and then down from the common ancestor to the party in question.

**Degree of relationship for A:** The closest common ancestor for both the decedent and A are the GGGPs. A is related to the decedent by the fifth degree.

**Degree of relationship for B:** The closest common ancestor for both the decedent and B is the GGPs. B is related to the decedent by the fifth degree.

**Degree of relationship for C:** The closest common ancestor for both the decedent and C are the GGPs. C is related to the decedent by the fifth degree.

**Degree of relationship for D:** The closest common ancestor for both the decedent and D are the GGPs. D is related to the decedent by the sixth degree.

**Degree of relationship approach:** Under the degree of relationship approach, those relatives of a closer degree take to the exclusion of those of a more remote degree. Here, A, B, and C are of the fifth degree, D is of the sixth degree. A, B, and C would take to the exclusion of D. A, B, and C would split the estate equally.

**Parentelic approach:** Under the parentelic approach, one simply keeps going out by parentelic lines until one finds the first collateral line with a live taker. The property is then distributed to the takers in that line. Here, there are no live takers in the parents' line or the grandparents' line, but there are live takers in the great-grandparents' lines (the third-line collaterals). Under the parentelic approach, once a collateral line with a live taker is found, the property is distributed in that line. Here, the property would go to the issue of the great-grandparents, *B, C,* and *D*.

(How much *B, C,* and *D* would take turns on the particulars of the state's intestate distribution scheme. Some jurisdictions split the property 50-50 between the maternal and paternal common ancestors and then distribute to their issue—in that case, *B* and *C* would take 25 percent each, and *D* would take 50 percent. Other jurisdictions would apply the per stirpes/per capita with representation/per capita at each generation default approach and make the first division below the common ancestor tier.)

**D. Degree of relationship with parentelic tiebreaker:** There is a third approach to property passing to collateral relatives—the degree of relationship with a parentelic tiebreaker. As the name indicates, the first step is to determine the degree of relationship of the possible takers. Those of a closer degree take to the exclusion of those of a higher, more remote degree. Then, if there are multiple takers sharing the lowest degree of relationship, under the parentelic tiebreaker, those in the closer parentelic/collateral lines take to the exclusion of those in the more remote parentelic/collateral lines.

**Application:** Analyzing the above fact pattern under the degree of relationship with a parentelic tiebreaker approach, *A, B,* and *C* are of the fifth degree of relationship while *D* is of the sixth degree. *A, B,* and *C* would prevail initially. But, because *B* and *C* are of a closer parentelic line (the *GGPs*' line, *D* is in the *GGGPs*' line), *B* and *C* would take to the exclusion of *A* under the parentelic tiebreaker. *B* and *C* would split the estate 50-50.

**E. Half-bloods:** Half-bloods are relatives who share only one common parent as opposed to the traditional relationship in which siblings share both parents.

**Classic scenario:** *H* and *W* are married with two children, *A* and *B*. *H* either dies or *H* and *W* divorce, and *W* remarries *H2*. *W* and *H2* have a child *C*. *A* and *B* are whole-blooded siblings, and *A* and *B* are half-blooded siblings with *C*.

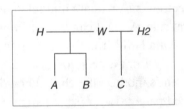

If *H, W,* and *H2* die, and then *A* dies intestate, with no surviving spouse or issue, *A*'s property will pass to his or her siblings. Inasmuch as *B* is a whole-blooded sibling, and *C* is only a half-blooded sibling, the issue is whether *B* should take more than *C*.

1. **Common law:** At common law, only whole-blooded relatives were entitled to inherit. Only *B* would inherit from *A*.

2. **UPC and modern trend majority:** The UPC and the majority of jurisdictions have abolished the old common law rule and treat half-bloods the same as whole-bloods. UPC §2-107. *A*'s intestate estate would be distributed equally between *B* and *C*.

3. **Modern trend minority:** A handful of jurisdictions permit a whole-blooded relative to take more than a half-blood (typically the half-blood takes either half a share, or takes only if there are no full-blooded relatives).

# VI. ISSUE: WHO QUALIFIES

**A. Issue as intestate takers:** The basic intestate distribution scheme gives a decedent's probate property first to his or her surviving spouse, and second to his or her issue/descendants. Often, the decedent's issue receive a share even if there is a surviving spouse. There are several ways one can qualify as an issue.

**Issue as chain of parent-child relationships:** One's issue are all generations of descendants from an individual—children, grandchildren, etc. But a line of descendants is nothing more than a line of parent-child relationships:

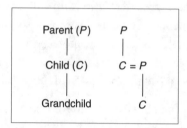

**B. Qualifying as an issue:** To qualify as an issue, a party must establish a parent-child relationship.

**C. Establishing parent-child relationship:** The starting point for analyzing whether a parent-child relationship exists is to apply the traditional, biological test. The woman who contributes the egg *and* gives birth to the child is the child's natural mother. The man who contributes the sperm is the natural father.

1. **Parents married:** Both at common law and under the modern trend, if a child is born and the natural parents were married, a parent-child relationship arises for inheritance purposes.

2. **Inheriting "from and through":** A parent-child relationship establishes inheritance rights in both directions as a general rule. A child can inherit *from* a parent if the parent dies intestate, and a parent can inherit *from* a child if the child dies intestate. Moreover, as a general rule, inheritance rights are not only from a person, but also *through* a person. If a child's parent dies, and thereafter the parent's mother (the child's grandmother) dies intestate, the child can inherit *through* the deceased parent. Likewise, a parent can inherit not only from a child, but also *through* a predeceased child under the appropriate circumstances. When discussing inheritance rights, the general rule is that a person can inherit from and through the other party.

   a. **Presumption:** A child born to a married couple is presumed to be the child of that couple. The wife is presumed to be the natural mother. The husband is presumed to be the natural father. As a general rule, the child can inherit from and through either natural parent (*NP*), and either natural parent can inherit from and through the child (*C*).

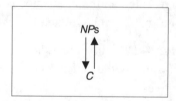

**b. UPC approach:** A handful of jurisdictions and the UPC require the natural parent (or, in some jurisdictions, the relatives of the natural parent) to openly treat the child as his or her own and not to refuse to support the child before that parent or relatives of that parent can inherit from and through the child, *even if the natural parents are married.* UPC §2-114(c).

**c. Posthumously born child:** A posthumously born child is a child conceived while the natural father is alive, but born after he dies. *If the couple was married,* the posthumously born child doctrine applies. It is an offshoot of the presumption that a child born to a married couple is a child of that couple. As long as the wife gives birth to a child within 280 days of a husband's death, a rebuttable presumption arises that the child is a natural child of the predeceased husband. If the child is born more than 280 days after the husband's death, the burden is on the child to establish that he or she is a child of the predeceased husband. (The Uniform Parentage Act §4 provides that any child born to a woman within 300 days of her husband's death is presumed to be a child of that husband.)

**D. Adoption:** The jurisdictions are split as to what effect, if any, adoption has on (1) a child's right to inherit from his or her natural parents, and (2) a child's right to inherit from his or her adopting parents. Pay careful attention to the statute you are covering. The focus here will be on the UPC approach, which is the general approach.

**1. General rule:** If a child is adopted, the general rule is that the adopting parents step into the shoes of the natural parents and a parent-child relationship is established between the adopted child and the adopting parents. Moreover, adoption severs the parent-child relationship between the natural parents and the child. The child (*C*) can no longer inherit from and through the natural parents (*NP*), and the natural parents can no longer inherit from and through the child. Instead, the child inherits from and through the adopting parents (*AP*), and the adopting parents inherit from and through the child. UPC §2-114(b).

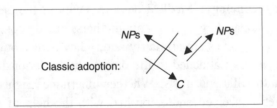

**2. Example:** In *In re Estates of Donnelly*, 502 P.2d 1163 (Wash. 1972), after Jean Louise's father died, her mother remarried and the stepfather adopted Jean Louise. Thereafter, Jean Louise's natural father's father died and his property passed via intestacy. The Washington statute expressly prfovided that an adopted child shall not be considered an "heir" of his natural parents, but it made no reference to the child's natural grandparents. The court construed the statute as adopting the general rule that adoption severs the right of the adopted child to inherit from or through the natural parents. Jean Louise could not inherit from her natural parental grandfather.

**3. Stepparent adoption exception:** A number of jurisdictions, including the UPC, modify the general rule concerning adoption when the adoption is by a stepparent (a spouse of a natural parent): (1) the adoption does not affect the parent-child relationship (and the inheritance rights) between the adopted child and the natural parent who is married to the adopting stepparent; (2) the adoption establishes a parent-child relationship between the adopting stepparent and the child, with full inheritance rights in both directions; and (3) the adoption does *not* completely sever the parent-child relationship with the natural parent of the same gender as the adopting stepparent. The natural parent loses his or her right to inherit from and through the child, but the child retains the right to inherit from and through the natural parent of the same gender as the adopting stepparent. UPC §2-114(b).

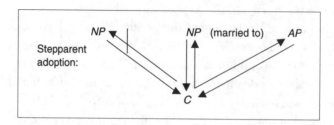

a. **Rationale:** While at first blush the rule may appear unfair to the natural parent of the same gender as the adopting parent, under family law, as a general rule, a natural parent must consent to his or her child being adopted if the child is a minor (the typical situation). A natural parent's consenting to the stepparent adopting his or her child is tantamount to the natural parent waiving his or her right to inherit from and through the child. The child, on the other hand, has no say in the adoption if he or she is a minor. Accordingly, the child's ability to inherit from and through the natural parent should not be affected.

b. **Example:** In *Estate of Donnelly,* above, if the state had adopted the stepparent adoption exception, because the adoption was by Jean Louise's stepfather, she still would have been able inherit *through* her natural father from his side of the family—she would have inherited from her paternal grandfather's estate.

### E. Nontraditional parent-child relationships

1. **Reproductive technology:** Medical advancements in the area of reproductive possibilities (donated sperm, donated eggs, surrogate mothers) greatly complicate the issue of who legally is the parent. These issues are primarily family law issues, but to the extent inheritance rights traditionally have been attached to the parent-child relationship, the family law issues naturally overlap into wills and trusts. Whether inheritance rights should be altered to take into account children conceived and/or birthed with the help of reproductive technology is unsettled and open for debate.

2. **Same-sex couples:** Where a woman has a child through artificial insemination, and then her lesbian partner adopts the child (if permitted in the jurisdiction), the same-sex couple adoption scenario poses problems. The general adoption rule provides that the adopting parent steps into the shoes of the natural parent of the same gender, and the adoption completely severs the parent-child relationship between the child and the natural parent of the same gender as the adopting parent (no doubt assuming a traditional heterosexual couple). In the same-sex couple scenario, however, the effect is that the adopting partner knocks out the natural mother—not the intended effect. To avoid this outcome, some courts permit the natural mother to adopt along with the adopting lesbian partner, thereby coming back in as an adopting parent.

3. **Adult adoptions:** When one thinks of an adoption, one naturally assumes that the adoptee is a minor child. Adoption is not limited to minors, however. As a general rule, adopted adults are treated the same as adopted children for intestate distribution purposes. (Whether adopted

adults are treated as qualifying issue for purposes of distributions under wills and/or nonprobate instruments is a question of the transferor's intent. See Ch. 11, III.D.)

**F. Equitable adoption:** Equitable adoption applies where the natural parents transfer custody of their child to a couple (or individual) that promises to adopt the child but then fails to complete the proper paperwork to adopt the child legally. The doctrine is based on the equitable maxim that "equity regards as done that which ought to be done." As applied in this scenario, equity will treat the child as a child of the adoptive parent for purposes of distributing the adoptive parent's *intestate* property.

1. **Traditional requirements:** Although the rationale for the doctrine is based in equity, the doctrinal requirements are based in contract. Equitable adoption requires (1) an agreement between the natural parents and the adoptive parents to adopt the child; (2) the natural parents fully perform by giving up custody of the child; (3) the child fully performs by moving in and living with the adoptive parents; (4) the adoptive parents partially perform by taking the child in and raising the child as their own; and (5) the adoptive parent dies intestate.

2. **Child's right to take:** If the requirements of the doctrine are established, the child is entitled to receive his or her intestate share of the adoptive parent's probate estate.

3. **Agreement to adopt:** The agreement to adopt, the first requirement, need not be in writing. It can be either oral or implied.

4. **Theoretical perspective:** There are two ways to view the equitable adoption doctrine. One is that it establishes a parent-child relationship, but one which is different from a legally adopted parent-child relationship. As a general rule, under equitable adoption the child can inherit *from,* but not *through,* the adoptive parent. The adoptive parent cannot inherit from or through the child. Moreover, the doctrine does not affect the child's relationship or inheritance rights with the child's natural parents. If one argues equitable adoption establishes a parent-child relationship, the inheritance rights that accompany it look very little like the inheritance rights that accompany the typical parent-child relationship.

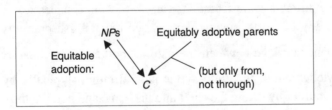

In light of the limitations on the parent-child relationship that arise from the equitable adoption doctrine, one way to think of the doctrine is that it does not establish a parent-child relationship; rather, it merely provides a cause of action for the child against the adoptive parent for breach of contract (the promise to adopt), with damages measured by the intestate share the child would have received if the parent had adopted the child.

5. **Modern trend:** In *O'Neal v. Wilkes*, 439 S.E.2d 490 (Ga. 1994), the court applied equitable adoption in a very technical manner and denied the claim. The court held the first requirement was not satisfied because the aunt who had physical custody of the child and who entered into

the agreement with the adopting parents lacked legal custody and authority to enter into the agreement. The dissent argued (1) that in applying the doctrine, courts should remember its equitable nature and apply it to promote equity; and (2) that the doctrine should apply *anytime the child is led to believe that he or she was adopted*. In **Wheeling Dollar Sav. & Trust Co. v. Hanes**, 250 S.E.2d 499 (W. Va. 1978), the court ruled while the existence of a contract to adopt is very convincing evidence, if a claimant can prove by clear and convincing evidence that his or her status is identical to that of a formally adopted child, except for the absence of a formal adoption, a finding of equitable adoption is proper without proof of a contract to adopt.

**G.  Child born out of wedlock:** The inheritance rights of a child born out of wedlock vary depending upon whether the jurisdiction applies the common law or the modern trend.

**1.  Common law:** At common law, a child born out of wedlock was considered an "illegitimate" child. As such, the child was considered a child of no one. The child could not inherit from or through either natural parent, and neither natural parent could inherit from or through the child.

**2.  Modern trend:** The modern trend repudiates the common law approach, but a child born out of wedlock is still not treated the same as a child born to a married couple. Under the modern trend, a child born out of wedlock automatically has a parent-child relationship with his or her natural mother (assuming no surrogate mother) and can inherit from and through the natural mother. Inheritance from and through the natural father, however, typically requires proof of paternity.

**a.  Paternity issues:** Proving paternity is primarily a family law issue that naturally overlaps with inheritance rights. Without going into all the details of paternity law, the following briefly summarizes the different ways one can establish paternity. Because issues of paternity tend to take the course into family law, professors vary on how far they want to venture into paternity. You should take your cue from your professor's classroom discussion of paternity issues and whether he or she distributes all or parts of the Uniform Parentage Act.

**b.  Establishing paternity:** Jurisdictions vary as to what is necessary to establish paternity. In most states, any of the following can be used to establish paternity:

- Subsequent marriage between the natural mother and the natural father; or

- Acknowledgment of the child by the natural father (typically by writing filed with the clerk of court or by taking the child into his home and holding the child out as his own); or

- Adjudication of paternity during the father's lifetime based on a preponderance of the evidence; or

- Adjudication of paternity after the father's death based on clear and convincing evidence.

**c.  Uniform Parentage Act:** The Uniform Parentage Act automatically establishes a parent-child relationship between the child and the natural mother, with the child being entitled to inherit from and through the natural mother. But the Uniform Parentage Act requires proof of paternity between a child and natural father before the child is entitled to inherit from and through the natural father. Proving paternity turns on whether or not a presumption of paternity arises.

- If a presumption of paternity arises, the child can bring an action to establish paternity (and inheritance rights) at any time.

- If no presumption of paternity arises, the action to establish paternity must be brought within three years of the child reaching the age of majority or it is barred.

- A presumption of paternity arises if the father acknowledges the child by taking the child into his home while the child is a minor and holding the child out as his own; or if the father acknowledges his paternity in writing and files the writing with the appropriate administrative agency or court.

**d. UPC:** With respect to a child born out of wedlock, under the modern trend, a majority of jurisdictions and the Uniform Probate Code require the natural parent (or, in some jurisdictions, the relatives of the natural parent) to openly treat the child as his or her own and not to refuse to support the child before that parent or relatives of that parent can inherit from and through the child. UPC §2-114(c).

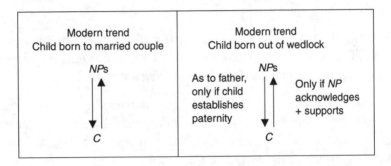

**e. Example:** In *Estate of Stern v. Stern*, 311 S.E.2d 909 (N.C. Ct. App. 1984), Edward Stern's natural parents never married, but they lived together and raised Edward together. Edward's mother died when he was six, after which he was raised by his father. His father died in 1979, leaving his estate to "my son" Edward. When Edward died intestate in 1980, with no surviving spouse or issue, the father's family claimed a right to share in the intestate distribution of Edward's estate. The applicable North Carolina statute provided that for a putative natural father and/or the paternal heirs to inherit from and through an intestate illegitimate child, the putative father either has to be adjudged to be the natural father or he has to have acknowledged the child in a writing filed with the clerk of court. Inasmuch as neither method of establishing paternity existed here, the court denied the paternal heirs any right to inherit from Edward's estate.

**f. Posthumously conceived children:** Common law treats a posthumously *born* child (conceived while the natural father is alive but born after his death) as alive from the moment of conception if it were to the child's benefit. With the development of modern reproductive technology, it is now possible to have a posthumously *conceived* child (conceived after a natural parent's death). The issue is whether the posthumously *conceived* child should be treated as a child of the predeceased natural parent for purposes of distributing his or her estate.

**i. Intestacy—uniform law:** The Uniform Status of Children of Assisted Conception Act §4(b) provides that a natural parent who dies before the artificial conception of a child is not treated as a parent of the child.

ii. **Intestacy—case law:** In *Woodward v. Commissioner of Social Security*, 760 N.E.2d 257 (Mass. 2002), after learning that the husband had leukemia, the Woodwards "banked" some of the husband's sperm, concerned that the leukemia treatment might leave him sterile. Unfortunately, the treatment was unsuccessful, and he died. Two years later, the wife conceived through artificial insemination using the husband's preserved semen, giving birth to twin girls. She applied for surviving "child" benefits and surviving "mother" benefits under two Social Security survivor benefits programs. The Social Security Administration rejected the claims based on its interpretation of Massachusetts law on the childrens' inheritance rights. The issue was certified to the Massachusetts court. The court ruled that posthumously conceived children may enjoy inheritance rights of "issue" under the state's intestacy scheme where the surviving parent or child's legal representative demonstrates (a) a genetic relationship between the child and the decedent; (b) that the decedent affirmatively consented to the post-humous conception and to the support of any resulting child; (c) that the action to establish paternity inheritance rights is brought in a timely manner; and (d) that notice is given to all interested parties.

iii. **Probate testate and nonprobate:** If a natural parent wants a posthumously conceived child to be treated as his or her child, the parent can expressly so provide in his or her will or nonprobate instrument (inter vivos trust).

**H. Advancements:** The doctrine of advancement addresses the issue of whether inter vivos gifts a decedent made to an heir should count against the heir's share of the decedent's probate estate. (If the donor dies testate, the doctrine of satisfaction applies; the issue and policy considerations are very similar. Satisfaction is covered in Chapter 6.)

1. **Common law:** Under the common law approach, if a parent makes an inter vivos gift to a child, an irrebuttable presumption arises that the gift constitutes an advancement that counts against the child's share of the parent's intestate estate.

   a. **Hotchpot:** All inter vivos gifts to the child are added back (on paper—the child is not forced to give the gift back) into the parent's probate intestate estate to create the "hotch-pot." Then the hotchpot is divided equally among the decedent's heirs. Any advancement received by a child is counted against that child's share of the hotchpot. The child actually receives from the parent's intestate estate only his or her share of the hotchpot minus any advancement the child has received.

   b. **Rationale:** Intestate property passes to one's children equally because it is assumed the parent loved his or her children equally and wanted to treat them equally upon his or her death. While that assumption is reasonable as applied to a parent's probate property, it is questionable whether it should it be extended to include inter vivos gifts a parent made to his or her children. The logic underlying the advancement doctrine is that only by including inter vivos gifts can it be said that the children were truly treated equally.

   c. **Example:** Decedent died intestate with three children, *A, B*, and *C*. Decedent gave *A* inter vivos gifts totaling $25,000. Decedent gave *B* inter vivos gifts totaling $50,000. Decedent gave *C* inter vivos gifts totaling $75,000. Decedent died with a probate estate of $150,000. How much does each child take?

**Analysis:** Under the advancement doctrine, the inter vivos gifts are added back, on paper, to the actual probate estate to create the hotchpot. The hotchpot here is $300,000 (the actual probate estate, $150,000, plus the inter vivos gifts: $25,000 + $50,000 + $75,000). Then the hotchpot is divided equally among the children. $300,000 divided by 3 is $100,000 each. Because A received $25,000 inter vivos, A receives only $75,000 from the actual probate estate (leaving $75,000 in the actual probate estate). Because B received $50,000 inter vivos, B receives only $50,000 from the actual probate estate (leaving $25,000 in the actual probate estate). Because C received $75,000 inter vivos, C receives only $25,000 from the actual probate estate (exactly what is left, leaving nothing in probate).

**d. Advancement exceeds share:** If a child receives inter vivos gifts that exceed what he or she is entitled to receive from the hotchpot, the child does not have to give any of the inter vivos gifts back to the parent's probate estate, but the child will not be permitted to share in the distribution of the parent's estate.

**e. Child predeceases:** If a child predeceases the parent, and the child received an inter vivos gift, under the common law approach the advancement doctrine still applies to the share of the parent's estate going to a child's issue.

**f. Criticisms:** The common law advancement doctrine has been heavily criticized. It inherently involves a high cost of administration (hearings to calculate exactly what was given to whom, when, and how to value it) that invariably led to siblings fighting with siblings when they should be consoling each other.

2. **Modern trend/UPC approach:** Under the modern trend/UPC approach, the advancement doctrine has been modified to try to reduce the potential for litigation, costs of administration, and family fighting. Inter vivos gifts do not constitute an advancement unless there is a writing indicating that the donor intended the gift to constitute an advancement. UPC §2-109.

   **a. Writing requirement:** (1) If the *donor* creates the writing, the writing must be made *contemporaneously* with the inter vivos gift; (2) if the *donee* creates the writing, the writing may be made *anytime*. UPC §2-109(a).

   **b. Donee predeceases:** Unlike the common law approach, if the donee predeceases the donor, and the inter vivos gift to the donee qualified as an advancement, the advancement does *not* count against the share of the donor's estate going to the donee's issue unless the writing expressly provides so. UPC §2-109(c).

   **c. Scope:** Although the UPC/modern trend arguably reduces the scope of the doctrine by providing that it applies *only* if there is a writing expressing or acknowledging such intent, the modern trend also expands the doctrine by providing that it may apply to any heir, not just to a child. UPC §2-109(a).

   **d. Valuation:** If an inter vivos gift qualifies as an advancement, it is valued as of the time the donee receives possession or enjoyment of the property, whichever occurred first. UPC §2-109(b).

I. **Expectancies:** When there is only one parent left alive, most children expect to receive some property from that parent's estate when that parent dies. Anytime any heir apparent has such an expectation, it is called an "expectancy."

1. **Not a property interest:** An expectancy is not a property interest. The heir needs to survive the decedent to take anything, and even if the heir were to survive the decedent, the decedent can defeat the expectancy by transferring the property inter vivos or by executing a will that devises the property to others.

2. **Transferability:** Because an expectancy is not a property interest, the general rule is that it is not transferable. If, however, an heir apparent agrees to transfers his or her expectancy for valuable consideration and thereafter tries to avoid enforcement of the agreement on the grounds that an expectancy is not transferable, a court of equity will enforce the agreement if it finds it fair and equitable under the circumstances.

**J. Transfers to minors:** Under the intestate distribution scheme, if a decedent dies intestate and is survived by issue, there is a good chance that some of the property may be distributed to a minor. The problem is that minors lack the legal capacity to transfer property. The law has devised a number of options for managing property for a minor.

1. **Guardianship:** The first, and arguably the oldest, is guardianship—or guardian of the property. The guardian's job was exactly as its name implies: to guard and preserve the ward's property until the minor reached the age of capacity.

   **Criticisms:** Guardians had minimal powers over the property. They had to go to court for authorization to deal with the property. The guardian was permitted to use only the income generated from the property, not the property itself, absent court approval. Guardians had to account regularly to the probate court. The result was a very inefficient arrangement with high administrative costs.

   **Modern trend:** The modern trend has modified guardianship and transformed it into a conservatorship. Under a conservatorship, the conservator takes title as trustee for the minor and has all the powers a trustee would have over the property. The conservator still has to account to the court, but usually only once a year. The result is a far more efficient arrangement for managing a minor's property. UPC Article V.

2. **Uniform Gifts/Transfers to Minors Act:** A second arrangement for managing a minor's property is as a custodian under the Uniform Gifts to Minors Act, or its successor, the Uniform Transfers to Minors Act. Under either, a custodian has discretionary power to use the property for the benefit of the minor, as the custodian deems appropriate, without court approval. UPC §2-109(a). UTMA §14(a). Upon the minor's turning 21, the custodian must disburse any remaining property to the minor. The custodian has no duty to account to the court, only to the minor upon turning 21. A custodianship arguably is more efficient than a guardianship, but is most appropriate for small to moderate size gifts.

3. **Trusts:** The third arrangement that can be used to hold and manage a minor's property is a trust. The terms of the trust control the scope of the trustee's powers over the property, the trustee's ability to use the principal and/or income for the benefit of the child, the trustee's duty to account, and when the trust is to terminate and the property to be distributed. The trust is the most flexible way to hold and manage property for a minor, but typically there are higher upfront costs involved in creating the trust and the trust may have high administrative fees depending on the trustee's fees. It is most appropriate when the size of the gift to the minor is large.

4. **Comparisons:** Of the three possible arrangements, the trust and custodianship have substantial benefits over guardianship. Both the trust and the custodianship arrangements, however, require a written instrument expressly opting for that arrangement. Absent such a writing, the default in a jurisdiction will be either guardianship or conservatorship, if the jurisdiction follows the modern trend.

# VII. SURVIVAL REQUIREMENT

A. **Introduction:** To be eligible to receive property from a decedent, a taker must "survive" the decedent. How long the taker must survive the decedent, and the burden of proof the taker has to satisfy, varies from jurisdiction to jurisdiction, and within any given jurisdiction it may vary based upon the type of property involved—probate intestate, probate testate, or nonprobate. *If the claimant fails to meet the survival requirement, treat the claimant as if he or she predeceased the decedent.*

B. **Scope—applies to *all* takers:** The survival requirement applies to all takers, regardless of the type of property involved: nonprobate, probate testate, or probate intestate. Some jurisdictions apply the same survival requirement to all three types of property; some apply different requirements to the different types of property. Close reading of the controlling statute is necessary to determine a jurisdiction's approach.

**Heirs vs. heirs apparent:** To qualify as an heir (an intestate taker), the heir must survive the decedent. Though laypeople often refer to people as their "heirs," technically this usage is inappropriate. Because an heir must survive the decedent, a person who is alive has no heirs, only "heirs apparent."

C. **Common law:** Under the common law approach, to qualify as an heir the party had to prove by a preponderance of the evidence that he or she survived the decedent by a millisecond. Whether a person survived the decedent is a question of fact.

**Historical perspective:** The preponderance of the evidence approach proved workable at early common law because the potential for simultaneous death scenarios was low. With the development of machines such as cars, trains, and airplanes that substantially increased the potential for simultaneous death scenarios, the preponderance of the evidence standard came under increasing criticism.

D. **Uniform Simultaneous Death Act:** As initially adopted, the Uniform Simultaneous Death Act (USDA) basically codified the common law rule. The Act provided that where "there is no sufficient evidence" as to who survived whom, the party claiming a right to take is to be treated as having predeceased the decedent.

1. **Criticism of common law and USDA:** Under a typical intestate scheme, if both spouses die intestate with no children, all the couple's probate property ends up on the second-to-die spouse's side of the family. If both spouses die together, the issue becomes which spouse survived the other. Instead of the two families grieving together, they end up suing each other to see which family receives all the couple's property. The common law rule has been criti-cized: (1) for its high costs of litigation (the "winner take all" outcome coupled with the low burden of proof invites litigation in simultaneous death situations); (2) for its unfairness (all the

couple's property ends up on one side of the family); and (3) because it encourages unseemly behavior (families suing each other when they should be comforting each other).

   **2. Example:** In *Estate of Villwock*, 418 N.W.2d 1 (Wis. App. 1987), Roy and June Villwock were critically injured when they were in a head-on car crash. While both were being transported together to the hospital, Roy suffered cardiopulmonary failure minutes before June. After continued CPR at the hospital failed to revive them, June was pronounced dead at 8:23 P.M., and Roy at 8:34 P.M. Following a hearing, the probate court determined that Roy died in the ambulance when he suffered irreversible heart and lung failure while June was still alive and conscious. His will left all his property to his wife, and it contained no express survival requirement. Roy's daughter from a prior marriage sued, claiming that there was insufficient evidence that June survived him. Applying the USDA standard, the court held that there was sufficient evidence to support the finding that June survived Roy and that they did not die simultaneously.

   **3. Determining time of death:** To determine whether one person survived another, one needs to know when each party died.

      **a. Common law:** Under the common law approach, a person is dead when there is irreversible cessation of circulatory and respiratory functions.

      **b. Criticism:** With the advent of modern medical technology, that standard became unworkable. People can be put on artificial life support systems to keep their hearts beating and lungs breathing.

      **c. Modern trend:** Under the modern trend, where circulatory or respiratory functions are artificially maintained, death occurs when there is irreversible cessation of total brain activity.

**E. The clear and convincing evidence standard:** To try to minimize simultaneous death litigation, some states have raised the bar on the survival requirement. To qualify as a survivor, a claimant must prove by clear and convincing evidence that he or she survived the decedent.

**Criticism:** The clear and convincing evidence survival standard has been criticized for not raising the bar enough. The difference between preponderance of the evidence and clear and convincing evidence arguably is not enough to deter family members from suing each other when substantial money is at stake.

**F. UPC 120-hour approach:** The UPC requires that to qualify as a taker (surviving heir, devisee, or life insurance policy beneficiary), the taker must prove by clear and convincing evidence that he or she survived the decedent by 120 hours (five days). UPC §§2-104 and 2-702. The most recent version of the USDA requires the same.

**G. The mechanics of the survival requirement:** The mechanics of applying the survival requirement is a two-step process: (1) did the claimant ***actually*** survive the decedent, and (2) did the claimant ***legally*** survive the decedent?

The first step is purely a question of fact based upon the fact pattern. The second prong is an artificial analysis based upon the statutory requirement that the heir must survive by a requisite period of time. Even if the claimant actually survives the decedent, if the claimant does not "legally" survive the decedent (meet the statutory survival requirement), the claimant is treated as if he or she predeceased the decedent.

1. **Apply separately to each decedent:** In applying the survival requirement, be sure to start the analysis all over again when analyzing who gets the second-to-die decedent's property. Otherwise one can get caught in an abstract catch-22 where one reasons that because the second-to-die is treated as predeceasing the first-to-die, the first-to-die must take the second-to-die's property.

2. **Example:** Pete and Gerri are married with no children. While taking a romantic drive down the Big Sur coastline, Gerri looks a bit too long at the sunset and drives off the road. The car sails off the cliff onto the rocks below. Pete is killed instantly. Gerri dies two days later. Assume both Pete and Gerri died intestate. Pete is survived by his father, Frank. Gerri is survived by her mother, Maude.

   **Analytical steps:** Start with the decedent who died first. Check to see if the claimant actually and legally survived the decedent. Then, when analyzing who gets the second-to-die's property, start the analysis all over again.

   a. **Common law/USDA approach:** Pete died first. Because Gerri can prove by a preponderance of the evidence that she survived him (here by two days), she takes his probate intestate property. Then Gerri died two days later. Because Pete failed to survive her, Gerri's intestate property (including the property she got from Pete) will go to her mother, Maude.

   b. **The clear and convincing evidence approach:** Pete died first. Because Gerri can prove by clear and convincing evidence that she survived him (here by two days), she takes his probate intestate property. Then Gerri died two days later. Because Pete failed to survive her, her property (including the property she took from Pete) will go to her mother, Maude.

   c. **UPC approach:** Analyze the spouses in the order of their actual deaths.

      i. **Analysis of the first spouse to die:** Pete died first. (1) Can Gerri prove that she *actually* survived Pete? Yes, she survived by two days. (2) Can Gerri prove that she *legally* survived Pete—can she prove by clear and convincing evidence that she survived Pete by 120 hours (5 days)? No. She died two days later. For purposes of distributing Pete's estate, Gerri is treated as if she predeceased him. All his probate property will pass to his father, Frank.

      ii. **Analysis of the second spouse to die:** Who takes Gerri's probate property? Because we treated her as predeceasing Pete, does she have a surviving spouse? No. Start the analysis all over again when analyzing who gets a decedent's property. When analyzing who gets Gerri's probate property, ask whether Pete (1) actually survived Gerri, and (2) legally survived Gerri. Here, Pete did not actually survive Gerri, so she has no surviving spouse. Her probate property will pass to her mother, Maude.

H. **Failure to meet survival requirement:** Whichever standard is applied, if the claimant fails to meet the survival requirement, the claimant is treated as if he or she predeceased the decedent.

I. **Wills and nonprobate instruments:** As applied to probate testate and nonprobate property, the statutory survival requirement is a default rule that applies if the written instrument does not have its own express survival requirement. If the written instrument has an express survival requirement, it will apply.

# VIII. BARS TO SUCCESSION

**A. Introduction:** The material so far has focused on determining who takes the decedent's property when he or she dies intestate, and how much they get. The doctrines in this section address the issue of whether there are situations in which an otherwise eligible taker should nevertheless be barred from taking.

**B. Homicide:** Where a party who otherwise is entitled to take from a decedent kills the decedent, the equitable principle that one should not profit from one's own wrongdoing argues against permitting the killer from taking *any type* of property from the decedent.

  **1. Judicial approaches:** If the jurisdiction does *not* have a statute addressing the issue, the courts are split over how to treat the issue:

    **a.** The decedent's property passes to the killer because that is the statutory probate scheme, and if the court were to alter the scheme the court would be legislating;

    **b.** The killer is barred from taking the decedent's property because equity demands that one should not profit from one's own wrongdoing; or

    **c.** Legal title to the decedent's property passes to the killer, but a constructive trust is imposed to prevent unjust enrichment and the court orders the property to be distributed to the next in line to take.

  **2. Example:** In *Bradley v. Fox*, 129 N.E.2d 699 (Ill. 1955), one joint tenant murdered the other. The defendants challenged the constitutionality of an Illinois statute that provided that a murderer shall not inherit from or acquire any interest in the estate of the deceased person on the grounds that as applied to joint tenancy property it offends the constitutional prohibition against forfeiture. The court ruled that despite the property fiction that joint tenants own the entire property, each joint tenant must share the property. While acknowledging that some courts have deprived the killer of the entire estate or half of it, others have imposed a constructive trust on the entire estate for the benefit of the heirs of the victim, while others have imposed a constructive trust modified by a life estate in half of the property—the Illinois court decided that the result most in line with Illinois public policy was that the murder destroyed the right of survivorship and the murderer retained only the title to his undivided one-half interest as a tenant in common with the victim's heirs.

  **3. Statutory/UPC approach:** A majority of the jurisdictions and the UPC have an express statute that provides that a killer shall not take from his victim. UPC §2-803. Most of the statutes provide that the killer should be treated as if he or she predeceased the decedent.

  **4. Intentional and felonious killing:** The general rule, both judicially and statutorily, is that for the killing to bar (either outright or through the constructive trust) the killer from taking from the decedent, the killing must be intentional and felonious.

    **a. Manslaughter:** In cases of manslaughter, it is critical to distinguish the two types of manslaughter. *Voluntary* manslaughter is intentional killing and comes within the scope of the homicide doctrine—the killer would be barred from taking. *Involuntary* manslaughter is unintentional killing and does not come within the scope of the homicide doctrine—the killer would not be barred from taking.

**b. Self-defense:** Killing in self-defense is not felonious and does not trigger the homicide doctrine.

**c. Assisted suicide:** Mercy killings and assisted suicides technically are intentional and felonious killings and come within the scope of the homicide doctrine, though there is much debate over whether the doctrine should include such acts.

5. **Burden of proof:** Whether a killer should be able to take from his or her victim is a civil issue, not a criminal issue. A criminal conviction will have res judicata effect upon the civil issue (UPC §2-803(g)), but an acquittal will not be the final word because the burden of proof in a criminal case is proof beyond a reasonable doubt, while the burden of proof in a civil case is merely preponderance of the evidence. If the defendant is acquitted on homicide charges, but civilly found liable for the decedent's intentional and felonious wrongful death, the killer will be barred from participating in the distribution of the victim's estate.

6. **Remedy:** The general rule is that if the doctrine applies, in distributing the victim's property, treat the killer as if he or she had predeceased the victim.

7. **Killer's issue:** The general rule is that application of the homicide doctrine means that the killer is treated as if he or she predeceased the victim. If a relative predeceases the decedent, and the relative is survived by issue, often the relative's share passes to his or her issue. With respect to property passing under intestacy, this occurs pursuant to the per stirpes/per capita doctrines. With respect to probate testate property (and in some jurisdictions non-probate property), this occurs pursuant to the lapse and anti-lapse doctrines (to be studied later). The jurisdictions are split over whether the homicide doctrine should apply to the killer's issue to bar them from taking if they would otherwise take under these doctrines (and in some states, such as California, it varies depending on whether the victim died testate or intestate).

   **UPC approach:** The UPC treats the killer as if he or she had disclaimed the property (UPC §2-803), which arguably permits the killer's issue to take the killer's share under anti-lapse and the per stirpes/per capita doctrines if they would otherwise qualify (if they meet the requirements of those doctrines).

8. **Scope of doctrine:** The general rule is that the homicide doctrine applies to all types of property: nonprobate, probate testate, and probate intestate. UPC §2-803.

   **Joint tenancy:** If the victim and the killer held property in joint tenancy, by operation of law the UPC converts the joint tenancy into tenancy in common. UPC §2-803(c)(2). The killer keeps his or her interest, and the victim's interest is distributed as if the killer had predeceased the victim.

9. **Statute covers probate property only:** Where the statute expressly covers probate property only, one can argue that a constructive trust should be imposed on the nonprobate property. The argument would be based on the equitable principle that one should not benefit from one's own wrongdoing. The constructive trust would be in favor of those who would have taken if the killer had predeceased the victim.

C. **Abandonment/Elder abuse:** A number of states have other doctrines that will bar a taker from receiving if the taker is guilty of misconduct short of homicide. Some states bar a taker if they are guilty of abandonment. Other states bar a taker from receiving if they are guilty of the new offense of elder abuse. Elder abuse involves acts that amount to physical abuse, neglect, or fiduciary abuse of the decedent while he or she was an elder or dependent adult. Cal. Prob. Code §259.

**D. Disclaimers:** Distributions under intestacy, devises under a will, and nonprobate transfers are simply different ways of making a gift. What makes these gifts unique is that for all practical purposes these gifts are testamentary gifts—gifts made by the donor at time of death. To have a valid gift, there must be intent to make a gift, delivery, and acceptance. While acceptance is generally presumed, a disclaimer is simply a way of expressing one's intent that he or she declines to accept a testamentary gift.

1. **Treat as if predeceased:** If a party disclaims, as a general rule the legal significance is that the party disclaiming is treated as if he or she predeceased the decedent. The property in question is then distributed as if the party who disclaimed predeceased the decedent. The property is distributed to the next eligible taker under the various rules governing who takes in the event a taker predeceases the decedent.

2. **Benefits of disclaiming:** There are a variety of reasons a party may disclaim his or her testamentary gift:

   a. **Redistribute property:** Disclaimers are often called a form of "post-mortem estate planning." Disclaimers can be used to adjust "who takes" and "how much they take" after the death of the decedent. For example, if a decedent dies intestate survived by a spouse and two children, in many states the children are entitled to receive up to 50 percent of the decedent's estate. If the children are both adults, they may disclaim their interests to increase the share going to the surviving spouse. If both disclaim, they will be treated as if they predeceased the decedent, and as long as they have no issue, the decedent will now be treated as if he or she had no surviving issue, in which case more (potentially all) of the decedent's property will pass to his or her surviving spouse.

   b. **Avoid gift tax consequences:** One of the benefits of disclaiming is that it can avoid estate and gift tax consequences. If one accepts the property and then gives it to the next taker in line, there may be gift tax consequences to the transfer. If, however, one disclaims and the legal effect is simply to pass the property in question to the next taker in line, the disclaimer has no gift tax consequence.

   c. **Avoid creditors:** As a general rule, creditors are entitled to reach any property that the debtor holds that is transferable. If an heir or devisee is facing creditors' claims, such that any inheritance or devise would, for all practical purposes, go directly to the creditors, the heir or devisee can elect to disclaim the property in question to avoid the property going to the creditors. If the taker disclaims, the legal significance is that the disclaimer is tantamount to rejecting the gift. If the gift is rejected, it was never accepted, so the taker never had a property interest in the property in question. If the taker never held a property interest in the property, the taker's creditors never had a right to reach it.

   **Federal government as creditor:** Where the federal government is a creditor of the disclaimant (for tax purposes or under Medicaid reimbursement provisions), the property disclaimed often is subject to the claim of the federal government.

3. **Scope:** Careful attention should be paid to a disclaimer statute to see if it applies to only probate property (traditional approach) or if it also can be used to disclaim nonprobate property (modern trend approach).

4. **Execution requirements:** Most disclaimer statutes have technical rules concerning what must be done for the disclaimer to be effective. Most require that the party disclaiming do so in writing within nine months of the decedent's death.

**Example:** In *Estate of Baird*, 933 P.2d 1031 (Wash. 1997), Phyllis Baird, who suffered from Alzheimer's disease, died intestate, survived by a son, James, and a daughter. Almost two years before Phyllis died, James brutally assaulted his wife Susan, for which he was sentenced to 20 years. On the day he was sentenced, James purported to disclaim "any and all interest" he "may have" in his mother's estate. Thereafter Susan was awarded a judgment of $2.75 million, and a week later, James filed for bankruptcy. Susan's claim represented 95 percent of the outstanding creditor claims in the bankruptcy proceeding. Two months later Phyllis died intestate. James' children from a prior marriage claimed James' $500,000 interest in Phyllis' estate pursuant to his "anticipatory disclaimer." The court ruled that the disclaimer was invalid because the interest did not arise until Phyllis died, and therefore James was not a beneficiary when he executed the disclaimer. Whether the disclaimer would have been effective to defeat Susan's claim if James had waited until after Phyllis died is unclear. Most courts would have permitted it to defeat Susan's claim where there is no bankruptcy filing or the beneficiary executes it *before* filing for bankruptcy; but the courts are split where the disclaimer is executed *after* filing for bankruptcy.

---

## *Quiz Yourself on* INTESTACY: THE DEFAULT DISTRIBUTION SCHEME

Where the question is split to reflect different jurisdictional approaches, you should answer only the approach(es) that you will be expected to know for your exam.

4. Goldie and Curt have been living together for 15 years. They have two children, and Goldie has a child from a prior relationship. Many years from now, Goldie drowns accidentally while filming a sequel entitled "On Silver Pond." She is survived by Curt and her three children.

   **a.** Who takes her probate property under the typical statute of descent and distribution if she dies intestate?

   **b.** Who takes her probate property under the UPC statute of descent and distribution if she dies intestate?

5. Juwon and Leslie met while serving in the armed forces. They were married a few years later, but never got around to executing wills. Both were assigned to the Pentagon. When the plane crashed into the Pentagon on Septmber 11, Leslie was killed instantly. Juwon suffered severe burns over 90 percent of his body and died three days later. Leslie was also survived by her mother, Mae, and Juwon was survived by his father, Freddie.

   **a.** Who takes Leslie's and Juwon's property under the traditional common law approach?

   **b.** Who takes Leslie's and Juwon's property under the modern tren/UPC approach?

**6.** Assume the following family tree and that A, B, C, D, F, and X predecease the decedent:

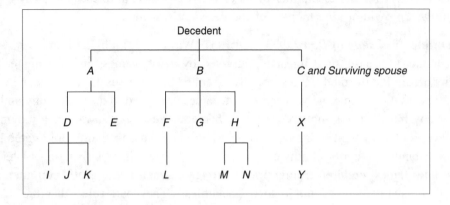

**a.** Who takes how much under the per capita approach?

**b.** Who takes how much under the per stirpes approach?

**c.** Who takes how much under the per capita at each generation approach?

**d.** Do you need to answer all three of the subquestions, or only the approach that your jurisdiction follows?

**7.** Assume the following family situation. The only people alive when the decedent dies are those identified by the bold letters: *A, B, C,* and *D.*

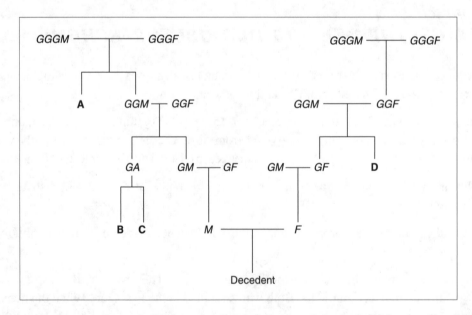

**a.** Who takes the decedent's estate if he or she dies intestate and the jurisdiction applies the degree of relationship with a parentelic tiebreaker approach?

**b.** Who takes the decedent's estate if he or she dies intestate and the jurisdiction applies the UPC approach?

**8.** H and W are married and have two children. Thereafter, they divorce, and H marries W2. W2 adopts A and B. Thereafter W2 becomes pregnant. H dies unexpectedly during the seventh month of W2's pregnancy, and W2 dies 2 months later while giving birth to C. One year later, A dies intestate, with no surviving spouse or issue. Who takes A's property under the modern tren/UPC approach?

9. Tracy is a wild and crazy kind of guy, enlisting in the Navy so he can have them pay to ship him around the world. He is an "old fashioned" kind of sailor, liking to believe that he has a girl in every port. Lulu claims that Tracy is the father of her child, but Tracy refuses to acknowledge that the child is his. Tracy moved on, and Lulu raised the child, Sunshine, on her own without any help from Tracy. Sunshine grew up to have a very successful musical career, only to die in a plane crash. Tracy has stepped forward and now asserts his right to inherit from his daughter, Sunshine. Who takes Sunshine's property under the modern trend/UPC approach?

10. Molly is a single mom. Her husband died years ago, and she has struggled to raise their two children, Alice and Bob. Alice has been an ideal child, excelling in school and graduating from college. Molly gave Alice $100,000 while Molly was alive, to help offset the expenses of attending a private college. Bob, on the other hand, has been an underachiever, not even graduating from high school. Molly died unexpectedly last week, with an estate of $300,000. How should Molly's estate be distributed:

    a. Under the common law approach?

    b. Under the modern trend/UPC approach?

11. O.J. and Nicole are married. They own Brentwood estates as joint tenants. They both have life insurance policies, with the other as sole beneficiary. They also have wills leaving all their probate property to their surviving spouse. Nicole is found dead one night, her throat slashed. Nicole is survived by O.J. and her parents. O.J. is tried for her murder, but he is acquitted. In a related civil case, however, he was found responsible for her wrongful death. What is the most likely result as to who gets her property?

12. Harry and Whilma are married. The have two grown children, Ann and Bill. Ann has two children, Ned and Mary. Bill has one child, Fred. Harry also has a child, Pat, from a prior marriage. Pat has one grown child, Tom. Harry dies intestate. Pat always liked Whilma and is concerned that she might not have enough money to get by now that Harry is dead. Pat disclaims his right to take any property from Harry's estate. Who takes how much under the modern trend/UPC approach?

---

## Answers

4. **a.** When a decedent dies intestate, the order of takers is (1) surviving spouse, and (2) issue. Although Curt survives her, he will not qualify as a spouse unless the jurisdiction recognizes common law marriages. If the jurisdiction recognizes common law marriages, Goldie and Curt's relationship would probably qualify as a common law marriage. Assuming it does, under a typical descent and distribution statute Curt will take 33 percent of her property because more than one child also survives her. The remaining 66 percent would be divided equally among her three children. If the jurisdiction does not recognize common law marriages, Goldie has no surviving spouse and all her property passes equally to her three children.

**b.** Under the UPC approach, the threshold question is still whether the jurisdiction recognizes common law marriage. If the jurisdiction recognizes common law marriages, Goldie and Curt's relationship probably would qualify as a common law marriage. Assuming it does, Curt would qualify as a surviving spouse. Under the UPC approach to intestate distribution, how much Curt takes is determined by who her surviving issue are and who his surviving issue are. Here, all of her issue are not also his issue, as one has a different father. Accordingly, under the UPC, he would take the first $100,000 and 50 percent of the rest. The three children would split the remaining 50 percent equally. If the jurisdiction does not recognize common law marriages, and it has adopted the UPC approach to intestate distribution, Curt would not qualify as a surviving spouse. All Goldie's probate property would pass equally to her three children.

**5. a.** At common law, to qualify as a taker one had to prove by a preponderance of the evidence that he or she survived the decedent by a millisecond. Under the common law approach, Juwon would qualify as a surviving spouse. Because Leslie is also survived by her mother, Juwon would take 50 percent of Leslie's property, with the remainder going to Leslie's mom, Mae. When Juwon dies three days later, he does not have a surviving spouse. Leslie actually died three days before he did. All of Juwon's property (including the 50 percent that he took from Leslie's estate) will go to his father, Freddie.

**b.** Under the modern trend/UPC approach, to qualify as a taker under intestacy, one has to prove by clear and convincing evidence that he or she survived the decedent by 120 hours (5 days). Although Juwon actually survived Leslie, he did not legally survive her—he cannot meet the statutory survival requirement. Juwon will be treated as if he predeceased Leslie, and all of Leslie's property will pass to her mother, Mae. When Juwon died, Leslie had actually predeceased him. He has no surviving spouse, so all his property will pass to his father, Freddie.

**6. a.** Under the per capita approach, divide at the first generation where there is a live taker. All the decedent's children, *A*, *B*, and *C*, predeceased the decedent, so the first division is at the grandchildren's generation. The number of shares is one share for each party who is alive at that tier, and one share for each party who is dead at that tier but survived by issue. *E*, *G*, and *H* would take shares because they are alive. *D*, *F*, and *X* would take shares as deceased but survived by issue. Divide the estate into six shares. Under per capita, the dropping shares drop by bloodline. *D*'s one-sixth would drop to *I*, *J*, and *K* equally (one-eighteenth each). *E* would keep his one-sixth. *F*'s one-sixth would drop to *L*. *G* would keep her one-sixth. *H* would keep her one-sixth. And *X*'s one-sixth would drop by bloodline to *Y*.

**b.** Under the per stirpes approach, always divide at the first generation, whether anyone is alive at that tier or not. The number of shares is one share for each party who is alive at that tier, one share for each party who is dead at that tier but survived by issue. *A*, *B*, and *C* will each take a share. Under per stirpes, the dropping shares drop by bloodline. *A*'s one-third will fall to *D* and *E* (one-sixth each), and *D*'s one-sixth will fall to *I*, *J*, and *K*, who will take one-eighteenth. *E* will take one-sixth. *B*'s one-third will fall to *F*, *G*, and *H* equally (one-ninth each) because each is either alive or dead but survived by issue. *F*'s one-ninth will fall by bloodline to *L*. *G* will keep her one-ninth. *H* will keep her one-ninth. *C*'s one-third will fall to *X*, who is dead but survived by issue, so the one-third will fall to *Y*.

**c.** Under the per capita at each generation approach, divide at the first generation where there is a live taker. All the decedent's children, *A*, *B*, and *C*, predeceased the decedent so the first division will be at the grandchildren's generation. The number of shares is one share for each party at that tier who is alive, and one share for each party who is dead at that tier but survived by issue. *E*, *G*, and *H* would take shares as alive, *D*, *F*, and *X* would take shares as dead but survived by issue. Under per capita at each generation, pool the dropping shares and divide them equally among the eligible takers at the next tier (the issue of the predeceased issue). There are three dropping shares, the shares for *D*, *F*, and

*X.* Their three one-sixth shares are pooled so that one-half of the decedent's estate is dropping to the great-grandchildren. That one-half will be divided equally among their collective issue: *I, J, K, F,* and *Y* would take one-tenth each.

**d.** Although statutorily each jurisdiction has a default approach, an individual can opt out of that approach by expressing an intent for a different approach in a written instrument that validly passes property at death (a valid will or will substitute). You need to be able to apply all three approaches, regardless of which approach your jurisdiction has adopted, because the testator/transferor can always opt out of the default.

7. **a.** Under the degree of relationship with a parentelic tiebreaker approach, the first step is to count the degree of relationship between each claimed taker and the decedent. *A* is related to the decedent by the fifth degree (Decedent to *M* = 1; *M* to *GM* = 2; *GM* to *GGM* = 3; *GGM* to GGGM = 4; and GGGM to *A* = 5). B and C are related to the decedent by the fifth degree (Decedent to *M* = 1; *M* to *GM* = 2; *GM* to *GGM* = 3; *GGM* to *GA* = 4; and *GA* to B/C = 5). D is related to the decedent by the fourth degree (Decedent to F = 1; F to GF = 2; GF to GGF = 3; GGF to D = 4). D will take all the decedent's property as the closest relative under the degree of relationship approach (there is no need to use the tiebreaker component here because there is only one relative claiming in the closest degree).

**b.** Under the UPC approach, if there is not a live taker within the grandparents' line or closer, the property escheats to the state. The state would take it all.

8. The order of takers under intestacy is surviving spouse, issue, parents, and issue of parents. Here, the facts say that *A* has no surviving spouse or issue. *A*'s natural parents are *W* and *H*. *H* predeceases *A,* so *H* is not an eligible taker. *W* survives *A,* but *W2* adopted *A* and *B.* Normally adoption establishes a parent-child relationship between the adoptive parent and the child and severs completely the relationship between the natural parent and the child. But if the adoption is by a stepparent, there is a widely recognized exception that provides that the adoption severs the right of the natural parent who is not married to the stepparent to inherit from the child, but the child can still inherit from that natural parent. Here, though, because it is the child who predeceased the natural parent, the exception is not applicable and the general adoption rule controls. *W,* the natural parent, cannot inherit from *A,* and both of *A*'s legal parents (*H* and *W2*) predeceased *A.* The next possible takers are the issue of *A*'s parents. *B* is a whole-blooded sibling. Although *H* died before *C* was born, because *H* and *W2* were married, it is presumed that *C* is *H*'s child. Relative to *A* and *B, C* is a half-blooded sibling. Under the modern trend/UPC approach, there is no distinction between half-blooded and whole-blooded siblings. *B* and *C* will split *A*'s estate equally.

9. Under the modern trend/UPC approach, before a natural parent or relative of a natural parent can inherit from or through a child, the natural parent must acknowledge and support the child. Tracy neither acknowledged nor supported the child. He will not be entitled to take from her estate if she dies intestate. Lulu would take all of her property.

10. **a.** Under the common law approach, any inter vivos gifts made from parent to child were presumed to be advancements that should count against the child's share of the parent's estate. Here, assuming Alice could not rebut the presumption, the $100,000 would qualify as an advancement. The advancement amount is added back into the decedent's estate ($100,000 + $300,000) to create the hotchpot ($400,000). The hotchpot is then divided among the heirs, with the advancement amount credited against the share of the recipient of the advancement. Here, the hotchpot would be split 50-50 between Alice and Bob, $200,000 each. Alice's advancement would be counted against her share of the hotchpot, and she would take only $100,000. Bob would take the remaining $200,000.

**b.** Under the modern trend, there is a presumption against inter vivos gifts counting as advancements unless there is a writing expressing such intent on the donor's part. Here, there is no evidence of any such writing. The $100,000 was merely an inter vivos gift. Molly's estate of $300,000 would be divided equally between Alice and Bob, with each taking $150,000.

11. Under the homicide doctrine, if one is civilly responsible for the intentional and felonious murder of the decedent, the killer is not entitled to receive any of the decedent's property, be it nonprobate, probate testate, or probate intestate. The general rule is to treat the killer as if he or she predeceased the decedent. The issue of whether someone intentionally and feloniously killed the decedent, for purposes of determining distribution of the decedent's property, is a civil issue to be determined by a preponderance of the evidence. The civil finding that O.J. was responsible for Nicole's wrongful death is probably sufficient to bar O.J. from taking the proceeds of her life insurance policy or from taking under her will. As for the joint tenancy, it is converted into tenancy in common. O.J. will keep his half, and her half will fall into probate where it will be distributed with the rest of her probate property as if he predeceased her.

12. Under the modern trend/UPC approach, one of the variables in determining the surviving spouse's share is whether the decedent has surviving issue, and if so, whose issue they are. Where not all the decedent's issue are also the surviving spouse's issue, the surviving spouse takes the first $100,000 plus 50 percent of the rest of the decedent's probate estate. The issue will split the remaining 50 percent. Here, Whilma would take the first $100,000 and 50 percent of the rest of Harry's probate property. Ann, Bill, and Pat would split the remaining 50 percent. But Pat has disclaimed. The question becomes what effect, if any, Pat's disclaimer has on who takes how much. The legal effect of a disclaimer is to treat the party who disclaims as if he or she predeceased the decedent. At first blush, it might look like all Harry's surviving issue are now issue of Whilma, so she should take all Harry's property. But Pat's child, Tom, steps up to take Pat's share by representation. Pat's disclaimer does not have the consequences Pat intended because Pat did not take into consideration that Pat's child would take Pat's share by representation. Whilma still takes only the first $100,000 and 50 percent of the rest, and the other 50 percent will be split equally among Ann, Bill, and Tom.

---

## Exam Tips on
## *INTESTACY: THE DEFAULT DISTRIBUTION SCHEME*

The intestate distribution scheme is core wills and trusts material. The intestate distribution scheme is the default. On an exam, intestacy issues can be raised expressly by the facts telling you that the decedent died intestate (without a will), or implicitly as a result of your properly analyzing that a will is invalid or was revoked. The doctrines that affect how much a taker takes are also often tested.

### The intestate distribution scheme

☞ You need to be very comfortable with *who* takes and *how much* they take under the intestate scheme you are studying. The order of takers is straightforward. Focus on how to calculate how much they take, and the variables that control how much they take.

## Surviving spouse: who qualifies

Focus on the creation and termination of the marriage relationship. It is relatively easy to spot an issue dealing with who qualifies as a spouse. Were the parties married or putative spouses; and/or did the court enter a final divorce decree before death?

## Surviving spouse: calculating share

The surviving spouse's share can vary from jurisdiction to jurisdiction, and great care should be taken to read the controlling statutory language. Start with the different possible shares that the surviving spouse can take, and then for each possible share, couple it with the variable(s) that determine when he or she takes that amount.

☛ How much the surviving spouse takes turns on who else survives the deceased spouse—children/issue, parents, or issue of parents. Watch carefully to see if the word *child* or *issue* is used in your statutory scheme. (If the statutory shares turn on the number of children, check to see if predeceased children count if issue survives them.)

☛ In most statutes, in determining the surviving spouse's share, the only issue who are relevant are the deceased spouse's issue, not the surviving spouse's issue. The UPC, however, changes that approach. You have to sweat the details of the statutory language that controls how much a surviving spouse takes. There are no short cuts.

## Issue: Calculating shares

Where a decedent dies intestate and more than one of his or her children predecease the decedent (either actually or are treated as if they predeceased), state and apply the default approach in your jurisdiction for who takes (per capita, per stirpes, or per capita at each generation). If the decedent dies testate or with a nonprobate instrument, look to see if he or she expressed an intent to apply an approach other than the jurisdiction's default.

☛ If your professor includes multiple-choice questions on the exam, these are core doctrines that are tailor-made for multiple-choice type questions.

## Shares of ancestors and remote collaterals

This material is rarely tested on a traditional essay-type fact pattern. If your professor spends time in class showing you how to calculate degrees of relationships and parentelic lines, this is easy to test in a multiple-choice question.

## Issue: who qualifies

This material is tested fairly often because it overlaps nicely with calculating a surviving spouse's share. If the surviving spouse's share turns on the number of issue or children, this material goes directly to that variable.

☛ Although this material is tested fairly often, most professors will not get too creative because this material has the potential of crossing over too far into family law.

To raise this issue, watch for either a nontraditional family situation or a nontraditional birth situation. In particular, watch for (1) child born out of wedlock; (2) child born after death of parent; (3) parent refuses to acknowledge/support child; (4) child was adopted (if so, by whom); or (5) an incomplete adoption.

Equitable adoption is a favorite rule to test in this area. It applies only if the claimed equitably adoptive parent died intestate. If he or she died testate or with a nonprobate instrument, the question is a question of the testator/transferor's intent, arguably not an equitable adoption doctrine question (though it may be relevant if there is not clear evidence of the testator/transferor's intent). In addition, as a general rule equitable adoption permits the party invoking it to inherit "from" the equitably adoptive parent, not "through" the equitably adoptive parent. (Remember to argue the modern trend approach in the alternative if the doctrine fails under the traditional approach.)

Advancement is easy to test and easy to spot. You have to see the decedent making an inter vivos gift to someone who later qualifies as an heir when the donor dies intestate.

☛ Lead with the rule your jurisdiction follows (common law vs. UPC). The UPC approach requires a writing for the doctrine to apply. If the donor creates the writing, it need not be signed, but it must be contemporaneous. Watch for a nice crossover issue/"argument-in-the-alternative" here. If the writing is by the donor, but it is not contemporaneous, but it is signed and in the donor's handwriting, while it will fail for advancement purposes, raise and analyze whether it qualifies as a holographic will.

## Survival requirement

The survival requirement material is core wills and trusts material that is tested often. The rules in this area vary. You need to know which approach applies to which type of property in your jurisdiction.

A survival issue should be easy to spot. Either you will see two or more people dying within seven days of each other, or you will see a written instrument that has an express survival requirement.

☛ If you spot a survival issue, always deal with the person who actually died first. Analytically, in applying the rule, the party claiming that he or she survived (1) has to actually survive the decedent, and (2) has to legally survive the decedent—the latter being where the statutory survival requirement comes in.

☛ Start the process over again when dealing with the second person to die. Even if you treated the second-to-die as predeceasing the first-to-die for purposes of distributing the first person's property, when analyzing who takes the second-to-die's property start the process all over again—do not treat that person as predeceasing anyone.

## Bars to succession

If homicide is tested, it is easy to spot—the decedent had to have been murdered. The tricky part of homicide is remembering the nuances of the doctrine: It applies only to voluntary manslaughter, not involuntary; it is a civil issue, so the burden of proof is preponderance of the evidence; it generally applies to all types of property—nonprobate, probate testate, and probate intestate.

☛ If the doctrine applies, treat the killer as if he or she predeceased the decedent (except for the special ruling covering joint tenancy). If the killer has surviving children, analyze whether the killer's issue take his or her share. The jurisdictions are split, so pay special attention to the statutory language in your jurisdiction.

Disclaimers appear often on exams because it is a great "overlap" issue. Disclaimers are easy to spot because there has to be a writing expressing the intent to disclaim the property in question. (Rarely is creation of the disclaimer an issue. Few professors spend much time on the requirements for validly creating one. The key is their effect.)

☛ Watch for overlap issues. For example, assume the decedent had two children. One of the children predeceased the decedent, survived by a child. The other child survives the decedent and has three children. The decedent died intestate, and the surviving child disclaims. As applied to that child, the issue is simple. The disclaiming child is treated as predeceasing the decedent and his or her share will go to his or her children. But the disclaimer raises a tough overlap issue. In light of the disclaimer, the decedent now has no surviving child. Assuming the jurisdiction applies the per capita or per capita at each generation approach, where should the court make the first division? The per capita doctrines say at the first division where there is a live taker, but where is that when the only live child disclaims? Disclaimers can be used to raise a number of challenging over-lapping issues.

## CHAPTER 3

# LIMITATIONS ON THE TESTAMENTARY POWER TO TRANSFER

## *ChapterScope*

Even if a person were inclined to opt out of intestacy by executing a will, if he or she is married (and/or has children), there are limits to the testamentary power to transfer his or her property to ensure that a decedent adequately provides for his or her spouse (and/or family). This chapter examines the spousal (and family) protection doctrines that limit a person's power to transfer property at death. In particular, the chapter examines the surviving spouse's right to support, and the surviving spouse's right to share in the marital property, and the omitted spouse and/or child doctrines.

- **The elective share (or forced share):** Under the separate property system, although each spouse owns his or her earnings acquired during marriage, upon death the surviving spouse is entitled to a share of the deceased spouse's property regardless of the terms of the deceased spouse's will. How much property the surviving spouse is entitled to, and what property is subject to the elective share, varies from jurisdiction to jurisdiction.

  - **Common law:** At common law, the elective share entitled the surviving spouse to a share of the deceased spouse's *probate* estate, regardless of the terms of the deceased spouse's will. A spouse could avoid the elective share by putting his or her assets in a nonprobate instrument.

  - **Modern trend/UPC approach:** The modern trend/UPC approach expands the reach of the elective share to permit the surviving spouse to claim an elective share against not only the deceased spouse's probate estate, but also against the deceased spouse's "augmented estate"—the deceased spouse's nonprobate assets, and possibly even inter vivos gifts.

- **Community property:** Under the community property system, earnings acquired by either spouse during the course of the marriage are owned equally by the spouses. Each spouse owns an undivided one-half interest in each community property asset. Upon the death of a spouse, the surviving spouse owns his or her one-half of each community property asset outright, and the deceased spouse's half of each community property asset goes into probate where he or she can devise it to anyone.

- **Omitted spouse:** Where an individual executes a valid will, thereafter marries, and thereafter dies without revoking or revising the will, a presumption arises that the testator did not intend to disinherit the new spouse. The presumption is rebuttable if (1) the will expresses the intent to disinherit that spouse; (2) the testator provided for that spouse outside of the will and intended for the transfer to be in lieu of the spouse taking under the will; or (3) the spouse waived his or her right to claim a share of the deceased spouse's estate.

- **Omitted child:** Where an individual executes a valid will and thereafter has a child, and thereafter dies without revoking or revising his or her will, a presumption arises that the testator did not intend to disinherit the new child. The presumption is rebuttable if (1) the will expresses the intent to disinherit that child; (2) the testator provided for the child outside of the will and intended for that transfer to be in lieu of the child taking under the will; or (3) the testator had one or more children when the will was executed and devised substantially all of his or her estate to the other parent of the omitted child.

- **Child mistakenly thought dead:** If the testator fails to provide for a child in a will because the testator mistakenly believes that the child is dead, the child receives the share he or she would receive under the omitted child doctrine.

---

# I. SPOUSAL PROTECTION SCHEMES: AN OVERVIEW

**A. Introduction:** There are two different types of spousal protection: (1) *support* for the rest of the surviving spouse's life, and (2) an outright *share of the marital property,* regardless of who acquired the marital property.

1. **Support:** Through a combination of state and federal law, in virtually every state, a surviving spouse has rights for support under (1) the social security system, (2) ERISA (Employee Retirement Income Security Act of 1974), (3) the homestead exemption, (4) the personal property set-aside, and (5) the family allowance.

2. **Share of marital property:** There are basically two property approaches to marital property—the separate property approach and the community property approach. The overwhelming majority of the jurisdictions follow the separate property approach. Only eight jurisdictions follow the community property approach.

   a. **Separate property approach:** Under the separate property approach, any property acquired by either spouse, including his or her earnings, is that spouse's separate property. A spouse has no rights in the other spouse's separate property absent divorce or death. The spousal protection doctrine that grants a surviving spouse a share of the marital property in a separate property jurisdiction is called the elective share. Upon the death of one spouse, under the elective share doctrine, the surviving spouse has a right to claim a share of the deceased spouse's property regardless of the terms of the deceased spouse's will.

   b. **Community property approach:** Under the community property approach, all property acquired during the marriage as a result of the time, energy, and/or labor of either spouse is community property (and any property acquired with such property). Each spouse has an undivided one-half interest in each community property asset. Upon one spouse's death, each community property asset is divided in half. The surviving spouse's half is his or hers immediately and outright, thereby ensuring that each spouse has a share of the marital property regardless of which spouse acquired it. The deceased spouse's half goes into probate where he or she can devise it to whomever he or she wishes.

# II. SURVIVING SPOUSE'S RIGHT TO SUPPORT

**A. Spousal support:** Although the states are split over the surviving spouse's right to *share* in the deceased spouse's property (the elective share approach vs. the community property approach), the jurisdictions agree that surviving spouses, and maybe dependent children, are entitled to *support* from the deceased spouse. The surviving spouse is entitled to the following despite attempts by the deceased spouse to defeat such rights.

1. **Social security:** All workers are required to participate in social security, and it provides benefits upon retirement to the worker and his or her surviving spouse. Only a surviving spouse can receive the worker's survivor's benefit—a stream of income for life—that is, support. The worker spouse cannot transfer the benefit to anyone.

2. **Private pension plans:** Under ERISA, a surviving spouse must have survivorship rights in the worker spouse's retirement benefits, typically an annuity (a stream of income for life—that is, support). Unlike social security, under ERISA a surviving spouse can waive his or her rights in the worker spouse's private pension plan, but such waivers are not favored and there are strict requirements that apply to such waivers (prenuptial agreements do not qualify).

3. **Homestead:** The homestead right is to ensure that a surviving spouse has somewhere to live. The details of the homestead exemption vary greatly from state to state. Some states grant the surviving spouse a life estate (support) in the family home or farm, while other states merely grant the surviving spouse a sum of money to provide for housing. (The UPC recommends a lump sum payment of only $15,000.) Some states require the decedent to claim the homestead exemption while alive, while other states permit the homestead exemption to be claimed as part of the probate process.

4. **Personal property set-aside:** The surviving spouse is entitled to claim certain tangible personal property items regardless of the deceased spouse's attempts to devise them. Again, the details of the right vary from state to state. Some states have a statutory list of tangible personal property to which the surviving spouse is entitled; other states have a monetary limit on how much the surviving spouse may claim.

5. **Family allowance:** A surviving spouse (and minor children, depending on the jurisdiction) needs money to live on during probate. The surviving spouse has a right to receive a family allowance during probate (but not for life). Some states give a fixed allowance to all surviving spouses, some jurisdictions give an amount that takes into consideration the standard of living the surviving spouse was accustomed to at the time the deceased spouse died.

    a. **Commonwealth approach:** England and a number of its former colonies provide that surviving spouses (and others who were dependent upon the decedent for financial support) are entitled to a reasonable amount of support for life, regardless of their level of need. The English approach has been criticized as being too discretionary, involving too high a cost of administration, and for denying the surviving spouse a right to share in the deceased spouse's property.

    b. **Dower and curtesy:** At early common law, the principal method of providing spousal support was either dower or curtesy.

    i. **Dower**: Dower provided a surviving wife with a life estate in one-third of all her husband's qualifying real property—property in which the husband held an inheritable and/or devisable interest during the marriage. Once dower attached to a parcel of land, the husband could not unilaterally terminate it by transferring the land. The right would spring to life upon the husband's death unless the wife also consented to the transfer by signing the deed, even if title were held in only the husband's name.

    ii. **Curtesy:** Curtesy provided a surviving husband with a life estate in all the wife's qualifying real property, but only if children were born to the couple. Qualifying real property was the same as with dower, as were the rules as to when the right attached and that it could not be terminated unilaterally.

    **iii. Modern trend:** Virtually all jurisdictions have abolished dower and curtesy in favor of the elective share. In the handful of jurisdictions that still retain the doctrines, curtesy is identical to dower. Moreover, in the few states that retain dower, the elective share is also available and almost always results in a greater financial award for the surviving spouse.

# III. SURVIVING SPOUSE'S RIGHT TO A SHARE OF THE MARITAL PROPERTY

**A. Overview:** If an unmarried individual acquires property, it is his or her separate property. If the individual marries, many argue that marriage is a partnership, and that by getting married the parties have agreed to share, to some degree, the burdens and benefits of marriage, including the property acquired by either spouse during the marriage.

**B. Traditional scenario:** Even assuming that marriage is a legal sharing of burdens and benefits, in practice the sharing usually is not a true 50-50. Often children are an integral part of a marriage. Because only women can give birth to children, historically this led most couples to agree, either expressly or as a result of custom, that the wife would focus more of her time and labor within the home, while the husband would focus more of his time and labor outside the home. To the extent the efforts outside the home generate more material recognition (earn more money), the norm was for the husband to acquire more money/property in his name than the wife.

**C. Policy issues:** The issue is (1) *what* credit, if any, should the nonwage-earning spouse (historically the wife) receive for contributing to the partnership and enabling the wage-earning spouse (historically the husband) to focus on earning money; and (2) *when* should that credit be recognized.

**D. Overview of the elective share:** The traditional English, common law view was that the act of marriage had no effect upon the characterization of the property acquired by either spouse. Any and all property earned by either spouse during the marriage remained his or her separate property. Only upon termination of the marriage (divorce or death), if the nonwage-earning spouse was not adequately provided for would the state intervene and "force" the wage-earning spouse to give a share of his or her property to the nonwage-earning spouse. The separate property system's "at time of death" spousal protection scheme is commonly known as "the elective share" or "the forced share."

**E. Overview of community property:** Community property arguably is truer to the "marriage is a partnership" model. The moment any marital property is acquired, the community owns the asset. Each spouse owns an undivided one-half interest in each marital property asset. Upon the death of one spouse, the surviving spouse owns his or her half outright, and the deceased spouse's half goes into probate estate where he or she can devise it to whomever he or she wishes.

**Marital property:** Community property applies only to marital property. Marital property is property acquired as a result of the time, energy, or labor of either spouse during the marriage. Property acquired before marriage, and gifts acquired by either spouse during the marriage, are that spouse's separate property.

# IV. THE ELECTIVE SHARE DOCTRINE

**A. Jurisdictional variations:** More than any other area of wills and trusts, the jurisdictions differ over the exact details of their elective share doctrines. The differences can be in the amount that the surviving spouse is entitled to, the variables that determine the amount (length of marriage, family situation, surviving spouse's net worth, property subject to the elective share doctrine, etc.), or the property subject to the elective share.

1. **Coverage note:** If your professor is teaching your jurisdiction's probate code, read and analyze your elective share statute very carefully. The discussion here will focus on the UPC provisions and the major aspects of the doctrine that you should keep in mind when reading your jurisdiction's particular elective share statute.

2. **Share vs. support:** Virtually all elective share statutes grant the surviving spouse a *share* of the deceased spouse's property, but a handful permit the deceased spouse to satisfy his or her statutory requirements by granting the surviving spouse a *life estate* in a specific fraction of the deceased spouse's property. In such cases, arguably the elective share is nothing more than an enhanced support right, not a true share.

**B. Introduction:** The elective share doctrine is the time of death spousal protection approach adopted by separate property states. During the marriage, each spouse owns all of his or her earnings as his or her separate property. The separate property system intervenes only when the marriage is terminated—in divorce or death. The elective share typically gave the surviving spouse the right to claim a share of the deceased spouse's probate property (typically one-third if the testator had surviving issue, or one-half if no surviving issue). The elective share applies regardless of the length of the marriage.

**C. Scope of doctrine:** Inasmuch as the elective share doctrine gives the surviving spouse the right to a forced share, if necessary, of the deceased spouse's property, the issue becomes *how much of the deceased spouse's property* is subject to the elective share.

**D. Traditional:** The original formulation of the elective share, and the formulation still in effect in a number of states, provides that the surviving spouse is entitled to a share of the deceased spouse's *probate* estate only.

**Rationale:** Historically, most of a decedent's property passed via probate, so tying the elective share to the deceased spouse's probate estate made sense. In addition, under the separate property system, absent cause (divorce or death), each spouse is free to do with his or her property whatever he or she wants, including making inter vivos transfers.

**E. Nonprobate avoidance:** The traditional approach to the elective share doctrine accepts that inter vivos transfers by the deceased spouse are not subject to the elective share, only the decedent's testamentary transfers—property that the decedent owns at time of death. This distinction, however, arguably assumes a classic inter vivos transfer—made to a third party, with the transferor retaining no interest in the property following the transfer.

1. **Nonprobate transfers:** Property placed in an inter vivos trust does not pass through probate, thus avoiding the elective share under the traditional approach.

2. **Example:** Assume a spouse creates an inter vivos trust, transfers substantially all his or her property to the trust, and retains a life estate interest in the trust (and possibly even the power

to revoke or appoint the property). Despite the fact that the spouse has virtually the same right to enjoy the property in the trust that he or she would have if the property were not in trust, under the traditional approach the property in the trust would be deemed not subject to the elective share because the future interest in trust property passed inter vivos pursuant to the terms of the trust, not through probate and not at time of death.

**F. Judicial responses:** As the use of such nonprobate avoidance arrangements grew, pressure grew for changes to the elective share doctrine to close such loopholes. The courts have struggled with articulating a workable response—to identify those inter vivos transfers that are not really inter vivos transfers for purposes of the elective share doctrine. Different approaches have been articulated by different jurisdictions, though sometimes it is hard to tell the difference. Some states have adopted one of the approaches statutorily. All these approaches have been criticized as being either incomplete or having high administrative costs.

**1. The illusory transfer test:** The most common judicial response to the nonprobate avoidance problem has been to adopt the "illusory transfer test" approach. The test focuses on how much of an interest the decedent retained after setting up the nonprobate arrangement. If the decedent retained too much control over the property while in the nonprobate arrangement, the transfer would be treated as a testamentary transfer subject to the elective share. The problem is that how much of an interest the deceased spouse must retain varies from jurisdiction to jurisdiction, and often each case turns on its particular facts.

**Example:** In *Newman v. Dore*, 9 N.E.2d 966 (N.Y. 1937), Ferdinand Strauss died with a valid will that created a trust for the benefit of his wife of one-third of his probate property, with his wife having the right to receive the income from the trust for life. At that time New York law provided that as long as the testator left one-third of his or her estate in trust to pay the income to the surviving spouse for life, the deceased spouse had satisfied his or her legal duty to "share" his or her property with his or her surviving spouse, and the surviving spouse was prevented from claiming an outright one-third elective share. Then, three days before dying, Mr. Strauss transferred all his real and personal property to an inter vivos trust that made no provision for his surviving spouse. Mr. Strauss retained not only the income for life and the power to revoke the trust, but also the right to control the trustees. The court focused on the substance of the conveyance, not its form, and ruled that the conveyance was an illusory transfer—meaning the settlor never intended to divest himself of the property. The court declined to set forth a precise test for how much interest and/or control the settlor must divest himself or herself of to make the transfer a valid inter vivos transfer and not illusory (and not subject to the elective share).

**2. The present donative intent test:** Some jurisdictions have reworded the illusory transfer test so that it focuses more on whether the deceased spouse had a real and present donative intent at the moment that he or she created the nonprobate transfer. The courts focus on the circumstances surrounding the transfer, especially how much of an interest the party gave away, to determine whether any real interest passed at the time the arrangement was created. Some courts focus on the nature and extent of the control the settlor gave up over the property. (Most courts applying this approach have found the commonly used inter vivos revocable trust with retained life estate to be a valid nonprobate transfer, but there is an emerging modern trend that tends to hold the revocable inter vivos trust with retained life estate subject to the elective share claim.)

**Example:** In *Sullivan v. Burkin*, 460 N.E.2d 572 (Mass. 1984), the husband and wife separated but did not divorce. The husband created an inter vivos trust, to which he transferred his real estate (his principal asset) to himself as sole trustee. He retained a life estate interest in the income, the right to withdraw principal upon written request to the trustee, and the right to revoke. Upon his death, the property in the trust was to be distributed to two friends. His will (disposing of only 15 percent of his wealth) likewise made no provision for his separated wife. She invoked her right to an elective share and argued that it included the property in the trust. The court held that the trust was a valid inter vivos trust and as such the surviving wife had no right to claim an elective share in the property in the trust. The court went on the announce, however, that henceforth, assets in an inter vivos trust created during the marriage would be subject to the elective share if the deceased spouse alone retained a power to revoke or general power of appointment (exercisable by deed or will). (In *Johnson v. La Grange State Bank*, 383 N.E.2d 185 (Ill. 1978), however, the court held that the degree of control retained by the settlor was not determinative but merely was one of the factors to be considered.)

3. **The intent to defraud test:** The intent to defraud test focuses on the deceased spouse's state of mind regarding his or her surviving spouse: Did the deceased spouse intend to defraud his or her surviving spouse by creating the nonprobate property arrangement in question? The jurisdictions are split on how to determine whether the deceased spouse intended to defraud the surviving spouse of his or her elective share rights in the property.

   a. **Subjective approach:** Some jurisdictions take a subjective approach: Did the deceased spouse *actually intend* to defraud the surviving spouse of his or her right to an elective share in the property by creating the nonprobate transfer? The obvious criticism of this approach is the difficulty of proving subjective intent.

   b. **Objective approach:** A handful of jurisdictions take an objective approach to whether the nonprobate transfer in question defrauded the surviving spouse of his or her right to an elective share in the property.

4. **Effect of holding inter vivos transfer subject to elective share:** As a general rule, if an inter vivos transfer is found to be an illusory transfer subject to the surviving spouse's elective share claim, the inter vivos transfer is not invalid, but the value of the assets transferred is added back into the deceased spouse's probate estate to determine the amount of the surviving spouse's elective share. Some of the inter vivos transfer may be invalidated, however, if necessary to fund the elective share.

G. **Statutory/UPC response:** In many states, the legislature addressed the problem by drafting legislation that expands the scope of the property subject to the elective share.

1. **1969 UPC augmented estate:** The 1969 version of the UPC adopted what became known as the "augmented estate" approach to the elective share. The surviving spouse was entitled to receive one-third of the deceased spouse's augmented estate.

   a. **The augmented estate:** The augmented estate included not only the decedent's probate estate, but also certain nonprobate and gratuitous inter vivos transfers *made during the marriage*: (1) any transfers where the deceased spouse retained the right to possession or income from the property; (2) any transfers where the deceased spouse retained the power to revoke or the power to use or appoint (dispose of) the principal for his or her own benefit; (3) any joint tenancies with anyone other than the surviving spouse; (4) gifts to third parties within two years of the deceased spouse's death in excess of $3,000 per donee per year; (5) property given to the surviving spouse either inter vivos or via nonprobate transfers (including life estate interests in trusts). Life insurance proceeds to someone other than the surviving spouse were expressly excluded.

**Property given to surviving spouse:** Property given to the surviving spouse inter vivos or through nonprobate transfers is included in the augmented estate to prevent a surviving spouse who has been adequately provided for by such transfers from claiming an elective share to take more than his or her fair share.

**b. Funding:** To protect the deceased spouse's estate plan as much as possible, the augmented estate is funded first by crediting any property he or she received under the will against the elective share amount. Any remaining property due is taken pro rata from the other will beneficiaries (though a few jurisdictions take it from the residuary gift).

**c. Community property component:** The 1969 version of the UPC limited the augmented estate to those nonprobate transfers made *during the marriage.* If the transfer occurred prior to marriage, even if the transfer otherwise would have constituted a transfer subject to the augmented estate, the property subject to the premarriage transfer was not included in the augmented estate. By limiting the augmented estate to transfers made during the marriage, the 1969 version of the UPC arguably began to introduce community property principles into the separate property system.

**2. 1990 UPC marital property approach:** The 1990 version of the UPC elective share doctrine strove to achieve an elective share that would result in approximately the same amount of the deceased spouse's property going to the surviving spouse as would have gone under community property. Several major changes were adopted to the elective share doctrine to try to achieve this result under separate property rules.

**a. Sliding scale:** The 1990 version of the UPC abandons the fixed percentage elective share and provides instead a gradually increasing share depending on the length of the marriage. The surviving spouse starts out entitled to 3 percent of the deceased spouse's augmented estate and the share increases approximately 3 percentage points a year until the spouse is entitled to 50 percent of the deceased spouse's augmented estate after 15 years of marriage. UPC §2-202(a) (as amended in 1993).

**b. Augmented estate:** The 1990 version of the augmented estate no longer focuses only on the deceased spouse's property, but includes both spouses' property. If neither couple had any separate property when they married, this approach mirrors community property. Unlike the 1969 version of the UPC, however, the 1990 version includes transfers made before marriage if the deceased spouse retained substantial control over the property. The 1990 version of the UPC also reverses the 1969 UPC and expressly includes life insurance proceeds paid to someone other than the surviving spouse.

**c. Community property differences:** The 1990 version of the UPC augmented estate arguably is broader than the community property notion of marital property. Under community property, the core concept of marital property is earnings acquired by either spouse during the marriage. Property acquired before marriage and gifts acquired during marriage are that spouse's separate property and the other spouse has no rights in that property. Under the

1990 UPC approach to the augmented estate, property acquired before marriage and gifts acquired during marriage may be subject to the elective share.

**H. Funding the elective share with a life estate:** It is not uncommon for the first spouse to die to leave the surviving spouse only a life estate in all or part of his or her property. The general rule is that if the surviving spouse claims the elective share, the elective share is satisfied first by counting the property the deceased gave under his or her will to the surviving spouse. The issue is whether permitting a life estate interest to count toward the elective share is incompatible with the principle of the elective share. A life estate is intrinsically "support" in nature, while the elective share is intended to ensure that the surviving spouse receives a fair, outright share of the marital property.

  **1. General rule:** If the surviving spouse elects to claim the elective share and takes against the will, most jurisdictions do *not* permit any life estate interests left in the will to the surviving spouse to count against the elective share.

  **2. UPC:** Under the 1969 version of the UPC, if the surviving spouse claimed an elective share, any life estate left to the surviving spouse did *not* count against the elective share amount. In 1975, the UPC was revised to provide that any life estate interests left in the will to the surviving spouse *did* count against the surviving spouse's elective share. In 1993, the UPC reversed itself yet again and returned to the original position that any life estate interests in the rejected will should *not* count against the elective share. UPC §2-209.

  **3. Valuation:** If the life estate counts toward the elective share, under the 1975 version of the UPC the life estate was valued at 50 percent of the property in which the surviving spouse was granted the life estate. In 1990, the UPC was amended to remove the 50 percent valuation method and no substitute method was inserted.

**I. Exercise of the elective share—personal right:** The general rule, and UPC approach, is that only the surviving spouse can elect to claim the elective share. If the surviving spouse dies before asserting the claim, the surviving spouse's estate, heirs, and creditors have no standing to claim the share even if the time to assert it has not expired.

  **1. Incompetent spouse:** If the surviving spouse lacks the capacity to decide whether to exercise the elective share, a guardian of the spouse can decide, "in the best interests" of the surviving spouse, for the surviving spouse, with the probate court's approval. In some jurisdictions, what constitutes the best interests of the surviving spouse is a purely economic question—whether the spouse would take more under the elective share. In a majority of jurisdictions, however, the guardian is given greater discretion and is permitted to take the totality of the circumstances surrounding the deceased spouse and the surviving spouse into consideration.

  **2. UPC approach:** The 1969 version of the UPC authorized the probate court to claim the elective share for an incompetent spouse only if necessary to provide adequate support for the surviving spouse for the rest of his or her life. This approach reflects a "support" approach to the elective share. In 1990, the UPC was amended to provide that if the elective share is exercised for an incompetent spouse, the share of the elective share that exceeds the share the spouse was taking under the deceased spouse's will is placed in a custodial trust, with the surviving spouse having a life estate, and a remainder in the devisees under the will (so as to minimize the effect on the deceased spouse's estate plan). UPC §2-212.

  **3. Medicaid eligibility:** Although the general rule is that the elective share is personal to the surviving spouse and cannot be exercised by anyone other than the surviving spouse, an exception exists when it comes to Medicaid eligibility. The elective share and the property that would satisfy the elective share are assets that may be included in determining an individual's eligibility for Medicaid. Courts have ordered guardians of an incompetent spouse to claim the elective share so as not to jeopardize the spouse's Medicaid eligibility (thereby acting in the best interests of the spouse).

**J. Waiver:** The general rule is that a surviving spouse may waive his or her right to an elective share (and to the homestead allowance, personal property exempt property, and the family allowance) at any time, as long as the waiver is in writing, signed by the waiving spouse, and that it was executed after fair disclosure of the other party's financial situation. The waiver is not enforceable if the surviving spouse can prove (1) that it was not made voluntarily, or (2) that it was unconscionable when executed (if the amount the waiving spouse is to receive is wholly disproportionate to the amount of the other spouse's property and to the amount the waiving spouse would take under the law), and before executed, the surviving spouse did not know nor reasonably could have known the deceased spouse's financial situation and the surviving spouse did not voluntarily and expressly waive the right to know such information.

**Example:** In *Geddings v. Geddings*, 460 S.E.2d 376 (S.C. 1995), the Geddings were married in 1979. Both had been married before, and both had children from their prior marriages. In 1988, Mrs. Geddings signed a document entitled "Waiver of Right to Elect and of Other Rights." The document acknowledged that each had executed a will, that each wanted the bulk of their property to go to their respective children, that each waived the right to claim an elective share in the other's estate, and that each had made a full, fair, and complete disclosure to each other of all presently owned assets. The evidence at trial was that while Mrs. Geddings had disclosed her financial situation to Mr. Geddings, there was no evidence that he had disclosed his financial situation to her—and there was substantial evidence that he was secretive about his financial affairs. The court held the waiver void because Mrs. Geddings had not received the required fair disclosure.

**K. Malpractice liability:** An attorney who fails to advise a client about the elective share and the effect it would have on the client's testamentary scheme can be liable under malpractice for any damages caused.

**L. Conflict of laws:** The standard conflict of laws rule is that the laws of the state where the real property is located control disposition of the real property, including whether the surviving spouse is entitled to receive an elective share in the real property. The UPC, however, provides that the laws of the state where the decedent was domiciled at the time of death control whether the surviving spouse is entitled to receive an elective share in real property located in another state. UPC §2-202(d).

**M. Spousal abandonment:** The general rule is that spousal abandonment is not grounds for barring the surviving spouse from claiming an elective share. A handful of states, however, bar the abandoning spouse from claiming an elective share.

**N. Same-sex couples:** To date, no court has extended the elective share doctrine to include same-sex couples that lived in a spousal-like relationship.

    **1. Contract claim:** In some states, a surviving same-sex partner might have a claim against the deceased partner based on contract law. Whether the contract must be express (oral vs. written—vs. implied) varies from jurisdiction to jurisdiction.

    **2. Domestic partners:** Some state legislatures are granting same-sex couples many of the same rights as married couples, but without permitting them to marry. In Hawaii, same-sex couples can register as "reciprocal beneficiaries" and receive elective share rights. In California, same-sex couples can register as "domestic partners" and receive the same inheritance rights as spouses with respect to separate property. Starting January 1, 2005, domestic partners will be granted community property rights and the same inheritance rights as spouses with respect to it.

3. **Defense of Marriage Act:** In 1996, Congress enacted the Defense of Marriage Act. The Act defines "marriage" for federal purposes as applying only to heterosexual couples and provides that despite the Full Faith and Credit Clause of the Constitution, states are not required to recognize same-sex marriages entered into in other states.

# V. COMMUNITY PROPERTY

A. **Introduction:** The essence of community property is that all marital property is owned by the community the moment it is acquired. Marital property is any property acquired during marriage as a result of the time, energy, or labor of either spouse. As a practical matter, community property is any earnings acquired by either spouse during marriage (and any property purchased with such earnings). Property acquired by gift, devise, or inheritance during marriage or by either spouse before marriage is separate property.

1. **Transmutation:** The spouses can convert the legal characterization of property by agreement. Separate property can be converted to community property, and vice versa. The jurisdictions are split over what evidence is necessary to prove a transmutation (writing vs. clear and convincing nonwritten evidence, etc.).

2. **Death:** Upon the death of one spouse, each community property asset is divided 50-50. The surviving spouse owns his or her share outright. The deceased spouse's share goes into probate, where the deceased spouse can devise it as he or she wishes.

3. **Stepped up basis:** Upon the death of a spouse, his or her property receives a stepped up basis for purposes of calculating capital gains following subsequent sale of the property. If the property is held concurrently but not as community property (i.e., joint tenancy or tenancy in common), only the deceased spouse's share receives a stepped up basis to its fair market value at the time of the spouse's death. If, however, the property is held as community property, the whole asset receives a stepped up basis (both the deceased spouse's half and the surviving spouse's half).

B. **Community property vs. elective share:** One of the principal differences between the elective share and community property is their timing. Under community property, the spousal protection scheme attaches the moment the marital property is acquired. Under the elective share approach, the spousal protection doctrine does not arise until one of the spouses dies and the surviving spouse elects to claim his or her statutory amount instead of taking under the deceased spouse's will.

C. **Fundamental differences:** There are, however, a number of key differences between the two approaches, at least as developed historically, that should be noted upfront.

1. **Rights during marriage:** Under the separate property approach, the nonwage-earning spouse has no rights in the wage-earning spouse's property during the marriage. Under the community property approach, the moment each dollar is earned during the marriage, the nonwage-earning

spouse has an equal right to half of it. The latter arguably puts the spouses on a more equal status during the marriage.

2. **Scope of property covered:** Historically, the elective share applied to *all* the deceased spouse's probate property, not just to the spouse's marital property. Community property, on the other hand, applies only to marital property acquired during the marriage, and not to either spouse's separate property.

3. **Fractional shares:** Historically, the elective share was limited to 33 percent of the deceased spouse's property. Community property, on the other hand, grants an immediate 50 percent interest in each marital asset to the nonwage-earning spouse.

4. **Short marriage:** If the marriage is very short, and the deceased spouse had a sizeable separate property estate when he or she got married, the surviving spouse is better off under the elective share approach.

5. **Order of deaths:** If the nonwage-earning spouse dies first, he or she is worse off under the elective share approach. Under community property, he or she can still share in the marital property and devise half the community property as he or she deems appropriate. Under the separate property approach, however, he or she has no rights in the separate property acquired by the wage-earning spouse during the marriage. All the nonwage-earning spouse can devise is his or her own separate property.

D. **Partnership model:** Many argue that community property is truer to the principles underlying the "marriage is a partnership" model. Under community property, the spouses are held to have agreed that the community owns any and all property acquired by the labor of either spouse, with each spouse having an undivided half interest in each asset. The partnership, however, does not extend to the spouse's separate property.

E. **Migrating couples:** Migrating couples pose problems for the spousal protection doctrines. The problems arise because (1) real property is governed by the laws of the state where it is located; (2) personal property is characterized at the time it is acquired as either separate or community property based on the laws of the spouses' domicile at the time of acquisition; and (3) the time of death spousal protection a surviving spouse is entitled to depends on the spouses' domicile at the time of death of the first spouse.

1. **Separate to community example:** Assume a traditional relationship where all the couple's marital property is acquired by and titled in the wage-earning spouse's name. If the couple lives in a separate property jurisdiction, the property is the wage-earning spouse's separate property. If the couple retires and moves to a community property state, and shortly thereafter the wage-earning spouse dies, the spousal protection scheme is community property. The surviving spouse is entitled to 50 percent of their community property, but they have no community property. The characterization of their property is not changed because the couple moved to a community property jurisdiction. Legally the spouse is protected, but as a practical matter there is no protection. The nonwage-earning spouse slips through the cracks of the spousal protection systems.

   a. **Quasi-community property:** Quasi-community property is separate property that would have been characterized as community property if the couple had been domiciled in a community property jurisdiction when the spouse acquired the property. When a spouse with quasi-community property dies, the quasi-community property is treated like community property for distribution purposes. The surviving spouse immediately receives a one-half interest in the quasi-community property that is his or hers outright. The deceased spouse can devise only half of the quasi-community property. Quasi-community property protects the migrating couple.

    **b. Order of deaths:** Quasi-community property is not the same as community property. Quasi-community property applies only to the property owned at death by the deceased spouse, not by the surviving spouse. If the nonacquiring spouse dies first, he or she has no right to devise any of the surviving spouse's property (even if the surviving spouse has property that would have been characterized as quasi-community property if he or she had died first). Quasi-community property gives the nonwage-earning spouse property rights in the property acquired during the marriage by the other spouse only if the wage-earning spouse dies first.

**2. Community to separate example:** Assume a traditional relationship where all the couple's marital property is acquired by and titled in the wage-earning spouse's name. If the couple lives in a community property jurisdiction, the property will be treated as community property. Each spouse owns an undivided one-half interest in the property regardless of how it is titled. If the couple retires and moves to a separate property jurisdiction, and shortly after moving, the wage-earning spouse dies, the spousal protection scheme is the elective share. The nonwage-earning spouse will receive his or her half of the community property outright, and the deceased spouse's half will go into probate. The surviving spouse can then claim an additional one-third or one-half interest in the deceased spouse's probate property (depending on the jurisdiction and family situation). When moving from community property jurisdictions to separate property jurisdictions, the surviving spouse may be able to "double dip" in the spousal protection schemes.

    **a. Legislative reform:** The Uniform Disposition of Community Property Rights at Death Act, adopted in many, but not all, separate property jurisdictions, provides that a deceased spouse's community property that is brought into the state is not subject to the elective share doctrine.

    **b. Transmute property:** One might think that the couple should transmute their community property to separate property upon moving from a community property to a separate property jurisdiction. That would avoid the potential problem of the surviving spouse double dipping in the spousal protection doctrines. But by transmuting the property, the couple would lose the tax benefits of the double stepped up basis that community property receives upon the death of the first spouse. The lost tax savings could be huge.

**F. "Widow's election"—putting a spouse to an election:** Community property jurisdictions do not recognize an elective share, but they do permit a deceased spouse to put a surviving spouse to an election. Despite the similarity in terminology, the doctrines are not similar at all. Putting a spouse to an election is simply a variation on the idea that a decedent can make a conditional gift. The deceased spouse conditions a devise to the surviving spouse on the surviving spouse agreeing to the deceased spouse being permitted to give away some of the surviving spouse's property. One of the principal issues is how clear must the deceased spouse be that he or she is putting the surviving spouse to an election. Historically, spouses were put to an implied election anytime the deceased spouse's will appeared to give away some of the surviving spouse's property. Under the modern trend, the courts have tightened up the intent necessary to put the surviving spouse to an election, holding that the intent must be clear.

# VI. THE OMITTED/PRETERMITTED SPOUSE

**A. Overview:** People disagree over whether the omitted spouse doctrine, historically known as the "pretermitted" spouse doctrine, is a spousal protection doctrine or a corrective doctrine, a doctrine designed to correct what is presumed to be a mistake by the decedent.

**B. Traditional scenario:** The omitted spouse doctrine applies where a testator executes a will, thereafter gets married, and dies without revising or revoking his or her will. The issue that arises is whether the testator intended to disinherit his or her spouse, or whether the testator intended to revise his or her will to provide for his or her new spouse, but died before getting around to it.

    **1. Spousal vs. nonspousal capacity:** The classic omitted spouse scenario assumes that the testator's will does not provide at all for the person who ends up being his or her spouse. But even if the will does provide for the person who ends up being the testator's spouse, unless the testator thought the person was going to be his or her spouse when he or she executed the will, the gift in the will to the person who became the testator's spouse generally will not defeat the doctrine; but some courts apply the statutory language narrowly and strictly and refuse to apply the doctrine if the surviving spouse is provided for in the will but not in his or her capacity as a spouse.

    **2. Example:** In *Herbach v. Herbach,* 583 N.W.2d 541 (Mich. Ct. App. 1998), Walter Herbach executed his will in 1982. It gave $50,000 to his "friend" Eileen. Thereafter Walter and Eileen married. Walter died without revising his will. Eileen claimed pretermitted spouse. The court held she was provided for in the will and refused to consider whether she was named in the will in some capacity other than as a spouse.

**C. Omitted spouse presumption:** Where the testator (1) marries after executing his or her will and (2) dies without revising or revoking his or her will, this combination creates a presumption that the testator "accidentally disinherited" his spouse—i.e., meant to amend his or her will to provide for his or her new spouse, but died before doing so.

**D. Rebuttable presumption:** The presumption that the testator accidentally disinherited his or her spouse is rebuttable, but the traditional omitted spouse doctrine provided that the presumption could be rebutted only by showing that (1) the failure to provide for the new spouse was intentional and that intent appears from the will; (2) the testator provided for the spouse outside of the will and the intent that the transfer outside of the will be in lieu of the spouse taking under the will is established by any evidence, including oral statements by the testator and/or the amount of the transfer; or (3) the spouse validly waived the right to share in the testator's estate.

**Will evidences intent to omit:** The courts have construed the first method of rebutting the presumption, that the will evidences the intent to disinherit, very narrowly. Most courts have held that a general disinheritance clause, and even a general clause disinheriting any future spouse, is insufficient to defeat the presumption. The will must demonstrate the express intent to omit this specific spouse, and the clause must have been executed when the testator was contemplating marrying this specific spouse.

**E. Omitted spouse's share:** If the presumption that the failure to provide for the new spouse was not intentional is not rebutted, the typical omitted spouse statute gives the omitted spouse his or her intestate share of the testator's probate estate.

**F. UPC:** The UPC tracks the basic provisions of the traditional pretermitted spouse doctrine, but it has a few revisions worth noting.

1. **Intent to omit:** The UPC broadens the evidence that can be used to prove that the spouse's omission from the will was intentional to include evidence (1) from the will, or (2) other evidence that the will was made in contemplation of the testator's marriage to the surviving spouse, or (3) a general provision in the will that it is effective notwithstanding any subsequent marriage.

2. **Omitted spouse's share:** The UPC grants an omitted spouse the right to receive no less than his or her intestate share of the deceased spouse's estate from that portion of the testator's estate, if any, that is not devised to a child of the testator or the child's descendants (directly or through anti-lapse) if (1) the child is not a child of the surviving spouse, and (2) the child was born before the testator married the surviving spouse. The effect of this provision is that if the testator devises all his probate estate to his child or descendants from a prior relationship or marriage, the surviving spouse will not receive an omitted spouse's share despite otherwise meeting the requirements of an omitted spouse.

**G. Elective share vs. omitted spouse:** It is hard to make many detailed comments about the difference between the elective share and the omitted spouse share because the elective share varies so much from jurisdiction to jurisdiction, but close attention should be paid to the differences between the two in your jurisdiction. In particular, you should watch for the following:

1. **Overlap:** The typical omitted spouse will also qualify for an elective share. If the spouse's decision is based solely on the bottom line, it is important that you know how to calculate the exact amount of the share he or she would receive under the respective doctrines. The modern trend approach to the elective share often includes nonprobate property as well, making it look more attractive, unless the UPC sliding scale has been adopted and the marriage has been a short one.

2. **UPC:** Under the UPC approach to the omitted spouse doctrine, where the testator has a will that devises all or substantially all his or her property to a child or descendants of a child not of the surviving omitted spouse, for all practical purposes the surviving spouse is forced to claim an elective share because the omitted spouse's share under these circumstances will be so small.

**H. Malpractice liability:** If the client advises the attorney, during the estate planning process, that he or she is planning on getting married, and the attorney fails to expressly note that the will was made in contemplation of marriage, the beneficiaries whose shares are reduced to fund the omitted spouse's share can sue the attorney for malpractice. Moreover, if the attorney does not know that the client is contemplating marriage when the will is drafted and executed, but learns thereafter the testator has married, the attorney has an ethical obligation to advise the client of the omitted spouse doctrine and of the effect the doctrine would have on the testamentary scheme expressed in the will. ABA Model Code of Responsibility, Disciplinary Rule 2-104(A)(1).

**I. Modern trend—application to revocable trusts:** A few states have modified the omitted spouse doctrine to provide that it arises only if the marriage occurs after execution of all the deceased spouse's wills and revocable trusts, and the omitted spouse's share is of the property included in the probate estate and revocable trusts.

# VII. THE OMITTED/PRETERMITTED CHILD

A. **Overview:** The omitted child doctrine, historically known as the "pretermitted" child doctrine, parallels the omitted spouse doctrine. Because a testator can completely omit a child (except in Louisiana), but cannot completely disinherit a spouse (due to the elective share/community property spousal protection doctrines), the omitted child doctrine arguably is more of a presumed intent/corrective doctrine than a protective doctrine.

B. **Traditional scenario:** The omitted child doctrine applies where a testator executes a will, thereafter has a child, and dies without revising or revoking his or her will. The issue is whether the testator intended to omit his or her new child, or whether the testator intended to revise his or her will to provide for his or her new child, but died before getting around to it.

1. **Gift:** The classic omitted child scenario assumes that the testator did not provide at all in his or her will for the child born after execution of his or her will. If the will contains a provision that gives a share to children born after execution of the will, as a general rule that child will not qualify as an omitted child.

2. **Children alive at execution:** Some states extend the omitted child statute to include not only children born after execution of the will, but also children born *before* execution of the will but not named in the will.

   **Affirmative disinheritance:** Where the omitted child statute covers living children as well, most courts require affirmative disinheritance (specific reference to the child). A negative disinheritance (a blanket statement that the testator has no children, or that no children are to take under the will) is generally held not to be sufficient. Generic clauses giving a nominal amount to any child who might qualify to take are likewise generally held insufficient to bar the doctrine.

C. **Omitted child presumption:** Where the testator has a child after executing his or her will and dies without revising or revoking his or her will, this combination creates a presumption that the testator meant to amend his or her will to provide for his or her new child, but died before getting around to it.

D. **Rebuttable presumption:** The presumption that the testator accidentally disinherited his or her child is rebuttable, but the traditional omitted child doctrine provided that the presumption could be rebutted only by showing that (1) the failure to provide for the new child was intentional and that intent appears from the will; (2) the testator provided for the child outside of the will and the intent that the transfer outside of the will be in lieu of the child taking under the will is established by any evidence, including the amount of the transfer; or (3) the testator had one or more children when the will was executed and devised substantially all his or her estate to the other parent of the omitted child.

1. **"Missouri" type statute:** Under what is known as the "Missouri" type of omitted child statute, the intent to omit the child must be determinable solely from the terms of the will. Extrinsic evidence is not admissible.

2. **"Massachusetts" type statute:** Under what is known as the "Massachusetts" type of omitted child statute, extrinsic evidence is admissible to help determine whether the omission of the child was intentional or not.

**3. Example:** In *Estate of Glomset,* 547 P.2d 951 (Okla. 1976), John and Margie Glomset executed joint and reciprocal wills leaving everything to each other, and in the event the two died in a common disaster, all to John's son, John Jr. John failed to mention his 40-year-old daughter, Carolyn, in his will. John died a year later, and Carolyn claimed a share of his estate as a pretermitted heir. The court found that Carolyn was not named in the will, and therefore she qualified as a pretermitted heir. Although the dissent argued that the wording of the Oklahoma statute should be characterized as a "Massachusetts-type" statute for which extrinsic evidence should be admissible, the majority ruled that because there was no ambiguity in the will, extrinsic evidence was not admissible to determine if Carolyn's omission was accidental or intentional.

**E. Omitted child's share:** If the presumption that the failure to provide for the new child was not intentional is not rebutted, the typical omitted child statute gives the omitted child his or her intestate share of the testator's probate estate.

**F. Overlooked child:** A number of states have expanded the traditional omitted child doctrine to include a living child who is omitted if the child is omitted because (1) the testator does not know about the child, or (2) the testator mistakenly believed the child was dead. (More states cover only the latter, a handful cover both.) As a general rule, the overlooked child receives his or her intestate share just like a pretermitted child.

**G. UPC:** The UPC tracks the basic provisions of the traditional pretermitted child doctrine, but it has a few revisions worth noting.

**1. Adopted children:** The UPC expressly provides that it applies to children born or adopted after execution of the will.

**2. Intent to omit:** Unlike the UPC omitted spouse doctrine, the UPC omitted child doctrine does not broaden the scope of the evidence that can be used to prove the intent to omit a new child. The UPC sticks with the traditional rule that the evidence that the failure to provide for the child was intentional must come *from the will.*

**3. Other children:** Under the traditional approach, if the presumption arose that a child was accidentally omitted, the presumption could be overcome if the testator had one or more children when the will was executed and devised substantially all his or her estate to the other parent of the omitted child. The UPC, however, does not permit such evidence to defeat the child's claim to an omitted share, but rather uses it in calculating how much the child should receive.

**4. Omitted child's share:** The omitted child's share under the UPC depends on whether the testator has other children living at the time he or she executes the will.

**a. No children:** If the testator had no children when he or she executed the will, the omitted child receives his or her intestate share, unless the testator devised all or substantially all his or her estate to the other parent of the omitted child and the other parent survives the testator and is entitled to take—in which case the omitted child takes nothing.

**b. One or more children:** If the testator has one or more children living at the time he or she executes the will, and the will devised property to one or more of the then-living children, the omitted child's share (1) is taken out of the portion of the testator's estate being devised to the then-living children; (2) should equal the share or interest the other children are receiving, had the testator included all omitted children with the children receiving shares and given each an equal share. (Gifts to the then-living children are to abate pro rata.)

**5. Overlooked child:** The UPC expressly includes a child who is overlooked in the will because the testator thought the child was dead when he or she executed the will. The UPC does not extend omitted child status to the child overlooked because the testator does not know about the child.

**H. Omitted issue of deceased child:** Most omitted child statutes cover omitted children only. Some statutes, however, expressly provide that they apply not only to omitted children, but also to the omitted issue of a child who died before the testator. The omitted issue of the child who died before the testator take their intestate share.

**I. Modern trend—application to revocable trusts:** A few states have modified the omitted child doctrine to provide that it arises only if the birth occurs after execution of all the deceased spouse's wills and revocable trusts, and the omitted child's share is of the property included in the probate estate and revocable trusts.

# VIII. LIMITATIONS ON CHARITABLE GIFTS

**A. Mortmain statutes:** Mortmain statutes limit the testamentary gifts a decedent can make to charitable recipients. The rationale was that as one got older and closer to death, one might "irrationally" think about trying to "buy" one's way into a better afterlife—at the expense of family members. Mortmain statutes varied by jurisdiction, some putting monetary limits on testamentary gifts to charities, others restricting gifts to charities made within a prescribed time period before death, and yet others employing some combination of these two approaches. In addition, some statutes added that they applied only if certain "close" family members survived the testator.

**B. Modern trend—abolition:** In virtually every jurisdiction, the mortmain statute has been either legislatively repealed or judicially invalidated as unconstitutional under the Equal Protection Clause (for lacking a "fair and substantial relationship" to the legislative objective).

---

## *Quiz Yourself on*
## *LIMITATIONS ON THE TESTAMENTARY POWER TO TRANSFER*

**13.** List the five different rights to support to which a surviving spouse is entitled as a general rule upon the death of his or her spouse. _____

**14.** Bob marries Carol. They have one child, Sunshine. On April 1, 2000, Bob dies intestate with a gross probate estate of $200,000. Bob's funeral expenses, administration expenses, and debts total $50,000. Carol is trying to determine what she would get if she claimed her elective share. As a result of Bob's death, Carol received $600,000 in life insurance proceeds from a policy on which Bob had paid the premiums. In addition, prior to his death, and during the marriage, Bob made the following transfers:

- 1/1/85 Transferred $150,000 in trust for the benefit of Mom, but he retained the power to revoke the trust during his lifetime.

- 1/1/95 $600,000 Purchased Malibuacres—Bob put up all the consideration, but took title in joint tenancy with his brother, Bill.

- 6/1/97 Irrevocable gift to Lulu $20,000.

- 1/1/98 Irrevocable gift to Lulu $20,000.

- 6/1/98 Irrevocable gift to Lulu $25,000.

- 1/1/99 Irrevocable gift to Lulu $30,000.

- 5/1/99 Transferred $150,000 in trust for his benefit for life, remainder to Lulu, and retained the power to revoke.

- 6/1/99 Irrevocable gift to Lulu $30,000.

- 1/1/2000 Irrevocable gift to Lulu $35,000.

(Answer the question below that constitutes the approach your jurisdiction takes. If your jurisdiction's approach is not among the possible questions, do your best to answer it on your own and then check the answer for the approach closet to your state's approach.)

**a.** What is Carol's right to an elective share if (1) the elective share is one-third of the net estate if the decedent is survived by one or more children, otherwise one-half of the net estate; and (2) the jurisdiction limits the elective share to the deceased spouse's probate estate? _____

**b.** What is Carol's right to an elective share if (1) the jurisdiction follows the same fractional shares as above, and (2) it also follows the "illusory transfer" approach to what constitutes the decedent's estate? _____

**c.** What is Carol's right to an elective share if (1) the jurisdiction follows the same fractional shares as above, and (2) it also follows the 1969 UPC approach to what constitutes the decedent's estate? _____

15. Suzy and Kevin are starving students. They get married and live in Missouri, a noncommunity property state. Suzy works outside the home earning their marital property, and Kevin stays at home raising the children. They decide to retire. At the time, they have a total of $500,000 in savings in Suzy's name alone. Shortly after moving to a community property state, Suzy dies with a will devising all her property to the American Heart Association. Assuming the state has no special statute governing migrating couples and their property, and Kevin asserts his rights to a share of the marital property, how much does the American Heart Association take? _____

16. In problem 15 above, what if after moving to the community property jurisdiction, it was Kevin who died with a will devising all his property to the American Heart Association? Suzy survives him, and the jurisdiction has adopted quasi-community property. How much does the American Heart Association take? _____

17. Sunshine and Dude, two penniless hippies residing in a community property state, get married. Dude hits it big on the surfing circuit. During the marriage, he earns $1,000,000 in his name alone. Sunshine spends all her time volunteering to fight global warming. Concerned that melting icebergs will submerge the coastal state where they live, the two retire to Missouri, a separate property jurisdiction. Shortly after establishing domicile in Missouri, Dude dies of boredom. His will devises all his property to the Heal the Bay Association. Assuming Missouri has no special statute governing

migrating couples and their property, and assuming Sunshine asserts her rights to the couple's marital property, how much will the Heal the Bay Association take?    _____

**18.** In problem 17 above, what if Missouri has adopted the Uniform Disposition of Community Property at Death Act?    _____

**19.** Gloria has a will that devises all her property to the National Organization for Women. The will includes an express clause disinheriting any and all other individuals who might claim they are entitled to a share of her estate, including any future spouses. Not long after, to the shock of everyone, she marries Fred. Thereafter, she dies without revoking or revising her will, but she takes out a $1,000,000 life insurance policy that provides that the proceeds are to be paid to Fred upon her death. Following Gloria's death, Fred claims he is an omitted spouse entitled to a share of Gloria's property. Is Fred entitled to a share of Gloria's property:

**a.** Under the traditional approach to the omitted spouse doctrine?    _____

**b.** Under the UPC approach to the omitted spouse doctrine?    _____

**20.** Peter and Carolyn are married with no children. Peter executes a will leaving all his property to Carolyn. Thereafter, Carolyn gives birth to a child, Chad. Shortly after, Peter dies without revising his will. Is Chad entitled to any of Peter's probate property:

**a.** Under the traditional approach to the omitted child doctrine?    _____

**b.** Under the UPC approach to the omitted child doctrine?    _____

**21.** What if in problem 20 above, Peter and Carolyn had two children (Ali and Benji) at the time Peter executed his will, and Peter's will left 70 percent of his estate to Carolyn and the rest to Ali and Benji. Thereafter, Peter and Carolyn had another child, Chad. Is Chad entitled to any of Peter's probate property:

**a.** Under the traditional approach to the omitted child doctrine?    _____

**b.** Under the UPC approach to the omitted child doctrine?    _____

---

## Answers

**13.** As a general rule, a surviving spouse's rights to support include rights under social security; rights under ERISA; rights under the homestead exemption to a place to live; rights under the personal property set-aside to certain tangible personal property; and rights to a family allowance to live on during probate (either a set statutory amount or an amount tied to the family's standard of living at the time the deceased spouse died).

**14. a.** This approach represents the traditional elective share approach because it is limited to the deceased spouse's probate estate. The share depends upon the family situation. Here, Bob is survived by one child, so his wife, Carol, is entitled to 33 percent of his net probate estate. Bob's gross probate estate is $200,000, but he has expenses and debts totaling $50,000. Bob's net probate estate is $150,000. Carol can claim 33 percent of that, or $50,000.

**b.** There is no consensus as to what constitutes an illusory transfer. The essence of the doctrine is that inter vivos transfers that, as a practical matter, do not transfer any *real* interest until the transferor dies should not be treated as inter vivos transfers for purposes of the elective share doctrine (i.e., considered part of the decedent's estate when calculating the elective share). As applied to this fact pattern, the most likely result is that in addition to Bob's net probate estate ($150,000), the 5/1/99 revocable trust, in which Bob retained a life estate interest, remainder to Lulu, would be brought back in and added to the net probate estate (to total $300,000 now). Whether the 1/1/85 trust in favor of his mother would be brought back in is less clear. On the one hand, he retained the power to revoke, so he had control over the assets until he died (like a will, he could have changed the beneficiaries until death). On the other hand, Bob had no interest in the income or principal, only the power to revoke. He established the trust for the benefit of his mother. (These considerations begin to raise the arguments that led to the development of the intent to defraud test—the property is brought back in only if the decedent had the intent to defraud his or her surviving spouse of his or her elective share, though the jurisdictions are split over whether this is a subjective or objective test.) If the court were to conclude that the revocable trust in favor of mom constitutes an illusory transfer, for purposes of the elective share doctrine his estate would be $450,000, and Carol would take one-third or $150,000. If the court were to conclude that the trust should not be brought back in, Bob's estate for elective share purposes would be $300,000—and Carol would be entitled to $100,000. (Property held in joint tenancy is generally held not to constitute an illusory transfer—the other party acquires substantive and substantial inter vivos right, and the gifts to Lulu were completed inter vivos transfers that generally would not be considered part of Bob's assets still under the illusory transfer approach.)

**c.** The 1969 UPC approach takes the augmented estate approach. In addition to the probate estate, the augmented estate includes a number of transfers made without consideration, including (1) transfers where the decedent retained the power to revoke; (2) any transfer in joint tenancy where the other joint tenant is not the spouse; (3) any transfers within two years of death exceeding $3,000 per donee, and (4) property received by the surviving spouse as a result of the decedent's death. Here, in addition to Bob's net probate estate ($150,000), under the 1969 UPC approach, the augmented estate would include (1) both of his revocable trusts—to mom and Lulu ($300,000); (2) Malibuacres, the joint tenancy with his brother ($600,000); (3) the gifts to Lulu within two years of Bob's death that exceeded $2,000 a year (6/1/98 $25,000 + 1/1/99 $30,000 + 6/1/99 $30,000 + 1/1/2000 $35,000 = $120,000); and (4) the life insurance proceeds Carol received ($600,000). The total augmented estate is $1,770,000. Carol's one-third is $590,000. Property that passes to the surviving spouse (the life insurance and probate estate share) is counted first in funding her share. Because Carol has already received more than her elective share amount, she takes no additional property under the 1969 UPC approach.

15. Because Missouri is a noncommunity property jurisdiction, all the money that Suzy earns is her separate property. When they move to the community property jurisdiction, the characterization of the property does not change. Assuming the jurisdiction has no special statutes governing migrating couples (i.e., no quasi-community property doctrine), when Suzy dies, Kevin is entitled to half of their community property. Because they have no community property, Kevin takes none of the property. The American Heart Association would take all $500,000.

16. Quasi-community property gives the surviving spouse community property rights in the deceased spouse's property that would have been characterized as community property if the couple had been domiciled in a community property jurisdiction when the property was acquired. Here, Kevin has no property in his name. Quasi-community property does not attach to Suzy's separate property. The American Heart Association would take nothing under Kevin's will because he has no property in his name and no rights to the property in Suzy's name.

**17.** When a couple moves from a community property jurisdiction to a separate property jurisdiction, there is the potential for the surviving spouse to "double dip." Here, because Dude's $1,000,000 was earned during marriage in a community property state, it is community property. When they move to Missouri, a noncommunity property state, the characterization of the property does not change. Upon his death, Sunshine takes her half of the community property outright, and Dude's half goes into probate. Because the couple's marital domicile at time of death was a separate property jurisdiction, Sunshine can also claim her elective share rights in Dude's probate property. Assuming the share is 50 percent of the deceased spouse's probate estate, Sunshine could claim another $250,000. The Heal the Bay Association would take only $250,000.

**18.** Under the Uniform Disposition of Community Property at Death Act, the deceased spouse's share of their community property is not subject to the elective share doctrine. Here, Dude's half of the community property in his probate estate would not be subject to Sunshine's elective share claim. The Heal the Bay Association would take $500,000.

**19. a.** Under the omitted spouse doctrine, because Gloria married Fred after she executed her will and she died without revoking or revising her will, a rebuttable presumption arises that Fred's disinheritance was accidental. One way to rebut the presumption is to show that the decedent provided for the spouse outside of the will and the transfer was intended to be in lieu of the surviving spouse taking under the will. Here, shortly after she married Fred, Gloria took out a $1,000,000 life insurance policy and designated Fred as the beneficiary. When Gloria died, Fred received the $1,000,000. A strong argument can be made that Gloria intended this transfer outside of the will to be in lieu of Fred's taking under her probate estate. Although there is no direct evidence that this is what Gloria intended, the size of the nonprobate transfer and the fact that she purchased the policy shortly after marrying Fred should be enough to convince the court that Gloria intended the life insurance proceeds to be in lieu of Fred taking under her will.

**b.** Under the UPC, if the will expressly provides that the testator is intentionally omitting all future spouses, this clause effectively overcomes the presumption that the spouse was omitted accidentally. Fred would be barred from claiming an omitted spouse's share under the UPC approach because of the express general disinheritance clause in the will.

**20. a.** Under the traditional approach, Chad would be entitled to his intestate share of Peter's estate. Under the omitted child doctrine, when Chad was born after Peter had executed his will, and Peter died without revising or revoking his will, a presumption arose that Chad was accidentally omitted. The traditional methods of rebutting the presumption do not apply here (the will does not express a specific intent to omit this child, there is no transfer outside of the will to Chad, and although Peter transferred all his property to the other parent of the omitted child, he had no children at the time he executed the will).

**b.** Under the UPC, Chad is not entitled to any of Peter's estate as an omitted child. Under the UPC, if the testator has no children at the time he or she executes the will, and the testator leaves all or substantially all of his or her property to the other parent of the omitted child, and the other parent survives the decedent and takes under the will, the child does not take a share of the decedent's probate estate.

**21. a.** Under the traditional approach, although the presumption would arise that the child was accidentally omitted, the presumption is rebutted here. The testator had one or more children when the will was executed and the testator devised substantially all of his or her estate to the other parent of the omitted child. It is presumed that the testator decided to let the other parent of the child decide how best to care for the omitted child.

**b.** Under the UPC approach, the presumption would arise that Chad is an accidentally omitted child. Under the UPC approach, if the testator had one or more children when the will was executed, and the testator devised property to one or more of the then-living children, the omitted child is entitled to a share of the property being distributed to the then-living children. The omitted child's share is the share the child would have received if all omitted after-born children (or adopted) children are included with the children who are taking under the will. Here, Chad would take one-third of the property being devised to Ali and Benji (30 percent of Peter's estate). Each child would end up with 10 percent of the estate.

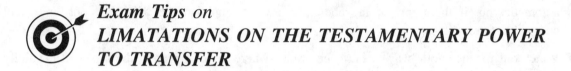

## *Exam Tips on* LIMATATIONS ON THE TESTAMENTARY POWER TO TRANSFER

The material in this chapter can be divided into three major areas: (1) a surviving spouse's right to support; (2) a surviving spouse's right to share in the couple's marital property (elective share and community property); and (3) the omitted spouse/omitted child doctrines.

### Surviving spouse's right to support

The details of a surviving spouse's right to support are generally beyond the scope of the typical wills and trusts course. If you see a spouse die with a surviving spouse, state that the surviving spouse has a right to support, and then quickly list the five forms of support.

### Surviving spouse's right to share in the couple's marital property

The key is coverage. When most professors reach this section of the book, the professor covers only that material that corresponds to the approach in that jurisdiction. Pay close attention to your professor's classroom coverage of this material.

☛ If the professor covers some of the comparative material, close attention in class will best tell you how much of the other approach you need know.

### The elective share

More than any other doctrine, the elective share varies from state to state. The core concepts of the elective share doctrine are its temporal component (no inter vivos rights, just testamentary), its fractional share, and the property subject to it (probate estate only vs. augmented estate—if the latter, focus on what is included in the augmented estate).

### Community property

The core concepts of the community property approach are the scope of community property (property/earnings acquired during marriage, not premarriage property or gifts during marriage), and that at death community property is treated much like tenancy in common (split the property 50-50, the deceased's half goes into probate where he or she is free to devise it as he or she sees fit).

☞ Migrating couples are a great way to test how well the students understand some of the key differences between the two systems.

☞ If you are in a community property jurisdiction, the details of quasi-community property are important. Quasi-community property applies only to the property owned by the deceased spouse, not the surviving spouse.

## Omitted spouse/omitted child

This is core wills and trusts material and is tested often. These issues should be easy to spot, because the triggering fact is either marriage or birth of a child after execution of the will, and then the testator dies without revoking or revising his or her will.

☞ Watch for codicils—and republication by codicil overlaps. Republication is not necessarily automatic, but if the terms of the codicil expressly republish the will, the court may feel compelled to republish.

☞ Watch out for the subtle way to raise the issue—where there appears to be a new will validly executed after the marriage/birth, but for some reason the "new will" is invalid. Not only will this mean that the original will still controls, but also because the attempted new will is invalid, the omitted spouse/child doctrine will still apply.

☞ If the presumption arises, give the rules for how it can be overcome (the limited ways), and then check to see if any apply.

☞ If the will purports to disinherit all future spouses/children, the general (non-UPC) rule is that the disinheritance must be specific—it must be written with an eye toward this particular person. Conversely, just because a spouse takes a gift, if he or she does not take in a spousal capacity, the presumption still arises.

☞ Pay close attention to whether your jurisdiction permits extrinsic evidence concerning whether the omission was intentional (the UPC permits extrinsic evidence for omitted spouses, not for omitted children).

☞ With respect to omitted children, the jurisdictions are split over the significance of whether the testator had one or more children at the time he or she executed the will. Pay close attention to how your jurisdiction deals with this situation.

☞ With respect to omitted children, pay close attention to how the share is calculated and funded. Some states permit the child to take his or her intestate share from the decedent's probate estate, while the UPC approach limits the share to a share of the property being devised to the other children.

CHAPTER 4

# TESTAMENTARY CAPACITY

## *ChapterScope* ───────────────────────

The traditional method of opting out of intestacy is to execute a will. This chapter examines the first requirement for creating a valid will: testamentary capacity. Even if a testator has testamentary capacity generally, if the will or any part thereof is caused by a defect in capacity (insane delusion, undue influence, or fraud), the court will strike that part of the will.

■ **Testamentary capacity:** The testator must have the ability to know (1) the nature and extent of his or her property; (2) the natural objects of his or her bounty; (3) the nature of the testamentary act he or she is performing; and (4) how all of these relate to constitute an orderly plan of disposing of his or her property.

■ **Insane delusion:** A false perception of reality that the testator adheres to against all reason and evidence to the contrary. A *majority* of courts hold that if a *rational person* could not reach the same conclusion under the circumstances, the belief is an insane delusion. A *minority* of courts holds that if there is *any factual basis to support* the belief, the belief is *not* an insane delusion.

■ **Undue influence:** Where another person substitutes his or her intent for the testator's intent. The plaintiff bears the burden of proving that (1) the testator was susceptible; (2) the defendant had the opportunity; (3) the defendant had a motive; and (4) causation.

  ▪ A *presumption of undue influence* will arise in many jurisdictions, shifting the burden of proof to the defendant, if the plaintiff can prove (1) the defendant and the testator were in a confidential relationship; (2) the testator was of weakened intellect; and (3) the defendant takes the bulk of the testator's estate.

  ▪ **No contest clauses:** A testator may include a clause in the will that provides that if the beneficiary challenges the will or any provision in the will, the beneficiary is barred from taking under the will. No contest clauses are generally valid, but narrowly construed, and may not be enforced (depending on the jurisdiction) if (1) there is probable cause to support the challenge, or (2) the challenge is based on forgery, revocation, or misconduct by a witness or the drafter.

■ **Fraud:** An intentional misrepresentation, made purposely to influence the testator's testamentary scheme, which causes the testator to dispose of his or her property in a way which he or she otherwise would not have (causation).

  ▪ *Fraud in the execution* occurs if a person intentionally misrepresents the nature of the document that the testator is signing (either completely or in part). *Fraud in the inducement* occurs if a person intentionally misrepresents a fact to the testator to induce the testator to execute a will (or amend a provision in a will or to revoke a will) in reliance upon the misrepresentation.

# I. GENERAL TESTAMENTARY CAPACITY

**A. Introduction:** The traditional method of opting out of the intestate distribution scheme is to execute a will. The first requirement for a valid will, in every jurisdiction, is that the testator has the requisite testamentary capacity.

**1. Policy justifications:** It is so well accepted that a testator must have capacity that it often goes unquestioned. The policy justifications are primarily intuitive.

- A person who lacks capacity is not recognized as an individual for a whole host of purposes. Consistency dictates that capacity is required to execute a valid will.

- Requiring capacity assures testators that the intent expressed when they have capacity will be protected from the risk that they may lose capacity later in life.

- The requirement of capacity protects testators from unscrupulous third parties who may try to take advantage of a testator of weakened capacity.

- The requirement of capacity protects family members. Most people assume that testators normally will provide for their families. If a testator fails to leave most or all of his or her property to family members, that *may* be evidence that the testator lacked capacity. The capacity requirement has been criticized for elevating family protection above testamentary freedom.

**2. Temporal application:** The testator must have the requisite capacity at the time he or she performs a testamentary act—executes a will or revokes a will.

**Lucid interval:** If a person who usually lacks testamentary capacity executes a will during a lucid moment, the will is valid even though the testator lacked capacity for some period of time before and/or after executing the will (though the testator's condition immediately before and after executing the will is relevant to the issue of testator's capacity at the moment of execution).

**B. Requirements:** To execute a will, or to revoke a will, the testator must be *at least 18 years old and of sound mind.*

**1. Sound mind:** Sound mind requires that the testator have the *ability* to know (a) the nature and extent of his or her property; (b) the natural objects of his or her bounty; (c) the nature of the testamentary act he or she is performing; and (d) how all of these relate together to constitute an orderly plan of disposing of his or her property.

**a. *Ability* to know:** The testator need only have the *ability* to know the information covered by the requirements. He or she need not *actually* know the information.

**b. Low threshold:** When viewed from the perspective of the ability to know, it becomes readily apparent that the test for sound mind is extremely low. De facto, there is a strong presumption that one has testamentary capacity.

**2. Example:** In ***Barnes v. Marshall,*** 467 S.W.2d 70 (Mo. 1971), Dr. Marshall died July 29, 1968. His daughter challenged a will and two codicils executed shortly before his death on the grounds that he lacked testamentary capacity. Three lay witnesses testified that starting as early as 1940 Dr. Marshall claimed to be the only person on earth who could speak with the Lord, that the Lord had given him special powers, and that the Lord had told him to run for president, and if elected, to "kill the damn bankers and the crooks and the thieves that were robbing the people." A lay witness also testified that in talking about these people Dr. Marshall would become highly emotional—he would pound his fists on the table, use profanity, turn red with rage, his eyes would bug out, and the veins in his neck would stick out. Dr. Rowling saw the testator in 1940 and concluded that Dr. Marshall was then suffering from manic-depressive psychosis, an incurable mental disease, which only gets worse. Dr. Rowling also concluded Dr. Marshall was not of sound mind on particular days in 1968 when he executed the will and codicils. In response to a hypothetical question, Dr. Hartman, a specialist in psychiatry and neurology, concluded that Dr. Marshall was of unsound mind when he executed the instruments and was incapable of generalized logical thinking. The defendants presented evidence that the testator was calm, quiet, collected, and of sound mind the day the will was executed. The court concluded that testator's stated views on government, religion, morals, and finances went beyond peculiarities and eccentricities and were sufficient evidence from which a jury could reasonably find that he lacked sound mind when he executed the will and codicils. Moreover, evidence of testator's mental condition *prior* to the execution is admissible if it tends to show his condition at the time of execution.

3. **Standing:** The general rule is that a party has standing to contest the validity of a will, or provision in a will, only if that party will financially benefit if his or her challenge is successful.

4. **Testamentary capacity vs. contractual capacity:** One must have contractual capacity to enter into a valid and binding contract. Contractual capacity is higher than testamentary capacity.

   a. **Rationale:** Contractual capacity is concerned with one improvidently disposing of one's assets during one's lifetime. The risk is that the person may become destitute and therefore dependent on the state for support. The state has a legitimate interest in not wanting to pay the cost of caring for those who could have cared for themselves. Testamentary capacity, on the other hand, is concerned with the level of capacity necessary to transfer one's assets at time of death. The state has less of an interest in the possible consequences of testamentary transfers.

   b. **Appointment of conservator:** If one lacks contractual capacity, a conservator is appointed to handle the person's affairs. Because testamentary capacity is lower than contractual capacity, the mere appointment of a conservator does not mean that the person necessarily lacks testamentary capacity as a general rule. More facts would be necessary to determine if the person lacked testamentary capacity.

5. **Testamentary capacity vs. marriage capacity:** Testamentary capacity is higher than the capacity necessary to marry. The right to marry is a fundamental right. It is accorded special status that limits the state's ability to regulate it. Accordingly, the level of capacity necessary for a valid marriage is below testamentary capacity.

> Summary: Contractual capacity > testamentary capacity > capacity to marry

6. **Attorney's ethical duty:** A lawyer has an ethical duty to assess the capacity of an individual before drafting a will for the person. It is unethical to draft a will for a person who lacks capacity. But the attorney is authorized to rely upon his or her own judgment in determining whether the person has the requisite testamentary capacity.

7. **Attorney's legal duty:** In *Gonsalves v. Superior Court,* 24 Cal. Rptr. 2d 52 (Cal. App. 1993), testatrix executed her will weeks just after undergoing surgery for colon cancer and just a month before she died. The doctor's and social worker's hospital notes uniformly described the testatrix as alert, coherent, and in full possession of her mental faculties. Testatrix executed a will that disinherited her niece. The niece sued the attorney, claiming that the attorney had a legal duty to determine the testatrix's legal capacity before permitting her to execute the will. California had adopted the modern trend approach to professional liability, which permits intended beneficiaries who lose their testamentary rights because an attorney fails to prepare the will properly to sue the attorney. Nevertheless, the court held that an attorney who fails to investigate his or her client's testamentary capacity is not liable to a former beneficiary who is disinherited by the will the attorney prepared. The former beneficiary should challenge the will directly (for lack of capacity).

8. **Defects in capacity:** Even if a person has general testamentary capacity, a person may suffer from a "defect" in capacity that may invalidate part or all of the will. There are three possible defects in capacity that may nullify part or all of the will: (1) insane delusion, (2) undue influence, or (3) fraud.

9. **Remedy:** If the testator suffers from a defect that causes him or her to dispose of the testator's property in a way that he or she otherwise would not have, the court will strike as much of the will as was caused by the defect.

## II. INSANE DELUSION

A. **Definition:** An insane delusion is a false sense of reality to which a person adheres despite all evidence to the contrary.

1. **Delusion:** A delusion is a false perception of reality. At one level, one could argue that a delusion is nothing more than a form of a mistake.

2. **Mistake:** As a general rule, courts do not correct mistakes—if they did, every time a person was left out of a will that he or she expected to be in, the person could claim there must have been a mistake and ask the court to rewrite the testator's will to include the person. There is general agreement that courts should not rewrite testators' wills. The process is too speculative, involves high costs of administration, and opens the door to fraudulent claims.

B. **Jurisdictional split:** Two different doctrinal approaches have evolved with respect to what constitutes an insane delusion.

1. **Majority:** A majority of jurisdictions apply the *rational person test* to determine what constitutes an insane delusion. If a rational person in the testator's situation could not have reached the same conclusion, the belief is an insane delusion.

2. **Minority:** A minority of the jurisdictions apply the *any factual basis to support test* to determine what constitutes an insane delusion. If there is any factual basis to support the testator's belief, it is not an insane delusion.

3. **Protection of testator's intent:** The any factual basis approach is more protective of the testator's intent. If there is any factual basis that supports the testator's belief, there is no room for a jury to substitute its belief. Under the rational person approach, even if there is some factual basis to support the testator's belief, if the jury thinks the belief is too bizarre, the jury can substitute its belief.

4. **Traumatic event:** Although not an explicit part of either test, the cases tend to indicate that if there is a traumatic event in a person's life that alters how he or she views the world, or at least part of the world, the contestant has a better chance of convincing the jury and/or court that the testator suffered from an insane delusion.

5. **Example:** In *In re Honigman,* 168 N.E.2d 676 (N.Y. App. 1960), testator and his wife were faithfully married for 40 years. At the age of 70, after undergoing surgery for prostate cancer, he became obsessed with the belief that his wife was being unfaithful. He told anyone who would listen that she was having sex with everyone she met; that she hid men in the closet and under the bed; and that she hauled men up into their second-floor bedroom window by tying bed sheets together and pulling them up. Testator executed a will that left his wife the bare minimum permitted under the law and the rest to his siblings. He told his attorney that his wife was independently wealthy and he wanted to take care of his siblings. After his death, his wife challenged the will, claiming that his belief that she was being unfaithful was an insane delusion. In support of the belief, the siblings presented evidence that the wife always answered the phone; that one day the wife received a sentimental anniversary card addressed only to her from a male friend and it was not the testator and his wife's anniversary; and that one day when the testator was leaving, the wife asked when he would be back. The testator became suspicious, so he hid near the house and watched the same male friend of theirs who sent the anniversary card enter the house.

   a. **Rational person analysis:** The question is whether a rational person in the testator's position could reach the same conclusion. After 40 years of faithful marriage, the testator's belief appears to be the result of his coming out of the surgery not quite the same man. While it is theoretically possible that his wife may suddenly have begun a life of promiscuous extramarital sex, the testator's claims seem rather preposterous under the circumstances.

   b. **Any factual basis analysis:** The question is whether there is any factual basis to support the testator's belief. The key here is how much nexus there must be between the belief and the allegedly supportive evidence. The testator's siblings offered three bits of evidence that arguably support the belief, but only indirectly at best. The siblings have an argument though.

   c. **Court's holding:** Applying the rational person test, the court held that the contestants had presented sufficient evidence from which the jury could conclude that the testator suffered from an insane delusion.

C. **Causation:** Even if the testator suffers from an insane delusion, the insane delusion is irrelevant unless it can be shown that it caused the testator to dispose of his or her property in a way that the testator otherwise would not have.

1. **Majority:** Most jurisdictions require *"but for" causation:* But for the insane delusion, the testator would not have disposed of his or her property as he or she did.

2. **Minority:** A minority of jurisdictions requires only that the insane delusion *might have affected* the disposition of the testator's property.

3. **Protection of testator's intent:** The "might have affected" test for causation is so low as to be almost always satisfied. The "but for" test arguably is more protective of testator's intent, requiring a showing that the testator would not have disposed of his or her property as he or she did if the testator did not have the insane delusion.

4. **Example:** In *In re Honigman,* above, assuming the court concludes that the testator's belief that his wife was being unfaithful constitutes an insane delusion, there is still the issue of causation.

    a. **Majority approach:** The question is whether *but for* the alleged insane delusion, would the testator still have disposed of his property as he did. The testator arguably left his property to his relatives because they were poor and his wife was independently wealthy, not because of his belief that she was being unfaithful. Under the but for test, there is a strong argument there is no causation.

    b. **Minority approach:** The issue is whether the testator's belief that his wife was being unfaithful *might* have affected his decision not to leave more than the bare minimum to her. The might have affected test is so low, the contestants will almost always have presented enough evidence for it to go to the jury.

    c. ***Honigman* approach:** In the *Honigman* case, New York followed the might have affected approach, and the jury concluded that the belief might have affected the testator's will. The court struck the entire will.

5. **Fact sensitive:** Both the majority and the minority approaches to whether a belief constitutes an insane delusion are extremely soft, fact sensitive doctrines. The more preposterous the belief, the more likely it is to be called an insane delusion.

6. **Religious/spiritual beliefs:** As a general rule, courts and juries are reluctant to apply the doctrine to religious/spiritual beliefs. This is intuitively understandable. In light of the principle of separation of church and state, most people are uncomfortable with the idea of courts and juries evaluating how "reasonable" a person's religious/spiritual beliefs are, or whether there is any factual basis to support the beliefs.

7. **Unnatural disposition:** Because the doctrine of insane delusion is so fact sensitive, some have argued that it permits juries to substitute their intent for the testator's intent. This is particularly true where the testator's intent constitutes an "unnatural disposition"—not what a typical person would do under the circumstances. Although an unnatural disposition does not itself constitute an insane delusion, at a minimum it opens the disposition to attack, thereby forcing the estate to defend against the claim.

    a. **Example:** In *Matter of Estate of Bonjean*, 413 N.E.2d 205 (Ill. App. 1980), the decedent specifically disinherited her living sisters and brother, devising her property to the son of a predeceased brother and to her deceased husband's relatives. There was ample evidence that the testatrix was a troubled woman, unhappily married for 19 years—a marriage that ended when her husband took his own life in 1971 following one of their arguments. She blamed herself for his death, checking herself into a mental institution several times over the course of the next year for severe guilt, grief, and depression. She attempted to take her own life several times. In 1973, her brothers and sisters tried unsuccessfully to have her involuntarily committed, after which she became increasingly antagonistic toward them. From 1975 to 1977, the testatrix held a job, maintained excellent relations with her co-workers, but had little contact with her siblings. In 1977, the testatrix committed suicide. The court held that the act of attempting or committing suicide is not, per se, proof of lack of sanity or insane delusion. Nor did the testatrix's feelings toward her siblings lack a rational basis. While the siblings may have thought that they were acting in the testatrix's best interest, the testatrix's hostility could be rationally explained as a natural reaction to what she perceived as a threat to her liberty. The court declined to set aside the will.

b. **Trial vs. appeal:** At least one study found that where there is an unnatural disposition, a jury is likely to find the testator lacked capacity for one reason or another, only to have the court of appeals reinstate the will in approximately half the cases where the jury found the will invalid.

c. **Potential for litigation:** Anytime there is an unnatural disposition in a will, the will arguably is subject to attack for lack of or defect in capacity. At a minimum, the beneficiaries under the will are looking at the costs of trial, the potential embarrassment of the testator's eccentric beliefs being made public, and in light of the jury's natural sympathy with the contestants, the possible costs of an appeal. In light of the inevitable costs of defending the will, most beneficiaries will agree to settle for a percent of the gift under the will under a cost-benefit analysis that even if they were to prevail, the costs of defending the will would be greater.

d. **Family protection:** In light of the jury's sympathy for family members where there is an unnatural disposition in the testator's will, many argue for a stronger approach to family protection doctrines. Many European countries grant children a right to take from a parent's probate estate.

# III. UNDUE INFLUENCE

A. **Introduction:** The second possible defect in testamentary capacity that may render a will invalid is undue influence.

B. **Definition:** Undue influence is "substituted intent"—when one influences the testator to the extent that the will expresses the influencer's intent, not the testator's intent. Some courts have defined it as "coercion." Other courts have specifically rejected that approach, instead holding that it occurs when a beneficiary has gained an unfair advantage by means that reasonable people would regard as improper. The issue is how high a bar one wants to set for a plaintiff alleging undue influence.

**Proof:** Rarely is there direct evidence of undue influence. At best there is circumstantial evidence.

C. **Traditional rule statement:** The prevailing view is that the traditional undue influence doctrine has four elements:

■ **Susceptibility:** Was the testator susceptible to the undue influence?

■ **Opportunity:** Did the defendant have the opportunity to exert undue influence?

■ **Motive:** Did the defendant have a motive for exerting undue influence?

■ **Causation:** Did the undue influence cause the testator to dispose of his or her property in a way that the testator would not have otherwise?

1. **Burden of proof:** Under this approach, the party challenging the will bears the burden of proof. Some courts require clear and convincing evidence of the alleged undue influence, others just a preponderance of the evidence.

2. **Causation:** Note the nature of the four elements. The first three are, by nature, factual. It is relatively easy to marshal facts that reflect directly upon them. Invariably, the analysis comes down to the final requirement—causation. It is the toughest to prove. Rarely are there facts that go directly to it. The issue is whether the alleged facts combined to cause the testator to dispose of his or her property in a way that the testator would not have otherwise. It is usually the determining element.

   **Example:** In *In re Estate of Kamesar,* 259 N.W.2d 733 (Wis. App. 1977), the testator died in 1974 at the age of 84. During his life, the testator made substantial gifts to two of his children, Armon and Jeanette, but not to the third, Bernice. In 1971, he executed a will that left the bulk of his estate to his second wife and his daughter Bernice, expressly disinheriting Armon and Jeanette because he had provided for them during life. The latter sued to invalidate the will, alleging it was the result of Bernice's undue influence. Testator lived in Milwaukee. His son Armon lived there as well and managed his father's financial affairs until 1971 when he moved to California where Jeanette lived. Bernice, who had lived abroad, moved back to Milwaukee in 1968, and she managed her father's financial affairs from 1971 until his death. There was testimony that the testator's mental condition was failing as he got older. The court found that although Bernice had ample opportunity to influence the testator, the objectors did not establish that he was susceptible, that Bernice had the disposition, or that his will was the "coveted result" of her actions (as opposed to the testator's attempt to compensate for the larger inter vivos gifts he had given to Armon and Jeanette). The court affirmed the trial court's ruling to admit the will to probate. (The court's discussion of the presumption of undue influence is set forth below.)

D. **Burden shifting approach:** Because there is rarely direct evidence of undue influence, and the defendant is in the best position to present whatever evidence is available, most jurisdictions have a "burden shifting approach" to undue influence. If the elements of the burden shifting doctrine are satisfied, a presumption of undue influence arises, and the burden shifts to the defendant to rebut the presumption.

1. **Rule statement:** The burden shifting doctrine varies from jurisdiction to jurisdiction. In many jurisdictions, the presumption of undue influence will arise if:

   ▪ there was a *confidential relationship* between the defendant and the testator;

   ▪ the defendant *receives the bulk of the testator's estate;* and

   ▪ the testator was of *weakened intellect.* (Some jurisdictions put more emphasis on whether the defendant was *active in the procurement or execution of the will,* either substituting it for the third requirement or adding it as a fourth requirement.)

   In some jurisdictions the presumption of undue influence will arise if:

   ▪ there was a *confidential relationship* between the defendant and the testator; and

   ▪ *suspicious circumstances* surround the making of the will.

2. **Example:** In the *Kamesar* case, above, Armon and Jeanette argued a presumption of undue influence arose because there was a confidential relationship between Bernice and her father, the testator, and because there were suspicious circumstances surrounding the making of the will. The court found that because of Bernice's role in managing her father's financial affairs there was a confidential relationship between Bernice and the testator. Nevertheless, although Bernice called the attorney, made the appointment to see him to have the will signed, drove the testator to the attorney's office, and communicated the terms of the will (that she was to be the sole beneficiary), the court found that there was nothing suspicious about these activities; rather, these activities were of the type customarily undertaken by testator's children. The court concluded that there were no suspicious circumstances surrounding the making of the will and affirmed the trial court's admitting the will to probate.

3. **Burden of proof:** If these requirements are satisfied, the burden will shift to the proponent of the will to rebut the presumption of undue influence. Most courts hold the proponent must overcome the presumption by a preponderance of the evidence, while other courts say that where the presumption of undue influence is stronger (cases involving alleged attorney misconduct or attorney's conflict of interest), the burden of proof to rebut it is likewise heavier—clear and convincing evidence.

4. **Confidential relationship:** There is no bright line for what constitutes a confidential relationship, but at a minimum the testator has to confide in, place trust in, and/or rely upon the other party, particularly where the testator is in a weakened condition or dependent upon the other party.

5. **Comparison:** In essence, the presumption doctrine provides that where the plaintiff can prove the first three elements of the traditional doctrine *by this particular evidence,* then a presumption of causation arises, and the burden shifts to the defendant to show no undue influence.

6. **Fact sensitive:** Just as with insane delusion, undue influence is an extremely soft, fact sensitive doctrine.

7. **Nontraditional relationships:** Because undue influence is such a soft, fact sensitive doctrine, there is the potential for abuse. In applying the doctrine, juries may be affected by how they perceive the testator's relationship with the party alleged to have committed undue influence. The more nontraditional the relationship, the more potential the jury will impose its own values in assessing the nature of the relationship. Just as with insane delusion, a fairly high percentage of jury findings of undue influence are reversed on appeal.

E. **Deterring challenges:** Alleged defects in capacity are among the most common grounds for challenging a will (or trust). Assuming one were anticipating a challenge, there are a number of estate planning tools that one might consider using to reduce the likelihood of such a suit, and to decrease the chances that such a suit would be successful.

1. **No contest/*in terrorem* clause:** A no contest or *in terrorem* clause basically says if a beneficiary under the instrument sues contesting the instrument, the beneficiary loses whatever he or she is taking under the instrument.

   a. **Public policy considerations:** No contest clauses are something of a double-edged sword. No contest clauses may deter strike suits and protect testator's intent, which is good. But no contest clauses may actually be shielding a party's wrongful conduct, which is bad.

**b. Construction:** Because of the mixed public policy concerns, the general rule is that no contest clauses are valid, but are construed narrowly and not enforceable in certain situations. An action to construe a will is not considered a will contest.

**c. Enforceability:** To say that a no contest clause is unenforceable means that even if a beneficiary contests and loses, the beneficiary still takes their original gift under the will. The jurisdictions are split as to when no contest clauses are unenforceable.

   **i. Majority/UPC approach:** A majority of jurisdictions and the UPC refuse to enforce a no contest clause if there is probable cause to support the will contest, whatever the nature of the contest. UPC §§2-517 and 3-905.

   **ii. Rationale:** If there is probable cause to support the claim, the risk that the no contest clause is being used to shield wrongful conduct is too great to ignore. The legal system wants such contests brought and investigated to ensure that the will is not the product of wrongful conduct.

   **iii. Minority approach:** In a minority of jurisdictions, a no contest clause is unenforceable, regardless of the amount of evidence supporting the claim, if the claim is one of forgery, revocation, or misconduct by one active in the procurement or execution of the will. This approach arguably is more protective of no contest clauses, creating a narrower exception to their enforcement.

**2. Inter vivos trusts:** Another way a person can try to protect his or her estate plan is to use an inter vivos trust instead of a will. As a practical matter, using an inter vivos trust increases the chances that the testamentary scheme will survive a challenge.

**Benefits:** If a will is challenged and held invalid, no transfers have to be "undone"—all that happens is that the transfers proposed in the will are not given effect. If an inter vivos trust is challenged after the settlor's death and held invalid, the court faces the task of undoing potentially years worth of inter vivos transactions. As a practical matter, courts are more unlikely to hold an inter vivos trust to be invalid years after its creation than they would be to hold a will invalid before it is given effect.

**F. Gifts to attorneys:** Gifts to the client's attorney, particularly if the attorney drafted the instrument, smack of impropriety. Such gifts naturally raise questions as to whether it was truly the client's intent—or whether the gift was the result of undue influence or fraud on the part of the attorney. Attorneys are skilled in the subtle art of persuasion, so the client may never realize what is happening; the attorney owes a fiduciary duty to the client and such gifts appear to conflict with that duty; and as the drafter-taker it would be easy for the attorney to fraudulently slip the gift into the will.

**1. Majority approach:** The general rule is that anytime an attorney who drafts an instrument receives a substantial gift under it, a *presumption of undue influence* arises unless the attorney is related to or married to the client.

**Heightened burden:** Most jurisdictions require a heightened burden of proof to overcome the presumption—requiring clear and convincing evidence that the gift was truly the testator's intent.

**2. Minority approach:** Some jurisdictions are so concerned about gifts to the drafting attorney that they create an *irrebuttable presumption of undue influence.*

**Exceptions:** The irrebuttable presumption cannot be overcome by evidence. The presumption can only be avoided if the attorney comes within one of two exceptions: (1) if the attorney is related to or married to the testator, or (2) if the will was reviewed by an independent attorney who advised the testator about the potential for undue influence to make sure the gift was the free and voluntary act of the testator.

3. **Example:** In *In re Will of Moses*, 227 So. 2d 829 (Miss. 1969), the testatrix, an older woman, was having sexual relations with her younger, male attorney. The testatrix decided to change her will to leave the bulk of her estate to her attorney. She went to an independent attorney, who drafted a will that she properly executed that expressed her wishes, but the attorney failed to investigate the nature of her relationship with the beneficiary or to advise her about the appearance of undue influence. The court held that due to the attorney-client relationship between the testatrix and the beneficiary, a special presumption of undue influence arose even though he did not draft the will. Moreover, the presumption was not overcome because although the testatrix went to an independent attorney, the attorney did not advise her about the potential for undue influence to make sure the gift was her free and voluntary act.

**Criticism:** Critics have argued that in *Moses* the court was more concerned with the nontraditional sexual relationship than it was with the attorney abusing his fiduciary relationship with a client by receiving a gift. Note again the potential for improper use of the doctrine due to its soft, fact sensitive nature.

4. **Rationale:** Most jurisdictions found it necessary to create a special presumption of undue influence for the attorney who takes under a client's testamentary instrument because the existing doctrines did not do a good job of covering the problem.

   a. **Presumption of undue influence doctrine:** Under the general presumption of undue influence doctrine, the attorney-client relationship constitutes a confidential relationship. It is easy to argue that the testator is of weakened intellect, relative to the attorney—particularly if the client is elderly or physically debilitated. But the gift must constitute the bulk of the testator's estate. A shrewd attorney could avoid application of the presumption of undue influence doctrine by making sure he or she did not get too greedy—by making sure that the gift, while substantial, did not constitute the bulk of the testator's estate.

   b. **Basic undue influence doctrine:** Under the basic undue influence doctrine, where the attorney who drafts a will takes under it, it is relatively easy to prove susceptibility (testator confided in attorney and relied upon attorney's advice in drawing up will); opportunity (attorney had access to client's innermost thoughts about estate plan, finances, had fiduciary relationship with client, ability to influence testator's thinking); and motive (money). As usual, however, the difficult element is causation. The attorney would argue there was no substituted intent—that the gift was the client's true intent in appreciation of years of service.

5. **Ethical considerations:** In addition to invalidating the gift, the interested drafter may be subject to ethical discipline. Rule 1.8(c) of the Model Rules of Professional Conduct provides that a lawyer "shall not prepare an instrument giving the lawyer or a person related to the lawyer . . . any substantial gift from a client, . . . except where the client is related to the donee." The comments to the rule recognize that before a client makes a gift to his or her

attorney, the client should have the detached advice of an independent attorney. Disciplinary actions for violating the rule range from suspension to disbarment.

# IV. FRAUD

A. **Rule:** Fraud occurs where someone intentionally misrepresents something to the testator, with the intent of influencing the testator's testamentary scheme, and the misrepresentation causes the testator to dispose of his or her property in a way that he or she would not have otherwise.

   **Misrepresentation:** A person must intentionally misrepresent something to a testator, knowing it to be false when he or she makes the misrepresentation.

B. **Fraud in the inducement:** Fraud in the inducement occurs when a person misrepresents a fact to the testator, for the purpose of inducing the testator to execute a will with certain provisions, or for the purpose of inducing the testator to revoke a will. The key is the misrepresentation does not go to the terms of the will per se, but rather concerns a fact that is important to the testator and may induce the testator to dispose of his or her property differently in light of the misrepresentation.

C. **Fraud in the execution:** Fraud in the execution occurs when a person misrepresents the nature of a document the testator is signing. Fraud in the execution occurs when either a person tricks another into signing a document that purports to be the signer's will, but the signer does not realize it, or when the testator realizes he or she is signing his or her will, but the person misrepresents some of the contents of the will.

D. **Mens rea:** The misrepresentation must be made knowingly and for the purpose of influencing testator's testamentary scheme. If the misrepresentation is made as a practical joke or as a conscious exaggeration, and the testator changes his or her testamentary scheme based upon the misrepresentation, technically the fraud doctrine should not apply.

E. **Causation:** The fraud must cause the testator to dispose of his or her property in a way that he or she would not have otherwise.

   **Example:** In ***In re Roblin's Estate***, 311 P.2d 459 (Or. 1957), the testator and his wife had two children, a son and a daughter. The son became a peripatetic. His mother sent him money and paid his bills to the point where the testator moved out of the home. When the mother died, she devised her probate estate equally to her two children (approximately $700 each), but she gave the son an additional $12,300 worth of property through nonprobate means. When the daughter visited the testator, and he asked about the mother's estate, the daughter replied that the mother had left everything except a diamond ring to the son. The father immediately asked the daughter to find him a lawyer, whom the father instructed to prepare a will leaving all his property to the daughter. The son sued, alleging fraud. The court concluded that the daughter's statement was only a conscious exaggeration expressing her disappointment that lacked the intent to deceive. Moreover, the court found that the relationship between the father and son was already strained to the point where it was unclear whether the daughter's statement caused the father to draft the will as he did even if the statement had been found to be fraudulent. The court dismissed the son's will contest action.

F. **Remedy:** The remedy for fraud depends on the effect of the fraudulent misconduct.

1. **Fraudulent provisions:** The norm is that the fraud will cause the testator to execute a will he or she otherwise would not have. In such cases, the remedy is to strike as much of the will as was affected by the fraud—or if necessary, strike the whole will.

2. **Fraudulent failure to revoke:** If the fraud causes the testator not to revoke a will (or clause) that he or she otherwise would have revoked, the appropriate remedy is to strike the will (or clause) that the testator would have revoked but for the misconduct.

3. **Fraudulent failure to execute:** If the fraud causes the decedent not to execute a will that he or she otherwise would have, although the court will not execute the will for the decedent, the court can impose a constructive trust on the parties who take the decedent's probate property and order the property distributed to the parties who would have taken the property had the decedent executed the will that the misconduct prevented the decedent from executing.

   a. **Constructive trust:** The practical effect of this remedy is to give effect to the will that the decedent did not execute. The constructive trust remedy is rare, but courts have imposed it, where appropriate, to prevent unjust enrichment by those who would otherwise receive the decedent's property. As a general rule, the unjust enrichment must result from some party's misconduct.

   b. **Example:** In *Latham v. Father Divine*, 85 N.E.2d 168 (N.Y. 1949), testatrix's will left almost all her estate to Father Divine. The plaintiffs alleged that the testatrix intended to revoke that will and execute a new will leaving her estate to them, but the testatrix was prevented due to Father Divine and his followers' fraud, undue influence, and physical force. The court ruled that the plaintiffs' complaint stated a case for relief in equity, and that if proved, entitled the plaintiffs to a constructive trust ordering the beneficiaries under the testatrix's will to transfer the property to the plaintiffs.

G. **Tortious interference with an expectancy:** Where a third party has committed misconduct in the testamentary process, those who would have taken but for the misconduct can also sue the third party for tortious interference with an expectancy.

   1. **Misconduct:** The plaintiffs will have to prove that the third party committed fraud or undue influence.

   2. **Advantages:** Inasmuch as the plaintiff must prove fraud or undue influence, the plaintiff could just sue under those doctrines, but the tort action has advantages over a suit in probate for fraud or undue influence.

      a. **Not a will contest:** If a will contains a no contest clause, and a beneficiary sues for fraud or undue influence, the challenge would come within the scope of the no contest clause and the beneficiary may lose his or her gift under the will if he or she were to lose the challenge. If, however, the beneficiary sues claiming tortious interference with an expectancy, that tort action does not challenge the validity of the will and thus does not trigger the no contest clause. By suing in tort, even if the plaintiff were to lose, he or she could still take under the will as a beneficiary despite a no contest clause.

      b. **Punitive damages:** By suing in tort, the plaintiff is eligible to claim punitive damages. If the plaintiff sues for fraud or undue influence, the typical remedy is simply to strike those parts of the will affected by the fraud or misconduct.

    **c. Longer statute of limitations:** As part of the probate process, notice is given to creditors to bring their claims within a shortened statute of limitations or their claims will be forever barred. Claims against a will likewise must be brought within a shortened time period or they are forever barred. The tort statute of limitations, however, does not begin to run until the party discovers or should have discovered the misconduct.

---

## *Quiz Yourself on* TESTAMENTARY CAPACITY

**22.** George is an elderly gentleman and very successful businessman, but he has been very lonely since the death of his wife. His children are grown and live out of town. One evening, George meets Anna Nicoli, a woman young enough to be his daughter. Anna Nicoli, an ex-playboy bunny, uses her persuasive powers to convince George that what he feels is true love. George proposes to Anna Nicoli, and she agrees. They run off to Las Vegas where they are married. They spend the rest of the night celebrating, including drinking so much alcohol that George does not know what he is doing. Anna pulls out a will, has George declare that it expresses his testamentary wishes, and has him sign it in front of two of her bridesmaids (her best friends). Later that night, George slips into a coma and never recovers, dying several days later. Who takes George's probate property?

**23.** While vacationing in Scotland, Ned is out boating on Loch Ness, when out of the blue his boat capsizes and he almost drowns. When he comes to, he tells everyone that the Loch Ness monster caused the accident. He swears until he is blue in the face that he saw the beast as the boat capsized. His buddies razz him that he just can't handle a boat in choppy waters. When he dies, his wife and kids are shocked to learn that he left all his property to the Society for the Discovery of the Loch Ness Monster. His wife wants to challenge the will. What is the wife's best claim for challenging the will, and what are her chances of succeeding?

**24.** Pattie is kidnapped by a group of ecosystem revolutionaries called the Redwood Liberation Army. During her kidnapping, she is subjected to a series of psychological brainwashing techniques, including beatings and food and light deprivation. After weeks of such torture, Pattie becomes a follower of the movement and denounces her family's publishing empire as being a waste of our natural resources. She properly executes a will leaving all her property, including her share of the family's publishing empire, to Ima Treehugger, the leader of the Redwood Liberation Army. Sadly, during a "tree sit-in," Pattie is stung to death by a swarm of killer bees. Ima offers Pattie's will for probate. Pattie's family wants to challenge the will. What are their best arguments, and what is the most likely result?

**25.** Nogood Nolan is an attorney. His office is across the street from Retirement World, a seniors-only retirement community. Every day Nolan goes to Retirement World for breakfast, lunch, and dinner, befriending old men and women who have been moved there by their children who do not have enough time to care for them. After befriending them, he convinces them that their children really do not care for them, and that he is their best friend. He persuades them to execute a new will, giving a substantial gift to him. He refers them to a good friend of his whose office is in the same suite as Nolan's. This attorney has a standard "Nogood Nolan" will that gives the testator's family half the estate, and the other half to Nolan. The will includes a no contest clause. After one elderly woman dies, and her family learns of her new will and gift to Nolan, the family considers suing to challenge the gift to Nolan.

**a.** What would be their best claim?

**b.** What else should they argue in the alternative?

**c.** If they lose, is the no contest clause enforceable?

26. Jill loves animals. She has a will that leaves everything to the Humane Society (an organization that takes care of lost pets), but she is very concerned about what is going to happen to her pets when she dies. She is "pet guardian" of two dogs (she prefers that term to "pet owner," thinking that the latter implies that pets are mere property with no rights). Knowing Jill's opinions about animals, one of her neighbors, Jim, tells Jill that if she leaves her property to him, he will use her money to take care of her dogs until they die, and then he will give what is left to the Humane Society. Jill executes a new will that leaves all her property to Jim. When Jill dies, Jim has the dogs put to sleep and uses the money to buy a new house for himself. The Humane Society wants to sue. What is their best claim, and what is the most likely result?

---

## Answers

22. The threshold issue is whether George has a valid will. George arguably lacked general testamentary capacity at the time that he executed the will. If George was so drunk that he did not know what he was doing when he signed the will, he did not have the ability to know the nature and extent of his property, who were the natural objects of his bounty, the nature of the testamentary act that he was performing, and how all of that fit together to form an orderly plan of disposition. The court will likely hold that George lacked testamentary capacity at the time he executed the will. The will is invalid. Assuming this is George's only will, he would die intestate. The first taker under intestacy is the decedent's surviving spouse. While George's will is invalid, it is much harder to set aside a marriage. Marriage is a fundamental right. The mental capacity necessary for a valid marriage is lower than that necessary for a valid will. Moreover, there is no evidence that George was drunk when he got married. The most likely result is that the court will find that the marriage is valid. Although Anna Nicoli is not able to take under the will because it is invalid, she is entitled to take a surviving spouse's share under intestacy. Assuming that the court applies the UPC approach, because George has surviving issue who are not Anna Nicoli's issue, Anna Nicoli will take the first $100,000 and 50 percent of the remainder, and George's issue will split the remaining 50 percent.

23. While there is no evidence that Ned lacks testamentary capacity generally, a strong argument can be made that he is suffering from an insane delusion. Under the majority approach, an insane delusion is a belief that a reasonable person in the testator's situation could not reach. A strong argument can be made that a reasonable person could not reach the conclusion that the Loch Ness monster really exists. In addition to showing that the testator suffered from an insane delusion, those challenging the will must also show causation—that the insane delusion caused the testator to dispose of his or her property in a way that he or she otherwise would not have. Ned's belief in the Loch Ness monster appears to be the only reason that he left his property to the Society for the Discovery of the Loch Ness Monster, so if the belief constitutes an insane delusion, causation should not be a

problem. Under the minority approach, a belief is not an insane delusion if there is any factual basis to support it. People claim to have seen the Loch Ness monster, and there are even pictures that purport to show it. Under the minority approach, arguably there is evidence to support the belief that the Loch Ness monster really exists. Ned's wife and children have a stronger argument and a better chance of prevailing under the majority approach to insane delusion than they do under the minority approach.

**24.** The best chance Pattie's family has to have the will declared invalid is to claim undue influence. Undue influence is substituted intent, arguably a form of mental coercion. Pattie's family will bear the burden of proving undue influence. They could proceed first under the presumption of undue influence doctrine. The typical burden shifting approach requires that (1) the testator was of weakened intellect, (2) the alleged undue influencer received the bulk of the testator's property, and (3) the alleged undue influencer was in a confidential relationship with the testator. Pattie arguably was in a state of weakened mental capacity and intellect as a result of her kidnapping and captivity. Ima received all of Pattie's property. The issue is whether Ima and Pattie had a confidential relationship. That is questionable, though one could argue that Ima forced a confidential relationship upon Pattie during her treatment. If the court were to find a confidential relationship existed between the parties, a presumption of undue influence would arise and Ima would have the burden of rebutting it.

In the alternative, Pattie's family could argue the basic four-factor undue influence doctrine. They would have to show that Pattie was susceptible to undue influence, that Ima had both the opportunity and motive to exert undue influence, and causation. Pattie was susceptible to undue influence as a result of her kidnapping, captivity, and treatment. Ima had the opportunity to unduly influence Pattie by secluding her during her kidnapping and wielding great control over Pattie, including whether Pattie was fed. Ima had sufficient motive to exert undue influence, both money and the public relations coup of being able to say that the daughter of such a well-known industrialist had turned on her family's operations. And lastly, Ima's actions caused Pattie to dispose of her property in a way that she otherwise would not have. Before Ima kidnapped and brainwashed Pattie, there is no evidence that Pattie had ever had any dealings with the Redwood Liberation Army or that she would have left her property to them.

In the alternative, Pattie's family could also argue that Pattie lacked testamentary capacity generally, but that is a more difficult argument because Pattie appears to be functional and to otherwise understand what she is doing.

**25. a.** Because of the no contest clause, their best claim is to sue for tortious interference with an expectancy. One of the principal benefits of the doctrine is that it does not constitute a will contest, so it does not come within the scope of a no contest clause. Even if the family were to lose, they would still be entitled to take their half of the estate.

To succeed under a tortious interference with an expectancy claim, however, the family would have to show undue influence. This is a close call. Under the burden shifting approach, although Nolan and the testatrix were friends, it is unclear whether their relationship was close enough to qualify as a confidential relationship. It is also unclear whether the testatrix was of weakened intellect. The testatrix is elderly, but there was no other evidence to show that her mind had deteriorated. And last, although Nolan received a substantial gift, arguably he did not receive the bulk of the testatrix's estate. Meeting the requirements under the burden shifting approach to undue influence would be difficult.

Under the traditional approach to undue influence, susceptibility is tough to show under these facts, other than that she was elderly, living alone, and somewhat isolated from her family. Opportunity is similar—other than the time he spent with her at breakfast, lunch, and dinner, Nolan's contacts with her were minimal. As an attorney, however, he is trained in the art of subtle persuasion, a factor that might be relevant to both opportunity and susceptibility. Motive is the easiest to prove—Nolan stands to gain financially. But causation is tough. It is unclear whether Nolan substituted his intent for hers, or whether she simply wanted to thank him for his friendship. This is a close call that could go either way.

The family might also assert a claim of interested drafter, if the jurisdiction recognizes it. The doctrine varies from jurisdiction to jurisdiction. There is no evidence that Nolan actually drafted the will, but he arguably was active in the procurement of the will (it is unclear what the relationship is between Nolan and the drafting attorney, but if they are partners or closely affiliated professionally that might be enough to come within the scope of the interested drafter doctrine). There is no evidence that the drafting attorney inquired as to the nature of the relationship or advised the testatrix about her testamentary scheme to ensure that it was her independent wish.

Though there are several arguments the family can make, the outcome is far from clear.

**b.** See the different claims raised and discussed in answer **a**.

**c.** As discussed in answer **a**, if the claim is one of tortious interference with an expectancy, even if the family loses, the no contest clause would not be enforced against them because the claim is not a will contest. If the claim is a straight undue influence claim and they lose, whether the no contest clause would be enforced against them depends on which approach the jurisdiction takes to the exceptions to no contest clauses. Under the majority/UPC approach, the no contest clause is unenforceable as long as there is probable cause to support the claim. Because most courts find that testamentary gifts to an attorney raise at least the appearance of impropriety, it is likely that a court would find that there is probable cause to support the family's claim here and would not enforce the no contest clause. Under the minority approach, the no contest clause is enforceable unless the claim is one of forgery, revocation, or misconduct by one active in the procurement or execution of the will. If the jurisdiction recognizes the last ground, the no contest clause should not be enforced because Nogood encouraged the woman to have a new will executed. The family should not lose their gifts under the will.

26. The Humane Society's best claim would be to claim fraud, fraud in the inducement in particular. To prove fraud in the inducement, the claimant must show that someone knowingly made a false statement to the testator, with the intent of inducing the testator to execute a will that disposed of his or her property based on the statement, and the misrepresentation caused the testator to dispose of his or her property in a way that he or she would not have otherwise. Here, the key is whether at the time that Jim represented to Jill that he would use the money to care for the dogs and then give the money to the Humane Society, he did not intend to honor that statement. If he never intended to honor the statement, he knowingly made a false representation. He arguably made such a statement to induce Jill to leave her property to him, and arguably that is what caused her to change her will and leave her property to him. The most likely result is that the court will find that Jim's statements amounted to fraud in the inducement and will impose a constructive trust, ordering Jim to transfer the money to the Humane Society.

## Exam Tips on
# TESTAMENTARY CAPACITY *(Entire Chapter)*

You should raise and discuss the material in this chapter only if you think one of the parties to the fact pattern could bring a claim involving testamentary capacity in good faith.

Unlike most of the wills and trusts doctrines, the doctrines in this chapter are very soft, fact sensitive doctrines that usually can go either way. From an exam writing perspective, it is more important to focus on how you marshal the facts and make your arguments pro and con, than it is to worry about reaching a "right" conclusion.

## General testamentary capacity

☛ If you see facts raising capacity concerns, the key is whether the testator had the requisite capacity *at the moment* he or she performed the testamentary act. (Capacity applies to executing wills and codicils and performing acts of revocation.)

☛ If testamentary capacity is going to be tested, much more often it is tested through one of the "defects in capacity" doctrines.

## Insane delusion

There is some overlap among the defect doctrines. One way to distinguish an insane delusion is that both undue influence and fraud involve misconduct by a third party, while an insane delusion usually arises independently from the testator's own beliefs.

☛ Watch for a belief that is unusual or extreme. The more extreme, the more likely the professor expects you to raise and analyze it as a possible insane delusion.

    ☞ you have an insane delusion issue, lead with the rule statement for your jurisdictions. Be sure to raise and analyze *causation*. Just as with the underlying doctrine, raise and argue the different approaches on behalf of the competing parties.

## Undue influence

Undue influence is another soft, fact sensitive doctrine. Lead with the rule statement, and then apply the different doctrinal requirements to the facts. How well you marshal and argue the facts pro and con, and analyze them, are the keys.

☛ There are arguably four different ways to claim undue influence (depending on the jurisdiction): (1) the traditional four-element approach, (2) the burden shifting three-element approach, (3) the interested witness doctrine, and (4) the interested drafter doctrine. On an exam, a party asserting undue influence would probably analyze the doctrines in the exact opposite order, because that order gives the claimant the best chances of the result he or she wants. Argue in the alternative if the facts permit.

☛ No contest clauses are tested often and are easy to spot in a traditional fact pattern. There has to be an express no contest clause. Lead with the basic rule statements concerning enforceability. Sweat the details of the approach your jurisdiction applies. These typically are statutory rules, so there is no need to argue in the alternative.

## Fraud

Fraud is fairly simple to spot. If you see someone make a misrepresentation to the testator, raise and analyze the fraud issue. State whether it is fraud in the execution or fraud in the inducement. Even if there is fraud, there also has to be causation.

☞ Tortious interference with an expectancy is a nice doctrine that you should raise and analyze anytime you claim either undue influence or fraud. Raise it and argue it in the alternative. Include in your discussion of the rule the advantages of this tort doctrine over the pure wills doctrines (in particular, if there is a no contest clause in the document).

## CHAPTER 5

# WILLS EXECUTION, REVOCATION, AND SCOPE

## *ChapterScope* _____

This chapter examines some of the core issues in the course—the requirements for a validly executed will, a validly revoked will, and the scope of a will.

- **Attested wills:** To have a valid attested will, the will must be in *writing, signed,* and *witnessed.* Each jurisdiction adds a plethora of other detailed requirements.

  - The jurisdictions are split over how strictly the testator must comply with formalities in their Wills Act. Most jurisdictions require *strict compliance,* but the modern trend favors either *substantial compliance* or the *dispensing power* approach.

- **Holographic wills:** Holographic wills need not be witnessed, but the will has to be handwritten, signed by the testator, and express testamentary intent (the intent that the document be the decedent's will).

- **Codicils:** A will that amends an existing will is called a codicil.

- **Scope of the will:** There are several doctrines that permit testamentary intent that is not expressed in a will to be given effect as long as there is a validly executed will.

  - **Integration:** Those pieces of paper physically present when the will is executed and that the testator intends to be part of the will constitute the pages of the will.

  - **Republication by codicil:** A codicil has the effect of reexecuting, republishing, and thus, as a general rule, redating the underlying will.

  - **Incorporation by reference:** A document not executed with Wills Act formalities may be given effect along with the will if the document was in existence at the time the will was executed, the will expresses an intent to incorporate the document, and the will adequately identifies the document.

  - **Facts of independent significance:** A will may refer to a fact or event that is to occur outside of the will, and that fact or event may control either who takes under the will or how much a beneficiary takes, as long as the referenced fact has its own significance independent of its effect upon the will.

- **Revocation of wills:** A validly executed will (attested or holographic) can be revoked *by a subsequent will; by act; by presumption; or by operation of law.*

  - **Revival:** If testator executes will #1, and thereafter executes will #2 that revokes will #1, and thereafter revokes will #2, will #1 is revived, if (1) will #1 is reexecuted with Wills Act formalities, or (2) in some jurisdictions, all that is necessary to revive will #1 is that the testator intended to revive will #1.

  - **Dependent relative revocation:** If the testator revokes a will, in whole or in part, based upon a mistake, and the testator would not have revoked but for the mistake, the revocation will not be given effect.

■ **Contracts relating to wills:** A person may contract to execute a particular will, to make a particular devise, or not to revoke a particular will or devise. If the contract is valid under contract law (consideration), it will be enforced against the testator's estate before the decedent's estate is distributed.

# I. EXECUTING A VALID WILL

**A. Overview:** Whether a will has been properly executed is a function of two variables: (1) the jurisdiction's statutory Wills Act formalities; and (2) the jurisdiction's judicial philosophy as to what degree of compliance with the Wills Act formalities is acceptable.

**B. Statutory requirements:** Every jurisdiction has a statute that sets forth the requirements that an individual must comply with to execute a valid will. These statutory requirements are commonly referred to as the jurisdiction's Wills Act formalities. The Wills Act formalities vary from state to state, and the requirements depend upon whether the will is a traditional attested (i.e., witnessed) will or a holographic will. For a traditional attested will, at a minimum there has to be a writing that is signed and witnessed.

**Functions served:** The writing, signature, and witnessing requirements serve a number of different functions to ensure that the document expresses the decedent's final wishes and is the document the testator intends to be probated as his or her will.

**1. Evidentiary:** The Wills Act formalities serve an evidentiary function by ensuring that the document offered for probate truly reflects the testator's last wishes as to who should take his or her property.

**2. Protective:** The Wills Act formalities serve a protective function by making it more difficult for fraudulent claims to be brought and by protecting testator's intent as expressed in the properly executed will.

**3. Ritualistic:** The Wills Act formalities serve a ritualistic function by impressing upon the testator the finality of the act he or she is performing.

**4. Channeling:** The Wills Act formalities serve a channeling function by encouraging individuals to consult an attorney to draft and supervise the execution of their wills, thereby facilitating the probating of the will and decreasing administrative costs.

**C. Judicial philosophy:** The other variable that controls whether a will has been validly executed is the judicial philosophy as to how strictly the testator must comply with the Wills Act formalities. The jurisdictions are split over the degree of compliance required. Common law required strict 100 percent compliance with the Wills Act formalities, while the modern trend favors either substantial compliance or a dispensing power approach.

# II. COMMON LAW APPROACH TO ATTESTED WILLS

**A. Introduction:** The traditional common law approach to an attested will is (1) statutorily to have lots of detailed and technical Wills Act formalities, and (2) judicially to require strict compliance with each and every one of those Wills Act formalities.

**B. Statutory requirements:** All states permit attested wills—a will that is witnessed. At a minimum, there must be a writing that is signed and witnessed, but invariably there are a number of other requirements. How many, and what they are, vary from state to state.

**Typical statute:** The typical common law Wills Act takes the basic three requirements (writing, signature, and witnesses) and expands them into a plethora of requirements. The following is a typical common law Wills Act broken down to show its many formalities:

> (1) A writing (2) signed (3) at the foot or end thereof (4) by the testator, (5) or by another (6) in his presence (7) and by his direction, (8) such signature made or acknowledged (9) by the testator (10) in the presence (11) of two or more witnesses (12) present at the same time (13) and such witnesses shall attest [sign] (14) and shall subscribe [sign at the end of] the will (15) in the presence of the testator.

**C. Judicial approach:** The traditional common law judicial approach to the statutory Wills Act formalities is to require *absolute* strict compliance with each Wills Act requirement, no matter how clear the testator's intent that this document be his or her last will. If there is *any* deficiency in the execution ceremony, the document is not a valid will.

   **1. Testator's intent:** The common law combination of statutorily having numerous, detailed Wills Act formalities and judicially requiring strict compliance meant that a testator who was not careful could end up with his or her clear testamentary intent not being given effect for failure to comply perfectly with each Wills Act formalities.

   **2. Example:** In *Morris v. West,* 643 S.W.2d 204 (Tex. App. 1982), two witnesses, present at the same time, watched the testator properly sign his will and codicil in the attorney's conference room, but then the witnesses walked down a hall to the secretarial office where they signed the instruments in each other's presence while the testator remained in the conference room. The conference room and the secretarial office are separated by the lawyer's private office. The witnesses then returned to the conference room where the testator's attorney signed the self-proving affidavit in his capacity as notary public. The court held that the will was not properly executed because the witnesses did not sign the will in the testator's presence.

**D. Typical formalities:** Although the Wills Act formalities vary from jurisdiction to jurisdiction, there are a number of requirements that are common to most of the statutes. These requirements have given rise to a number of ancillary rules.

   **1. Writing:** As a general rule, oral wills are not permitted—there must be a writing.

   **2. Signature:** The writing must be signed. A signature is anything the testator intends as his or her signature. There is no requirement that the individual sign his or her full name, but if a person intended to sign his or her full signature and does not complete it, the general rule (at least under the strict compliance approach) is that the partial signature will not qualify as the person's signature.

   **A mark:** A mark, even an *X,* may qualify as the testator's signature if that is what the testator intended as his or her signature. In some jurisdictions, for an *X* to qualify, there must be a witness who saw the person make the mark, the witness must write the name of the person who made the mark under the mark, and the witness must sign as the person who wrote the name of the other person.

   **3. Signature by another:** The will may be signed by someone other than the testator, as long as the person signs the testator's name, in the testator's presence, and at the testator's direction. The testator's direction must be express; it will not be implied.

**4. Witnesses:** Most jurisdictions require that the testator sign or acknowledge in the presence of at least two witnesses, present at the same time. The witnesses must sign the will, and in most jurisdictions the witnesses must know that what they are signing is the testator's will.

**5. Acknowledgment:** Under most statutes, the testator need not sign in front of the witnesses as long as the testator acknowledges, in front of the witnesses present at the same time, that the signature already on the document is the testator's signature.

**6. Presence:** The testator must sign or acknowledge in the presence of the witnesses, and under the traditional approach, the witnesses must sign in the presence of the testator. (The presence requirement thus needs to be defined very carefully to take into account *who* has to perform *what* in the presence of *whom*.) There are two approaches to the presence requirement.

    **a. Line of sight test:** Under the traditional approach, the witnesses, present at the same time, must *see or have the opportunity of seeing* (if the party were to look or slightly alter his or her position) the testator sign or acknowledge his or her signature, and the testator must *see or have the opportunity of seeing* the witnesses sign the will.

    **Example:** In the *Morris* case above, the court applied the line of sight test when the witnesses signed the will and codicil in the secretarial area and the testator remained in the conference room. The court found that it would have required more than the testator slightly altering his position to have been able to see the witnesses signing the will. The witnesses did not sign in the testator's presence.

    **b. Conscious presence test:** Under the modern trend approach, presence is defined by whether the party, in whose presence the act has to be performed, can tell from sight, sound, and general awareness of the events, that the required act is being performed. The conscious presence approach is broader than line of sight, opening up the temporal and physical scope of the presence doctrine.

    **Example:** In *Cunningham v. Cunningham,* 83 N.W. 58 (Minn. 1900), Cunningham, who was ill and confined to his bed, summoned his doctors and asked one to draw his will, which he did. Dr. Adams then read the will to Cunningham, he approved it, sat up on the side of the bed, and properly signed it as both doctors stood at the side of the bed and watched. The doctors then took the instrument and stepped to a table in the sitting room about 10 feet from Cunningham. There the doctors signed the will in the presence of each other, returned to the bed, and returned the instrument to Cunningham. From where Cunningham sat he could not see the table where the doctors signed the will, but he could have had he moved two or three feet. The court applied the conscious presence test and held that while Cunningham did not and could not see the doctors sign the will, the signing was within the sound of his voice, he knew it was being signed, it took less than two minutes, the witnesses then returned the will to him and pointed out their signatures, and he reviewed and approved it. The court said the whole affair was one single and entire transaction that was valid and only an extremely technical construction of the presence requirement, without the slightest reason for being so, would invalidate the will.

**7. Order of signing:** Because the witnesses are required to witness the testator sign or acknowledge his or her signature, there appears to be an implicit order of performing.

**a. Traditional approach:** Some courts have held this implicit order of performing is mandatory. The testator must sign the will before either witness signs. If a witness signs before the testator, the witness must resign after the testator signs or acknowledges, or the witness's signature is invalid.

**b. Modern trend:** A witness may sign the will before the testator signs or acknowledges as long as all the parties sign the will as part of one ceremony—and as long as no one leaves the room during the execution ceremony. (This argument may be difficult to make under the UPC approach because it expressly requires the witnesses to sign "after" witnessing the testator perform. UPC §2-502(a)(3).)

8. **Writing below signature:** With respect to attested wills, if there is writing physically below the testator's signature, two variables must be analyzed: (1) whether the jurisdiction requires the will to be "subscribed"—that is, signed at the end; and (2) *temporally,* when was the writing added.

   **a. Subscribe requirement + writing added *after* will signed:** If the jurisdiction requires that the will be subscribed, writing below the signature raises the issue of whether the will was subscribed. The key is *when* the writing below the signature was added. If it was added temporally after the will was properly executed and subscribed, the original will is valid and only the writing that was added later in time and physically below the signature is null and void (assuming it does not qualify as a codicil in its own right—an issue to be discussed later).

   **b. Subscribe requirement + writing added *before* will signed:** If the jurisdiction requires that the will be subscribed, and the writing below the signature was added temporally before the will was signed, the will was not signed at the end. Under the traditional strict compliance approach, the whole will would be invalid. (Under the modern trend, a court might simply strike the provision below the signature and hold that whatever is above the signature is still valid.)

   **c. Need not subscribe + writing added *after* will signed:** If the jurisdiction does not require that the will be subscribed, and the writing below the signature was added temporally after the will was executed, the writing is not considered a part of the will. The will as it existed when it was executed is given effect, but the writing added later cannot be given effect (unless it qualifies as its own codicil).

   **d. Need not subscribe + writing added *before* will signed:** If the jurisdiction does not require the will to be subscribed, as long as the writing below the signature was added temporally before the will was executed, the whole will is valid, including the writing physically below the signature.

9. **Delayed attestation:** If the statute requires the witnesses to sign in the testator's presence, the witnesses must sign the will at the same time as the testator, in the testator's presence. If the statute does not expressly require the witnesses to sign in the testator's presence, the modern trend permits the witnesses to sign the will later (delayed attestation), even after the death of the testator, as long as the witnesses sign within a reasonable time period.

   **Reasonable time period:** What constitutes a reasonable time period is unclear. The witnesses should sign the will while their recollection of the execution ceremony is still fresh enough that they can remember whether the execution ceremony was valid. A general recollection that they thought it was valid, arguably, is not sufficient.

10. **Testamentary intent:** Testamentary intent is the intent that the document in question is to serve as the party's last will and testament when he or she dies. At the time a person executes the instrument, the person must intend that following his or her death, the document is to be probated as his or her will. For attested wills, the typical execution ceremony has such a strong ritualistic component that it virtually guarantees that the executed document has testamentary intent. In the appropriate fact pattern, however, testamentary intent can be the determining element even for traditional, witnessed wills.

11. **Videotaped wills:** To date no court has upheld a videotaped will. The typical videotaping scenario lacks any ritualistic function, lacks direct evidence as to whether the person intended the taped statement to constitute his or her last will and testament, and has the potential for high administrative costs.

12. **Attestation clause:** Attestation clauses are not required for a valid will, but they facilitate the probating of the will. Historically, before a will was admitted to probate, the witnesses would be called to court to testify as to the execution process to establish that the will was properly executed. An attestation clause, or self-proving affidavit, creates a rebuttable presumption that the will was properly executed, often eliminating the need to call the witnesses to court before probating the will.

**Example:** In *Matter of Estate of Collins,* 458 N.E.2d 797 (N.Y. 1983), respondents challenged the validity of a document offered for probate as testatrix's will on the ground that there was not sufficient evidence of its due execution. Although neither of the witnesses had any real recollection of the execution ceremony in question, the court held that the properly created attestation clause was sufficient to create a presumption that the will was properly executed, a presumption that was not rebutted.

E. **Interested witness:** The witnessing requirement implicitly assumes that the witnesses will assess the testator's capacity at the time of execution, assess the execution ceremony, and protect the testator. These functions arguably require that the witnesses be "disinterested"—that they not take under the will. If a witness has a financial interest under the will, the witness would have a conflict of interest. Historically, the requirement has been that there must be at least two *disinterested* witnesses. If there are not, the remedy has evolved over time, with jurisdictions split over which remedy is appropriate.

1. **Invalidate will:** At common law, an interested witness was not permitted to testify in court. If the interested witness were one of the necessary witnesses to the will, without his or her testimony the whole will would fail. (But invalidating the whole will arguably is harsh—it deprives other beneficiaries in the will of their gifts.)

2. **Void interested witness's gift:** By voiding the gift to the interested witness, the witness' ability to testify is restored. With the witness' credibility restored, the will can be probated, but the witness's gift is voided. (But even this remedy arguably is harsh. The witness has a conflict of interest only to the extent that the witness stands to take more under this will than he or she would take if this will were not valid.)

**Example:** In *In re Estate of Watts,* 384 N.E.2d 589 (Ill. App. 1979), there were three witnesses to Laura Watts' will, but two of them took under the will. Because there were not two disinterested witnesses, the decedent's heirs at law sued under the interested witness doctrine. The two parties who were both beneficiaries and witnesses argued that as to each, the testimony of the nontaking witness and the other taking witness was sufficient to make each beneficiary witness a nonnecessary witness as to their respective gifts under the will. The court rejected the argument, voided the gifts to each of the beneficiaries/witnesses, and because one of the gifts was the residuary clause, the voided gifts passed via intestacy to the decedent's heirs.

3. **Purging approach:** The purging approach adopts the argument that a witness has a conflict of interest only to the extent he or she stands to take *more* under the will than he or she would otherwise and purges the interested witness only of their *excess* interest under the will. To determine the excess interest, calculate (1) how much the witness would take if the will were not valid, and (2) how much the witness stands to take under the will. If the latter amount is greater, purge the witness of the excess interest. (When calculating how much the witness would take if the will were not valid, do not automatically use the intestate scheme. The testator may have a prior will that would control who takes how much.) The old version of UPC §2-505, adopted in a significant number of states, adopted the purging approach.

4. **Rebuttable presumption of misconduct:** An interested witness gives rise to only a rebuttable presumption of misconduct. If the interested witness rebuts the presumption, he or she gets to keep their whole gift under the will. If the interested witness cannot rebut the presumption, apply the purging approach.

5. **Abolish the doctrine:** The most recent version of the UPC completely abolishes the interested witness doctrine on the theory that it does more harm than good by trapping innocent interested witnesses. If one suspects that an interested witness is guilty of wrongdoing, the party can still challenge the gift under the appropriate doctrines (undue influence, fraud). Revised UPC §2-505.

F. **Swapped wills:** In the swapped wills scenario, two individuals (typically spouses) have "mirror" wills prepared for their execution. The testamentary schemes in the wills mirror each other—they are basically the same. When the two go to execute the wills, however, the wills are accidentally switched, so each party signs the will that was intended for the other party. The mistake often is not discovered until after the death of the first party. The issue is whether the will the person signed, but which was not drafted for him or her to sign, can be probated as a valid will.

1. **General rule:** Under the traditional common law approach, the will is invalid. The testator signed the wrong document. Most courts apply the strict compliance approach and rule the will is a nullity and refuse to probate it. This approach is consistent with the general rule that courts will not correct mistakes.

2. **Modern trend:** Under the modern trend, the courts are more concerned with testator's intent and less concerned with Wills Act formalities. Under the modern trend, a number of courts have stretched some existing doctrines to validate an accidentally swapped will.

   a. **Misdescription doctrine:** The misdescription doctrine was developed to help construe a validly executed will that contains a misdescription. Under the misdescription doctrine, the court takes extrinsic evidence to determine the extent of the misdescription and then strikes the words that constitute the misdescription. The court will *not*, however, insert any words or rewrite the will. The court will only strike the words that constitute the misdescription and then check to see if there are enough words left to give effect to testator's intent.

In the swapped will scenario, some courts have used the misdescription doctrine to strike all the words that do not make sense in light of the fact that the testator signed the wrong document, and then checked to see if there were enough words left to make sense of the document and to determine who is to take what. Most courts will not apply the misdescription doctrine to the swapped wills scenario, because in the swapped wills scenario it is being used to *validate* a will, which is not the doctrine's intended use of *construing* an otherwise valid will.

**Which will:** Where the parties sign the wrong wills, it is best to offer for probate the will the decedent signed. It arguably meets all the Wills Act formalities (writing signed and witnessed). If the document that was drafted for, but not signed by, the decedent is offered, the proponents are asking the court to validate a document that the decedent did not sign it—a greater stretch for the court.

b. **Two wills as one:** In *In re Snide,* 418 N.E.2d 656 (N.Y. 1981), the court basically treated the execution scenario as one big execution ceremony, ordered the will probated, and simply changed the names in the will to reflect the true intent of the decedent as expressed in the other will.

c. **Scrivener's error doctrine:** Scrivener's *error* has the same effect upon testator's intent as scrivener's *fraud.* If the attorney had intentionally swapped the wills, that would be fraud in the execution. A court would impose a constructive trust to protect and give effect to the testator's intent. Academics have argued that it should not matter whether the will was accidentally swapped or intentionally swapped—either way testator's intent is frustrated unless a court imposes a constructive trust to save it. Recently, a court adopted the scrivener's error doctrine for the first time, but in a different context (see Ch. 6, II), though the doctrine would appear to cover swapped wills as well.

# III. MODERN TREND APPROACH TO ATTESTED WILLS

A. **Introduction:** The modern trend, as typified by the UPC, has tried to make it easier for testators to execute a valid will by addressing both variables that control whether a will has been properly executed. First, the modern trend approach has reduced the number of requirements in the Wills Act. Second, the modern trend has encouraged courts not to require strict compliance, but rather to apply substantial compliance or dispensing power as the judicial approach to the degree of compliance with the Wills Act formalities.

B. **UPC requirements:** The Uniform Probate Code has tried to simplify the execution process by (1) reducing the number of requirements, and (2) loosening up on several of the requirements that remain. UPC §2-502 requires:

> (1) a writing; (2) signed (3) by the testator or (4) in the testator's name by another (5) in the testator's conscious presence (6) and by the testator's direction; and (7) signed (8) by at least two individuals, each of whom (9) signed within a reasonable period after he [or she] witnessed either (10) the signing of the will or (11) the testator's acknowledgment of the will. [Not the exact version of the UPC, paraphrased to highlight the differences with the traditional common law approach.]

**C. UPC formalities:** The UPC eliminates several common law Wills Act formalities and loosens up on several other requirements.

   **1. Need not sign at end:** There is no requirement in the UPC that the testator sign the will at the end or foot of the will.

   **2. Signed by another:** The UPC expressly provides that where another signs for the testator, in the testator's presence and at the testator's direction, the test for requirement that the other sign in the testator's presence is the conscious presence test—a looser standard than the line of sight approach to presence. UPC §2-502(a)(2).

   **3. Acknowledgment:** The UPC loosens the acknowledgment option by providing that the testator may acknowledge either his or her signature *or the will.* UPC §2-502(a)(3). At common law, if the testator were going to acknowledge, the testator had to open the will to where he or she had previously signed the will so that the witnesses could see the signature. This burden could trip up the careless testator. The UPC significantly lowers the threshold for a valid acknowledgment by permitting the testator to acknowledge the signature *or the will.*

   **4. Separate witnesses:** The UPC does not require the witnesses to be present at the same time for any reason, even when the testator signs or acknowledges. UPC §2-502(a)(3).

   **5. Witnesses' execution:** The UPC provides that the witnesses need to sign within a reasonable time after witnessing the testator sign or acknowledge. UPC §2-502(a)(3). This language implicitly rejects the requirement that the witnesses have to sign in the presence of the testator and arguably endorses the delayed attestation approach.

   **6. Witnesses' presence:** The UPC does not require the witnesses to sign the will in either the testator's presence or the presence of each other. UPC §2-502(a)(3). Many traditional Wills Act statutes required the witnesses to sign in each other's presence.

**D. UPC judicial philosophy:** The modern trend, as reflected by the UPC, has been to encourage the courts not to insist on strict compliance with the Wills Act formalities requirements, but rather to apply a substantial compliance approach or even a dispensing power approach if the execution ceremony fails to meet the Wills Act requirements.

   **1. Substantial compliance:** Under substantial compliance, even if a will is not executed in strict compliance with the jurisdiction's Wills Act formalities, the court is empowered to probate the will if (1) there is clear and convincing evidence the testator intended this document to constitute his or her last will and testament, and (2) there is clear and convincing evidence the will substantially complied with the statutory Wills Act formalities. UPC §2-503 (1990 version).

      **a. Example:** In *In re Will of Ranney,* 589 A.2d 1339 (N.J. 1991), the testator properly signed the will in front of two witnesses present at the same time, but the witnesses signed the self-proving affidavit instead of the will. The self-proving affidavit technically is not a part of the will. Applying strict compliance, the New Jersey Supreme Court held that the will was not properly executed, but the court went on to adopt the substantial compliance doctrine and remanded the case.

      **UPC self-proving affidavit:** The UPC permits a combined attestation clause and self-proving affidavit that requires the testator and witnesses to sign their names only once, thereby avoiding the potential for the mistake that occurred in the *Ranney* case. UPC §2-504. (Only a minority of jurisdictions have adopted it.)

b. **Criticism:** Professor Langbein, arguably the father of substantial compliance in the United States, rather quickly criticized his own proposal. After studying its use in Australia, Professor Langbein concluded that the courts put too much emphasis on the requirement that there be clear and convincing evidence that the will substantially complied with the Wills Act formalities. Professor Langbein advocated a dispensing power/harmless error approach as a better alternative.

2. **Dispensing power/harmless error:** Under the dispensing power/harmless error approach, if a will is not executed in strict compliance with the jurisdiction's Wills Act formalities, the court is empowered to probate the will if there is clear and convincing evidence that the decedent intended the document to constitute his or her last will and testament. UPC §2-503 (1997 version). (The doctrine was initially called the dispensing power approach, but more recently has been renamed the harmless error doctrine.) The dispensing power/harmless error approach is substantial compliance without the second prong.

a. **Scope:** The dispensing power/harmless error doctrine authorizes courts to "dispense" with those Wills Act formalities that they deem appropriate as long as there is clear and convincing evidence the decedent intended the document to be his or her will. As applied to the writing, signature, and witness requirements, many have argued that (1) the witness requirement is the least important—thus the easiest to be dispensed with, and (2) the writing requirement is the most important—thus one that should not be dispensed with under almost any scenario.

b. **Pros and cons:** Although strict compliance may have its weaknesses (occasionally frustrating testator's intent even where clear), it has its strengths (bright line test, easy to apply, lower costs of administration, and less potential for fraud). Substantial compliance, and even more so harmless error, increases the power of the courts to give effect to testator's intent, but both doctrines have their own weaknesses (softer, more fact sensitive doctrines that will increase costs of administration and the potential for fraud).

3. **Majority approach:** Although the academic community favors substantial compliance and dispensing power/harmless error, the states favor strict compliance. A minority of jurisdictions has followed the UPC lead and adopted the dispensing power/harmless error approach, though some of them have modified the doctrine to statutorily indicate that the signature requirement cannot be dispensed.

# IV.  HOLOGRAPHIC WILLS

A. **Distinguishing feature:** The distinguishing feature of holographic wills is that there is no requirement that the will be witnessed.

1. **Jurisdictional split:** Only about half the states, primarily in the West and South, recognize holographic wills because the absence of witnesses raises a number of concerns: whether the testator had capacity when the will was executed; increased potential for fraud and undue influence; whether the decedent really intended for this writing to be his or her last will; how to resolve conflicts between multiple wills; and higher costs of administration.

2. **UPC approach:** The UPC recognizes holographic wills. UPC §2-502.

**B. Requirements:** In light of the concerns raised by the lack of witnesses, most states that recognize holographic wills compensate by adding additional requirements, the most important of which is that the will must be in the testator's handwriting.

1. **Writing:** As with attested wills, holographic wills must be in writing.

2. **Signed:** As with attested wills, holographic wills must be signed. Anything the testator intends as his or her signature qualifies as a valid signature. Unlike attested wills, however, only the testator can sign a holographic will. Most states do not require the holographic will to be signed at the end (if it is not, however, it raises questions about whether the person wrote his or her name intending it to be his or her signature vs. for identification purposes).

3. **Dated:** Some states require that holographic wills be dated. The UPC does not require the holographic will to be dated to be valid. UPC §2-502.

4. **Handwritten:** To offset the lack of witnesses, holographic wills must be in the testator's handwriting. This decreases the potential for fraud in the execution. The jurisdictions are split over how much must be in the testator's handwriting. Some jurisdictions require that the *entire* document must be in the testator's handwriting; most require only that the *material provisions* be in the testator's handwriting.

   a. **Entirely:** If the jurisdiction requires that the holographic will be entirely in the testator's handwriting, any printing or other marks on the document may invalidate the whole will under a strict compliance approach to the requirements.

   b. **Material provisions:** The material provisions are the provisions that affect the disposition of testator's property: the "who" gets "what," or the administrative provisions (i.e., appointment of a personal representative or guardian), and *maybe* testamentary intent (the intent that the document constitutes the party's last will).

   c. **UPC approach:** The UPC requires only that the material provisions be in the testator's handwriting, not the entire instrument. UPC §2-503(b).

5. **Testamentary intent:** Testamentary intent is the intent that this document constitutes the person's last will—the intent that this document be probated as the decedent's will. Because holographic wills are not witnessed, there is no ritualistic function. The requirement that the document express testamentary intent is to ensure that only writings that the decedent intended to serve as a will are probated—as opposed to drafts or idle thoughts or instructions to one's attorney. The key is use of words that indicate the document is to have significance following the person's death. Words such as *save this* support a finding of testamentary intent, though the word *estate,* standing alone, has been held too ambiguous to establish testamentary intent.

   a. **Example:** In *Fischer v. Johnson,* 441 S.W.2d 132 (Ky. 1969), the decedent, who had previously executed a formal will, wrote in his own handwriting a document addressed to his attorney that indicated who was to take what when he died. The document did not provide very much for his in-laws, and it explained why he decided not to give them more. The document expressly stated "Put these explanations in my Will if you think it advisable." Following the decedent's death, the handwritten letter was offered for probate as his will. The court characterized the document as a letter giving instructions to his attorney and not a will because it lacked testamentary intent.

**b. Material provisions:** If the jurisdiction requires only that the material provisions be in the testator's handwriting, a subissue is whether testamentary intent is a material provision. If it is, testamentary intent must be discernable exclusively from the handwritten portions of the document. (This issue arises most often with commercially printed form wills where the decedent fills in the blanks indicating who is to get what, but does not write in his or her own handwriting any words that express the intent that the document serve as his or her will due to the preprinted words clearly expressing such an intent.)

   **i. Strict compliance:** Some courts have held that testator's intent must be discernable exclusively from the testator's handwriting. The court "whites out" any material not in the testator's handwriting and then assesses what is left to see if testamentary intent can be established.

   **ii. UPC contextual approach:** The UPC has expressly disavowed, as overly formalistic, the approach that the testamentary intent must be discernable exclusively from the testator's handwriting. Under the "contextual approach," testamentary intent can be derived from the handwritten material and/or the printed material. UPC §2-502(c).

   **iii. Example:** In *In re Estate of Muder,* 765 P.2d 997 (Ariz. 1988), the decedent purchased a commercially printed form will, filled in the blanks giving different assets to different individuals, and then signed the form will. Because only one witness signed the will, the issue was whether the writing expressed the requisite testamentary intent to be a valid holographic will. The court ruled that the handwritten provisions on the commercially printed form will may draw testamentary context from both the printed and the handwritten language on the form. The court held the document qualified as a valid will.

**6. Judicial approach:** Holographic wills present an interesting dilemma for courts in terms of what degree of compliance with the holographic requirements the court should demand. On the one hand, because holographic wills eliminate the witness requirement, the remaining requirements are so important that absolute strict compliance arguably should be required. On the other hand, because holographic wills are intended to permit the layperson to execute his or her will without the cost of an attorney, the courts arguably should apply a looser standard. The courts appear torn between the two approaches.

**C. Conditional wills:** Conditional wills are wills that contain an express clause conditioning their being given effect upon some event occurring. Although conditional wills are valid and permitted, it is often unclear whether a clause in a will was intended to be an express condition precedent to the will being given effect or merely an explanation for why the person got around to executing a will. Courts tend to view conditional wills with disfavor and favor construing such clauses, when possible, as mere explanations for why the decedent executed the will. Such clauses tend to appear more often in holographic wills than in attested wills.

**D. Nuncupative/oral wills:** A handful of states permit nuncupative/oral wills under certain limited circumstances. A nuncupative will is one created under peril of death. Where permitted, it can devise only a limited amount of personal property. Likewise, some statutes grant members of the armed forces in actual combat or away at sea the power to dispose of limited amounts of personal property via oral wills. Typically, the oral will must be declared in the presence of two witnesses, who then typically must comply with a plethora of additional requirements if the oral will is to be given effect. Often such oral wills are valid only if the testator dies within a prescribed period after making the oral will. The additional requirements and restrictions on oral wills are so numerous that one could argue that for all practical purposes oral wills are no longer a viable option. The Uniform Probate Code does not recognize nuncupative or oral wills.

# V. SCOPE OF A WILL

**A. Integration:** The scope of a will starts with the threshold issue of determining what constitutes the pages of the will. The doctrine of integration provides that those pieces of paper that are physically present at the time of execution and that the testator intends to be part of the will constitute the pages of the will.

**Example:** In *Estate of Norton,* 410 S.E.2d 484 (N.C. 1991), proponents offered a writing as the last will of the decedent. The first six pages, entitled "Last Will and Testament of Lawrence Norton," were stapled together and contained provisions typically found in a will. While the decedent had signed the lower right-hand corner of each of the pages, the pages did not bear the signatures of any witnesses or notary public. The seventh page was entitled "Codicil to Last Will and Testament of Lawrence Norton" and it purported to devise certain real property. This page was signed by the decedent and two witnesses, along with a second page following this page. These two pages were stapled together and stapled to the six other pages with a legal cover on top of all eight pages. These documents were then put into a single envelope on the outside of which was written "Will" and then typewritten "of Lawrence Norton and Codicil of Lawrence Norton." The court held that the six pages did not qualify as a valid will in their own right (not properly attested) and there was no evidence that they were physically present when the "Codicil" was executed. The six pages that were stapled together were not part of the decedent's will. (See below for the incorporation by reference analysis.)

**B. Republication by codicil:** A codicil is a will that merely amends an existing will. (See section VI. C. 3 below for a fuller discussion of codicils.) Executing a codicil to a will "reexecutes" and "republishes" the underlying will.

    **1. Republication by codicil:** As a general rule, a codicil automatically redates the underlying will. The codicil can either redate the underlying will expressly (via an express clause expressing such an intent) or implicitly (in the absence of an express clause, the courts presume that the testator intended to redate the underlying will).

    **Exception:** There will be a handful of scenarios where redating the underlying will may be counterproductive to the testator's apparent wishes. In such situations, the parties can argue that the testator did not intend to redate the will in light of the adverse consequences that would follow. Courts are generally receptive to this argument where there is no express republication clause in the codicil, but not where there is an express republication clause (although one can argue that such clauses are boilerplate and do not really express testator's intent).

    **2. Preexisting will:** Classifying a will as a codicil implicitly presumes a preexisting valid will. If the purported will is not valid, the "codicil" cannot be a codicil but rather will be its own freestanding will (even if it does not dispose of all the testator's property). As a will, it will not reexecute and republish the invalid will, but it may still be possible to use the valid will to give effect to the testamentary wishes expressed in the invalid will through incorporation by reference (see section C below).

**Exception:** A handful of jurisdictions do not recognize incorporation by reference (e.g., New York). In those states, some courts will stretch republication by codicil to reexecute and republish an invalid underlying will, but only if the invalid will went through a valid execution ceremony but is invalid for some other reason (e.g., lack of or defect in capacity at the time the underlying will was executed).

3. **Curative powers:** If there were potential problems with the original will execution ceremony that do not affect its validity in whole (e.g., interested witness, or undue influence claim as to part of the will), these problems may be cured by the republication by codicil doctrine. As long as the problem is not present when the codicil is executed, the codicil's execution is deemed to reexecute and republish the underlying will, thereby curing the possible problem in the will.

C. **Incorporation by reference:** A valid will can incorporate by reference a document that was not executed with Wills Act formalities, thereby giving effect to the intent expressed in the incorporated document, as long as (1) the will expresses the intent to incorporate the document; (2) the will describes the document with reasonable certainty; and (3) the document being incorporated was in existence when the will was executed. UPC §2-510.

1. **Intent and describe requirements:** The courts tend to apply a rather low threshold to the first two requirements. If the will references another document, arguably that is enough to constitute the intent to incorporate it. If the court is persuaded that this is the document to which the testator was referring, most courts will find that the will describes the document with reasonable certainty despite the will's description of the document not being 100 percent accurate.

2. **Document in existence requirement:** The courts strictly apply the requirement that the document had to have been in existence at the time that the will was executed. Exact dating is not necessary, but the plaintiff bears the burden of proving by a preponderance of the evidence that the document was in existence when the will was executed. If the document changes over time, only the document as it existed at the time the will was executed can be incorporated by reference.

3. **Example:** In *Clark v. Greenhalge,* 582 N.E.2d 949 (Mass. 1991), testatrix's 1977 will named Greenhalge as executor and principal beneficiary, and provided that he was to receive all her tangible personal property except for those items designated to be given to others "by a memorandum" she would create and make known to Greenhalge. Thereafter testatrix created a memorandum *and* a notebook in which she made entries giving certain items of tangible personal property to certain beneficiaries. The memorandum was created in 1972 and amended in 1976. The notebook was titled "List to be given [testatrix] 1979" and contained an entry giving a picture to Ms. Clark. The testatrix told Ms. Clark of her intent to add the picture to the list in early 1980. Testatrix died in 1986, and Greenhalge refused to honor the purported gift of the picture via the list. Greenhalge argued that the will expressed the intent to incorporate *only* the memorandum. The court held that the language of the will was broad enough to include both the memorandum *and* the notebook, and that the will described the notebook with reasonable certainty. As for whether the entry in question had been entered in

the notebook when the will was executed, the court noted that the testatrix executed two codicils to her will, one in May 30, 1980, and a second on October 23, 1980. (The court did not analyze whether the precise entry had been made in the notebook by the date of the second codicil, apparently because it was displeased with the way the executor had behaved.)

4. **Example:** In the *Estate of Norton* case, above, the court declined to give effect to the six-page stapled document under incorporation by reference because there was not sufficient evidence that this was the document the decedent intended to incorporate. The court emphasized that the decedent's will made no express reference to the six-page document and that the decedent had executed numerous wills prior to his death. A strong dissent argued there was sufficient evidence to incorporate the six pages.

5. **UPC's tangible personal property list:** The UPC's tangible personal property list permits a testator to give away his or her tangible personal property via a list not executed with Wills Act formalities, even if the list is created *after* the will is executed, as long as the will expressly states such an intent. UPC §2-513. In essence, the doctrine modifies incorporation by reference by waiving the requirement that the document be in existence at the time the will is executed as long as the document only disposes of the testator's tangible personal property.

In *Clark v. Greenhalge,* above, if Massachusetts had adopted the tangible personal property list doctrine at the time, the doctrine would have mooted the issue of whether the entry in the notebook giving the picture to Ms. Clark had been made in the notebook at the time the will was republished by the codicil.

D. **Facts of independent significance:** Under the doctrine of facts of independent significance, a will may dispose of property by reference to facts outside of the will (the referenced fact can control either who takes or how much a beneficiary takes) as long as the referenced fact has significance independent of its effect upon the testator's probate estate. UPC §2-512. (In some jurisdictions the doctrine is known as "acts" of independent significance. The UPC calls it "events" of independent significance.)

1. **Conceptually difficult:** Conceptually, the doctrine of facts of independent significance is difficult because it permits a testator to "change" his or her will without having to execute a codicil. The counterargument is that the will is not really being changed—the language of the will just referenced a fact outside of the will, which was performed for reasons independent of its effect on the will, and the fact just happens to control either who takes or how much a beneficiary takes under the testator's will.

2. **Example:** The testatrix's will provides: "I give $1,000 to each of my sons-in-law, I give all the stuff in my garage to my brother, Bob, and I leave $10,000 to each of the persons I will identify in a letter I will leave for my executor." At the time the testatrix executed her will, she had two daughters, neither of whom were married. Thereafter, both daughters married, the testatrix bought a new lawnmower that she stored in the garage, and the testatrix wrote a letter to her executrix telling her to give $10,000 to Carolyn and $10,000 to Kristin. When the testatrix dies, who takes what?

**Analysis:** One could argue that the testatrix should have executed a codicil after each of the events referenced in the will occurred expressly stating what was to happen. But the facts of independent significance doctrine provides that as long as the fact referenced in the will has its own significance independent of its effect upon the testator's probate property, the referenced fact can control who takes how much without the testator having to execute a codicil.

    **a. First clause:** The referenced fact in the first clause is each daughter getting married. Getting married is an act that has its own independent significance apart from the fact that it affects the testatrix's will. The gifts to the sons-in-law are valid without the testatrix having to execute a codicil.

    **b. Second clause:** The referenced fact in the second clause is the act of putting things in and taking things out of the testatrix's garage. Storing items and using items are legitimate inter vivos purposes that show that the referenced fact has its own independent significance apart from its effect upon the testatrix's will. Bob gets the new lawnmower without the testatrix having to execute a codicil.

    **c. Third clause:** The referenced fact in the third clause that controls who will take $10,000 is the creation of a letter addressed to the executor. The letter does *not* have its own independent significance apart from its effect upon who takes under the testatrix's will. The referenced fact, the letter, is intended to and actually does serve only one purpose, to control who takes under the testatrix's will. The letter has no independent significance. Carolyn and Kristin do not take any money.

  **3. Writing as independent act:** The creation of a writing, even a testamentary writing, can qualify as a fact of independent significance as long as the referenced writing has its own independent significance apart from its effect on the will.

    **Example:** In *In re Tipler's Will,* 10 S.W.3d 244 (Tenn. App. 1998), testatrix executed a valid will that left the bulk of her estate to her husband. Two days later, testatrix executed a valid holographic codicil that provided in the event her husband predeceased her, his will would control the disposition of her estate. At the time she executed her will, her husband did not have a will. Thereafter he executed a valid typed will, and thereafter he predeceased her. Upon her death, her heirs at law challenged the testatrix's attempt at disposing of her estate via her husband's will. The testatrix could not incorporate her husband's will by reference, because his will was not in existence at the time she executed her will. The court, however, upheld the testatrix's incorporating the distribution plan of her husband under the facts of independent significance doctrine: Testatrix referenced her husband's will in her will, and her husband's will had its own significance independent of its effect upon her estate—his will distributed *his* probate property.

**E. Temporal perspectives:** Republication by codicil, incorporation by reference, and facts of independent significance are doctrines that expand the scope of the will by giving effect to writings or events outside of the will. The doctrines, however, have different "temporal" perspectives.

  **1. Backward looking:** Republication by codicil and incorporation by reference look back in time. Republication by codicil looks back in time by requiring that a valid will was executed *before* the codicil is executed. The codicil then republishes and redates the underlying will. Incorporation by reference looks back in time by requiring that the document to be incorporated be created *before* the will was executed.

**2. Forward looking:** Although facts of independent significance can look back in time, typically they looks forward. With rare exception, the referenced fact will be to an act or event to occur in the future, after the will is executed. Whenever a will references an act or event to occur in the future that affects who takes or how much they take, facts of independent significance is the only doctrine that can give effect to the gift.

**F. Pour-over wills:** The most common estate planning combination today is a pour-over will and trust. A pour-over will devises property to a trustee of an inter vivos trust to hold and distribute pursuant to the terms and conditions of the inter vivos trust (the will "pours" the probate property over to the trust). Because a document *not* executed with Will Act formalities (the trust) controls who takes the probate property, the pour-over clause must be validated. Traditionally, there were two doctrines that could be used to try to validate a pour-over clause: facts of independent significance and incorporation by reference. Today, a third option exists: UTATA (Uniform Testamentary Additions to Trusts Act). Validating pour-over clauses is discussed in detail in Ch. 7, VIII.

# VI. REVOCATION

**A. Revocability of wills:** Wills are executed inter vivos, but are not effective until death. If the testator changes his or her mind after executing a will, the testator can revoke it, replace it, or amend it at any time. A will may be revoked (1) by act, (2) by writing, (3) by presumption (a subset of revocation by act), and (4) by operation of law.

**B. Revocation by act:** A will may be revoked by a *physical* act as long as the act is destructive in nature (burning, tearing, etc.) and is performed with the intent to revoke. The act may be performed by the testator or by another, but if by another, the act must be performed in the testator's presence and at the testator's direction. UPC §2-507(a)(2).

**1. Common law:** The traditional and majority rule requires the destructive act to affect some part of the printed words of the will.

**2. Modern trend/UPC:** The UPC rejects the common law approach. The UPC requires only that the destructive act affect some part of the will. UPC §2-507(a)(2).

**C. Revocation by writing:** A will may be revoked by a subsequent writing expressing the intent to revoke, but only if the subsequent writing qualifies as a valid will—either attested or holographic. UPC §2-507(a)(1). A subsequent will can revoke a prior will expressly or implicitly by inconsistency.

**1. Express revocation:** Express revocation is when there is a clear and express statement of the intent to revoke the prior will ("I hereby revoke my prior will"). A will that does no more than express the intent to revoke a prior will is a valid will.

**2. Revocation by inconsistency:** Revocation by inconsistency occurs when a later will disposes of the decedent's property in a way that is inconsistent with a prior will. Because the later expression of the testator's intent controls over the prior, the prior will is deemed revoked to the extent of any inconsistencies. UPC §2-507(a)(1).

**3. Will vs. codicil:** If a subsequent will completely revokes a prior will, the subsequent will becomes the testator's sole will. If, however, the subsequent will only partially revokes or amends the prior will, the subsequent will is a *codicil*. The prior will still stands and is valid to the extent it is not revoked by the codicil. (To the extent neither will is inconsistent with the other will, a testator can have multiple wills.)

**Example:** In *Wolfe's Will,* 117 S.E. 804 (N.C. 1923), the testator properly executed a will that gave a certain tract of land to Ms. Luffman. Less than a month later, the testator executed a second will that gave "all my effects" to his sisters and brothers, equally. The court ruled that absent evidence to the contrary, it is presumed that the word "effects" applies only to personal property, and thus the two instruments were not inherently inconsistent. Ms. Luffman took the land.

4. **Codicils—execution:** First and foremost, a codicil is a will—it must be executed with the requisite Wills Act formalities. A codicil is a will that merely amends an existing will rather than completely replacing it. UPC §2-507(b)-(d). Holographic codicils to attested wills are valid, and attested codicils to holographic wills are valid.

   **Exception—codicils to holographic wills:** An important exception to the general rule that codicils must qualify as a valid will in their own right is that courts have held that handwritten amendments (*interlineations*) to a holographic will constitute a valid holographic codicil, even if the interlineations (the handwritten amendments) would not qualify as a valid holographic will in their own right.

5. **Revocation of codicil/will:** Revocation of a codicil does not revoke the underlying will. Revocation of a will revokes all codicils thereto.

6. **Writing as revocation by act:** The act of writing can qualify as revocation by act. If a testator writes "VOID" across her will, but does not sign it after writing "VOID," the act of writing "VOID" does not qualify as a valid revocation by writing because it does not qualify as a valid will (not signed). But the act of writing "VOID" does qualify as a destructive act. Assuming the testator had the intent to revoke at the time she performed the act, which is implicit in the nature of the act, the act of writing "VOID" qualifies as revocation by act.

7. **Example:** In *Thompson v. Royall,* 175 S.E. 748 (Va. 1934), the testatrix had her attorney take out her will and codicil to revoke them. The attorney suggested that rather than destroying them, she keep them as memoranda. So, on the back of the manuscript cover to the will, the attorney handwrote, in the presence of the testator and another, "This will null and void...". The testatrix signed the notation. The testatrix died three weeks later. The will and codicil were offered for probate. The writing did not qualify as *revocation by writing* because the writing did not qualify as a valid will (not attested because not witnessed and not holographic because the material provision—the intent to revoke—was not in the testator's handwriting). The writing did not qualify as *revocation by act* because the writing did not touch any of the printed words of the will as required under the traditional common law approach.

   **Modern trend:** The writing may qualify as a valid *revocation by act* because the act arguably affected some portion of the will (if the manuscript cover were construed to be part of the will). The writing may also qualify as *revocation by writing*. The testatrix died three weeks after creating the writing in the presence of two witnesses. Under the modern trend, delayed attestation is permitted as long as it occurs within a reasonable time period. The witnesses could be brought in and asked to sign the notation as witnesses, thereby qualifying it as a valid attested will.

**D. Revocation by presumption:** If a will was last in the testator's possession and cannot be found following the testator's death, a rebuttable presumption arises that the testator revoked the will by act. If the presumption cannot be overcome, the will is deemed revoked. If the presumption is rebutted, the will is deemed "lost" and extrinsic evidence will be admitted to prove its terms. If the terms can be established by clear and convincing evidence (almost any evidence is admissible), the "lost" will should be probated.

**1. Rationale:** Testators know that their will is a very important document. If the testator takes the will home with him or her, the presumption is that he or she will safeguard the will—keep it in a safe place with his or her other important papers. If the will cannot be found after the testator's death, the more likely explanation is that the testator revoked it by act rather than that the testator lost it. (Notice that, technically, revocation by presumption is a subset of revocation by physical act.)

**2. Strength of the presumption:** The strength of the presumption that the testator revoked the will depends on the particular facts of the case—how much control the decedent had over the will and whether others had access to it—particularly parties who stand to benefit if the will were deemed revoked. If those supporting the will offer a more plausible explanation for why the will cannot be found, the issue becomes one for the trier of fact.

**Example:** In *First Interstate Bank of Or. v. Henson-Hammer,* 779 P.2d 167 (Or. App. 1989), the testator executed a will that created a testamentary trust for the benefit of his daughter (his only heir) during her life, and upon her death, the principal was to be distributed to her children equally. The testator left a copy of the will with his attorney, sent a copy to the bank that was to be trustee, and he took the original. Following his death, the will last in his possession could not be found. The court found that the presumption arose that the testator destroyed the will with the intent to revoke it. The daughter claimed this presumption could be overcome only with clear and satisfactory evidence. The court noted that the strength of the presumption depends on the facts of each case. The court ruled that because the daughter had access to the will while in the testator's possession and because she stood to benefit if the will were revoked, the strength of the presumption was relatively weak. The court found there was sufficient evidence (the testator's reaffirmation of his estate plan shortly before his death and his concerns that the daughter's husband might receive some of the property if left outright to the daughter) to overcome the presumption.

**3. Duplicate originals:** Duplicate originals are multiple originals of the same will, each one properly executed. A photocopy of an executed will is not a duplicate original. The testator must properly execute each version of a duplicate original.

    **a. Revocation by act or by writing:** Affirmative evidence that the testator properly revoked one duplicate original by act or by writing will automatically revoke all duplicate originals.

    **b. Revocation by presumption:** The jurisdictions are split over whether the presumption doctrine should apply to revoke all duplicate originals if the one the testator took home cannot be found, but the other duplicate original can be found.

        **i. Revokes all duplicate originals:** If the presumption doctrine applies to one duplicate original, it applies to all duplicate originals. The reasoning underlying this approach is that revocation by presumption is a subset of revocation by act. Valid revocation by act revokes all duplicate originals, so valid revocation by presumption of one should revoke all duplicate originals.

ii. **Not revoke all duplicate originals:** The presumption doctrine will not revoke duplicate original wills unless *none* of the duplicate originals can be found following the testator's death. The reasoning underlying this approach is that presumption assumes that testators who take their wills home with them will take care to safeguard them. If there is a duplicate original, however, testators are less likely to safeguard the duplicate original they took home with them. If the will the testator took home cannot be found, it is just as likely that he or she lost it as that they destroyed it with the intent to revoke.

4. **Example:** In *Harrison v. Bird,* 621 So. 2d 972 (Ala. 1993), the testatrix executed duplicate wills, leaving one with her attorney and taking the other home with her. Thereafter, the testator called the attorney and advised him that she wanted to revoke her will. The attorney tore the will he had into pieces in the presence of his secretary and mailed the pieces to the testatrix. The court held that the attorney's tearing the will into pieces was not a valid revocation by act because it was not done in the presence of the testatrix. But, because the pieces of the will that were mailed to the testatrix could not be found after her death, the presumption doctrine arose. The court ruled that the presumption doctrine revoked *all* duplicate originals, even if one or more can be found following the testatrix's death.

5. **Partial revocation by physical act:** The jurisdictions are split over whether partial revocation by physical act should be permitted because (1) it increases the potential for fraud, and (2) a partial revocation intrinsically is also a new gift. By revoking only part of a will, the revoked part has to go somewhere. If it goes anywhere else in the will, it arguably is a new gift. New gifts should be executed with Wills Act formalities—so the reasoning goes.

a. **If jurisdiction does not recognize:** Those jurisdictions that do not recognize partial revocation by physical act simply ignore the act in question and give effect to the will as originally written.

b. **Modern trend/UPC approach:** Many states and the UPC do recognize partial revocation by physical act (UPC §2-507), but the states are split over how to treat the revoked gift. The majority permits the revoked gift to fall to the residuary and increase the residuary, but the partial revocation cannot increase a gift outside of the residuary. A few states, concerned that the "new gift" was not made with Wills Act formalities, hold that the revoked gift may pass via intestacy only. The UPC provides that the partial revocation should be given effect regardless of its effect, even if the partial revocation increases a gift outside of the residuary.

E. **Revival:** Assuming a testator validly executes will #1, and thereafter validly executes will #2 that expressly or implicitly revokes will #1, and thereafter validly revokes will #2 intending to give effect to will #1, the jurisdictions are split over what the testator must do to "revive" will #1.

1. **English approach:** Under the English approach, will #1 was never revoked so it is still valid and can be probated. The English approach takes literally the statement that a will is not effective until the testator dies. Taken literally, will #2 would have revoked will #1 only if will #2 had remained in effect until the testator died. Because the testator revoked will #2 before he died, will #2 never become effective, so it never revoked will #1. So there is no need

to "revive" will #1 because it was never revoked. A handful of states follow the English approach.

2. **American approach:** Despite the general rule that a will is not effective until the testator dies, for purposes of revoking an existing will, the general American rule is that a will is effective the moment it is properly executed. The moment the testator properly executes will #2, it revokes will #1. If thereafter the testator revokes will #2, will #1 is not automatically revived. The testator must do something to "revive" will #1. The jurisdictions are split over what the testator must do to revive will #1.

3. **Minority approach:** A minority of states requires the testator to reexecute will #1 to revive it (or incorporate it by reference into a valid new will). Only by going through the Wills Act formalities again can testamentary life be given to will #1.

4. **Majority/UPC approach:** A majority of the states and the UPC think that requiring the testator to go through the Wills Act formalities again is too burdensome. Instead, all the testator has to do to revive will #1 is to intend to revive will #1. UPC §2-509. This statement is a bit misleading, however, because the states limit what evidence the courts can take of the testator's intent to revive depending on how the testator revoked will #2.

   **Proving intent to revive:** If the testator revoked will #2 by act, the courts will take almost any evidence of testator's intent to revive will #1, even the testator's own alleged statements. UPC §2-509(a). If, however, the testator revoked will #2 by writing a new will (will #3), the intent to revive will #1 must be set forth in the new will (will #3). UPC §2-509(c).

5. **Will #2 as will vs. codicil:** Where will #2 wholly revokes will #1, the UPC follows the majority American approach discussed above. Where will #2 only partially revokes will #1, however, (i.e., where will #2 is a codicil) the UPC follows the English approach. The part of will #1 that was revoked by will #2 is presumed to be automatically revived, and the burden of proof is on the party trying to prove that the testator did *not* intend to revive the revoked provisions of will #1. UPC §2-509(b).

F. **Dependent relative revocation:** Even if a will is validly revoked (in whole or in part), the courts will ignore the revocation if (1) the revocation was based upon a mistake, and (2) the testator would not have revoked if testator had known the truth. In addition, the courts tend to apply the doctrine only if (1) there is a failed alternative testamentary scheme, or (2) if the mistake is set forth in the writing that revoked the will and the mistake is beyond the testator's knowledge.

1. **Revocation by act:** The classic dependent relative revocation scenario is where the testator revokes a gift by act (valid revocation) on the belief that a new will or codicil is valid, but the new will or codicil is not valid (mistake of law). The intended beneficiary stands to take nothing because the original gift has been validly revoked and the new gift fails due to the mistake of law. Dependent relative revocation reasons that it is better to save the original gift if that is what the testator would have wanted if he or she had known that the new will/codicil was invalid.

   a. **Example:** Pete has a valid typed will that provides in part as follows: "I give $10,000 to Lulu." Thereafter, Pete decides that Lulu deserves more. He takes out the will and draws a line through the $10,000 and handwrites above the lined out gift "$20,000." Thereafter he dies. How much, if anything, does Lulu take?

**b. Analysis:** When Pete drew the line through the original gift of $10,000, Pete validly revoked the gift by act. When Pete handwrote in "$20,000," he was attempting a holographic codicil that fails. Lulu stands to take nothing. She should invoke dependent relative revocation. There was a valid revocation (the line through the $10,000), based upon a mistake (the belief that the holographic codicil would be valid), and arguably the testator would not have revoked but for the mistake (Pete was trying to increase the gift, so clearly he would prefer the original gift over no gift). The failed alternative testamentary scheme is the attempt at a new will/codicil that failed due to a mistake of law. Where the revocation is by act, almost invariably the mistake will be a mistake of law because the testator's attempt at a new will/ codicil will fail for some legal reason.

**c. Example:** In *Schneider v. Harrington,* 71 N.E.2d 242 (Mass. 1947), the testatrix's will left her estate: "one third (1/3) to my niece Phyllis; one third (1/3) to my sister Margaret; and one third (1/3) to my sister Amy." There was no residuary clause. Thereafter, testatrix apparently drew a line in pencil through the whole clause making the gift to Amy and drew lines through the numbers (1/3) in the first two clauses, writing in above them (1/2) (but not drawing a line through the words "one third" in the first two clauses). The court found the gift to Amy was validly revoked. The court found that the attempt to change the gifts in the first two clauses to 1/2 each was invalid because not properly executed. Amy invoked dependent relative revocation and argued that her gift was revoked only because of the testatrix's mistake of law that the attempted holographic interlineations would be valid, and if the testatrix had known that the interlineations would not be valid, she would not have revoked at all. The court agreed, finding that the revocation was inextricably linked to the interlineations and that the testatrix would not have wanted Amy's one-third to fall to intestacy. The court applied dependent relative revocation and ordered that the revocation be ignored.

**2. Revocation by writing:** The less common dependent relative revocation scenario is where the revocation is by writing. For dependent relative revocation to apply, most courts require that the mistake be set forth in the writing and that the mistake be beyond the testator's knowledge.

**a. Example:** Pete's valid will provides in part as follows: "I give $10,000 to Lulu." Thereafter, Pete hears that Lulu married Fred, a marriage that angers Pete. Pete properly executes a codicil that provides as follows: "I hereby revoke my gift to Lulu in light of her marriage to Fred." In fact, Lulu never married Fred.

**b. Analysis:** Pete's codicil validly revoked the gift to Lulu. Here, Pete thought Lulu had married Fred when in fact she had not. Where the revocation is by writing, the mistake must be set forth in the revoking writing, and it must be beyond the testator's knowledge. Here, the codicil expressly stated that the reason Pete was revoking was because of his belief that Lulu had married Fred, and the mistake is beyond Pete's knowledge. There is no reason to believe that Pete should have known whether Lulu and Fred were actually married.

**3. Tendencies:** Almost invariably, where the revocation is *by act*, the mistake will be a *mistake of law* in that the testator attempted a new will/codicil that is invalid. Almost invariably, where the revocation is *by writing*, the mistake will be a *mistake of fact* that must then be set forth in the valid revoking instrument. It is possible, however, to have a valid revocation by writing where the mistake will be a mistake of law—but the mistake will still have to be set forth in the writing (the new gift fails because it violates the Rule against Perpetuities, or it violates public policy, etc.).

**Example:** In *Carter v. First United Methodist Church of Albany*, 271 S.E.2d 493 (Ga. 1980), testatrix had a valid will dated 1963, and she expressed to her attorney her desire to change her will. After her death, her 1963 will was found folded together with a handwritten document dated 1978 that was captioned as her will but was unsigned. Pencil marks had been made across the dispositive provisions of the 1963 will. Because the will was last in testatrix's possession, the presumption arose that the testatrix made the pencil marks with the intent to revoke—thereby revoking the will by presumption. The 1978 document was not valid because it was not signed. The testatrix appears to die intestate. The beneficiaries under the 1963 will invoked dependent relative revocation. The beneficiaries convinced the court that the testatrix revoked the 1963 will because she believed that the 1978 instrument was a valid new will, establishing both the mistake and the failed alternative scheme. The court stated that the 1978 instrument made only "a somewhat different disposition of her property," apparently indicating that the testatrix would have preferred the 1963 testamentary scheme over intestacy. The court probated the 1963 will.

**Alternative analysis:** Some courts have held that pencil marks do not show finality of intent and are not sufficient, in and of themselves, to constitute a valid revocation. The court could have found that the 1963 will was never properly revoked.

**G. Revocation by operation of law—divorce:** The overwhelming majority rule is that divorce automatically and irrebuttably revokes all provisions in a testator's will in favor of the ex-spouse, unless the will expressly provides otherwise. UPC §2-804.

  **1. Rationale:** After a typical divorce, the law presumes that the ex-spouses no longer love each other, they no longer consider each other natural objects of their bounty, and they no longer wish to leave any of their property to each other.

  **2. Traditional scope:** The traditional approach, and still majority approach, is to apply the revocation by operation of law doctrine only to wills, not to the will substitutes—life insurance, joint tenancy, pension plans, and other nonprobate arrangements.

  **3. Modern trend/UPC scope:** The UPC applies the revocation by operation of law doctrine not only to wills, but also to the will substitutes—life insurance, joint tenancy, pension plans, and other nonprobate arrangements. UPC §2-804.

  **4. Beneficiaries affected:** The jurisdictions are split over which beneficiaries come within the scope of the revocation by operation of law doctrine—just the ex-spouse or also the ex-spouse's relatives. The UPC takes a fairly broad approach, revoking provisions in favor not only of the ex-spouse, but also revoking provisions in favor of the ex-spouse's relatives. UPC §2-804(b)(1).

  **5. Domestic partners:** Some states permit domestic partners to obtain inheritance rights by registering. Some of those states apply the revocation by operation of law doctrine to the partners. If the parties terminate their partnership, the termination automatically revokes all provisions in the will in favor of the ex-domestic partner.

  **6. Revocation by marriage, birth of child:** To the extent the omitted spouse and omitted child doctrines give the new spouse or child a share of the testator's property before giving effect to the will, the doctrines indirectly revoke the will by operation of law. But in those scenarios, it is not so much that any particular provision of the will is being revoked, but rather a "new gift" is being read into the will that may have the effect of reducing or eliminating some of the gifts already in the will.

# VII. CONTRACTS CONCERNING WILLS

A. **Introduction:** Under probate administration, creditors take first—before beneficiaries under a will or heirs under intestacy. Creditors have extended valuable consideration to the decedent and are entitled to recover that to which they are entitled before beneficiaries or heirs who are merely donees.

   1. **Potential for fraud:** The principle that creditors take before beneficiaries or heirs creates a potential for fraudulent claims. Individuals who thought they were going to be beneficiaries under a testator's will, but are not, might try to turn their frustration into a claim that they "contracted" with the testator and are entitled to take from the decedent's estate as a creditor.

   2. **Contract requirements:** Contracts relating to wills, contracts to make a will (or provision) or not to revoke a will (or provision) must meet the standard contract requirements—offer, acceptance, and consideration.

   3. **Remedy—constructive trust:** If a contract concerning a will is established, and the testator breaches the agreement by executing a different will, the probate court will still probate the will the testator executed. Moreover, the damaged contract beneficiaries are not entitled to specific performance, but a constructive trust based on the contract will be imposed on the testator's probate property.

B. **Writing requirement:** Under contract law, the Statute of Frauds generally controls whether a contract needs to be in writing. As applied to contracts concerning wills, however, because of the potential for fraudulent claims and the fact that the other party to the alleged contract is dead, some jurisdictions require contracts concerning wills to be in writing even if not required under the Statute of Frauds.

   1. **Equitable estoppel:** Under traditional common law principles, oral agreements between parties that one would leave property to the other upon the first party's death did not have to be in writing. This approach, however, facilitates fraudulent claims of contracts concerning wills.

   2. **Clear and convincing evidence:** Some states have tried to reduce the potential for fraudulent claims concerning wills by requiring clear and convincing evidence to establish contracts concerning wills.

   3. **Modern trend/UPC:** The Uniform Probate Code has tried to reduce the potential for fraudulent claims even further by requiring that contracts concerning wills must be evidenced by some writing signed by the decedent. UPC §2-514.

C. **Contracts not to revoke:** A contract not to revoke a will arises when a party agrees not to revoke a will or a provision in a will.

   1. **Joint wills:** A joint will is a single will that serves as the last will and testament of two parties, typically husband and wife. The joint will must be properly executed by each party. It typically provides that upon the death of the first party, all his or her property goes to the surviving party, and upon the death of the surviving party, the property goes to some agreed-upon beneficiary or beneficiaries.

2. **Mutual wills:** Mutual wills, also known as mirror wills, are similar to joint wills, only instead of there being only one will, there are two wills—but each will has the same testamentary distribution scheme. Like joint wills, mutual wills typically arise between husband and wife. Each spouse has his or her own separate will that typically provides that upon the spouse's death, all to the surviving spouse, if one, otherwise to their children (or some other agreed-upon beneficiary).

   a. **Ambiguity:** The issue that naturally arises out of joint wills and/or mutual wills is whether they implicitly contain a contract not to revoke, so that upon the death of the first party, the testamentary scheme the parties agreed upon becomes binding on the surviving party. Ultimately, it is a question of the parties' intent. Historically, most courts required clear and convincing evidence of the claimed contract not to revoke. While older cases were more likely to imply a contract not to revoke, more recent cases are reluctant to imply a contract to revoke.

   **Example:** In *Lawrence v. Ashba,* 59 N.E.2d 568 (Ind. App. 1945), Mr. and Mrs. Lawrence executed mutual wills, each of which gave all the first decedent spouse's property to the surviving spouse, and upon the surviving spouse's death, all to the children of Mrs. Lawrence from a prior marriage. There was no express contract not to revoke clause. After Mrs. Lawrence died, Mr. Lawrence disposed of his property inconsistent with the original testamentary scheme. After Mr. Lawrence's death, Mrs. Lawrence's children sued, claiming breach of a contract not to revoke. The court found that in light of the evidence, particularly that the wills contained substantially identical provisions, that the same lawyer prepared them, that the wills were executed at the same time in front of the same witnesses with full knowledge of each other's provisions, it was sufficient to constitute clear and convincing evidence of a contract not to revoke.

   **Example:** In *Oursler v. Armstrong,* 179 N.E.2d 489 (N.Y. 1961), Charles Oursler had two children by his first wife and two by his second wife, Grace. In 1951, Charles and Grace executed mutual wills at the same time before the same witnesses, each of which left all of the first-to-die's property to the surviving spouse, and if there were none, all to the four children equally. Charles died in 1952. Grace died in 1955, but in January of that year she executed a new will that left all the property to her children, excluding his children by his first wife. The excluded children sued, claiming a contract not to revoke. The court found the evidence failed to establish an express or implied contract not to revoke.

   b. **Modern trend/UPC:** The UPC provides that executing a joint will or mutual wills does not create even a presumption of a contract not to revoke. UPC §2-514. The surviving party is free to dispose of all the property, including the property received by virtue of the first party's death, as he or she sees fit.

3. **Property affected:** The scope of the property subject to the contract not to revoke should be addressed in the contract, but in the absence of clear drafting, the courts tend to hold that the standard contract not to revoke applies not only to the property the surviving party received from the deceased party, but also to the surviving party's property—both the property the surviving party held at the time of death of the first party and the property subsequently acquired by the surviving party.

4. **Right to use:** The surviving party is deemed to have a life estate in the property subject to the contract not to revoke, with the right to reasonable consumption.

5. **Survival requirement:** Under general wills rules, a beneficiary has to survive the testator to take. Under general contracts doctrines, the beneficiary to a contract does not have to survive the other party to the contract to claim his or her benefits under the contract. As applied to beneficiaries of the contract not to revoke, as a general rule the courts hold that the beneficiaries claim in their capacity as will beneficiaries unless and until there is a breach of the contract not to revoke. If there is no breach, the beneficiaries must survive the decedent to take. If there is a breach, at that moment their status changes to creditors claiming under the contract and they need not survive the decedent to claim their benefits under the contract.

6. **Example:** In *In re Estate of Wiggins*, 350 N.E.2d 618 (N.Y. App. Div. 1976), husband and wife executed a joint will that expressly provided that the survivor had the right to consume the principal during his or her lifetime, *except the right to dispose of the same by will.* Mr. Wiggins died in 1948, and Mrs. Wiggins executed two codicils shortly before she died in 1969. The court ruled that the clause in question constituted a contract not to revoke, that it applied to the collective assets of both spouses acquired during their lifetimes, that the contract became enforceable upon the death of the first spouse, and that Mrs. Wiggins' property was to be distributed pursuant to the joint will despite the codicils.

D. **Contract rights vs. spousal protection rights:** Where there is a contract not to revoke, and the parties to the contract are husband and wife, if after the first spouse's death the surviving spouse remarries, the contract not to revoke comes into conflict with the omitted spouse doctrine and the elective share doctrine. (See Ch. 3.)

1. **Order of takers:** As a general rule, (1) creditors take before beneficiaries in the will, (2) spouses claiming spouse protection take before beneficiaries in the will, and (3) creditor's claims are satisfied before spousal protection claims are satisfied. The issue is whether creditors claiming under a contract not to revoke are entitled to the same status as other creditors, or whether spouses are entitled to protection before the beneficiaries of the contract not to revoke.

2. **Contract beneficiaries:** The complexity of this issue stems from the fact that the third-party beneficiaries of the contract not to revoke are also beneficiaries under the will. If the surviving spouse dies without remarrying, the beneficiaries take under the will in their capacity as beneficiaries. If, however, the surviving spouse remarries and breaches the contract not to revoke, the will beneficiaries can now claim as creditors. The breach of the contract permits them to try to change their place in line from will beneficiaries (who normally take last) to creditors (who normally take first). Inasmuch as the will/contract not to revoke beneficiaries wear two hats, their place in line depends first on whether there was a breach of the contract not to revoke.

3. **Breach:** Some contracts not to revoke state that *anything* that alters the agreed-upon distribution scheme constitutes a breach of the contract. Under this language, the mere act of remarrying may constitute a breach because it alters the agreed-upon testamentary distribution scheme by subjecting the estate to spousal protection claims. Other contracts not to revoke are worded such that the contract is breached only if the surviving spouse revokes the will. Under this language, the surviving spouse's remarriage does not constitute a breach of the contract not to revoke, and the new spouse should be entitled to take before the will beneficiaries because the beneficiaries can claim only in their capacity as will beneficiaries.

a. **Jurisdictional split:** The jurisdictions are split over who should take first where the surviving spouse remarries and the new spouse's claims constitute a breach of the contract not to revoke.

 i. **Majority:** A majority of jurisdictions enforce the terms of the contract not to revoke and let the contract beneficiaries take before the new spouse. These jurisdictions justify their approach on a number of different grounds.

 ii. **Minority:** A minority of the jurisdictions invokes the principle that contracts that discourage or restrain the right to marry are void as against public policy. These courts protect the new surviving spouse and let the new spouse take first by voiding the contract not to revoke because it violates public policy.

b. **Example:** In *Shimp v. Huff*, 556 A.2d 252 (Md. 1989), Lester and Clara Shimp executed a joint will that contained a contract not to revoke. Clara died, and thereafter Lester married Lisa Mae. Lester did not execute a new will. Upon Lester's death, the joint will was offered for probate, but Lisa Mae claimed her spousal protection rights (a family allowance and her elective share). The court noted that Lester did not execute a new will after marrying Lisa Mae, and thus he did not breach the contract not to revoke. Accordingly, the court recognized that the beneficiaries under the joint will were merely legatees and not contract creditors, thereby giving the surviving spouse a superior right to the probate assets. But the court acknowledged that this reasoning had the perverse result of making the contract beneficiaries better off if the contract had been breached. Thus, the court invoked public policy considerations in favor of marriage and protecting the spouse to support its ruling that a surviving spouse is entitled to spousal protection before the beneficiaries under a contract not to revoke.

---

## *Quiz Yourself* on
## WILLS EXECUTION, REVOCATION, AND SCOPE

**27.** Pete is hit by a car and rushed to the hospital. He is lucid, but has sustained serious internal injuries and it is not clear whether he will make it. Lulu, his girlfriend, hears about the accident and rushes to be by his side—bringing with her a draft of his will that leaves everything to her. Lulu calls in two nurses, and in front of both of them, Pete declares that the document is his last will and testament and disposes of his property as he wishes. He picks up the pen, starts to sign his first name, when suddenly the door to his hospital room opens and his wife, Bertha, walks in. She is livid to see Lulu there. All hell breaks loose, and in the commotion, Pete forgets to complete his signature. Lulu takes the document out to the nurses' station, where she has the nurses sign their names.

 **a.** Is the will valid under the traditional common law approach? _____

 **b.** Is the will valid under the modern trend approach? _____

**28.** Tess has a properly executed, typed will. When the will is found after her death it is discovered that physically below her signature line is a handwritten sentence that provides as follows: "I also give $1,000 to my friend Betty." Is the will valid? Is the gift to Betty valid? _____

**29.** Tim has a heart attack. He remains conscious and alert. His girlfriend, Wi, and his neighbor, Joe, put him in the back seat of his car (in the seat behind the driver's seat). Joe gets in back with Tim.

Wi jumps in front and starts driving to the hospital. Tim's attorney had sent Tim a draft of a new will. His old will gave all his money to UCLA, his alma mater. His new will gives half to Wi, and half to UCLA. As Wi was running around the house looking for the car keys, she had the presence of mind to grab the draft of the new will. While racing Tim to the hospital (but keeping her eyes on the road at all times), Wi passes the new will back to Tim and asks him to execute it. Tim declares that the document is his last will and testament and signs it. Joe, who is sitting next to Tim and watching all this, then signs it. Joe then passes it up to the front seat, where Wi signs it at the first stoplight. Tim survives the heart attack, only to die from the hospital food (food poisoning). Who takes his property? _____

30. Gerri and Dick have been married for years. Her will leaves everything to Dick, and in the event he predeceases her, to her mom. Gerri thought she and Dick were happily married, until she discovers that he is having an affair with Anna Nicoli. Gerri is crushed. She handwrites her mom a dated letter in which she pours out her heart, describing the anguish she is going through as she debates filing for divorce. The letter has a sentence that reads: "And to think that I have a will that leaves all of my property to that jerk. It should go to you." Gerri signs the letter, "your loving daughter." A week later, Anna Nicoli kills Gerri. Who gets Gerri's property? _____

31. Dude is deathly afraid to fly. Anna Nicoli asks him to go to Hawaii with her. She promises to make it worth his while. Dude decides the offer is too good to pass up. Before getting on the plane, he handwrites, dates, and signs the following instrument: "If the plane crashes and I die, I want all my property to go to my alma mater, Chico State." Dude successfully makes it to Hawaii and back, only to drive off the road while daydreaming about the time he spent with Anna Nicoli in Hawaii. Dude dies from his injuries. Chico State offers the writing for probate. His heirs oppose it. Assuming the jurisdiction recognizes holographic wills, who gets Dude's property? _____

32. Gerri and Dick have been married for years. Her typed will leaves everything to Dick, and in the event he predeceases her, to her mom. Gerri thought she and Dick were happily married, until she discovers that he is having an affair with Anna Nicoli. Gerri takes out the envelope containing the will and writes across the envelope, in big letters, "VOID." Gerri is killed in a car crash a week later. Who takes her property? _____

33. Tami executed a will leaving her property to her alma mater, Loyola, and took it home with her. A month later, a violent earthquake struck the area, totally destroying Tami's house and killing her. Following her death, her family could not find her will. Who takes Tami's property? _____

34. What difference, if any, would it make if Tami had executed duplicate original wills in the previous question? _____

35. Tom properly executes a will. The will provides in part as follows: "I give $10,000 to my favorite research assistant, Raquel, and I give the rest, residue and remainder of my estate to my church." Following Tom's death, his will is found, but there is a line drawn though the sentence giving the gift to Raquel. Who takes what? _____

36. Toni has a properly executed will that provides in part as follows: "I give my best friend Gail, $10,000. I give the rest of my estate to my alma mater, the University of Chicago." Thereafter, Toni hears that her best friend is dating her ex-boyfriend, Frankie. Toni takes out her will, and with a pen draws a line through her gift to Gail. She tells everyone she revoked the gift to Gail because she is dating her ex-boyfriend. Toni is so depressed she commits suicide. It turns out that although Gail is

dating someone named Frankie, it is not the Frankie Toni used to date. What is Gail's best argument that she is entitled to take? What are her chances of prevailing? _____

37. Jalo had a valid will that left all her property to Puffy. Thereafter, she broke up with Puffy and started seeing Ben. Shortly after she started seeing Ben, she properly executed a new will that left all her property to Ben. Not long thereafter, however, she grew tired of Ben and went back to Puffy. At the time, she handwrote, dated, and signed an instrument that provided as follows: "I hereby revoke my will leaving my property to Ben. Jalo." She told everyone that the reason she was revoking her second will was that she really loved Puffy and wanted him to have her property. Shortly thereafter, she died on the operating table during elective surgery. Who takes her property? _____

38. Surfer Dude has a valid will that leaves his "surfboard to Jane, and the rest of my property shall go as directed in a letter I will send to my executor, Hulama." Thereafter, Surfer Dude types and signs a letter telling Hulama that he wants all his property to go to the Heal the Bay organization. Thereafter, Surfer Dude executes a valid codicil appointing Jake his executor. Thereafter, Surfer Dude dies from an infection he contracts as a result of surfing in polluted waters. Who takes his property? _____

39. Paul and his sister Kristin went to UCLA, and they hated their dreaded rival USC. They often talked about how they would leave their estates to the UCLA Athletic Department to help fight their rivals. Paul was several years older than his sister, and he wanted to make sure that she was taken care of first. Paul properly executed a will that provided that he left everything to his sister Kristin for life, and upon her death his property should be distributed according to the residuary clause of Kristin's will. Unbeknownst to Paul, Kristin had not drafted her will yet. It was not until two years after Paul executed his will that Kristin properly executed her will that left everything to UCLA. Who takes Paul's property when he dies? _____

40. Tommie promised to leave all his property to Anna Nicoli if she would take care of him for the rest of his life. Anna Nicoli did for six months, only to discover when Tommie died at the end of the six months that he had a properly executed will leaving all of his property to his church. Anna Nicoli sues to enforce the terms of her agreement with Tommie. Who takes Tommie's property? _____

41. Pete and Gerri are married. They have four lovely children. They execute mirror wills that have an express clause waiving the testator's right to revoke the will. Each will leaves all of the testator's property to the surviving spouse, if one, otherwise to the children equally. Many years later, Pete dies, and Gerri moves in with Rick—fulfilling his lifelong dream. Gerri executes a new will leaving all her property to Rick. Who takes her property when she dies? _____

---

# Answers

27. **a.** Under the traditional common law approach, Pete's will was not validly executed. There are a couple of problems with the document Lulu is offering as Pete's will under the common law approach. First, it arguably was not properly signed. Although anything the testator intends to qualify as his signature constitutes a valid signature, there is a general presumption that when a person begins to sign his or her name, he or she intends to sign the whole name. If the person does not sign the whole name, but stops of his or her own volition, then arguably whatever the person wrote he or she intended

to constitute his or her whole signature. Where, however, the person is interrupted during the signing of his or her name, the presumption is that the person intended to sign the whole name and did not intend for anything short to qualify as his or her signature. Here, it is assumed that Pete intended to sign his whole name. When his wife walked in and interrupted the signature, Pete may have reconsidered and decided not to sign the document. Under the traditional common law approach, the more likely result is that the court would hold that Pete did not properly sign the document.

Moreover, under the traditional common law approach, witnesses were required to sign the will in the testator's presence. Here, the nurses did not sign the will in Pete's room; they signed the document back at the nurses' station. There is no evidence that Pete was anywhere nearby when they signed the will. Because the nurses did not sign the document in Pete's presence, the will was not properly executed and is invalid.

**b.** Under the modern trend approach, the will arguably is still invalid, though a much stronger argument can be made that it should be considered a valid will. Under the modern trend, the witnesses do not have to sign the will in the testator's presence. Delayed attestation is permitted as long as the witnesses sign within a reasonable time of witnessing the testator perform. Under the modern trend, the fact that the nurses signed the document a bit later at the nurses' station is acceptable.

The issue under the modern trend is whether the will was properly signed. Just as was true at common law, whatever the testator intended to qualify as his signature will qualify. The issue with respect to a partial signature, however, is still the same. Where the testator is interrupted during signing, a presumption arises that he or she did not intend for the partial signature to constitute his or her signature because when the person started to sign he or she intended to sign his or her full name. That is particularly applicable here where the reason the testator stopped signing is because his wife, who would have been disinherited to the full extent permitted by law, entered the room. Maybe seeing her made him reconsider. Under the modern trend, if one were to apply strict compliance, most likely the will would be invalid.

In some jurisdictions, the modern trend favors substantial compliance and/or dispensing power. Under both of those doctrines, however, the will proponents still have to prove by clear and convincing evidence that the decedent intended this document to be his or her last will. Because we presume Pete intended to sign his whole name, it is questionable whether there is clear and convincing evidence that he intended this document to be his last will. What constitutes clear and convincing evidence, however, is fact sensitive and somewhat subjective. Different people disagree over what constitutes clear and convincing evidence. Pete did start to sign his name, which arguably constitutes clear and convincing evidence that he intended the document to be his will. But when his wife, who was being disinherited, entered the room, he stopped and did not complete his name. Arguably he did not complete his signature because he had second thoughts and no longer wanted to disinherit her. It is unclear how the case would come out. Although the will proponents have a stronger argument under these doctrines, the equities and public policy considerations favoring a spouse may be the deciding factor.

**28.** The analysis depends on whether (1) the jurisdiction follows the common law approach to the Wills Act formalities (which typically requires that the will be signed at the end) or the modern trend approach (which does not require the will to be signed at the end); and (2) when the handwritten clause was added to the document, *temporally* before or after the document was signed?

If the jurisdiction requires the will to be "subscribed" (signed at the end), and the handwritten sentence was added temporally *before* the testator signed the will, the whole will is invalid because the will was not signed at the end. If the jurisdiction requires the will to be subscribed, and the handwritten sentence was added temporally *after* the testator signed the will, the original will should be valid but the handwritten material added temporally after the will was executed is invalid.

If the jurisdiction follows the modern trend and does not require the will to be signed at the end, and if the handwritten sentence was added temporally *after* the testator signed the will, the will is valid, but the handwritten sentence was not part of the original will and is not valid unless it qualifies as a holographic codicil. Because it was not signed, it most likely does not qualify as a holographic codicil (an argument can be made under the dispensing power approach that it might qualify as a valid holographic codicil).

If the jurisdiction does not require the will to be signed at the end, and if the handwritten sentence was added temporally *before* the testator signed the will, the handwritten material is a valid part of the original will and both the will and the handwritten material are valid and can be given effect.

29. The first issue is whether the will was properly executed. The testator has to sign the will in the presence of two witnesses. The traditional common law approach to the presence requirement is the line of sight approach. The modern trend takes the conscious presence approach. Here, Joe satisfies either test, but Wi arguably would not satisfy the line of sight test. Sitting in the driver's seat, she was not capable of seeing what Tim was doing in the back seat right behind her. The facts specifically say that she kept both eyes on the road at all times because she was speeding Tim to the hospital. Under the line of sight test, the will arguably was not properly executed.

Under the modern trend approach, the will arguably was properly witnessed. Although Wi did not actually see Tim sign the will, from the totality of the circumstances she realized that Tim was executing the will: She knew that Tim had had a heart attack, she knew that when she passed the will back to him it had no signatures on it, she heard him declare that he wanted the document to be his will, and that when the document was passed back up to her it had Tim's signature on it. Under the modern trend, the will arguably was signed in her presence even though she did not see it being signed.

But Wi is an interested witness. At early common law, this would void the whole will. Tim's property would pass to UCLA pursuant to the prior will. The general rule, however, is that an interested witness does not void the will but rather it creates an irrebuttable presumption of wrongdoing on the part of the interested witness. Some jurisdictions void the whole gift to the witness; others take the purging approach. Under the purging approach, the interested witness is purged of the excess interest he or she stands to gain if this will were valid. Here, Wi stood to take nothing under the prior will, and half of Tim's estate under the new will, so she would be purged of the full 50 percent that she stood to take under this will. Under these approaches, the issue then becomes what happens to the failed gift to Wi. Under the common law approach, when part of the residuary clause fails it falls to intestacy—here to Tim's heirs under intestacy. Under the modern trend approach to partial failure of the residuary clause, the failed part passes to the other residuary takers—here to UCLA.

Under the modern trend, in some jurisdictions an interested witness creates a *rebuttable* presumption of wrongdoing. Here, Wi probably could rebut the presumption, thereby entitling her to take the full gift, half of Tim's estate. Under the UPC, the interested witness doctrine has been abolished. The burden is on the parties who suspect wrongdoing to bring a claim of wrongdoing and prove it. Under this approach, Wi would take her devise in the will.

**30.** Gerri's property will go to Dick unless the writing she sent to her mother qualifies as a holographic will. Assuming the jurisdiction recognizes holographic wills, there is a writing (the letter), it is dated (if the jurisdiction requires), the whole document is in her handwriting (so it does not matter if the jurisdiction requires only the material provisions or the whole document to be in the testator's handwriting), and it is signed (it is assumed the testatrix intended "your loving daughter" to be her signature). The issue is whether the document has testamentary intent—the intent that this document be taken down and probated as the decedent's will. Although testamentary intent is a rather soft, fact sensitive doctrine, here it appears the document falls short. It is unclear whether Gerri's comment that her property "should" go to her mother is enough to indicate an intent to change her testamentary scheme and to have this document qualify as her new will. The letter describes the anguish she was going through. Arguably Gerri had not made up her mind as to how she wanted to react, both inter vivos (whether she should file for divorce) and at time of death (whether she wanted to revoke her gift to Dick). In cases where the courts have held such letters to have adequate testamentary intent, usually there is also a phrase indicating the intent that the document is to have future significance (such as "save this" or "keep this, it may help you in the future"). Although a close call, arguably the letter lacks the necessary testamentary intent to qualify as a valid holographic will.

*Note:* The homicide doctrine is not applicable. It applies only to the killer. Here, Anna Nicoli killed Gerri, not Dick, and there is no evidence that Dick was in any way involved in Gerri's death. If there were evidence that Dick were involved, Gerri's heirs might have been able to invoke the homicide doctrine against him.

**31.** The writing qualifies as a valid holographic will. It is dated, completely in the testator's handwriting, is signed, and expresses testamentary intent (the document expresses the intent that it controls who takes Dude's property when he dies, that Dude intended for this to be his will). The issue is whether this is a conditional will that was to be effective only if Dude died in a plane crash. Most courts construe such clauses more as an explanation of why the testator is executing the will, rather than a condition precedent to the will being valid. The more likely result is that the will is valid.

**32.** The issue is whether the will was properly revoked. The two principal means of revoking a will are by act or by writing. If by writing, the writing has to qualify as a valid will. Here, the word *void* is not enough to qualify as a valid will. There were no witnesses, so it cannot qualify as a traditional attested will. There is no signature, so it cannot qualify as a holographic will (there also is an issue as to whether it adequately expresses testamentary intent that is moot because it was not signed). For revocation by act, the act has to be destructive in nature and done with the intent to revoke. Here, the act of writing "VOID" arguably is sufficiently destructive, and it was performed with the intent to revoke (Gerri no longer wanted her estate to go to Dick in light of his affair). The issue is whether the act qualifies because it is on the envelope. At common law approach, the act had to affect the printed words of the will. Writing on the envelope fails to affect the printed words of the will. Under the modern trend, the act need only affect some part of the will. The envelope is not part of the will. Even under the modern trend, the most likely result is that the will was not revoked. Dick takes her property.

**33.** Here, because the will was last in Tami's possession and cannot be found following her death, the presumption that she revoked it arises. The presumption, however, is rebuttable if there is a more plausible explanation for why the will cannot be found. Here, the explanation would be that the will was destroyed when Tami's house was destroyed. That is probably sufficient to overcome the presumption. Although the presumption has been overcome, there is no will to probate. Under the lost will doctrine, the court will take extrinsic evidence as to the terms of the will, and if the terms can be established by clear and convincing evidence, the court will probate the lost will.

**34.** Although some jurisdictions apply the presumption doctrine only if none of the duplicate originals can be found, others apply it even if other duplicate originals can be found. Here the presumption doctrine does not apply at all, so the question is irrelevant.

**35.** Under a variation on the presumption doctrine, when the will was last in the testator's possession and is found after the testator's death with a destructive or mutilating mark on it, a presumption arises that the testator made the mark with the intent to revoke. Here, the presumption would arise that the testator made the mark. Inasmuch as the mark affects only part of the will, the issue arises as to whether the jurisdiction recognizes partial revocation by act. If the jurisdiction does not, Raquel takes $10,000, and the residue would pass to the testator's church. If the jurisdiction recognizes partial revocation by act, there is still a subtle issue. The facts do not indicate if the mark was made with pen or pencil. Some courts have held that where the mark is made with pencil, that does not show enough finality of intent to constitute the intent to revoke. If the mark were made with pencil, Raquel might still take her gift of $10,000. If the mark were made with pen, and the jurisdiction recognizes partial revocation by act, the gift to Raquel would be revoked. Because a partial revocation is inherently a new gift, those jurisdictions that strictly apply the Wills Act formalities reason that where there is partial revocation, the gift that is revoked must pass through intestacy. The general rule, however, is the gift will fall to the residuary clause. The testator's church would take the revoked gift as well as the rest of the residuary.

**36.** Gail will claim that she is entitled to take under dependent relative revocation (DRR). Under DRR, the claimant must show that there was a revocation based upon a mistake, and but for the mistake, the testator would not have revoked. In addition, the courts typically apply the doctrine only where there is either a failed alternative scheme or the mistake is set forth in the revoking instrument. Here, Toni validly revoked the gift by drawing a line through the gift with the intent to revoke. The revocation was based upon a mistake, the wrongful belief that the Frankie Gail was dating was Toni's ex-boyfriend. Because that appears to be the only reason Toni revoked the gift to Gail, it is reasonable to conclude that but for the mistake, Toni would not have revoked the gift to Gail. But the courts typically apply the doctrine only where there is a failed alternative scheme or where the revoking instrument sets forth the mistake. Therefore, Gail is not entitled to relief under DRR. Toni revoked by act, so the only way Gail can prevail under the prevailing judicial approach to DRR is if there is a failed *alternative* scheme. There is no failed alternative scheme here. Gail's claim would fail. Under the majority approach to partial revocation by act, the gift would fall to the residuary clause. Under the minority approach, the revoked gift would pass through intestacy.

**37.** The handwritten instrument qualifies as a valid holographic will. There is a writing, all the terms of the writing are in the testator's handwriting, the document expresses testamentary intent (the intent to revoke an existing will affects a testator's testamentary scheme and thereby expresses testamentary intent), and it is signed. The holographic will here is will #3 and it revokes will #2—the classic revival scenario. Under the English approach, will #1 is effective because will #2 never revoked will #1, it just "covered" it. The general American approach is that the moment will #2 was executed it revoked will #1. The jurisdictions are split on what is necessary to revive will #1 if will #2 is revoked. If the jurisdiction requires the testator to reexecute will #1, will #1 cannot be revived under these facts, and Jalo died intestate. If all the testator has to do to revive will #1 is to intend to revive will #1 when he or she revokes will #2, the key is how did the testator revoke will #2. If the testator revoked will #2 by act, the courts will take any evidence of the testator's intent to revive will #1. If, however, the testator revoked will #2 by will #3, the intent to revive will #1 must be set forth in will #3. Here, Jalo revoked will #2 by will #3. The intent to revive will #1 must be set forth in will #3—which it is not. Despite Jalo's oral declarations as to her intent to revive will #1, the document would not be revived under revival. (Nor would the court give effect to will #2 under DRR.)

38. The issue is whether the court can give effect to Surfer Dude's testamentary wishes as expressed in his letter to Hulama. The letter does not qualify as a will. There is no evidence that there were any witnesses to its execution, so it cannot qualify as a valid attested will. The letter is typed, so it cannot qualify as a valid holographic will. The Heal the Bay organization can argue incorporation by reference. Although the reference in the will to the letter satisfies the intent to incorporate and describe with reasonable certainty requirements, the letter was created after the will was executed so it cannot be incorporated by reference. But Surfer Dude executes a codicil. Under republication by codicil, the codicil is presumed to reexecute and redate the underlying will to the date of the codicil. By redating the will to the date of the codicil, the letter to Hulama is now in existence when the will is republished and can be incorporated by reference. Jane gets Surfer Dude's surfboard. The Heal the Bay organization gets the rest of his property. (Facts of independent significance cannot be used to give effect to the letter because it has no independent significance apart from its effect upon Surfer Dude's probate estate.)

39. UCLA will not be able to claim Paul's property under incorporation by reference. Although the reference in Paul's will that his property should be distributed pursuant to the residuary clause of his sister's will arguably satisfies the intent to incorporate requirement and it describes the document with reasonable certainty, Kristin's will was not in existence when Paul executed his will. Nor did Paul execute any codicils to his will that would permit redating the will. Under facts of independent significance, however, the will may refer to facts outside of the will that may control who takes or how much they take as long as the referenced fact has its own significance independent of its effect upon the will. Here, the referenced fact is the residuary clause of Kristin's will. Kristin's will has its own significance independent of its effect upon Paul's will—disposing of Kristin's property. The court can give effect to the clause in Paul's will referencing the clause in Kristin's will under facts of independent significance.

40. Who takes Tommie's property turns on whether the jurisdiction follows the common law approach or the modern trend/UPC approach. At common law, oral contracts to make a will were enforceable (some jurisdictions require clear and convincing evidence). Here, the agreement between Tommie and Anna Nicoli arguably is enforceable. Under the modern trend/UPC approach, however, there has to be a writing signed by the decedent evidencing the terms of the agreement. Here, there is no such writing. Anna Nicoli would not be entitled to enforce the terms of their agreement, but she would be entitled to bring a claim for quantum meruit for the value of the services she did render.

41. Although the mere execution of mutual wills or a joint will does not give rise to a contract not to revoke, here the mirror wills expressly provided that the parties agreed to waive their power to revoke. When Gerri executed a new will in favor of Rick, she breached her contract not to revoke. The children will be able to sue as third-party beneficiaries under the contract not to revoke in the original will. The court will probate the new will in favor of Rick, but the court will impose a constructive trust on Rick ordering him to transfer Gerri's property to the children under the contract not to revoke.

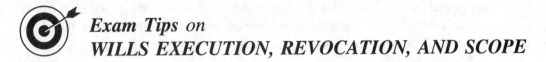

## Exam Tips *on*
## WILLS EXECUTION, REVOCATION, AND SCOPE

This chapter presents core wills material that is tested with great frequency.

### Executing a valid will

If you get a will execution issue, remember to raise and discuss the two variables that control whether a will has been properly executed: the jurisdiction's statutory Wills Act formalities, and the jurisdiction's approach to what degree of compliance is required.

☞ You should know every requirement of the Wills Act in your jurisdiction. Every requirement is a potential issue. There are, however, a few scenarios that are tested more often.

☞ If you see anything other than the testator's full name, you have a signature issue.

 ☞ It is presumed that the testator intended whatever he or she wrote to be his or her signature, unless there is evidence that the testator was interrupted while signing. If the testator was interrupted, the presumption is that if the testator did not complete what he or she intended when he or she started, whatever is there is not a complete signature.

☞ The witness requirement is tested often. There are several aspects to the witness requirement that make it a favorite.

 ☞ Know whether your jurisdiction applies the line of sight or the conscious presence test. Know *who* has to do *what* in *whose* presence.

 ☞ Watch for a delayed attestation scenario where one witness signs the will and then something happens and the second witness fails to sign right away. Under the modern trend, the will is not necessarily invalid. If the testator dies within a relatively short time thereafter, be sure to raise and note that the second witness can still be called in to sign the will to save it.

 ☞ If a witness steps away for any part of the testator's performance, and then returns, most likely you will have to start the execution analysis all over again—if the whole execution ceremony was not completed before the witness left, whatever the parties do after the wayward witness returns has to qualify as a valid execution ceremony in its own right.

 ☞ If a witness signs the will before the testator, at common law that act was a nullity and the analysis would have to start all over beginning when the testator signs the will.

 ☞ A fairly common execution scenario is when a typed will is found and there is handwritten material physically below the testator's signature block. This simple scenario is deceptive in that it can raise a plethora of issues: (1) where on the will must it be signed; (2) when was the material added; (3) assuming the material does not qualify as part of the original will, can it be qualified as its own holographic will; and (4) can the court use the typed material above in analyzing whether the holographic instrument has testamentary intent?

☞ Inasmuch as there are five different approaches to the interested witness doctrine, know which approach your jurisdiction has adopted and its effect when applied.

☞ The swapped wills scenario is a nice overlap testing scenario because it can test the common law approach (invalid), the misdescription doctrine overlap (to try to cure the execution ceremony), and the new scrivener's error doctrine.

## Modern trend approach to attested wills

Know the key modern trend changes to the typical common law Wills Act formalities. Unless your jurisdiction has adopted substantial compliance or dispensing power by statute, lead with strict compliance when analyzing whether the testator has complied with the Wills Act formalities. If the execution ceremony fails, argue and apply in the alternative that the court should adopt substantial compliance or dispensing power.

☛ Under both curative doctrines, there still must be clear and convincing evidence that the testator intended the document to be his or her will. While the doctrines permit the court to relax the execution requirements, they do not permit the court to relax the testamentary intent requirement. If you have doubt as to whether the testator intended this to be his or her will, arguably the will is still not valid under these curative doctrines.

## Holographic wills

If your jurisdiction recognizes holographic wills, you need to sweat the details of the statute because they can vary greatly from jurisdiction to jurisdiction.

☛ The most litigated and tested element of the holographic will doctrine is the requirement that the document has testamentary intent. Define the requirement before applying it.

☞ In applying it, be sure to include whether the jurisdiction takes the contextual approach or not (if your jurisdiction has not taken a position on the issue, argue it in the alternative). Testamentary intent is very fact sensitive. Include the key words from the writing that you think are relevant to the issue. Always include the alternative characterization of the instrument (what would the party opposing the instrument call it if not a will).

☞ Remember that holographic codicils to holographic wills have their own special rule.

## Revocation

Be able to distinguish a codicil from a new will. This is important under both the common law and the modern trend in a whole host of different contexts (e.g., scope of revocation effected by second instrument, effect of revocation of second instrument).

If the subsequent will has a residuary clause, almost invariably it will be a whole new will. If, however, the subsequent will does not have a residuary clause, but the prior will had one, the subsequent will invariably will be a codicil.

☛ Revocation by act is easy to spot—some destructive act must be performed to some part of the will. Make sure there is evidence of the intent to revoke, and revocation is a testamentary act that requires capacity at the time the act is performed. Watch the facts carefully to see which part of the will is affected (tests the common law vs. modern trend approach).

☛ If someone other than the testator performs the revocation by act, the same presence concerns and issues can arise as discussed under the execution material.

☞ Strict compliance is applied to the revocation by act requirements, just as it is to the execution requirements. If the revocation fails under strict compliance, you can argue that the court should adopt substantial compliance and dispensing power judicially.

☞ If the will was last in the testator's possession and cannot be found after his or her death, this gives rise to a presumption that the will was destroyed by act.

   ☞ If the will was last in the testator's possession and it is found following his or her death, but with destructive marks across the will, based upon the presumption doctrine, the presumption arises that the testator made the marks with the intent to revoke.

☞ Many students get confused over the relationship between the revocation by presumption doctrine and the lost will. If the presumption doctrine applies and the presumption is not rebutted, the will is revoked (the lost will doctrine would not apply then). If the presumption doctrine does not apply, or it applied but the presumption was rebutted, the will is not revoked—but it cannot be found. The lost will doctrine will apply, and the will should be probated if there is clear and convincing evidence of its terms.

   ☞ *Partial* revocation by physical act is a subset of the revocation material that is often tested. Know whether your jurisdiction recognizes the doctrine, and, if so, what happens to the revoked gift (or be prepared to argue all three approaches in the alternative).

☞ Dependent relative revocation is one of the most difficult doctrines covered in the course. The doctrine is fairly easy to spot. The triggering facts are that you have to see a valid revocation based upon a mistake (of fact or law, does not matter).

   ☞ Where the revocation is by act, watch for an attempt at a new will that fails. If the testator revoked the original will because he or she thought the new will was valid, you have both your mistake (of law) and your failed alternative scheme. Assuming you can show causation, apply dependent relative revocation to give effect to the original will.

   ☞ Where the revocation is by writing, make sure the mistake is set forth in the revoking will. Where the mistake is a mistake of law (the new will expressly revokes the old, but the new gift violates the Rule against Perpetuities and is void), the mistake typically will not be patent but will be implicit in the wording of the doctrine.

☞ A classic dependent relative revocation scenario involves partial revocation by act. Watch for a testator who scratches out part of a typed will and then handwrites a clause or sentence on the original will purporting to amend the will. Analyze the act of scratching out part of the typed will as a revocation. Analyze the handwritten interlineations as a possible holographic codicil. If not a valid codicil, analyze under dependent relative revocation.

   ☞ The final requirement of dependent relative revocation is that the testator would not have revoked the original will but for the mistake. Under dependent relative revocation, the court has only two options: give effect to the valid revocation or ignore the revocation and give effect to the original gift. If the testator's true intent is closer to the original gift than it is to giving effect to the revocation, apply dependent relative revocation—assuming the other requirements are met. If the testator's true intent is closer to the result that would occur if the court gave effect to the valid revocation, do not apply dependent relative revocation—even if all the other requirements are met.

☛ Revival is a fairly simple doctrine that is generally easy to spot. You must have at least two wills, and the testator must revoke will #2. When the testator revokes will #2, that automatically gives rise to a revival issue. The subtle way to raise the revival issue is to make will #2 a codicil. If there is a will and a codicil to the will, and the testator revokes the codicil, you have a revival issue.

☛ Under the "revive as long as intended" approach to revival, *how* the testator revoked the second will determines what evidence is admissible to prove the intent to revive.

☛ The revocation by operation of law issues tested most often go to its scope: Does it also apply to the will substitutes (not under the common law approach); does it apply to other family members (not under the majority rule).

## Scope of the will

Republication by codicil, incorporation by reference, and facts of independent significance are core doctrines that are heavily tested.

☛ Republication by codicil not only redates the underlying will, it also reexecutes it. If there is a problem with the will, republication by codicil may clean up the problem.

     ☞ While republication by codicil generally redates the will, watch for scenarios where that is inconsistent with the testator's apparent testamentary intent, and argue against redating the will.

     ☞ If there appears to be a republication by codicil issue, but the underlying document does not qualify as a valid will, switch to incorporation by reference.

☛ Incorporation by reference is another basic doctrine often tested. Because the courts apply such a low threshold to the first two requirements, almost invariably the element at issue will be whether the document to be incorporated was in existence when the will was executed.

     ☞ The burden of proof is on the party trying to incorporate the document. If the document is undated, the party trying to incorporate will fail unless there is something about the codicil that shows its "relative" date to be before the will.

     ☞ The document can be incorporated only as it existed on the date the will was executed. Watch for scenarios where the document being incorporated is changed later.

     ☞ If there is difficulty showing that the document was in existence on the date the will was executed, or if the document was revised after execution, watch for a codicil that would redate the will and thereby clear up the apparent problem with the dates.

☛ If you see generic language in a will that refers to something outside of the will that will affect either who takes or how much they take, that is the classic scenario for testing facts of independent significance.

     ☞ Analytically, the key is to identify the controlling "referenced" fact in the will. Then ask if that fact has its own independent significance (usually its own inter vivos significance) apart from its effect upon the will. If it does, apply the doctrine and permit the clause to dispose of the property; if it does not, the clause is invalid.

## Contracts relating to wills

Know which approach your jurisdiction takes to whether contracts relating to wills must be in writing, and what type of writing.

☞ If you see a joint will, or mutual wills where there is great coordination and apparent reliance by the parites, raise and discuss the contract not to revoke issue. If there is a valid contract not to revoke and a breach, remember to probate the breaching will, but the court will impose a constructive trust on the takers under the will.

☞ If the parties are spouses, and after the death of the first, the surviving spouse remarries, read the fact pattern carefully to see what is necessary to breach the contract not to revoke, and know which approach your jurisdiction takes to spousal protection vs. contract beneficiaries issue.

## CHAPTER 6

# CONSTRUING WILLS

*ChapterScope* ─────────────────────────────────

This chapter examines issues that may arise in probating and giving effect to a will. In particular, the chapter deals with doctrines that address the fact that changes can occur between the time when a will is executed inter vivos and when it becomes effective at time of death.

- ◼ **Admissibility of extrinsic evidence:** The general rule is that extrinsic evidence is admissible only if there is an ambiguity in the will.

  - ▪ **Patent vs. latent ambiguities:** Common law distinguished between patent and latent ambiguities, and admitted extrinsic evidence to help construe the ambiguity only if the ambiguity was a latent ambiguity. The modern trend has abolished the distinction between latent and patent ambiguities and admits extrinsic evidence anytime there is an ambiguity in the will.

  - ▪ **Scrivener's error doctrine:** Under the modern trend, if there is clear and convincing evidence of a scrivener's error, and clear and convincing evidence of its effect upon testator's intent, extrinsic evidence is admissible to correct the error.

- ◼ **Ademption:** Under the common law approach, if the testator makes a specific gift and the item that is the subject of the specific gift is not in the testator's estate at time of death, under the identity approach an irrebuttable presumption arose that the gift was revoked. Under the modern trend/UPC approach, a presumption against revocation arises and the beneficiary is entitled to any replacement property the testator owns at time of death or, if none, the monetary equivalent of the gift.

  - ▪ **Avoidance doctrines:** Because ademption is such a harsh doctrine, a number of avoidance doctrines have arisen: (1) classify the gift as general, not specific; (2) change in form, not substance; (3) construe the will at time of death, not execution.

  - ▪ **Softening doctrines:** In addition, doctrines that soften the impact of ademption have arisen: (1) if the testator is owed an outstanding balance as a result of the transfer of the specific gift, the outstanding balance goes to the beneficiary; (2) if the specific gift was transferred while a conservator or durable power of attorney agent was acting for the testator, the beneficiary is entitled to the monetary equivalent of the net sale price.

- ◼ **Satisfaction:** At common law, if a testator makes an inter vivos gift to his or her child, and the child is also a beneficiary in the testator's will, a rebuttable presumption arises that the inter vivos gift counts against the child's testamentary gift. Under the modern trend/UPC, if a testator makes an inter vivos gift to anyone who is also a beneficiary under his or her will, the gift does not count against the beneficiary's testamentary gift unless there is a writing evidencing such an intent.

- ◼ **Lapse:** Where a beneficiary predeceases the testator, the gift is said to lapse and it fails. Failed specific gifts and failed general gifts fall to the residuary clause; failed residuary gifts fall to intestacy.

■ **Anti-lapse statutes:** Anti-lapse statutes provide that where there is a lapsed gift, if (1) the predeceased beneficiary meets the requisite degree of relationship to the testator, and (2) the predeceased beneficiary has issue who survive the testator, the gift will go to the issue of the predeceased beneficiary (3) as long as the will does not express an intent that anti-lapse should not be applied.

■ **Class gifts:** A class gift has a built-in right of survivorship so that if one member of the class predeceases the testator, his or her share is simply redistributed among the surviving members of the class. When it is not clear whether a gift to multiple individuals is a class gift, courts focus on four factors: (1) how the beneficiaries are described, (2) how the gift is described, (3) whether all the individuals share a common characteristic, and (4) the testator's overall testamentary scheme.

# I. ADMISSIBILITY OF EXTRINSIC EVIDENCE: GENERAL RULE

**A. Scope of chapter:** The chapter is titled Construing Wills and it focuses on wills. The modern trend adopted in a handful of jurisdictions, however, applies the will construction doctrines examined in this chapter to nonprobate instruments as well, particularly trusts and contracts with payable-on-death clauses.

**B. Extrinsic evidence:** The key to analyzing whether extrinsic evidence should be admitted is to ask *why* the extrinsic evidence is being offered. If it is being offered to help determine the validity of a will (whether it was properly executed, whether the decedent had the requisite testamentary capacity, whether the decedent suffered from a defect in capacity, whether the will was properly revoked, etc.), the extrinsic evidence is admissible. If, however, the extrinsic evidence is being offered to help construe an admittedly valid will, the courts are reluctant to admit such evidence absent an ambiguity.

**C. Common law:** At common law, courts were very reluctant to admit extrinsic evidence to help construe a will. To the extent the testator had gone to all the trouble and expense of executing a will, the will arguably constituted the best evidence of testator's intent.

**Policy considerations:** The common law position was that once the testator had properly executed a will, the court's job was to protect that intent. Admitting extrinsic evidence would only increase the potential for fraudulent claims and increase the costs of administration.

**D. Plain meaning rule:** The common law position against admitting extrinsic evidence manifested itself in the plain meaning rule: In construing and giving effect to a will, the words used in the will should be given their plain meaning. As a general rule, extrinsic evidence would not be admissible to show that the testator used the words to mean something other than their plain meaning. Extrinsic evidence was admissible to help construe a word or phrase in a will if there was an ambiguity.

1. **Majority approach:** Although the plain meaning rule is coming under increasing criticism, and there is a modern trend approach that rejects it, the plain meaning rule remains the majority approach.

2. **Example:** In *Mahoney v. Grainger*, 186 N.E. 86 (Mass. 1933), the testatrix instructed her attorney that she wanted to leave the residue of her estate to her 25 or so first cousins equally.

She told her attorney her first cousins were her nearest relatives. In fact, her maternal aunt was her nearest relative. Rather than naming each of the testatrix's first cousins in the will, the attorney drafted the will so it left the residue of her estate to her "heirs at law," thinking that the first cousins would take as the nearest relatives. The testatrix properly executed the will. Following the testatrix's death, the maternal aunt claimed the residue as the nearest heir at law. The first cousins offered extrinsic evidence to show that the testatrix intended that the residue was to go to the first cousins. The court applied the plain meaning rule and found that the phrase heirs at law was not ambiguous. The extrinsic evidence was not admissible to establish a meaning for the phrase *heirs at law* that was inconsistent with the plain meaning of that phrase.

   **a. Criticism:** The assumption underlying the plain meaning rule is that the meaning the reader attributes to a word is the same meaning the testator attributed to the word. Inasmuch as the testator wrote the will, and probate is about determining and giving effect to the testator's intent, the testator's meaning arguably should control, not the reader's construction.

   **b. Counterargument:** Admitting extrinsic evidence opens the estate to fraudulent claims and increases costs of administration (increased litigation).

**3. Personal usage exception:** If the testator has always referred to a person by a name other than the person's true name (i.e., a nickname), and the testator uses that name in the will, courts will take extrinsic evidence to show that the testator always called the person by that name and to show that the person called by the nickname is the person who is supposed to take the gift, not the person whose true name actually matches the name used in the will (assuming someone else has that name).

**E. Patent vs. latent ambiguity:** At common law, the courts would admit extrinsic evidence to help construe a latent ambiguity, but not to help construe a patent ambiguity.

   **1. Patent ambiguity:** A patent ambiguity is an ambiguity that is apparent from the face of the will. It is apparent from the four corners of the will; no extrinsic evidence is necessary to realize that there is an ambiguity.

   **Extrinsic evidence:** At common law, if an ambiguity was a patent ambiguity, extrinsic evidence was not admissible to help construe the ambiguity.

   **2. Latent ambiguity:** A latent ambiguity is an ambiguity that is not apparent on the face of the will. Recourse to circumstances outside of the will is necessary to show that there is an ambiguity. The latent ambiguity does not become apparent until the court attempts to give effect to the decedent's will—to determine who is to take what.

   **Extrinsic evidence:** The very nature of a latent ambiguity is such that extrinsic evidence is necessary to establish the ambiguity. At common law, the courts would admit extrinsic evidence both to establish and to help construe a latent ambiguity.

   **3. Construing vs. rewriting:** Although a court will take extrinsic evidence to establish and help construe a latent ambiguity, as a general rule courts will not add words to a will or "rewrite" the will. If the ambiguity cannot be resolved, the gift will fail.

   **4. Latent ambiguity doctrines:** A number of latent ambiguity scenarios arose with such frequency that specific ambiguity doctrines were developed to deal with them.

**a. Equivocation:** An equivocation is where the language in the will fits more than one object or person equally well. The court will take extrinsic evidence to determine which of the objects or people was the intended object or person.

**Example:** In *Siegley v. Simpson*, 131 P. 479 (Wash. 1913), testator's will left $6,000 to "my good friend Richard H. Simpson." The legacy was claimed by Richard H. Simpson and Hamilton Ross Simpson. Although the latter's name did not match the name in the will exactly, nevertheless the court said that the names were similar enough that the language in the will constituted an equivocation. The court then took extrinsic evidence to determine the identity of the person named in the will. The testator had met Richard H. Simpson only once in 20 years, referred to him as "Mr. Simpson," and did not even know that his full name was Richard H. On the other hand, Hamilton Ross Simpson was the testator's good friend, the two had worked together closely for years, and the testator had told associates that he had provided for Hamilton Ross Simpson in his will. In light of the extrinsic evidence, the court concluded that when the testator used the name Richard H. Simpson in the will, he really intended Hamilton Ross Simpson.

**b. Misdescription:** Misdescription arises where the description of an object or person in the will appears fine on the face of the will, but when the court goes to apply it, there is no object or person that matches the exact description, but there is an object or person that almost matches the description. The classic example of a misdescription is a typographical error when numbers or names get inverted.

   **i. Mechanics:** Consistent with the courts' general rule that they will not rewrite wills, courts will take extrinsic evidence to establish the misdescription and to determine which words in the will to strike, but courts will not insert any words to correct the description. The court will strike the misdescription and then look to see if the remaining words adequately describe the object or person so that the clause in the will can be given effect.

   **ii. Example:** In *Estate of Gibbs*, 111 N.W.2d 413 (Wis. 1961), Mr. and Mrs. Gibbs died approximately one month apart from each other. Each had a provision in their will devising 1 percent of their respective estates to "Robert J. Krause, now of 4708 North 46th Street, Milwaukee, Wisconsin." Robert W. Krause, who was a 30-year employee of Mr. Gibbs and friend of the family for many years, claimed the gifts. Robert J. Krause, who lived at the address listed in the will, also claimed the gift. He *may* have met Mrs. Gibbs once when he worked as a cab driver, but the incident in question predated the reference to Robert Krause in Mr. Gibb's first will. The court concluded that it was appropriate to admit extrinsic evidence to establish that the middle initial and address were misdescriptions and to disregard both. The property was given to Robert W. Krause.

**c. Personal usage exception:** One can argue that the personal usage exception is a form of a latent ambiguity. It is analogous to an equivocation except that the court treats the personal usage that the testator gave to the object or person as equal to the proper name of the object or person.

**F. Omission:** Under the common law approach, if material was omitted from a will, extrinsic evidence was not admissible to establish or correct the omission. At best the omission constituted a patent ambiguity so no extrinsic evidence was admissible. Moreover, in the case of an omission, there is not language in the will that is ambiguous, there simply is language missing from the will.

1. **Example:** In ***Knupp v. District of Columbia***, 578 A.2d 702 (D.C. 1990), testator's properly executed will failed to name a residuary taker. Testator's prior two wills left the residue of his estate to his good friend Knupp, who claimed that he was the intended beneficiary under the will in question. The drafting attorney submitted an affidavit admitting that it was his fault there was no residuary taker and stating that the testator had instructed him to leave the residue to Knupp. The court ruled that because there was no ambiguity in the will, the extrinsic evidence was not admissible.

2. **Exceptions:** A handful of modern trend courts have admitted extrinsic evidence to correct an omission under the rationale that the omission constitutes an ambiguity.

G. **Modern trend:** The modern trend is much more open to trying to ascertain and give effect to the testator's intent. It repudiates a number of the common law doctrines.

1. **Plain meaning rule:** The modern trend has repudiated the plain meaning rule. The modern trend will consider extrinsic evidence of the circumstances surrounding the testator at the time he or she executed the will in analyzing what the testator's intent was when he or she executed the will and whether there is an ambiguity in the will.

   **Example:** In ***Estate of Kremlick***, 331 N.W.2d 228 (Mich. 1983), testator left part of the residue of his estate to "the Michigan Cancer Society." The Michigan Cancer Society, an affiliate of the Michigan Cancer Foundation, claimed the devise. The American Cancer Society offered extrinsic evidence to establish that the language was ambiguous and that the testator intended the American Cancer Society as the beneficiary. The evidence showed the testator had made substantial inter vivos donations to the American Cancer Society, that it had helped his wife while she was dying of cancer, and that at the time of her death the testator asked that memorials be made to the American Cancer Society. The court ruled that this was the type of evidence that trial courts should admit to both establish and resolve an ambiguity.

2. **Latent vs. patent:** The modern trend also repudiates the patent vs. latent distinction, admitting extrinsic evidence anytime there is an ambiguity.

H. **Modern trend admissibility analysis:** Under the modern trend, there are several steps involved in determining whether extrinsic evidence is admissible for construction purposes, and if so, what extrinsic evidence is admissible.

1. **Ambiguity requirement:** Under the modern trend, the general rule is that there still must be an ambiguity before extrinsic evidence is admissible to help construe the will. At common law, the ambiguity had to be a latent ambiguity. Under the modern trend, any ambiguity will justify admitting extrinsic evidence.

2. **Ambiguity defined:** An ambiguity is any express language in a will that is reasonably susceptible to two or more interpretations.

3. **Admissible evidence:** Just because an ambiguity exists in the will, not all extrinsic evidence is admissible—only extrinsic evidence that is consistent with one of the possible reasonable interpretations of the ambiguity is admissible.

**Example:** In *Estate of Russell*, 444 P.2d 353 (Cal. 1968), the testator's valid holographic will provided in pertinent part as follows: "I leave everything I own Real & Personal to Chester H. Quinn & Roxy Russell." Testator's heirs offered extrinsic evidence to prove that Roxy Russell was a dog. The court ruled that the fact that Roxy Russell was a dog was a latent ambiguity and extrinsic evidence was admissible to establish that fact. Dogs, however, are not eligible beneficiaries, so the gift to Roxy would fail and, under the law of the jurisdiction at that time, fall to intestacy. Chester offered extrinsic evidence to prove that the testator did not want any of her property to pass through intestacy, that he was to take all the testator's property, and that he was to care for the dog. The court adopted the modern trend, repudiating the plain meaning rule and the latent-patent distinction. Nevertheless, the court held that the words of the will were not reasonably susceptible to the interpretation that Chester's extrinsic evidence attempted to put on the express words of the will and that the extrinsic evidence in question should not have been admitted.

# II. SCRIVENER'S ERROR

A. **Rule:** Where there is clear and convincing evidence that there was a scrivener's error, and clear and convincing evidence of its effect upon testator's intent, extrinsic evidence is admissible to establish and correct the mistake. The doctrine of scrivener's error is a new doctrine that was adopted for the first time just recently.

B. **Rationale:** Several arguments have been advanced in support of the doctrine.

   1. **Theoretical argument:** For years academics have argued that it was incongruous to distinguish scrivener's fraud from scrivener's error. In both cases, the effect of the scrivener's actions is to frustrate testator's intent. If the scrivener fraudulently committed the act in question, a court will admit extrinsic evidence to prove the fraud and impose a constructive trust to correct it; but if the scrivener merely negligently committed the act, historically the courts would fail to correct the mistake and leave the frustrated beneficiaries to sue for malpractice. To the extent the two scenarios are functionally equivalent, they should be treated the same. The courts should take extrinsic evidence and come to the aid of testator's intent in both situations.

   2. **Testator's intent:** While there is a risk that admitting extrinsic evidence may undermine testator's intent if fraudulent claims are brought, excluding extrinsic evidence may undermine testator's intent if the document as offered for probate does not accurately reflect testator's intent due to a scrivener's error.

   3. **Will execution:** When a testator validly executes a will, it creates a strong presumption that the will accurately reflects the testator's testamentary intent. The presumption, however, is rebuttable. If there is clear and convincing evidence of a scrivener's error, and clear and convincing evidence of its effect upon testator's true intent, extrinsic evidence should be admissible to overcome the presumption.

   4. **Example:** In *Erickson v. Erickson*, 716 A.2d 92 (Conn. 1998), the testator executed a will leaving the residue of his estate to Dorothy, and two days later he married her. Under the state's laws, however, if after making a will a testator gets married, the marriage automatically revokes the will unless the will expressly provides for the marriage. The testator died without changing his will, and his children from his first marriage invoked

the statute to void the will, thereby claiming a share of his estate through intestacy. Dorothy offered extrinsic evidence to establish the attorney erred in having the will executed two days before the marriage and not expressly acknowledging the impending wedding in the will. The testator's children objected to the evidence because there was no ambiguity in the will. The court adopted the scrivener's error doctrine, ruling that if there is clear and convincing evidence of the scrivener's error and clear and convincing evidence of its effect upon testator's intent, the evidence should be admitted.

**5. Scope:** The *Erickson* case arguably raises more questions about the scope of the doctrine than it answers. Is the case an aberration or the wave of the future? Is the doctrine limited to cases involving the validity of the instrument or does it also apply to construction cases? Is the doctrine limited to situations where it can be applied without rewriting the will, or will it open the doors to courts rewriting wills to correct the scrivener's error? Will the doctrine be applied only to instruments that were validly executed but are invalid for other reasons, or will it also be applied to wills that were not validly executed because of the scrivener's error? Will the doctrine be limited to situations where the scrivener is an attorney, or will it apply regardless of who is the scrivener, even to holographic wills?

**C. Modern trend:** A handful of recent cases have ignored the traditional rule that courts do not correct mistakes and have corrected drafting mistakes by attorneys. Most have done so simply based on the equities of the case and the evidence of the mistake, without articulating a broad doctrine to explain or justify their actions. An exception is the doctrine of "probable intent" adopted by New Jersey.

**Probable intent:** The doctrine of probable intent provides that if there is an unforeseen change in circumstances after a will is executed that is not provided for in the will, and the unforeseen change materially frustrates testator's intent as expressed in the will, the court will take extrinsic evidence of the circumstances surrounding the testator, paying particular attention to family considerations. The court will put itself in the testator's situation and decide what it thinks the testator probably would have done under the circumstances.

**D. Reforming donative documents:** The Restatement (Third) of Property authorizes courts to reform any donative document, even where there is no ambiguity, to conform to the donor's intent if there is clear and convincing evidence (1) that a mistake of fact or law affected the specific terms of the document, and (2) of the donor's intent. Restatement (Third) of Property, Donative Transfers §12.1. The language of the Restatement (Third) arguably includes wills, trusts, and other testamentary instruments.

# III. CHANGES IN TESTATOR'S PROPERTY

**A. Introduction:** A will is executed inter vivos but does not take effect until the testator dies. In between, there can be changes in the testator's property that create a number of construction issues. Most of the doctrines that have developed to deal with the more common scenarios turn on the type of gift involved.

**1. Characterization of gift:** There are basically three types of gifts that a testator can make: a specific gift, a general gift, or a residuary gift. Characterizing a devise is ultimately a question of testator's intent.

2. **Specific gifts:** A specific gift is a gift where the testator has a specific item in mind when he or she makes the gift—typically an item that he or she currently owns. The testator intends for that specific item, and arguably only that specific item, to satisfy the gift. Almost invariably the gift is modified by the word "my."

**Example:** If the will says "I give my car to Alice," the gift would be construed as a specific gift of the car that the testator owned when he or she executed the will.

3. **General gifts:** A general gift is a gift of a general pecuniary value that can be satisfied by using *any item* that fits the description of the gift.

   a. **Example:** The classic example of a general gift is a gift of money. If the will says, "I give $1,000 to Bill," the gift would be construed as a general gift. The testator is making a pecuniary gift. Any thousand dollars will do—no specific bills were intended. A general gift can be measured by any means the testator selects. If the will says "I give a 1995 Saturn GLS to Cindy," that gift would probably be construed as a general gift. If the testator owns a 1995 Saturn GLS when he or she dies, that car can be used to satisfy the gift. If the testator does not have an item that matches the general gift in his or her estate at the time of his or her death, the executor has a legal duty to purchase an item that matches the general gift and give it to the beneficiary.

   b. **Demonstrative gifts:** Demonstrative gifts are general gifts from a specific source. For example, the will says, "I give Dave $1,000 from my checking account at Wagon Wheel Bank." The gift starts out looking like a general gift ($1,000), but then it looks like a specific gift ("from *my* checking account at Wagon Wheel Bank"). Demonstrative gifts are classified as a subset of general gifts and should be treated as a general gift for construction purposes.

4. **Residuary gifts:** A residuary gift is a gift that gives away all the testator's property that has not otherwise been given away. The classic example of a residuary gift is: "I give the rest, residue, and remainder of my property to Elaine." While that is the classic way to state a residuary gift, no magic words are necessary. A residuary gift is any gift that gives away all the testator's property except whatever was given away specifically or generally ("I give all of my property to Bob.").

B. **Ademption:** The most common construction issue concerning the testator's property arises when the testator makes a specific gift in his or her will and thereafter the item in question is transferred. The issue is what, if anything, should the beneficiary take.

1. **Common law:** The common law doctrine of ademption states that where the testator makes a specific gift, and thereafter the item that is the subject of the specific gift is transferred, an irrebuttable presumption arises that the testator revoked the gift.

2. **Identity approach:** Under the identity approach to ademption, if the will makes a specific gift, the executor is to go through the testator's probate estate to see if he or she can "identify" that item in the estate. If he or she can, the beneficiary takes the item. If the executor cannot find the item, the gift is adeemed (revoked), and the court will not take extrinsic evidence as to why the item cannot be found or what was (or might have been) testator's intent with respect to the item.

a. **Voluntary vs. involuntary transfer:** Under the identity approach to ademption, it does not matter why the property that was the subject of the specific gift is no longer in the testator's probate estate. The identity approach applies to both voluntary and involuntary transfers of specific gifts.

b. **Efficiency vs. intent:** The identity approach arguably exalts efficiency over testator's intent. The concern is that opening up the probate process to self-serving extrinsic evidence as to what the testator allegedly intended every time property that is subject to a specific gift is transferred would increase costs of administration and increase the potential for fraudulent claims. The identity approach puts the burden on testators to revise their wills if they transfer a specific gift but want the beneficiary still to take a gift.

3. **Example:** In *In re Estate of Nakoneczny*, 319 A.2d 893 (Pa. 1974), testator's will, executed in 1956, devised "3039 Preble Avenue" to his son, Paul. At the time the testator owned the premises, which he used as a restaurant, barroom, and living quarters. In 1968, the Urban Redevelopment Authority acquired the building, and the testator used the proceeds to purchase certain bonds that he still held when he died. The court found the gift to be a specific devise, applied the identity approach, concluded the gift was adeemed, and denied the son's claim to the bonds.

**Will substitutes:** The modern trend is for courts to apply ademption to the will substitutes, particularly inter vivos revocable trusts.

C. **Avoidance:** Because ademption is such a harsh doctrine, courts have developed a number of avoidance doctrines (varying from jurisdiction to jurisdiction) to justify not applying ademption where one might think it would otherwise apply.

1. **Incomplete disposal:** If any part of the specific gift remains in the testator's estate when the testator dies, first and foremost the beneficiary is entitled to receive whatever is left of the specific gift.

2. **Avoidance doctrines:** There are three principal avoidance doctrines.

a. **Characterize gift as general, not specific:** The ademption doctrine applies only to specific gifts. Where the wording of a gift is ambiguous, if the beneficiary can convince the court that the gift is a general gift, the executor has a legal duty to go out and acquire the item to satisfy the gift, thereby avoiding ademption.

b. **Change in form, not substance:** The "change in form, not substance" doctrine provides that if the item that is the subject of the specific gift is in the estate, but there has been a change in the item that goes to its form, not its substance, the court should give the beneficiary the item. This doctrine gives some flexibility to the ademption doctrine.

**Example:** Testatrix's will provides that she gives "my checking account at Megabank to Alice." Thereafter, the testatrix grows tired of the endless fees at Megabank and moves the checking account to Wagon Wheel Bank where she gets truly free checking. When the testatrix dies, Alice should take the checking account at Wagon Wheel Bank because moving the checking account from one bank to another is merely a change in form, not substance.

c. **Construe at time of death:** The general rule is that a will should be construed relative to the circumstances surrounding the testator at time of execution. If testator's will says,

"I give my car to Alice," the gift would be construed to be a specific gift of the car that testator owned at the time he or she executed the will. If testator sold the car and purchased a new car, under a strict application of the ademption doctrine, the specific gift is adeemed. If, however, the beneficiary can persuade the court to construe the gift at time of death, the beneficiary would take the car that the testator owned at time of death.

**Change in value:** Courts are reluctant to construe the will at time of death if the effect is to give the beneficiary a gift that is worth substantially more.

3. **Fact sensitive:** Each of the avoidance doctrines is a very soft, fact sensitive, judicial doctrine. If a court dislikes the ademption doctrine, the avoidance doctrines often can be construed broadly to avoid application of the ademption doctrine. If a court likes the ademption doctrine, the avoidance doctrines often can be construed narrowly to enforce the ademption doctrine.

D. **Conservatorship exception:** Under the modern trend, states are increasingly providing by statute that if the property subject to the specific gift was transferred during conservatorship or by an agent acting under a durable power of attorney for an incapacitated principal, the ademption doctrine does not apply. The beneficiary receives the general pecuniary value of the specific gift. The exception applies whether the transfer by the agent/conservator was voluntary or involuntary.

**Effect:** The effect of the exception is to convert all specific gifts into general gifts. The beneficiary is entitled to the general pecuniary value of the specific gift measured as of the moment it is transferred.

E. **Outstanding balance doctrine:** A softening doctrine to ademption provides that (1) if the item that is the subject of the specific gift is transferred voluntarily (sale/gift) or involuntarily (fire/theft, etc.), and (2) when the testator dies, there is still an outstanding balance due the testator as a result of the transfer, then (3) the beneficiary of the specific gift that was adeemed takes the outstanding balance in lieu of the specific item.

F. **Jurisdictional differences:** The identity approach to the ademption doctrine represents the traditional and still overwhelming majority approach to the doctrine. Not all states, however, have adopted all the modern trend avoidance, exception, and softening doctrines. Careful attention needs to be paid to the law in each jurisdiction to determine the exact scope of the ademption doctrine and to determine which avoidance, exception, and softening doctrines the jurisdiction has adopted.

G. **UPC:** The most recent version of the UPC rejects the identity approach to ademption. It adopts a "testator's intent" approach that opens the door to extrinsic evidence on what the testator intended, or would have intended, as to the specific gift. In addition, the most recent version of the UPC adopts a replacement property doctrine, along with the other modern trend avoidance and softening doctrines. The net effect is to limit greatly the scope of the ademption doctrine to the point where it is arguably more likely that the specific gift will *not* be adeemed even where it cannot be found in the testator's estate at time of death. The comments to the UPC acknowledge this change when they state that the new version of the UPC creates a "mild presumption" against ademption.

1. **Replacement property exception:** The UPC expressly provides that where a testator owns property at death that was acquired to replace property that was a specific gift in his or her will, the beneficiary of the specific gift gets the replacement property. UPC §2-606(a)(5).

2. **Outstanding balance doctrine:** The UPC expressly adopts the outstanding balance doctrine. Whether the property is transferred voluntarily or involuntarily, if the testator is owed money at time of death as a result of the transfer of the property subject to the specific gift, the outstanding balance is given to the beneficiary of the specific gift. UPC §2-606(a)(1)-(3).

3. **Testator's intent approach:** If neither the replacement property doctrine nor the outstanding balance doctrine apply, the UPC provides that the beneficiary of the specific gift is entitled to money equal to the value of the specifically devised property as of the date of its disposition if the beneficiary can establish that (1) ademption would be inconsistent with the testator's plan of distribution, or (b) the testator did not intend for ademption to apply. UPC §2-605(a)(6).

4. **Conservatorship exception:** The UPC also adopts the modern trend exception that if the property subject to the specific gift was transferred during conservatorship or by an agent acting under a durable power of attorney for an incapacitated principal, the ademption doctrine does not apply. UPC §2-605(b).

5. **Extrinsic evidence:** With the adoption of the replacement property doctrine and the testator's intent doctrine, the UPC has opened the ademption doctrine up to extrinsic evidence to a much greater extent than the avoidance/exception/softening doctrines.

   **Public policy considerations:** The UPC approach is willing to accept increased costs of administration and increased potential for fraud for the sake of trying to ascertain the testator's true intent.

H. **Stocks:** Gifts of stock are challenging because of the nature of stock. With most forms of property, the owner has exclusive control over the property so that any changes in the property are largely within the owner's control. With stock, that is not the case. The corporate entity, and even other corporate entities, can influence the stock owned by the testator through stock splits, stock dividends, mergers, acquisitions, etc.

1. **Common law:** The traditional common law approach focuses on whether the gift of stock is a specific or general gift. If the gift of stock is specific, and the change is due to a stock split, the beneficiary takes the additional shares. If the gift of stock is a general gift, the beneficiary does not take the additional shares following a stock split.

2. **Modern trend:** The modern trend rejects the separate versus general gift analysis, reasoning that even if the gift of stock is a general gift, the intent was to give a percentage interest in the company. The only way to give the intended percentage interest is to take into consideration stock splits and to give the beneficiary the increased number of shares to achieve the desired percentage interest in the company.

3. **UPC:** The UPC approach rejects the common law specific vs. general gift distinction (based on the language used in the will) and instead focuses on whether at the time the testator executed the will he or she owned stock that matched the description of the gift of stock in the will. If so, and thereafter the testator acquired additional stock as a result of his or her ownership of the devised stock and action initiated by a corporate entity, the beneficiary gets the benefit of whatever changes occurred between date of execution of the will and date of death of the testator, even if the stock in the estate is stock of a completely different corporate entity. UPC §2-605.

**I. Satisfaction:** If after executing a will, the testator makes an inter vivos gift to a beneficiary under the will, the issue is whether the inter vivos transfer should count against the beneficiary's testamentary share of the estate.

   **1. Common law:** If the beneficiary were a child of the testator and the property transferred inter vivos were of "like kind" to that devised under the will, a rebuttable presumption arose that the testator wanted the inter vivos gift to count against the child's share under the will (either complete or partial satisfaction).

   **2. Modern trend/UPC:** The modern trend/UPC approach reverses the presumption. Inter vivos gifts to a beneficiary under a will (any beneficiary, not just to the testator's children) are presumed *not* to be in satisfaction (partial or complete) absent a writing expressing such an intent. The writing can be the will making the testamentary gift, a writing by the testator at the time of the inter vivos gift, or a writing created by the donee anytime. UPC §2-609.

   **3. Scope:** Satisfaction applies to general gifts only. If the testamentary gift in question was a specific gift, when the testator gave the specific gift inter vivos to the beneficiary under the will, ademption would apply. Some authorities tend to blur this distinction, however, by calling satisfaction *ademption by satisfaction.*

   **4. Advancement vs. satisfaction:** The doctrines of advancement and satisfaction address the same generic issue: whether inter vivos gifts to one taking from the decedent's estate should count against the party's testamentary share. Advancement deals with the issue when the decedent dies intestate; satisfaction deals with the issue when the decedent dies testate.

   **5. Example:** In *Matter of Estate of Wolff*, 349 N.W.2d 33 (S.D. 1984), testator owned approximately 2,800 acres of land. In 1971, the testator properly executed a will that devised the property to his three sons (Arthur, Erwinn, and Jacob Jr.) equally. Thereafter, inter vivos, he conveyed approximately one-third of the land to Arthur, and another one-third to Erwinn. Decedent wrote Jacob Jr. a letter in which he indicated that he had already "sent Arthur and Erwinn the Deed for their land" and referred to the remaining land as "your land." Testator died without revising his will. Arthur and Erwinn claimed a share in the remaining land held by the testator. The court ruled that the letter adequately indicated testator's intent that the land transferred inter vivos to Arthur and Erwinn constituted an ademption (by satisfaction) of their share, and that Jacob Jr. took all the remaining land in question.

**J. Abatement:** If the testator gives away more in his or her will than he or she has to give, the doctrine of abatement provides for which gifts are to be reduced first.

   **1. General approach:** The general approach, based on testator's presumed intent, is that the residuary clause is reduced first, then general gifts, and specific gifts last. This order is based on the assumption that the more precise the nature of the gift, the more important it must have been to the testator.

   **2. Example:** In *In re Estate of Potter*, 469 So. 2d 957 (Fla. Dist. App. 1985), testatrix's will left her residence outright to her daughter, and she provided in her inter vivos trust that upon her death the trustee was to give her son a cash disbursement equal to the value of the house. When she died, there were not enough assets in the trust to make the disbursement to the son. The court found that the will's reference to the trust was sufficient to incorporate the trust by reference, but that while the testatrix may have had a general intent to treat her children equally, the gift of the residence to the daughter constituted a specific gift, the bequest of cash to the son constituted a general gift, and under abatement, the general gift is abated first.

3. **Criticism:** Often the testator presumes that the residuary clause will be the biggest gift and saves it for the most important beneficiary, typically his or her surviving spouse. Reducing the residuary gift first arguably is inconsistent with the testator's overall testamentary scheme in such situations.

4. **Minority approach:** Some states adopt the general approach, but then include a statutory provision giving the courts the flexibility to alter the order of abatement where it appears inconsistent with the testator's overall testamentary wishes.

K. **Exoneration of liens:** Where a will devises property that is burdened by debt (a mortgage or lien typically), the issue is whether the beneficiary should take the property free and clear of the debt (thereby reducing the gift to the residuary taker) or whether the beneficiary should take the gift subject to the debt. The issue is one of testator's intent. If the will fails to indicate testator's intent on the issue, a default rule is needed.

1. **Common law:** At common law, the presumption was that the beneficiary was to take the devised property free and clear of any debt.

2. **Modern trend/UPC:** The modern trend/UPC approach reverses the presumption. The presumption is that the testator intended the beneficiary to take the property subject to the accompanying debt (i.e., to receive only the testator's equity in the devised property). A general clause in a will to pay all the testator's just debts is not enough to overcome the modern trend presumption. An express reference to the debt in question is necessary. UPC §2-607.

# IV. CHANGES IN THE BENEFICIARY

A. **Survival requirement:** All jurisdictions have as a default rule the requirement that one taking from a decedent must survive the decedent. (See Ch. 2, VII, for a detailed discussion of the survival requirement.)

B. **Lapse:** If a beneficiary fails to survive the testator, the gift is said to lapse. A lapsed gift fails.

**Rationale:** It is presumed that the testator intended the beneficiary *personally* to benefit from the gift. If the beneficiary predeceases the testator and there were no lapse doctrine, the gift would pass to the beneficiary's estate to be distributed either to the predeceased beneficiary's heirs or to a devisee under the predeceased beneficiary's will—neither of whom the original testator may have met. The reasonable assumption is that if the named beneficiary predeceases the testator, the testator would prefer that the gift be revoked.

C. **Failed gifts:** Although the most common reason a gift fails is that it lapses, a gift may fail for a variety of reasons: The gift may be to an ineligible taker (pets are not eligible takers—gifts to pets fail), or the gift may violate the Rule against Perpetuities. Whatever the reason, if a gift fails and it is not "saved," it falls in a cascading scheme.

1. **Specific gifts:** If a specific gift fails, it falls to the residuary clause, if there is one, otherwise to intestacy.

**2. General gifts:** If a general gift fails, it falls to the residuary clause, if there is one, otherwise to intestacy.

**3. Residuary gift:** If a residuary gift fails *completely*, it falls to intestacy.

**4. Part of residuary gift:** If there are multiple takers in the residuary gift, and the gift fails as to one or more of them but not as to all of them, the jurisdictions are split as to what happens to the part of the residuary gift that fails.

   **a. Common law:** Under the "no residue of a residue" rule, if part of the residuary gift failed, that part fell to intestacy.

   **b. Modern trend/UPC:** The modern trend reasons that if the testator included a residuary clause, the testator's intent was for *all* the testator's property to pass via the will and for nothing to pass through intestacy. As long as any part of the residuary gift is valid, that part catches whichever part of the residuary fails.

   **Rule statement:** If part of the residuary gift fails, the other part catches it. The part that fails is distributed among the other beneficiaries in the residuary gift. UPC §2-604(b).

**D. Saving failed gifts:** There are two principal doctrines that can be used to try to save a failed gift: the anti-lapse doctrine and the class gift doctrine.

**E. Anti-lapse statutes:** The presumption that the testator would prefer that the gift fail where the beneficiary predeceases the testator arguably does not apply where the beneficiary is sufficiently related to the testator and the beneficiary has issue who survive the testator. In that situation, anti-lapse presumes that the testator would prefer that the gift go to the predeceased beneficiary's issue rather than fail. The presumption can be rebutted, but only by an express contrary intent expressed in the will. Virtually all states have adopted the anti-lapse doctrine statutorily, but the details of the statutes can vary greatly from state to state, as discussed below.

**1. Basic rule statement:** Anti-lapse statutes provide that (1) where there is a lapse, and (2) the predeceased beneficiary meets the statutory degree of relationship to the testator, and (3) the predeceased beneficiary has issue who survive the testator, the lapsed gift goes to the issue of the predeceased beneficiary (4) unless the will expresses a contrary intent. UPC §2-605 (1969 version).

**UPC rule statement:** The UPC drafters have adopted several different versions of the anti-lapse doctrine, the most recent of which is extremely complicated and not well received to date. The UPC discussion below will focus on the 1969 version. It is widely adopted and representative of what most states are doing.

**2. Lapse requirement:** While the lapse doctrine arose to cover scenarios where the beneficiary *actually* predeceased the decedent, it has been expanded to cover scenarios where the beneficiary *is treated as* predeceasing the decedent: if the beneficiary disclaims; if the beneficiary fails to meet an express survival requirement; if the beneficiary feloniously and intentionally kills the testator, etc.

   **a. Void gifts:** A gift is *void* if the beneficiary was dead when the will was executed; a gift *lapses* if a beneficiary was alive when the will was executed, but died before the testator. Both void gifts and lapsed gifts are failed gifts.

**b. Common law:** As originally developed, the anti-lapse doctrine applied to lapsed gifts only, not to void gifts.

**c. Modern trend/UPC:** The modern trend/UPC approach is to apply the anti-lapse doctrine to any qualifying beneficiary who predeceases the testator regardless of whether the beneficiary died before or after execution of the will. UPC §2-605 (1969 version).

3. **Requisite degree of relationship:** Although virtually all states have adopted the anti-lapse doctrine, the doctrine varies from state to state depending on how closely related the predeceased beneficiary has to be to the testator. Some states limit the doctrine to devises to beneficiaries who are descendants of the testator, while other states define the requisite degree of relationship broadly to include a much larger pool of beneficiaries (California includes any beneficiary who is related to the testator or the testator's spouse, current or former). Careful attention must be paid to the degree of relationship required by each statutory articulation of the doctrine.

   **UPC:** The UPC requires that the predeceased beneficiary be a grandparent or a lineal descendant of a grandparent to qualify for the anti-lapse doctrine. UPC §2-605 (1969 version). A 1990 amendment expanded the scope of predeceased beneficiaries covered to include stepchildren.

4. **Survived by issue:** The predeceased beneficiary must have issue who survive not only the predeceased beneficiary, but also the testator. The UPC requires that the issue survive the testator by 120 hours. UPC §2-605 (1969 version).

5. **Contrary intent:** The anti-lapse doctrine is based on presumed intent. If the beneficiary is related closely enough to the testator and is survived by issue, the testator is presumed to have preferred that the gift go to the issue of the predeceased beneficiary rather than fail. This presumption is a rebuttable presumption, but the contrary intent *must be expressed in the will*.

   **a. Low threshold:** Most courts and/or statutes have created a very low threshold for what constitutes an express contrary intent. The general rule is that (1) *any* express words of survival, or (2) any express gift over in the will to another beneficiary in the event of the first beneficiary's death constitutes a sufficient "express contrary intent" to bar application of the anti-lapse doctrine.

   **b. Criticism:** Increasingly wills are boilerplate documents. The boilerplate language typically includes an express survival requirement ("To ____, if she survives me."). If the express survival requirement is simply part of the drafting lawyer's form will, it arguably should not be sufficient to bar anti-lapse.

   **c. UPC:** The 1990 version of the UPC agrees with the criticism of the general rule and provides that mere words of survival ("if he survives me" or "my surviving issue"), without more, are not sufficient to constitute an express contrary intent barring application of anti-lapse. UPC §2-603(b)(3) (1990 version).

   **Criticism:** The 1990 version of the UPC has been heavily criticized by commentators and practicing attorneys alike for imposing the UPC's presumptions as to what an individual would want over the express words of the testator's own will, thereby exposing practicing attorneys to an increased potential for malpractice claims when drafting such clauses.

**d. Example:** In *Estate of Rehwinkel*, 862 P.2d 639 (Wash. App. 1993), the testator's residuary clause provided that he devised his estate "to those of the following who are alive at the time of my death . . .". The clause went on to list his brother, sister, and a number of his nieces and nephews. One of his named nieces died a month before the testator. The niece's son claimed a share of the testator's estate under the anti-lapse statute. The court held that the conditional clause introducing the beneficiaries constituted an express contrary intent barring application of anti-lapse.

**e. Gift to multiple beneficiaries and all predecease:** In *In re Estate of Burns*, 100 N.W.2d 399 (S.D. 1960), testatrix's will left the residue of her estate to her three sisters, "and in case of the death of any of said persons, that said rest and residue shall be divided between the survivors of said persons[.]" All three sisters predeceased the testatrix, and only one had surviving issue. The surviving issue claimed the property under anti-lapse, a claim opposed by the testatrix's 21 heirs. The court acknowledged that whether a gift to multiple beneficiaries or the survivor of them constitutes an express contrary intent that bars the application of anti-lapse is a question about which there is a split of authority. The court adopted the view that since the provision failed to address the scenario where *all* the named beneficiaries predeceased the decedent, the provision did not bar applying anti-lapse to that scenario.

**6. Scope:** The traditional and still majority approach applies the lapse and anti-lapse doctrines to wills only. Under the modern trend, however, a few states have statutes that apply the doctrines to most of the will substitutes—trusts, insurance policies, and contracts with payable-on-death clauses generally, but not joint tenancies.

**7. Spouses:** The general rule (and UPC approach) is that anti-lapse does *not* apply to spouses.

**Partial failure of residue overlap:** The modern trend "residue of the residue" rule can cause trouble when overlapped with the general anti-lapse rule. If the residuary clause is to multiple beneficiaries, and one is the testator's spouse, if the spouse predeceases the testator, the gift to the spouse lapses. Assuming the spouse is not covered by the anti-lapse rule, the gift fails. Under the common law "no residue of a residue" rule, the predeceased spouse's share of the residuary clause falls to intestacy where the testator's heirs take the gift. But under the modern trend residue of the residue rule, the predeceased spouse's share passes to the other residuary takers.

**F. Class gifts:** Class gifts are gifts to more than one individual that intrinsically include a right of survivorship. The right of survivorship means that if the gift fails as to one member of the class, his or her share does not "fall" out of the class, but rather the failed share is redivided among the other members of the class. The shares of the surviving members of the class are recalculated.

**1. Transferor's intent:** Whether a gift to multiple individuals is a class gift with a built-in right of survivorship or just a gift to multiple individuals is determined by testator's intent.

**2. Analysis:** Where it is not clear whether the testator intended a gift to multiple individuals to be a class gift, courts typically look to four factors to help construe testator's intent: (1) how did the testator describe the beneficiaries; (2) how did the testator describe the gift; (3) do the beneficiaries share a common characteristic; and (4) what is the testator's overall testamentary scheme?

a. **Description of beneficiaries:** Typically a gift to multiple beneficiaries will refer to them either collectively (as a group) or individually by name. Where the reference is to the beneficiaries collectively, that argues in favor of finding that the testator intended the gift to be to a class gift. Where the testator identifies each of the beneficiaries by name, that argues against finding that the testator intended the gift to be a class gift.

b. **Description of gift:** Typically a gift to multiple beneficiaries will describe the gift either in the aggregate or in separate shares. Where the gift is described in the aggregate, that argues in favor of finding that the testator intended the gift to be a class gift. Where the gift is described in distinct shares, that argues against the finding that the testator intended the gift to be a class gift.

c. **Common characteristic:** Intrinsic to the notion of a class gift is that there is something special about those individuals that separates them from other individuals—that they share a common characteristic that distinguishes them and separates them from everyone else. If they all share a common characteristic, that argues in favor of finding that the testator intended the gift to be a class gift. If there is no common characteristic, that argues against finding that the testator intended the gift to be a class gift.

**Prevalence:** Even where there is a common characteristic, if there are others who share the same common characteristic and they are not included in the gift, some courts have concluded that their exclusion from the gift cuts against a finding that the testator intended the gift to be a class gift.

d. **Overall testamentary scheme:** This factor asks whether, in light of everything else the testator tried to do with his or her property, it makes more sense to apply a right of survivorship to the gift (i.e., to find that the gift is a class gift). This factor is extremely fact sensitive. The court has to take the totality of the testator's testamentary scheme into consideration. There are two aspects of the testator's estate plan that should be examined in particular under this factor.

   i. **Express right of survivorship:** A number of courts have held that if there is a gift in the will to multiple individuals that has an express right of survivorship in the gift, the failure to include an express right of survivorship in another gift to multiple individuals indicates that the testator did not intend for the latter gift to be a class gift. The counterargument, however, is that the testator thought it so obvious that the latter gift was a class gift that he or she thought there was no need to include an express right of survivorship.

   ii. **Alternative takers:** It is always important to determine who would take the failed gift if it were not a class gift. Once that is determined, the courts analyze whether there is anything about the testator's overall testamentary scheme that indicates that the testator would not want that person to take the property in question. If so, that argues in favor of finding that the testator intended the gift to be a class gift.

3. **Factors, not requirements:** The four factors the courts focus on are only factors. All four do not have to be satisfied for a court to conclude that the testator intended a class gift. The more factors that cut in favor of finding that the testator intended a class gift, the better. But in the end, it is a question of testator's intent, and the factors are relevant only to the extent that they shed light on that issue.

4. **Anti-lapse and class gifts:**  Both anti-lapse and the class gift doctrine can be applied to save a lapsed gift to a class member, but the doctrines save the gift in favor of different takers. With anti-lapse, the saved gift goes to the issue of the predeceased class member. With the class gift doctrine, the saved gift goes to the other members of the class. The overwhelming majority of states and the UPC apply anti-lapse first to a lapsed gift to a class member. UPC §2-605 (1969 version). If anti-lapse cannot save the lapsed gift, apply the class gift doctrine to try to save the lapsed gift.

5. **Example:**  In *In re Moss*, 2 Ch. 314 (Eng. C.A. 1899), the testator's will gave all his interest in the Daily Telegraph newspaper to his wife and his niece, E.J. Fowler, as trustees, to pay the income to his wife during her lifetime, and upon her death, to remain in trust for the benefit of E.J. Fowler and the children of his sister Emily Walter who shall reach the age of 21. The residuary clause of his will devised the rest of his property to his wife. E.J. Fowler predeceased the testator. The court reasoned that a gift to a single individual and a class of persons should be construed as a class gift, so that if the share to the individual lapsed, his or her share should be divided equally among the other members of the class. The testator's overall testamentary scheme supported this conclusion. By putting his newspaper interest in trust and giving his wife only a life estate interest in the income, the testator clearly indicated he did not want his wife to take a share outright. If the gift to E.J. failed and was not saved by the class gift doctrine, E.J.'s share would fall to the residuary and go outright to his wife. Not applying the class gift doctrine arguably would be inconsistent with his overall testamentary scheme to limit his wife's interest in the Daily Telegraph newspaper to a life estate.

   **Gifts to an individual and a class:**  There is no consensus on how to characterize gifts to an individual and class, such as was the case in *In re Moss*. The American Law of Property states that such a gift is presumed *not* to be a class gift to a single class, but rather is a gift to an individual and a class separately. The Restatement of Property says the opposite—the gift is presumed to be a single class composed of the individual and the subclass. Go figure.

---

## *Quiz Yourself on* *CONSTRUING WILLS*

42. Anna wants to leave her pink velvet couch to the nice lady who works at the local pastry shop in Beverly Hills. Anna fondly refers to her as "Mrs. Sugar," and the woman at the pastry shop has grown to adore the name and answers to it when Anna comes in. Anna dies one night after overeating at a Hollywood party. Her properly executed will devises "my pink velvet couch to Mrs. Sugar." The real name of the woman who works at the pastry shop is Mrs. Jones. A woman named Patty Sugar comes forward and claims she is entitled to the pink velvet couch because she is Mrs. Sugar. Mrs. Jones wants to offer as evidence a birthday card that Anna gave her a few months before she died addressed to "Mrs. Sugar." Is the evidence admissible, and who takes the couch?

43. While being treated at the New Beginnings rehabilitation center in Malibu, Chandler forms a close friendship with a woman named Jennifer. A week after his discharge from the center, Chandler dies.

His properly executed will devises "$100,000 to Jennifer from New Beginnings." There are five women named Jennifer enrolled at New Beginnings, and all five claim the money. What result?

_____

**44.** Rachel's properly executed will states, "my engagement ring to my sister Monica, if she survives me, everything else to Phoebe." Monica dies, survived by two sons, Ross and Joey. Thereafter, Rachel dies. Who gets the ring? _____

**45.** Homer, a single father, has a will that states, "all of my property to my children." Homer has three children, Bart, Lisa, and Maggie. Tragically, Bart dies in a skateboarding accident. Upon hearing of Bart's death, Homer has a heart attack and dies. Bart is survived by two children, Crusty and Bob. Who takes Homer's estate? _____

**46.** Justin's will states, "my custom-made red leather pants to Britney." After wearing the red leather pants a few times, Justin's stylist tells him that red leather is out and off-white is in. Justin does not want to be out of style, so he burns the red leather pants and has off-white leather pants custom-made to replace them. Thereafter, Justin has a heart attack at dance practice and dies. What, if anything, does Britney take? _____

**47.** Martha's will leaves "300 shares of IBM stock" to her stockbroker, Bob. After some tough times in the stock market, IBM stock goes up dramatically and splits 3 for 1. The next day, Martha accidentally dies after inhaling toxic potpourri with which she was experimenting. How many shares of IBM stock does Bob take? _____

---

# ANSWERS

**42.** Under the common law approach, the general rule of construction is the plain meaning approach. The words of a will are to be given their usual and plain meaning, and extrinsic evidence is not admissible to prove a different meaning was intended. An exception to the common law plain meaning rule is the personal usage exception. Where the testator uses a personal phrase or name to refer to a person, and uses that personal phrase or name in the will, extrinsic evidence is admissible to show that the testator used that phrase or name to mean something different from what it appears. Here, Anna called the woman in the pastry shop by a personal phrase that only they understood. Extrinsic evidence should be admissible to show the personal usage and to establish the identity of the woman that Anna wanted to take the couch—Mrs. Jones. Under the modern trend, the plain meaning has been rejected and extrinsic evidence is admissible anytime there is an ambiguity, be it patent or latent. The extrinsic evidence should be admissible to help construe the words of the will in light of the circumstances surrounding the testator at time of execution—that Anna used the nickname "Mrs. Sugar" to refer to the woman in the pastry shop. Mrs. Jones should take the couch under the modern trend as well.

**43.** Under the common law approach, extrinsic evidence is admissible if there is a latent ambiguity in the will, but not if there is a patent ambiguity. A latent ambiguity is one that is not apparent from the face of the will. Typically it becomes apparent when the court attempts to give effect to the will. Here, although the reference to "Jennifer from New Beginnings" appears clear upon first reading, when the probate court attempted to give effect to the clause it discovered that there were five women named Jennifer enrolled at New Beginnings. Where more than one person or thing matches the language used in the will, that is called an equivocation. An equivocation is a latent ambiguity. Even at common law, extrinsic evidence was admissible to prove the latent ambiguity and to help the courts construe the language in the will. Under the modern trend, extrinsic evidence is admissible anytime there is an ambiguity, latent or patent. An ambiguity is language in the will that is reasonably susceptible to two or more interpretations. Here, the reference to "Jennifer from New Beginnings" is reasonably susceptible to multiple interpretations. The court will take extrinsic evidence of the circumstances surrounding the testator at time of execution in attempt to help construe the language and determine which Jennifer was intended to take the gift.

**44.** A beneficiary under a will must survive the testator. If the beneficiary does not, the gift lapses—it fails, unless it can be saved. Anti-lapse provides that where there is a lapse, but the beneficiary is sufficiently related to the testator and has issue who survive the testator, it is presumed that the testator would rather the gift go to the issue of the predeceased beneficiary, unless there is a contrary intent expressed in the will. Here, Monica predeceased Rachel, so the gift lapses unless it can be saved by anti-lapse. The requisite degree of relationship between testator and beneficiary depends on the wording of each state's statute, but most states cover siblings. If the statute covers descendants only, anti-lapse would not apply. Assuming Monica meets the statute's degree of relationship requirement, she is survived by issue. Unfortunately, there is an express contrary intent that blocks the anti-lapse doctrine. The express phrase "if she survives me" has been construed by the courts applying the common law approach as an express intent that anti-lapse not apply. Under the modern trend/UPC approach, however, such an express survival clause is not sufficient to constitute an express intent that anti-lapse not apply. Under the modern trend/UPC approach, the court would apply anti-lapse and give the ring to Monica's issue, Ross and Joey.

**45.** When Bart dies before Homer, Bart's gift lapses and the gift fails. There are two ways a failed gift can be saved—by anti-lapse or by the class gift doctrine. In most jurisdictions, anti-lapse applies to class gifts, so check for anti-lapse first. Under anti-lapse, there must be a lapse, the predeceased beneficiary must meet the statutory degree of relationship requirement (varies by jurisdiction), the predeceased beneficiary must have issue who survive the testator, and there must be no express intent in the written instrument that anti-lapse not apply. Bart's death before Homer, the testator, constitutes a lapse. Bart is Homer's son, so he meets the degree of relationship requirement in every state. Bart has issue who survive Homer, Crusty and Bob. And there is no express intent in the will that anti-lapse should not be applied. Crusty and Bob would take Bart's share. Maggie would take one-third; Lisa would take one-third; and Crusty and Bob would split one-third (one-sixth each).

If the jurisdiction does not apply anti-lapse to a class gift, the class gift doctrine may save the gift for the other members of the class. Whether a gift constitutes a class gift depends on the testator's intent. Where that intent is not clear, the courts typically look at four factors: (1) how the beneficiaries are described—by name or by group; (2) how the gift is described—in the aggregate or in shares; (3) whether the beneficiaries share a common characteristic; and (4) the testator's overall testamentary scheme. Here, Homer described the beneficiaries as a group—"my children," which favors a class gift. Homer described the gift in the aggregate—"all my property," which favors a class gift. The beneficiaries share a common characteristic— they are all Homer's children and there is no evidence Homer has any other children who were excluded, which favors a class gift. And Homer's overall testamentary scheme appears to have been to leave all his property to his children, which arguably favors a class gift here. Most likely, the gift would be construed to be a class gift, and under the right of survivorship that is built into each class gift, Bart's share would go to the other members of the class, Maggie and Lisa (one-half each), if the jurisdiction does not apply anti-lapse to class gifts.

**46.** Justin's gift of "my custom-made red leather pants" constitutes a specific gift. He intends for one specific item to satisfy that gift. When he burns the pants, the question is what effect, if any, that has on the gift. Under the traditional common law approach to ademption, there was an irrebuttable presumption that by disposing of the item subject to the specific gift before he died, Justin intended to revoke the gift. Under ademption, Britney would take nothing. Because of the harshness of the ademption doctrine, however, many jurisdictions have developed avoidance doctrines. One such doctrine is the "change in form, not substance" doctrine. Under that doctrine, the beneficiary can argue that the gift really is still in the testator's estate, it is just that the gift has changed slightly in form, but not in substance. Here, though, Justin burned the pants. Although there is another pair of custom-made leather pants in Justin's estate, they are a different pair, not the same pair that has changed slightly. Under the traditional strict approach to ademption, Britney probably would fail on her change in form, not substance argument and she would not take (though if she can convince the court that the change from red to white is merely a change in form, not substance, and the court overlooks the fact that it is a completely different pair of pants, she might prevail).

Under the modern trend/UPC approach to ademption, there is a slight presumption against ademption. The UPC has adopted the replacement approach to ademption. If the testator disposes of the item that was the subject of the specific gift, but acquires property to replace the specifically devised property, the beneficiary takes the replacement property if still owned at death. Here, Justin burned the red pants and replaced them with white pants. Britney would take the replacement pants—the white leather pants.

**47.** Under the traditional common law approach, where there is a stock split, whether the beneficiary gets the additional shares owned at the testator's death as a result of the stock split depended on whether the gift of stock was construed as a specific gift or general gift of stock. If specific, the beneficiary tended to take the additional shares. If general, the beneficiary did not take the additional shares. Here, there is no evidence that Martha owned any shares of IBM stock at the time she executed her will, and the wording of the gift does not refer to any specific shares of IBM stock. The gift would most likely be construed to be a general gift, and under the traditional common law approach Bob would take only 300 shares of IBM stock upon Martha's death. Under the modern trend, the courts tend to give the beneficiary the additional shares whether the gift is specific or general. Bob would take 900 shares as a result of the stock split to ensure that he takes the same proportional interest in IBM that Martha intended prior to the stock split.

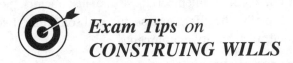

## *Exam Tips on* CONSTRUING WILLS

### Interpreting wills

The threshold issue is *why* the extrinsic evidence is being offered. If the evidence goes to the validity of the will, invariably the courts admit the evidence. If the evidence goes to the construction of the will, it is not admissible unless there is an ambiguity in the will.

☞ If the extrinsic evidence is being offered to help construe the will, you need to know: (1) whether your jurisdiction applies the plain meaning rule, and (2) whether your jurisdiction still applies the latent-patent distinction.

☞ If your jurisdiction follows the modern trend, apply the steps in the analysis. If there is an ambiguity, only extrinsic evidence that is consistent with one of the possible reasonable interpretations is admissible, and the courts favor evidence of the circumstances surrounding the testator at time of execution as opposed to alleged oral declarations (easy to fabricate).

☞ Even where extrinsic evidence is admissible to help construe a will, as a general rule the courts will not rewrite a will, they will only construe the ambiguous language. What constitutes "construing" and what constitutes "rewriting" can be a very difficult question. The interpretation desired by the claimant must not vary too far from the express words of the will, or it is subject to being construed as a rewrite, not a mere construction.

### Scrivener's error

The scrivener's error doctrine is a new doctrine. The problem is that there is only one case adopting and applying the doctrine so far, and that case can be spun a number of different ways, leaving many questions unanswered. Because it is new, be on the watch for issues raising some of the unanswered questions raised by the case.

### Changes in the beneficiary

Core wills material—lapse/anti-lapse/class gifts/failed gifts. These doctrines constitute some of the most tested material in the course—lapse in particular, because it is a great "overlap" issue. Whatever you conclude on the lapse issue, be sure to check if it affects your analysis of another issue raised by the fact pattern. (Examples: overlap between lapse and the per capita doctrine; or lapse and the advancement's doctrine; etc.).

☞ Watch for the more subtle ways to raise the lapse issue: the beneficiary dies before the will is executed (lapse vs. void, common law vs. modern trend); or the beneficiary dies after execution of the will, but then the testator executes a codicil; or the beneficiary survives the testator but is treated as if he or she predeceased the testator.

☞ If you have a lapse issue, be sure to raise and discuss anti-lapse. The final element, no express contrary intent, is a particularly tricky element. The express contrary intent must be in the instrument making the testamentary gift.

☞ Failed gifts can also be saved by the class gift doctrine. If you see a gift to more than one individual, you should stop and analyze whether the gift constitutes a class gift. Focus on the four elements in analyzing whether the gift is a class gift. Remember these are just factors, not requirements. Three is probably good enough to qualify the gift as a class gift, and sometimes two is all that it takes. Be prepared to make detailed, fact sensitive arguments.

☞ If a gift to a class member lapses, know which approach your jurisdiction takes to which doctrine should be applied first to try to save the gift: anti-lapse or the class gift doctrine.

☞ If a gift is not saved by anti-lapse, or the class gift doctrine, or the residue of the residue-rule, the gift fails. You need to know the cascading scheme of who takes if a gift fails, because it underlies this whole batch of material and is necessary to ascertain who will argue which approach when it appears that a gift is failing.

### Changes in testator's property

Ademption is another key doctrine that every student should know and that shows up frequently on exams.

☞ A tricky area of the law of gifts is where language in the will appears to indicate a general gift, but when the testator executed the gift, he or she owned a specific item that matched the gift exactly. If you get such a scenario, argue both sides. The outcome may turn on which legal conclusion is most beneficial to the beneficiary. In the more common scenario, the item will no longer be in the testator's estate, so classifying the gift as a general gift is more beneficial (i.e., avoids ademption). Sometimes, however, it will be more beneficial to classify the gift as specific (if the gift is of stock and thereafter there is a stock merger). (This is also a good overlap issue for whether extrinsic evidence should be admitted to help resolve the conflict.)

☞ Ademption applies only to specific gifts. Know which approach your jurisdiction takes to ademption: the harsh common law approach or the kinder and gentler UPC approach.

☞ If your jurisdiction applies the harsh identity approach to ademption, run through the avoidance and softening doctrines. One or more can usually be argued in good faith.

☞ If your jurisdiction applies the UPC approach, look first to see if there is any replacement property in the testator's estate at time of death. If not, argue for the monetary equivalent. Be prepared to use extrinsic evidence to support your claim that the testator did not intend for the gift to be adeemed.

☞ If you see a beneficiary under a will receiving an inter vivos gift from the testator, there is a high probability that either ademption or satisfaction will apply, depending on whether the gift was specific or general.

☞ Gifts of stock is another area that is tested often. Know which approach your jurisdiction applies (the common law, the modern trend, or the UPC approach), and the differences between the different approaches.

☞ The wrinkle in the abatement area to watch for is whether your jurisdiction grants the flexibility to vary the normal abatement order if it appears inconsistent with the testator's overall testamentary scheme.

## CHAPTER 7

# NONPROBATE TRANSFERS: WILL SUBSTITUTES

## *ChapterScope* _____

This chapter briefly examines the traditional methods of avoiding probate and planning for incapacity before death.

- ■ **Inter vivos gifts:** If a party transfers title to property, real or personal, to a donee inter vivos, the party has no interest in the property when he or she dies and so the property does not go into the decedent's probate estate.

- ■ **Life insurance contracts/contracts with payable-on-death clauses:** Although life insurance contracts effectively pass property at the time of the insured's death, the insurance proceeds are deemed "nonprobate" assets. The modern trend/UPC extends this nonprobate exception to all third-party beneficiary contracts with payable-on-death clauses.

- ■ **Joint tenancies:** The right of survivorship means that upon the death of one joint tenant, his or her share is extinguished and the shares of the remaining joint tenants are recalculated. No property passes, so there is nothing to pass through probate.

  - ▪ **Multiple party bank accounts:** Banks often force multiple parties to use the joint tenancy account even if that is not what the parties intended. Upon the death of one of the depositors, the courts will take extrinsic evidence of the parties' true intent and treat the account accordingly. The modern trend presumes that inter vivos the parties own in proportion to the contributions and at death there is a right of survivorship.

- ■ **Inter vivos trusts:** The trustee holds legal title. The beneficiaries hold equitable title. There is no need to transfer legal title upon the death of any of the beneficiaries—even if the trust is revocable and the settlor is the life beneficiary. The property placed in an inter vivos trust is nonprobate property.

  - ▪ **Revocability:** If a trust is silent as to its revocability, it is irrevocable. If the trust is revocable and it expressly provides for a particular method of revocation, only that method will suffice (if the trust does not provide for a particular method of revocation, any method that demonstrates settlor's intent to revoke should suffice).

  - ▪ **Creditor's rights:** When a life tenant's interest is extinguished, creditors of the life tenant have no right to reach the property. Under the modern trend, however, where the settlor is the life beneficiary of a revocable trust, creditors of the settlor can reach the property in the trust even after the settlor's death.

- ■ **Pour-over wills:** Where a will has a pour-over clause giving probate property to the trustee of the testator's inter vivos trust, the pour-over clause must be validated under either the Uniform Testamentary Additions to Trusts Act (UTATA), facts of independent significance, or incorporation by reference.

■ **Planning for incapacity:** Good estate planning includes planning for the possibility that the person may become incapacitated before he or she dies. With respect to property issues, the most common tool to deal with that possibility is the durable power of attorney. With respect to personal decisions about one's health care, the tools are either a living will or a durable power of attorney for health care decisions.

# I. INTER VIVOS GIFTS

A. **Introduction:** Where a donor transfers full title to an asset inter vivos, the donor no longer holds any interest that would pass into his or her probate estate upon death. Often, however, there are issues as to whether the donor made a valid and complete transfer inter vivos—particularly where the donor retains possession until death.

B. **Real property—Statute of Frauds:** The Statute of Frauds provides that for a party to transfer his or her interest in real property there should be a writing signed by the party to be charged (in gift cases, the donor). The writing must express the grantor's intent to transfer and reasonably describe the parties and the property. There must be delivery, and there must be acceptance by the grantee. Most jurisdictions recognize an exception to the Statute of Frauds under the doctrine of part performance.

1. **Part performance:** Real property may be transferred by part performance where the grantee (1) takes possession and (2)(a) makes substantial improvements to the property, or (2)(b) pays part of the purchase price. In such cases a court of equity is empowered to order specific performance and order the property transferred to the grantee. Where the doctrine is invoked after the death of the alleged grantor, the courts typically require clear and convincing evidence to support the claim.

   **Example:**   In *Mertz v. Arendt*, 564 N.W.2d 294 (N.D. 1997), John and Emilie Mertz had six children. John Jr., the youngest, remained home with his parents and helped farm the land after the older ones had moved away. John Sr. quit farming the land, and John Jr. started farming the land, in 1957. John Jr. claimed that in 1958 or 1959 his parents agreed to give him the farm so that it would stay in the family. The parents continued to live on the farm. Emilie died in 1974, and John Sr. died in 1993. John Jr. was the only party who farmed the tillable land from the late 1950s until 1994 when his father's personal representative took possession of the land; John Jr. was the only party who paid the taxes on the land during this period (the parents actually paid the taxes, but John Jr. reimbursed them); John Jr. insured the property and listed himself as owner; John Jr. made a number of substantial improvements (cleared rocks, built a dam, rebuilt a well, installed a water tank, reshingled a granary). The court found that there was an executed parol gift from the parents to John Jr. Accordingly, the farm did not constitute an asset in John Sr.'s probate estate.

2. **Delivery:** Delivery is the grantor's intent to relinquish dominion and control over the property, to presently divest him- or herself of title. Because delivery relates to the grantor's state of mind, often there is only circumstantial evidence, that is, circumstantial evidence arising out of how the parties treat the written instrument that purports to transfer title to the property.

**a. Presumptions:** If the grantor retains possession of the instrument, a rebuttable presumption arises that no delivery has occurred. If the grantor gives the grantee possession of the instrument, a rebuttable presumption arises that delivery has occurred. If the instrument is recorded, a rebuttable presumption arises that delivery has occurred.

**b. Post-death delivery:** Absent consideration, delivery must occur inter vivos. Where the instrument is given to a third party inter vivos to deliver to the grantee upon the occurrence of some event, including the grantor's death, the delivery is a valid inter vivos transfer as long as the grantor did not retain the power to recall the instrument after giving it to the third party. If the grantor did not retain the power to recall the instrument, the grantor is deemed to have relinquished control and dominion inter vivos when he or she gave the instrument to the third party—even if the instrument is not given to the grantee until after the grantor's death.

**c. Example:** In *Lenhart v. Desmond*, 705 P.2d 338 (Wyo. 1985), in 1974, Mr. Desmond executed a deed conveying his real property to his only child, Elizabeth, in case he died so she could have it. He placed the deed in his safe deposit box. He told Elizabeth of his intentions, of the deed, and gave her access to the safe deposit box. Mr. Desmond was in an automobile accident, and Elizabeth had to access insurance documents in the safe deposit box. Thereafter, Mr. Desmond learned that the deed was gone and that it had been recorded by Elizabeth without his consent. Mr. Desmond sued to have the deed declared invalid. The court found that there had been no delivery. Although the recording created a presumption of delivery, Mr. Desmond had adequately rebutted the presumption.

**C. Personal property:** To transfer title to personal property inter vivos, there must be intent, delivery, and acceptance.

**1. Intent:** The donor must presently intend to relinquish control and dominion over the property.

**Gratuitous promise to make a gift in the future:** The present intent to make a donative transfer must be distinguished from a gratuitous promise to make a gift in the future. The latter does not constitute an enforceable intent. The donor is free to change his or her mind, and if he or she dies before delivery, the property in question remains the promisor's and passes into his or her probate estate.

**2. Delivery:** The property must be delivered to the donee. Where manual delivery is possible, common law required it; where manual delivery was impossible or impractical, constructive or symbolic delivery is acceptable. Constructive delivery is delivery of something that gives control over the item. Symbolic delivery is delivery of something that symbolizes the item (typically a piece of paper).

**a. Example:** In *Gruen v. Gruen*, 496 N.E.2d 869 (N.Y. 1986), Victor Gruen wrote a letter to his son on April 1, 1963, informing the son, who was away from home studying at Harvard, that he (Victor) was giving him (the son) a valuable Klimt painting for his birthday, but that he (Victor) wanted to retain possession of it for his lifetime. Thereafter in May, Victor sent his son a second set of letters, one of which stated that his lawyer said the earlier letter should not have stated that he (Victor) wanted to retain possession for his lifetime, and the other was a "substituted" gift letter expressing the intent to give the painting to the son without reference to Victor retaining it for his lifetime. Nevertheless, Victor retained possession until his death, at which time Victor's wife (the son's stepmother) claimed that no inter vivos gift had occurred, and she was entitled to the painting. The court found that Victor had the requisite donative intent to give an inter vivos gift despite retaining possession of the painting. Victor had a present intent to convey a future interest to the son (a remainder). Inasmuch as the gift was of a future interest, actual delivery arguably was impossible and illogical. The letter constituted symbolic delivery. Acceptance was presumed.

     **b. Delivery to intermediary third party:** Where the donor transfers the property to an intermediary third party, the issue is whether the donor has relinquished control over the property. If the third party is deemed merely an agent of the donor, the donor has not relinquished control and no delivery has occurred (if the donor dies, the agency ends automatically by operation of law, and the property will pass into the donor's estate as probate property). If the third party is deemed a trustee, the donor has relinquished adequate control over the property (even if the trust is revocable), and the donee can enforce the terms of the trust on the trustee after the donor's death if necessary to receive the property.

**3. Acceptance:** Acceptance by the donee is presumed as long as the item is of value.

**4. Checks:** Because checks are orders to pay that are subject to stop payment instructions, the party who executed the check is deemed not to have relinquished control and dominion over the money until the check is cashed. If the donor dies before the check is cashed, most courts hold no delivery has occurred.

**D. Gifts causa mortis:** Gifts causa mortis, also known as "deathbed" gifts, are gifts made in contemplation of an impending death.

**1. Conditional:** A gift causa mortis is a conditional gift. The donor must intend that if he or she does not die as expected, the gift is automatically revoked (if the donor does not have this intent, the gift is deemed a traditional inter vivos gift and is analyzed pursuant to that doctrine).

**2. Revocable:** The donor is deemed to retain the power to revoke the gift while he or she is still alive. (Gifts causa mortis differ from traditional inter vivos gifts in this respect—the latter are generally considered irrevocable.)

**3. Survival requirement:** If the donee predeceases the donor, the gift causa mortis automatically fails, and the property is considered the donor's property.

**4. Scope:** Only gifts of personal property can be transferred under the gifts causa mortis doctrine. Real property is beyond the scope of the doctrine.

**5. Creditors' rights:** If the donor's estate does not have enough assets to meet the claims of the donor's creditors, the creditors may reach the property that was the subject of a gift causa mortis.

**6. Example:** In *Scherer v. Hyland*, 380 A.2d 698 (N.J. 1977), Catherine Wagner and the plaintiff lived together for 15 years. Four years prior to her death, Catherine was in a serious car accident that greatly restricted her mobility and caused her to suffer from severe depression. The morning she received her settlement check for $17,400 for damages arising out of her accident, she endorsed the check, left it on the kitchen table, locked the apartment, and committed suicide by jumping off the roof of the apartment building. Catherine left a note in which she "bequeathed" all her property to the plaintiff, including the check. The note did not qualify as a will. In light of the clear evidence of Catherine's donative intent, the court found that her actions were sufficient to constitute delivery to support a gift causa mortis.

7. **Gifts to minors:** Because minors lack legal capacity to transfer property, special considerations arise when the donee is a minor. See Ch. 2, VI.J for a discussion of the different legal arrangements that are available to deal with the situation.

# II. OVERVIEW OF NONPROBATE TRANSFERS

A. **Introduction:** Historically, there were four types of legal arrangements that, for all practical purposes, passed property at time of death but were not subject to the Wills Act formalities. The four were life insurance contracts; joint tenancies; certain possessory estates and future interests (legal life estates and remainders); and inter vivos trusts.

**Justification:** Why these four particular arrangements were deemed not subject to the Wills Act formalities is debatable. Some argue that the property interest technically passes inter vivos and nothing really passes at time of death—so there is no testamentary transfer that is subject to the Wills Act formalities. Others argue that the formalities associated with the creation of each of these arrangements adequately serves the functions underlying the Wills Act formalities so there is no need to apply them.

B. **Controlling law:** Each of the four recognized will substitutes arguably falls within a particular area of law other than the law of wills. Life insurance policies are a subset of the law of contracts. Joint tenancies and possessory estates and future interests are a subset of the law of property. Inter vivos trusts are a subset of the law of trusts.

1. **Creation:** Inasmuch as these will substitutes do not have to be created with Wills Act formalities, the issue of whether any of these will substitutes were properly created is beyond the coverage of the law of wills and thus beyond the scope of this outline (except for the inter vivos trust, which is covered later).

2. **Construction:** There is a growing debate over whether the will substitutes should be subject to the *"wills-related" doctrines*—in particular the will construction doctrines. For example, if the beneficiary of an insurance contract dies before the insured, should contract law control the issue of whether the beneficiary has to survive the transferor, or should the wills-related doctrines control (lapse and anti-lapse)?

   a. **Common law:** The traditional common law approach held that inasmuch as these will substitutes are subsets of other areas of law, the rules and doctrines of those other areas of law control.

   b. **Modern trend:** The modern trend is to subject the will substitutes to the wills-related construction doctrines.

      **Rationale:** Most people use will substitutes to avoid the costs, hassles, and delays of probate, not to avoid the wills-related doctrines. The wills-related doctrines were specifically developed to deal with construction issues that can arise between the time of creating an instrument that purports to transfer the property at time of death and the time of death of the party creating the instrument. The wills-related doctrines are better suited to deal with these construction issues.

C. **Scope:** At common law, there were only the four categories of will substitutes. If the instrument purporting to transfer a property interest at death did not qualify as one of these four types of property arrangements or as a valid will, the written instrument was an invalid attempt at transferring property at time of death without complying with the Wills Act formalities, no matter how clear the individual's intent in the instrument.

# III. CONTRACTS WITH PAYABLE-ON-DEATH CLAUSES

A. **Introduction:** The classic example of a contract with a payable-on-death clause is a life insurance policy. The insured enters into an agreement with an insurance company. The agreement provides that upon the insured's death, the company will pay the benefits under the policy to a beneficiary designated in the policy. For all practical purposes, the agreement effectively transfers property to a designated beneficiary upon the insured's death, but the written agreement between the insured and the insurance company need not be created with Wills Act formalities.

1. **Common law:** At common law, the only type of contracts that were exempt from the Wills Act formalities were life insurance contracts. If the contract were any other type of contract with a payable-on-death clause, no matter how clear the party's intent that the property in question should be transferred to the identified beneficiary upon the party's death, the written instrument was an invalid attempt at transferring property at time of death if it did not qualify as a will.

2. **Modern trend/UPC:** The modern trend/UPC approach expands the historical will substitute exemption for life insurance contracts and applies it to *any and all* contracts with payable-on-death clauses (employment contracts, promissory notes, deposit agreements, pension plans, retirements accounts, etc.). UPC §6-101.

3. **Example:** In ***Kansas City Life Ins. Co. v. Rainey***, 182 S.W.2d 624 (Mo. 1944), the decedent purchased an "Investment Annuity Policy" from the Kansas City Life Insurance Company for $50,000 for the benefit of his wife. When she predeceased him, he changed the beneficiary to his secretary. Upon his death, his executor claimed that the contract did not qualify as a life insurance policy because no element of risk was involved. The court ruled the policy was not a testamentary transfer because it was an inter vivos contract with a third-party beneficiary. The court ordered the money to be paid to the secretary.

4. **Revocability:** Beneficiaries of a payment-on-death clause do not receive an irrevocable property interest inter vivos. The transferor who creates the payment-on-death clause is presumed to have the right to cancel or change the payment-on-death clause (absent consideration).

5. **Construction:** The modern trend/UPC approach applies the wills-related rules to the will substitutes. The wills-related rules are primarily those rules of construction that arise out of changes that can occur between when the instrument is created and when the transferor/ testator dies.

**Survival requirement:** Although the modern trend/UPC approach is generally to apply the wills-related rules to the will substitutes, an exception to this trend is the survival requirement. The UPC expressly applies a survival requirement to life insurance contracts. It is silent as to contracts with payable-on-death clauses generally. UPC §§2-104, 2-702, 6-101.

6. **Superwills:** A superwill is a will that can change the beneficiaries of the will substitutes. Under the modern trend, an individual might have a plethora of written instruments that could qualify as valid will substitutes. The issue is whether a subsequently executed will should have the power to revise these instruments. For public policy reasons, almost all jurisdictions have rejected the idea of a superwill.

   a. **Rationale:** One of the principal benefits of the will substitutes, particularly life insurance contracts, is that they permit the quick and relatively easy transfer of property to the intended beneficiary upon the transferor's death. There are none of the hassles, delays, and expenses associated with probate. If, however, the nonprobate instrument were subject to change by a superwill, the nonprobate transfer could not occur until the party responsible for making the transfer was confident that there was not a valid superwill changing the beneficiary or the gift.

   b. **Counterargument:** The party responsible for making the transfer could still make the transfer immediately upon the death of the transferor, but the recipient could be required to post a letter of credit or execute an indemnity agreement protecting the party responsible for making the transfer.

7. **UPC:** The UPC has adopted the superwill doctrine *only* if the contract permits the beneficiary of the policy to be changed by a subsequently executed will. UPC §6-101. The UPC is silent as to what the rule should be if the contract is silent.

# IV. MULTIPLE PARTY BANK ACCOUNTS

A. **Intent vs. paperwork:** The courts have long recognized that a person might have several different reasons for opening a multiple party bank account, but historically banks would offer the depositor only one option: a joint tenancy bank account. Even at common law, courts would take extrinsic evidence to determine the depositor's true intent and treat the property in the multiple party bank account consistent with the depositor's true intent.

B. **Depositor's intent:** There are three possible reasons that a depositor may open a multiple party bank account (or add another party's name to an existing account, thereby making the account a multiple party bank account).

1. **Joint tenancy account:** A depositor may create a multiple party bank account because he or she intended to create a joint tenancy account. The moment the account is opened, or the moment the other party's name is added to an existing account, the other party takes a proportional interest in the account inter vivos, and upon death, a right of survivorship exists such that the property will pass nonprobate.

2. **Convenience/agency account:** A convenience or agency account is where a depositor adds a second party to an account as a convenience to the depositor, to facilitate paying bills, etc. As such, the second party is acting as an agent for the depositor; the second party is merely helping out. The depositor does not intend that the second party receive any interest in the

account. Inter vivos the second party can access the account, but only to use it for the benefit of the depositor (not for the second party's own benefit), and upon death, there is no right of survivorship.

   3. **Payable-on-death account:** The depositor may intend a payable-on-death account to avoid probate. The depositor does not intend for the other party on the account to take any interest inter vivos, but at time of death, the depositor intends a right of survivorship. Any money remaining in the account is to go to the other party.

   a. **Common law:** Even if the depositor's true intent was to create a payable-on-death account, at common law payable-on-death accounts were an invalid attempt at a testamentary transfer without complying with Wills Act formalities. The assets remaining in the account upon the depositor's death would fall to probate.

   b. **Modern trend/UPC approach:**  Payable-on-death bank accounts are one of the many possible payable-on-death arrangements permitted under the modern trend/UPC approach.

C. **Bank's perspective:** While there were three different possible reasons that a depositor might want to create a multiple party bank account, historically banks offered only one multiple party bank account option—a joint tenancy account.

   1. **P.O.D. accounts:** At common law, banks could not offer payable-on-death accounts, even if that is what a depositor wanted, because they were not valid will substitutes.

   2. **Agency accounts:** While banks could offer a convenience or agency account, such an account exposes banks to liability in the event the bank knew or should have known that the agent was misappropriating funds or if the bank permitted the agent to continue to access the account after the agency was terminated (an agent's authority typically is terminated upon the principal becoming incapacitated or dying).

   3. **Joint tenancy accounts:** As long as the paperwork provides that the account is a joint tenancy account, the bank is protected. Thus, banks often force depositors interested in creating multiple party bank accounts to use the paperwork stating the account is a joint tenancy account even if that is not the depositor's true intent.

D. **Extrinsic evidence:**  Even at common law, the courts quickly realized that banks routinely forced depositors interested in creating multiple party bank accounts to use a joint tenancy account, even if that was not the depositor's true intent. Because the joint tenancy account may have been involuntarily created, the courts take extrinsic evidence to determine the depositor's true intent and then treat the account accordingly.

   1. **Temporal focus:** The key is what the depositor's intent was at the time the multiple party bank account was created. The depositor's subsequent comments and/or actions may be relevant to the issue of his or her intent at the time the account was created.

   2. **Burden of proof:** If the depositor executes paperwork that expressly states that the account is a joint tenancy account, the paperwork creates a presumption that the account is a "true" joint tenancy account. To overcome the presumption, most jurisdictions require clear and convincing evidence of a different intent.

   3. **Example:** In *Franklin v. Anna National Bank of Anna*, 488 N.E.2d 1117 (Ill. App. 1986), Mr. Whitehead, an elderly man with failing eyesight, asked Mrs. Goddard to help care for

him. Mr. Whitehead added Mrs. Goddard's name to his bank account. Mrs. Goddard testified her name was added so that she could access the account when they needed money and so she would own the money after his death. The bank had the parties execute the paperwork for a joint tenancy account. Mrs. Goddard never deposited any money into the account, she never made any withdrawals from the account, and she never had possession of the passbook for the account. When Mrs. Franklin took over caring for Mr. Whitehead, Mr. Whitehead instructed the bank to remove Mrs. Goddard's name and add Mrs. Franklin's name to the account. The letter asking the bank to make the change expressly stated: "In case I can't see she is to take care of my bill or sick." The court found there was clear and convincing evidence that when Mr. Whitehead added Mrs. Goddard's name, he intended an agency account. Mrs. Goddard did not receive any interest in the account.

**E. Criticism:** The common law approach of taking extrinsic evidence to determine the true intent of the depositor has been widely criticized for promoting litigation. Almost anytime there is a multiple party bank account there is the potential for litigation, usually between family members.

**Paperwork conclusive:** Some courts have gone so far as to hold that the joint tenancy paperwork is conclusive and extrinsic evidence is inadmissible to show a contrary intent.

**F. UPC approach:** The UPC provides that inter vivos, it is presumed that the parties to a multiple party bank account own in proportion to their contributions, and that upon the death of any party, it is presumed that there is a right of survivorship. The presumptions control the distribution of the money in the account unless there is clear and convincing evidence of a contrary intent. UPC §§6-201 through 6-227.

1. **Survival requirement:** The UPC imposes an express survival requirement for parties to a multiple party bank account. UPC §6-212. There is no express survival requirement for other contracts with payable-on-death clauses.

   **P.O.D. accounts:** The UPC permits P.O.D. multiple party bank accounts. If the account is a P.O.D. account, the UPC applies the wills-related doctrines of lapse and anti-lapse to the beneficiary. UPC §§6-212, 2-706. In addition, if the account is a P.O.D. account, the beneficiary cannot be changed by will. UPC §6-213(b).

2. **Criticism:** The UPC "presumption" approach does little to reduce the potential for litigation; it merely changes the presumed characterization of the account from a joint tenancy account to what amounts to a payment-on-death account.

3. **Example:** In the *Franklin* case, above, under the UPC approach, the presumption would arise that neither Mrs. Goddard nor Mrs. Franklin received any interest in the bank account inter vivos, and the presumption would arise that the party whose name was on the account at the time of Mr. Whitehead's death was entitled to any remaining money in the account. There is, however, clear and convincing evidence that Mr. Whitehead intended an agency account. Any money remaining in the account at time of death should fall to his probate estate.

**G. Totten trusts:** Totten trust accounts are very similar to payment-on-death bank accounts. Totten trusts rationalized as a form of inter vivos trusts (though not subject to general trust rules). The depositor sets up a totten account by depositing money in an account in the name of the depositor "for the benefit of" the beneficiary. Legal title remains in the name of the depositor, but equitable title is in the name of the beneficiary. The bifurcation of the legal and equitable title constitutes the intent to create a trust.

**Example:** In *Green v. Green*, 559 A.2d 1047 (R.I. 1989), George Green opened eight bank accounts, each of which he took in his name in trust for the benefit of one of his three children from a prior marriage. Following George's death, his surviving spouse challenged the accounts, claiming that they were not valid trust accounts. The court ruled that the accounts were valid totten trusts and awarded the money to the surviving beneficiary named on each account. The court stated that whether an account constituted a valid totten trust or an invalid attempt at avoiding probate was a question of the depositor's intent. The court ruled that when a depositor opens an account in his or her name in trust for another, it creates a prima facie case supporting the creation of a valid totten trust and shifts the burden to the party opposing that characterization. Here, the prima facie case was not rebutted, and the children took.

1. **Revocability:** The trust is deemed revocable as a general rule so that withdrawals by the depositor are permitted without constituting a breach of trust (though general trust law holds a trust is irrevocable unless there is an express clause stating that it is revocable). Some jurisdictions also permit oral revocation of a totten trust.

   **Example:** In *In re Rodgers' Estate*, 97 A.2d 789 (Pa. 1953), Elizabeth Rodgers opened an account at the Beneficial Saving Fund Society and entitled it "Elizabeth M. Rodgers in trust for sister Martha B. Rodgers." Following Elizabeth's death, her heirs claimed that she had revoked the "tentative trust." Her attorney testified that during the process of drafting her will, Elizabeth acknowledged that her sister was too infirm to take care of herself and her affairs, and that she wished to establish a testamentary trust to hold the property, including her money at the Beneficial Saving Fund Society. The court held this was sufficient evidence that Elizabeth had revoked the tentative trust orally, and the court went on to hold that the testamentary scheme established in the will also evidenced her intent to revoke the tentative trust because without the funds in the account there was not sufficient money to fund the testamentary trust.

2. **Testamentary modification:** An express clause in the settlor's will changing the beneficiary of a totten trust is permitted in some jurisdictions (though generally wills cannot change the terms of a will substitute).

3. **Survival requirement:** Most jurisdictions require the beneficiary of a totten trust account to survive the depositor (though generally at common law there is no survival requirement for beneficiaries claiming under trusts or other will substitutes).

4. **Commentary:** Totten trusts are unique. They should be segregated from the other nonprobate property arrangements because of their unique rules.

# V. JOINT TENANCIES

A. **Basic characteristics:** Joint tenancies are a form of concurrent ownership whereby multiple parties own the property in question both in whole and in shares. The key characteristic of a joint tenancy is its right of survivorship. Under the right of survivorship, upon the death of one party to the joint tenancy, his or her share is *extinguished* and the shares of the surviving joint tenants are recalculated. This process of recalculating shares continues until there is only one owner surviving, at which time the concurrent ownership ends and the party owns it outright with no right of survivorship. When there is only one remaining party, the property is no longer nonprobate property. Upon that party's death, it will fall into his or her probate estate.

**B. Probate avoidance:** If a joint tenant dies and he or she is not the lone surviving joint tenant, his or her share is extinguished. His or her share was tantamount to a life estate. The deceased joint tenant has no interest in the property that can fall to probate. No interest *passes* when a joint tenant dies. The joint tenants owned in whole from the outset. The surviving joint tenants' shares are simply recalculated.

**C. Devisability:** Although a joint tenancy can be severed inter vivos and converted into a tenancy in common (with inheritable and devisable shares), the mere execution of a will does not sever a joint tenancy, even if the will makes express reference to the deceased joint tenant's interest in the property. The right of survivorship extinguishes the joint tenant's interest before the will has any effect upon the property.

**D. Creditor's claims:** Because a joint tenant's interest in the property is extinguished upon his or her death, there is nothing left for creditors of a deceased joint tenant to reach. Each joint tenant's interest is tantamount to a life estate, and when the life estate is extinguished, the party has no remaining interest in the property for creditors to reach. Creditors of a joint tenant must assert their claims while the joint tenant is alive.

# VI. REVOCABLE DEEDS

**A. Introduction:** A revocable deed typically states that it transfers the real property to a grantee, but the grantor retains the right to possess the property until he or she dies and the power to revoke the deed inter vivos. Such arrangements have troubled the courts.

**B. Common law:** At common law, the courts were particularly protective of the Wills Act formalities and particularly suspicious of revocable deeds. The courts reasoned that for all practical purposes no property interest passed inter vivos. Inasmuch as the property interest was being passed upon the grantor's death, the transfer constituted a testamentary transfer that would be valid only if the written instrument constituted a valid will. The typical revocable deed does not qualify as a valid will and is invalid under this approach.

**Example:** In *Butler v. Sherwood*, 135 N.E. 957 (N.Y. App. Div. 1922), the decedent executed an instrument that purported to convey all her real property to Edward Sherwood in exchange for $1 and other valuable consideration. The instrument recited that it was to take effect only upon her death, only if he survived her, and she retained the power to revoke the instrument. She delivered the instrument to Edward inter vivos. The court found the document to be an attempt at a gift despite the recited consideration, that the gift was not to take effect until her death, and as such it was testamentary in character. The court applied the Wills Act formalities and found the instrument void.

**C. Modern trend:** The modern trend, with its intent-based approach, generally holds that the revocable deed constitutes a valid inter vivos transfer. The modern trend construes the revocable deed as creating a legal life estate and remainder inter vivos. Title passes inter vivos though possession is delayed until death—but the title transfer constitutes an inter vivos transfer not subject to the Wills Act formalities. Moreover, the power to revoke merely makes the remainder a contingent remainder; the interest still passes inter vivos. The modern trend upholds revocable deeds as valid inter vivos conveyances.

## VII.  INTER VIVOS TRUSTS

**A.  Introduction:**  A trust is nothing more than another way to make a gift. Conceptually, the key to understanding a trust is to remember that it is a bifurcated gift. (Trusts are covered in great detail in Chapter 8—this is merely a brief introduction.)

**Parties:**  While the traditional gift involves only two parties, a donor and a donee, a gift in trust involves three parties: a settlor, a trustee, and the beneficiaries. There are three parties because when a gift is made in trust, title to the property in question is bifurcated. Legal title is given to the trustee, who holds and administers the property for the benefit of the beneficiaries, who hold the equitable title. The donor is called the settlor.

**B.  Theoretical perspective:**  There are several different types of inter vivos trust. They arguably run the spectrum from those that clearly are inter vivos transfers to some that look very testamentary in nature. Whether all such trusts should be recognized as valid will substitutes is raised most notably where the settlor is also trustee and life beneficiary, and retains the power to revoke.

1.  **Classic trust:**  At one end of the spectrum is the classic inter vivos trust. Assuming the settlor, trustee, and beneficiaries are all different parties, and assuming the trust is irrevocable, the classic trust is clearly an inter vivos transfer that is not subject to the Wills Act formalities. The settlor transfers the property to the trust inter vivos. Following the transfer, the settlor no longer has any interest in the property. The trust holds legal title to the property, not the settlor. When the settlor dies, no property interest is transferred by the settlor.

    **Example:**  Sally transfers $1,000 to Tess, as trustee, to hold for the benefit of Bob during his lifetime, and upon his death, any remaining money is to be distributed outright to Betty. Assuming the transfer is irrevocable, Sally, the settlor, retains no interest in the property. It is like any other inter vivos gift Sally may make. Moreover, when Bob dies any property distributed to Betty is not a testamentary transfer because the future interest was given to her when the trust was created.

2.  **Settlor is trustee and life beneficiary, and retains power to revoke:**  While the classic inter vivos trust does not look testamentary at all, at the other end of the spectrum is the inter vivos trust where the settlor is also the trustee and life beneficiary, and retains the power to revoke. This type of trust takes the issue of whether a gift in trust is a testamentary transfer that should be subject to the Wills Act formalities to the limit.

    a.  **Instrument constitutes a will:**  To the extent the settlor wears all three hats (settlor, trustee, and life beneficiary) and retains the power to revoke, arguably the trust instrument is functionally indistinguishable from a will. If it is indistinguishable from a will, it should be subject to the Wills Act formalities.

    b.  **Instrument constitutes a valid inter vivos trust:**  Even where the settlor is also trustee and life beneficiary and retains the power to revoke, a property interest is still conveyed inter vivos to the beneficiaries holding the future interest. Unlike a will, where the beneficiaries receive no rights or interest inter vivos, beneficiaries in a trust are owed a fiduciary duty; they immediately receive rights that they can enforce against the trustee if the trustee breaches any of the numerous onerous burdens the trustee owes the beneficiaries. The fact that the trust is revocable does not defeat the fact that the property interest has been conveyed inter vivos. Typically the future interest is a remainder. Where the trust is revocable, the remainder is a contingent remainder—but a contingent remainder is still a property interest the moment it is created even though full enjoyment is delayed until the interest becomes possessory.

    **c. Case law:** In *Westerfeld v. Huckaby*, 474 S.W.2d 189 (Tex. 1971), settlor executed two declarations of trust in which she appointed herself trustee and retained a life estate interest and a power to revoke. Thereafter she executed two quitclaim deeds transferring certain real property to the trusts. Following her death, her executor challenged the validity of the trusts. The court acknowledged that while older cases and authorities had held such an arrangement invalid, there had been a marked shift in opinion supporting such an arrangement as a valid inter vivos trust. The court adopted the modern trend and upheld the trusts.

    **Wills Act formalities:** In the alternative, some argue that even if a revocable trust where the settlor is also trustee and life beneficiary is functionally indistinguishable from a will, the process one has to go through to create such a revocable inter vivos trust satisfies the functions underlying the Wills Act formalities and therefore should qualify as a will substitute on that basis.

    **3. Other trust arrangements:** While the two trust examples above arguably represent the different ends of the trust spectrum, there are many other possible trust arrangements that fall in between these two.

**C. Doctrinal perspective:** Revocable inter vivos trusts are widely recognized as valid will substitutes that do not have to comply with the Wills Act formalities, even where the settlor is also the trustee and life beneficiary.

**Example:** In *Farkas v. Williams*, 125 N.E.2d 600 (Ill. 1955), Farkas purchased stock on four different occasions, each time taking title in his name "as trustee for Richard J. Williams." Concurrently with each purchase, Farkas signed four declarations of trust where he conveyed himself the life interest, remainder to Williams, and retained the power to revoke by selling the stock. Farkas died intestate. His heirs claimed the inter vivos trusts were invalid testamentary dispositions that failed to comply with the Wills Act formalities. The court upheld the inter vivos trusts, reasoning that some interest passed inter vivos to Williams even though the trusts were revocable, and in the alternative, the process Farkas went through in creating the inter vivos trusts adequately served the functions underlying the Wills Act formalities.

**D. Trust law coverage:** The basic law of trusts is covered in great detail in Chapter 8. Please refer to that chapter for treatment of the law of trusts (requirements to create, beneficiary's rights, creditor's rights, revocability, modification, and termination).

# VIII. POUR-OVER WILLS AND INTER VIVOS TRUSTS

**A. Introduction:** The inter vivos trust and pour-over will combination is the most common estate planning scheme today. The revocable inter vivos trust's principal advantage is that it avoids probate, but only as to those assets placed in the trust inter vivos. Unlike a will, which automatically reaches out and applies to all the decedent's probate assets at death, an inter vivos trust applies only to those assets transferred to the trust inter vivos. People acquire and dispose of assets on such a rapid basis that it is virtually impossible to put all one's assets in an inter vivos trust, even if one were so inclined. Most settlors put their larger assets, and those assets that they do not use on a regular basis, in the trust. They use a pour-over will for their other assets and for their newly acquired assets.

**B.  Pour-over wills:** A pour-over will is a will that contains an express clause giving some or all of the decedent's probate property to the trustee of the decedent's inter vivos trust, to hold and distribute pursuant to the terms of the trust. Typically the pour-over clause is the residuary clause, but it need not be.

**Standard  clause:** A typical pour-over clause provides as follows: "I give the rest, residue, and remainder of my estate to the trustee of my inter vivos trust, to hold and distribute pursuant to its terms."

**C.  Validity:** The effect of a pour-over clause is that a document that was not executed with Wills Act formalities (the inter vivos trust) will control who takes some or all of the decedent's probate property. This violates both the spirit and the letter of the Wills Act formalities that any disposition of the decedent's probate property must comply with the Wills Act formalities. Before a pour-over clause can be given effect, the pour-over clause must be validated.

**Inter  vivos vs. testamentary funding:** As to those assets transferred to the inter vivos trust during the settlor's lifetime, the inter vivos trust is a well-recognized will substitute and its terms will be given effect regardless of the validity of any pour-over clause. As to the decedent's probate assets being transferred to the trust via a pour-over clause, that transfer constitutes a testamentary transfer that is subject to the Wills Act formalities. Before the inter vivos trust can apply to the decedent's probate property, the pour-over clause must be validated.

**D.  Common law:** At common law, there were two possible "will expanding" doctrines that could be used to try to validate a pour-over clause—facts of independent significance and incorporation by reference.

    **1.  Facts of independent significance:** Facts of independence significance provides that a will can reference a fact outside of the will, and the fact can control either who takes or how much they take, as long as the referenced fact has its own significance apart from its effect upon the disposition of the decedent's probate property.

        **a.  Pour-over clause:** As applied to a pour-over clause scenario, the "fact" referenced in the will is the reference to the trust. The question becomes whether the trust has its own significance apart from its effect upon the decedent's probate property. As long as the trust is funded inter vivos, and has some property in it at the time of the decedent's death, the trust has its own significance—holding and managing of the property placed in the trust inter vivos.

        **b.  Temporal sequence:** Under facts of independent significance, it does not matter when the inter vivos trust is created (before or after the execution of the will), as long as the trust is created inter vivos and has property in it at the time of the decedent's death.

        **c.  Trust amendments:** Under facts of independent significance, amendments to the trust are valid and can be given effect, regardless of when they are created.

**d. Probate court supervision:** Inter vivos trusts generally *are not* subject to probate court supervision. Testamentary trusts generally *are* subject to probate court supervision. With facts of independent significance, as for the property placed in the trust while the party is alive, the trust is an inter vivos trust. As for the property being poured into the trust via the pour-over clause, arguably those assets should likewise be treated as an inter vivos trust not subject to probate court supervision. But some probate courts retained jurisdiction over the assets being poured over, in essence treating the trust as a testamentary trust, subjecting it to the court's supervision and requiring the trustee to account to the court.

**Costs:** As a general rule, there are greater costs and administrative burdens associated with testamentary trusts as opposed to inter vivos trust. Typically the trust is subject to probate court supervision for the life of the trust, and the trustee has a duty to account to the probate court on a regular basis.

2. **Incorporation by reference:** Incorporation by reference permits a will to incorporate and give effect to the provisions of a document that was not executed with Wills Act formalities as long as (1) the will expresses the intent to incorporate the document, (2) the will describes the document with reasonable certainty, and (3) the document was in existence at the time the will was executed.

   **a. Pour-over clause:** As applied to a pour-over will scenario, incorporation by reference incorporates the inter vivos trust *instrument* into the will and gives effect to it—thereby permitting the terms of the inter vivos trust instrument to control who takes the decedent's probate property and how much they take.

   **b. Temporal requirement critical:** Although there are three requirements for incorporation by reference, as applied to the pour-over will scenario, invariably the element at issue will be whether the inter vivos trust *instrument* (as opposed to the trust itself) was in existence at the time the will was executed.

   **Analysis:** The courts apply a low threshold to the first two requirements. By stating in the will that the testator devises the property "to the trustee of my inter vivos trust, to hold and administer pursuant to the terms of the trust," the testator has adequately expressed the intent to incorporate the trust instrument into the will and has described it with reasonable certainty (assuming the decedent has only one trust instrument). In the typical pour-over clause setting, the element at issue will be whether the trust instrument was in existence at the time the will was executed. The burden of proof is on the party seeking to incorporate the inter vivos trust instrument.

   **c. Funding:** Incorporation by reference incorporates the trust *instrument,* not the *trust*—so there does not have to be any funding in the trust. If there is property in the trust inter vivos, one should probably use facts of independent significance to validate the pour-over clause because it has more benefits associated with it.

   **d. Trust amendments:** One of the disadvantages of using incorporation by reference to validate a pour-over clause is that the doctrine incorporates the trust instrument *as it existed at the time the will was executed.* Any subsequent amendments to the inter vivos trust instrument cannot be incorporated and given effect (unless the will is reexecuted or republished by republication by codicil).

**e. Probate court supervision:** If incorporation by reference is used to validate a pour-over clause, the trust instrument is incorporated into the will. The effect is that the trust will be deemed a testamentary trust, with the added costs and administrative burdens inherent in the probate court's supervision.

**E. Uniform Testamentary Additions to Trust Act (UTATA):** In light of the benefits of the pour-over will and inter vivos trust combination, and the hassles and limitations of the common law validation doctrines, estate planners brought pressure for legislative action to facilitate validating the pour-over will and inter vivos trust testamentary scheme. The result was UTATA—the Uniform Testamentary Additions to Trusts Act. UTATA arguably gives the estate planner and client the best of both worlds. As long as the transferor meets the UTATA requirements, the transferor does not have to put a penny into his or her inter vivos trust, the pour-over clause will be valid, all amendments to the trust will be valid even if executed after the date of the will, and after the probate property is poured over to the trust pursuant to the pour-over clause, the trust will be treated as an inter vivos trust that is not subject to probate supervision.

**1. UTATA requirements—original version:** The original (and widely adopted) version of UTATA required (1) that the will refer to the trust, (2) that the terms of the trust be set forth in a writing separate from the will, and (3) that the trust instrument be executed *prior to or concurrently* with the execution of the will.

**a. Observation:** The original UTATA requirements are basically the same as incorporation by reference only with the added requirement that the trust instrument must be signed prior to, or concurrently with, the execution of the will.

**b. Analysis:** In analyzing the UTATA requirements and the typical pour-over will scenario, the key element typically is going to be the requirement that the trust has to be executed (signed) prior to or concurrently with the execution of the will. The pour-over clause by its nature will satisfy the first requirement, that the will refer to the trust. The requirement that the terms of the trust be set forth in a separate document provides a bright line between a testamentary trust and a UTATA/inter vivos trust. If the settlor wants a testamentary trust, which would be subject to probate court supervision, the settlor should put the terms of the trust in the will. If, however, the settlor wants the benefits of a trust but without the costs and administrative burdens of probate court supervision, the settlor has to put the terms of the trust in a document separate from the will. The key requirement is that the trust instrument must be signed prior to, or concurrently with, the execution of the will.

**c. UTATA benefits:** If the settlor/testator meets the requirements of UTATA, the trust will be deemed an inter vivos trust for purposes of probate court supervision, thereby saving the trust money and facilitating its administration even though not a penny was put in the trust inter vivos. Second, all amendments to the trust are valid regardless of when they are executed.

**2. Revised UTATA:** The revised version of UTATA eliminates the requirement that the trust instrument must be executed *prior to, or concurrently with, the execution of the will,* thereby making it even easier to validate a pour-over clause under UTATA. As long as the trust instrument is signed by the settlor anytime before he or she dies, if the will refers to the trust instrument and the terms of the trust are set forth in a separate document, the pour-over clause will be valid and the trust will be considered a UTATA trust not subject to probate court supervision. The UPC has adopted the revised version of UTATA. UPC §2-511.

3. **UTATA trust—inter vivos vs. testamentary trust:** Before the adoption of UTATA, when classifying a trust based upon when it was created, there were only two possible types of trusts: inter vivos trusts and testamentary trusts. To have an inter vivos trust, property had to be transferred to the trust inter vivos. The traditional testamentary trust was set forth in the decedent's will and was funded when the settlor/testator died. UTATA is a hybrid trust in that it can be wholly unfunded until time of death (which makes it look like a testamentary trust) yet the express provisions of UTATA state that for purposes of probate court supervision, it is treated like an inter vivos trust and is not subject to probate court supervision. To the extent other doctrines draw a distinction between inter vivos trusts and testamentary trusts, the issue is how should the UTATA trust be classified and treated for purposes of those doctrines.

    a. **Divorce:** All jurisdictions have statutes that provide that upon divorce all provisions in each spouse's will in favor of the ex-spouse are automatically revoked by operation of law. Most statutes apply only to the ex-spouse's will and not to any will substitutes. Because a testamentary trust is considered part of the will, the doctrine applies to testamentary trusts. Inasmuch as inter vivos trusts are will substitutes, the statute does not apply to inter vivos trusts. The issue is whether a UTATA trust should be treated like a testamentary trust that is subject to the divorce doctrine or an inter vivos trust that is not subject to the doctrine.

    b. **Example:** In ***Clymer v. Mayo***, 473 N.E.2d 1084 (Mass. 1985), Clara Mayo executed a will and a revocable inter vivos trust. The will gave her personal property to her husband, and the residue of her probate property to the trustee of her trust, to hold and distribute pursuant to the terms of the trust. Clara changed her life insurance policy and pension plans to make the proceeds payable to the trustee, to hold and distribute pursuant to the terms of the trust. Thereafter Clara and her husband divorced, and Clara died without revising any of her estate planning documents. Clara's heirs claimed that the pour-over clause was invalid because the trust was wholly unfunded at death and that they were entitled to receive her property. Clara's ex-spouse admitted that he was not entitled to take under her will due to the revocation by operation of law doctrine, but claimed that he was still entitled to take under the terms of the trust because the revocation by divorce doctrine in that jurisdiction applied to wills only. The court applied UTATA and held that there was no problem validating the pour-over clause and trust. The trust was executed concurrently with the will and did not have to be funded inter vivos. The court also held that because the decedent considered the will and trust one integrated testamentary scheme, the UTATA trust should be treated like a testamentary trust for purposes of the revocation by operation of law doctrine—at least where the trust was wholly unfunded at time of death.

4. **Common law doctrines post-UTATA:** UTATA does not render the common law validation doctrines meaningless. The key is to validate the pour-over clause to give effect to the testator's intent that the property be distributed pursuant to the terms of the trust. UTATA facilitates validating a pour-over clause and has the most benefits associated with it, but if the pour-over will cannot be validated under UTATA, the pour-over clause will fail unless the clause can be validated using one of the common law doctrines. If the trust was funded inter vivos, use facts of independent significance. If the trust was not funded inter vivos, try incorporation by reference.

**Example:** Tom calls his attorney, Alice, and asks her to prepare an inter vivos trust and pour-over will. The pour-over clause gives the residue of his estate to his trustee to hold and distribute pursuant to the terms of the trust. Alice does as Tom requests. Tom executes the will, but forgets to sign the trust instrument. Thereafter Tom dies. Because the trust instrument was not signed, the pour-over clause cannot be validated under UTATA (either the original or the revised version). Because Tom did not transfer any property to the trust inter vivos, the pour-over clause cannot be validated under facts of independent significance. Because the will referred to the trust and the trust instrument was in existence when the will was executed, the pour-over clause can be validated under incorporation by reference. The trust will be considered a testamentary trust subject to probate court supervision, but the probate property will be held and distributed pursuant to the terms of the trust.

5. **Failure to validate pour-over clause:** If the pour-over clause cannot be validated under UTATA, facts of independent significance, or incorporation by reference, the pour-over clause fails. If the pour-over clause fails, the property in question cannot be distributed pursuant to the terms of the trust. If the pour-over clause is the residuary clause of the will, and it fails, the property will fall to intestacy. If the pour-over clause is not the residuary clause, and it fails, the property in question will fall to the residuary clause if there is one, if not, to intestacy.

**Example:** Tom handwrites a valid, dated holographic will that gives all his property to the trustee of his inter vivos trust, to hold and distribute pursuant to the terms of the trust. A week later, Tom types up a trust instrument, dates it, but he fails to sign it or to transfer any property to it. Tom dies. Because the trust instrument was never signed, the pour-over clause cannot be validated under UTATA (either the original or the revised version). Because Tom did not transfer any property to the trust inter vivos, the pour-over clause cannot be validated under facts of independent significance. Because the trust instrument was not in existence when the will was executed, the pour-over clause cannot be validated under incorporation by reference. The pour-over clause fails. The property will pass via intestacy to Tom's heirs.

F. **Revocable trusts:** There are a number of pros and cons associated with using revocable inter vivos trusts, though most argue the pros outweigh the cons for the typical individual.

1. **Inter vivos:** Using an inter vivos trust to hold and manage one's assets while one is alive offers a variety of potential benefits. These benefits include professional management of the trust property and segregation of the trust assets from other assets. For tax purposes, however, as long as the settlor retains the power to revoke the trust, the trust property is legally treated as if it were still the settlor's property regardless of the terms of the trust.

2. **Time of death:** The principal time of death benefit of using a revocable inter vivos trust is that the property transferred to the trust inter vivos avoids probate—thereby avoiding its hassles and delays. In addition, using an inter vivos trust saves probate court costs, executor's fees, and attorney's fees; increases privacy (wills are public documents, trusts generally are not); can avoid ancillary probate; might (depending on the jurisdiction) permit one to avoid family protection doctrines; gives one greater choice of law options; facilitates "dead hand" control; and decreases the chances of a challenge to the decedent's testamentary scheme expressed in the trust. Inter vivos trusts, however, do not have the shortened statute of limitations for creditors' claims that probate does.

# IX. PLANNING FOR THE POSSIBILITY OF INCAPACITY

**A. Introduction:** People are living longer and longer, and with the evolution of modern medicine, it is becoming increasingly likely that one may lose legal capacity well before one's death. Proper estate planning should include planning for the possibility of incapacity. Such planning should take into consideration the individual's wishes with respect to how his or her property should be managed, and the individual's wishes with respect to his or her health care and disposition of his or her body.

**B. Asset management:** There are several possible tools one can use to plan for managing one's assets during incapacity.

**1. Inter vivos revocable trust:** Arguably the best legal tool available for providing for the possibility of one's incapacity is the inter vivos revocable trust. The settlor can appoint him- or herself as the initial trustee, and then expressly appoint a successor trustee in the event the settlor is unable or unwilling to serve as trustee. This can avoid the expense and emotional stress often involved in instituting guardianship or conservatorship proceedings.

**2. Durable power of attorney:** A power of attorney authorizes one to act for another. It creates a principal-agent relationship where the terms of the power dictate the scope of the agent's power to act for the principal. The standard power of attorney automatically terminates upon the incapacity of the principal. The durable power of attorney continues despite the incapacity of the principal. It is a relatively simple and cheap method of planning for one's incapacity.

**a. Differences from trust:** Unlike a trustee, an agent's power under a durable power of attorney automatically terminates upon the principal's death; the property subject to the durable power of attorney does not avoid probate; and an agent does not have legal title to the property subject to the power, making many third parties more reluctant to deal with an agent.

**b. Scope:** Most states require that a durable power of attorney be created in writing. The writing can either incorporate by reference a statutory list of powers or it can be drafted to suit a principal's particular wishes. Even if a power of attorney is worded broadly enough to appear to authorize actions that may be inconsistent with the principal's interests, the instrument should be construed narrowly to prohibit such actions absent express authorization for the questionable action.

**C. Health care management:** Modern medicine is steadily prolonging the dying process. This development raises serious financial and ethical issues. Some people have ethical and personal objections to artificially prolonging the dying process. While one has capacity, one has the power to control the health care one receives, including the right to refuse medical treatment. Prudent estate planning now includes planning for incapacity to ensure that one's wishes with respect to one's health care are respected.

**1. Living wills:** A living will is a document that directs that extraordinary medical treatment shall not be undertaken when there is no reasonable expectation of recovery. Living wills are heavily regulated by statute, and care should be taken in drafting and executing living wills to ensure compliance with such statutes.

**Disadvantages:** The principal disadvantage of a living will is that it has to anticipate possible scenarios and provide in advance for what the individual would want done in these situations.

Living wills lack flexibility when the actual situation does not fit neatly into the express terms of the instrument.

2. **Durable power of attorney for health care decisions:** The durable power of attorney for health care decisions appoints an agent to make health care decisions for one after one becomes incapacitated. The instrument can give general directives to the agent that must be followed, but the durable power of attorney for health care decisions has the added benefit of flexibility. By giving the power to an agent, the agent can take the principal's wishes and all the circumstances into consideration before making a decision as to what the principal would have wanted under the particular situation.

3. **Disposition of one's body:** All states have adopted some form of the Uniform Anatomical Gift Act, permitting one to give one's body, or any part thereof, to any authorized health care provider for medical research or transplantation. The Act permits the decedent to identify a specific individual who is to receive his or her body or any part thereof for transplantation. The gift may be made by will or by a donor card signed by the individual (some states require that the card be witnessed).

---

## *Quiz Yourself on*
## *NONPROBATE TRANSFERS: WILL SUBSTITUTES*

**48.** Luke and Hans decide to make a movie together as partners. Their signed, typewritten agreement includes a provision that in the event of the death of one, all his interest goes to the surviving partner, if one, otherwise to his parents equally. During filming, Hans falls in love with Lea and marries her. Unfortunately, shortly thereafter Hans accidentally trips over some little green character and hits his head, killing Hans instantly. Hans died testate with a will giving all his property to his wife Lea. Who takes Hans' interest in the movie? _____

**49.** Ozzie and Sharon are married. He has a life insurance policy that designates Sharon as beneficiary. Thereafter, Ozzie and Sharon develop marital problems, and Ozzie moves out. He meets Anna Nicoli and is immediately captivated by her abilities. He properly executes a new will that expressly provides that he leaves the proceeds of his life insurance policy to Anna Nicoli and the rest of his property to his children. Thereafter Ozzie dies. Who takes the proceeds of his insurance policy? _____

**50.** Pete is a single wills and trusts professor. He has been invited to teach in Europe for the coming year. Before leaving the country, he put his colleague's name (Bob) on his bank account as a joint tenant so that Bob could pay Pete's bills while Pete was out of the country. Unfortunately, Pete is killed while participating in the running of the bulls (he was trampled by the people running—even in death denied the glory of saying that he was gored to death). Pete had no will. Who takes the money in his bank account? _____

**51.** Bubba and Emily own Malibuacres as joint tenants with right of survivorship. Bubba properly executes a valid will that provides in part that he devises his interest in Malibuacres to his mom, Mia, and the rest of his property to his grandmother, Gia. When Bubba dies, who takes his interest in Malibuacres? _____

**52.** Jerry executes a will that provides that it leaves all his property to the trustee of his trust, to hold and distribute pursuant to the terms of the trust. Thereafter, Jerry has his attorney draw up a trust instrument that is for the benefit of Elaine during her lifetime, and upon her death, the property is to be distributed outright—one-half to George and one-half to Kramer. Jerry executes the trust instrument at his attorney's office, but on his way to his accountant to transfer property to the trust, Jerry is hit and killed by a mail truck. Who takes Jerry's property? _____

**53.** Groucho properly executes a valid will that leaves all his property to the trustee of his trust, to hold and distribute according to the terms of this trust. A month later, Groucho drafts (but does not sign) a trust instrument that provides that the trust is for Harpo's benefit during his life, and upon his death, the principal is to be split between Chico and Zeppo. A month later, Groucho executes a codicil to his will, changing his executor to Zeppo. A month later, Groucho drafts (but does not sign) an amendment to his trust, giving an outright gift of $100,000 to Mrs. Claypool. A week later, Groucho makes an appointment with his attorney to sign the trust and trust amendment (and fund it), but the night before his appointment he falls asleep while smoking a cigar and dies from the ensuing fire. Who takes his property? _____

---

## Answers

**48.** At common law, a written agreement that purported to transfer a property interest at time of death was valid only if it qualified as a valid will or as a valid nonprobate transfer. The partnership agreement between Luke and Hans is not a valid will because there is no evidence that there were any witnesses so it cannot be an attested will, and it was typed, so it cannot be a holographic will. While one might try to argue that it qualifies as a joint tenancy, the alternative gift over in each partner's parents shows that the parties did not intend to create a joint tenancy. The agreement is a contract with a payable-on-death clause. At common law, such contracts and clauses were valid will substitutes only if they qualified as a life insurance contract. Because the partnership agreement is not a life insurance agreement, the payment-on-death clause is invalid. Hans' interest in the movie would fall into probate where it would be distributed to Lea pursuant to the terms of his will. Under the modern trend/UPC approach, all contracts with payment-on-death clauses are valid. Here, the court would enforce the partnership agreement and give Hans' interest to Luke as a valid nonprobate transfer.

**49.** The life insurance policy is a valid will substitute. The general rule is that the beneficiary of a life insurance policy can be changed only in accordance with the terms of the life insurance contract. The standard life insurance contract does not permit change of beneficiary by a properly executed will. The attempt to change the beneficiary is an attempt at what has been called a *superwill*. The general rule is that such superwills are not effective to change the beneficiary of a payment-on-death clause. Sharon would still take. The UPC permits superwills where the contract permits the will to change the beneficiary of the payment-on-death clause, but there is no evidence here that the contract permitted Ozzie to change the beneficiary by will.

**50.** Because banks routinely ask people to use the paperwork for a joint tenancy bank account, even if that is not what the parties intended, the courts will take extrinsic evidence to determine the true intent of the parties when a multiple party bank account is created. At common law, the paperwork created a presumption that the depositor intended a joint tenancy account, but if there is extrinsic evidence that the depositor intended a different account (either an agency account or a payment-on-death account), the court will treat the account accordingly. (Some jurisdictions require clear and convincing evidence of an intent other than that indicated by the paperwork.) Here, Pete put Bob's name on the account so that Bob could pay Pete's bills while Pete was gone. Pete intended to create an agency account, not a true joint tenancy. Bob was to have no interest in the account inter vivos or upon Pete's death. The money in the account will fall into Pete's probate estate where it will pass to his heirs.

Under the modern trend/UPC approach, it is presumed that the parties own in proportion to their contributions to the account inter vivos, and upon the death of one of the parties to a multiple party bank account, it is presumed that there is a right of survivorship. The presumption can be overcome only by clear and convincing evidence. Here, arguably there is clear and convincing evidence that Pete intended only an agency account—which has no right of survivorship. Even under the modern trend/UPC approach, the money in the account should fall into Pete's probate estate where it will pass to his heirs.

51. The key characteristic of joint tenancy is the right of survivorship—when one joint tenant dies, his or her interest is extinguished. When one joint tenant dies, nothing "passes" to the surviving joint tenants; rather their shares are merely recalculated to reflect that the deceased joint tenant's share has been extinguished. Executing a will does not sever a joint tenancy. Here, Bubba's will has no effect on the joint tenancy in Malibuacres. When Bubba died, his interest in Malibuacres was extinguished, and Emily owns it outright. Bubba's will passes no interest in Malibuacres.

52. The issue is whether the pour-over clause in the will is valid. There are three possible ways to validate a pour-over clause: UTATA, facts of independent significance, or incorporation by reference. If the jurisdiction has adopted the revised version of UTATA, the will must reference the trust, the terms of the trust must be set forth in a document other than the will, and the trust must be signed. The trust need not be funded inter vivos. Here, the will references the trust, the trust terms are set forth in a deed of trust separate from the will, and Jerry executed the trust, so the pour-over clause can be validated under the revised version of UTATA. Even though the trust was not funded inter vivos, the trust will not be subject to probate court supervision. Elaine takes a life estate in the trust, and upon her death the property will be distributed outright—one-half to George and one-half to Kramer.

If the jurisdiction follows the original (and widely adopted) version of UTATA, the will must reference the trust, the trust terms must be set forth in a document other than the will, and the trust must be signed prior to, or contemporaneously with, the will. Here, the will references the trust, the terms are set forth in a deed of trust separate from the will, but Jerry did not execute the trust instrument until after he executed the will. The pour-over clause cannot be validated under the original version of UTATA. Facts of independent significance will work only if the trust was funded inter vivos. Jerry was on his way to his accountant to transfer some property to the trust when he was hit and killed. No property was transferred to the trust inter vivos, so the pour-over clause cannot be validated under facts of independent significance. Under incorporation by reference, the will must express the intent to incorporate the document, the will must describe the document with reasonable certainty, and the document must be in existence when the will is executed. Here, the pour-over clause expresses the intent to incorporate the trust instrument and describes the trust instrument with reasonable certainty. But the trust instrument was not in existence when the will was executed. The pour-over clause cannot be validated. Because the pour-over clause is the residuary clause of his will, the property will fall to intestacy where it will be distributed to Jerry's heirs.

**53.** The issue is whether the pour-over clause in the will is valid. There are three possible ways to validate a pour-over clause: UTATA, facts of independent significance, or incorporation by reference. Under UTATA, the will must reference the trust, the terms of the trust must be set forth in a document other than the will, and the trust must be signed (the original and widely adopted version of UTATA requires that the trust be signed prior to, or concurrently with, the execution of the will). Here, Groucho never executed the trust. Facts of independent significance will work only if the trust was funded inter vivos. No property was transferred to the trust inter vivos, so the pour-over clause cannot be validated under facts of independent significance. Under incorporation by reference, the will must express the intent to incorporate the document, the will must describe the document with reasonable certainty, and the document must be in existence when the will is executed. Here, the pour-over clause expresses the intent to incorporate the trust instrument and describes the trust instrument with reasonable certainty. The trust instrument was not in existence when the will was executed, but Groucho executed a codicil to the will. Under republication by codicil, the codicil is deemed to reexecute and redate the will to the date of the codicil. By redating the will, the trust instrument was in existence when the codicil was executed. The trust instrument can be incorporated by reference. The amendment to the trust, however, cannot be given effect because it was not in existence when the codicil was executed. The pour-over clause can be given effect under incorporation by reference, the trust will be a testamentary trust subject to probate court supervision, and the beneficiaries under the trust will take the property pursuant to the terms of the trust (but Mrs. Claypool takes nothing.)

---

## Exam Tips *on*
## *NONPROBATE TRANSFERS: WILL SUBSTITUTES*

### Inter vivos gifts

If inter vivos gifts are tested, it is usually: (1) the delivery requirement (and the different approaches to it); and/or (2) the intent to make a present transfer of the property interest (as opposed to a gratuitous promise to make a gift in the future). These two requirements may overlap in some scenarios.

☛ Because gifts causa mortis fit naturally into a time of death scenario, some professors like to test gifts causa mortis rather than inter vivos gifts. Remember that gifts causa mortis differ from typical inter vivos gifts in several respects and focus on those differences.

### Overview to the will substitutes

At the macro level, the key to the nonprobate transfer issues is that if the transfer qualifies as a valid nonprobate transfer, give the property to the intended beneficiary. If the transfer does not qualify as a valid nonprobate transfer, the property falls to probate where it will be distributed pursuant to the testator's will, if one, otherwise via intestacy.

☛ A second potential issue is whether the wills-related construction doctrines (covered in the last chapter) apply to the will substitutes in your jurisdiction. If so, professors often overlap these areas by testing the wills-related rules in a nonprobate setting.

## Contracts with payable-on-death clauses

The principal issue with contracts with payable-on-death clauses is whether your jurisdiction recognizes them as a valid will substitute. The transferor's intent is usually very clear, but if the jurisdiction does not permit them, the transfer fails and the property falls to probate despite the clarity of the transferor's intent.

☞ Watch for a will that makes an express reference to property subject to a valid will substitute, particularly a payable-on-death beneficiary. As a general rule, a will cannot change the beneficiary of a nonprobate instrument, though the UPC permits it for life insurance contracts if the contract expressly permits it.

## Multiple party bank accounts

Start with the presumption (common law vs. modern trend) and then analyze whether there is sufficient evidence of a contrary intent to overcome the presumption.

## True joint tenancies

If you have a joint tenancy issue, state (1) that the key characteristic is the right of survivorship, and (2) that upon the death of one joint tenant his or her interest "is extinguished" and the shares of the surviving joint tenants are recalculated (as opposed to saying that upon the death of one joint tenant his or her interest "passes" to the surviving joint tenants). Thus, a will does not sever a joint tenancy.

## Revocable Deeds

Revocable deeds are rarely tested in their own right. They are easy to spot (you must have a revocable deed) and fairly easy to analyze (the only issue is whether the jurisdiction applies the common law vs. modern trend approach).

## Inter vivos trusts

This material is primarily of historical and theoretical importance. Doctrinally, virtually all jurisdictions recognize inter vivos trusts as valid will substitutes even if the trust is revocable and the settlor is also the trustee and life beneficiary. As long as someone else holds the future interest, the trust is valid.

## Pour-over wills and inter vivos trusts

The pour-over wills material is critical. Not only is it the most common estate planning technique used today, it also overlaps the two major parts of the course—wills and trusts.

☞ Pour-over clauses always constitute an issue—the pour-over clause must be validated. The pour-over will is easy to spot. There must be a clause in the will expressly giving the property in question to the trustee of the testator's trust, to hold and distribute pursuant to the terms of the trust.

☞ If the will goes on to state the terms of the trust, the clause is not a pour-over will but rather the clause is creating a testamentary trust. There is no pour-over issue to analyze.

☞ If the will does not set forth the terms of the trust, the clause constitutes a pour-over clause that must be validated.

☛ In attempting to validate a pour-over clause, lead with UTATA; if that fails, try facts of independent significance; if that fails, try incorporation by reference last; if that fails, the pour-over clause is invalid and that gift fails.

☞ In applying UTATA, the key element typically will be whether the trust instrument was signed. Pay close attention to which version of UTATA your jurisdiction follows.

☞ If the pour-over clause qualifies under UTATA, be sure to include a statement of its benefits: The trust does not have to be funded at all inter vivos, yet for purposes of probate court supervision, it will be treated as an inter vivos trust; and all subsequent amendments to the trust are valid regardless of when they are executed.

☞ In applying facts of independent significance to validate a pour-over clause, the key requirement typically is whether the trust was funded inter vivos. In applying incorporation by reference to validate a pour-over clause, the key requirement typically is whether the trust *instrument* was in existence at the time the will was executed. (The trust instrument need not be signed at that time, nor must the trust be funded inter vivos.)

☛ While UTATA clearly states that a UTATA trust is not subject to probate court supervision, and thus is treated more like an inter vivos trust rather than a testamentary trust for purposes of probate court supervision, that does not necessarily mean that a UTATA will be treated like an inter vivos trust for all doctrines where it makes a difference whether the trust is an inter vivos trust or a testamentary trust.

☞ If a doctrine distinguishes between inter vivos and testamentary trusts, whether a UTATA trust will be treated as an inter vivos trust or a testamentary trust will be a question of first impression where the courts will consider the public policy considerations underlying the doctrine in question. The best way to handle the issue is to start by asking whether the UTATA trust was wholly unfunded until time of death. If so, absent countervailing public policy considerations, the UTATA trust should be treated as a testamentary trust. If the UTATA trust was funded inter vivos and has property in it at time of death, the UTATA trust should be treated as an inter vivos trust, absent countervailing public policy considerations.

## CHAPTER 8

# TRUSTS:
# CREATION, LIFE, AND TERMINATION

## *ChapterScope* ▬▬▬▬▬▬▬▬▬▬▬▬▬▬▬▬▬▬▬▬▬▬▬▬▬▬▬▬▬▬

This chapter examines the key components of an express trust—the requirements for creating a valid express trust; the different types of trusts; the rights of the beneficiaries during the life of a trust; creditors' rights; and how a trust can be modified or terminated prematurely.

- ■ **Express trust requirements:** To have a valid express trust: (1) the settlor must have the intent to create a trust; (2) the trust must be funded; (3) the trust must have ascertainable beneficiaries; and (4) the terms of the trust must be in writing if the trust property includes real property or if the trust is a testamentary trust.

- ■ **Trust life:** Once a trust is validly created, the primary issue during the life of the trust is the extent of the beneficiaries' interest in the trust. The beneficiaries' interest can be either mandatory or discretionary, and it can be in either the principal or the income.

  - ▪ **Mandatory trust:** If the trustee *must* distribute all the income on a regular basis, the trust is a mandatory trust.

  - ▪ **Discretionary trust:** If the trustee has *discretion* over when to distribute the income and/or principal, or how much to distribute, the trust is a discretionary trust. Because of the trustee's fiduciary duties to the beneficiaries, however, the trustee still has a duty to inquire and a duty to act reasonably and in good faith in exercising his or her discretion.

- ■ **Creditors' rights:** A creditor's ability to reach the beneficiary's interest in the trust depends on whether the creditor is a creditor of a beneficiary who is not the settlor or creditor of a beneficiary who is also the settlor.

  - ▪ **Creditors of beneficiary who is not the settlor:** A creditor of a beneficiary steps into the beneficiary's shoes and acquires the same rights the beneficiary had—no more and no less.

  - ▪ **Spendthrift trust:** If the trust includes a spendthrift clause, the general rule is that the beneficiary's creditors cannot reach the beneficiary's interest in the trust.

    - ▪ **Exceptions:** Not all creditors are subject to spendthrift clauses. As a general rule, children entitled to child support, ex-spouses entitled to alimony, creditors who provide basic necessities, and the government, are creditors who are not subject to a spendthrift clause but rather can step into the beneficiary's shoes.

  - ▪ **Creditors of beneficiary who is also the settlor:** It is against public policy to permit a person to shield his or her assets from creditors. Accordingly, creditors of a settlor can reach the settlor's interest in the trust to the full extent that the trustee *could* use the trust for the benefit of the settlor. Moreover, spendthrift trusts in favor of a settlor are null and void.

- ■ **Revocation:** The general rule is that a trust is irrevocable unless the trust expressly provides that it is revocable. If the trust is revocable and it sets forth a particular and exclusive method of

>vocation, that and only that method of revocation will suffice. Otherwise, anything that <br>
>dequately expresses the settlor's intent to revoke will suffice.

**ermination and modification:** A trust ends naturally when all the trust principal is disbursed pursuant to the terms of the trust. Under special circumstances, however, the terms of the trust may be terminated prematurely or modified by court order.

- **Termination:** At common law, under the Claflin doctrine, the courts would order a trust to be terminated prematurely, even if the trustee objected, if (1) all the beneficiaries consented, and (2) there was no unfulfilled material purpose.

- **Modification:** At common law, the courts would order the terms of a trust to be modified if (1) all the beneficiaries consented, and (2) there was an unforeseen change in circumstances that materially frustrated settlor's intent. The trust would be modified to promote the settlor's presumed intent under the circumstances.

# I. INTRODUCTION: CONCEPTUAL OVERVIEW

A. **Introduction:** Most students begin the course with no conceptual understanding of what a trust is or what it does. Without some conceptual understanding, it is difficult to understand the law of trusts. As you cover the material, focus on the conceptual nature of a trust as much as the law of trust.

B. **Terminology:** The law of trust has its own terminology.

- **Settlor:** The party who creates the trust (also known as the trustor).

- **Trustee:** The party to whom the settlor transfers the trust property; the trustee holds legal title to the trust property and manages the property for the duration of the trust.

- **Beneficiaries:** The parties who hold the equitable interest in the trust (typically bifurcated over time); the parties to whom the trustee owes a fiduciary duty.

- **Declaration of trust:** If the settlor is also the trustee, the expression of the intent to create the trust, and the terms of the trust, is called a declaration of trust. (Although the term *declaration of trust* implies the expression is oral, it usually is in writing and must be if the trust holds real property.)

- **Deed of trust:** If someone other than the settlor is the trustee, the expression of the intent to create the trust, and the terms of the trust, is called a deed of trust. (Although the term *deed of trust* implies the expression is written, at common law it could be oral if the trust involved only personal property.)

- **Res/corpus:** The trust property is often referred to as the trust res, or trust corpus, or more modernly, simply the trust property.

- **Inter vivos trust:** An inter vivos trust is a trust created while the settlor is alive. A trust is created when it is funded—when property is transferred to the trust/trustee.

- **Testamentary trust:** If the trust is created when the settlor dies (either in the settlor's will or funded via the settlor's will), it is a testamentary trust.

**C. Trust purpose:** One of the reasons it is so hard for students to conceptualize the prototypical trust is that a trust can serve so many different purposes. A will has but one principal purpose—to dispose of the testator's property upon death. A trust, on the other hand, can serve an endless number of purposes. A trust serves the settlor's intent, whatever that may be. It is the most flexible legal instrument available. Each trust must be read carefully to determine its purpose.

**D. Trust structure:** While there is no prototypical trust purpose, there is a prototypical trust structure, and that structure is what defines the essence of a trust. The prototypical trust structure is that *A* transfers property to *B* for the benefit of *C* (and possibly others). That is a trust. One party (the settlor) transfers property to a second party (the trustee), who holds and manages the property for the benefit of one or more third parties (the beneficiaries).

**E. Bifurcated gift:** A trust is merely another way of making a gift. A gift occurs when a donor transfers property to a donee. A trust is a "bifurcated gift." The gift in trust is bifurcated in that legal title to the property is given to the trustee, while the equitable interest is given to the beneficiary. The equitable interest is the right to use and benefit from the property. The extent of the beneficiary's equitable interest in the property is defined by the terms of the trust, and the terms of the trust are determined by the settlor when he or she sets up the trust.

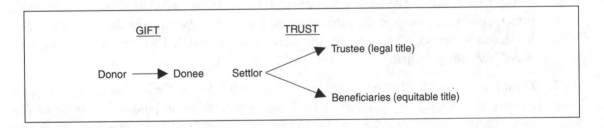

The trustee holds and manages the trust property for the benefit of the trust beneficiaries. Once title is bifurcated between the legal and the equitable interests, the trustee owes the beneficiaries a whole host of fiduciary duties.

**F. Ongoing gift:** The statement that the trustee "holds and manages" the trust property implicitly indicates another difference between the classic gift and a gift in trust. The classic gift is a two-party transaction. The moment the property is given to the donee, the gift is over. It has no "on-going" life. A trust, on the other hand, is a three-party transaction. The statement that the trustee "holds and manages" the trust property implicitly indicates that a trust has an ongoing life after the settlor transfers the property to the trust. The trustee holds and manages the trust property during the life of the trust.

   **1. Bifurcate trust property:** Because the trustee holds and manages the trust property over time, the trust property typically becomes bifurcated between the trust principal (the property the settlor transferred to the trust) and the trust income (the money generated by the trust principal while the trustee is holding and managing the trust). A beneficiary's interest can be in the trust income and/or the trust principal.

   **2. Bifurcate equitable interests:** In addition, at the equitable level, invariably the equitable title is bifurcated over time. The beneficiary who currently holds the right to benefit from the trust right now holds the possessory equitable interest. The party who currently holds the right to benefit from the trust in the future holds the future equitable interest. The simplest bifurcation is a life estate and remainder.

**"Equitable" vs. "legal" possessory estates and future interests:** If someone wants to break up property interests over time, doing so in trust (equitable possessory estates and future interests) is much preferred to doing so by deed (legal possessory estate and future interests). By bifurcating the interests in trust, one party, the trustee, holds legal title to the property in trust and power to manage the property. This greatly facilitates dealing with the property.

G. **Example—gift vs. trust:** Alice gives Betty $1,000. That is a classic inter vivos gift. Betty can do whatever she wants with the gift. On the other hand, if Alice gives Betty $1,000, to use for the benefit of Cindy during her lifetime, and upon her death, any remaining principal is to be given to Deb, that is a classic trust. Betty cannot use the property for her own benefit. She can use the property only for the benefit of Cindy and Alice. Cindy has a life estate interest, and Deb has the remainder interest.

H. **Visualize:** One way to visualize a trust is that it is nothing more than a legal receptacle, a legal "bucket," that holds the trust property during the life of the trust. The settlor creates the bucket by expressing the intent to create a trust. The settlor funds the trust by putting property into the trust, the legal bucket. The trustee holds the bucket, managing the property in the bucket for the benefit of the beneficiaries. The trustee will reach into the bucket and distribute income or disburse principal to one or more of the beneficiaries—pursuant to the terms of the trust (i.e., pursuant to the settlor's intent). Typically the life beneficiary is entitled to the income, the remainder beneficiary the principal.

I. **Trust purposes:** The trust may be the most flexible instrument the law has conceived. A trust can be used for virtually any purpose. A trust can be used to avoid probate; it can be used to hold property for a minor; it can be used for a variety of estate planning/tax purposes; it can be used to try to influence the beneficiaries' behavior; it can be used for an endless variety of purposes. The key is to read each trust carefully to ascertain the particular purpose or purposes of each trust.

J. **Basic trust rules:** There are a few basic rules relating to trusts that are critical to understanding the larger law of trusts.

1. **Same party can wear all three hats:** Although there are three distinct parties to a trust—settlor, trustee, and beneficiary—the same person can wear all three hats at the same time—can be settlor, trustee, and beneficiary at the same time—as long as there is another trustee or another beneficiary.

   **Merger:** If the same party is both trustee and beneficiary, and there is no other trustee or beneficiary, the legal title and the equitable title are said to merge, and the trust is terminated (bifurcation of the legal and equitable titles is essential to a trust). Bifurcation creates a fiduciary duty between the trustee and the beneficiaries. If the same person is both trustee and beneficiary, one cannot hold oneself to a fiduciary duty, so the trust merges and terminates.

2. **A trust is not created until it is funded:** A trust is not created until it is funded. A trust is not funded until property is transferred to the trust/trustee. Funding is distinct from the expression of the intent to create a trust. Where the trustee is a third party (someone other than the settlor), property has to be transferred to the trustee, with the intent that the trustee

hold and manage it for the benefit of someone else. Executing a deed of trust does not constitute funding.

3. **A trust will not fail for want of a trustee:** Where the settlor clearly expresses the intent to create a trust and provides for funding, a trust will not fail for want of a trustee. If the trustee declines to serve (a named trustee is not required to serve but rather must accept the appointment), dies, or is unable to continue, or if the settlor forgot to name a trustee, a court will appoint a successor trustee. (Once a trustee accepts the position, due to the fiduciary duties inherent in the office, the trustee can leave the position only with court approval or the consent of all beneficiaries.)

   **Exception:** If the court concludes that the powers given to the trustee were personal, to be exercised by only that trustee, the court will decline to appoint a successor trustee, and the trust will fail. The courts construe this exception narrowly, however, and rarely apply it.

4. **Cotrustees must agree on action:** If a private trust appoints cotrustees, the general rule is that all the trustees must consent to any proposed action. An individual trustee or subgroup cannot act alone. The trust instrument, however, can provide that the trust can act upon a vote of a majority of the trustees.

   **Uniform Trust Code:** The Uniform Trust Code rejects the common law rule and permits action based on the vote of a majority of the cotrustees.

K. **Remedial trusts:** Remedial trusts arise by operation of law and thus are not subject to the requirements to create a valid trust. They are used as equitable remedies by courts to order one party who is currently holding property to transfer the property to another party whom the court concludes has a stronger equitable claim to the property.

1. **Resulting trust:** A resulting trust arises anytime a trust fails in whole or in part. The courts use it to require the party holding the property (typically the trustee) to return the property to the settlor (or the settlor's estate if the settlor is dead).

2. **Constructive trust:** Constructive trusts are used to prevent unjust enrichment. Historically, the courts required (1) a confidential or fiduciary relationship between the transferor and the transferee, (2) a promise (express or implied) by the transferee, (3) that the transferor transferred property to the transferee in reliance upon the promise, and (4) that the transferee refuses to honor the promise—thereby constituting unjust enrichment. Under the modern trend, the courts tend not to emphasize the elements as much as the equitable notion that the constructive trust is used to prevent unjust enrichment.

# II. REQUIREMENTS TO CREATE A VALID EXPRESS TRUST

A. **Overview:** There are four requirements to create a valid express trust: (1) the settlor must have the intent to create a trust; (2) there must be funding—property transferred to the trust/trustee; (3) the beneficiaries must be ascertainable; and (4) possibly a writing.

**Practical application:** Just as the requirements for a valid inter vivos gift are easy to satisfy, so too are the requirements for the creation of a valid express trust.

**B. Theoretical comparison:** The requirements to create a valid express trust are similar to the requirements to make a gift. In fact, the requirements arguably are the same—only altered slightly to reflect the differences between an outright gift and a gift in trust.

**1. Gift requirements:** To make an outright gift, there must be the intent to make a gift and delivery (acceptance is presumed). At common law, if manual delivery was practical, manual delivery was required. If manual delivery was impractical or impossible, constructive or symbolic delivery was acceptable. (Constructive delivery is delivery of something that gives control over the property being gifted; symbolic delivery is delivery of something that stands for or 'symbolizes' the property.)

**2. Express trust requirements:** The express trust requirements arguably are the same as for a gift, only altered slightly to reflect the inherent nature of a trust.

    **a. Intent:** To make a gift in trust, the settlor must have the intent to make a gift in trust. The only difference in the intent requirement is that the intent must be that the gift be in trust as opposed to outright.

    **b. Delivery:** The second requirement for a gift, delivery, has to be altered to reflect the fact that a gift in trust is a bifurcated gift. As applied to the trust, the delivery requirement is that the property must be delivered to the trustee (funding). Where the property is delivered to the trustee with the intent that the gift be a trust, equitable title is automatically transferred to the beneficiaries by operation of law.

    **c. Ascertainable beneficiaries:** The beneficiaries must be ascertainable so the court knows who has standing to enforce the terms of the trust and the fiduciary duties the trustee owes the beneficiaries.

    **d. Writing:** The final *possible* requirement, writing, is not really a trust requirement. If the trust involves real property, the Statute of Frauds requires that the trust be in writing. If the trust is a testamentary trust, the Wills Act requires that the trust terms be in writing. The writing requirement is no different than it is for an outright inter vivos gift of real property or any other testamentary gift.

**C. Observation:** The doctrinal requirements for a valid trust are rather straightforward. There are, however, a handful of challenging conceptual issues with respect to some of the elements, particularly the first two—intent and funding. Because these issues can be a bit confusing, they tend to distort some students' perception of the material. Trust law is easier to understand if you keep these two elements in perspective.

**D. Intent:** The first requirement for a valid express trust is the intent to create a trust. The intent to create a trust (to make a gift in trust) exists anytime one party transfers property to another party with the intent to vest the beneficial interest in a third party. No technical words are necessary, but if the settlor uses any of the basic trust terms ("in trust" "trustee"), that is presumed indicative of the intent to create a trust.

**1. Fuzzy at the margins:** Because the intent to create a trust is merely a variation on the intent to create a gift, sometimes it is hard to tell the difference between the two. There are two scenarios in particular where it is important to distinguish between the two: (1) precatory trusts; and (2) failed gifts.

2. **Precatory trust:** A precatory trust arises where there is an outright gift from a donor to donee, but the donor includes some language that expresses the *hope*, or the *wish*—but *no legal obligation*—that the property be used for the benefit of another. A precatory trust is not a trust at all, but merely a "gift with a wish." The key is whether the language used in conjunction with the transfer indicates the intent to vest the beneficial interest in the third party (in which case the transfer is a trust) or whether the language expresses merely the *hope or wish* that the recipient of the property uses it for a third party (in which case the transfer is merely a gift, a precatory trust).

   **Example:** In *McKinsey v. Cullingsworth*, 9 S.E.2d 315 (Va. 1940), testatrix's holographic will provided that she left all her property to "Vennor" (Vernon S. Cullingsworth). The will also stated "and you take care of Lula as best you can." Lula claimed that the language adequately expressed the testatrix's intent that Vernon was to take as a trustee, to hold and use the property for the benefit of Lula. The court ruled that the language in question was merely precatory and that Vernon took the property in question. (But in *Levin v. Fisch*, 404 S.W.2d 889 (Tex. Civ. App. 1966), the court ruled that in light of the evidence surrounding the testator at the time she executed her will, the word *desire* as used in the will was a positive directive and imposed a legal obligation.)

3. **Failed gifts:** Where a donor has the intent to make a gratuitous inter vivos gift, but the gift fails for want of delivery (typically the donor will die before making delivery), the donee may try to save the gift by recharacterizing the donor's intent as the intent to create a trust. The donee will argue that when the donor expressed the intent to create a trust, the donor also appointed him- or herself trustee, thereby "delivering" the property from him- or herself as settlor to him- or herself as trustee. Because a trust will not fail for want of a trustee, the donee will then ask the court to appoint a successor trustee and instruct him or her to transfer the property to the donee—thereby satisfying the delivery requirement for the gift, but only by recharacterizing the failed inter vivos gift as an intent to create a trust.

   a. **General rule:** A leading trust authority (1 Austin W. Scott, Trusts §31 (William F. Fratcher, 4th ed. 1987) and the Restatement (Third) of Trusts §16(2) (T.D. No. 1, 1996), along with most courts, reject the argument that an inter vivos gift that fails for want of delivery can be saved by recharacterizing the donor's intent as an intent to declare a trust.

   b. **Reliance:** Where a donee changes his or her position in reliance upon a promised gift such that it would be inequitable not to enforce the gift, a court of equity will compel the donor to complete the gift, not because the incomplete gift is being converted into a declaration of trust, but rather a constructive trust is being imposed on the donor to prevent unjust enrichment. Austin W. Scott, Trusts §31.4 (William F. Fratcher, 4th ed. 1987).

E. **Funding:** The second requirement for a valid trust is that the trust must be funded—some property must be transferred to the trust/trustee. There are two key components to the funding requirements: (1) the act of funding, and (2) what type of property interest will qualify as an adequate property interest for purposes of funding the trust.

   1. **Act of funding:** To fund the trust, the property must be transferred to the trust.

      **Example:** In *Farmers' Loan & Trust Co. v. Winthrop*, 144 N.E. 686 (N.Y. 1924), Helen Bostick executed a deed of trust, with Farmers' Loan and Trust Co. as trustee, funded the trust, and expressly indicated that she reserved the right to deliver additional funds to the trust. When she executed the deed of trust, she was awaiting the transfer of over $2 million in property, a settlement of a matter pending in court. Thereafter, Helen executed a power of attorney authorizing Farmers' Loan and Trust to collect any and all property she may be entitled to when the settlement decree was entered. The decree was entered on March 16, 1920. Stocks worth $856,880 were distributed by hand to her attorney on April 27, 1920, but an additional $1,470,473 in securities was not ready for delivery that day. Helen died that night. The securities were delivered on July 13, 1920. The court ruled that Helen had the intent to gift the securities to the trust. The securities delivered to her attorney before she died were transferred to the trust, but upon her death the power of attorney automatically terminated and no delivery of the remaining securities occurred inter vivos. Those securities passed into her probate estate and were distributed pursuant to her will.

2. **Third party as trustee (transfer in trust or deed of trust):** Where the trustee is someone other than the settlor (the classic trust structure), funding is rather easy conceptually and practically. Some property must be transferred to the trust/trustee (or a written deed of trust must be transferred to the trustee and it must list the property subject to the trust that is being transferred with the deed of trust).

3. **Settlor as trustee (declaration of trust):** Where the settlor is the trustee, funding the trust arguably requires the settlor to "transfer" property from him- or herself as settlor to him- or herself as trustee. But some courts have held that it is impossible for a settlor to transfer property to him- or herself, reasoning instead that the settlor-trustee retain legal title (not as settlor but rather as trustee), but the settlor must transfer equitable title to a beneficiary. What is necessary to properly transfer the equitable interest to a beneficiary depends on the type of property being transferred to the trust.

   a. **Personal property:** If the property being transferred to the trust is personal property, and the settlor is the trustee, the declaration of trust often will be deemed to simultaneously transfer the equitable interest to the beneficiary as long as the declaration of trust adequately refers to the property. No writing is required to either create the trust or to transfer the equitable interest.

   b. **Overlap with intent:** Where (1) the trustee is the settlor, and (2) the funding and the trust property is personal property, the overlap between the intent to create a trust requirement and the funding requirement increases the potential for questionable claims of declarations of trust and funding, especially where a donor/settlor has died and a frustrated beneficiary is looking for a way to get his or her gift. The courts tend to heighten the threshold of evidence necessary for each requirement. With respect to the funding requirement, the courts tend to require the claimed "declaration of trust" to identify expressly the property subject to the trust and/or the courts look for evidence that the claimed settlor separated the "trust" property from the rest of his or her other property (one of the trustee's duties is to segregate the trust property from the rest of the trustee's property).

   c. **Example:** In *Taliaferro v. Taliaferro*, 921 P.2d 803 (Kan. 1996), Will C. Taliaferro executed a revocable inter vivos trust instrument that appointed himself trustee and granted himself a life estate interest. The trust expressly provided that the trustee accepted and held in trust all the personal property described in schedule A (certain bank stock, an insurance policy, and his tangible personal property). The trial court ruled that although the settlor clearly expressed his intent to create a trust and clearly identified the property to be used to fund the trust, there was no evidence that the property in question was transferred to the trust, and thus the trust was invalid. The Kansas Supreme Court ruled that a court of equity will consider a declaration of trust as equivalent to an actual transfer of legal interest. As long as the settlor adequately expresses the present intent to transfer an equitable interest to a beneficiary via a declaration of trust, there is no need to prove a transfer of legal title. The court held that the equitable interest was adequately transferred upon execution of the declaration of trust.

    **d. Real property:** If the property being transferred to the trust is real property, and the settlor is the trustee, the declaration of trust must be in writing, and there must be a writing that satisfies the Statute of Frauds to transfer the real property in question to the trust (though the writing does not have to be recorded).

**4. Adequate property interest:** Funding requires that some property interest must be transferred to the trustee. Virtually anything one thinks of as a property interest will qualify: real property, personal property, money (even as little as a dollar or a penny), leasehold interests, possessory estates, future interests (even contingent remainders), life insurance policies, etc. There are two interests, however, that as a general rule the courts have held do not constitute an adequate property interest for purposes of holding that the trust has been funded: expectancies and future profits.

    **a. Future profits:** Although the courts are in agreement that for purposes of funding a trust, future profits *do not* constitute an adequate property interest, a number of courts have held that for purposes of making an inter vivos gift, future profits *do* constitute an adequate property interest.

    **b. Trusts:** In *Brainard v. Comm'r*, 91 F.2d 880 (7th Cir. 1937), in December 1927, the taxpayer orally declared, in the presence of his wife and mother, a trust of his stock trading during 1928 for the benefit of his family. Taxpayer agreed to assume personally any losses, but any profits were to be distributed to his family members after paying himself reasonable compensation for his services. There was no evidence that taxpayer owned any stock at the time he declared the alleged trust, and he had no property interest at that time in any possible future profits. The court held that the declaration constituted nothing more than a gratuitous undertaking to create a trust in the future when the property was realized and was coupled with the intent to create a trust. There being no validly created trust in December 1927, when the profits were realized in 1928 they were taxable to the taxpayer as his property before being transferred to the trust.

    **c. Realized profits:** Although future profits are not an adequate property interest to create a trust, once the profits are realized, if the party still has the intent to hold them in trust, the moment the profits are realized they will be deemed transferred to the trust and will be sufficient to fund and create the trust at that moment.

    **d. Grantor trusts—taxation:** In *Brainard,* the taxpayer was trying to avoid taxes by shifting the income generated by his stock trading from himself, as settlor, to the income beneficiaries, who were in lower tax brackets. Such tax avoidance is no longer available. Where the settlor/grantor retains sufficient dominion and control over the trust, under what are known as the "Clifford regulations," the trust is known as a grantor trust and the settlor is deemed owner of the income generated by the trust for tax purposes.

**F. Ascertainable beneficiaries:** The third requirement for a valid trust is that there must be ascertainable beneficiaries. The moment a settlor intends to create a trust and transfers property to the trustee, the equitable interest is transferred to trust beneficiaries automatically, by operation of law. The trustee needs to know to whom he or she owes a fiduciary duty; the courts need to know who has standing to enforce the terms of the trust and the fiduciary duty. Thus the requirement that the beneficiaries must be ascertainable.

**1. Unborn children exception:** Trusts created in favor of the settlor's unborn children are upheld despite the fact that the settlor's unborn children are not ascertainable when the trust is created. The public policy justification is to encourage settlors to create such trusts. The courts will monitor the trustee's actions until the children are born to ensure that he or she is properly performing his or her fiduciary duties.

**2. Charitable trusts exception:** The requirement that trust beneficiaries have to be ascertainable applies to private trusts, not to charitable trusts (this is covered in greater detail in Ch. 9, I.D).

**3. Ascertainable:** Ascertainable means that you must be able to *identify the beneficiaries by name*. If their names are not expressly set forth in the trust, the trust must contain a formula or description of the beneficiaries that permits the court to determine who they are by *objective* means. The trust may grant the trustee discretion in selecting the beneficiary as long as there is an ascertainable standard to which the trustee can be held accountable by a court taking extrinsic evidence.

   **a. Example:** In *Moss v. Axford*, 224 N.W. 425 (Mich. 1929), testatrix's residuary clause gave her property to Henry Axford "with the instructions to pay the same to the person who has given me the best care in my declining years and who in his sole opinion is the most worthy of my said property." The court ruled that the language in question was mandatory and declared Mr. Axford to be a trustee. The court also ruled that although the will did not name the beneficiary, the requirement that the property be given to "the person who has given me the best care in my declining years" was sufficiently clear to enable the court by extrinsic evidence to identify the beneficiary. The court upheld the devise in trust to Mary Piers, the person the trustee designated, because Mary cared for the testatrix from the time she executed the will until she died. (But in *Morice v. The Bishop of Durham*, 32 Eng. Rep. 947 (Chancery 1805), testatrix left the residue of her personal estate to the Bishop of Durham, upon trust, to distribute the same to such objects of benevolence and liberality as the Bishop, in his discretion, shall approve. The Bishop admitted he took no beneficial interest. The court ruled that the gift did not qualify as a charitable trust, and as a private trust it failed for want of ascertainable beneficiaries. The property passed into intestacy.)

      **i. Power of appointment:** Powers of appointments are covered in Chapter 10, but three key differences are that (1) with a power of appointment, the holder owes no fiduciary duty to the possible appointees; (2) exercise of the power is purely discretionary; and (3) the possible appointees of a power do not have to be ascertainable. All that is necessary under a power is that the person to whom any property is distributed has to reasonably meet the description set forth in the power. If it is unclear whether the testator intended a power of appointment or a trust, some courts will construe the language to constitute a power of appointment in the interest of furthering the decedent's intent.

   **ii. Transform failed trust into power:** Professor Scott, one of the top scholars on the law of trusts, argued that anytime a trust in favor of a class that was not ascertainable failed, the trust should automatically be transformed into a power of appointment. The Restatement (Second) and (Third) of Trusts have adopted Scott's argument, but only a handful of courts have adopted the rule.

**b. Familial terms:** Courts routinely hold that familial terms such as children, issue, nephews, and nieces are objectively ascertainable. Some courts have even held the terms relatives and relations as referring to one's heirs under the state's descent and distribution scheme and thus as objectively determinable.

4. **Honorary trusts:** Trusts for the benefits of a pet, or trusts to maintain one's gravesites, while honorable, technically fail for want of ascertainable beneficiaries. One of the principal purposes for the ascertainable beneficiaries requirement is to determine who has standing to come into court and hold the trustee accountable. Neither a pet nor a gravesite has standing to come into court and sue a trustee. If the beneficiary of a trust is not an ascertainable person, the trust fails for want of ascertainable beneficiaries. But the trust may be saved as an honorary trust.

   **a. Rule statement:** Where the purpose of a trust is such that it is impossible to have ascertainable beneficiaries, so that the trust should fail for want of ascertainable beneficiaries, if the purpose is specific and honorable, and not capricious or illegal, the trust may continue as long as the "trustee" is willing to honor the terms of the "honorary trust." If the trustee stops honoring the terms of the honorary trust, he or she will not be permitted to keep the property. A resulting trust will be imposed and the property will be ordered distributed to the proper takers.

   **b. Rationale:** While honorary trusts technically fail to meet the requirements for a valid trust, the courts decided to permit such trusts because of the honorable purpose of the trust (to care for one's pets, to maintain one's gravesite), but only as long as the party designated as the "trustee" was willing to "honor" the terms of the trust, even though there is no beneficiary to enforce the terms of the trust.

   **c. Example:** In *In re Thompson*, Eng. Rep. 805 (Ch. 1933), testator bequeathed money to his friend George Lloyd to be used by him for the promotion and furtherance of fox-hunting. Although the court found that the trust did not qualify as a charitable trust, and although the trust lacked ascertainable beneficiaries, the court upheld the trust as an honorary trust.

   **d. Rule against Perpetuities:** One problem with honorary trusts is that in theory such trusts intrinsically violate the Rule against Perpetuities (covered in Chapter 11). If the administration of the trust can continue for longer than the maximum period allowed under the Rule against Perpetuities, the trust is invalid *from the moment of its attempted creation*. Under the traditional application of the Rule against Perpetuities, most honorary trusts would be invalid.

   **Modern trend:** There are a variety of modern trend approaches to the Rule against Perpetuities that soften the impact of the rule. Under the "wait-and-see" approach, the rule is not tested in the abstract, but rather the courts actually let the time period run and wait and see if the administration of the trust actually continues for longer than the maximum period allowed under the Rule against Perpetuities. Under the wait-and-see approach, the honorary trust is allowed to continue for at least 21 years.

**e. Honorary vs. charitable:** Charitable trusts are not subject to the Rule against Perpetuities; so if the honorary trust qualifies as a charitable trust, favor the latter characterization. But charitable trusts have to be for the good of the community at large, or a large subset thereof, and most honorary trusts are for the benefit of a *particular* pet or gravesite. As such, most honorary trusts will not qualify as charitable trusts, but one should always check.

**G. Writing:** The fourth and final *possible* requirement for a valid trust is that it must be in writing. Under the common law approach, whether a trust must be in writing is not a function of the law of trusts per se, but rather a function of the Statute of Frauds and the Wills Act formalities. Absent state statutes expressly requiring all trusts to be in writing (which some states have adopted), whether a trust has to be in writing to be valid is a function of (1) whether the trust is an inter vivos trust or a testamentary trust; and (2) what type of property the trust holds.

**1. Inter vivos trusts:** As a general rule, inter vivos trusts do not have to be in writing unless the trust holds real property. If the trust is to hold real property, under the Statute of Frauds, the declaration of trust or deed of trust must be in writing.

**a. Common law:** The common law strictly applied the Statute of Frauds regardless of the consequences. Under the Statute of Frauds, the terms of an *oral trust involving real property* cannot be enforced against the transferee because oral conditions are not permitted to vary the terms of a deed.

**Example:** Assume *A* conveys real property to *B*, for the benefit of *C*, but (1) the agreement between *A* and *B* that the property is for the benefit of *C* is oral, and (2) the deed from *A* to *B* makes no reference to the agreement. Under the Statute of Frauds, evidence of the oral understanding between *A* and *B* is not admissible to alter the deed. Without the evidence, *B* will own the property outright—not as a trustee, but as a donee, free and clear of any trust. As applied to oral attempts to create inter vivos trusts of land, the common law approach was harsh.

In ***Fairchild v. Rasdall***, 9 Wis. 350 (1859), the plaintiffs alleged that the decedent, desiring to arrange his affairs so he could leave the country after dangerously wounding another man and fearing arrest, conveyed his real property to his brother in a deed absolute on its face; but plaintiffs also alleged that the brother orally agreed to hold the property in trust for the use and benefit of the deceased and his heirs. The court stated that it was convinced that the conveyance was made by the decedent under the circumstances alleged, but it ruled that pursuant to the Statute of Frauds, the evidence of the oral agreement was inadmissible. The court ordered the complaint dismissed, but it expressed the hope that the brother, as a matter of conscience, would reconvey the property to the deceased's family.

**b. Modern trend:** The modern trend (adopted by the Restatement (Third) of Trusts §24) finds the common law outcome constitutes unjust enrichment of the intended trustee and corrects the situation by imposing a constructive trust and ordering the purported trustee to distribute the real property to the intended beneficiaries—not in trust, but outright. (Often the settlor is the intended beneficiary, so the constructive trust ends up looking much like a resulting trust.)

**c. Equitable basis:** Although one could argue that the modern trend should be imposed anytime an oral inter vivos trust of real property fails for want of writing, the courts have shown a greater willingness to impose the constructive trust where there is some additional equitable basis for imposing the constructive trust. In particular, if the purported trustee has procured the transfer as a result of fraud or undue influence, or if the purported trustee stood in a confidential relationship with the transferor, or if the transfer was made with an eye toward the transferor's impending death, the courts will impose a constructive trust.

**d. Remedial trusts:** The Statute of Frauds does not apply to the remedial trusts (constructive trust or resulting trust) because they are not true trusts in the full sense of the words but rather are judicial, remedial trusts that arise by operation of law. Under the remedial trusts, the original trust is not upheld and enforced; the purported trustee is simply ordered to transfer the real property in question immediately to the appropriate party or parties.

**Example:** In *Sullivan v. Rooney*, 533 N.E.2d 1372 (Mass. 1989), the plaintiff and defendant had a thirteen or fourteen-year relationship, for seven of which they lived together in a house they had purchased. Each thought of the purchase as a joint transaction that would belong to both of them, but on the way to the Registry of Deeds, the defendant informed the plaintiff that for them to qualify for Veterans' Administration financing, he would have to take title in his name alone. The deed was executed and recorded in his name alone. Both parties contributed to the expenses of the home (he the mortgage, taxes, utilities, and insurance; she the food, household supplies, and much of the furniture). The defendant repeatedly promised to put the house in joint ownership, but he never did. The court found that the defendant would be unjustly enriched if he were permitted to retain sole ownership of the house upon the dissolution of the relationship. The court imposed a constructive trust on one-half of the property for the benefit of the plaintiff based on the fiduciary relationship between the parties and the defendant's breach of his duty.

**e. Unclean hands:** Constructive trusts are an equitable remedy. Equity regards as done that which ought to be done. If the settlor created the oral trust for real property for improper reasons (the settlor was trying to hide his or her assets from creditors or from an impending divorce, etc.), even under the modern trend the courts generally will not come to the aid of one who has "unclean hands." The purported trustee will be permitted to keep the real property free of any trust.

**f. Recent statutory developments:** Florida and New York have recently enacted statutes requiring trusts with "testamentary aspects" to be enacted with Will Act formalities, whether the trust holds personal and/or real property.

2. **Testamentary trusts:** Testamentary trusts, which typically are created in a testator's will, must be in writing pursuant to the Wills Act formalities. Where a testamentary trust fails for want of a writing, the issue is whether the relief should be a constructive trust or a resulting trust. The answer turns on whether the failed testamentary trust is deemed a secret trust or a semi-secret trust.

   a. **Secret trust:** A secret trust is a testamentary trust that fails because the terms of the trust are not set forth in the will. On the face of the will, the secret trust looks like an outright gift to a devisee. It is a "secret" trust because there is nothing on the face of the will that indicates that the testator intended the devisee to take the property as a trustee, not as a devisee, with the beneficial interest in some third party. Inasmuch as the courts have to admit extrinsic evidence to determine that the devisee was supposed to take as a trustee, the courts use the extrinsic evidence to impose a constructive trust on the devisee, ordering the devisee to transfer the property to the intended beneficiaries.

**b. Semi-secret trust:**  A semi-secret trust is a testamentary trust that fails because the terms of the trust are not set forth in the will. It is a "semi-secret" trust because there is something in the express language of the will that indicates, or at least hints at, the fact that the devisee was not intended to take the property for his or her own benefit. The courts do not need extrinsic evidence to realize that the devisee is not to take the beneficial interest, so the courts will not *take any* extrinsic evidence to identify the intended beneficiaries. The gift to the devisee as trustee fails. The courts impose a resulting trust and give the property back to the settlor/testator. Typically the property then falls to the residuary clause, or if the failed testamentary trust was the residuary clause, to intestacy.

**c. Modern trend:**  The modern trend, as reflected in the Restatement (Second) and (Third) of Trusts, §§55 and 18, respectively, takes the position that a constructive trust in favor of the intended beneficiaries should be imposed in both the secret and semi-secret trust situation. The majority of the courts, however, still follow the old common law distinction, imposing a constructive trust on secret trusts and a failed gift/resulting trust analysis on semi-secret trusts.

# III.  LIFE OF TRUST: EXTENT OF BENEFICIARIES' INTERESTS

**A. Introduction:**  Once a trust has been validly created, there is one principal issue during the life of the trust—what is the extent of each beneficiary's interest in the trust. When analyzing the beneficiaries' interests in the trust, the trust property has to be bifurcated between the income and the principal (the latter being the property transferred to the trust, and the former being the money the principal generates). In assessing each beneficiary's interest in the income and/or the principal, the beneficiary's interest can be either mandatory or discretionary. Once a trust has been validly created, it is critical that each beneficiary's interest be analyzed.

**B. Mandatory trust:**  A mandatory trust is one where the beneficiary's interest in the income is mandatory—the trustee must distribute the income to the beneficiary (typically according to a fixed schedule set forth in the express terms of the trust).

**Overview:**  Mandatory trusts, and mandatory interests, cause relatively few problems because either the trustee performs pursuant to the mandatory terms of the trust or the trustee does not. In contrast, discretionary trusts are full of "soft" doctrines that lend themselves to litigation over interpretation and application.

**C. Discretionary trust:**  A discretionary trust is one where the beneficiary's interest in the income and/or principal is discretionary—the beneficiary has no right to receive payments of income and/or principal. Any such payments are at the discretion of the trustee (typically according to some standard set forth in the express terms of the trust).

**1. Introduction:**  At first blush, it seems somewhat incompatible to say that a beneficiary has an equitable interest in a trust, that the trustee owes the beneficiary a fiduciary duty, and at the same time to describe the beneficiary's interest as merely a discretionary interest. The courts have been very careful to articulate the scope of a discretionary interest to ensure that a beneficiary has more than a mere expectancy.

2. **Duty to decide:** Where a beneficiary's interest in a trust is discretionary, it is, to a certain degree, at the mercy of the trustee. But the trustee must exercise his or her discretion pursuant to the terms of the trust, even if that decision is not to make a payment to the beneficiary. In assessing the trustee's decision-making process, the courts have kept in mind the fiduciary duty that the trustee owes the beneficiary.

3. **Duty to inquire:** Consistent with the fiduciary duty the trustee owes the beneficiary, before the trustee can exercise his or her discretion with respect to whether to make a payment to the beneficiary, the trustee has a duty to inquire as to the beneficiary's status and needs. If the trustee fails to inquire, the trustee will be deemed to have breached his or her fiduciary duty to the beneficiary.

   **Scope of duty:** In defining and apply the duty to inquire, the courts are guided by the fact that the trustee owes the beneficiary a fiduciary duty to do all that he or she does in the beneficiary's best interests. Under the duty of inquiry, the trustee must exercise due diligence in attempting to gather the relevant information, and where the initial attempts are unsuccessful or incomplete, the trustee has a duty to follow up. Where the trustee fails to do so, it is relatively easy for the courts to find that the trustee has failed to properly exercise his or her discretionary power.

4. **Scope of discretion:** After having gathered all the appropriate information about the beneficiary, in deciding whether to make a payment, the trustee has a duty to act reasonably and in good faith.

   a. **Duty to act reasonably:** The duty to act reasonably is an objective standard—to act as a reasonable trustee would act. The duty to act reasonably requirement permits a fair degree of judicial oversight of a trustee's discretionary decisions.

   b. **Duty to act in good faith:** The duty to act in good faith is a subjective standard. The trustee acts in good faith as long as he or she honestly thought that he or she was acting in the best interests of the beneficiaries and the trust in making his or her decision.

5. **Absolute discretion:** The trustee's duty to act reasonably and in good faith in making a discretionary decision is a default standard. A settlor may modify the duty by express language in the trust instrument. It is not uncommon for the trust to authorize the trustee to act in his or her "sole discretion," or "sole and absolute discretion." The courts have construed such language as not granting truly absolute and uncontrolled discretion, for if such were the case, there would be nothing left of the trustee's fiduciary duty; and without a fiduciary duty, there would be no trust, just a precatory trust. Instead, the courts have construed such language as virtually eliminating the duty to act reasonably, but the trustee still must act in good faith.

6. **Settlor's purpose:** A settlor also can, and often does, provide a purpose or standard that the trustee must keep in mind when exercising his or her discretion. The standard must be set forth in the express terms of the trust. Each clause granting a beneficiary a discretionary interest must be read carefully to see if there is a statement of a standard, or purpose, that the trustee is to keep in mind when making his or her decision. Such standards, if present, are given great weight when considering whether the trustee properly exercised his or her discretion.

**Comfortable support and maintenance:** One of the most common standards that settlors include in their discretionary trusts is that the trustee has the discretion to make whatever payments he or she deems advisable for the beneficiary's "comfortable support and maintenance." The phrase "comfortable support and maintenance" has become a term of art expressing the intent that the beneficiary is to be kept at the standard of living that he or she was accustomed to at the time that he or she became a beneficiary of the trust.

7. **Beneficiary's resources:** Whether a trustee is to consider a beneficiary's other resources in deciding whether to make a payment to the beneficiary is a question of settlor's intent. In essence the issue is whether the settlor intended to provide a floor level of income for the beneficiary regardless of the beneficiary's other resources or whether the settlor intended to provide a safety net only in the event the beneficiary's other resources were inadequate. Where the settlor's intent is not clear, most courts hold that the presumption is that the settlor intended to provide for the beneficiary regardless of the beneficiary's other resources—i.e., the trustee is *not* to take into consideration a beneficiary's other resources absent the trust expressly authorizing it.

8. **Example:** In *Marsman v. Nasca*, 573 N.E.2d 1025 (Mass. App. 1991), Sara created a testamentary trust that provided that the trustees were to pay the income to her husband (Cappy) at least quarterly, and "after having considered the various available sources of support for him, my trustees shall, if they deem it necessary or desirable . . . , in their sole and uncontrolled discretion, pay over to him, . . . such amount or amounts of the principal thereof as they deem advisable for his comfortable support and maintenance." During Sara's lifetime, Sara and Cappy lived well. Following Sara's death, Cappy lost his employment and his standard of living fell substantially. When Cappy brought his plight to the trustee's attention, the trustee gave Cappy a minimal distribution of principal ($300) and asked Cappy to explain in writing the need for the principal. Cappy failed to reply, and the trustee failed to follow up. The court ruled that the trustee had breached his duty to inquire into Cappy's situation, and that the trustee had breached his or her discretion in not disbursing more principal to Cappy. Despite the broad discretion in the trust, the court found that Cappy's standard of living had been reduced substantially and, in light of the settlor's intent that the principal was to be used to maintain Cappy's comfortable support and maintenance, the trustee had breached the duty to distribute principal under the trust.

9. **Exculpatory clauses:** Discretionary trusts often include an exculpatory clause protecting the trustee against liability for breach of trust absent "willful neglect" or the like. Such clauses are like no contest clauses in that they are double-edged swords: they can deter frivolous lawsuits by frustrated beneficiaries who do not like a trustee's decision under a discretionary trust; but they can also reduce a trustee's incentive to pay attention to a beneficiary. Such exculpatory clauses are generally upheld, but the courts construe them narrowly. If a court concludes that an exculpatory clause was put in the trust because of the trustee's overreaching or abuse of fiduciary or confidential relationship, the clause will be deemed null and void. Such clauses are also unenforceable if the court concludes that the breach of trust was committed intentionally, in bad faith, or in reckless disregard for the beneficiary's interest. (New York voids exculpatory clauses granting immunity to trustees for failure to exercise reasonable care as against public policy.)

**Example:** In *Marsman v. Nasca*, above, the trustee inserted an exculpatory clause into the trust protecting the trustee absent "willful neglect or default." The trustee testified that he discussed the clause with the settlor during the drafting process, and the settlor approved the clause. Although the trustee drafted the trust and suggested the clause, the court ruled that was insufficient to render the clause null and void. While the trustee's conduct concerning Cappy constituted a breach of duty, the court implicitly found that the breach was not intentional, in bad faith, or in reckless disregard for the beneficiary's interest.

**D. Support trust:** A support trust is a trust that requires the trustee to pay as much income (and, if expressly provided in the trust, principal as well) as necessary for the beneficiary's support.

1. **Creation:** The key to classifying a trust as a support trust is the formula that controls how much the trustee can distribute to the beneficiary, not the use of the word *support* per se. Where the payment is limited to the amount necessary for the beneficiary's support (or "support and education" or "maintenance"), the trust qualifies as a support trust. If the trustee is required to distribute all the income to the beneficiary for his or her support, the trust is not a support trust because the amount to be paid is not limited to the amount necessary for the beneficiary's support.

2. **Mandatory:** A support trust is a form of a mandatory trust. The trustee is required to distribute as much income as necessary for the support of the beneficiary.

**E. Sprinkle/spray trust:** A sprinkle or spray trust requires the trustee to distribute the property in question, but the payment is to be made to a group of individuals and the trustee has discretion as to whom to make the payments and how much each is to receive. The trustee has the power to "sprinkle" or "spray" the property among the eligible beneficiaries. Sprinkle/spray trusts are something of a hybrid. From the beneficiaries' perspective, the trust is discretionary—no beneficiary has a right to receive any of the property. From the trustee's perspective, the trust is mandatory—the trustee must distribute the property, but as to whom and how much, the trust is discretionary.

**F. Unitrust:** Under a unitrust, a life beneficiary is given a fixed annual percentage interest in the total worth of the trust, regardless of whether the property needed to satisfy that fixed interest comes from the income or the principal. The trustee is then free to pursue any investment that he or she thinks will produce the greatest benefit for the trust, regardless of the amount of income the investment produces, because the trustee has the power to disburse not only income but principal to the life beneficiary to satisfy the life beneficiary's fixed annual percentage interest in the unitrust.

**G. Perpetual dynasty trust:** An increasing number of jurisdictions are abolishing the Rule against Perpetuities. This permits trusts to last forever. Where a settlor takes advantage of this and creates a trust that will last forever for the benefit of one's issue, the trust is typically called a perpetual dynasty trust. The standard distributive provisions of such trusts grant the trustee discretionary powers over both the income and the principal, thus granting the trustee the flexibility to manage the trust to permit the corpus to remain intact, if not grow, while creating a stream of income for settlor's descendants.

# IV. LIFE OF TRUST: CREDITORS' RIGHTS/SPENDTHRIFT CLAUSES

**A. Introduction:** A creditor's ability to reach a beneficiary's interest in a trust depends first on whether the beneficiary is the settlor or someone other than the settlor. As a general rule, it is against public policy to use a trust to try to shield one's assets from one's creditors. Creditors of a beneficiary who is also the settlor have a greater ability to reach that beneficiary's interest in the trust than a creditor would if the beneficiary is not the settlor. When the material refers to a beneficiary, assume the norm, that the beneficiary is not the settlor, unless the material expressly provides otherwise.

**B. Creditors' rights generally:** As a general rule, a creditor can reach a debtor's property as long as the property interest in question is transferable. As applied to trusts, absent special provisions in the trust, generally a beneficiary's interest is freely transferable, whether the beneficiary's interest is discretionary or mandatory.

**C. Scope of creditors' rights:** In light of the fact that a beneficiary's interest in a trust is freely transferable, creditors of a beneficiary can reach the beneficiary's interest in the trust. For all practical purposes, the creditor steps into the shoes of the beneficiary and receives whatever interest the beneficiary has in the trust—no more and no less.

1. **Mandatory trust:** If the trust is a mandatory trust, the creditor can force the trustee to distribute the income to the creditor pursuant to the terms of the trust just as the beneficiary could have. The trustee must distribute the income to the creditor.

2. **Discretionary trust:** If the trust is a discretionary trust, just as the beneficiary could not force a trustee to distribute property to the beneficiary (absent a showing of abuse of discretion), nor can a creditor of a beneficiary of a discretionary trust force a trustee to distribute property (absent a showing of abuse of discretion as applied to the beneficiary in question, not the creditor).

   a. **Example:** In *United States v. O'Shaughnessy*, 517 N.W.2d 574 (Minn. 1994), Lawrence P. O'Shaughnessy was beneficiary of two trusts established by his grandfather. The trusts provided that the trustees "*may pay*" principal or income to Lawrence as they saw fit during his lifetime. The United States government served a notice of levy against the trustees, claiming that Lawrence's interest in the trust constituted a property interest that the government, as a creditor, was entitled to reach to satisfy a federal income tax deficiency against Lawrence. The court ruled that where a beneficiary's interest in a trust is merely discretionary, neither the beneficiary nor a creditor of the beneficiary has the right to force the trustee to make any payments to him or her.

   b. **Court order:** In some jurisdictions, a creditor of a beneficiary of a discretionary interest can get a court order directing that if and when the trustee decides to exercise his or her discretion in favor of making a payment to the beneficiary, the trustee must make the payment to the creditor. Some settlors avoid such provisions by an express clause in the trust permitting the trustee to make payments directly to any third parties that provide support to the beneficiary. Such language permits the trustee to choose which creditors will receive any payments the trustee decides to make—current creditors or past creditors. The courts are split on the validity of such provisions, though the more recent cases tend to hold payments to third parties subject to the creditors' claims.

   c. **Example:** In *Wilcox v. Gentry*, 867 P.2d 281 (Kan. 1994), Ron and Nancy Wilcox obtained a judgment against Isabell Gentry for $40,000 actual damages and $11,667 punitive damages. Isabell was the beneficiary of a discretionary trust that had no spendthrift clause. The trust authorized the trustee to make payment either to Isabell or on her behalf to third parties. Ron and Nancy garnished the trust seeking satisfaction of their judgment. The trial court held that payments made directly to Isabell were subject to the garnishment, but not payments made on her behalf to third parties. On appeal, the Kansas Supreme Court ruled that once the trustee has been served by the creditor, any payments are subject to the creditor's claims whether the payments are made directly to the beneficiary or on the beneficiary's behalf to a third party.

**D. Spendthrift clauses:** A settlor can modify a beneficiary's ability to transfer his or her interest by including what is known as a spendthrift clause in the trust that expressly restricts the beneficiary's power to transfer his or her interest. A standard spendthrift clause will bar a beneficiary's ability to transfer his or her interest voluntarily (by sale or gift) or involuntarily (creditors reaching). (In New York, a beneficiary's interest is presumed nontransferable unless the trust expressly provides otherwise.)

**1. Voluntary transfers:** A spendthrift clause does not have to restrict both voluntary and involuntary transfers by a beneficiary. A spendthrift clause that bars only voluntary transfers by a beneficiary but leaves open involuntary transfers, thereby permitting a beneficiary's creditors to reach the property, is permitted.

**2. Involuntary transfers:** A spendthrift clause that bars only involuntary transfers by a beneficiary, but leaves open voluntary transfers, is deemed against public policy and is null and void. If the beneficiary has the benefit of the right to transfer his or her interest voluntarily, the beneficiary must also have the risk of creditors having the right to involuntarily reach the beneficiary's interest.

**E. Validity:** There is an ongoing debate over both the validity of spendthrift clauses and the scope of spendthrift clauses.

**1. Arguments against:** It is unfair to permit one to enjoy the benefits of being a beneficiary without permitting creditors of that beneficiary to reach that property. Moreover, because the rich are much more likely to use trusts than are the poor, permitting spendthrift clauses in trusts unfairly favors the rich over the poor.

**2. Arguments in support:** The property in trust is not really the beneficiary's property. The beneficiary has no legal interest in the property, only an equitable interest. The scope of a beneficiary's interest in a trust is purely a question of the settlor's intent, and there is no reason why a settlor should not be permitted to limit a beneficiary's interest by barring the beneficiary's ability to transfer his or her interest. A creditor can still reach the beneficiary's interest once the property has been distributed to the beneficiary, the creditor just cannot reach the property while it is still in the trust.

**3. General rule:** The general rule is that spendthrift clauses are valid and enforceable, even as applied to remainder interests in trust.

**F. Exceptions:** Although spendthrift clauses are generally valid, most jurisdictions have either statutorily or judicially adopted doctrines that limit their application and effect.

**1. Judicial exceptions:** In many jurisdictions, for public policy reasons, courts have held that certain categories of creditors are not subject to spendthrift clauses: (1) ex-spouses entitled to spousal support (alimony); (2) children entitled to child support; (3) creditors who provide basic necessities; and (4) tax claims by the state or federal government. In essence, these creditors can pierce the spendthrift clause and reach the beneficiary's interest in the trust.

   a. **Example:** In *Bacardi v. White*, 463 So. 2d 218 (Fla. 1985), Luis and Andriana Bacardi divorced, and Luis agreed to pay monthly alimony of $2,000. Shortly after the divorce was final, Luis stopped paying. Andriana obtained two judgments: $14,000 for unpaid alimony and $1,000 for incidental attorney's fees. She served a writ of garnishment on the trustee of a spendthrift trust created by Luis' father for Luis' benefit. The trustee invoked the spendthrift clause. The court ruled that the public policy requiring a former spouse to pay alimony or child support outweighed the public policy in favor of spendthrift clauses. The court limited its ruling, however, stating that garnishment of the trust interest should be a last resort, and its holding applied only to mandatory interests, not discretionary interests unless the trustee decides to exercise that discretion and make a disbursement.

   b. **Tort creditors:** A majority of jurisdictions still apply spendthrift clauses to tort creditors. An emerging modern trend, however, subjects a beneficiary's interest to the claims of intentional or gross negligence tort creditors.

      **Example:** In *Sligh v. First Nat'l Bank of Holmes County*, 704 So. 2d 1020 (Miss. 1997), Will Sligh was paralyzed as a result of injuries sustained in an accident caused by a drunk driver, Gene Lorance. Gene had no assets other than his life interest in two spendthrift trusts established by his mother prior to the accident. Will filed a writ of garnishment against the trustee of the trusts. The trustee admitted it was indebted to Gene in the amount of $313,677, but claimed the interest was not subject to seizure. The court ruled that the public policy protecting spendthrift individuals from personal pauperism, and in support of the right of donors to dispose of their property as they wish, was not as strong as the claim of tort judgment creditors where the creditors are intentional or gross negligence tort creditors.

2. **Statutory limitations:** A number of states have adopted the above judicial exceptions and/or statutorily limited the amount of the beneficiary's interest in the trust that can be protected against creditors' claims by a spendthrift clause. Such statutes usually take one of three approaches. The first limits the amount of a beneficiary's interest that can be shielded from creditors' claims by a spendthrift clause to the amount necessary for the beneficiary's support and education. The second type of statute permits a creditor to reach a fixed percentage (usually less than a third) of a beneficiary's interest in the income. And the third type of statute typically has a fixed dollar amount cap on the amount of money that can be shielded from creditors' claims by a spendthrift clause.

   a. **ERISA:** An employee's pension benefits, and the employee's ability to depend upon those assets being there when needed, are so important that ERISA mandates that such benefits are nontransferable. Thus, an employee's interest in a pension trust is not reachable by his or her current creditors.

   b. **Bankruptcy creditors:** The Bankruptcy Code provides that a beneficiary's interest in a trust passes to the bankruptcy trustee only if the beneficiary's interest is transferable. If the trust has a spendthrift clause, the beneficiary's interest is not reachable in bankruptcy.

G. **Support trusts:** Even in the absence of a spendthrift clause, if the trust is a support trust, the beneficiary does not have the right to transfer his or her interest. The effect of saying that the interest is nontransferable is to imply a spendthrift clause.

**Basic necessities:** Because a support trust is to ensure that the beneficiary receives support, creditors who provide basic necessities (whatever is necessary for support) are not subject to the implied spendthrift clause and can reach the beneficiary's interest in the support trust.

**H. Self-settled trusts/settlor as beneficiary:** The general rule is that one cannot use a trust to shield one's assets from one's creditors. The general creditors' rights rules set forth above assume that the beneficiary is someone other than the settlor. If the beneficiary is the settlor, creditors have greater rights to reach the beneficiary's interest in the trust.

1. **Mandatory interest:** If the settlor retained a mandatory interest in the trust, creditors of the settlor can reach the mandatory interest in the trust. If the trustee fails to make the payment to them, they can force the trustee to make the payment to them.

2. **Discretionary interest:** If the settlor retained a discretionary interest in the trust, creditors of the settlor can reach the discretionary interest in the trust to the full extent that the trust permits the trustee to use the trust for the benefit of the settlor. In essence, the creditors can force the trustee to exercise his or her discretion to the full extent permitted under the terms of the trust for the benefit of the settlor.

3. **Spendthrift clause:** As a general rule, spendthrift clauses are null and void as applied to creditors of a beneficiary who is also the settlor. It is against public policy to permit one to shield one's assets in a spendthrift trust.

   **Exceptions:** Alaska and Delaware do permit spendthrift trusts in favor of a beneficiary who is also the settlor if (1) the trust is irrevocable; (2) the trust interest is discretionary; and (3) the trust was not created to defraud creditors.

4. **Power to revoke:** The jurisdictions are split as to whether a settlor's power to revoke is a property interest that the settlor's creditors can reach.

   a. **Common law:** At common law, the power to revoke is not a property interest—it is merely a "power." As such, creditors of a settlor of a revocable trust cannot reach the power or force the settlor to exercise the power in their favor.

   b. **Modern trend:** The modern trend expands creditors' rights to permit creditors to reach a settlor's power to revoke.

   **Rationale:** A settlor's power over trust property subject to a power to revoke is functionally indistinguishable from one's power over money in one's bank account. In addition, the modern trend also thinks it unfair to permit one to shield one's assets merely by putting them in a revocable trust that benefits others.

5. **Post-death:** Where a settlor retains a life estate in his or her revocable trust, the jurisdictions are split over whether the settlor's creditors can reach his or her interest in the trust following the settlor's death.

   a. **Common law:** Under the common law approach, if a settlor retains a life estate, upon the settlor's death, the life estate is extinguished. The settlor no longer has an interest in the trust, so there is nothing for the settlor's creditors to reach.

   b. **Modern trend:** The modern trend analogizes the assets in a revocable inter vivos trust to the settlor's other assets, and reasons that to the extent the settlor had the right to use and benefit from those assets during his or her lifetime, his or her creditors should have a right to reach those assets following settlor's death. Under the modern trend, the settlor's creditors are permitted to reach the property in the trust to the extent the settlor had the power to use those assets during his or her life. If the settlor retained the power to revoke the whole trust, all the trust assets are subject to the claims of the settlor's creditors.

   i. **Judicial vs. statutory:** Most jurisdictions that have adopted the modern trend have done so statutorily, though a few have done so judicially. The Uniform Trust Code adopts the modern trend.

   ii. **Probate estate:** Most jurisdictions that have adopted the modern trend require the settlor's creditors to exhaust the settlor's probate assets before being able to reach the settlor's trust assets. Only when the settlor's probate assets are insufficient to satisfy the claims can the creditors reach the assets in the settlor's revocable trust.

   c. **Example:** In *State St. Bank & Trust Co. v. Reiser*, 389 N.E.2d 768 (Mass. App. 1979), Dunnebier created a revocable inter vivos trust and transferred the stock of five closely held corporations to the trust. Thereafter Dunnebier obtained an unsecured loan for $75,000. During the loan application process, Dunnebier represented to the bank that he held controlling interest in the five closely held corporations. (The court found that Dunnebier had not done so fraudulently.) Thereafter, Dunnebier died unexpectedly. His probate assets were insufficient to pay his creditors. The bank sued to reach the assets in his revocable inter vivos trust. The court adopted the modern trend and held that to the extent Dunnebier had power over the assets in the revocable inter vivos trust during his lifetime, those assets should be available to creditors following the settlor's death. The court required the creditors to exhaust the decedent's probate assets first.

I. **Public health benefits:** Public health benefits, like Medicaid and state-sponsored health programs, are usually limited to people who are without the resources to pay for their own health services. People have tried to use trusts (discretionary trusts in particular) to shield their assets from their medical expenses, thereby qualifying for public assistance. Whether such legal maneuvering is successful turns primarily on whether the applicant who is the beneficiary of the trust contributed to the creation of the trust or whether someone other than the applicant/ beneficiary created the trust.

   1. **Applicant created trusts:** If the applicant created or contributed to the creation of the trust (or the applicant's spouse created the trust), the rules tend to favor including the trust property among the applicant's resources for determining the applicant's eligibility for Medicaid and the state-sponsored health programs. If the applicant has the power to revoke, the whole trust is considered the applicant's property for purposes of determining eligibility. If the trust is irrevocable, the trust property is considered the applicant's property to the full extent that any part of the trust could be used for the applicant's benefit. These rules do not apply if the trust (1) is a testamentary trust created by the applicant's spouse (by his or her will), or (2) is created for a disabled individual and it provides that it will reimburse the government for all unreimbursed medical costs upon the applicant's death.

   **Example:** In *Cohen v. Comm'r of Div. of Med. Assistance*, 668 N.E.2d 769 (Mass. 1996), the grantor of an irrevocable trust, to which the grantor transferred substantial assets and of which the grantor (or spouse) is a beneficiary, claimed eligibility for Medicaid assistance because the trust, while according the trustee substantial discretion in most respects, expressly denies the trustee any discretion to make any sums available to the grantor if such availability would make the grantor ineligible for public assistance. The court found that the primary purpose of such trusts is to defeat the Medicaid ineligibility standards. Inasmuch as the trustee has substantial discretion to pay the beneficiary the full amount of the trust for other purposes, that full amount available to the beneficiary shall be used for purposes of determining the beneficiary's eligibility for Medicaid assistance.

2. **Third-party–created trusts:** If the applicant had no role in the creation of the trust, the beneficiary's interest in the trust is considered part of the applicant's resources only to the extent the beneficiary could compel the trustee to make a payment of income or principal (typically in a mandatory or support trust, but not in a discretionary trust). As a provider of basic necessities, the government generally is not subject to a spendthrift clause.

# V. TRUST MODIFICATION AND TERMINATION

A. **Natural termination:** A trust ends naturally pursuant to its terms and/or when its purpose is complete. A trust ends when all of the trust res is completely disbursed. A trust's terms will provide for when the trust res (principal) is to be disbursed.

**Example:** In *Frost Nat'l Bank of San Antonio v. Newton*, 554 S.W.2d 149 (Tex. 1977), the testatrix established a testamentary trust, with one-third of the income to be paid to her husband, Rexford Cozby, and two-thirds of the income to be used to pay for the education of his great-nieces and great-nephew. Any excess income from the two-thirds of the trust after paying the educational expenses was to be distributed to Louise Purvis and Karolen Newton. The trust specifically provided it was to terminate upon the death of the survivor of Rexford Cozby, Karolen Newton, and Louise Purvis—though the trustee had the right to terminate the trust before then if the trustee determined that the income was insufficient to justify continuing the trust. Rexford Cozby predeceased the testatrix, and after the great-nieces and great-nephew had completed their education, Karolen and Louise petitioned to terminate the trust on the grounds that its purpose, to provide for her husband and the education of his great-nieces and great-nephew, was complete and all other purposes were merely incidental. The court declined to try to determine what were the "primary" purposes as opposed to the "incidental" purposes of the trust; it ruled that the trust purpose was not complete because it specifically provided that excess income was to be distributed to Karolen and Louise, and that it was not to terminate until the death of the survivor of Rexford, Karolen, and Louise or until the trustee, in its discretion, determines that the income of the trust is insufficient to justify its continuation.

B. **Premature termination:** Despite the express provisions of a trust dealing with its purpose and/or termination, a trust may be modified or terminated prematurely. The issue of trust modification and/or termination turns on who has an interest in the trust, and what is the extent of his or her interest.

C. **Revocable trusts:** If the settlor retains the power to revoke the trust, the settlor can single-handedly terminate the trust. The power to terminate implicitly includes the power to modify—the settlor can revoke the trust and create a new trust with modified terms and conditions. The settlor can terminate or modify regardless of the objections of the beneficiaries and/or the trustee. The settlor must comply with the requirements for revoking the trust.

1. **Revocability:** The overwhelming majority rule is that inter vivos trusts are presumed to be irrevocable unless the terms of the trust expressly state that the trust is revocable. California is one of a handful of states that presumes all inter vivos trusts are revocable unless the trust expressly states it is irrevocable.

2. **Revocation—particular method:** Where a trust sets forth an express, *particular* method of revocation, *only* that method of revocation will be valid. In many well-drafted trusts, a standard provision is that the trust may be revoked only by written instrument delivered to the trustee.

   a. **Rationale:** The guiding principle of trust law is that settlor's intent controls. If the settlor sets forth a particular method of revoking a trust, it is presumed that the settlor intended that to be the exclusive method of revoking the trust. The issue is how particular must the method be before it is deemed the exclusive method.

   b. **Criticism:** The standard revocation clause, that the trust is revocable by writing delivered to the trustee, arguably is boilerplate language added by the draftor more to protect the trustee from claims of improperly distributing trust assets after the trust was revoked than to limit the settlor's ability to revoke the trust. Nevertheless, most courts presume that the settlor read and intended every clause of the trust and hold the clause constitutes the exclusive method of revoking.

   c. **Example:** In *Connecticut Gen. Life Ins. Co. v. First Nat'l Bank of Minneapolis*, 262 N.W.2d 403 (1977), John Aughenbaugh created a revocable life insurance trust that provided that it was revocable "by written instrument executed by the Donor and delivered to any trustee...during Donor's lifetime." The trust was for the benefit of his then wife and three Aughenbaugh children. Thereafter John divorced, remarried, and executed a new will that expressly provided that it revoked all previous wills and trusts. John gave his new will to his new wife, Marilyn. John died shortly thereafter. The court stated that the general rule is that a trust that is revocable inter vivos cannot be revoked by a will after the settlor dies. Moreover, here, the trust set forth an express and exclusive method of revocation with which the settlor did not comply. The trust was not revoked.

3. **Revocation—no particular method:** If the trust is revocable, but silent as to the method of revocation, the power may be exercised in any manner that adequately expresses the intent to revoke. The trust can be revoked by writing (even if the writing does not qualify as a will), by act (destructive act coupled with intent), by presumption (arguably), and even orally (unless real property is involved).

   a. **Example:** In *Barnette v. McNulty*, 516 P.2d 583 (Ariz. App. 1973), Mr. Barnette executed a form trust that declared himself trustee of all his stock in Van Pack of Arizona, Inc., a company he owned and operated. The trust was for the benefit of his wife, and upon his death, the stock was to be distributed to her. The stock, however, was not transferred on the books of the corporation nor was the assignment on the back of the stock certificate executed by Mr. Barnette. Thereafter marital problems developed. Mr. Barnette met with his attorneys to discuss both his marital problems and his will. He told his attorneys that Van Pack was his company, his separate property, that his wife had no interest in it, and that he wanted it to go to his son upon his death. One of the attorneys drafted a will that Mr. Barnette properly executed that specifically referred to the company as Mr. Barnette's separate property. Mr. Barnette and his wife filed for divorce, but Mr. Barnette died shortly after filing, with his wife at his bedside. First, the court ruled that Mr. Barnette created a valid inter vivos trust, funded with his stock. The owner of shares of stock may make him- or herself trustee of the stock for another by oral or written declaration of trust without delivery of any document. The trust, however, expressly gave Mr. Barnette the power to revoke without notice to, or the consent of, the beneficiary. All the settlor has to do in such cases is communicate to the trustee his or her decision to revoke. Such intent to revoke can be established by the settlor's communications with the beneficiaries or third parties. The court found that Mr. Barnette's statements to his attorneys showed his intent to revoke the trust (the court also found that inasmuch as his will did not become effective until he died, its provisions would not have been sufficient to revoke the trust).

**b. Divorce:** In many jurisdictions an inter vivos revocable trust is not revoked by divorce, while a will is automatically revoked by operation of law.

**D. Modification or termination by consent (estoppel):** In theory, there are three parties who could have an interest in a trust: the settlor, the trustee, and the beneficiaries. If all three groups agree to modify or terminate the trust, the trust can be modified or terminated. If any of the parties subsequently changes his or her mind and sues any of the other parties, the suing party will be estopped based on his or her initial consent.

**1. Settlor and beneficiaries consent:** If the settlor and all the beneficiaries consent, even if the trustee objects, the trust can be modified or terminated. The trustee has no beneficial interest in the trust. At best, the trustee can assert the settlor's intent, as expressed in the terms of the trust, as grounds for objecting to modification or termination. If, however, the settlor is alive and consents, the trustee has no right to speak for the settlor.

**a. Example:** In ***Johnson v. First Nat'l Bank of Jackson***, 386 So. 2d 1112 (Miss. 1980), Mary Johnson inherited a substantial sum of money upon her father's death when she was 25 years, and, being rather unsophisticated in managing money, she created an irrevocable trust under which she was the sole beneficiary. A few years later she changed her mind and petitioned to terminate the trust; the trustee objected. The court ruled that where the settlor is the sole beneficiary, the settlor may revoke an irrevocable trust. The trial court had no right to consider whether revocation was in the best interests of the settlor/beneficiary.

**b. Getting consent of all beneficiaries:** Before a court will order modification or termination of the trust, *all* the beneficiaries must consent. There are doctrines facilitating getting consent from beneficiaries who lack the capacity to consent or from future beneficiaries who might not even be born yet.

**c. Guardian ad litem:** One method of getting the consent of minors or unborn beneficiaries is to petition the court for an appointment of a guardian ad litem to represent the interests of the minor or unborn beneficiaries.

**i. Traditional approach:** Traditionally, guardians ad litem took a rather strict and conservative approach to representing the minor or unborn beneficiary, asking only whether the proposed modification would increase or decrease the economic value of the interest the guardian was appointed to protect. The guardian would ignore family considerations.

    **ii. Modern trend:** The courts have encouraged guardians ad litem to take into consideration noneconomic factors, such as family harmony and the settlor's apparent primary intent to take care of other family members.

    **iii. Example:** In *Hatch v. Riggs Nat'l Bank*, 361 F.2d 559 (D.C. Cir. 1966), appellant created an irrevocable spendthrift trust, with all the income to be distributed to her during her life, and upon her death, the property was to be distributed as she appointed in her will, and in the absence of such appointment, to her heirs. Thereafter settlor decided to modify the trust to provide that the trustee was to distribute an additional $5,000 a year to her out of the principal. The settlor argued that under the doctrine of worthier title she was the sole beneficiary and settlor, and as such she was empowered to agree to the proposed modification. The court ruled that the jurisdiction did not recognize the doctrine of worthier title, but ruled that a guardian ad litem could be appointed to represent the interests of her unborn or unascertainable beneficiaries, and if such guardian consented, the trust could be modified. (Following the court's ruling, a guardian ad litem was appointed and did consent to the modification, which was ordered over the trustee's objection.)

**d. Virtual representation:** Some courts have held that under the doctrine of virtual representation, if the interests of the minor or unborn beneficiaries are virtually identical to those of living adult beneficiaries, the living adult beneficiaries will be deemed to speak not only for themselves, but also for the interests of the minor or unborn beneficiaries by virtual representation.

**e. Modern statutory trends:** The modern trend has been to either try to facilitate getting the consent of all the beneficiaries by reducing the pool of beneficiaries who have to consent, or by permitting the court to order modification even in the absence of all the beneficiaries consenting. The new Uniform Trust Code permits the court to order modification without requiring the consent of all the beneficiaries. Uniform Trust Code §411(a) (1999 draft).

**2. Trustee and beneficiaries consent:** Assuming the settlor has no interest in the trust (an irrevocable trust), if all the beneficiaries consent and the trustee consents, the trust can be modified or terminated. The trustee owes a fiduciary duty to the beneficiaries to comply with the terms of the trust, and modification or termination arguably constitutes a breach of that duty. But if all the beneficiaries consent, each will be estopped later if one tries to sue the trustee. The settlor has no interest in the trust and as such has no right to sue the trustee if the trustee consents with the beneficiaries to the termination of the trust.

**3. Beneficiaries consent—trustee objects:** If all the beneficiaries consent, but the trustee objects, and the settlor is dead, the jurisdictions are split over whether the beneficiaries have the power to modify or terminate the trust over the trustee's objections.

**a. English approach:** Under the English approach, "dead hand" control generally is not permitted. After the death of the settlor, the beneficiaries are deemed the owners of the trust property for purposes of modification and termination of the trust. If all the beneficiaries consent, the trust is modified or terminated regardless of the terms in the trust or the trustee's objections.

**b. Traditional American approach:** The traditional American approach is more protective of settlor's intent. Under the general American approach, the trustee has the right, to some degree, to object to a modification or termination by invoking the settlor's intent as expressed in the terms of the trust.

**i. Rationale:** The creation of trusts for the benefit of others is considered a good that should be encouraged. The assumption is that by protecting a deceased settlors intent as expressed in the trust, future settlors will be encouraged to create trusts because they will know that as a general rule the courts will protect and uphold their intent even after their death (if the trustee objects). The trust is a creature of settlor's intent—settlor's intent controls. The trust owns the property, pursuant to the settlor's intent, as set forth in the terms of the trust, and the trustee should be permitted to protect that intent.

**ii. Counterargument:** The courts should be somewhat suspicious of the trustee's objection because of the trustee's vested interest in continuing to receive his or her trustee fees. Because of the conflict of interest, the courts developed a doctrine to discern when the trustee was objecting for legitimate reasons as opposed to when the trustee was objecting for illegitimate reasons.

**4. The Claflin doctrine:** Consistent with the traditional American approach of being more protective of settlor's intent, under the Claflin doctrine the trustee can block premature termination of the trust, even if all the beneficiaries consented, but only if the trust has an unfulfilled material purpose. If, however, there is no unfulfilled material purpose, and all the beneficiaries consent to the premature termination of the trust, the trustee cannot block its termination.

**a. Unfulfilled material purpose:** Under the Claflin doctrine, what constitutes an unfulfilled material purpose is whatever a court concludes is an unfulfilled material purpose. The test is very fact sensitive, turning on the language and apparent purpose of each trust. There are a handful of scenarios where virtually every court has held the trust intrinsically includes an unfulfilled material purpose: (1) discretionary trusts; (2) spendthrift trusts; (3) support trusts; and (4) trusts where the property is not to be disbursed until the beneficiary reaches a specific age. If the court determines that the dispositive provisions of the trust constitute merely a succession of interests that have no material purpose, premature termination will be ordered if all the beneficiaries consent.

**b. Example:** In *American Nat'l Bank of Cheyenne v. Miller*, 899 P.2d 1337 (Wyo. 1995), the settlor created an irrevocable trust for her benefit during her lifetime; upon her death, $200 a month was to be paid to her daughter and her daughter's husband (or the survivor of them) to assist with the educational expenses of their three children, and upon the death of the survivor of her daughter and her daughter's husband, the principal was to be divided into as many equal shares as there were living children of her daughter, with each child to get his or her principal distributed over time until each child reached age 35; when the youngest child reached age 35, the balance of the trust was to be distributed to the scholarship fund the settlor had established at the University of Wyoming. Thereafter the settlor died, the daughter died, and all her children reached the age of 35. The daughter's husband assigned his interest to their three children (the trust had no spendthrift clause) and the children and the University of Wyoming agreed to terminate the trust. The court held that all the material purposes of the trust had been fulfilled, that all the beneficiaries had consented, and it ordered the trust to be terminated despite the trustee's objection.

**c. Settlor's consent:** Even if the trust expresses an unfulfilled material purpose that the trustee invokes to block premature termination of the trust, if the settlor is alive and consents with all the beneficiaries, the settlor's consent will control over the trustee's attempt to block. In essence, the settlor's consent constitutes a waiver of the unfulfilled material purpose.

**d. Modern trend:** A number of states have statutes that facilitate premature termination of a trust, even where there is an unfulfilled material purpose, under a variety of conditions (for good cause; court determines in beneficiaries' best interest; court determines unborn or unascertained beneficiaries not adversely affected; changed circumstances would otherwise defeat settlor's intent).

**e. Probate settlement:** Where there is litigation during probate, and the heirs and trust beneficiaries reach a settlement that includes terminating the trust, most (but not all) courts will enforce the settlement and terminate the testamentary trust despite its terms (even if there is an unfulfilled material purpose).

**Example:** In *Adams v. Link*, 145 A.2d 753 (Conn. 1958), testatrix created a testamentary trust that provided for the payment of the net income to two beneficiaries for life, and upon the death of the survivor of the two, the principal was to be distributed to the New York Association for the Blind. One of the life beneficiaries predeceased the testatrix. Upon the death of the testatrix, her heirs challenged the admissibility of the will to probate, and the life beneficiary, the residuary beneficiary, and the testatrix's heirs at law entered into a compromise agreement that provided for the termination of the trust. The trustee objected. The court ruled that the trust had an unfulfilled material purpose (to provide a stream of income for the life beneficiary for the remainder of her life), and the court declined to apply a more liberal rule just because the petition was part of a probate settlement agreement.

**E. Modification based on unforeseen change in circumstances:** At common law, even if the trustee objects, if there is an unforeseen change of circumstances that would defeat or substantially frustrate settlor's intent, and all the beneficiaries consent, the court will order modification of the trust.

**1. Settlor's intent:** Under the common law doctrine of modification, the assumption is that the modification is to *further* the settlor's intent.

**2. Unforeseen change:** The requirement that the change in circumstances must be unforeseen is a very soft, fact sensitive inquiry.

**a. Common law:** At common law, the courts were generally more protective of settlor's intent, even against attempts at modification. The courts tended to apply a rather high threshold for what constituted an unforeseen change in circumstances.

**b. Modern trend:** Under the modern trend approach, there is a noticeable shift toward giving the beneficiaries greater control over the property in the trust after the settlor's death. This translates into a low threshold for what constitutes an unforeseen change in circumstances. An unusually high rate of inflation or increased medical costs can be enough to constitute an unforeseen change.

**c. Beneficiary's advantage:** The mere fact that the proposed modification would be more advantageous to one or more beneficiaries is not enough to warrant modifying a trust even if all the beneficiaries agree.

3. **Substantially impair:** Whether an unforeseen change in circumstances would "defeat or substantially impair" the settlor's intent is a very soft, fact sensitive inquiry.

   **a. Common law approach:** At common law, the courts were generally more protective of settlor's intent. The courts tended to apply a rather high threshold before finding that the change defeated or substantially impaired settlor's intent.

   **b. Modern trend approach:** The modern trend favors granting beneficiaries greater power over the trust. The modern trend takes a rather low threshold for what constitutes defeating or substantially impairing settlor's intent.

4. **Tax benefits:** A handful of states, and both the Restatement (Third) of Property, Donative Transfers and the Uniform Trust Code, authorize modification of trusts to further a settlor's apparent tax minimizing objectives.

   **Example:** In *Walker v. Walker*, 744 N.E.2d 60 (Mass. 2001), the settlor created a revocable trust during his life that was intended to eliminate, or to minimize to the fullest extent possible, any adverse tax consequences to his estate and the estate of the trust beneficiaries (in particular the estate of his surviving wife, Virginia). The trust, however, gave Virginia in her capacity as sole trustee unbridled discretion to pay principal from the nonmarital deduction trust to herself as beneficiary—thereby constituting a general power of appointment that would include all the property in the nonmarital deduction trust in her gross estate upon her death. The court agreed with the parties that this was inconsistent with the settlor's overall intent and ordered the trust reformed to ensure that the discretion to pay principal did not constitute a general power of appointment and that the property would not be included in Virginia's gross estate for estate tax purposes.

5. **Administrative modification:** As a general rule, courts are more willing to modify administrative provisions under the unforeseen change in circumstances doctrine than they are to modify distributive provisions. The rationale is that the distributive provisions go to the heart of the settlor's intent, while the administrative provisions are merely the means of achieving those objectives. Pursuant to this reasoning, modifying administrative provisions is less violative of settlor's intent.

**F. Trustee's removal:** The traditional approach is that settlor's intent controls. If the settlor selected a particular trustee, that trustee cannot be removed, even if all the beneficiaries consent, unless the trustee is unfit to serve or commits a breach of trust.

**Uniform Trust Code:** The Uniform Trust Code increases the grounds for which a trustee can be removed, though it does not go so far as to give the beneficiaries the power to change trustee if all beneficiaries consent. Under the Uniform Trust Code, the trustee can be removed if there is a material breach of trust; infighting among cotrustees substantially impairs its administration; the trust has underperformed persistently and substantially relative to comparable trusts; or due to changed circumstances, change of trustee would be in the beneficiaries' best interests.

## Quiz Yourself on
## TRUSTS: CREATION, LIFE, AND TERMINATION

**54.** What are the requirements to create a valid private trust? _____

**55.** In front of several witnesses, Sally orally tells Bob that she intends to give him her computer next month. A week later, she dies. Bob claims that Sally's statement constitutes a declaration of trust and that he is entitled to the computer despite her death. Is Bob entitled to the computer? _____

**56.** In front of several witnesses, Sally declares that she holds her computer for Bob's benefit and that she will deliver it to him next month. A week later, she dies. Bob claims that Sally's statement constitutes a declaration of trust and that he is entitled to her computer despite her death. Is Bob entitled to her computer? _____

**57.** Charlie's dad gives him $10,000. As he hands the money over, he says, "I hope you use this to help the poor of Malibuville." Instead, Charlie spends the money on Lulu, one of Heidi's friends. Has Charlie misused the money? _____

**58.** After a rather long and productive night of working very closely with his assistant, Lulu, Professor Wendel writes her a note that provides in pertinent part, "I want to show my appreciation for your services in helping me finish my contractual obligations to Aspen. I hereby declare myself to be the trustee of the profits of my Wills and Trusts Emanuel's, if I ever finish writing it, with 25 percent of the profits being held in trust for your benefit, Lulu." Professor Wendel finally finishes the Emanuel's, but dies before it is published. Is Lulu entitled to any of the profits, if there are any? _____

**59.** Professor Wendel makes a fortune on his student study aid (obviously a hypothetical). To thank his students, he puts a provision in his will that provides in pertinent part that he give "$100,000, in trust, to Lulu, my trustee, to distribute equally among my favorite students." Following his death, the takers under his residuary clause sue to invalidate the gift. Who takes the $100,000? _____

**60.** Michael's will provides in pertinent part that upon his death he leaves $50,000 to his sister, Janet, to use to take care of Bubbles, his pet monkey. Following Michael's death from a mysterious skin ailment, the takers under his residuary clause challenge the gift to Janet. What is the most likely outcome? _____

**61.** Lisa is engaged to Nicholas. Worried that their relationship might not make it, and concerned that if they divorce the court may award part of her prize possession, Gracelandacres, to Nicholas, she transfers Gracelandacres to her old friend Michael shortly before she marries Nicholas. Lisa and Michael orally agree that Michael will hold Gracelandacres while Lisa is married, and that Michael will convey Gracelandacres back to Lisa after five years or following her divorce from Nicholas, whichever comes first. Only months after their marriage, Lisa and Nicholas file for divorce. Following the divorce, Lisa asks Michael to convey Gracelandacres back to her. Michael refuses. Lisa sues to recover Gracelandacres.

   **a.** What is the most likely outcome under the common law approach? _____

   **b.** What is the most likely outcome under the modern trend? _____

**62.** Richard learns that he has terminal cancer. Accepting the inevitable, he contacts his good friend, Ian, and asks Ian if he will do him a favor. Richard tells Ian that he wants to leave him $25,000 to use to take the cast of his last movie to London where they will have a grand party to celebrate his life. Ian agrees. When Richard dies, his will provides in pertinent part, "I leave $25,000 to Ian to use for the purpose we have agreed upon." The takers under his residuary clause challenge the gift.

    **a.** Who takes the $25,000 under the common law approach? _____

    **b.** Who takes the $25,000 under the modern trend approach? _____

**63.** Robert's father sets up a trust that provides in pertinent part that "the trustee shall distribute the income to Robert quarterly, and the trustee may distribute to Robert as much of the principal as trustee deems necessary, in her sole and absolute discretion, for his comfortable support and maintenance." Each quarter, the trustee mails Robert a questionnaire inquiring as to his situation. Robert is addicted to drugs and is in rehab. He fails to return several questionnaires, and claims financial hardship in some of the others, but fails to support his claim with details because he is too embarrassed to admit to his addiction and the financial problems it is causing. The trustee declines to disburse any principal to him. Thereafter, when Robert's condition improves, he sues the trustee claiming abuse of discretion and breach of fiduciary duty in not disbursing any principal to him. The trustee responds that because Robert's interest in the principal is merely discretionary, and the trustee has absolute discretion, Robert has no right to any principal so there was no breach of trust or duty. What is the most likely result? _____

**64.** Father sets up a trust for the benefit of his sons, Alec, Steven, William, and Fred. The trust provides in pertinent part that "the trustee shall distribute the income equally to the sons at least quarterly, and the trustee may distribute principal to any of the sons if the trustee deems it appropriate." Thereafter Alec divorces Kim. The court orders him to pay alimony and child support. Thereafter Alec buys a new yacht (dealer financed) and sets sail, never to be seen again. The yacht dealer, Alec's ex-wife, and his children sue the trustee to reach Alec's interest in the trust to satisfy his debts.

    **a.** What is the most likely result? _____

    **b.** What difference would it make if the trust contained a spendthrift clause? _____

    **c.** What difference, if any, would it make if Alec had created the trust? _____

**65.** Bill properly created an inter vivos trust for the benefit of his intern, Monica. Thereafter, Bill tore up the trust, declaring that he did not want "that woman" to take any of his property. Bill dies in a freak accident (he accidentally choked on a cigar). Has the trust been properly revoked? _____

**66.** Sally creates an inter vivos revocable trust and funds it with her house. The trust is for Sally's benefit during her life, and upon her death, the property is to be given to her dad. The terms of the trust provide that it may be amended or revoked only by a writing delivered to the trustee expressing the intent to revoke. The trust appoints her sister, Toni, as trustee. Thereafter Sally's dad abandons her mom. Sally is livid at her dad and concerned about her mom's financial situation. Sally properly executes a will that expressly provides that she revoke her trust and gives her house to her mom. A few days later, Sally dies unexpectedly in a car crash. Who takes the house? _____

**67.** George W. is the son of a widely respected family. A couple of years ago, the family had George W. put all his principal assets (including his profits from some questionable stock deals) in an inter vivos revocable trust that provided for his benefit during his lifetime, and upon his death, the trust was for the benefit of his parents. George W. has been surprisingly successful—so successful that he decides to purchase a baseball team. When George W. applied for the loan to purchase the baseball team, he listed his assets as his own, forgetting to mention that the assets had been transferred to the inter vivos revocable trust (George W. did not intend to defraud the bank; he has always had trouble remembering names and details). Shortly after the bank gave George W. a substantial unsecured loan, George W. cut his finger on a dangling chad. The cut became infected, and before the doctors could do anything, he died. There are not enough assets in George W's probate estate to repay the loan to the bank. Can the bank reach his assets in the inter vivos revocable trust? _____

**68.** Ted's will established a trust for the benefit of his children. The trustee was to pay the income to them for 20 years, and then the principal was to be disbursed to them equally. Shortly after his death, the relationships among Ted's children turned frosty. One of the children proposed terminating the trust and splitting the money. The others agreed, but the trustee objected. Can the children force premature termination of the trust? _____

---

## Answers

**54.** To have a validly created private trust, there must be: (1) the intent to create a trust, (2) the trust must be funded with property, (3) there must be ascertainable beneficiaries, and (4) if the trust is an inter vivos trust that holds real property, the trust terms must be in writing; or if the trust is a testamentary trust, the trust terms must be in writing.

**55.** Sally's statement arguably does not constitute a valid declaration of trust, and Bob is not entitled to the computer. Sally's statement arguably constitutes merely a gratuitous promise to make a gift in the future, not a present declaration of a trust. The distinction is a difficult one, but here there is no express reference to a trust or trustee, and the focus of the statement appears to be in the future, not the present. It is unlikely that a court would hold that this statement constitutes the necessary intent to create a trust. It is merely a gratuitous promise to make a gift in the future, a gift that fails for want of delivery.

**56.** Sally's statement constitutes a valid declaration of trust, and Bob is entitled to Sally's computer. Sally's statement constitutes a present declaration of a trust. She expressed the present intent that she held the property in question for the benefit of another—classic intent to create a trust. Because she is both settlor and trustee, her statement that she held the computer for Bob's benefit constitutes adequate evidence of funding. Pursuant to the statement, she transferred the computer from herself as settlor to herself as trustee. The trust has an ascertainable beneficiary, Bob. And because the trust was created inter vivos and held only personal property, the trust does not have to be in writing to be valid. A trust will not fail for want of a trustee. The courts will appoint a successor trustee who will be bound by the terms of the trust—to distribute the computer to Bob next month.

**57.** No, Charlie's dad's statement imposes only a moral obligation, not a legal obligation. Where the qualifying language attached to the gift imposes only a moral obligation, there is only a precatory trust, not a true trust. A precatory trust imposes no legal obligations on the donee. The donee is free to use the property as he or she sees fit. It is only a gift with a wish attached. There is no intent to create a trust, no trust, and no breach of trust.

**58.** Although Professor Wendel has the intent to create a trust (as evidenced by his declaring himself trustee and declaring that he hold the future profits "in trust"), the beneficiary is ascertainable (Lulu), and the terms of the trust are in writing (the note), under traditional trust law the trust fails for want of funding. Professor Wendel has attempted to fund this trust with the future profits from his book. Classic trust law holds that future profits are not an adequate property interest to constitute funding. Without funding, the trust fails and the future profits are not subject to the terms of the trust.

**59.** Professor Wendel has the intent to create a trust, as evidenced by the phrase "my trustee, in trust." Professor Wendel has funded the trust through the clause in his will transferring $100,000 to the trustee of the trust. The trust is a testamentary trust, so the terms must be in writing, which they are by being set forth in the will. The trust fails, however, for want of ascertainable beneficiaries. There must be an objective method of identifying the beneficiaries. Here, the alleged beneficiaries are Professor Wendel's "favorite students." There is no objective way to ascertain who the intended beneficiaries are. Whenever a trust fails, a resulting trust is imposed and the property will be ordered transferred back to the settlor. Here, Lulu will be ordered to return the $100,000 to Professor Wendel, where the property will fall to his probate estate and to his residuary clause.

**60.** The gift to Janet arguably was an attempt to create a private trust. (The trust is not a charitable trust because the gift is not for the care of animals generally, just for this particular monkey.) Janet was to hold and manage the property not for her own benefit, but for the benefit of Bubbles. The trust is a testamentary trust, funded via the provision in his will with $50,000. As a testamentary trust, it must be in writing—as it is because its terms are set forth in the will. The problem, however, is that technically the trust fails for want of ascertainable beneficiaries. Where, however, the purpose of a private trust is such that it is impossible to have ascertainable beneficiaries, and the purpose is not capricious or illegal, the courts usually permit the "trust" to continue as an honorary trust as long as the "trustee" is willing to honor the terms of the gift. If Janet is willing to use the money to care for the monkey, the courts will permit the arrangement as long as Janet is willing to carry out Michael's wishes. (There is a Rule against Perpetuities issue, but that is beyond the scope of the material at this point.)

**61.** **a.** Lisa intended to create an inter vivos trust when she conveyed Gracelandacres to Michael. Michael was not to hold the property for his own benefit, but rather he was to hold it for Lisa's benefit. The trust was funded when she transferred the property to Michael, and she constitutes an ascertainable beneficiary. But inter vivos trusts of land must be in writing. The agreement between Lisa and Michael was oral. The common law took the Statute of Frauds seriously. The deed conveying Gracelandacres from Lisa to Michael could not be conditioned by any oral understanding between the parties. Any attempts by Lisa to introduce evidence of their oral understanding would be barred by the Statute of Frauds under the common law approach. Michael would keep the property.

**b.** The modern trend does not like the notion that the Statute of Frauds could be used to perpetrate what amounts to a fraud. Under the modern trend, extrinsic evidence is generally admissible to prove an alleged oral trust with respect to real property. The attempted trust is still invalid, but once the oral agreement is established, the court can impose a constructive trust and order the property transferred to the intended beneficiaries. Resulting trusts and/or constructive trusts are equitable trusts (remedies) that arise by operation of law and as such are not subject to the Statute of Frauds. But inasmuch as both are equitable remedies, the party seeking relief must not be guilty of unclean hands. Here, Lisa is guilty of unclean hands in that she transferred Gracelandacres to Michael in an attempt to hide the asset in the event of divorce. If the court finds that Lisa is guilty of unclean hands, even under the modern trend Michael will be permitted to keep Gracelandacres.

**62.  a.** The agreement between Richard and Ian constitutes the necessary intent to create a trust—Ian has agreed to receive and use the property for the benefit of others, the cast of the movie. The trust is to be funded through the gift in the will, and the beneficiaries are ascertainable, the cast of his last movie. The problem is, because the trust is being funded through the gift in his will, the trust is a testamentary trust. Testamentary trusts must be in writing, and the necessary terms of this trust are not in writing. The trust fails. At common law, if the express words of the will hinted at the intent to create a trust, but the trust failed for want of writing, the trust was called a "semi-secret" trust. If the failed testamentary trust were a semi-secret trust, the courts imposed a resulting trust—the property would be ordered back to the decedent's probate estate. Here, the property would be distributed to the residuary takers under Richard's will.

**b.** The analysis is basically the same under the modern trend—the trust is still invalid for want of a written instrument. The modern trend, however, no longer distinguishes between secret trusts and semi-secret trusts. In both cases, the courts tend to grant a constructive trust and order the property distributed to the intended beneficiaries. Here, that would be the cast of Richard's last movie.

**63.** Even where a beneficiary's interest in a trust is discretionary, the trustee still owes the beneficiary certain duties. First, the trustee must exercise his or her discretion, and before he or she can do so, he or she must inquire as to the beneficiary's situation and needs. Where the beneficiary fails to reply or returns an incomplete reply, the duty is on the trustee to follow up. Here, the trustee failed to follow up when Robert failed to reply, thereby breaching the duty to inquire. In addition, once the trustee has all the necessary information, the trustee has a duty to act reasonably and in good faith in deciding whether to exercise his or her discretion under the terms of the trust. This standard can be altered by the settlor, but even where the trust purports to grant the trustee absolute discretion, the discretion cannot be absolute (if it were, the trust would be merely a precatory trust). The trustee still must act in good faith with an eye toward the purpose of the trust. Here, the trust specifically provided that the trustee had the power to invade the principal if necessary to maintain Robert's comfortable support and maintenance. This phrase has become a term of art that means the beneficiary is to be kept at the standard of living he or she had at the time he or she became a beneficiary. The facts say that Robert's addiction has caused him financial problems. If these problems have affected his standard of living, the trustee has abused his or her discretion in not disbursing any of the principal to Robert. The most likely result under the facts is that the court will find that the trustee has breached the duty of inquiry and abused his or her discretion in not disbursing any of the principal to Robert.

**64.  a.** The general rule is that creditors of a beneficiary can reach a beneficiary's interest in a trust. The creditors step into the beneficiary's shoes and acquire the beneficiary's interest in the trust, but not more. Here, all the creditors can reach Alec's interest in the trust. Because Alec's interest in the income was mandatory, the creditors can force the trustee to distribute Alec's share of the income to them, but because his interest in the principal was discretionary, they cannot force the trustee to exercise the trustee's discretion to disburse any of the principal to them.

**b.** The general effect of a standard spendthrift clause is to make a beneficiary's interest in the trust nontransferable and thus creditors of the beneficiary cannot reach the beneficiary's interest in the trust. Not all creditors, however, are subject to spendthrift clauses. Here, assuming a yacht is not a basic necessity, the yacht dealer would be subject to the spendthrift clause and cannot reach Alec's interest in the trust. Alec's ex-wife entitled to alimony and his children entitled to child support are not subject to the spendthrift clause as a general rule and they would be able to reach his interest in the trust. They could force the trustee to distribute Alec's share of the income to them, but they could not force the trustee to distribute any principal to them.

**c.** Where the settlor is also a beneficiary, and the creditors are creditors of the settlor/beneficiary, spendthrift clauses are null and void and creditors can reach the maximum amount the trustee could pay to the settlor/beneficiary under the terms of the trust. Here, even if the trust had a spendthrift clause, all the creditors could force the trustee not only to distribute Alec's share of the income to them, but if that were not enough to satisfy the debts, the creditors could force the trustee to exercise his or her discretion and disburse principal to them until their debts were satisfied.

**65.** Where a trust is silent as to its revocability, the general rule is that the trust is irrevocable (though California is a notable exception—California assumes a trust is revocable unless it expressly provides that it is irrevocable). Here, the facts do not say if the trust is revocable. Applying the general rule, the trust would be irrevocable. Despite Bill's intent and his actions, the trust was not revocable and thus was not revoked.

**66.** Where a trust is revocable, if the terms of the trust set forth a particular method of revocation, only that method of revocation will be effective. Here, the trust specifically provided that the trust was revocable upon delivery of a written instrument expressing that intent to the trustee. Although Sally properly executed a valid will that expressed the intent to revoke the trust, there is no evidence that the will was delivered to Toni, the trustee, during Sally's lifetime. Absent evidence that the will was delivered to Toni during Sally's lifetime, Sally has not complied with the terms of the trust concerning revocation, and the trust was not validly revoked. The house goes to Sally's dad.

**67.** George W.'s interest in the trust was a life estate, with a remainder in his parents. Under the traditional common law approach, when a life estate ends, the party no longer has any interest in the asset in question. Under the common law approach, when George W. died, he no longer had any interest in the trust for the bank to reach in an attempt to satisfy his debt. The modern trend, however, provides that where a settlor retains a life estate in his or her inter vivos trust, such an interest is analogous to one's interest in the rest of one's property. If the settlor could enjoy the benefits of the property during his or her lifetime, his or her creditors should be able to reach the property even after the settlor's death. Under the modern trend, the bank could reach the assets in George W.'s inter vivos revocable trust.

**68.** Under the Claflin doctrine, if all the beneficiaries consent to premature termination of the trust, but the trustee objects, the trustee can block the termination only if the trust has an unfulfilled material purpose. Here, there does not appear to be an unfulfilled material purpose. The children should be permitted to terminate the trust.

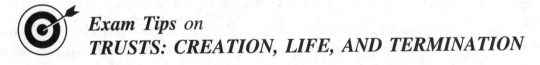

## *Exam Tips* on
## *TRUSTS: CREATION, LIFE, AND TERMINATION*

### Requirements for a valid private trust

Creation of a valid private trust is much easier than the material makes it look. Rarely is creation an issue in the real world. Don't let the material distort your understanding of it.

☞ The first requirement, the intent to create a trust, is the most difficult to understand and thus one of the more favorite elements to test. The issue is almost always whether the person had the intent to make an outright gift or the intent to make a gift in trust, but there are a number of different possible intent scenarios.

☞ First, if you see a transfer of property from one party to another with qualifying language that is ambiguous, the issue is whether the language constitutes merely a precatory trust or a true trust. The key is who is to have the beneficial interest in the property, the recipient (gift) or someone else (trust).

☞ Second, if there is a declaration of intent but no transfer of property, the issue is whether the party has adequately expressed the intent to create a trust, thereby appointing him- or herself trustee, or if the party has merely expressed a gratuitous intent to make a gift in the future (which typically will fail for want of delivery). If the party uses classic trust terminology, the intent to create a trust is present. Otherwise, analyze the language very carefully to see if there is a present intent to transfer an interest to a third party (trust) or merely a promise to transfer some property in the future (promise to make a gift in the future).

☞ The second requirement, that the trust be funded with some property interest, is doctrinally simple, but theoretically complicated. Doctrinally, any property interest will qualify, except expectancies and future profits. Theoretically, the distinction is hard to justify.

☞ The third requirement, ascertainable beneficiaries, is simple. There must be an objective method of naming the beneficiaries. If, however, the purpose of the trust is such that it is impossible to have ascertainable beneficiaries, think honorary trust.

☞ The final requirement, writing, is rather straightforward. The wrinkle on this requirement, and the area tested most often, is what remedy should be awarded if the trust fails for want of a written instrument. If a testamentary trust, at common law whether the court ordered a resulting trust or a constructive trust turned on whether the failed testamentary trust was a secret trust or a semi-secret trust. If an inter vivos trust of land failed, at common law the "trustee" got to keep the property. Under the modern trend the courts impose a constructive trust to take the property from the "trustee"—unless the "settlor" was guilty of unclean hands in creating the arrangement.

## Life of the trust

Once the trust is created, the key issue during the life of the trust is what is the extent of each beneficiary's interest. A beneficiary's interest is either mandatory or discretionary. The extent of a beneficiary's interest depends on settlor's intent as expressed in the terms of the trust. Properly analyzing the extent of a beneficiary's interest requires careful reading of the express language of the trust.

☞ Mandatory interests pose few issues. The trustee must perform as directed.

☞ Discretionary interests contain a whole host of issues and are tested much more often. To say that an interest is discretionary only begins to touch on the subissues involved in discretionary trusts.

☞ Know the subduties inherent in a discretionary trust: the duty of inquiry; the duty to act reasonably and in good faith in exercising the discretion—unless modified by the settlor in the express terms of the trust (but a trustee cannot have absolute discretion because that would be a precatory trust); and the duty to take any express purpose set forth in the trust into consideration when deciding.

☛ Creditors' rights are a favorite area to test because they are derivative of beneficiary's interests—so a professor can test both areas at once. The key to analyzing creditors' rights is who is the beneficiary: the settlor or someone other than the settlor.

☞ If the beneficiary is someone other than the settlor, the creditor steps into the beneficiary's shoes and acquires the same rights as the beneficiary but not more. A spendthrift clause blocks a creditor's ability to step into the beneficiary's shoes—the creditor must wait until the property is distributed to the beneficiary. However, not all creditors are subject to a spendthrift clause.

☞ Support trusts are a favorite area to test because of their wrinkles. First, use of the word *support* does not necessarily make a trust a support trust unless the level of distribution is limited to as much as necessary for support. Second, a support trust inherently includes a spendthrift clause. And third, only creditors who provide basic necessities can pierce the spendthrift clause.

☞ If the beneficiary is the settlor, public policy does not permit one to shield one's assets behind a trust. Creditors not only can step into the beneficiary's shoes, they can force the trustee to exercise his or her discretion to the full extent permitted under the terms of the trust, and spendthrift clauses are null and void.

## Modification and premature termination

The method of revocation material is tested often because it differs from the wills revocation material.

☛ Just because you see a settlor tearing up an inter vivos trust and declaring his or her intent to revoke it, unless the fact pattern also tells you that the trust expressly provided that it was revocable, you should raise the issue and presume that in the absence of such a fact in the fact pattern, it is more likely than not that the trust was irrevocable and the settlor's actions are a nullity.

☛ If there is a provision stating that the trust is revocable, read carefully to see if it sets forth an exclusive method of revocation.

☛ Modification and termination issues are fairly easy to spot because one or more beneficiaries have to ask the trustee to change the dispositive provisions of the trust. Distinguishing between the two issues is also fairly easy because it goes to the scope of the change the beneficiaries are requesting: if a slight change—modification, if total distribution—termination.

For modification, all beneficiaries have to consent and there has to be an unforeseen change in circumstances that is materially frustrating settlor's intent.

☞ Common law was more protective of settlor's intent and strictly applied the doctrinal requirements. Modern trend favors the beneficiaries and takes a broader interpretation of the doctrinal requirements (which leads to a great theoretical question of who really owns the property in trust).

☞ A wrinkle issue is how all the beneficiaries can consent if some are minors or unborn—discuss the guardian ad litem and virtual representation doctrines.

☞ Premature termination is a bit more complicated just because there are different scenarios in which it can arise. Focus on who is objecting and whether they have the power to block the premature termination.

## CHAPTER 9

# CHARITABLE TRUSTS

*ChapterScope* ————————————————————————————

This chapter examines the requirements for, and benefits of, charitable trusts.

■ **Charitable purpose:** A trust is a charitable trust if it has a charitable purpose. A purpose is charitable if it is for: (1) the relief of poverty; (2) the advancement of education; (3) the advancement of religion; (4) the promotion of health; (5) governmental or municipal purposes; or (6) any other purposes the accomplishment of which is beneficial to the community at large. Benevolent trusts (trusts that perform kind acts) are not charitable trusts unless they accomplish one of the specific charitable purposes.

■ **Benefits:** There are two principal advantages, from a trust law perspective, of classifying a trust as a charitable trust:

  ▪ **Rule against Perpetuities:** Because charitable trusts serve charitable purposes that benefit the community at large, they are ***not*** subject to the Rule against Perpetuities.

  ▪ **Ascertainable beneficiaries:** Because charitable trusts have to serve the community at large, or at least a good segment of the community at large, there is no requirement that the trust have ascertainable beneficiaries.

  ▪ **Cy pres:** Where a trust with a general charitable purpose expresses a particular charitable purpose, and it becomes impossible, impractical, or illegal to carry out that particular charitable purpose, rather than imposing a resulting trust, modify the trust purpose to another particular charitable purpose within the general charitable purpose.

  ▪ **Administrative deviation:** If accomplishing the trust purpose has become impossible or impractical for administrative reasons, apply administrative deviation and modify the administrative provisions to remove the obstacle before modifying the settlor's intent with cy pres.

■ **Charitable trust supervision:** The attorney general of each state has the duty of supervising the administration of each charitable trust. This is an extreme burden, so many courts have granted standing to members of the community who bear a particular relationship to the trust to bring suit against the charitable trustee for breach of trust.

————————————————————————————

# I. CHARITABLE PURPOSE

**A. Rule statement:** The distinguishing characteristic and key requirement of a charitable trust is that the trust be for a charitable purpose.

**B. Charitable purposes:** What constitutes a charitable purpose is not a completely fact sensitive inquiry. The courts typically have limited the concept to one of six delineated purposes. The trust purpose must be (1) to relieve poverty; (2) to advance education; (3) to advance religion; (4) to promote health; (5) governmental or municipal purposes; or (6) other purposes which if accomplished would be beneficial to the community. (The courts tend to construe this last charitable purpose very narrowly, often requiring an overlap with at least one of the other five charitable purposes.)

1. **Benevolent trusts:** Benevolent trusts are trusts that perform kind acts or do "good things." Benevolent trusts are not charitable trusts unless the kind acts qualify as one of the recognized charitable purposes.

2. **Example:** In *Shenandoah Valley Nat'l Bank v. Taylor*, 63 S.E.2d 786 (Va. 1951), settlor's trust provided that the income was to be distributed on the last day of school preceding Easter and Christmas break to the children in the first, second, and third grades at a local elementary school, to be used by the children to further their education. The timing of the payments indicated that the true purpose of the trust was to be a benevolent trust, not a charitable trust. There were no enforceable restrictions on how the children used the money, and in light of the timing of the payments, the children would not use it on education. Where a trust conveys mere financial enrichment, the trust qualifies as a charitable trust only if from a totality of the circumstances, it becomes apparent that the intended beneficiaries are poor or in necessitous conditions. There was no evidence that these children were poor. As a benevolent trust, the trust failed because it violated the Rule against Perpetuities.

3. **Unrestricted gift vs. restricted gift vs. charitable trust:** Where a gift is made to a charitable entity, questions may arise as to the nature of the gift. The gift itself may constitute an unrestricted gift that the entity may use as it deems best consistent with its charitable purpose; the gift may constitute a restricted gift, which means that the gift can be used only for the purpose for which it was donated; or the gift may constitute a charitable trust with the entity acting as trustee. The presumption is that a gift to a charitable entity is an unrestricted gift unless the intent that the gift constitute either a restricted gift or a charitable trust is clearly expressed.

   **Example:** In *Lefkowitz v. Cornell Univ.*, 316 N.Y.S.2d 264 (N.Y. App. Div. 1970), in 1945 Curtiss-Wright Corporation donated a wind tunnel and research facilities to Cornell University in exchange for Cornell's agreement to continue research and development on some of Curtiss-Wright's inventions at a reasonable charge. Cornell created Cornell Aeronautical Laboratories, Inc. (CAL), to which it transferred the laboratory and wind tunnel in exchange for all 100 shares of CAL. Cornell continued to operate CAL on a nonprofit basis until 1968 when it decided to sell CAL for $25 million. The state attorney general sued to block the sale to a for-profit entity on the grounds that the gift from Curtiss-Wright constituted a charitable trust. The court held that the gift constituted an unrestricted gift because there was not clear intent that the parties intended either a charitable trust or a restricted gift.

C. **Rule against Perpetuities:** One of the principal benefits of a charitable trust is that it is not subject to the Rule against Perpetuities.

   1. **Modern trend:** With most jurisdictions now following the "wait-and-see approach" to or abolishing the Rule against Perpetuities, this benefit is not as great as it used to be.

   2. **UPC:** The UPC expressly provides that a trust that fails for want of a charitable purpose may continue for up to 21 years if the trustee is willing to honor the purpose and the purpose is lawful. UPC §2-907(a).

**D. Beneficiaries:** While private trusts require that there be ascertainable beneficiaries, a charitable trust, by its nature, must be for the community at large, or at least a significant subset of the community at large. In assessing who benefits from a charitable trust, it is important to distinguish between direct beneficiaries and indirect beneficiaries.

   **1. Direct vs. indirect beneficiaries:** A charitable trust can benefit a single or limited number of individuals, as long as a larger pool of the community at large has a chance to be that individual, or as long as that individual is being supported in an activity that constitutes a charitable service that will benefit the larger community.

   **Examples:** A trust to educate a specific individual is generally not a charitable trust, but where the trust is to put a specific individual through medical school on condition that the individual return to the rural community that is supporting the trust to provide medical care to the community, the trust is held to constitute a charitable trust. Trusts to educate a group or class of individuals, such as the valedictorians of a particular school, are generally upheld as charitable trusts.

   **2. Governmental:** Trusts to improve governmental functions, or the structure of the government, are charitable trusts; but trusts for the benefit of a political party are not.

**E. Trustees:** The general rule for private trusts is that they are authorized to act only if all the trustees consent to the proposed action. (The modern trend is to permit the trust to act upon a vote of the majority of the trustees.) Unlike private trusts, charitable trusts have always been permitted to act based upon a vote of a majority of the trustees.

# II. CY PRES

**A. Overview:** Because charitable trusts are not subject to the Rule against Perpetuities, they can last forever. But it is possible that the specific charitable purpose for which they were created may become impossible or impractical (e.g., a charitable trust for the cure of a particular illness for which a cure is found). If a trust purpose becomes impossible or impractical, the general trust rule is the trust fails and a resulting trust is imposed to give the trust property back to the settlor (absent an express clause saying what is to happen if the trust fails). With respect to charitable trusts, however, the courts developed the doctrine of cy pres instead of immediately applying a resulting trust.

**B. Cy pres:** Where a trust with a general charitable purpose expresses a particular charitable purpose, and it becomes impossible, impractical, or illegal to carry out that particular charitable purpose, rather than imposing a resulting trust, modify the trust purpose to another particular charitable purpose within the general charitable purpose.

   **1. Example:** In *Estate of Crawshaw*, 819 P.2d 613 (Kan. 1991), the testator devised the residue of his estate to two residuary beneficiaries: 15 percent outright to the Salvation Army, the remaining 85 percent to Marymount College, in trust, to be used to provide educational loans to its nursing and other students. The will appointed Marymount trustee of the trust. Two months later, Marymount ceased operations. Three months later Marymount and the bishop for that diocese established the Marymount Memorial Educational Trust Fund (MMETF). The Salvation Army argued the gift to Marymount failed, and as the other beneficiary in the residuary clause, it was entitled to all the residuary estate. Marymount sought cy pres. After considering the provisions of the will and extrinsic evidence, the court found that the testator had a general charitable purpose. The court agreed that MMETF could serve as trustee of and administer the testator's trust, but only as long as it agreed to use the funds, to the maximum extent possible, consistent with the testator's original purpose, which was to benefit students, particularly nursing students.

2. **Express gift over clause:** Most courts hold that where the settlor expressly provides for what should happen to the property in the event the charitable trust fails, cy pres does not apply.

**Example:** In *Simmons v. Parsons College*, 256 N.W.2d 225 (Iowa 1977), the testator's will created two trusts for needy students at Drake University and Parsons College. The will provided that in the event either college was unable to administer the trust, the assets in question should go to his heirs at law. After the testator executed his will, but before he died, Parsons College stopped operating as an educational institution. Drake University argued that cy pres should be applied to permit it to serve as trustee of all the assets. The court ruled that in light of the testator's express clause addressing what should occur if either college was unable to administer its trust, application of cy pres would be inappropriate; and thus the trust property should go to the testator's heirs at law.

3. **Philanthropic inefficiency:** A lively academic debate has arisen over whether "inefficient" use of charitable trust resources to support the original trust purpose is grounds to apply cy pres to put the trust resources to more productive use. Implicit in this issue is the question of who really owns the property in a charitable trust—the community or settlor's intent as expressed in the trust.

   a. **Example:** Testatrix devised the residue of her estate (oil stocks worth $9 million) in trust to support the relief of poverty and other charitable purposes in Marin County (one of the richest counties in the country). Within a decade, the stock was worth over $300 million. The trustee, a community trust foundation administering trusts throughout the San Francisco Bay area, petitioned the court to apply cy pres, claiming that the unforeseen change in value of the trust res, coupled with the limited area where the trust funds could be used, constituted inefficient use of the trust income. The court ruled that concepts of inefficiency and ineffectiveness are not relevant to whether a settlor's charitable purpose has become "impractical."

   b. **Uniform Trust Code:** The Uniform Trust Code authorizes a court to apply cy pres if the particular charitable purpose becomes unlawful, impractical, impossible, *or wasteful*. UTC §408(b).

4. **Administrative deviation:** Where the administrative provisions of a trust cause the purpose to become illegal, impossible, or impractical, the doctrine of administrative deviation provides that the administrative provisions of the trust should be modified before modifying the trust purpose—thereby preserving settlor's intent.

**Example:** In *Matter of Estate of Wilson*, 452 N.E.2d 1228 (N.Y. 1983), two private trusts were established to help defray the educational expenses of young men. In *Matter of Wilson*, the superintendent was to certify the young men with the highest grades in chemistry to a private trustee so that the boys could qualify for trust benefits. In *Matter of Johnson*, the local board of education acted as the trustee and selected the "bright and deserving young men." In both cases, the participation of the public official was challenged as constituting state action implicating the equal protection provisions of the Fourteenth Amendment. The lower courts ordered administrative deviation to remove the role of the public official. The intermediate court of appeals held that judicial application of administrative deviation constituted state action that violated the Fourteenth Amendment, and it applied cy pres instead to remove the gender discrimination. The New York Court of Appeals ruled that application of cy pres is inappropriate unless the court first finds that the specific charitable purpose has become impossible or impracticable. In light of the fact that the only obstacle to the settlors' original charitable purpose was the participation of the public officials in the administration of the trusts, administrative deviation to remove that participation was the proper remedy.

5. **Discriminatory trusts:** Many older charitable trusts limited who qualified as a beneficiary based on either gender or race (or both). There has been much litigation over whether such restrictions constitute illegal discrimination. Some courts have applied cy pres to modify the terms of the trust to eliminate the racial or gender restriction; some courts have applied administrative deviation to eliminate the state action involved in the trust administration while permitting the discrimination (see *Wilson*, above); and some courts have terminated the trust rather than apply cy pres.

**Example:** In *Evans v. Abney*, 396 U.S. 435 (1970), in 1911, U.S. Senator Bacon of Georgia devised real property in trust to the city of Macon, Georgia, for the creation of a park (Baconsfield) exclusively for white people. In time, the city decided to permit all races to use the park, but the board of managers of the park appointed under the will sued to have the city replaced as trustee. The Georgia court accepted the city's resignation as trustee and appointed new trustees to continue the original trust purpose. The U.S. Supreme Court reversed, holding that due to the public nature of Baconsfield, it was subject to the equal protection and due process provisions of the Fourteenth Amendment. The Georgia court then ruled that the purpose of the trust had become impossible. The Attorney General of Georgia sought application of cy pres, to save the trust by striking the racial restriction and opening the park to all. Bacon's heirs opposed the motion. The proponents argued that failure to apply cy pres would be tantamount to applying a harsh penalty for applying the protections of the Fourteenth Amendment. The U.S. Supreme Court ruled that the issue was one of settlor's intent, and here Bacon's will clearly expressed a specific charitable intent and the intent that the property was not to be used for any other purpose. The Court declined to apply cy pres. The property was distributed to Bacon's heirs. (In *Trammell v. Elliott*, 199 S.E.2d 194 (Ga. 1973), the court applied cy pres to strike the discriminatory language, distinguishing the Evans case on the grounds that the will in question did not express a specific intent that conclusively negated a general charitable intent.)

# III. ENFORCING THE TERMS OF A CHARITABLE TRUST

A. **Standing:** An issue that naturally arises is who has standing to enforce the terms of a charitable trust and the trustee's fiduciary duty.

B. **State attorney general:** The general rule is that the state's attorney general represents the interests of the community and has exclusive standing to enforce the terms of the trust and the fiduciary duty against the charitable trustee.

C. **Individuals with special interest:** Depending upon the trust, some members of a community may receive more direct benefits from a charitable trust than do other members of the community.

Some courts have seized upon this point to expand the scope of who has standing to enforce the terms of a charitable trust to recognize that members of the community who have a "special interest" in the trust also have standing to sue to enforce the terms of the trust and the trustee's fiduciary duty. The plaintiff must show that he or she has a special interest in the trust—that he or she is eligible for a benefit that other members of the community are not.

1. **Modern trend:** Recognizing that state attorney general offices are overwhelmed with other responsibilities, courts are increasingly defining what constitutes a special interest more broadly, thereby facilitating private parties' ability to bring suits against trustees of charitable trusts.

2. **Uniform Trust Code:** The Uniform Trust Code expressly rejects the old common law rule and gives settlors standing to enforce the terms of their charitable gifts even in the absence of an express retention of an interest. UTC §408(d).

---

## *Quiz Yourself on* *CHARITABLE TRUSTS*

**69.** Sammy sets up a trust, the pertinent provisions of which state that the trust is to promote education, and that the income from the trust is to be distributed in equal shares to the sixth graders at Mother Theresa's Elementary School (an inner-city school located in the poorest part of the city), the day before the end of each semester. Sammy's heirs sue, claiming that the kids use the money to purchase candy and that the trust violates the Rule against Perpetuities. Does the trust qualify as a charitable trust? _____

**70.** Ali sets up a trust, the pertinent provisions of which provide that the income is to go to the law school Ali attended to pay the salary of "a wills and trust professor who knows what he or she is doing." Ali's heirs sue, claiming that the trust violates the Rule against Perpetuities. Does the trust qualify as a charitable trust? _____

**71.** Elizabeth funds a trust with the royalties from her movies and perfume. The trust provides in pertinent part that the income is to be used to support research to help find a cure for AIDS. Not long after Elizabeth's death, a leading biotech company finds a cure for AIDS. The takers under Elizabeth's residuary clause sue, asking the court to order a resulting trust and give the trust principal to them. Are the residuary takers under her will entitled to the property? _____

---

## *Answers*

**69.** The trust fails as a charitable trust that advances education, but it qualifies as a charitable trust that relieves poverty. Where a trust conveys mere financial enrichment upon its beneficiaries, to qualify as a charitable trust the court must find, from a totality of the circumstances, that the intended beneficiaries were poor or in necessitous circumstances. Here, Mother Theresa's Elementary School is located in the poorest part of the city. The court should find that the trust has a charitable purpose—the relief of poverty.

**70.** The trust has a charitable purpose, the advancement of education, but it appears to benefit only one person—the professor whose salary the income will pay. But by helping the law school to hire a qualified wills and trusts professor, the law students will benefit, and by benefiting the law students, the community at large arguably will benefit by being served by better trained lawyers. The indirect beneficiaries are the law students and the community at large. The trust qualifies as a charitable trust.

**71.** The court could impose a resulting trust and order the property distributed to the residuary takers, but the more likely result is that the court will apply cy pres. Elizabeth had a general charitable purpose (the promotion of health by curing communicable diseases), and although the particular charitable purpose (finding a cure for AIDS) is now impossible because it has been achieved, there are other communicable diseases that need curing. The court will probably apply cy pres and modify the terms of the trust to permit the income to be used to help find a cure for another communicable disease.

# *Exam Tips* on
# *CHARITABLE TRUSTS*

### Charitable trusts—charitable purpose

Whether a trust qualifies as a charitable trust is basically a two-step process. First, the purpose of the trust must be charitable. Second, a charitable trust arguably should not have ascertainable beneficiaries because it is for the benefit of the community at large. Trusts that appear to have a charitable purpose but that are for the benefit of a single individual or narrow group of individuals arguably do not qualify as a charitable trust.

☛ In assessing whether the trust is for the benefit of the community at large, distinguish between direct and indirect beneficiaries.

### Cy pres

If it becomes impossible or impractical to achieve the purpose of a charitable trust, apply the cy pres doctrine before applying the resulting trust doctrine.

☛ Cy pres is a two-step process. First, based on the original specific purpose of the trust, identify its more general charitable purpose (typically one of the five specific charitable purposes). Second, pick another specific charitable purpose within its general charitable purpose that is closely related to the trust's original specific purpose.

    ☞ As a practical matter, many courts appear more likely to apply cy pres the longer a charitable trust has been operating. Some courts will apply the doctrine even where the trust has an express gift over clause in the event the specific charitable purpose becomes impossible or impractical, though that is of questionable practice.

☛ Before applying cy pres, check analytically to see if administration deviation applies.

    ☞ The issue of ineffective philanthropy raises fascinating theoretical issues, but doctrinally the courts have declined to hold that it constitutes grounds to apply cy pres.

## CHAPTER 10

# POWERS OF APPOINTMENT: DISCRETIONARY FLEXIBILITY

## *ChapterScope*

This chapter examines an important tool that estate planners commonly use to add flexibility to the administration of a trust—giving a power of appointment to a trust beneficiary.

- **Power of appointment:** A power of appointment is similar to a power to revoke in the hands of a beneficiary other than the settlor. A power of appointment gives the donee the power to override the distributive terms of the trust and to direct the trustee to distribute some or all of the trust res outright to the appointees.

  - **General power:** A general power of appointment permits the donee to exercise the power (i.e., to appoint the property) in favor of the donee, the donee's estate, the donee's creditors, or creditors of the donee's estate.

  - **Special power:** A special power of appointment is one that cannot be exercised in favor of the donee, the donee's estate, the donee's creditors, or creditors of the donee's estate.

  - **Inter vivos vs. testamentary:** In creating the power, the donor can also specify *when* the power may be exercised—only inter vivos, only upon the donee's death (testamentary), or either.

- **Creditors' rights:** Creditors of a donee do not have much right to reach the property subject to the donee's power. If the power is a *special power*, creditors cannot reach the property subject to the power. If the power is a *general power*, creditors cannot reach the property subject to the power unless the donee exercises the power. If the donee exercises the power, the creditors can reach the property that was appointed. (In a few states, creditors of a donee holding a general power of appointment can reach the property subject to the power.)

- **Creation:** If one party intends to give another party a discretionary power to appoint property, the first party has created a power of appointment. No technical words are necessary to create a power.

- **Release:** A donee may release the power in whole or in part (either in whose favor the property may be appointed or when the power may be exercised).

- **Exercise:** A power of appointment is exercised anytime the donee intends to exercise the power. The instrument creating the power may stipulate how express the donee must be. The majority rule is that a basic residuary clause does not exercise a general or special testamentary power of appointment, though the jurisdictions are split on the issue.

  - **Allocation:** Where the holder of a special power creates an instrument that purports to (1) blend the appointive property with his or her own property, and then (2) dispose of all the property, the allocation doctrine "unblends" the property to ensure that only eligible appointees take the appointive property.

- **Capture:** Where the holder of a general power creates an instrument that purports to (1) blend the appointive property with his or her own property, and then (2) dispose of all the property, and (3) one or more of the gifts fail, the donee will be deemed to have appointed the failed gift to him- or herself (or estate), and the appointive property will be distributed accordingly.

- **Failure to exercise:** If a donee fails to exercise the power of appointment, the appointive property will be distributed pursuant to the donor's instructions in the event the power was not exercised. Where the donor has not made express provision for such an event, the property will be returned to the donor (or the donor's estate), unless the power was a special power of appointment to an ascertainable limited group, in which case the property may be distributed equally among the possible appointees.

# I. INTRODUCTION

A. **Conceptual overview:** In the context of a trust, the party who holds a power of appointment has the ability to direct a trustee to distribute some or all of the trust property regardless of the distributive provisions of the trust. While a power of appointment may be given to anyone, if a power to appoint property held in trust is created, the power is usually given to one of the trust beneficiaries.

1. **Observation:** A power to revoke is a form of a power. It gives the settlor the right to direct the trustee, regardless of the distributive provisions of the trust, to give some or all of the trust res back to the settlor. A power of appointment is similar, only a power of appointment is held by someone other than the settlor (typically a trust beneficiary), and the power can be structured so as to limit to whom the property can be distributed (i.e., in whose favor the power can be exercised) and when the power can be exercised (inter vivos or testamentary).

2. **Discretionary:** Like a power to revoke, a power to appoint is purely discretionary. The holder owes no fiduciary duty to anyone. It is the discretionary nature of the power of appointment that helps distinguish it from other legal relationships.

3. **Purpose:** Powers of appointment add flexibility to an estate plan. When a settlor creates a trust and decides who should take what and when, the settlor is making assumptions about the future. Often the future does not unfold as one assumes. While the settlor is alive and retains the power to revoke, the settlor can revoke and/or amend the trust to change the trust to reflect the changed circumstances. But after the settlor dies, or the trust becomes irrevocable, if things change, by giving a beneficiary a power of appointment, the beneficiary has the power to override the terms of the trust if change warrants it. By creating a power of appointment, the settlor is giving someone the power to override the trust if the holder deems it appropriate.

   **Example:** Sally creates a trust for her benefit for life, and upon her death, the principal is to be distributed equally among her children. If one of the children were in a bad accident and paralyzed for life, Sally might want to alter her distributive scheme to use more of the property to help that child. If Sally were alive and the trust were revocable, she could revoke the trust, in whole or in part, to make sure she had enough money to provide for the child. If Sally were dead, however, her distributive scheme would be set in stone unless she had granted someone a power of appointment. If she had, the party could exercise the power to override the trust's distributive scheme to ensure that the disabled child had enough resources.

**B. Terminology:** There is special terminology that accompanies a power of appointment.

- **Donor:** The party who creates the power of appointment.

- **Donee:** The party who holds and has the right to exercise the power of appointment.

- **Appointive property:** The property that is subject to a power of appointment; the property that the donee may appoint.

- **Objects:** The class of individuals to whom the property may be appointed; the group of eligible appointees in whose favor the power may be exercised.

- **Appointee(s):** The individual or individuals to whom the property is actually appointed; the individual(s) in whose favor the power is actually exercised.

- **Takers in default:** The individuals who are identified in the instrument creating the power who are to take the property if the donee fails to exercise the power.

**C. Types of powers:** There are two key variables with respect to each power of appointment that control the scope of the power. Special attention should be paid to (1) in whose favor the power can be exercised—whether the power is general or special, and (2) when it can be exercised—inter vivos, testamentary, or either.

1. **General power:** A general power of appointment is one that may be exercised in favor of the donee, the donee's estate, creditors of the donee, or creditors of the donee's estate.

   **Comment:** One way to think about a general power of appointment is that it may be exercised in favor of anyone in the world. Because the donee can appoint the property to him- or herself, the donee can turn around and gift the property to anyone in the world.

2. **Special power:** A special power of appointment is one that the donee can exercise in favor of anyone except the donee, the donee's estate, creditors of the donee, or creditors of the donee's estate.

   **Comment:** While the definition of a special power of appointment makes the class of objects sound large, as a practical matter, the instrument creating the power will identify a rather small class of objects—one that *must* exclude the donee, the donee's estate, creditors of the donee, and creditors of the donee's estate.

3. **Inter vivos power:** An inter vivos power of appointment is one that must be exercised, if at all, by a writing or deed executed by the donee inter vivos.

4. **Testamentary power:** A testamentary power of appointment is one that must be exercised, if at all, by the donee at death—typically in his or her will.

**D. Creditors' rights:** The general rule is that a creditor may reach a debtor's property, if necessary, to satisfy a debt. A power of appointment is generally considered a personal right and not a property interest. Creditors cannot reach the power. Creditors of a donee may, however, be able to reach the appointive property if the power is exercised.

1. **Special power:** A donee of a special power of appointment has no right to appoint the property to him- or herself or to use it for his or her benefit. The donee is merely an agent for the donor, with the power to appoint the property for the benefit of others. Creditors of a donee of a special power of appointment have no right to reach the appointive property, either before it is appointed or after it has been appointed.

2. **General power:** The traditional common law view of a general power of appointment was that it was not a property interest; it was merely an offer to the donee to have some power over the donor's property. The donor was still considered the owner of the property until the power was exercised. Under the traditional view of a general power of appointment, the donor had offered a gift to the donee, but there was no acceptance until the general power was exercised.

   a. **Failure to exercise:** The appointive property is considered the donor's property until the power has been exercised. Under the traditional view, if the donee does not exercise the power, creditors of the donee cannot reach the property subject to the power of appointment.

   b. **Exercised:** If the donee exercises the general power of appointment, the courts treated the exercise as if the property momentarily passed through the donee's hands, and during that instant, the creditors of the donee's interest attaches to the appointive property. If the donee exercises the power in favor of anyone, even if not him- or herself, creditors of the donee can reach the appointed property.

      **Modern statutory trend:** In some states, by statute, creditors of a donee of a general power of appointment can reach the appointive property even absent an exercise of the power by the donee. The rationale is that holding a general power of appointment is tantamount to ownership over the assets, thereby subjecting them to creditors' claims. Such statutes often require the creditors to exhaust the donee's other property first.

   c. **Elective share claims:** Under the traditional approach, the appointive property would not be subject to the elective share doctrine. The Uniform Probate Code's augmented estate, however, expressly includes property over which the decedent held a general power of appointment. The surviving spouse is entitled to claim a portion of the appointive property under the elective share. UPC §2-205(1)(i).

3. **Tax consequences:** The Internal Revenue Code has its own rules for powers.

   a. **General power:** For tax purposes, the holder of a *general* power of appointment is generally treated as the owner of the property over which he or she holds the power. If the property generates income, it is treated as the donee's income for income tax purposes. If the donee appoints the property, the property is subject to gift taxes. If the holder of a general power dies holding the power, the appointive property is included in his or her estate for federal estate tax purposes.

      **Life estate in surviving spouse with general power:** If the decedent leaves his or her surviving spouse a life estate interest in property, with a general power of appointment, the transfer will qualify for the marital deduction and is not taxable for federal estate tax purposes when the first spouse dies, but the property will be taxable as part of the federal gross estate of the second spouse to die.

**b. Special power of appointment:** For tax purposes, the holder of a special power of appointment is generally *not* treated as the owner of the property over which he or she holds the power of appointment. The income generated by the appointive property is not treated as the donee's income, and the appointive property is not included in the donee's estate for federal estate tax purposes.

4. **Malpractice liability:** A lawyer who fails to take full advantage of the tax savings opportunities present in using powers of appointments may be liable in malpractice for tax liability that could have been avoided.

# II. CREATING A POWER OF APPOINTMENT

**A. Intent:** A power of appointment is created as long as one has the intent to create a discretionary power in one party, over property held by another party, to direct the one holding the property to transfer the property. No technical words are necessary to create a power of appointment, only the intent to create a discretionary power.

**B. Donee:** A power of appointment can be created only in a living person.

**C. Power to consume:** If a party is given a life estate, with a power to consume the principal, the power to consume will be deemed to constitute a general power of appointment if the power to consume is not limited to an ascertainable standard relating to the health, education, support, or maintenance of the holder of the power to consume.

# III. RELEASING A POWER OF APPOINTMENT

**A. Release:** Because a power of appointment is a discretionary power, with no fiduciary duty attached to it, a donee has no duty to exercise it. Failure to exercise the power occurs if the donee dies without exercising it. Included within the right not to exercise the power, however, is the right to release the power at any time. The release may be complete or partial. If partial, it is important to note whether the release relates (1) to *the property* that may be appointed; (2) to *whom* the property may be appointed; or (3) to *when* the power may be exercised.

**B. Testamentary power:** A testamentary power is exercisable only upon the donee's death. The primary purpose of making a power testamentary is to make sure that the donee waits as long as possible before exercising the power of appointment. By waiting until death, the donee will be forced to take into consideration all the changes that occur during his or her lifetime before deciding whether, and how, to exercise the power.

1. **Contract to exercise:** If a donee of a testamentary power of appointment enters into an inter vivos contract that promises to exercise the testamentary power in a certain way upon the donee's death, the contract is null and void. The contract violates the donor's intent in creating the testamentary power. The effect of the contract, if enforceable, would be to exercise the power inter vivos. Any attempt at exercising a testamentary power inter vivos is null and void. This rule applies to all powers of appointment that are not presently exercisable. Nevertheless, any appointment made pursuant to such a contract that otherwise complies with the power of appointment is not invalid because of the contract.

      **a. Example:** In ***Benjamin v. Morgan Guar. Trust Co.***, 609 N.Y.S.2d 276 (N.Y. App. Div. 1994), the donee entered into an inter vivos agreement to exercise her testamentary power of appointment in favor of two hospitals and then executed a will that properly exercised the power in favor of the hospitals. Following the donee's death, the plaintiffs sought to invalidate the exercise because of the inter vivos agreement. The court ruled that while the agreement was unenforceable, the appointments were within the scope of the power and valid.

      **b. Restitution:** Although an inter vivos contract to exercise a testamentary power is unenforceable, if the donee fails to exercise the power as agreed, the contracting party has a cause of action against the donee for restitution, of the value given, from the donee's personal assets.

  **2. Release:** Although a testamentary power of appointment may not be exercised inter vivos, a testamentary power of appointment may be released inter vivos.

  **3. Contract vs. release:** Although an inter vivos contract to exercise a testamentary power of appointment is unenforceable, if the substantial effect of the contract is the same as the effect of a release of the power, many courts (but not all) will enforce the agreement not as a contract but as an inter vivos release of the testamentary power.

  **4. Example:** In ***Seidel v. Werner***, 364 N.Y.S.2d 963 (N.Y. Sup. Ct. 1975), the decedent held a testamentary power of appointment. The decedent contracted inter vivos to make, and not revoke, a will that exercised his power of appointment in favor of his children, for their support and maintenance until they reached the age of 21, at which time they were to receive the principal equally. Just four months later, the decedent executed a will exercising his testamentary power of appointment in favor of his new wife. The court held the contract to exercise the testamentary power of appointment null and void. The children attempted to characterize the contract as a release of the testamentary power. The court analyzed the effect of a release and the effect of the contract and ruled that the two were not substantially the same. The court declined to construe the contract as a release, but the court held that the children were entitled to restitution from the decedent's probate estate.

# IV. EXERCISING A POWER OF APPOINTMENT

  **A. Intent:** The donor's intent will control what is necessary to validly exercise a power of appointment. Assuming the donee complies with the requirements inherent in each type of power (general vs. special; inter vivos vs. testamentary), whether a donee has exercised a power of appointment is a question of the donee's intent. Although no express reference to the power is generally required (unless the instrument creating the power expressly requires), failure to refer to the power expressly will constitute an ambiguity that often results in litigation over whether the donee intended to exercise the power.

  **B. Residuary clause:** The jurisdictions are split over whether a standard residuary clause in the donee's will that does not make any reference to a power of appointment exercises a testamentary power of appointment.

1. **Majority rule:** The majority rule is that a standard residuary clause that does not make any reference to a power of appointment does *not exercise* either a general or a special testamentary power of appointment that the testator may have held.

   a. **Extrinsic evidence:** Where the decedent held a power of appointment and his or her residuary clause does not make any reference to the power, the jurisdictions that follow the majority rule are split over whether this constitutes a sufficient ambiguity to permit courts to admit extrinsic evidence as to the decedent's intent that his or her residuary clause exercise the power of appointment.

   b. **Example:** In *In re Proestler's Will*, 5 N.W.2d 922 (Iowa 1942), Henry Proestler's will created a testamentary trust for the benefit of his wife, Mathilde. It also gave her a testamentary general power of appointment over $20,000. When Mathilde died, her will made no express reference to the power and gave the residue of her estate to her nephew, Werner. Werner offered oral testimony to establish that Mathilde intended for her residuary clause to exercise her testamentary power of appointment. The court held that the residuary clause did not express the intent to exercise the power and that the will was unambiguous— thus the extrinsic evidence was not admissible to help interpret the will.

2. **Minority rule:** A minority of jurisdictions holds that a standard residuary clause adequately expresses the testator's intent to exercise a general power of appointment that the testator held, but not a special power that the testator held.

   a. **Rationale:** A general power of appointment is so close to ownership of the property subject to the power that the donee often thinks of the appointive property as if it were his or hers. Hence, the residuary clause should be deemed to exercise a general power, but not a special power (because the donee of a special power does not think of the property as his or hers because the donee cannot appoint it to him- or herself). In addition, the minority approach assumes that most power holders would want to exercise a power of appointment.

   b. **Example:** In *Will of Block*, 598 N.Y.S.2d 668 (Sup. Ct. 1993), Dina Block died in 1981. Her will created a testamentary trust of one-half of her residuary estate for the benefit of her son, Paul, Jr., and his twin sons, Allan and John. The trust terminated upon Paul, Jr.'s death, and he was given a limited testamentary power of appointment to appoint the property between Allan and John, and in the event he failed to do so, the property would be devised equally to them. The twins' older half-brother, Cyrus, was not an eligible appointee. Paul died in 1987. His will, executed after his mother's death, made no express reference to the power. He left the residue of his estate to an inter vivos trust he established in 1974. The trust contained subtrusts for his sons: 35 percent for Allan and John each, and 30 percent for Cyrus. The court stated that a residuary clause is presumed to exercise a power of appointment unless the will expressly or implicitly evidences the intent not to exercise the power. The court ruled that (1) there was insufficient evidence to overcome the strong presumption in favor of the residuary clause exercising the power, and (2) all the property subject to the power should be deemed appointed to their subtrusts equally, not just 70 percent of the appointive property.

3. **UPC approach:** A residuary clause expresses the intent to exercise a power of appointment the testator held only if (1) the power is a general power of appointment and the creating instrument does not contain a gift over in the event the power is not exercised; or

(2) the testator's will manifests an intention to include the property subject to the power. UPC §2-608.

4. **Generic reference:** The cases disagree over whether a standard residuary clause with a generic reference to any powers of appointment the testator may hold is adequate to exercise a power of appointment (this assumes the document creating the power does not expressly require an express reference to the power when the power is exercised). The UPC requires the reference to be specific.

   a. **Blended residuary clause:** A "blended" residuary clause is one that includes within the residuary clause a generic reference to any power of appointment the testator may hold: "I hereby give the rest, residue, and remainder of my estate, including any property over which I hold a power of appointment, to . . .". Under the UPC, such a generic reference is not enough, in and of itself, to exercise any power of appointment the testator may hold. It may, however, raise an issue of intent that may permit extrinsic evidence on the question of testator's intent.

   b. **Example:** In *Estate of Hamilton*, 593 N.Y.S.2d 372 (N.Y. App. Div. 1993), Milton Hamilton's 1982 will created a trust for the benefit of his wife, Anita. Paragraph four of the will granted Anita a testamentary general power of appointment over the property in the trust, "exercisable only by specific reference to said power in [Anita's] last Will and Testament." In the event she failed to exercise her power, the will devised the property equally to Milton's two daughters. When Anita died, her will purported to exercise the power of appointment given to her in paragraph "Sixth" of her husband's 1966 will. Milton's 1966 will had been revoked by subsequent wills executed by Milton in 1975 and 1982. The court held that Anita did not exercise the power of appointment granted to her in her husband's 1982 will because her reference in her will was not a "specific reference" as required by the 1982 will. Thus, the remainder of the trust passed to Milton's two daughters.

5. **Lapse and anti-lapse:** Where a donee exercises a testamentary power of appointment, but the appointee predeceases the donee, the issue arises whether lapse and anti-lapse should be applied to the appointment.

   a. **General power:** As a general rule, the courts have applied lapse and anti-lapse where the appointee of a general power of appointment predeceases the donee—if the appointee meets the necessary degree of relationship to the donee.

   b. **Special power:** The appointee of a special power of appointment must be an eligible object as defined in the instrument creating the power of appointment. If the effect of applying anti-lapse would be that the appointive property would end up in the hands of issue who were not eligible takers under the express terms of the power, the traditional rule is that anti-lapse cannot be applied. The modern trend applies anti-lapse to objects of the special power of appointment class even if their issue are not express objects of the class.

C. **Limitations:** Although the expectation is that the holder of a power of appointment would appoint the property outright to an appointee, theoretically, that is not the only option. A donee could appoint the property in trust, or even create a new power of appointment. Whether such conditional appointments are valid is a question of the original donor's intent.

1. **General power:** The donee of a general power of appointment can appoint the property as he or she wishes—outright, in trust, or even subject to a new power of appointment.

2. **Special power:** Absent express authority in the instrument originally creating the special power, the general rule is that the donee is to appoint the property outright. The modern trend, however, permits the donee of a special power of appointment to appoint either in trust or even subject to a new power of appointment as long as both the donee and objects of the new power were included in the original class of objects.

   **Restatement (Second):** The Restatement (Second) of Property, Donative Transfers, permits the donee to create either a general power of appointment in an appointee who was a member of the original class of objects, or to create a special power of appointment in anyone as long as the class of objects is the same as the original class of objects.

3. **Appointments:** Where the power is a special power of appointment, and the class of objects is relatively small, the issue arises of whether the donee can appoint all the property to one member of the class.

   a. **Exclusive:** If the power is exclusive, the donee can appoint all the property to one member of the class.

   b. **Nonexclusive:** If the power is nonexclusive, each member of the class must receive some distribution of the appointive property (and in some jurisdictions, the amount cannot be a "sham" amount).

   c. **Donor's intent:** In determining whether the power is exclusive or nonexclusive, the starting point is the donor's intent. Particular attention is paid to the language used in creating the power. Words such as *to one or more* indicate an exclusive power, while *among* is usually held to constitute a nonexclusive power.

   d. **Default:** The jurisdictions are split over which approach should be the default that applies where the instrument is ambiguous. The Restatement (Second) of Property §21.1 adopts the exclusive approach as its default.

4. **Fraud:** A fraud on a special power of appointment occurs where the donee and an eligible appointee agree that the donee will exercise the power of appointment in favor of the class member on condition that he or she share some of the appointive property with a person who is not an eligible appointee.

   a. **Remedy:** Where the parties engage in fraud on a special power of appointment, the courts tend to hold that the entire appointment is void, even the portion that the eligible appointee was to retain.

   b. **Example:** In *In re Carroll's Will*, 8 N.E.2d 864 (N.Y. 1937), William Carroll's will created a testamentary trust for the benefit of his wife, and upon her death, the property was to be split into two equal shares, one for the benefit of his daughter, Elsa, and the other for the benefit of his son, Ralph. Each child was given a special testamentary power of appointment over the property in their trust. Elsa had the power to appoint the property among her relatives who survived her, and in the event she failed to exercise the power, the property was to pass to her surviving children or descendents, and if there were none, to the donor's surviving heirs or next-of-kin. During her lifetime, Elsa expressed an intent to leave some of the property to her husband, only to be informed that she could not because he was not an eligible appointee. Her last will and testament appointed $250,000 of the property to her cousin Paul Curtis, but prior to executing the will that exercised the power of appointment, she asked Paul to give $100,000 of the property she appointed to him to her husband, and she asked Paul to put their agreement in writing the day she executed the will. The court held that the appointment to Paul was in consideration of his prior agreement to give $100,000 of it to Elsa's husband, and that constituted a fraud on the special power of appointment. The court found the gift of $150,000 to Paul inseparable from the $100,000 gift to Elsa's husband, and the court voided the entire exercise of the power. The appointive property passed in default of exercise to her brother.

## V. ATTEMPTED APPOINTMENT THAT FAILS

**A. Allocation/marshalling:** If the donee of a special power of appointment expresses the intent to exercise the power of appointment, but inappropriately attempts to mix the appointive property with the donee's own property in the distributive clause (typically in a blended residuary clause), the doctrine of allocation "unblends" the property to ensure that only eligible objects receive the appointive property.

**Rationale:** In "unblending" the appointive property from the donee's own property, and making sure that the appointive property is allocated only to takers who are eligible takers, the court is simply construing the language in the donee's will so that it gives maximum effect to the intent expressed while honoring the requirement that only eligible takers can take the appointive property.

**B. Capture:** If the donee of a general power of appointment (1) expresses the intent to exercise the power of appointment, and (2) the donee *blends* the exercise with the distributive provisions of his or her own will (typically in a blended residuary clause), if any of the appointment gifts fail for any reason, the donee will be held to have appointed the failed gifts to him- or herself ("captured the appointive property"), and the failed appointive property will be distributed as a part of the donee's general assets.

## VI. FAILURE TO EXERCISE A POWER OF APPOINTMENT

**A. Donor's intent:** If a donee fails to exercise a power of appointment, the donor's intent controls what should happen to the appointive property where the power is not exercised.

**B. Takers in default:** If the instrument that created the power identifies one or more express takers in default if the power is not exercised, the expressly identified takers in default will take if the power is not exercised.

**C. No takers in default—general power:** If there are no express default takers, and the power is a general power of appointment, if the power is not exercised the property will revert to the donor (or the donor's estate if he or she is dead).

**D. No takers in default—special power:** If there are no express takers in default and the power is a special power of appointment, if the class of possible objects is relatively small and ascertainable, the court may imply that the donor intended that the appointive property be distributed equally among the members of the appointive class rather than revert to the donor (or his or her estate).

## *Quiz Yourself on*
# *POWERS OF APPOINTMENT: DISCRETIONARY FLEXIBILITY*

**72.** Judy creates a trust that provides in pertinent part that the trustee shall distribute the income quarterly to her daughter Liza, and upon Liza's death, Liza has the power to appoint the principal as she deems appropriate, and in the absence of appointment, the property shall go to the Make a Wish Foundation. What is Liza's interest in the trust? Assume at Liza's death her medical bills exceed her probate estate. May her creditors reach the property over which she holds the power to appoint? _____

**73.** Bill's will provides that he leaves his property to his wife, Yi, "for life, with full power in her to dispose of the property during her life as she may desire, and upon her death, the remaining property shall go to our kids equally." What is Yi's interest under Bill's will, and what is the significance of that interest at the time of her death? _____

**74.** Tom's mother creates a trust in which he holds a life estate and general testamentary power of appointment. The trust expressly provides that in the event Tom does not exercise the power of appointment, the property in question will go to his issue. Thereafter, Tom and Nicole divorce. As part of the divorce, Tom executes an agreement that promises to execute a will that properly exercises the testamentary power of appointment that he holds in favor of his children. When Tom dies, his will contains a provision that expressly exercises the power of appointment in his mother's trust in favor of Lulu. Nicole and the kids sue. Who takes the property subject to the power? _____

**75.** Rosemary's will left all her estate, in trust, to George for life. The will also gave George the power to appoint the property, inter vivos or upon his death, to whomever he desired. Thereafter, George executed a valid will that made no express reference to the power of appointment under his mother's will. The residuary clause of George's will left "the rest, residue, and remainder of my property to Chicago Memorial Hospital." When family members asked George during life about the power of appointment in his mother's will, he assured them that he had taken care of it in his will. Has George validly exercised the power of appointment? _____

**76.** Tom's mother creates a trust with $1 million in which he holds a life estate and a testamentary power to appoint the property among his relatives, as he deems appropriate. Tom's will provides in pertinent part as follows: "I give the rest, residue, and remainder of my estate, including any property over which I hold a power of appointment, as follows: one-fourth to Penelope, one-fourth to Princeton, and one-half to my kids." Assuming Tom's residuary estate consists of $3 million how will his estate be distributed? _____

**77.** Barbara creates an inter vivos trust for the benefit of her son, George W., during his life, and she gives him a testamentary power to appoint the property among his issue upon his death. George W. executes a valid will that provides in pertinent part that he gives all his property, including any property over which he holds a power of appointment, to the Republican Party. Who takes the property subject to the power? _____

## *Answers*

**72.** Liza's interest in the income is mandatory, and she has a general testamentary power of appointment over the principal. Here, the creating instrument expressly provides that Liza can appoint the property upon her death, making it testamentary, as she deems appropriate. This language would permit Liza to appoint it to her estate or creditors of her estate, making it a general testamentary power. The general rule is that the creditors of a donee holding a general power of appointment cannot reach the property subject to the power unless the donee exercises the power. If Liza's will exercised the power of appointment, her creditors can reach the property subject to the power even if Liza appointed the property to someone else. If, however, Liza did not exercise the power of appointment, under the general rule her creditors could not reach the property.

**73.** Yi has a life estate and, arguably, a power to consume. A power to consume constitutes an inter vivos general power of appointment. No technical words are necessary to create a power of appointment. Yi's ability to appoint the property in question to herself during her lifetime makes the power to consume a general power of appointment. The significance of that is that for federal estate tax purposes, property over which a decedent holds an unrestricted general power of appointment is included in the decedent's federal gross estate for estate tax purposes.

**74.** Inter vivos contracts with respect to how a donee will exercise a testamentary power of appointment are null and void as contrary to the donor's intent. Tom's inter vivos agreement that promised that he would exercise the power in favor of the kids is unenforceable as an inter vivos contract. Where the effect of an inter vivos contract is substantially the same as the effect of a release, the inter vivos contract can be construed as an inter vivos release. Here, Tom's issue are the express default takers if the power is not exercised, and they are also the takers under the inter vivos contract. Many courts would hold that the inter vivos contract constitutes an inter vivos release and enforce it as such, giving the property to Tom's children.

**75.** The general rule is that a bare residuary clause that makes no reference to any powers of appointment does not exercise a power of appointment. Under the majority approach, George's residuary clause would be presumed not to have exercised the power of appointment. (The jurisdictions are split as to whether George's statements to his family members that he had taken care of the power of appointment are admissible as evidence of his intent that the residuary clause did exercise the power.) Under the UPC, a basic residuary clause exercises a power of appointment if the power is a general power of appointment and the creating instrument contains no express gift over in the event the power is not exercised. Here, George's power was a general power of appointment because he could appoint the property to "whomever he desired"—including himself. In addition, Rosemary's will makes no provision for where the property should go in the event George fails to exercise the power. Under the UPC approach, George's residuary clause would be deemed to have exercised the power of appointment.

**76.** Because Tom is limited in appointing the property over which he holds a power of appointment to his relatives, Tom's power is a special power of appointment. Yet Tom attempts to blend the property over which he holds the power of appointment with the residue of his probate estate and give the combined property to a group of takers—some of whom are not eligible appointees. The doctrine of allocation provides that the property needs to be "unblended" and the appointive property allocated first to those who are eligible to take. Here, if the property is unblended, the appointive property is $1 million. That property is allocated first to his kids, who are the only eligible takers in the clause, to count toward their share of the combined property (they were to take $2 million of the $4 million).

The rest of Tom's property is then allocated to best fulfill his intent—another $1 million to his kids, $1 million to Penelope, and $1 million to Princeton.

**77.** George's power of appointment is a special power of appointment because he is limited in whose favor he can appoint the property and the class excludes himself, his creditors, his estate, and creditors of his estate. George has attempted to exercise the power of appointment in his residuary clause, but the taker under the clause is not an eligible appointee. George has not properly exercised the power of appointment. There is no express default taker in the trust creating the power. Before giving the property back to Barbara (or her estate as the case may be), most courts would find that the class of eligible appointees constitutes a limited enough group to imply a default gift in the class members. George's issue will take in default rather than returning the gift to Barbara.

---

## Exam Tips on
## POWERS OF APPOINTMENT: DISCRETIONARY
## FLEXIBILITY

### Powers conceptually

Spend some time getting comfortable conceptually with powers of appointment. One way to think about them is that they are nothing more than a power to revoke in the hands of someone other than the settlor/donor. The party holding the power can override all the other provisions of the instrument (typically a trust) and order the property (typically the principal) distributed immediately pursuant to the exercise of the power.

### Powers generally

Every power has two key characteristics: its scope (general vs. special) and when it can be exercised (inter vivos vs. testamentary or both). Most of the issues and doctrines turn on whether the power is general or special, and to a lesser degree whether it is inter vivos or testamentary. Every time you see a power, you should immediately stop and analyze it for its two key characteristics. (Creditors' rights are derivative of the type of power, and thus a common area to test because the professor can test two doctrines with one issue.)

### Creation—intent based

No special language is needed to create a power, though proper drafting would expressly refer to the power as a power. A general power to appoint, however, can also be created as a power to withdraw, appropriate, or consume—a more subtle way to raise the issue.

### Release of a power

Whether a power has been released can be raised indirectly by a donee of a testamentary power attempting to contract inter vivos as to how the donee will exercise the power testamentary. The release material can also be raised by a partial release of a general power, turning the general power into a special power; or to turn a power that could be exercised inter vivos or testamentary into a purely testamentary power.

## Exercise of a power

Absent express requirements in the instrument creating a power, whether a power has been exercised is a question of the donee's intent. The area where this causes the most problems, and is tested the most, is whether a standard residuary clause with no express reference to any power of appointment exercised a power of appointment.

☛ The states are split over this issue, often distinguishing between a general power and a special power. Know which approach you need to know—your state's approach, the general approach, or the UPC approach. If the residuary clause is presumed not to have exercised the power of appointment, address whether evidence of the donee's intent is limited to the face of the will or includes extrinsic evidence.

☛ Where you have a validly exercised power, but the property is not appointed outright, you need to discuss whether there are any limitations on how the power can be exercised that affects the purported exercise.

## Failed or improper exercise of a power of appointment

An area of powers that is tested often (because they overlap nicely with other doctrines) is the failed/improper exercise of the power. Watch for blended residuary clauses—they often raise issues of allocation or capture.

☛ Under the doctrine of allocation, allocate the property subject to the power to those who are eligible to receive it first, and then allocate the decedent's property as appropriate to fulfill the rest of the decedent's wishes. If there is more property subject to the power to appoint than there are eligible takers, as to that excess appointive property, the property has not been appointed.

☛ If the power of appointment is a general power of appointment, and the gift to one or more of the beneficiaries fails, under the capture doctrine, give the failed gifts to the other takers under the decedent's will (or intestacy) rather than having the property subject to the power of appointment pass under the instrument creating the power.

## Failure to exercise a power

If the power is a general power, if the donee fails to properly exercise the power and the capture doctrine does not apply, first check to see if the instrument creating the power expressly provides for a default taker, and if not, give the property back to the donor and let it pass as a failed gift.

If the power is a special power, and the donee does not properly appoint all the property, first check again for an express default clause, but if there is none, before giving the property back to the donor, if the class of possible appointees is a fairly limited and defined class, argue that the power constitutes an imperative power and give the property equally to the class of possible appointees.

CHAPTER 11

# CONSTRUING TRUSTS: FUTURE INTERESTS AND CLASS GIFTS

## *ChapterScope*

This chapter examines the issue of how to construe the equitable interests that are created when a trust is created. Almost invariably, the interests are some combination of possessory estate and future interests. A future interest is the present right to possession and enjoyment in the future.

- **Future interests:** If the settlor retains the future interest, it must be a reversion, a possibility of reverter, or a right of entry. If a beneficiary holds the future interest, it must be a vested remainder, a contingent remainder, or an executory interest.

- **Vested remainders favored:** Remainders can be vested or contingent. The common law courts favored construing an ambiguous remainder as vested.

  - **Benefits:** Vested remainders have several benefits over contingent remainders: (1) vested remainders accelerate to immediate possession regardless of how the preceding estate ends; (2) vested remainders are transferable; (3) if the party holding the remainder dies before the end of the preceding estate, a vested remainder passes to the holder's heirs or devisees; and (4) language divesting vested remainders is construed strictly.

- **Class gifts:** Where a gift is to a class, a variety of construction issues can arise.

  - **Rule of convenience:** Under the rule of convenience, a class closes automatically, by operation of law, as soon as one member of the class is entitled to possession of his or her interest. No one else can enter the class, even if he or she otherwise appears to be eligible to join the class.

  - **"Heirs":** Remainders to a particular party's "heirs" create problems concerning who is included (surviving spouse?) and when the class of heirs should be determined (when the individual dies or when the remainder becomes possessory).

    - **Common law:** Common law rules often voided express gifts to "heirs." Under the doctrine of worthier title, if a document purports to create a remainder in the settlor's heirs, the remainder is converted into a reversion in the grantor; and under the Rule in Shelley's case, if a document purports to create a remainder in the heirs of a life tenant, the remainder is given to the life tenant.

  - **"Issue":** Gifts to "issue" are ambiguous if the instrument fails to indicate whether the gift should be distributed per stirpes, per capita, or per capita at each generation.

  - **Gift of income to class:** A gift of income to a class is presumed to be in joint tenancy with right of survivorship, so if one member dies, his or her share is distributed among the other class members. The presumption is rebutted if the instrument expresses a contrary intent, either expressly or implicitly.

# I. FUTURE INTERESTS

A. **Trust's equitable interests:** At the equitable level, every trust is some combination of possessory estate and future interests. At common law, there were a whole host of technical drafting rules with respect to the future interests. If the future interest violated the rule, typically it was null and void (thereby defeating the settlor's intent).

   1. **Possessory estate:** The party who holds the possessory estate holds the present right to possess the property right now.

   2. **Future interest:** The party who holds the future interest holds the present right to possess the property at some point in the future.

   3. **Terminology:** Possessory estates and future interests typically are created in a trust, but they do not have to be. If the interests are not created in a trust, they are called "legal" possessory estates and future interests; if they are created in a trust, they are called "equitable" possessory estates and future interests. If the interests are not created in a trust, the party who creates the interests is typically called the grantor, and any party other than the grantor who receives an interest is a grantee. If the interests are created in a trust, the party who creates the interests is typically called the settlor, and any party other than the settlor who receives an interest is typically called a beneficiary. This material will assume the interests are created in a trust.

B. **Future interests in the settlor:** If a settlor retains a future interest, it must be one of three future interests: a reversion, a possibility of reverter, or a right of entry. (The most common future interest in the settlor is the reversion.)

   1. **Reversion:** If the settlor has the right to possess the property after a finite estate ends, the settlor holds a reversion.

      a. **Finite estates:** A finite estate is an estate that must end. At common law there were three possible finite estates: life estates, fee tails, and terms of years (the most common is the life estate).

      b. **Implied reversions:** Reversions can arise implicitly (by operation of law) if a settlor does not convey his or her entire interest. Whatever interest he or she does not convey is presumed retained, and if the retained future interest follows a life estate or other finite estate (the most common scenario), it is a reversion.

      **Example:** Bilbo, who owns Shireacres, creates an inter vivos trust that provides in pertinent part: "To Frodo for life." State the title. Frodo holds a life estate; the settlor, Bilbo, holds a reversion.

      c. **Vested:** Reversions are vested future interests. (Classifying a future interest as vested does not necessarily mean that it will become possessory, but there are benefits associated with vested interests—transferability, not subject to destructibility, etc.)

   2. **Possibility of reverter:** If the settlor conveys a fee simple determinable, the settlor will be deemed to have retained a possibility of reverter.

   3. **Right of entry:** If the settlor conveys a fee simple subject to a condition subsequent, the settlor will be deemed to have retained a right of entry in the event the condition subsequent occurs.

**4. Example:** In *Mahrenholz v. County Bd. of School Trustees,* 417 N.E.2d 138 (Ill. App. 1981), the Huttons conveyed real property "to be used for school purposes only; otherwise to revert to Grantors." The grantee stopped using the land for school purposes, and thereafter the grantors' son executed an instrument that purported to convey his interest. At the time, the state had a statute that barred transferring both rights of entry and possibilities of reverter. The court held that the initial conveyance constituted a fee simple determinable, making the future interest a right of entry. The moment the grantees ceased using the land for school purposes, the fee simple interest reverted to the grantors. The son's deed was effective to convey fee simple.

**C. Future interests in a grantee/beneficiary:** There are only two future interests that a beneficiary can hold: a remainder or an executory interest.

**1. Remainder:** If a beneficiary has the right to possession after a finite estate ends, the beneficiary holds a remainder.

**a. Must be express:** Unlike reversions, a remainder will arise only if the words of the instrument expressly grant the future interest following a finite estate to a beneficiary. Remainders will not be implied.

**b. Example:** Bilbo creates an inter vivos trust that provides in pertinent part: "To Frodo for life, then to Sam for life." State the equitable interests created. Frodo holds a life estate. The trust expressly provides that Sam holds the future interest following Frodo's finite estate, so Sam holds a remainder—in life estate.

**2. Vested vs. contingent:** Every remainder is either vested or contingent. A remainder is vested if (1) the holder of the interest is ascertainable, and (2) there is no express condition precedent, in the clause creating the remainder or the preceding clause, that has to be satisfied before the remainder can become possessory. If a remainder is not vested, by default it is contingent.

**a. Ascertainable:** Ascertainable means that the party who holds the remainder must be identifiable by his or her personal name.

**b. Condition precedent:** A condition precedent is an express condition in the instrument creating the remainder that could occur before the remainder becomes possessory. If the condition is set forth in the clause creating the remainder or the preceding clause, the remainder is a contingent remainder.

**c. Destructibility:** At common law, if a contingent remainder did not vest before or at the moment the preceding finite estate ends, the contingent remainder was destroyed.

**d. Reversion:** Whenever an instrument creates a contingent remainder, there must be a reversion in the settlor (express or implied) in the event the contingent remainder does not vest in time.

**Example:** "To Frodo for life, then to Frodo's children." Frodo has no children. State the title. Frodo has a life estate. Because his children are not ascertainable, the instrument grants them a *contingent* remainder. Because the remainder is contingent, the settlor holds a reversion.

**e. Alternative contingent remainders:** A remainder that takes possession only if a contingent remainder created earlier in the conveyance fails is called an alternative contingent remainder. The "express condition precedent" is the condition that the prior contingent remainder must fail.

    **i. Example:** "To Frodo for life, then to Sam if he makes it back from Mordor, but if Sam does not make it back from Mordor, then to Pippin." State the title. Frodo has a life estate, Sam has a contingent remainder, Pippin has an alternative contingent remainder (contingent on Sam not making it back from Mordor), and the settlor has a reversion.

    **ii. Example:** In *Webb v. Underhill,* 882 P.2d 127 (Or. App. 1994), testator's will devised his real property (Buck Hollow Ranch) to his wife Agnes for life as long as she remained unmarried, but if she remarried or died, the property shall revert to four of the testator's children, but if one or more of these four shall be dead, his or her share shall go to his or her lineal descendants. The court found that the language created alternative contingent remainders in the children alive at the time of the wife's remarriage or death, or his or her grandchildren. The court determined that the contingent remainders would vest only upon survival to the date of the wife's death or remarriage, if any.

    **iii. Reversion:** Because contingent remainders cannot accelerate into possession, if the preceding finite estate ends early and the first contingent remainder has not vested by or at that moment, both contingent remainders are destroyed, and the property reverts to the settlor. So even though alternative contingent remainders do not appear to require a default reversion, one is necessary.

    **iv. Premature termination:** A finite estate can end prematurely (before its natural termination) if there is forfeiture, renunciation, or merger. Forfeiture occurs if one commits certain crimes and has to forfeit his or her property. Renunciation occurs where one renounces one's interest. Merger occurs if one party holds successive vested interests (usually as a result of a transfer of one of the interests). The interests merge into the largest possible interest. If a life estate merges into a larger interest, the life estate is terminated.

**3. Remainders and class gifts:** Where a remainder is to a class of beneficiaries, the interest may be (1) vested as to all, (2) contingent as to all, or (3) vested as to some, but still open. If the class is vested as to some but still open so others can join the class, as new members join the class they are entitled to a share of the property (thereby partially divesting those members of the class who previously had vested).

**Example:** "To Harrison for life, then to Harrison's children." Assume Harrison has two children, Ben and Will. State the title. Harrison has a life estate. Ben and Will hold a vested remainder. But because Harrison may have more children, Ben and Will hold a vested remainder subject to partial divestment (because the class is still open and if Harrison has more children, they would partially divest Ben and Will of some of their interests).

**4. Vested remainders subject to divestment:** A vested remainder subject to divestment is created when there is an express condition precedent that may affect the remainder's possessory interest, but the condition precedent is set forth in a clause *after* the clause creating the remainder. If the condition occurs, the vested remainder is completely divested. In distinguishing contingent remainders from vested remainders subject to divestment, the key is the location of the condition precedent.

a. **Example:** Compare the following two conveyances.

"To Frodo for life, then to Sam if he returns the ring." State the title. Frodo has a life estate. Sam has a contingent remainder—contingent because there is an express condition precedent in the same clause creating the remainder that he has to satisfy before the remainder can become possessory—he has to return the ring first. Because Sam holds a contingent remainder, the settlor retains a reversion.

"To Frodo for life, then to Sam, but if Frodo gives the ring to Paul, then to Paul." State the title. Frodo has a life estate. Reading and analyzing comma to comma, Sam has a vested remainder. There is, however, an express condition precedent (a condition that could occur prior to the remainder becoming possessory) in the clause subsequent to the clause creating the remainder. If that condition occurs, Sam's remainder would be completely divested and the property would pass to Paul instead. Sam holds a vested remainder subject to divestment.

b. **Powers of appointment:** If a trust creates a life estate, gives someone a power of appointment, and expressly provides for default takers who will take in the event the power of appointment is not exercised, the express takers in default hold a vested remainder and the potential exercise of the power of appointment constitutes a condition, which if exercised would divest the vested remainder.

5. **Executory interests:** An executory interest is a future interest if it is held by a third party (someone other than the settlor), and it follows either (1) a vested remainder subject to divestment, or (2) a fee simple subject to an executory limitation (the latter is a fee simple determinable or a fee simple subject to condition subsequent, only the future interest following fee simple defeasible is held by a third party).

**Shifting vs. springing:** The executory interest is a *shifting* executory interest if the party holding the interest takes the right to possession from someone other than the settlor. The executory interest is a *springing* executory interest if the party holding the interest takes the right to possession from the settlor.

# II. PREFERENCE FOR VESTED REMAINDERS

A. **Vested vs. contingent:** Classifying a remainder as a vested remainder or a contingent remainder has a number of possible consequences.

B. **Destructibility:** Under the common law destructibility of contingent remainders, if a contingent remainder did not vest before or at the moment the preceding estate ended, the contingent remainder was destroyed (it became null and void).

1. **Scope:** The destructibility of contingent remainders applied only to legal contingent remainders in real property.

2. **Modern trend:** The modern trend abolishes the destructibility of contingent remainders doctrine.

C. **Accelerate to possession:** A vested remainder accelerates into possession the moment the preceding life estate ends, whether it ends naturally or prematurely. On the other hand, contingent remainders cannot become possessory until all the express condition precedents are satisfied. If a contingent remainder did not vest in time, at common law it was subject to being destroyed under the destructibility of contingent remainders.

1. **Disclaimers—modern trend:** If a life tenant were to disclaim, at common law the issue of whether the remainder would accelerate into possession turned on whether the remainder was contingent or vested. Under the modern trend, some courts have ruled that the issue turns on testator's probable intent if he or she had known that the life tenant would disclaim. Many jurisdictions have adopted disclaimer statutes that expressly provide that the disclaiming party is treated as if he or she predeceased the decedent. Whether a remainder accelerates into possession or not then depends on the effect of treating the disclaiming party as if he or she predeceased the decedent.

2. **Disclaimer execution:** The UPC and federal tax laws disagree over when a disclaimer must be executed to be effective.

   a. **Federal tax laws:** Under federal tax laws, for a disclaimer to be effective and not incur a gift tax, the disclaimer must be executed within nine months of the interest in question being created. As applied to a trust, the disclaimer must be filed within nine months of the trust being created, even if the interest is contingent.

   b. **UPC:** Under the UPC, a disclaimer is effective as long as it is executed within nine months of the interest vesting indefeasibly. As applied to contingent remainders contingent upon the remainderman surviving the life tenant, the remainderman can wait until the death of the life tenant to decide whether to disclaim. UPC §2-801.

D. **Transferability:** At common law, vested remainders were transferable, but contingent remainders and executory interests were not. The modern trend repudiates the distinction between vested and contingent remainders, making contingent remainders transferable.

1. **Spendthrift clause:** A settlor can prevent the transferability of both vested and contingent remainders by including a spendthrift clause in the trust.

2. **Transmissibility:** A property interest is transmissible if the party holding it has the power to devise it upon death, and in the event the interest is not properly devised, the interest is descendible—it will pass to one's heirs. Reversions, remainders (vested and contingent—as long as the contingency is not that the remainderman must survive to the time of possession), and executory interests are transmissible.

3. **Taxation:** A transmissible future interest constitutes a property interest for purposes of the federal estate tax. If a party holds a transmissible property interest when he or she dies, the interest is included in his or her probate estate for purposes of calculating the party's estate tax.

   a. **Valuation:** Where the transmissible interest is vested, its value turns on the life expectancy of the life tenant, and discounting that value to its present value based on interest rates. Where the transmissible interest is contingent, or subject to a power of appointment, or subject to depletion in favor of the life tenant, valuation is much more difficult, turning on the totality of the circumstances.

   b. **Avoidance:** A special power of appointment is not a property interest for purposes of calculating estate taxes. Accordingly, if a settlor wishes to avoid estate taxes being imposed on a transmissible future interest in the event a vested remainderman dies before his or her interest becomes possessory, the settlor can make the remainderman's interest contingent on surviving to the time of possession and granting the remainderman a special power to appoint the property among his or her heirs. Because the special power of appointment is not a taxable property interest, the remainderman has the same power at death, to pass it to his or her heirs, without an estate tax being imposed.

**E. Preference for vested remainders:** Where a remainder is created, and the language is ambiguous as to whether the remainder is to vest upon the death of the transferor or upon the death of the life tenant, the preference for a vested remainder means that the gift is construed so that the remainder vests upon the death of the transferor.

1.  **Example:** In *In re DiBiasio,* 705 A.2d 972 (R.I. 1998), testator created a testamentary trust, with a life estate in his surviving brothers and sisters. Upon the death of the last surviving sibling, the trustee was to make certain outright distributions of cash to certain heirs, and after making such distributions, the trust was to terminate, and any remaining trust assets were to be distributed to Joseph DiBiasio, individually and for his sole use free and clear of trust. Joseph survived the decedent, but died before the last of the testator's surviving siblings. The testator's other heirs claimed that Joseph's interest was a contingent remainder, contingent upon surviving the last surviving sibling. The court applied the traditional rule favoring early vesting and held that Joseph's interest vested upon his surviving the testator. The court ruled that upon Joseph's death his interest passed to his heirs, and not to the testator's heirs.

2.  **Remainderman predeceases life tenant:** If the remainderman dies before the life tenant, the issue that arises is what happens to the remainderman's interest.

    a.  **Transmissibility:** The traditional and general rule is that the remainderman's interest is transmissible—it passes into his or her probate estate where the remainderman has the option of devising it to whomever he or she wishes, and in the event he or she fails to devise it, it passes to his or her heirs.

    b.  **Lapse/anti-lapse:** Historically, the lapse and anti-lapse doctrines were limited to wills. Recently, a few courts have applied the doctrines to revocable trusts and remaindermen because revocable trusts are functionally indistinguishable from wills. The difference between transmissibility and lapse/anti-lapse is significant. If the interest is transmissible, if a remainderman dies before his or her interest becomes possessory, he or she can devise the remainder to whomever he or she wants, and in the event it is not devised, the interest passes to his or her heirs. Under lapse/anti-lapse, the predeceased remainderman has no interest unless he or she meets the requisite degree of relationship, and even then, the interest will go only to his or her issue, and if none, the remainderman's interest lapses (fails).

    c.  **Divide and pay over provision:** Where a trust creates one or more life estates, and then conveys a remainder outright to a class of remaindermen, the trust often provides that upon the death of the surviving life tenant, the trustee is to "divide and pay over" the property to the remaindermen. Some courts have implied a requirement that the remaindermen must survive the last life tenant to die before they can take. The majority of courts, however, have held such a "divide and pay over" clause insufficient, in and of itself, to express the intent that the remaindermen have to survive the life tenants.

**d. Transmissible interest:** If a party holds a transmissible future interest, but the party dies before the interest becomes possessory, the interest is treated like any other property the party owns. The transmissible property interest falls into probate, where it is subject to the probate process and estate taxes.

**Flexibility:** A party who holds a transmissible property interest, in essence, holds a general testamentary power of appointment. The party can devise the transmissible interest as he or she sees fit. The power to devise the interest means that the party holding the transmissible interest has the flexibility to alter the disposition of the property if circumstances warrant. If the interest were subject to lapse and anti-lapse, the power to devise would be lost, and with that, the flexibility to take into consideration any change in circumstances that may warrant altering the disposition plan.

3. **Express survival requirement:** Where a settlor includes an express survival requirement in his or her instrument, care needs to be taken to indicate whether the party in question must survive the settlor, the life tenant, or one or more of the remaindermen. Whom the party must survive is a question of settlor's intent, and therefore is a fact sensitive issue. If a general rule exists, however, it appears to be that where a party's interest is qualified by an express survival requirement, more often than not, the courts construe the survival requirement to mean the party must survive to the moment he or she is entitled to possession.

**Example:** In *Browning v. Sacrison,* 518 P.2d 656 (Or. 1974), testatrix's will devised 960 acres of land to his daughter, Ada, for life, with remainder over at Ada's death to his grandsons Franklin and Robert, or, if either of them be dead, all to the other. Franklin died before Ada. The court construed the phrase "or if either of them be dead" as referring to the time of Ada's death, not the testatrix's death. Franklin's interest constituted a contingent remainder, contingent upon surviving the life tenant, which he did not. (*Compare Matter of Krooss,* 99 N.E.2d 222 (N.Y. Ct. App. 1951), where the testator's will left his property to his wife for life, and upon her death, to his children equally, "absolutely and forever," but if either should die before his wife, his or her share to his or her descendants. One child died before his wife without surviving issue. The court, emphasizing the words "absolutely and forever" in the will, construed the will as creating a vested remainder upon the testator's death, subject to divestment only if the child (1) predeceased the life beneficiary (2) with surviving issue.)

4. **Divesting condition:** Where the conveyance contains an express condition that if the remainderman dies without issue his or her interest is divested and transferred to another party, ambiguity often arises as to whether the divesting condition is to apply only if the remainderman dies before the life tenant or if the divesting condition is to apply whenever the remainderman dies. Again, the issue is one of settlor's intent. Absent clear evidence of settlor's intent, most courts rule that the divesting condition applies only if the remainderman dies before the life tenant.

**Example:** Godfather transfers property in trust as follows: "To Godfather for life, and then to Michael, but if Michael dies without surviving issue, to Sonny." The general rule is that the divesting condition "dies without surviving issue" applies only if the remainderman dies before the life tenant—here, only if Michael died without surviving issue before the Godfather died.

5. **Rules in Clobberie's case:** Clobberie's case is an old English case that established three rules of construction concerning gifts to be paid upon a beneficiary reaching a specific age.

The exact wording of the gift is critical to determine which rule applies. Two of the three rules evidence the common law preference against imposing a survival requirement and in favor of vested interests, but one implies a survival requirement, resulting in a contingent interest.

**a. Rule 1:** Where one conveys (by will or trust) "all the *income* to [a beneficiary], with principal to be paid when she reaches a specific age or upon marriage,..." and the beneficiary dies before reaching that age or marrying, the beneficiary's interest in the principal is transmissible.

**Rationale:** The rationale is that the gift was complete upon execution of the instrument and only possession was to be delayed. Upon the death of the beneficiary, however, there is no need to delay distribution of the principal. It is paid to the beneficiary's estate upon his or her death.

**b. Rule 2:** Where one conveys (by will or trust) a sum of money "to [a beneficiary] *at*" a specific age, if the beneficiary dies before reaching that age, the gift fails.

**Rationale:** The court construed the language that the gift is paid "at" a specific age as constituting an express condition precedent that the beneficiary reaches that age. One way to justify the distinction under this conveyance is that there is no comma between the words identifying the beneficiary and the condition that the gift is to be made "at" a specific age. In contrast, in the other two rules, the gift is made to the person, then typically there is a comma, and then there is the clause indicating that possession is to be delayed until a specific age. An alternative justification is that the language "to be paid at" a specific age, more clearly indicates a completed gift, with just possession being delayed until that age, versus a gift "at" at specific age, which appears to indicate an intent that the gift not be made until the person reaches the specific age. The latter is not just delaying possession, but the whole gift is contingent upon reaching that age.

**Criticism/modern trend:** Too much is being read into the distinction between a gift "*to be paid at*" a specific age and a gift "at" a specific age. Under the modern trend, the courts construe the latter the same as the former—in both the gift is complete, only possession is delayed, and if the beneficiary dies before receiving possession, the gift is paid to his or her estate.

**c. Rule 3:** Where one conveys (by will or trust) a sum of money "to [a beneficiary], to be paid when the beneficiary reaches" a specific age, and the party dies before reaching that age, the beneficiary's interest is transmissible.

**Rationale:** The rationale is comparable to the rationale for the first rule. The language of the gift indicates a completed gift, with possession delayed until a specific age, as supported by the location of the comma.

**d. Class gifts:** The rules in Clobberie's case have been applied to class gifts as well as gifts to individuals.

**6. UPC revision:** The UPC has advocated a new approach to future interests in trust (revocable or irrevocable), advocating a lapse/anti-lapse type approach to all future interests in trust, unless the instrument expressly provides otherwise. UPC §2-707.

**a. Implied survival requirement:** UPC §2-707 requires holders of future interests to survive to the time of distribution. If a remainderman does not survive to the time for distribution, the UPC provides for a gift over to the remainderman's issue; and if there are none, the gift fails and is returned to the settlor's estate—unless there is an express default taker who is to take in the event the gift fails.

**b. Rationale:** The UPC provision is based on the transferor's presumed intent. The transferor's intent was to give the gift to the person. If the person were to die before receiving the property, the UPC assumes that the transferor would prefer not to make the gift because under the common law approach the interest is transmissible so the donee could devise the gift to anyone—maybe even someone the transferor did not like. If, however, the predeceased beneficiary is survived by issue, the UPC assumes that the transferor would want the gift to go to the beneficiary's issue rather than fail. Otherwise the UPC presumes that the transferor would prefer that the gift fail if the beneficiary dies before receiving possession. (Technically, the UPC does not rest its rationale on the settlor's presumed intent, but rather on avoiding the high administration costs of probating the future interest where the holder dies before distribution.)

**c. Criticism:** The UPC proposal has been heavily criticized and not widely adopted. Critics have offered several arguments against it. As for the official UPC rationale, the modern trend is not to reopen probate where the beneficiary dies before distribution, but to permit the court to order distribution directly to those entitled to take at distribution. As for the presumed intent arguments, there is no evidence to support the assumption that the transferor would prefer the gift to fail. Moreover, by eliminating the transmissibility of the interest, the beneficiary loses the flexibility to alter the gift if circumstances warrant. The UPC provision also creates complications where the express language of the conveyance requires the beneficiary to survive until the time of distribution. Traditional construction would void the beneficiary's gift completely. The UPC would give the gift to the beneficiary's issue (if any) despite the settlor's express intent. Lastly, under the UPC, if the gift fails, the takers are the settlor's heirs or devisees, but if the settlor is still alive, the gift is not given to the settlor but to the settlor's heirs apparent at the time the gift fails. The ripple effect of the UPC approach raises the concern that its costs are not worth its benefits.

# III. CLASS GIFTS

**A. Class closing rules:** A class, by definition, is a generic description of a group of individuals who share a common characteristic, for example, a gift "to *A*'s children." Often the description of the common characteristic is such that other people holding that characteristic may enter the class—*A* may have more children. At some point, however, the class must close.

**1. Naturally:** The most common way for the class to close is naturally—if the way for people to enter the class closes naturally. In the example "to *A*'s children," the class closes naturally if *A* dies. No one else can enter the class.

**2. Rule of convenience—introduction:** Common law quickly realized that for administrative purposes, an alternative to closing the class naturally had to be created. For example, if the conveyance was "to *B* for life, then to the children of *A*," if *B* died and *A* was still alive with two children, what was to be done with the property? Could *A*'s children who were alive take the property, subject to possible partial divestment if *A* had more children? Should the court hold the property and accumulate income, thereby depriving the living children of the benefit of their gift? To avoid these difficult administrative issues, the common law courts created a second method of determining when a class closed—the rule of convenience.

**a. Rule statement:** Under the rule of convenience, as soon as one member of the class legally has the right to receive, possess, and/or enjoy his or her share of the property, the class closes.

**b. Rule of construction:** Despite the rationale for the rule, the courts have deemed the rule of convenience a rule of construction based upon the transferor's presumed intent, and not a rule of law. The courts, however, are quick to apply it, making it look more like a rule of law in most cases than a rule of construction.

**c. Vesting:** Closing a class under the rule of convenience does not mean that all those who are included in the class will necessarily receive a share of the property. A class may close, but the class may still be contingent as to some members of the class. As to the latter, if any of them do not satisfy the express condition precedent, they will not share in the property.

**Class closure:** Compare the following provisions in a testator's will: "to *A* for life, then to the children of *B,* upon reaching the age of 18" vs. "to *A* for life, then to the children of *B* who reach age 18." In the first example, the gift to *A*'s children vests upon the birth of a child, with payment delayed until he or she reaches age 18. If *B* has a child, the class will close as soon as *A*'s life estate ends, regardless of how old the child is. In the second example, the express condition precedent that only *B*'s children "who reach age 18" take means that the interest will not vest until the first child of *B* reaches age 18. The class is *B*'s children, but the class will not close until one of them is entitled to distribution—not until one of them reaches age 18.

**d. Example:** In ***In re Evans' Estate,*** 80 N.W.2d 408 (Wis. 1957), testator's will provided that he devised $50,000 to his grandchildren, in trust, the income to accumulate until each grandchild becomes of age, at which time he or she is to receive the income annually until he or she reaches the age of 30, at which time he or she is to be paid his or her full share of the principal together with accumulated interest. Testator had four grandchildren when he executed the will, and two more were born before he died. Thereafter three more grandchildren were born before the oldest grandchild reached the age of 30. The court ruled that the grandchildren who were alive at the time the testator died held a vested interest, subject to divestment upon the birth of more grandchildren. The court went on to apply the rule of convenience. The class closed when the time for distribution to the first class member arrived—when the first grandchild reached the age of 30. The three grandchildren born after the testator's death qualified as members of the class because the oldest grandchild had not reached 30 yet.

**3. Direct gift:** Where a written instrument (typically a will) provides for an outright gift to a class of beneficiaries, the class closes upon the death of the transferor/testator.

**a. Exception:** The courts have ruled that where no member of the class was born before the transferor's death, it must be presumed that the transferor knew this and yet still made the gift. Accordingly, under these conditions, the rule of convenience should not be applied, and the class will be held open until it closes naturally—until the death of the designated party who controls access to the class. (In the example "to the children of *A*," if *A* had no children when the testator died, the class would stay open until it closed naturally—until *A*'s death.)

    **b. Rule in Wild's Case:** The devise "to *A* and her children" contains an inherent ambiguity as to who takes what interest. The common law approach established in Wild's Case, and based on common law rules of construction, is that *A* and her children take as tenants in common. Under the modern trend, some courts construe this type of gift as conveying a life estate to *A,* remainder to the children.

**4. Gifts of specific amount:** Where a written instrument (typically a will) provides for an outright gift of a specific amount to each class member, the class closes absolutely and completely at the time for distribution (typically the death of the transferor). No exception applies, even if no member of the class has been born by that time.

**5. Future interests:** Where a written instrument creates a future interest in a class, the first variable is whether the gift is of income or principal.

    **a. Gifts of income:** Where the gift is a periodic payment of income, the class closes upon each periodic date for distribution of the income. Because no beneficiary is entitled to distribution of any income until the designated date for distribution, the class cannot be closed until the designated date for distribution. The class automatically reopens for the duration of the next payment period.

    **b. Gifts of principal:** Where the gift is a one-time disbursement of principal, the earliest the class will close is upon the end of the preceding estate if at least one member of the class is entitled to distribution—if at least one member's interest has vested (even if that member is dead, if the interest is transmissible or passes via anti-lapse to his or her issue, the future interest has vested). If the gift is to the children of a designated person who has not had any children yet (the scenario for the exception to outright gifts), the rule appears to be that the exception that applied to outright gifts applies to future interests.

    **c. Distribution of income:** Where a trust fails to provide for how the income is to be treated, the default rule is against holding and accumulating the income. The income is distributable to the beneficiaries on a regular basis.

**B. Implied survival requirement:** Although courts generally do not imply a requirement that the party survives until the time of possession where the gift is to the settlor's children, siblings, or similar "single generation gifts," they often do imply such a survival requirement where the gift is to the settlor's heirs, issue, descendants, or similar "multiple generation gifts." The issue, however, is one of intent and where the grantor's intent is clear enough, it will control.

**Example:** In *Usry v. Farr,* 553 S.E.2d 789 (Ga. 2001), testator's will devised his real property to his wife, for life, and upon her death to his children "who may survive my wife, and to my grandchildren with restrictions as follows: Any of my children taking . . . shall have a life interest therein, . . . with any grandchildren who take hereunder taking the part which their father or mother would have taken. Upon the death of my last surviving child title in fee simple . . . shall vest in my grandchildren, per stirpes and not per capita." The testator had five grandchildren when he died, but one died before the last of the children to die. The court held that the testator's express survival requirement on the children and no express survival requirement on the grandchildren adequately expressed an intent that the interest of the grandchildren vested upon the testator's death. The interest of the grandchild who died before the last of children, being a vested remainder, passed to his issue. The dissent focused on the last clause of the gift, arguing that the language that the property "shall *vest* in my grandchildren" upon the death of the last surviving child expressed an intent that the grandchildren's interest was contingent until the death of the last surviving child.

**C. Express survival requirement—gifts to "surviving children":** If a will or trust provides for a gift to one's surviving children, and the instrument fails to expressly provide for what is to happen upon the death of one of the children before distribution of the property, the general rule is that the gift was expressly limited to the transferor's surviving children, and the surviving issue of any deceased children do not take.

   **1. Example:** In *Matter of Marine Midland Bank, N.A.,* 547 N.E.2d 1152 (N.Y. 1989), testator's will created a testamentary trust first for the benefit of his wife, for life, then one-half for the benefit of his brother Leonard and one-half for the benefit of his brother Roy. If either brother predeceased the life tenant, the trust expressly granted his interest to his "surviving child or children." Leonard died before the life tenant, survived by his daughter, Jacqueline, and by the widow and the issue of his predeceased son Daniel. Upon the death of the life tenant, the court applied the plain meaning approach and held that only Jacqueline qualified to take as a surviving child.

   **2. Extrinsic evidence:** A few courts have held that where the instrument is homemade, the transferor may not have understood the full legal significance of the phrase "surviving children" and will take extrinsic evidence to determine the transferor's true intent with respect to the use of the term.

   **3. Stepchildren:** Although ultimately a question of the transferor's intent, the general rule is that use of the term *children* or *issue* does not include stepchildren absent contrary intent expressed by the transferor.

**D. Adopted children:** While all states provide by statute that an adopted child constitutes a child of the adoptive parent(s) for intestate purposes, the question of whether an adopted child constitutes a "child" or "issue" for purposes of taking under a written instrument is a question of the transferor's intent. The intestate rule does not necessarily control. Where the written instrument expressly addresses the issue, the transferor's intent controls. In the absence of such a provision, it is a question of transferor's intent.

   **1. Common law:** At common law, only blood descendants qualified as "children" or "issue." Under this approach, an adopted child would not qualify as a beneficiary under a written instrument.

      **Adopting parent:** Where, however, the transferor was the adopting parent, even the common law assumed that when the transferor used the terms *child* or *issue,* he or she intended to include any adopted child.

   **2. Modern trend:** The modern trend, both judicially and statutorily, has been to presume that the use of the terms *child* or *issue* should be construed as including adopted children absent contrary intent. Where the change has been made judicially, however, some states have said that the modern trend applies only when certain terms are used; when adopted legislatively, the change applies only prospectively.

**Example:** In *Newman v. Wells Fargo Bank, N.A.,* 926 P.2d 969 (Cal. 1996), the testatrix's will created a testamentary trust. The trust provided that the income was to be distributed to her brothers and sisters, and upon the death of any brother or sister, to that person's living issue by right of representation. One of the testatrix's brothers was Earl Mitchell. Jon Newman, Earl's son, was adopted by his stepfather in 1946. At the time of the adoption, and in 1972 when testatrix executed her will, California law provided that adoption cut off all inheritance rights between the adopted child and his or her natural parents and relatives. The testatrix died later in 1972. In 1985, the California legislature amended its probate code to provide that inheritance by a stepparent did not sever the child's ability to inherit from and through his or her natural parents. When Earl died in 1993, the issue arose whether Jon qualified as Earl's issue for inheritance purposes under the testatrix's testamentary trust. The court applied the law that was in effect when the will was executed and when the testatrix died and thus ruled that Jon did not qualify.

3. **UPC:** The UPC approach provides that adopted children and children born out of wedlock are included in gifts in written instruments to the same extent they would be included if the gift were being distributed through intestacy. Terms that do not differentiate relatives by blood from relatives by affinity (aunts, uncles, nieces, and nephews) are construed as excluding relatives by affinity. Terms that do not distinguish between whole and half bloods (brothers, sisters, nieces, nephews) are construed as including both half and whole bloods. UPC §2-705.

4. **Adult adoptions:** Adult adoptions are permitted in almost all states. The courts are split on whether an adopted adult should receive the same inheritance rights as an adopted minor. Although the statutes granting inheritance rights typically do not draw a distinction between an adopted adult and an adopted minor, in a significant number of cases the courts have engrafted an exception on the statute where the adult is adopted solely to try to qualify as an heir under the instrument of a remote ancestor.

E. **Gifts to "heirs":** The problem with gifts of future interests to "heirs" is whether who qualifies as an heir should be determined (1) upon the death of the transferor, or (2) at the time of distribution of their interest. The question is one of the transferor's intent.

1. **Common law:** The common law preference for vested interests argues in favor of ascertaining who qualifies as an heir of a denominated person as of the date when the denominated person dies. If thereafter the heir dies before distribution, his or her vested interest is transmissible. The preference, however, is merely a rule of construction. The issue is one of the transferor's intent, not a rule of law.

   a. **Exception:** Where the instrument gives a life estate or defeasible fee to a person who is one of the transferor's heirs, and then goes on to give a remainder or executory interest to the testator's heirs, some authorities and courts have concluded that the transferor's intent was that the term *heirs* should be determined upon the death of the life tenant because the transferor arguably did not intend to give a possessory interest and a future interest to the same party.

   b. **Overall testamentary scheme:** Because the issue of *when* the transferor's heirs should be determined is a question of transferor's intent, the transferor's overall testamentary scheme may be relevant to the issue. Whether such an approach is helpful, however, is extremely fact sensitive.

2. **Modern trend/UPC:** The modern trend approach, as reflected in the UPC and some state statutes, is to determine who qualifies as an heir at the time when the property is to be distributed to the heirs.

   **Rationale:** If heirs are determined upon the death of the transferor, and an heir dies before distribution, his or her transmissible interest is subject to estate tax upon distribution. Under the modern trend, by determining who qualifies as an heir at time of distribution, if a party who otherwise qualified as an heir dies before distribution, he or she no longer has a transmissible interest—thereby avoiding estate taxes (but depriving his or her devisees or heirs of their interest).

3. **Doctrine of worthier title:** Pursuant to the common law doctrine of worthier title, where a settlor purports to create a future interest in the heirs of the settlor, give the future interest to the settlor and reclassify it as a reversion. The doctrine of worthier title is yet another example of the common law's preference for vested interests.

   a. **Rule of construction:** The doctrine of worthier title is a rule of construction, not a rule of law. If there is sufficient evidence to show that the settlor intended to create a future interest in his or her heirs, the doctrine does not apply.

   b. **Modern trend:** Under the modern trend, most jurisdictions have abolished the doctrine of worthier title.

4. **Rule in Shelley's Case:** Where real estate is conveyed by a single written instrument (be it a will, trust, or deed), and the instrument purports to create a contingent remainder in the heirs of a life tenant, give the remainder to the life tenant (which vests the remainder, and if there is no other vested interest between the life estate and the remainder, the interests will merge). The rule in Shelley's Case is yet another example of the common law's preference for vested interests.

   a. **Rule of law:** The rule in Shelley's Case is a rule of law. The rule applies regardless of the clarity of the transferor's intent to create a remainder in the heirs of the life tenant.

   b. **Modern trend:** Under the modern trend, most jurisdictions have abolished the rule in Shelley's Case.

F. **Per capita vs. per stirpes vs. per capita at each generation:** While the use of the terms *heirs* or *issue* or *descendants* indicates the intent that if an issue dies survived by issue, his or her share can be taken by his or her surviving issue, there is still ambiguity as to which approach should be taken to calculate the shares going to each "heir" or "issue" or "descendant"—per stirpes, per capita, or per capita at each generation.

1. **Majority:** The majority approach is that the court applies whatever is the default approach in the jurisdiction (the intestacy approach).

2. **Restatement (Second):** The Restatement (Second) of Property, Donative Transfers, presumes that the per capita approach applies to gifts to "issue" in written instruments regardless of the state's default approach to intestate distributions to issue. (Though a gift to "issue per stirpes" expresses an adequate contrary intent to overcome the presumed default; the property would be distributed to the issue per stirpes.)

3. **UPC:** The UPC position depends on the language used. If the gift is to "issue" or "issue by representation," the property should be distributed pursuant to the state's default/intestate approach. The latter construction may cause problems.

**"By representation":** Historically the phrase "by representation" was construed to mean per stripes. Restatement of Property §303. The UPC approach construes the phrase "by representation" as meaning the default approach (which under the UPC is per capita at each generation and in most jurisdictions is the per capita by representation approach). This change in construction may cause problems in jurisdictions that used to follow the historical approach. UPC §§2-708, 2-709.

4. **Nonmarital children:** Another ambiguity inherent in the use of the term *issue/descendant* is whether nonmarital children/issue are included.

   a. **Common law:** Common law presumes that the terms *issue* and *descendant* include only children born to a married couple, not nonmarital children. The question is one of transferor's intent, however, and the presumption is rebuttable.

   b. **Modern trend:** The modern trend presumes that marital and nonmarital children are included in the term *issue/descendant* if that term is used in a written instrument. The question is one of the transferor's intent, and the presumption is rebuttable. (In many modern trend jurisdictions, the change in law applies only to written instruments executed after the change in law, not to written instruments created before. In such jurisdictions, attention to the relevant dates is critical.)

G. **Income to class:** A gift of income to a class, with a gift over to others following the death of the last class member, inherently includes an ambiguity. The express gift over following the death of the last class member indicates that each member of the class takes only a life estate interest in the income. If one member of the class dies, an ambiguity arises as to what happens to that share. If the instrument does not expressly provide for what happens to the income upon the death of a class member, litigation is inevitable.

1. **Default:** The general rule is that a gift to a class is presumed to be in joint tenancy with right of survivorship. Under this approach, upon the death of one member of the class entitled to share in the distribution of the income, his or her share of the income is redistributed among the other members of the class entitled to receive the income.

2. **Intent:** The issue of what is to happen to the share that was being distributed to the deceased member of the income class is a question of settlor's intent. The instrument creating the gifts may expressly or implicitly indicate an intent that differs from the default general rule.

3. **Example:** In *Dewire v. Haveles,* 534 N.E.2d 782 (Mass. 1989), the testator created a testamentary trust that provided in part that all the income was to go to his grandchildren, and 21 years after the death of his last surviving grandchild, the trust was to terminate. The settlor had six grandchildren. During the time when the trustee was distributing the income to the grandchildren, one of the six died. The trust failed to provide for what was to happen to his share. The court noted the general default rule, but held it inapplicable. The court concluded that the testator must have intended the income to be distributed to the issue of the deceased grandchildren. The court found that the settlor's repeated statements that it was his desire to treat each grandchild equally supported this interpretation.

## Quiz Yourself on
## CONSTRUING TRUSTS: FUTURE INTERESTS AND CLASS GIFTS

**78.** Bilbo funds his inter vivos trust with Shireacres. The trust gives the property "to Frodo for life, then to Frodo's first child." Bilbo's will devises all his property to Gandalf.

   **a.** Assuming Frodo has no children, state the equitable interests. _____

   **b.** If Bilbo dies, and then Frodo dies childless, what happens to the property? _____

   **c.** If Frodo has a child, Eve, and then Bilbo dies, what happens to the property? _____

   **d.** If Bilbo dies, Frodo has a child, Eve, who dies with a will devising all her property to Ian, and then Frodo dies, what happens to the property? _____

**79.** Bilbo's inter vivos trust provides as follows: "To Frodo for life, then to Frodo's first child if he or she survives him, otherwise to Gandalf." Assume Frodo has a child, Eve. State the future interests. _____

**80.** Bilbo's inter vivos trust provides as follows: "To Frodo for life, then to Frodo's first child, but if thechild fails to survive him, then to Gandalf." Assume Frodo has a child, Eve. State the future interests. _____

**81.** Bilbo dies with a will that devises Shireacres "to Frodo for life, then to his firstborn child." Frodo has a child, Eve, and Frodo disclaims his interest. State the title. _____

**82.** Bilbo dies with a will that devises Shireacres as follows: "To Frodo for life, then to his firstborn child if he or she survives Frodo." Frodo has a child, Eve, and Frodo disclaims his interest. Who holds what interest in the property? _____

**83.** Godfather transfers Sopranoacres in trust as follows: "To Godfather for life, then to Sonny, but if Sonny dies before Godfather, to Sonny's surviving children." Assume Sonny has two children, Mariano and Vinnie.

   **a.** Who has what interest in the trust? _____

   **b.** Assume Sonny dies, and then Vinnie dies survived by Rosina, and then Godfather dies. Who has what interest in the property? _____

**84.** Bruce transfers Duetacres in trust as follows: "To Bruce for life, then to Gwyenth, but if Gwyenth dies without surviving issue, then to Gwyenth's brother." Assume Bruce dies, and many years later Gwyenth dies, without issue, devising all her property to the Royale Shakespeare Company. Who takes Duetacres? _____

**85.** Olivia devises $1,000 "to Selena at age 30." Tragically, Selena is shot and killed before reaching age 30. Her will devises her property to Sergio. Who takes the $1,000? _____

**86.** Olivia transfers property in trust "to Juan for life, then to Selena." Tragically, Selena is shot and killed before Juan dies. She dies with a will devising all her property to Sergio. Who takes the property upon Juan's death? _____

**87.** Mom sets up a trust that provides as follows: "Income to Brady for life, upon Brady's death, all the income is to be distributed to his children, and upon the death of the last surviving child, the principal is to be distributed equally to his grandchildren then living." Brady dies survived by eight children. Assume one of them, Marsha, dies survived by two children, Izzy and Tom. Who takes Marsha's share of the income? _____

**88.** Laverne's will bequeaths $15,000 "to the children of Sherlie who reach age 21." At the time of Laverne's death, Sherlie has two children, Andy (age 12) and Betty (age 7). Five years later, Sherlie has another child, Carl, and five years later, Sherlie has yet another child, Deb. Two years later, Betty dies. Carl and Deb both live to age 21. Who takes how much of the property? _____

---

## Answers

**78. a.** The instrument gives the future interest following Frodo's life estate to someone other than the settlor, so it is a remainder. Frodo has no children, however, so his first child is not ascertainable. The remainder in favor of Frodo's first child is contingent, which means Bilbo must hold a reversion.

**b.** If Frodo dies without any children, the contingent remainder would be destroyed at common law because it did not vest before or at the moment the preceding life estate ended. The reversion would become possessory, but Bilbo has devised the reversion to Gandalf, so Gandalf owns the property.

**c.** Because Eve is ascertainable and there is no express condition precedent that Eve has to satisfy before taking possession, Eve holds a vested remainder. Once the remainder vests, there is no longer any reversion interest in the settlor.

**d.** Eve held a vested remainder when she died, so her interest is devisable and inheritable. She devised it to Ian. When Frodo dies, Eve's vested remainder becomes possessory. Ian is entitled to the property following Frodo's death.

**79.** The trust expressly gives the future interest following Frodo's life estate to someone other than the settlor, so it is a remainder. Although Frodo's daughter is ascertainable, there is an express condition precedent that she has to survive Frodo. The remainder is a contingent remainder. Gandalf takes, if at all, at the end of Frodo's life estate, so he too holds a remainder. It too is contingent, contingent on Frodo's first child not surviving him. Because both remainders are contingent, Bilbo holds a reversion (in the event the life estate ends prematurely, if the first contingent remainder is not vested at that moment, both remainders were destroyed and Bilbo's reversion would take possession).

**80.** The future interest following Frodo's life estate goes to someone other than the settlor, so it is a remainder. Frodo's daughter is ascertainable and there is no express condition precedent in the clause creating the remainder or the preceding clause, so Eve holds a vested remainder. The express condition precedent in the clause following the clause creating the remainder (that Eve must survive Frodo) makes the vested remainder subject to divestment, which means that Gandalf must hold an executory interest (shifting because he is taking the right to possession from someone other than the transferor).

The only difference in the conveyance in this problem versus the conveyance in the prior problem is where the express condition that Frodo's first child must survive Frodo is placed in the conveyance. If the express condition precedent is in the same clause as the clause creating the remainder or the preceding clause, it makes the remainder a contingent remainder. If the express condition precedent is in a clause subsequent to the clause creating the remainder, it makes the remainder subject to divestment.

81. As initially devised, Frodo held a life estate. His firstborn child, Eve, held a vested remainder. When Frodo disclaims, his interest is extinguished and the vested remainder accelerates into possession. Eve is entitled to the property.

82. As initially devised, Frodo held a life estate. His firstborn child, Eve, held a contingent remainder because of the express condition precedent that the child has to survive Frodo. Because the remainder is continent, Bilbo held a reversion. When Frodo disclaims, his interest is extinguished and at common law, contingent remainders did not accelerate into possession. Strict application of the destructibility of the contingent remainder doctrine would destroy the contingent remainder and the property would revert to the transferor, Bilbo. Under the modern trend/UPC approach, the disclaimant is treated as having predeceased the transferor. As applied to the trust, Eve will be treated as if she survived Frodo and her interest will accelerate into possession. Eve takes the property.

83. a. Read and analyze comma to comma, clause by clause. As drafted, Godfather has a life estate, Sonny has a vested remainder in fee simple subject to divestment, and Sonny's children have a shifting executory interest.

b. The general rule is that where a future interest is given to "surviving children," the condition precedent that the takers have to "survive" is applied at the moment their interest becomes possessory. Here, although Vinnie survived Sonny, he did not survive to the moment of possession (when Godfather died). Vinnie would not share in the property—his issue Rosina would not take either. Mariano would be the sole taker.

84. The general rule is that where the divesting condition is "if the remainderman dies without surviving issue," the condition is applied only if the remainderman dies before the life tenant. Here, Gwyenth survives Bruce, so even if many years later she dies without surviving issue, the divesting condition will not apply. The Royale Shakespeare Company would take Duetacres.

85. At common law, under the Rule in Clobberie's case, gifts to a beneficiary "at" a specific age were considered contingent gifts. Under that approach, Selena's gift was contingent upon her reaching age 30. The gift fails and falls to the residuary clause, or if there is none, to intestacy. The modern trend construes such gifts as transmissible. Selena's will devised all her property to Sergio, so he would get the $1,000.

86. Selena held a vested remainder. At common law and under the prevailing approach, a vested remainder is a transmissible interest. Selena was free to devise her interest to Sergio, so he would take upon Juan's death. Under the heavily criticized and not widely adopted UPC approach, all future interests in trust are subject to the lapse and anti-lapse doctrines. Selena's death would constitute a lapse, and because she has no children, anti-lapse would not apply. Where there is no express alternative taker, the UPC gives the failed gift to the settlor's residuary devisees or heirs. Under the UPC, Selena's remainder would fail, and the gift would pass to the settlor's residuary devisees or heirs.

**87.** At common law, where income was gifted to a class, with distribution of the principal delayed until the death of the last member of the income class, upon the death of one member of the income class, his or her share was redistributed among the other members of the income class. Brady's seven surviving children would share Marsha's share of the income. Izzy and Tom would not take any of the income. Under the modern trend, the preference is to apply anti-lapse to the share of the income and give it to the issue of the deceased income class member. Izzy and Tom would take Marsha's share of the income.

**88.** The gift is to a class (the children of Sherlie), with an express condition precedent attached (who reach age 21). The class closes under the rule of convenience as soon as the first member of the class is entitled to possession of his or her share. The day Andy turned 21, the class closed. Carl was born before this date, but Deb was born after this date. Deb is excluded from the class even though she meets the class description because of the rule of convenience. When the class closed, there were three members in the class, so Andy would be entitled to his share, one-third or $5,000. Betty died at age 19. She did not meet the express condition precedent and does not receive any of the property. Upon her death, the class is reduced to two members, so Andy receives another $2,500 upon Betty's death to reflect that he holds a one-half interest in the class now. When Carl reaches age 21, Carl receives the other half of the gift.

---

# Exam Tips *on*
# CONSTRUING TRUSTS: FUTURE INTERESTS AND CLASS GIFTS

## Classifying future interests

Much of this material is really beyond the scope of this course. The first key is to identify who holds the future interest, the settlor or someone else. If the settlor holds the future interest, for purposes of this course it is usually a reversion.

☛ If a third party is to take the future interest, then the future interest has to be either a remainder or an executory interest. Anytime there is a remainder, it must be classified as either vested or contingent. Anytime there is a contingent remainder (or alternative contingent remainders), the settlor must hold a reversion.

## Preference for vested remainders

☛ Watch for life tenants who disclaim their interest—this raises the issue of whether the remainder will accelerate into possession. Common law applies the destructibility of contingent remainders, while the modern trend approach treats the disclaimant as having predeceased the transferor, increasing the chances that the contingent remainders will be treated as vested.

☛ Watch for fact patterns where the holder of a vested remainder dies before his or her interest becomes possessory. This raises the issue of whether the interest is transmissible or whether anti-lapse should apply.

☞ Watch for express conveyances of future interests to "surviving children (or issue)" and for divesting conditions if the remainderman dies "without surviving issue." Such phrases raise quirky, but easy to test, rules of construction.

   ☞ Where the future interest is to "surviving issue," the general rule is that the survival requirement is applied at the moment the issue have the right to claim possession.

   ☞ Where the vested remainder will be divested if the remainderman dies without surviving issue, the general rule is that the condition applies only if the remainderman dies before the life tenant.

☞ Watch for gifts to a beneficiary upon his or her reaching a specific age or event. The key to analyzing such gifts is if the gift expressly provides that it is to be "to A *at* age 30," as opposed to "to A, *upon reaching* age 30" or "to A, *to be paid at* age 30." The rules in Clobberie's case provide that the latter gifts are vested (and thus transmissible even if the beneficiary dies before reaching the specific age), while the first gift is considered contingent (and not transmissible if the beneficiary dies before reaching the age). Under the modern trend, all three phases are presumed transmissible unless the language clearly indicates the gift is contingent ("to A *if* she reaches age 30").

## Class gifts

Just because a gift is to more than one individual, the gift is not necessarily a class gift. Analyze the conveyance to see if the transferor intended a class gift.

☞ Watch for gifts to "issue" or "descendants"—the problem is which approach to apply if one or more of the children predeceases the donor survived by issue: per capita, per stirpes, or per capita at each generation.

☞ Watch for adopted children and class gifts. Apply the common law/modern trend split.

☞ Watch for gifts to "heirs" of a party who holds a remainder. Generally who qualifies as an heir is determined as of the date of the death of the party holding the remainder, even if the remainderman dies before the interest becomes possessory. The exception to this is if the life tenant is one of the heirs of the party holding the remainder. In such a case, don't determine who qualifies as an heir until the life tenant dies.

☞ Watch for gifts of a remainder to a class, where the class is still open when the preceding finite estate ends. Under the rule of convenience, close the class once one member of the class is entitled to possession.

   ☞ But closing the class does not mean that all members of the class will receive property. If there is an express condition precedent that the members of the class must also satisfy, the class member receives property only when he or she meets the express condition precedent (and may receive additional property if other class members do not meet the condition).

CHAPTER **12**

# THE RULE AGAINST PERPETUITIES

*ChapterScope* ───────────────────

This chapter examines the Rule against Perpetuities—the rule that regulates future interests.

- **The Rule against Perpetuities:** A future interest must vest, if at all, within the lives in being at the time of its creation plus 21 years, or the interest is void. The rule is applied in the abstract and is not based on probabilities.

  - **The fertile octogenarian:** In applying the Rule against Perpetuities, the common law courts assumed conclusively that a person was fertile until death. This presumption often causes problems for future interests in grandchildren.

  - **The unborn widow:** A person's widow cannot be identified until the designated person dies, so any future interest following a future interest to a "widow" needs to be analyzed carefully to see if it violates the Rule against Perpetuities.

  - **The slothful executor:** The potential for delayed and/or prolonged administration of a decedent's estate means that gifts to be made to generic takers upon distribution of a decedent's estate usually violate the Rule against Perpetuities.

- **Class gifts:** If a gift to a class violates the Rule against Perpetuities as to one member of the class, it violates the rule as to all members of the class. The courts, however, have recognized several exceptions to this rule:

  - **Gifts to subclasses:** If the future interest in question can be characterized as a gift to subclasses, apply the Rule against Perpetuities separately to each subclass.

  - **Gifts of specific amounts:** If each class member's share is a specific sum not indeterminate upon the final number of class members, the gift is valid as to those members whose share is definitively ascertainable within the perpetuities period.

- **Powers of appointment:** A general inter vivos power of appointment must become presently exercisable, if at all, within the Rule against Perpetuities time period, or the power is void. General testamentary powers of appointment and special powers of appointment are valid as long as the donee cannot have the ability to exercise the power after the perpetuities period. With respect to any interests created by the exercise of a valid general testamentary power or special power, the interests created are analyzed as if they were created by the instrument creating the power.

- **Saving clause:** Because of the difficulty in understanding the Rule against Perpetuities, the courts will enforce a "saving clause" that provides that despite the express terms of the trust, the trust will terminate at the latest upon the running of the perpetuities period.

- **Modern trend:** Because of the harshness of the Rule against Perpetuities, in particular the fact that it is applied in the abstract regardless of real life probabilities, the modern trend is to modify the rule. There are several different approaches to such modification:

  - **Cy pres:** Under the cy pres doctrine, where a future interest in a trust violates the Rule against Perpetuities, the court is empowered to modify the trust so that it will not violate the rule.

- **Wait-and-see:** Instead of applying the Rule against Perpetuities in the abstract, the courts wait and see if the future interest in question actually does not vest until after the perpetuities period.

- **Abolishing the Rule against Perpetuities:** Some states have abolished the Rule against Perpetuities, permitting trusts to last forever.

# I. INTRODUCTION

A. **Overview:** The Rule against Perpetuities is yet another example of the common law's preference for vested interests. The rule was conceived to regulate future interests. Future interests that run far into the future permit "dead hand" control when such control may not be in the best interest of those affected or the community. If the future interests were vested, they could effectively be eliminated through transfer and merger. But if the interests are not transferable, they could clog the title inefficiently for decades to come. The courts developed the Rule against Perpetuities to limit how long "dead hand" control through nonvested future interests would be permitted.

B. **Rule statement:** No interest is good unless it must vest, if at all, within the lives in being at the time of its creation plus 21 years.

C. **Conceptual understanding:** One way to think about the Rule against Perpetuities conceptually is that it is like a statute of limitations.

   1. **Statute of limitations:** Under a statute of limitations, if a party has a cause of action against another party, the plaintiff must bring his or her action, if at all, within the statutory period or the cause of action is barred (effectively null and void).

   2. **Rule against Perpetuities:** Under the Rule against Perpetuities, a future interest must vest, if at all, within the perpetuities period (lives in being at the time of creation plus 21 years) or the interest is "barred"—null and void.

      a. **Vesting:** Just as a statute of limitation does not require that a cause of action be brought within the statutory period, it just cannot be brought *after* the statutory period, the Rule against Perpetuities does not require that a future interest must vest, it only requires that if the future interest is going to vest, it cannot vest *after* the perpetuities period.

      b. **Perpetuities period:** A statute of limitations sets forth a fixed period of years in which a cause of action must be brought, if at all, or the cause of action is barred. The Rule against Perpetuities sets forth a formula for when the future interest must vest, if at all, or the interest is barred/null and void. The formula is any life in being at the time the interest was created plus 21 years.

         i. **Life in being:** The "life in being" prong of the formula is the life of any person who was alive at the time the interest was created—however many years any person who was alive at the time the interest was created lives.

         ii. **Measuring life:** Whoever is picked to fulfill the life in being prong of the perpetuities period is typically referred to as the "measuring life." However long he or she lived, his or her life is used to measure the number of years that serves as the base period of the perpetuities period, to which 21 years is added under the second prong of the perpetuities period.

**D. Scope:** Despite the express language of the Rule against Perpetuities that "no interest" is valid unless it must vest, if at all, within the perpetuities period, the common law courts applied the rule only to certain future interests: Contingent remainders, vested remainders subject to open, executory interests, and powers of appointment are subject to the Rule against Perpetuities. (Where a trustee has discretion over the distribution of the property, that interest is contingent. Such an interest does not vest until the trustee exercises his or her discretion. The rule also applies to other interests beyond the scope of this material.)

**E. Application:** Unlike a statute of limitations that waits to see if a party holding a cause of action brings the cause of action within the statutory period, the Rule against Perpetuities is applied abstractly the moment the transferor attempts to create the future interest. If there is even one scenario, no matter how improbable, where the future interest vests, but not until after the running of the perpetuities period, the interest is null and void from the moment the transferor attempted to create it. There cannot be one scenario where the interest vests, but only after the perpetuities period—the lives in being plus 21 years.

**F. Vesting requirement:** The Rule against Perpetuities requires that the interest must vest, if at all, within the lives in being at the time of the interest's creation plus 21 years. The vesting requirement means something different as applied to the future interests that are subject to the rule.

    **1. Contingent remainders:** As applied to contingent remainders, the interest can vest by either (1) vesting in interest (but not possession), or (2) vesting in possession.

    **2. Executory interests:** As applied to executory interests, the interest vests only by vesting in possession.

**G. Analytical steps:** There are two different analytical approaches that can be used to apply the Rule against Perpetuities to a future interest to see if the interest is valid.

    **1. The measuring life approach:** Under the measuring life approach, the key is to identify who constitutes the measuring life in analyzing whether the future interest violates the Rule against Perpetuities. Although in theory anyone alive at the moment the interest is created can serve as the measuring life, in practice the only lives that are relevant are those lives that can affect whether the future interest in question vests (either in interest or in possession). By focusing on those lives, one can analytically determine whether the interest must vest, if at all, within the perpetuities period.

    **2. The invalidating life approach:** Under the invalidating life approach, the analysis is turned on its head. Instead of trying to prove logically that the interest must vest, if at all, within the perpetuities period, the invalidating life approach tries to create a scenario that violates the rule—where the interest in question vests, but only *after* the lives in being plus 21 years perpetuities period. The idea under the invalidating life approach is to see if you can create a person in whom the interest will vest, but only after the lives in being plus 21 years.

    **3. Example 1:** Assume the following conveyance: "To *A* for life, then to *A*'s first child to reach age 15." *A* has two children, *B* age 10, and *C* age 13. The contingent remainder in *A*'s first child to reach age 15 is subject to the Rule against Perpetuities.

        **a. Measuring life approach:** Using *A* as the measuring life, the interest must vest, if at all, within *A*'s life plus 21 years or fail. If the interest were to vest in either *B* or *C*, the interest must vest within the next five years at the latest, so the interest must vest, if at all, within the perpetuities period. Assuming a worst case scenario, that *B* and *C* both die before reaching age 15, the only other way the interest could vest would be for *A* to give birth to a child, and that event would have to occur within *A*'s lifetime (the measuring life), and that child would have to vest within 15 years of his or her birth, thereby satisfying the requirement that the interest must vest, if at all, within the perpetuities period. The interest is valid.

b. **Invalidating life approach:** Under the invalidating life approach, the first step is to create a party in whom the interest will vest, but not until *after* the perpetuities period. Here, the interest can vest only in a child of *A*, so the invalidating life has to be a new child for *A*. Assume *A* gives birth to a new child, *X*. Then kill all the lives in being named in the problem when the interest was created—*A*, *B*, and *C*. Then see if it is possible to delay the vesting for another 21 years. The contingent remainder in question must vest, if at all, when *A*'s first child reaches age *15*. *X* either will or will not reach age 15 within 21 years of *X*'s birth. There is no way to delay the vesting until after the perpetuities time. The interest is valid.

4. **Example 2:** Assume the following conveyance: "To *A* for life, then to *A*'s first child to graduate from law school." *A* has two children, *B* and *C*. The contingent remainder in *A*'s first child to graduate from law school is subject to the Rule against Perpetuities.

a. **Measuring life approach:** If the interest were to vest in either *B* or *C*, the interest would be valid, because either are lives in being at the time the interest was created. But it is conceivable that neither will attend law school. It is also conceivable that *A* could have another child, *X*. After *X*'s birth, it is conceivable that *A* could die. *X* could graduate from law school, but not until more than 21 years after *A*'s death. It cannot be proved conclusively that the interest must vest, if at all, within the lives in being plus 21 years period. The interest is null and void from the moment of its attempted creation.

b. **Invalidating life approach:** Under the invalidating vesting life approach, the first step is to identify in whom the interest must vest, if at all. The interest here must vest, if at all, in one of *A*'s children. Create a new child for *A*, child *X*. Then kill all the lives in being when the interest was created—kill *A, B,* and *C*. Now that the lives in being prong of the perpetuities period is accounted for, ask whether it is possible to delay the vesting until more than 21 years after the death of the last life in being? Certainly. *X* could graduate from law school more than 21 years after the death of the last life in being. Because a scenario exists under which the interest vests, but not until after the running of the perpetuities period, the interest is void from its attempted creation.

5. **Example:** In ***Thomas v. Harrison,*** 191 N.E.2d (Ohio Prob. Ct. 1962), testatrix's will created a testamentary trust for the benefit of her son, Jean, his wife, and his issue. The trustees were given absolute discretion over the income and/or principal to alleviate the financial burdens of the beneficiaries, to provide educational support to the beneficiaries, or to accumulate any income not spent. Because the trust was discretionary, the court found the whole trust to be contingent as to all the beneficiaries. Applying the Rule against Perpetuities, the court hypothesized that it was possible that Jean could have more issue after the testatrix's death, that Jean, his wife, and his issue alive at the time the contingent interests were created could all die, and more than 21 years could pass before the trustees decided to exercise their discretion and distribute some of the trust property. The whole trust violated the Rule against Perpetuities and was void. The court ordered the property distributed to the testatrix's heirs at law.

**H. Creation:** The Rule against Perpetuities requires that the interest must vest, if at all, within the lives in being at the time the interest is *created* plus 21 years. A key step in the analytical process is determining when the interest is created. That varies depending on the nature of the written instrument used to create the interest.

   **1. Deed:** If the interests are created in a deed, the general rule is that the interests are deemed created when the deed becomes effective—when it is delivered.

   **2. Will:** If the interests are created in a will, the general rule is that the interests are deemed created when the will becomes effective—when the testator dies.

   **3. Irrevocable trust:** If the interests are created in an irrevocable trust, the general rule is that the interests are deemed created when the trust is created—when it is funded.

   **4. Revocable trust:** If the interests are created in a revocable trust, the general rule is that the interests are deemed created when the trust becomes irrevocable—typically when the settlor dies (assuming the settlor alone holds the power to revoke).

   **Example:** In *Cook v. Horn,* 104 S.E.2d 461 (Ga. 1958), O.J. Massee created a revocable inter vivos trust for his widow for life, and upon her death, the res was to be divided—one share for each of the settlor's children then living, one share for each of the settlor's children dead but survived by issue. The trusts for each of the living children was for the benefit of the child for his or her life, and upon his or her death for the benefit of his or her issue, provided that the share of any such issue under age 21 would be held in trust until he or she reached age 21. Likewise, the property for the issue of any predeceased child was to be retained in trust until said issue reached age 21. The settlor's children sued, claiming the issue in the settlor's grandchildren violated the Rule against Perpetuities. The court agreed that while such would be the case if the interests were vested the moment the trust was created, the court ruled that the interests were not to be vested until the trust became irrevocable. Under that approach, the interests were valid.

   **5. Powers of appointment:** Where the interest is a power of appointment or is created by a power of appointment, special rules apply that are covered later in this chapter.

**I. Periods of gestation:** At common law, a child was considered alive from the moment of conception. For purposes of applying the Rule against Perpetuities, this rule must be kept in mind. A child in utero is considered alive for purposes of determining who qualifies as a life in being, and a child in utero is considered alive for purposes of qualifying as a taker under the terms of a conveyance.

# II. CLASSIC RULE AGAINST PERPETUITIES SCENARIOS

**A. Introduction:** There are a handful of Rule against Perpetuities scenarios that have become classics because they evidence the principle that the rule is not concerned with probabilities, but rather with abstract analysis, no matter how unlikely the scenario.

**B. The fertile octogenarian:** The common law presumed that an individual is fertile and capable of having children no matter what one's advanced age. When coupled with the Rule against Perpetuities' abstract approach, the result is that a future interest that appears valid may be invalid.

1. **Example:** Testator's will provides as follows: "To my wife for life, then to her first child to have a grandchild." When the testator dies, his wife is 80, she has three children, *A, B,* and *C,* and no grandchildren. Under the common law irrebuttable presumption that a person is fertile until death, the testator's wife could have another child, *X,* a year after the testator died. The testator's wife and her children who were alive when the testator died could die without any of the children having a child. More than 21 years later, it is conceivable that *X* could have a child, the first grandchild of the testator's wife. A scenario exists where the interest could vest, but not until after the perpetuities period. The interest is void.

2. **Modern trend:** Under the modern trend, some states have either modified or abolished the common law presumption that an individual is fertile until death. Some states have established statutory ages during which a person is presumed fertile; others permit extrinsic evidence to prove that the designated person is no longer fertile. Some states also provide that the possibility that a person may adopt is not relevant to the Rule against Perpetuities analysis.

C. **The unborn widow:** Where a conveyance refers to a designated person's widow, there is a tendency to assume that the reference to the widow must be to the person's current spouse. Such, however, is not the case. The person could divorce and remarry (or the spouse could die and the designated person could remarry). Moreover, the designated person may remarry someone *who is not even alive when the future interest is created.* Although this scenario is highly improbable, it is conceivable. Where a conveyance grants a future interest to a widow, there is a good chance the future interest *following* the future interest to the unborn widow violates the Rule against Perpetuities.

1. **Example:** In *Dickerson v. Union Nat'l Bank of Little Rock,* 595 S.W.2d 677 (Ark. 1980), testatrix's will created a trust that provided that it was to continue until the death of the testatrix's two sons, Martin and Cecil, and Martin's widow (not named in the will), and until the youngest child of either son reached age 25. The court ruled the last interest violated the Rule against Perpetuities because abstractly it was possible that (1) Martin could marry a woman who was not born when the testatrix created the trust (when she died), and (2) that woman could have a child, and (3) Martin, Cecil, and all the other lives in being alive when the trust was created could die the next day, and (4) the interest in the youngest child to reach age 25 would not vest until after the lives in being at the time the interest was created plus 21 years.

2. **Alternative contingent remainder:** Where a conveyance creates a contingent remainder, and an alternative contingent remainder, in as much as both remainders are contingent, both are subject to the Rule against Perpetuities. Each is analyzed separately under the rule. Just because one violates the rule does not necessarily mean the other will violate the Rule against Perpetuities.

D. **The slothful executor:** It is not uncommon for a beneficiary under a will to die before the gift is distributed from probate. In an effort to avoid this risk, some testators have provided that the gift is contingent upon the beneficiary surviving until the time the property is distributed from probate. Although it is reasonable to assume that such a time must occur within the lives in being plus 21 years, it is conceivable that probating an estate can take longer than the lives in being plus 21 years to probate. The phrase "the slothful executor" has arisen to describe this risk. Where such a conveyance is created, the gift may violate the Rule against Perpetuities, and if it does, it is void.

1. **Example:** *T*'s will gifts the residue of her estate to "my issue living when probate of my estate is completed." It is conceivable that one of *T*'s issue living at the time of her death may have a child *X* (another issue of *T*), that all of *T*'s issue living when *T* died may die, and another 21 years may pass before probate of *T*'s estate may be complete. Under this scenario, the interest in *T*'s "issue living when probate of my estate is completed" vests, but not until after the lives in being at the creation of the interest plus 21 years. The gift violates the Rule against Perpetuities and is void.

2. **Example:** In *In re Campbell's Estate,* 82 P.2d 22 (Cal. Dist. App. 1938), testator's will devised the residue of his estate to the four chair officers of the San Diego Lodge 168 of the Order of Elks, "being the four chair officers in office at the time of distribution of my estate,...". The officers were elected annually. The court held that the devise violated the Rule against Perpetuities.

3. **Modern trend:** Some courts have construed such clauses as implicitly containing a "reasonable time" provision, either closing the class and vesting the interest when distribution reasonably should have been made or leaving the estate open for a reasonable time to see if it closes within a reasonable time.

E. **Effect of voiding interest:** While it is clear that any interest that violates the Rule against Perpetuities is void *ab initio* (from the moment of its attempted creation), it is not so clear what effect this has on other interests in the conveyance. The general approach appears to be to expunge the interest from the conveyance and then to give effect to the interests that are left in the conveyance that are valid.

1. **Example:** In *Lovering v. Worthington,* 106 Mass. 86 (1870), testator devised certain real property in trust and instructed the trustees to pay the income to his daughter, Nancy Gay, for life, then to pay the income to her children, for life, then the fee was to be distributed to the heirs at law of such children. The court found that the fee interest in the children of Nancy's children violated the Rule against Perpetuities and struck the interest. The life estate interest in the income in Nancy and the life estate in her children were still valid. The reversion in fee fell to the testator's heirs at law.

2. **Infectious invalidity:** The doctrine of infectious invalidity authorizes a court to invalidate valid interests as well as the invalid interests (up to and including all the interests in the instrument) if the court concludes that the testator/settlor would have preferred that approach.

## III. CLASS GIFTS AND THE RULE AGAINST PERPETUITIES

A. **All or nothing:** As applied to class gifts, as a general rule the Rule against Perpetuities requires that the class close and the interest vest as to *all* members of the class before the running of the perpetuities period or the gift is null and void as to every member of the class. The focus is on whether there is one possible scenario, no matter how implausible, where the interest would vest in a class member but only after the lives in being when the interest was created plus 21 years.

1. **Rule of convenience:** The rule of convenience applies to class gifts. As soon as one member of the class is entitled to receive his or her interest, the class closes.

**Example:** In *Picken v. Matthews,* 10 Ch. Div. 264 (1878), testator's will created a testamentary trust for the benefit of his daughter Helen's children by her first husband and the children of his daughter Charlotte who reach the age of 25 equally. Helen had three children at the time of the testator's death, one of whom had reached the age of 25, and Charlotte had two infant children. First, the court applied the rule of convenience to close the class on the testator's death. Having closed the class, the court went on to rule as to each child in the class, the interest would vest, if at all, within the Rule against Perpetuities time period. Because the court closed the class under the rule of convenience, the class gift did not violate the rule.

2. **Closing vs. vesting:** Closing the class is not necessarily the same as vesting the class. There may be an express condition precedent that the parties within the class must satisfy before their interest vests.

3. **Close and vest:** As applied to class gifts, the Rule against Perpetuities analysis requires the class to close and vest with respect to *each* member of the class within the perpetuities period or the gift is void as to the whole class as a general rule.

**Example:** In *Leake v. Robinson,* 35 Eng. Rep. 979 (Chancery 1817), testator's will created a testamentary trust, income to be paid to his grandson William Rowe Robinson for life, then to Robinson's issue, and in the event he had no issue, the trust res was to be divided and distributed among Robinson's brothers and sisters, equally, upon their attaining age 25 (or earlier to a sister if she married with her parents' consent before reaching age 25). At the time of the testator's death, Robinson had one brother and four sisters. Both of his parents were still alive, and they had two more sons before Robinson died without issue. First, the court ruled that the class consisted of all the brothers and sisters alive at Robinson's death (not just those alive when the testator died). Next, the court ruled that the interests of the beneficiaries did not vest until they reached the age of 25. In as much as the interests of the siblings not alive when the testator died might not have vested until 25 years after the death of the life in beings, the interests violated the Rule against Perpetuities and were void. The court ruled that the gift was one gift, one class, and if it failed as to one beneficiary, it failed as to all, even to those alive when the testator died.

B. **Subclasses exception:** Where a gift to a class can be construed as gifts to subclasses, the Rule against Perpetuities is applied separately to each subclass. If the gift to a subclass closes and vests as to all members of the subclass within the perpetuities period, the gift is valid as to that subclass. As to any subclass where the gift does not close and vest as to all members of the subclass, the gift fails as to all members of that subclass.

1. **Subclass:** A gift to a subclass exists when the conveyance describes the beneficiaries not as a single class, but rather as a group of subclasses. As to each subclass, if the share to which the separate subclass is entitled is determinable within the perpetuities period, the gift to that subclass will not violate the Rule against Perpetuities.

2. **Example:** In *Estate of Coates,* 652 A.2d 331 (Pa. Super. Ct. 1994), testatrix created a testamentary trust to pay the net income to her daughter Alice for life, then to Alice's children until the death of the last of them, then to her great-grandchildren per stirpes for as long as permitted by law, then the principal was to be divided into two equal shares, with one share to the Pennsylvania Hospital and the other to the Pennsylvania Academy of Fine

Arts. Testatrix's daughter had three children when she died, all of whom were alive when the testatrix died (and thus constitute lives in being). Following the death of the last grandchild, the hospital sued, claiming that the future interest in the great-grandchildren violated the Rule against Perpetuities. The court applied the doctrine of "vertical separability" to hold that even though testatrix's great-grandchildren were not to receive any income until all the grandchildren had died, their separate shares became fixed upon the death of each grandchild. The great-grandchild of each grandchild formed a separate class. The court also noted that this met the second requirement of the vertical separability test—that application of the doctrine not upset the decedent's overall testamentary scheme.

**C. Specific amount exception:** One of the typical characteristics of a class gift is that the share of each class member cannot be determined until the class closes and each member's interest vests. It is possible, however, to have a class gift with respect to who is to receive, but a fixed amount as to each member who does qualify. In such class gifts, the courts have ruled that because the gift to each member is fixed, as long as the gift to that class member vests before the perpetuities period, as to that class member, the gift is valid, even if gifts to other class members violate the Rule against Perpetuities.

# IV. POWERS OF APPOINTMENT AND THE RULE AGAINST PERPETUITIES

**A. Introduction:** When studying powers of appointment, the material emphasized that there are two key variables to each power: (1) in whose favor it can be exercised—general vs. special; and (2) when can it be exercised—inter vivos vs. testamentary. These two variables are also the keys to analyzing powers of appointment under the Rule against Perpetuities.

**B. Application:** The Rule against Perpetuities can apply to a power of appointment in two ways: (1) the power itself is treated as a property interest subject to the Rule against Perpetuities; and (2) the property interests created by the exercise of a power are subject to the Rule against Perpetuities.

**C. The power:** In applying the Rule against Perpetuities to a power, the analysis turns on (1) *which type* of power it is, and (2) *when* the power can be exercised.

**1. General power:** In assessing a general power of appointment, the key is whether it is an inter vivos or testamentary power.

**a. Inter vivos:** For purposes of the Rule against Perpetuities, a donee holding a presently exercisable general power of appointment is treated as if he or she owns the appointive property. As long as a general inter vivos power of appointment becomes exercisable or fails within the perpetuities period, the power is valid, even if it is not actually exercised until after the perpetuities period.

**b. Testamentary:** For purposes of the Rule against Perpetuities, a donee holding a general *testamentary* power of appointment is not treated as if he or she owned the property, but rather the donee is treated as an agent of the donor. If the general testamentary power of appointment can be exercised, under any possible scenario, *after* the running of the perpetuities period, the power is void from the moment of its attempted creation.

2. **Special power:** A donee holding a special power of appointment is likewise treated as an agent of the donor. If there is any scenario under which the special power of appointment can be exercised *after* the perpetuities period, the power is void from the moment of its attempted creation.

    a. **Discretionary power to distribute:** If a trustee is granted a discretionary power to distribute income from the trust, for purposes of the Rule against Perpetuities, the discretionary power is treated the same as a special power of appointment.

    **Series of powers vs. one power:** One of the leading authorities on trusts, John Gray, argued that the discretionary power is not a single power but rather a series of annual powers to distribute the income. The discretionary power would be valid and exercisable for 21 years after the death of the life tenant before it violates the Rule against Perpetuities. Courts that have addressed the issue, however, have not agreed for the most part, holding that the whole power is invalid if it can be exercised at all beyond the perpetuities period.

    b. **Practical effect:** A trustee's discretionary power over income should be limited to persons alive when it is created or the power runs the risk of being invalid.

D. **Interests created:** In analyzing the interests created under the Rule against Perpetuities, the key is the nature of the power that was exercised.

    1. **General inter vivos power:** For purposes of applying the Rule against Perpetuities, a donee holding a general inter vivos power of appointment is treated as if he or she owned the appointed property. In analyzing interests created by the exercise of the power, the perpetuities period starts with the exercise of the power.

    2. **General testamentary power or special power:** A donee holding a general testamentary power of appointment or a special power of appointment is treated, under the Rule against Perpetuities, as if he or she is acting as an agent for the donor. In analyzing the interests created by the exercise of the power, most courts hold that the perpetuities period is deemed to have started when the power was created. The interests created by the exercise of the power must vest, if at all, within 21 years of the death of some life in being when the power was created, or the interest is void. The apparent harshness of his approach is tempered somewhat by the second-look doctrine. A few hold that the perpetuities period starts when the power is exercised.

    a. **Second-look doctrine:** Under the second-look doctrine, the courts do not look just at the words of the donee's appointment and read them into the initial instrument creating the power. The courts also look at the facts surrounding the donee at the time of the exercise to see if in applying the Rule against Perpetuities to the actual interests created, the interests must vest, if at all, within 21 years of the death of some life in being when the power was created.

    b. **Example:** *T*'s will devises property "to *A* for life, remainder as *A* appoints in her will, outright or in trust." *A*'s will provides that "the appointive property shall be held in trust until the youngest of my children reaches the age of 25, then the property shall be distributed outright in equal shares to those then living." *A*'s power is a general testamentary power of appointment. Reading the terms of *A*'s appointment into the instrument creating the power, the conveyance reads "to *A* for life, then to *A*'s children until the youngest reaches the age of 25, then the property shall be distributed outright in equal shares to those then living." Applying the Rule against Perpetuities in the abstract, the remainder interest violates the rule and would be void. Under the second-look doctrine, however, the courts look at the facts surrounding the donee at the time the power was exercised to see if all *A*'s children who survived *A* were alive when *T* died. If so, each child would qualify as a life in being at the time the interest was created and the remainder would not violate the Rule against Perpetuities.

c. **Example:** In *Industrial National Bank of Rhode Island v. Barrett,* 220 A.2d 517 (R.I. 1966), Arthur Tilley's last will and testament created a testamentary trust that qualified for the full marital deduction. He gave his wife a general testamentary power of appointment over the corpus remaining at her death. Her will devised the property in question in trust to pay the income to her granddaughters, Aline and Evelyn, equally for life, and upon the death of either of them, to pay the income to her issue, per stirpes. The court rejected the general rule that an interest created by a general testamentary power of appointment counts the perpetuity period as starting from the creation of the power. The court reasoned that inasmuch as the donee had a general power of appointment at the time it was exercised, the donee is the practical owner of the property, not an agent. The court held the trust created by Mrs. Tilley's will valid.

d. **Delaware tax trap:** Life estates and special powers of appointment are not subject to federal estate tax. In most states, the Rule against Perpetuities limits the number of life estates with a special power of appointment one can create. In Delaware, however, there is no limit on the number of life estates with a special power of appointment that can be created. The generation-skipping transfer tax, however, limits the attractiveness of life estates with a special power of appointment as a tax avoidance scheme by imposing a generation-skipping transfer tax of 55 percent. Because that rate is equal to the highest possible estate tax, a donee may want to appoint by giving the next life tenant a general power of appointment, thereby incurring an estate tax that may be lower than the generation-skipping transfer tax.

e. **Takers in default:** Where a settlor creates a trust and a general testamentary power of appointment or a special power of appointment, and the donee does not exercise the power, the failure to exercise the power is treated analytically the same as the exercise of the power for purposes of analyzing whether the interest in the takers in default violates the Rule against Perpetuities (i.e., the second-look doctrine applies at the time when the power could have been exercised even if it is not exercised).

**Example:** In *Sears v. Coolidge,* 108 N.E.2d 563 (Mass. 1952), the settlor, Thomas Jefferson Coolidge, created an inter vivos trust in 1913 that provided for the distribution of income among a number of beneficiaries, and for the distribution of principal in equal share to his then-living issue. The time for distribution was the first to happen of either (1) upon the death of the last child, grandchild, or great-grandchild alive when he died, or (2) when the youngest grandchild living when he died reached age 50. Although the default takers under both provisions would have violated the Rule against Perpetuities if tested as of the moment the trust was created, the settlor retained the power to amend the trust until his death. The court ruled that the power to amend the trust was tantamount to a special power of appointment, and that for purposes of the Rule against Perpetuities it should be treated as such even if the power is not exercised. The court applied the second-look doctrine and analyzed the interests as of the settlor's death when the power could no longer be exercised. Under that analysis, the future interests did not violate the Rule against Perpetuities.

# V.  THE RULE AGAINST PERPETUITIES SAVING CLAUSE

**A.  Saving clause:**  A Rule against Perpetuities saving clause is a clause in the instrument creating the future interests that provides that in the event the trust has not yet terminated, it shall terminate 21 years after the death of the last living beneficiary alive when the trust was created, and the property shall be distributed to the then income beneficiaries in the same ratio as they are entitled to receive the income.

**B.  Validity:**  Saving clauses are valid and enforceable, thereby saving a conveyance that would otherwise violate the Rule against Perpetuities. (But care needs to be taken in drafting saving clauses so as not to terminate the trust too early.)

**Example:**  In *Estate of Holt,* 857 P.2d 1355 (Haw. 1993), George Holt died in 1929 with a will that created a testamentary trust. The will provided that the property was to be held in trust for as long as legally possible, and during such time the income was to be paid to his widow, then the income was to be paid to all his heirs in equal share per stirpes, and when the trust had to be terminated, the property should be distributed among his heirs at that time per stirpes. In *Holt I,* the court construed the provision concerning the distribution among his heirs to mean all persons who were his heirs at any time between the date of death of his widow and the termination of the trust. In the present case, the court ruled that the testator's 11 children who were alive at his death and alive at the death of his widow were the measuring lives for purposes of application of the Rule against Perpetuities. Their interests were fully vested as heirs at that time. The last of such children died in 1986 and the trust had to terminate 21 years later—2007. The court rejected the guardian ad litem's argument that the term *heirs* should include any grandchildren alive when the testator died but their interests were not fully vested as only heirs apparent who became heirs upon the death of their parent.

**C.  Malpractice liability:**  As a general rule, attorneys who draft instruments that violate the Rule against Perpetuities are liable to the intended beneficiaries. Although there is one case that held that violating the Rule against Perpetuities did not constitute negligence because the rule is so hard to understand and apply, the case has been heavily criticized and distinguished by other courts. In particular, the availability of saving clauses makes it even easier to hold an attorney liable for not including such a clause.

# VI.  REFORMING THE RULE AGAINST PERPETUITIES

**A.  Modern trend:**  During the last 50 years or so, the Rule against Perpetuities has come under considerable attack as needlessly complicated and unnecessarily harsh. A number of jurisdictions have either modified or abolished the rule.

1. **Construe to avoid violations of the rule:** A number of jurisdictions favor construing conveyances so as to avoid violations of the Rule against Perpetuities.

2. **Example:** In *Warren v. Albrecht,* 571 N.E.2d 1179 (Ill. App. 1991), testator's will devised certain real property in trust for the benefit of his grandson John Warren, until he reached the age of 30, at which time he acquired a life estate. Upon his death, his children were to take, and if any predeceased John, his or her share went to the other children, and if no children or descendants survived John, the property was to pass to John's sisters Emma and Goldy, or the survivor, and if neither survived, the property would pass to the testator's heirs at law. John's children quitclaimed their interests to him, and John argued that the will granted his sisters an executory interest that would not vest until and unless his children died without issue—a remote possibility that violated the Rule against Perpetuities. The court construed the interests in question as a contingent remainder in John's children, and alternative contingent remainders in all the other takers, thus avoiding the potential violation of the Rule against Perpetuities.

**B. The cy pres approach:** Cy pres is a doctrine that empowers a court to modify a *charitable* trust that otherwise would fail (the doctrine is covered in more detail in the next chapter). One approach to modifying the *effect* of the Rule against Perpetuities is to extend the doctrine of cy pres to permit courts to modify private trusts that would otherwise fail because they violate the Rule against Perpetuities.

**C. The wait-and-see approach:** The wait-and-see approach abolishes the abstract application of the Rule against Perpetuities and instead applies a statute of limitations approach. The wait-and-see approach lets the facts unfold and waits to see if the future interest involved is still not vested when the perpetuities period ends. The mere possibility of remote vesting is not enough to invalidate the interest; only if the interest actually has not vested at the end of the perpetuities period is the interest invalid.

1. **Widely adopted:** A majority of the states now follow the wait-and-see approach. These states, however, are split over (1) how to *measure* the wait-and-see period, and (2) what to do if the interest still violates the reformed perpetuities period.

2. **Traditional period:** Some of the states apply the wait-and-see approach for the traditional perpetuities period—the lives in being at the time the interest was created plus 21 years. If it violates the perpetuities period at the end of that period, the states are split yet again on what should be done to the interest.

   a. **Judicial reform:** Some states permit the courts to modify an otherwise violating interest so as to effectuate the transferor's intent as closely as possible.

   b. **Void:** Some states apply the traditional approach to an interest that has not vested after the wait-and-see approach—void the interest and strike it.

3. **The Uniform Statutory Rule Against Perpetuities:** The Uniform Statutory Rule Against Perpetuities adopts the wait-and-see approach, but modifies the "life in being plus 21 years" perpetuities period by offering a simpler "90 years" perpetuities period. If the interest has not vested at the end of the 90-year period, the interest is not invalid but rather the statute authorizes the courts to reform the conveyance to validate the interest in a manner that most closely follows the transferor's intent.

a. **Traditional period:** The Uniform Statutory Rule Against Perpetuities does not reject the traditional common law perpetuities period, it just provides an alternative perpetuities period—90 years. As long as the interest vests within *either* perpetuities period, it is valid. As a practical matter, more often than not, the 90-year period will be the applicable period.

b. **Generation-skipping transfer tax:** Trusts created before the generation-skipping transfer tax was enacted in 1986 are not subject to the tax. If a jurisdiction has adopted the Uniform Statutory Rule Against Perpetuities and applies it to interests created by the exercise of a special power of appointment *after* the adoption of the statute, the effect is to permit the trust to last longer, avoiding taxes longer. Treasury regulations permit such extended tax avoidance only if the special power of appointment is not exercised in a way that attempts to obtain the longer of the two perpetuities periods permitted under the statute.

4. **Example:** In *In re Trust of Wold,* 708 A.2d 787 (N.J. Super. Ct. 1998), the settlor created a trust in 1944 for the life of Elaine Wold, and upon her death, gave her a special testamentary power of appointment over the property. In 1991, New Jersey adopted the Uniform Statutory Rule Against Perpetuities. Elaine wanted to appoint the property in further trust for the benefit of her children for life, and upon the death of one of her children, for the benefit of the issue of that child. The court ruled that the Uniform Statutory Rule Against Perpetuities was not retroactive to interests created before the statute was adopted, but where an interest is created pursuant to a power of appointment, the interest is deemed created as of the *exercise* of the power, not the creation of the power. The Uniform Statutory Rule Against Perpetuities would apply to the trust created by Elaine.

5. **Dynasty trust:** A dynasty trust is a trust set up to take maximum advantage of the tax savings permitted under the generation-skipping transfer tax. Each person can transfer up to $1 million in trust, from generation to generation, through a succession of life estates (with right to income) with a special power of appointment, for as long as permitted by the state's perpetuities period, and such transfers will be exempt from estate taxes, gift taxes, and generation-skipping transfer tax for the duration of the trust. The duration will depend on whether the jurisdiction has retained the traditional Rule against Perpetuities period, the Uniform Statutory Rule Against Perpetuities period, or has abolished the doctrine completely. Because the $1 million exemption applies to the initial contribution, not to the size of the trust, a well-invested dynasty trust could grow to hundreds of millions of dollars, with no taxes being imposed.

D. **Abolition:** The third modern trend approach to the Rule against Perpetuities is to abolish it completely. All future interests are valid no matter when they will vest.

"**Dead hand" control:** If one of the principal purposes of the Rule against Perpetuities is to control the risk that a settlor's intent will control well after the time when the settlor could be presumed to have been able to reasonably foresee the future, abolishing the rule creates the potential for inefficient and inflexible "dead hand" control restricting property for centuries. But under the modern trend, most settlers include powers of appointment, thereby building in flexibility by permitting the life tenants to alter the terms of the trust if circumstances warrant. Moreover, the modern trend grants courts and beneficiaries greater power to modify, if not terminate, trusts prematurely. These developments offset somewhat the risks created by abolishing the Rule against Perpetuities.

# Quiz Yourself on
# THE RULE AGAINST PERPETUITIES

**89.** Michael creates an irrevocable inter vivos trust that provides in pertinent part as follows: "To Donald for life, then to my first child to reach age 25." Michael has three children at the time the trust is created, Huey (age 10), Dewy (age 15), and Luey (age 20). Who holds what interests in the trust? _____

**90.** Michael dies and his will devises Mickeyacres as follows: "To Donald for life, then to my first child to reach age 25." Michael has three children when he dies, Huey (age 10), Dewy (age 15), and Luey (age 20). Who holds what interests in Mickeyacres? _____

**91.** Laura deeds her white house as follows: "To Al, but if a woman is ever elected President of the United States, to Hilary." Who holds what interests in the property? _____

**92.** Laura deeds her white house as follows: "To Al, but if Hilary is ever elected President of the United States, to Hilary." Who holds what interests in the property? _____

**93.** Martin devises Malibuacres "To the children of Charlie who reach age 25." Who holds what interests in the property if:

**a.** Charlie is alive and he has two children, Andy, age 15, and Betty, age 5. _____

**b.** Charlie is alive and he has two children, Andy, age 30, and Betty, age 3. _____

**94.** Martin devises "$100,000 to each of Charlie's children, whenever they are born, who reach age 25." Charlie is alive and has two children, Andy, age 15, and Betty, age 5. Two years after Martin's death, Charlie has another child, Sunshine. Who, if anyone, is entitled to receive $100,000?

_____

**95.** Martin devises Malibuacres "to Charlie for life, remainder to such of Charlie's issue as he appoints by will." Charlie's will provides that Malibuacres is to be distributed "to my children who reach age 25." When Martin died, Charlie had two children, Andy, age 15, and Betty, age 5. Charlie dies seven years later without having any more children. Is the interest in Charlie's children valid? _____

---

## Answers

**89.** The instrument appears to create a life estate in Donald, contingent remainder in Michael's first child to reach age 25. Because the remainder is contingent, Michael retains a reversion. The contingent remainder is subject to the Rule against Perpetuities. Although it appears likely that one of Michael's children will reach age 25 within the perpetuities period, you cannot use any of them to definitively prove it because each could die before reaching age 25. There is no validating life among the lives in being. Under the invalidating life approach, the interest can vest only in one of Donald's children, so create a new child for Donald, Fred. The next day, kill everyone who was alive when the interest was created (Donald, Michael, Huey, Dewy, and Luey). Then count 21 years. Fred is only 21 years old.

It is possible Fred will live another 4 years, thereby becoming Donald's first nephew to reach age 25—vesting the interest after the Rule against Perpetuities period. The contingent remainder violates the Rule against Perpetuities and is void from the moment Michael attempted to create it.

90. This conveyance is very similar to the one in the prior problem, but here the interests are being created in Michael's will. This difference is critical. Because the interests are created upon Michael's death, the pool of validating lives is limited to Huey, Dewy, and Luey, because no one else can satisfy the express condition in the instrument given that Michael is dead and cannot have any more children. Using their lives as validating lives, you can conclusively prove that the interest must vest, if at all, during one of their lives or the interest will fail. The contingent remainder does not violate the rule.

    Under the invalidating life approach, the first step is to create (give birth to) a new person in whom the interest can vest. Here, the interest can vest only in one of Michael's sons. Because the interests were created in his will, Michael must be dead, so you cannot create a new son for him. Without being able to create a new son for him, you cannot delay the vesting until after the perpetuities period. The interest must be valid.

91. Al and his heirs hold the property until a woman is elected President of the United States, at which time his interest is to be divested and Hilary or her heirs or devisees will take the property. There is no validating life that definitely proves that Hilary's interest must take possession, if at all, during the perpetuities period. Many generations from now, well after the lives in being at the time the interests were created, a woman may be elected president, thereby divesting Al's heirs or devisees of the property and transferring it to Hilary's heirs or devisees. The key is that both Al's interest and Hilary's interest are transmissible. Under the invalidating life approach, create heirs for both Al and Hilary, kill Al and Hilary, count 21 years, and ask if it is conceivable that a woman may be elected President? Obviously. You have created a scenario where the executory interest becomes possessory but not until after the perpetuities period. The executory interest violates the Rule against Perpetuities and is void.

92. The express divesting condition ("if Hilary is ever elected President") is tied to a life in being. Hilary can be used as the validating life. The executory interest must become possessory, if at all, during Hilary's life. Alternatively, it is impossible to conceive of a scenario where the executory interest would become possessory, but only after the perpetuities period. Although you can create heirs for Al and Hilary, the moment you kill the lives in being at the time the interest was created, by killing Hilary you make it impossible for the executory interest to become possessory after the perpetuities period. The executory interest does not violate the Rule against Perpetuities and is valid.

93. **a.** The gift to Charlie's children who reach age 25 is void as against the Rule against Perpetuities. Both of Charlie's living children could die before the age of 25. Charlie could have another child, after Martin's death. Charlie could die shortly after that child's birth, and that child could be the first to reach age 25—but this would be after the perpetuities period. There is not a validating life and it is easy to conceive of a scenario where the interest vests but only after the perpetuities period.

    **b.** The gift to Charlie's children who reach age 25 does not violate the Rule against Perpetuities. Under the rule of convenience, as soon as one member of the class is entitled to receive possession of his or her share of the property, the class closes. Here, when Martin dies, Charlie's oldest child is 30. The class closes immediately upon Martin's death. Although Charlie could have more children, they would not be able to get into the class. It is impossible then to create a scenario where a share would vest but only after the perpetuities period. Although it will be longer than 21 years before Betty's interest vests, she counts as a life in being, and therefore her interest must vest, if at all, during the perpetuities period.

94. Where a set gift is given to each member of a class, the Rule against Perpetuities is not applied to the whole class but rather is applied individually to each gift to each class member. Here, Andy and Betty constitute lives in being when the gift was made, so the gifts to them are valid. The gift to Sunshine, however, is invalid. She was not alive when the gift was made, and it is easy to conceive of a scenario where if all the parties died shortly after her birth her interest would not vest until after all the lives in being at the time the gift was made plus 21 years.

95. Charlie holds a special testamentary power of appointment. The power is valid because Charlie was a life in being when the interest, the power, was created. Because the power is a special testamentary power of appointment, when Charlie exercises the power, treat the interests created by the *exercise* of the power as if they were created by the instrument *creating* the power. The original instrument can be rewritten to read: "To Charlie for life, then to his children who reach age 25." At first blush, the future interests in Charlie's children who reach age 25 would appear to violate the Rule against Perpetuities because it is possible to conceive of a scenario where Charlie has another child whose interest would vest after the perpetuities period. But under the second-look doctrine, in applying the Rule against Perpetuities, the court will take into account the facts that existed when the power was exercised. Charlie died without having any more children. As applied to that factual situation, the interests in Charlie's children who reach age 25 does not violate the Rule against Perpetuities because the only children alive when he died were the same children alive when Martin created the power. As applied to those children, the interest does not violate the Rule against Perpetuities.

## Exam Tips on
# THE RULE AGAINST PERPETUITIES

### The Rule against Perpetuities

Under the measuring life (or validating life) approach, a validating life is a person who was alive at the time the interests were created whose life can be used to prove logically and definitively that under the terms of the conveyance, the interest in question must vest, if at all, within the perpetuities period. If you can find such a life, the interest must be valid. If you cannot find such a life, the interest is invalid.

Under the invalidating life approach, if you can create one scenario, no matter how preposterous, where the interest in question vests in someone who was *not* alive at the time the interest was created, but not until *after* the perpetuities period, the interest violates the Rule against Perpetuities and fails.

☛ The Rule against Perpetuities is applied in the abstract the moment the interest is created. In applying the invalidating life approach, do not apply the common law destructibility of contingent remainders rule.

☛ Watch for *when* the interest is created. The rule applies the moment the interest is *irrevocably* created (wills vs. revocable trusts vs. irrevocable trusts vs. powers of appointment). This is a favorite area for professors to test because the answer turns on the instrument used to create the interest, not so much the Rule against Perpetuities.

## Spotting Rule against Perpetuities issues

There is a Rule against Perpetuities issue anytime you see, and only when you see, a contingent remainder, a vested remainder subject to open (or subject to partial divestment), an executory interest, or a power of appointment.

☞ If the condition or power is tied to someone who is alive at the moment the interest is created, the interest does not violate the Rule against Perpetuities. If the interest or power is not tied to someone who is alive when the interest or power is created, that is when there is a potential problem with the Rule against Perpetuities.

 ☞ Be particularly suspicious of contingent remainders where there is an express time period that is greater than 21 years and contingent remainders where the future interest in question is more than two generations removed from the transferor.

 ☞ When analyzing executory interests, if the divesting condition is not tied to a life in being, almost invariably the interest will be void (unless it is limited to parties who are alive when the interest is created and when the divesting condition occurs).

## Class gifts and the Rule against Perpetuities

Remember the general rule, that the interest is valid as to the whole class or void as to the whole class, and the two exceptions: (1) if the class can be construed as subclasses, apply the rule separately to each subclass; and (2) if the gift is a specific amount to class members, apply the rule individually to each member (what constitutes a subclass is often difficult to delineate and open to too much debate).

## Powers of appointment and the Rule against Perpetuities

If the power is general inter vivos power of appointment, the power is valid. The only issue is whether the interests created by the exercise of the power are valid. Treat the exercise of the power as a new conveyance and analyze the future interests created by the power as you would any other conveyance. If the power is general testamentary power of appointment, or a special power of appointment, there are two issues that need to be analyzed: (1) is the power valid, and (2) are the interests created by the exercise of the power valid?

☞ In analyzing whether the power is valid, if you can conceive of a scenario where the power in question can be exercised beyond the perpetuities period, the power itself is void from the moment the donor attempted to create it.

☞ In analyzing whether the interests created by the power are valid, treat the interests as if they were created by the instrument creating the power. Analytically, rewrite the instrument creating the power to include the interests created by the power. In applying the rule to that "rewritten" conveyance, the courts take into consideration the facts that exist when the power is exercised. If those facts limit the possible scenarios that would violate the rule, limit your analysis of the rule likewise.

## Saving clauses

If the instrument contains a saving clause, the interests will not violate the Rule against Perpetuities. Focus on who would take if the saving clause were applied.

## Modern trend approaches to the Rule against Perpetuities

If the fact pattern tells you that the jurisdiction has adopted one of the modern trend reformations of the Rule against Perpetuities, you should apply that approach.

☛ Cy pres is tantamount to reading a saving clause into the conveyance.

☛ Under the wait-and-see approach, which adopts the statute of limitations approach, it is important to note the distinction between the common law approach and the Uniform Statutory Rule Against Perpetuities flat 90-year approach. Under either, however, if the interest is invalid at the appropriate time, the general rule is to permit the court to reform the interest to best carry out the transferor's intent.

CHAPTER 13

# TRUST ADMINISTRATION AND THE TRUSTEE'S DUTIES

*ChapterScope* _____

This chapter examines the core issues that arise during the administration of a trust—the trustee's duties generally, the trustee's powers generally, and the trustee's investment powers and duties.

- **Trustee's duties:** During the administration of a trust, the trustee has a number of duties with respect to the trust beneficiaries, the trust property, and the investment of the trust assets.

  - **Duty of loyalty:** The trustee owes a duty of absolute loyalty to the beneficiaries. Everything the trustee does must be done in the best interests of the beneficiaries.

  - **Duty to care for the property:** The trustee must take proper care of the trust property. The trustee has the duty to take possession of and protect the trust property; the duty to earmark the trust property; and the duty to segregate the trust property from other property (particularly the trustee's own property).

  - **Duty not to delegate:** A trustee cannot delegate those activities and responsibilities that he or she can reasonably be expected to perform. Trustees may delegate ministerial activities—those that do not require the exercise of discretion.

  - **Duty of impartiality:** A trustee has a duty of loyalty to all the beneficiaries. The trustee must balance the competing interests of the different beneficiaries. The trustee has a duty to produce a reasonable income for the life beneficiary while protecting the remainder interest for the remainderman.

  - **Duty to inform and account to beneficiaries:** The trustee has a duty to provide beneficiaries with complete and accurate information when requested, and a duty to account either to the court or to the beneficiaries on a regular basis.

- **Trustee's powers:** At common law, the office of trustee had no inherent powers, only those that were either expressly granted to the trustee by the deed or declaration of trust or those implicitly provided in light of the express trust powers and/or purpose. The modern trend has been to expand the trustee's powers. At first, to simplify the granting of trust powers, states adopted long lists of statutory powers that the settlor could incorporate by reference. More recently, the trustee has been granted automatically all the powers a prudent person would need to manage the trust in light of its purpose.

- **Trust investments:** The issue of what constitutes an appropriate trust investment has, to a large degree, paralleled the issue of the trustee's powers.

  - **Traditional approach:** Traditionally, the presumed purpose of a trust was to *preserve* the trust property. Trustees were authorized to make such investments as a prudent man would with his own property with an eye toward preserving the principal while producing a reasonable income. Only relatively safe investments were deemed appropriate, and each investment decision was viewed individually.

■ **Modern trend:** The modern trend view of a trust is that it is a vehicle for holding and managing assets. The modern trend adopts the prudent investor rule. The risk of loss is assessed on a portfolio basis, not individual investments, and the trustee has a duty to diversify his or her investments. The focus is on total rate of return, not individual investments or investment decisions.

   ■ **Duty to delegate:** The prudent investor rule also modifies the duty not to delegate, providing that an unsophisticated trustee has a duty to delegate investment decisions to professionals who are in a better position to make the necessary investment analysis and decisions.

   ■ **Principal and income:** The prudent investor rule also modifies the traditional rules concerning allocation of income and principal. Because the focus is on total return, and not on income vs. principal, the trustee is authorized to reassign some of the return, if necessary, to make sure that both categories of beneficiaries are treated fairly.

   ■ **Trustee's liability to third parties:** At common law, the trustee was personally liable, both in contract and in tort, for contracts entered into by the trust or for torts committed within the course of managing the trust. The trustee was entitled to reimbursement if the actions were authorized, but if the trust assets were inadequate, the trustee was personally liable. The modern trend limits the trustee's personal liability by limiting claims against the trustee to claims in his or her representative capacity as a general rule.

# I. TRUSTEE'S FIDUCIARY DUTIES

**A. Duty of loyalty:** The golden rule of trust administration is that the trustee owes the trust beneficiaries the duty of absolute loyalty. Everything the trustee does must be done in the best interests of the beneficiaries. All the other trustee's duties arguably are merely logical subduties of this one supreme duty—absolute loyalty to the trust beneficiaries.

1. **Fiduciary:** It should be noted that a trustee is a fiduciary, but that there are other types of fiduciaries—in particular, executors/personal representatives are fiduciaries with respect to the administration of the probate estate. So while the material will focus on the trustee and the trustee's duties, there are other fiduciaries that owe similar duties in carrying out the responsibilities inherent in their position.

2. **Scope:** In applying the duty of loyalty to a particular act undertaken by the trustee, the courts have translated the duty of loyalty into a duty to act reasonably and in good faith. The good faith requirement is a subjective standard that addresses the trustee's state of mind—the trustee must have thought that what he or she was doing was in the beneficiaries' best interests. The requirement that the trustee act reasonably is an objective standard that permits judicial review and supervision of a trustee's actions even where the trustee acted in good faith.

3. **Duty against self-dealing:** Self-dealing arises where the trust and the trustee engage in a transaction. The trustee has a conflict of interest. The trustee has a personal interest in the transaction while at the same time the trustee has a duty to act only in the best interests of the beneficiaries. The beneficiaries' interests must prevail. The duty against self-dealing is

usually construed broadly to include transactions involving other members of the trustee's family (spouse, children, and parents).

a. **No further inquiry:** Where a trustee engages in self-dealing, an irrebuttable presumption of breach of the duty of loyalty arises. Once it is established that self-dealing has occurred, no further inquiry of the trustee's reasonableness or good faith is necessary or appropriate—per se it constitutes a breach of the duty of loyalty. The beneficiaries can either hold the trustee liable for any loss or compel the trustee to transfer any profit made to the trust, or undo the transaction.

b. **Corporate trustee holding own stock:** The general rule is that a corporate trustee cannot hold its own stock (or the stock of an affiliate) unless authorized by the beneficiaries to retain as an investment its own stock (or the stock of an affiliate) received from the settlor. If not authorized, the trustee must sell the stock within a reasonable time.

c. **Trust pursuit rule:** Among the remedies available to trust beneficiaries where there is a breach of trust is the ability of the trust beneficiaries to pursue the trust property and secure its return despite its transfer, unless the property is sold to a subsequent bona fide purchaser without notice of the breach of trust.

   **Example:** In *Hartman v. Hartle,* 122 A. 615 (N.J. Chan. 1923), the testatrix had five children. Her will appointed two of her sons-in-law executors of her estate and directed that her real property was to be sold and divided equally among the five children. The land was sold for $3,900 at public auction, and one of the testatrix's sons bought it for his sister, who was the wife of one of the executors. Two months later, the sister sold the land for $5,500. The court ruled that the duty against self-dealing applied to the spouse of the fiduciary. Absent court approval of the transaction, the sale was inappropriate. The sale could not be rescinded because of the subsequent sale to a bona fide purchaser without notice of the breach of trust, but the sister was forced to share one-fifth of the profit upon resale with the complaining beneficiary.

d. **Self-dealing exception:** The duty against self-dealing can be waived either by the settlor in the terms of the trust or by all the beneficiaries, following a full disclosure of the proposed transaction.

   **Judicial review:** Even where self-dealing is authorized, the transaction must still be reasonable and fair, and if it is not, the trustee will be liable for breaching the duty of loyalty.

4. **Duty to avoid conflicts of interest:** A conflict of interest arises where the trust deals with another party with whom the trustee has an interest that may affect the trustee's assessment of the proposed transaction. If the transaction involves a possible conflict of interest, but not self-dealing, the no further inquiry rule does not apply. The transaction is assessed to see if it is reasonable and fair under the circumstances.

a. **Example:** In *In re Rothko,* 372 N.E.2d 291 (N.Y. 1977), testator's will appointed three friends executors of his estate (which consisted primarily of almost 800 paintings). The executors contracted with an art gallery that agreed to purchase 100 of the paintings and to sell the rest on consignment. In analyzing the contracts, the court found that two of the executors had a conflict of interest. One of the executors was a director and officer of the art gallery. The contract resulted in the executor receiving greater financial remuneration and status, and the gallery giving favorable treatment to the executor's own art collection. The second executor had a conflict of interest because he was a struggling artist seeking to curry favor with the gallery so it would buy and sell his paintings, something that in fact happened during the contract negotiations. The court found that the contracts were neither fair nor in the beneficiaries' best interests. The court found that the third executor was aware of the breaches of trust being committed by the other executors and failed to act—a breach of trust, even where the third executor was acting on the advice of counsel. The advice of counsel gave the executor good faith, but the transactions were not reasonable, and the executor did not act reasonably in failing to properly assess the contracts.

   **b. Damages:** Where a trustee is authorized to transfer trust property, but improperly sells it for too low a price, the trustee is liable for the difference in the actual sale price and the price that should have been realized. Where a trustee sells property he or she was not authorized to sell, appreciation damages are appropriate. Appreciation damages constitute the difference between the sale price and the value of the property as of the date of the court's decree (thereby putting the beneficiaries back in the position where they would have been but for the unauthorized sale). In *In re Rothko,* above, the court ruled that where the sale of the trust property constitutes a breach of misfeasance other than just selling the property for too low a price, the fiduciary may be liable for appreciation damages. Transferees who take with notice of the breach of trust are liable for appreciation damages as well. In *In re Rothko,* the court imposed appreciation damages on the two executors who acted with the conflict of interest, as well as the art gallery.

**5. Cotrustee liability:** A trustee is liable for a breach of trust if the trustee (1) consents to the action that constitutes the breach, or (2) negligently fails to act to stop or try to stop the other trustees from engaging in the action that constitutes the breach. A trustee's fiduciary duties to the beneficiaries include monitoring the conduct of his or her fellow trustees. Failure to monitor the actions of one's cotrustees, or delegating one's nonministerial responsibilities to cotrustees, constitutes a breach of trust.

   **Right to contribution:** Cotrustees are jointly liable. A trustee generally has a right to contribution from cotrustees where he or she is found liable. Under the Restatement (Second) of Trusts, however, the right to contribution may be limited if the trustee either was more at fault or benefited personally from the breach; and the right to contribution is eliminated if the trustee acted in bad faith.

**6. Award of attorney's fees:** Where legal fees have been rendered for the benefit of the estate as a whole, resulting in an increase in all the shares of all the beneficiaries, reasonable compensation should be awarded from the funds of the estate.

   **Example:** In *Matter of Kinzler,* 600 N.Y.S.2d 126 (N.Y. App. Div. 1993), the testatrix's will provided that her estate was to be divided into three shares for her three daughters. Gloria and Louise received their shares outright, and the share for Beatrice was to be held in trust. Beatrice was the income beneficiary and her children held the remainder. Gloria and Louise were appointed cotrustees of the trust. The will was drafted by Gloria's husband, and he was appointed executor. The executor sold the decedent's house, in which the trust held a one-third interest, to Louise, a cotrustee of the trust. The court found these actions constituted self-dealing. The court found that the executor failed to exercise impartiality by refusing to distribute any income to Beatrice despite the terms of the trust. The court also found that the executor acted improperly in awarding himself compensation in advance for legal services rendered without obtaining prior court approval as required by statute. The court ordered the attorney-executor to refund over $11,000 to the estate, along with $16,000 in interest. The efforts of Beatrice's (and her children's) attorney had increased the size of the probate estate by $28,000, thereby enhancing the distributive shares of all the beneficiaries. The court awarded the attorney $7,000 in legal fees.

**B. Duty to care for trust property:** A trustee has a duty to care for the trust property as a prudent person would care for the property of another. The prudent person standard is a higher standard than the average reasonable person takes with respect to his or her own affairs.

1. **Duty to secure possession:** Intrinsic in the trustee's job to hold and manage the trust property is the duty to secure possession of the trust property in a timely manner. With testamentary trusts, the trustee has a duty to monitor the executor's actions and ensure that the trust receives what it is entitled to with no unreasonable delays.

2. **Duty to care for and maintain:** Having secured possession, logically the trustee has a duty to care for and maintain the trust property. Where the trust holds real property, the trustee should treat the property as an ordinary owner would treat similarly situated property. The trustee should insure the property, keep the property in good repair, and otherwise take whatever reasonable steps an ordinary owner would take to protect and care for the property.

   **Example:** In *In re Estate of Kurkowski,* 409 A.2d 357 (Pa. 1979), decedent died intestate survived by his wife and two sons from a prior marriage. His wife was appointed administratix of his estate. At the time of his death, the principal asset of his estate was Monroe Cycle Center, Inc., a business of which he was the sole shareholder and president. The administratix proceeded to take over the operations of the business, without court approval, and mismanaged it—operating it at a loss. She made no attempt to sell it or its assets, and testified that she had intended to continue to operate it indefinitely. When efforts to sell the business proved unsuccessful, she simply closed the doors with no plan for wrapping up the business. When she closed the doors, the corporate accounts reflected over $120,000 in assets. The court found that the administrator's duty to preserve and protect estate assets does not include the duty to carry on a business conducted by the decedent (for longer than a limited time for purposes of selling the business as a going concern or winding up business or finishing off existing contracts) without court approval. The court found that the administratix clearly breached her fiduciary duty and surcharged her $119,000.

3. **Duty to segregate and identify:** Where the trust property is personal property, in particular fungible assets (money, stocks, etc.), the trustee has a duty to separate the trust property from all other assets and to properly designate the property as trust assets to ensure that a trustee cannot "switch" trust assets and personal assets after the fact where the former outperform the latter.

   a. **Exception—bearer bonds:** A well-recognized exception to the duty to segregate and identify trust assets is where a trustee invests in bearer bonds.

   b. **Common law—strict liability:** At common law, if a trustee breached the duty to segregate and identify trust assets, the trustee was strictly liable for any damage the trust property may sustain, even if the damage was not caused by the breach.

c. **Modern trend—causation:** The modern trend is that a trustee is not liable for a breach unless the breach of the duty caused the damage to the trust property.

C. **Duty not to delegate:** At common law, a trustee could not delegate any discretionary responsibilities. The reasoning was that the settlor reposed great trust in the trustee and selected a trustee because the settlor assumed that the trustee personally would hold and manage the trust property. If the trustee were to delegate discretionary responsibility to another, such delegation would violate the settlor's intent.

1. **Exception—ministerial responsibilities:** Even at common law, there was an exception for ministerial responsibilities. Responsibilities that did not require the exercise of any discretion were generally deemed ministerial (e.g., cutting the grass, making repairs, maintaining and cleaning the property).

2. **Modern trend—duty to delegate:** The modern trend recognizes that some trustees are unqualified to undertake certain responsibilities inherent in holding and managing trust property—in particular, the duty to invest trust property properly. Under the Uniform Prudent Investor Act §171 and the Restatement (Third) of Trusts §171, the trustee may have a duty to delegate those responsibilities if a prudent person would delegate under similar circumstances. The trustee must act in the best interests of the beneficiaries in deciding whether to delegate discretionary responsibilities, including investment-making responsibilities, and to whom to delegate them.

   a. **Duty to supervise:** Even where the trustee is authorized to delegate either ministerial or discretionary responsibilities, the trustee has an ongoing duty (1) to properly define the agents' roles, and (2) to monitor and supervise the actions of the agents to whom the trustee delegates the responsibilities to ensure that the agents are acting within the delegated authority and are acting in the best interests of the beneficiaries. The trustee cannot abdicate or delegate unreasonably.

   b. **Example:** In *Shriners Hospitals for Crippled Children v. Gardiner,* 733 P.2d 1110 (Ariz. 1987), settlor created a trust, income to her daughter, grandchildren, and daughter-in-law, remainder upon the death of the last income life beneficiary to Shriners Hospital. Settlor appointed her daughter trustee and her grandson as successor trustee. The daughter had no investment experience, so she placed the funds with a brokerage house. The grandson was a stockbroker, so he made all the investment decisions. The grandson embezzled $317,234 from the trust. The remainderman, Shriners Hospital, sued the daughter as trustee for breach of trust in delegating the investment responsibilities. The court stated that while an inexperienced trustee has a duty to seek expert advice with respect to the trust investments, the trustee cannot delegate the investment decisions completely, but rather must exercise his or her own judgment after receiving such advice. Here, the daughter turned over the investment decision-making process completely to the grandson in breach of her duty. The court noted that it made no difference that the grandson was the successor trustee.

D. **Duty to be impartial:** The trustee's duty of loyalty extends to all beneficiaries, those holding the present interest (typically a life estate in the income) and those holding the future interest (typically a remainder in the principal). Because the beneficiaries have different property interests, their personal interests often conflict. The income beneficiaries prefer the trust principal be invested so that high levels of interest are generated (risky investments); while the remaindermen prefer the trust property be invested in safe investments that protect the principal (but generate little income).

1. **Rule statement:** The trustee's duty of loyalty to both present and future interests translates into a duty of impartiality between the competing interests—a duty to invest the property so that it produces a reasonable income while preserving the principal for the remaindermen.

2. **Inception assets:** Many jurisdictions permit a trustee to have a preference for retaining the trust's "inception assets"—the assets used to fund the trust that the settlor recommends the trustee retain. Such preference, however, is not an absolute right and is subject to the trustee's more general duty of impartiality among the beneficiaries.

3. **Duty to sell:** Even where the trust instrument authorizes the trustee to retain the trust assets in question, where such assets are either underperforming (principal appreciating significantly but producing little income) or overperforming (producing substantial income stream but principal depreciating), the trustee has a duty to sell the trust property in a timely manner (within a reasonable time period).

   **Judicial authorization:** Where one group of beneficiaries objects to the sale, or if a cotrustee blocks the sale, the duty to be impartial requires the trustee (or other cotrustees as the case may be) to petition the court for authority to sell.

4. **Power to reallocate proceeds:** If a trustee does not dispose of underperforming or overperforming property within a reasonable time, the trustee has a duty to reallocate the sale proceeds so that the beneficiaries adversely affected by the delayed sale are compensated for the damage to their interest caused by the delay.

   a. **Underperforming property:** Where underperforming property is not sold in a timely manner, the income beneficiaries are entitled to a share of the sale proceeds to reflect the income they lost during the delay when the property was not generating the income it should have been. The Restatement (Third) of Trusts §241 calculates their share by subtracting from the sale proceeds the income that would have been generated by that amount from the date the duty to sell arose.

      **Revised Uniform Principal and Income Act:** The Revised Uniform Principal and Income Act provides that where underperforming trust property is sold, the proceeds must be apportioned between the income beneficiaries and the remaindermen to offset the loss sustained by the income beneficiaries even if the duty to sell never arose.

   b. **Overperforming property:** Where overperforming property is not sold in a timely manner, the remaindermen are entitled to a share of the income generated during the delay. The share is determined by calculating the value of the property on the date the duty arose, minus the actual sale price when finally sold, and multiplied by a percentage to reflect return on the properly invested principal for appreciation and inflation. If the trustee fails to withhold some of the income generated during the delay, the trustee may be liable for the difference.

   c. **Example:** In *Dennis v. Rhode Island Hospital Trust Co.,* 744 F.2d 893 (1st Cir. 1984), settlor created a testamentary trust in 1920 and funded it with three downtown Providence commercial buildings. The trust provided that the income was to go to the settlor's living issue until 21 years after the death of her last surviving child, and then the principal was to be distributed to her then-living issue. The remainderman sued, claiming that the trustee routinely acceded to the income beneficiaries' requests that the trust be managed so as to produce the highest possible income without regard for the principal. The trustee failed to recognize that the buildings were depreciating in value despite the income being generated and took no steps to amortize the depreciation or keep abreast of the declining real estate market in the downtown area to determine when the property should have been sold. The trustees were surcharged for the loss of principal that occurred as a result of their failure to sell the overproducing property in a timely manner.

**E.  Duty to disclose:** The beneficiaries are the equitable owners of the trust property. The trustee is merely holding and managing the trust assets. Accordingly, the trust beneficiaries are entitled to receive (1) enough information about the terms of the trust to be able to assess the extent of their rights and to determine if a breach of trust has occurred, and (2) complete and accurate information about the nature and extent of the trust property, including access to trust records and accounts.

   **1.  Settlor authorizes withholding information:** Where the settlor expressly provides in the trust that the terms of the trust are to be withheld from the beneficiary, or information about the trust property is to be withheld, the law is not clear. At a minimum, each beneficiary is entitled to receive information about his or her interest in the trust (and copies of those pages of the trust), but it is open to debate whether the beneficiaries are entitled to receive a complete copy of the trust.

   **California—right to receive:** By statute, the state of California provides that upon the death of a settlor of a revocable trust, all beneficiaries and heirs of the settlor have the right to request a complete copy of the trust instrument.

   **2.  Duty to notify before acting:** The trustee has a duty to give advance notice to the trust beneficiaries where the trustee proposes to sell a significant portion of the trust assets unless the value of the assets are readily ascertainable or disclosure would be seriously detrimental to the beneficiaries' interests.

   **3.  Example:** In *Allard v. Pacific National Bank,* 663 P.2d 104 (Wash. 1983), the Stones set up trusts for their children, appointing Pacific National Bank as trustee. The sole asset of the Stone trusts was a fee interest in a quarter block in downtown Seattle subject to a 99-year lease entered into in 1952 with Seattle-First National Bank (Seafirst). In 1977 Seafirst assigned its leasehold interest to City Credit Union of Seattle (Credit Union). Credit Union offered to purchase the property from Pacific National for $139,000. Pacific National countered at $200,000, and Credit Union agreed. The trust gave Pacific National the power to sell the asset without the consent of the beneficiaries, and Pacific National argued that meant it did not have a duty to inform the beneficiaries prior to selling the asset. The court disagreed, reasoning that a trustee's fiduciary duty includes the responsibility to inform the beneficiaries fully of all facts that would aid them in protecting their interests. The trustee must inform beneficiaries of all material facts in connection with nonroutine transactions, prior to the transaction taking place, that significantly affect the trust and the beneficiaries' interests. The court ruled that Pacific National's failure to inform the beneficiaries of the proposed sale of the trust's sole asset constituted an egregious breach of fiduciary duty, and Pacific National breached its fiduciary duty by not attempting to get the best possible price for the property. National Pacific did not offer the property for sale on the open market nor did it ascertain the fair market value by getting an independent appraisal, either of which would have satisfied the duty.

**F. Duty to account:** A trustee has a duty to account on a regular basis for the actions he or she has taken as trustee so that his or her performance can be assessed relative to the terms and fiduciaries' duties created by the express terms of the trust.

1. **Testamentary trusts:** Testamentary trusts are created as part of the probate process and supervision over the trust is generally accorded to the probate court. Trustees have a duty to account to the probate court so that the court can assess the trustee's performance. Some courts will permit a provision in the trust releasing a trustee from his or her duty to account to the probate court (burdensome and expensive) as long as the trustee accounts directly to the beneficiaries (typically the income beneficiaries). Some jurisdictions hold such "no judicial accounting" clauses violate public policy because they fail to adequately protect the interests of the remaindermen.

2. **Inter vivos trusts:** Inter vivos trusts are not created as part of the probate process and hence are not naturally subject to probate court supervision—though judicial accounting is still possible. Because the trust was not created as part of the probate process, however, "no judicial accounting" clauses are usually held valid if the trust is an inter vivos trust. Clauses that give absolute immunity based on accountings accepted by life beneficiaries alone have not been universally accepted.

3. **Duty to review accounting:** When a trustee makes an accounting, either to the court or directly to the beneficiaries, the beneficiaries have a duty to check the accounting and to object in a timely manner. If the beneficiaries fail to object in a timely manner, they will be barred from complaining later.

4. **Fraudulent accounting:** Where a trustee files a fraudulent accounting, and the beneficiaries later discover the fraud, the beneficiaries will not be barred from reopening the accounting.

5. **Constructive fraud:** Where an accounting makes factual representations that turn out to be false, if the trustee made the representations without undertaking reasonable efforts to ascertain the accuracy of the factual representations, such false factual representations in the accounting constitute a "constructive" or "technical" fraud and constitute grounds for reopening an otherwise properly allowed accounting.

   a. **Investigation:** The doctrine of constructive or technical fraud does not make trustees guarantors of all factual representations in an accounting. Where such representations are made in good faith, following reasonable efforts to ascertain the accuracy of the representations, the trustee has fulfilled his or her duty.

   b. **Factual representations:** The doctrine of constructive or technical fraud applies only to factual representations in the accounting. Statements of judgment or discretion are not factual representations.

   c. **Discoverability:** If the factual falsehood is discoverable from an inspection of all the trust accounts, the trust terms, and the law, the doctrine of constructive or technical fraud does not apply.

6. **Improper payments:** Where an accounting reveals that a trustee has improperly distributed trust property to one who was not entitled to receive such property, the trustee is liable for

breach of trust unless the court approved the accounting. Where the court's approval was based upon a fraudulent accounting, reopening such accounting voids the court's approval of the accounting.

## II. TRUSTEE'S POWERS

A. **Common law:** At common law, a trustee possessed only those powers either expressly granted in the terms of the trust or those necessarily implied in light of the trust purposes.

B. **Judicial authorization:** A trustee can petition a court of equity for authorization to undertake an action not expressly or implicitly authorized under the terms of the trust. If the court authorizes the requested action, in essence, the court has granted the trustee the requested additional power.

C. **Modern trend:** The modern trend has been to facilitate the granting of powers to the trustee. The modern trend has taken two approaches toward this goal.

  1. **Statutory list:** Under this approach, the jurisdiction adopts a statute that sets forth a long list of powers it is presumed a trustee would need, thereby permitting settlors to incorporate the statutory list of powers by simply referring to the statutory provisions (incorporation by reference).

  2. **Inherent powers:** The alternative modern trend approach is statutorily to grant the trustee a broad set of powers unless the settlor expressly provides that the trustee is not to have one or more of the granted powers. Typically the statute will provide that a trustee is presumed to have all the powers a reasonable person would need to perform the acts necessary in light of the purposes of the trust.

## III. TRUST INVESTMENTS

A. **Introduction:** The issue of what constitutes an appropriate trust investment goes directly to the core of what is the purpose of a trust. Just as the function of a trust has changed over time from preserving property to managing the trust property, so too has the notion of what constitutes an appropriate trust investment. The rules limiting trust investments to "safe" investments have given way to permitting an acceptable level of risk to ensure an adequate return on the trust property.

**Example:** In *In re Trusteeship Agreement with Mayo,* 105 N.W.2d 900 (Minn. 1960), Dr. Mayo established two trusts for the benefit of Esther Mayo Hartzell, and upon her death, her surviving children. Each trust expressly provided that the trust assets were not to be invested in real estate or corporate stock. At the time the trusts were created (1917 and 1919), the combined assets totaled $1,186,000. By December 30, 1940, the assets had declined to $957,711. By 1958, the trust assets were worth $968,893, but taking into account inflation, the assets were worth only $456,139 in 1940 dollars—a reduction of approximately 50 percent. Petitioner asked the court to authorize investments in corporate stock—a common practice of corporate trustees to hedge against inflation. The court concluded that the settlor's primary purpose was to preserve the value of the trust corpus and changes in circumstances (the creation of the Securities and Exchange Commission to regulate and control corporate stock purchases) justified authorizing the trustees to deviate from the express terms of the trust and to invest in corporate stocks.

**B. Statutory lists:** Historically, the most common approach to what constituted an appropriate trust investment was a statutory list of appropriate investments. The legislature would identify categories of investments that were presumptively appropriate, but even then an investment in a particular entity or activity included within the list had to be otherwise reasonable and proper.

1. **Investments analyzed individually:** Under the traditional approach, each investment was viewed separately. If one investment out of a hundred was deemed inappropriate, the trustee was liable for any loss caused by the one inappropriate investment. The other investments' risk level and profits were completely irrelevant in assessing the propriety of a particular investment.

2. **Settlor's authorization:** If a settlor expressly authorizes investments that are not on a jurisdiction's statutory list, such investments are appropriate investments as long as otherwise reasonable and proper.

   **Judicial construction:** As a general rule, courts tend to construe narrowly provisions authorizing a trustee to invest in otherwise inappropriate investments—requiring the trustee to still act reasonably and properly.

**C. Model Prudent Man Investment Act:** The Model Prudent Man Investment Act abolishes statutory lists and permits any investment that a prudent man would make, barring only "speculative" investments. The act was first adopted in 1940 and now represents the majority view.

**Prudent person:** The most common statement of the prudent person standard is that the trustee should invest with the same care as a prudent person would of his or her own property, taking into consideration the dual goals of preserving the principal while generating a stream of income.

**D. Uniform Prudent Investor Act:** The Uniform Prudent Investor Act, adopted in 1994, builds on the prudent person approach. The Uniform Prudent Investor Act focuses on the actions that constitute a prudent investor and the duties that go hand in hand with those actions. It adopts a number of express provisions that constitute innovative approaches that repudiate the old common law approach. The Restatement (Third) of Trusts has adopted the prudent investor standard.

1. **Duty to diversify:** The prudent investor standard still requires the trustee to spread the risk of loss by diversifying the trust investments—unless it is prudent not to do so.

   a. **Adequate diversification:** How much diversification is necessary is not addressed in the act. Apparently that is a fact sensitive issue to be determined on a trust-by-trust basis, taking into consideration the purpose of the trust and the particular investments in question.

2. **Pooling trust funds:** The common law rule strictly required each trust fund to be segregated from both the trustee's own funds and other trust funds. Segregating trust funds, however, makes diversification of smaller trusts more difficult and increases transaction costs associated with trust investments (increases transaction costs that could be reduced by permitting one transaction for multiple trusts). The modern trend and majority rule permits pooling of trust funds to achieve efficiencies of scale and to facilitate diversifying trust investments. The modern trend likewise permits investments in mutual funds.

3. **Portfolio approach:** The Uniform Prudent Investor Act expressly adopts the portfolio approach to investments—individual investments are no longer assessed in isolation, but rather the total performance of the trust's investments is the standard. The duty to diversify

goes hand in hand with the portfolio approach. A well-diversified portfolio spreads the risk of loss across all the investments so that the aggregate level of risk is acceptable in light of the trust purposes. Under the portfolio approach, an individual investment that might look speculative in isolation can be reasonable if offset by other safe investments with low levels of risk associated with them. One of the keys to assessing the propriety of an investment under the portfolio approach is whether it is a compensated or uncompensated risk.

a. **Compensated risks:** Compensated risks are investments that are riskier than others but that have a corresponding higher rate of possible return associated with them. The investor is compensated appropriately for the enhanced risk. Compensated risks are appropriate investments under the portfolio approach as long as the overall risk level of the trust's investment portfolio is acceptable relative to the trust purposes. Putting an appropriate amount of a trust's funds into a start-up company with great growth potential is an example of a compensated risk.

b. **Uncompensated risks:** Uncompensated risks are those investments that are risky and do not have a corresponding market-enhanced compensation to reward the investor for taking the risk. Putting all one's investments in one stock, regardless of the level of risk associated with the stock, is an example of an uncompensated risk.

c. **Investment decisions:** Arguably the key considerations in assessing a trustee's investments under the portfolio theory approach are (1) the trustee's investigations and decision-making process in determining the trust's acceptable level of compensated risk, and (2) how that level is achieved through the combination of trust investments.

d. **Duty to delegate:** The prudent investor approach assumes that expert assistance in the investing decision-making process is beneficial, if not required. Delegating the investment process to an expert is viewed with favor, though the trustee still has a duty to properly investigate to whom the power should be delegated, to consult with the agent to ensure that he or she properly understand the trust's terms, purposes, and acceptable level of compensable risk, and to monitor the activities and decisions of the investment agent.

4. **Duty to avoid unnecessary costs:** Just as a reasonable person would take all appropriate steps to minimize the expenses associated with his or her investments, so too a trustee must take all reasonable steps to minimize the expenses associated with the trust, including investment expenses.

**Pooling trust funds:** A trustee's duty to be cost-conscious is consistent with the modern trend, which permits the pooling of trust funds to achieve economies of scale and to reduce transaction costs.

5. **Duty to consider tax consequences and inflation:** The contemporary trustee has to recognize that tax consequences and inflation are very real and significant factors that need to be taken into consideration when assessing the investment options of a trust. Because the trustee has to preserve the trust principal for the remainder beneficiaries, preserving the principal should include its "real value," taking inflation into account. Principal needs to grow at the rate of inflation if the purchasing power of the corpus is to be preserved. Moreover, different investments have different tax consequences for both the income beneficiaries and the remainder beneficiaries that need to be taken into consideration in structuring the appropriate level of compensated risk.

6. **Presumption against junior mortgages:** Although not per se a breach of trust, there is a presumption that second or other junior mortgages are too risky—the risk of foreclosure by the prior lien(s) and loss of equity by the trust is simply too great absent unusual circumstances.

   **Duty to diligently investigate:** Because of the risk that the property may depreciate, a trustee has a duty to diligently investigate the valuation of the property and the financial status of the mortgagor before purchasing a mortgage.

7. **Professional and corporate trustees:** Professional trustees and corporations are usually held to a higher standard of care in investing due to their presumed expertise. Individual trustees are usually held to a lower standard of care.

8. **Settlor authorization:** If a settlor expressly authorizes all investments, regardless of their legality, the courts tend to construe such provisions narrowly, granting a trustee some extra room for lapses in judgment, but not absolute immunity for improper investments under the prudent investor standard. Such exculpatory clauses also do not protect a trustee who acted in bad faith or recklessly in making trust investments.

   a. **Judicial construction:** Some commentators have criticized the courts as being too narrow in their interpretation of the Uniform Prudent Investor Act, complaining that the courts implicitly are still applying the traditional view that trustees have to practice safe investing instead of permitting the broader investments authorized by the act and/or the express terms of a trust instrument.

   b. **Example:** In *Estate of Collins,* 139 Cal. Rptr. 644 (Cal. App. 1977), settlor created a testamentary trust primarily for the benefit of his wife and children. The trust expressly authorized the trustees to purchase any type of property and investment, whether permitted by law or not. In addition, the trust stated that all discretions granted the trustees were absolute, as if they owned the property. One of the trustees had a client who was having difficulty securing a construction loan to be secured by a second deed of trust. The trustees did not have the property appraised to determine its equity, nor did the trustees check to see if there were other claims pending against the company. The trustees lent the company $50,000 (two-thirds of the trust property) without complying with the usual business practices for making such a loan. The company and borrowers filed for bankruptcy shortly thereafter, and the trust lost another $10,000 trying to recoup the initial $50,000. The trial court found that the trustees did not act in bad faith, that they acted with the same degree of prudence and care, and not speculatively, as reasonable people would act in the disposition of their own funds. The appellate court found the trustees violated the duty to diversify, the duty not to invest in second mortgages absent unusual circumstances, the duty to diligently investigate before purchasing mortgages under the prudent investor standard, and that the terms of the trust did not authorize such a blatantly improper investment.

E. **Allocating principal and income:** Typically the life beneficiaries of a trust are entitled to the income, and the remainder beneficiaries are entitled to the principal. The bifurcated interests mean that decisions concerning what constitutes income and what constitutes principal are critical to the interests of the different categories of beneficiaries.

   1. **Settlor's intent:** To the extent the settlor expressly provides for what is to constitute income and/or principal, or the settlor gives the trustee discretion in determining what is to constitute

income and/or principal, settlor's intent controls as a general rule. Historically, however, such expressions of intent were usually construed narrowly.

**Example:** In *Englund v. First National Bank of Birmingham,* 381 So. 2d 8 (Ala. 1980), testator created a testamentary trust, one-quarter of the net income to be distributed to his aunt, three-quarters to be distributed to his wife. Upon the death of his wife, the trustee was to divide the trust into as many shares as there were surviving children, with each child entitled to the net income and as much principal as the trustee deemed necessary or desirable for the child's support, education, and comfort. In addition, the trust authorized the trustee to determine whether property coming into its hands shall be treated as income or principal. In 1977, the trustee sold all the stock it held in Alabama By-Products and Alabama Chemicals, realizing $17 million in proceeds from the sale. Gage Englund, the income beneficiary, asked the trustee to designate $900,000 as income and to distribute the same to her. The trustee agreed to do so. The court held that the trust provision authorizing the trustee to designate the character of property coming into its hands applied only if the character of the receipt is unclear or doubtful. Because the character of these proceeds were clearly principal, and principal could be disbursed only if necessary for support, education, and comfort, the trust provision in question did not authorize the allocation.

2. **1962 Principal and Income Act:** The 1962 Principal and Income Act sets forth the traditional approach to allocating income and principal.

   a. **Income:** The assumption is that money generated on a regular or irregular basis as a result of the trust property or trust investments constitutes income. Classic examples include interest, rent, cash dividends on stock, net profits from a business, and royalties (though a fraction of royalties are allocated to principal).

   b. **Principal:** The assumption is that money generated as part of a conveyance (voluntary or involuntary) of trust property is considered principal (e.g., sale proceeds, insurance proceeds). In addition, stock splits and stock dividends are considered principal because such property has to be retained as principal to maintain the trust's percentage interest in the company. Bond principal payments and part of royalty payments are also considered principal.

   c. **Example:** In *Tait v. Peck,* 194 N.E.2d 707 (Mass. 1963), the trust held shares of Broad Street Investing Corp., a regulated investment company. The settlor's widow was the life beneficiary, entitled to the net income monthly, with the principal to be paid to others upon her death. In 1961, Broad Street paid to the trustees two cash dividends from income, and in December 1961, Broad Street delivered to the trustees 1,463 additional shares of Broad Street as "distributions of gain." Broad Street gives the shareholder the option of taking the capital gain distributions in cash or in stock. Where ordinary industrial companies give the shareholder that option, the rule is that the distribution is treated as income. But the court held that where a regulated investment company is involved, it is more like participating in a common trust fund to achieve risk diversification. The court held that the distributions of gain should be classified as principal.

3. **1997 Principal and Income Act:** Under the portfolio approach, the focus is on the total return to the trust portfolio. As long as the trust achieves an acceptable rate of return on its investments, it is irrelevant whether that return is generated in the form of income or principal as traditionally defined (though the traditional classifications schemes are retained). The trustee

has the power and discretion to reallocate the total return between the income and principal beneficiaries to ensure that the two groups are treated fairly while paying particular attention to the larger rate of return regardless of how the return is classified (income vs. principal).

**Settlor's intent:** The settlor may expressly provide that the trustee does not have the power to reallocate principal and income.

4. **Unitrust:** Under a unitrust, the life beneficiaries are entitled to a specified percentage of the value of the trust principal each year, so there is no need to distinguish income from principal. All property generated by the trust is assigned to principal, and at the appropriate intervals, the specified percentage of the trust principal is distributed to the appropriate beneficiaries.

# IV. TRUSTEE'S LIABILITY TO THIRD PARTIES

A. **Trustee's liability:** A trustee is a fiduciary, like a personal representative, and a trustee's liability to third parties for acts arising during the administration of the estate is analogous to a personal representative's liability to third parties for acts arising during the administration of the decedent's estate. For a discussion of the applicable rules and approaches, *see* Ch. 1, IV.H, "Creditor's claims arising post-death."

---

## *Quiz Yourself on* *TRUST ADMINISTRATION AND THE TRUSTEE'S DUTIES*

96. Nancy sets up a testamentary trust for Ronald's benefit during his lifetime, and upon his death, the principal is to be distributed to the presidential library. The trust appoints George trustee. George decides that some trust property needs to be sold to help support Ronald. The property is sold at public auction, but the bidding is light, so Jeb, George's brother, purchases the property to help out. Not long thereafter, the property is appraised for significantly more than the sale price. The presidential library sues, claiming breach of fiduciary duty in the sale of the property. At trial, the only expert witness testifies that the sale price was fair and reasonable. Who prevails and why? _____

97. Frank creates a testamentary trust for the benefit of Maria during her lifetime, and upon her death, any remaining principal is to be distributed to their kids, Robert and Raymond. The trust appoints Raymond trustee. Raymond invests the trust principal in the stock market, diversifying his investment. To facilitate dealing with the stock and to save administrative costs, Raymond took title to each stock certificate in his personal name. All his investments went up in value, except for his investment in Enron. Robert sues Raymond, claiming breach of duty. Who prevails and why? _____

98. Frank creates a testamentary trust for the benefit of Maria during her lifetime, and upon her death, any remaining principal is to be distributed to their church. The trust appoints their sons, Robert and Raymond, as cotrustees. Raymond goes on vacation to San Francisco (to see the new baseball stadium), and on his way out of town he authorizes Robert to administer the trust while he is away. While Raymond is gone, Robert invests all the money in Worldcom, a telecommunications company that later files for bankruptcy. The church sues Raymond, claiming breach of duty. Raymond's defense is that Robert purchased the stock. Who prevails and why? _____

99. Frank and Marie establish an irrevocable inter vivos trust that is for the benefit of their sons, Robert and Raymond, during their lifetimes, and upon the death of the survivor, the principal is to be divided equally among their issue. Raymond is appointed trustee, and he invests all the trust property in a minor league baseball team that makes money at first, but then loses money on paper each year while appreciating in value (outperforming the market). The trust expressly permits Raymond to invest in any investment he deems appropriate in sole and absolute discretion, and it expressly permits him to retain any investment even if not otherwise authorized by law. Robert sues, claiming breach of duty. Who prevails and why? _____

100. SpongeBill creates a trust for the benefit of Tom and Jerry. The trust appoints Dexter as trustee. Dexter invests the trust proceeds in a variety of companies, including a start-up biotech company that is considered extremely risky. The company fails rather quickly. Tom and Jerry sue, claiming breach of duty. Who prevails, and why? _____

―――――――――――

# *Answers*

96. The presidential library will probably prevail on the grounds that the sale to a family member of the trustee constitutes self-dealing. A trustee owes a duty of loyalty to the trust beneficiaries. To ensure the trustee's undivided loyalty, there is a duty against self-dealing that applies not only to the trustee, but in many jurisdictions, to the trustee's family members as well. Where there is self-dealing, under the no further inquiry rule, the fairness and reasonableness of the sale are irrelevant. The court will probably hold the sale illegal and void, and order the property transferred back to the trust.

97. Robert's strongest argument is to claim failure to earmark the trust property. The trustee has a duty to separate trust property from his or her own property and to clearly indicate which property is the trust property. At common law, if the trustee breached the duty and the trust property declined in value, the trustee was strictly liable for any loss in the trust property regardless of whether the trustee's breach of duty caused the loss. Under the modern trend, the trustee is not liable for any loss not caused by the failure to earmark. Robert would probably prevail under the common law approach, but he would have a much tougher time and probably would not prevail under the modern trend.

98. At common law, a trustee could delegate ministerial duties, but not discretionary duties (such as how to invest the trust property). This duty against delegation included delegation to cotrustees. Under the modern trend, the trustee may have a duty to delegate investment decisions, but only to investment experts (there is no evidence to suggest that Robert would qualify as an investment expert). Raymond arguably would be liable under both the common law and the modern trend, though under the modern trend/Uniform Trust Code, he may be entitled to indemnity from Robert because Robert is substantially more at fault.

99. Whether there has been a breach of the duty of impartiality turns on the approach the jurisdiction takes. The general rule is that a trustee has a duty of impartiality that requires the trust to produce a reasonable income while preserving the principal for the remaindermen. The duty is implied even where the trust expressly authorizes the trustee to retain certain property. Here, the trust is no longer producing any income. Continuing to hold on to the investment in the baseball team constitutes an abuse of the duty of impartiality. Following the sale of the investment, a portion of the sale proceeds

should be allocated to income and distributed to the income beneficiaries to make up for the delay in selling the investment.

Under the modern trend portfolio approach, the focus is on the annual total return regardless of the form of the return. The trustee is authorized to reallocate receipts to ensure that the income and remaindermen beneficiaries are treated fairly. Under this approach, if Raymond reallocated some of the capital appreciation each year to income and distributed it, there may be no breach of the duty of impartiality.

In addition, if the trust were a unitrust, with the income beneficiaries entitled to a fixed share of the trust principal each year, as long as Raymond distributed to the income beneficiaries their annual share of the trust principal each year, there is no breach of the duty of impartiality.

100. Whether there has been a breach of the trustee's duty with respect to investing the trust assets depends on the approach taken by the jurisdiction. At early common law, trustees were limited in their investment options by a statutory list that expressly listed those investments considered safe and appropriate. Any investment in a company or investment vehicle not listed in the statutory list was considered improper unless expressly authorized by the trust instrument. Under the facts, it is unlikely a start-up company would be on the statutory list, and there does not appear to be an express provision authorizing the investment in question. If the jurisdiction followed something akin to a statutory list, the court would likely hold that the investment constituted a breach of the trustee's duty concerning trust investments.

If the jurisdiction has adopted the Uniform Prudent Man Investment Act, the trustee is not limited to those investments listed in a statutory list, but rather is authorized to make any prudent investment that is not speculative. A strong argument can be made that an investment in a start-up biotech company is too speculative to be appropriate for a trust investment. If the jurisdiction follows the Uniform Prudent Man Investment approach, the court would likely hold that the investment constituted a breach of the trustee's duty concerning trust investments.

If the jurisdiction has adopted the Uniform Prudent Investor Act, with its portfolio approach, it is unclear whether the investment in the biotech company is appropriate, at least without knowing more information about the other investments Dexter made. Under the portfolio approach, the total return on the trust investments is the key. High-risk investments, even investments that arguably are speculative, are authorized as long as they constitute a compensated risk and there are offsetting safe investments to balance the overall investment risk of the portfolio.

## *Exam Tips on*
## *TRUST ADMINISTRATION AND THE TRUSTEE'S DUTIES*

### Duty of loyalty

Under the broad duty of loyalty, watch for fact patterns where the trustee or someone associated with the trustee benefits from dealing with the trust. Distinguish between whether it is the trustee or a family member benefiting, in which case the duty against self-dealing probably applies, or whether it is someone else associated with the trustee, in which case the duty against conflicts of interest probably applies (if the trustee might benefit indirectly from the transaction, that is usually a conflict of interest situation).

☛ Under self-dealing, apply the "no further inquiry" rule unless the trust authorizes the self-dealing or the beneficiaries authorized the self-dealing after full disclosure surrounding the transaction. Even then, the trustee is under a duty to act reasonably and in good faith in engaging in the transaction.

☛ If the transaction involves an alleged conflict of interest, apply only the "reasonably and in good faith" standard.

☞ The beneficiaries may be entitled to appreciation damages if the breach involves some misfeasance other than simply selling the trust property for too low a price.

☛ If the trust has more than one trustee, watch for the issue of cotrustee liability (note the common law vs. Uniform Trust Code split on issue).

## Duty to care for trust property

If the trust property sustains a loss that is not the direct result of a questionable transaction that the trustee entered into, that usually raises the issue of whether the trustee has exercised proper care over the trust property. At common law these duties were strict liability duties. The modern trend requires causation. This split is tested often.

## Duty not to delegate

☛ The duty not to delegate can be tested two ways. First, if someone other than a trustee performs a function related to the trust property, the issue is whether it was appropriate for that person to perform the function.

☞ At common law, the rule was fairly easy to state and apply; discretionary duties could not be delegated, while ministerial duties could. While there is some gray area as to what constitutes discretionary vs. ministerial, if the function went to the heart of the trust or constitutes a critical function concerning the trust property, the function was discretionary and could not be delegated.

☞ Under the modern trend, the issue is complicated because not only is the trustee permitted to delegate certain investment-making decisions, the trustee may have a duty to delegate the power—but the trustee must still exercise care in selecting the agent and properly supervise the agent.

☛ The second and subtler way to test the duty not to delegate is where one trustee implicitly or expressly delegates functions to other trustees. The rule is the same for cotrustees—they can delegate ministerial duties to cotrustees, but not discretionary duties.

## Duty of impartiality

Duty of impartiality issues are easy to spot and analyze. Either the trust principal will be appreciating but it is not generating a reasonable stream of income, or the trust will be producing a healthy stream of income but the principal is depreciating. In either scenario, the trustee is favoring one class of beneficiaries over the other.

☛ The duty is breached even if the trust expressly permits the trustee to retain the assets in question.

☛ The hard part is to articulate the remedy—particularly where the breach has been ongoing. Whether a generic statement of reallocating assets will suffice or whether you need to know the details of how to reallocate the assets will depend upon your professor's coverage of this material.

☞ Under the modern trend, Uniform Prudent Investor Act, the traditional duty of impartiality is modified to reflect the focus on total return as opposed to principal vs. income. The trustee is empowered to reallocate receipts to ensure the beneficiaries are being treated fairly.

☞ The issue is moot under the unitrust, where the income beneficiary is entitled to a fixed percentage of the trust principal each year.

## Duty to keep beneficiaries informed and to account to beneficiaries

The duty to inform is straightforward. If tested, the wrinkle to watch for is where the trustee claims the settlor authorized withholding information.
The constructive fraud doctrine is an important doctrine to keep in mind when analyzing accounting issues.

## Trustee's powers

This material is fairly straightforward. If tested, the issue typically is whether a trustee has the power to do something that appears implicit in light of the express powers and the trust purpose. If there is doubt, a trustee can get court approval for the contemplated act.

## Trust investments

A trustee's powers and duties concerning trust investments are the "hot" area of trust administration (and thus of testing too).

☛ The historical context is important. The law has moved from the common law statutory lists, to the prudent investor standard (duty not to speculate), to the modern trend portfolio theory. Implicit in the historical evolution has been the shift from each investment decision to the overall return on the trust portfolio. Diversification has become increasingly important, as has the trustee's duty to create a paper trail supporting the reasonableness of his or her actions.

☛ One constant is that under all approaches, exculpatory clauses are construed strictly and are not given effect where they appear to protect trustees who acted with reckless indifference to the beneficiaries' interest or in bad faith.

## CHAPTER 14

# ESTATE AND GIFT TAXES

## *ChapterScope*

This chapter examines the principal provisions of the gift and estate tax system, and some of the more common methods of trying to avoid or minimize such taxes.

- ■ **Federal gift tax:** Inter vivos gifts that exceed the annual gift tax exclusion constitute a taxable gift during that year. Depending on the amount of cumulative taxable gifts, a donor may owe federal gift taxes.

- ■ **Federal estate tax:** Depending on the value of a decedent's net property holdings at death and the amount of his or her inter vivos gifts, a decedent may owe federal estate taxes at death. There are several steps in determining whether a decedent owes a federal estate tax.

  - ▪ **Calculate decedent's gross estate:** The decedent's gross estate consists of the value of virtually all property the decedent owned and transferred at time of death via probate or nonprobate means. The nonprobate property includes property transferred by right of survivorship, transfers where the decedent retained a life estate or control of the beneficial rights, revocable transfers, transfers where the decedent retained a reversionary interest, selected transfers within three years of death, and property over which the decedent held a general power of appointment.

  - ▪ **Calculate decedent's taxable estate:** To calculate the decedent's taxable estate, miscellaneous deductions are allowed from the decedent's gross estate. The principal deductions are for charitable contributions, a decedent's debts, loans, mortgages, and the marital deduction.

    - ▪ **Marital deduction:** One spouse can transfer an unlimited amount of property to the other spouse without any gift or estate tax as long as the transfer meets the requirements for the marital deduction, the key requirement being that the interest must be something other than a life estate or other terminable interest.

  - ▪ **Calculate estate tax before credits:** The estate tax is calculated on a "cumulative" basis, taking into consideration the decedent's taxable estate and inter vivos gifts. The tax is computed utilizing a graduated rate schedule with various adjustments to make sure that inter vivos gifts are not taxed twice.

  - ▪ **Apply tax credits:** A variety of tax credits are applied to the tentative estate tax to determine if the decedent owes a federal estate tax. The most important tax credit is the unified estate/gift tax credit.

- ■ **Generation-skipping transfer tax:** Where a transferor attempts to transfer property to a transferee who is more than one generation below the transferor, a federal generation-skipping transfer tax is imposed. The tax imposed is the highest possible federal estate tax rate, but various exemptions and exclusions apply.

# I. OVERVIEW

**A. Gift vs. estate taxes:** The government imposes a number of different taxes on an individual or on property, depending on the situation. The focus here is on those taxes imposed as part of the dying process that affect the transfer of property at death. It is important that one has upfront at least a conceptual understanding of each.

1. **Gift tax:** The gift tax system focuses on inter vivos transfers that lack consideration—inter vivos gifts. The tax is imposed where a donor makes a taxable gift. IRC §2501(a). The tax is imposed on the donor, but if the donor is unable to pay the tax, the donee is liable for the tax. The tax is implicated if there is a taxable gift. Each donor is entitled to make annual gifts up to a set amount to each individual donee before there are gift tax implications. Under the Tax Reform Act of 1976, the annual exclusion per donor was $10,000. The annual gift tax exclusion is now indexed for inflation (the exclusion increased in 2002 to $11,000 per year, per donee). Depending on the amount of cumulative taxable gifts, a donor may owe federal gift taxes.

2. **Estate tax:** The estate tax system focuses on testamentary transfers that lack consideration—at-death transfers. The tax is imposed on the decedent's taxable estate at time of death. The taxable estate is the decedent's gross estate less deductions. The gross estate includes (1) the property in his or her probate estate, (2) most nonprobate transfers, and (3) other transfers if the decedent retained sufficient control and/or power over the property even after its apparent inter vivos transfer. Deductions to arrive at the taxable estate include charitable devises, decedent's debts, loans and mortgages, and the marital deduction. The estate tax is calculated on a "cumulative" basis, taking into consideration the decedent's taxable estate and inter vivos gifts. The tax is computed utilizing a graduated rate schedule with various adjustments to make sure that inter vivos gifts are not taxed twice. Each individual, however, is granted a unified estate/gift tax credit that has the effect of permitting an individual to pass up to a set amount of property at death (and/or during life) free of any estate (or gift) tax. For many years this unified tax credit permitted each individual to pass $600,000 before any taxes were due, but recent legislative activity is phasing in an increase in the amount that can be passed tax-free. In 2002 and 2003 the amount of property that can be passed free of any federal estate tax is $1 million, and this is scheduled to increase incrementally to $3.5 million in 2009.

   a. **Exemption vs. credit:** Although it is often easier to think and speak of the amount of property that one can pass tax-free at death as an exemption from the estate tax system, technically the IRS calculates the exemption by granting a tax credit to the decedent. For example, the $1 million tax exemption is achieved by granting the decedent a unified tax credit of $345,000.

   b. **Abolition:** Under the Economic Growth and Tax Relief Reconciliation Act of 2001 (the 2001 Tax Act), the estate tax system will not apply to the estates of decedents dying after December 31, 2009. The 2001 Tax Act also repeals the generation-skipping transfer tax, but not the gift tax. The 2001 Tax Act contains a sunset clause, however, that, unless affirmatively changed by future legislation, will make all these changes, including the repeal of these taxes, evaporate after 2010 (returning the tax laws to the way they were prior to the 2001 Tax Act).

**c. Inheritance tax distinguished:** An inheritance tax system also focuses on testamentary transfers that lack consideration—at-death transfers. Unlike an estate tax, however, an inheritance tax is imposed on the amount a recipient receives, not on the decedent. The amount of the tax depends not only on the amount the recipient receives. In many jurisdictions, it also depends on the relationship between the recipient and the donor. The closer the relationship, the lower the inheritance tax. There is no federal inheritance tax, but some states have inheritance taxes.

3. **Unified gift and estate tax scheme:** The Tax Reform Act of 1976 unified the gift and estate tax schemes. Inter vivos and testamentary transfers are generally taxed at the same rates and the estate tax exemption/tax credit amount is applicable to an individual's inter vivos taxable gifts and the decedent's taxable estate. Large inter vivos gifts that trigger gift taxes do not result in the donor paying a gift tax that year, but rather the tax due as a result of the inter vivos gift is charged against the individual's unified estate/gift tax credit. Charging inter vivos gift tax amounts against the individual's unified credit means that the practical amount that the individual can pass at death free of the estate tax is reduced. While the gift and estate tax schemes are still unified, the 2001 Tax Act creates a divergence between the two with, starting in 2004, differing amounts transferable before the actual payment of taxes and, starting in 2010, differing rates of tax.

4. **Generation-skipping transfer tax:** Prior to 1986, it was possible to pass property in trust from one generation to another, via a series of life estates and special powers of appointment, with the property being passed from generation to generation escaping both estate tax and gift tax for as long as permitted under the Rule against Perpetuities (commonly called "dynasty trusts"). The Tax Reform Act of 1986, however, closed this loophole. It imposes a generation-skipping transfer tax on transfers where the beneficiary is more than one generation below the transferor's generation. As applied to dynasty trusts, it imposes a transfer tax upon the death of a life tenant if the next in line taker is a grandchild of the settlor or a more remote descendant. The Tax Act of 1986 imposes a tax on generation-skipping transfers at a flat rate equal to the highest estate tax rate after the effective application of various exemptions and exclusions.

**Scheduled repeal:** The 2001 Tax Act repeals the generation-skipping transfer tax system for generation-skipping transfers that occur after December 31, 2009 (subject to the same sunset clause discussed above).

# II. THE FEDERAL GIFT TAX SCHEME

A. **Taxable gift:** Two variables need analyzing when calculating whether an inter vivos gift triggers gift tax consequences: (1) whether the transfer is a gift, and (2) whether the amount exceeds the annual gift tax exclusion (or is otherwise excluded from gift tax).

1. **Gift defined:** The Internal Revenue Code does not fully define what constitutes a gift, but it is *not* determined by the intent of the transferor at the time of transfer. Rather, a gift for gift tax purposes is one where the transferor has not received adequate consideration in money or money's worth and when the transferor has abandoned sufficient dominion and control over the property being transferred to put it beyond recall or the right to demand the beneficial enjoyment of the property.

2. **Retained powers:** If the transferor retains the power to revoke, appoint, or change the owner, the transferor has not abandoned sufficient dominion and control over the property for the transfer to be deemed a completed gift. (These powers arise, if at all, more often than not where the transfer is the creation of a trust.)

   a. **Third-party consent required:** Where the transferor retains the power to revoke, appoint, or change the owner or beneficiary only upon the consent of a third party, for gift tax purposes, the issue is whether the third party is an adverse party (a beneficiary who would be adversely affected). Where the third party is adverse, the gift is complete despite the retained power. Where the third party is not adverse, the transferor has not relinquished sufficient dominion and control over the property for the transfer to be a gift.

   b. **Limited by ascertainable standard:** Where the transferor retains the power to appoint or change the owner or beneficiary (e.g., the transferor has the power to invade the principal and use it for another's benefit), but such power is limited by an express ascertainable standard (e.g., only for purposes of the person's health, education, support, or maintenance), the transferor has relinquished sufficient dominion and control over the property for the transfer to be considered a gift.

   c. **Termination of power inter vivos:** If the transferor terminates or releases the power inter vivos and the effect is that the transferor will now be deemed to have abandoned dominion and control over the property, the act of terminating or releasing the power constitutes the act that triggers gift tax consequences, valuing the amount of the gift at such time.

   d. **Termination of power upon death:** Where the transferor retains the power to revoke, alter, or appoint, and the power is not exercised but terminates with the death of the transferor, the termination of the power does not give rise to gift tax consequences. The property in question, however, will be considered part of the transferor's gross estate for estate tax purposes—thereby possibly implicating estate taxes (but not gift taxes), valuing the property at the transferor's death.

   e. **Tax implications:** If a gift has not been made, the transferor is still liable for the income generated by the property. If the settlor creates a revocable trust, and the trust provides that the income is to be paid to someone other than the settlor, the power to revoke means that no gift has been made. The settlor is liable for the income tax on the income generated by the property in trust. IRC §§676, 677.

3. **Retained interest:** Where the transferor retains an interest in the property, for example where the settlor is also a beneficiary, the issue is whether the interest is mandatory or discretionary.

   a. **Mandatory:** Where the settlor grants him- or herself a mandatory interest in the property in trust, there is no gift.

   b. **Gifts of future interests:** Where the holder of a future interest transfers his or her interest to a donee, a gift has been made. The fact that the gift is a future interest and not a possessory interest does not defeat the fact that the transferor has relinquished dominion and control over the property interest. The fact that it is a future interest will affect its valuation, but not the fact that a gift was made.

    **i. Contingent future interests:** Likewise, if the future interest is a contingent future interest, or if the future interest is subject to divestment, the future interest is still a property interest subject to being transferred as a gift. Its uncertain nature affects its valuation, but not its status as a property interest subject to being gifted to another.

    **ii. Example:** In *Smith v. Shaughnessy,* 318 U.S. 176 (1943), petitioner funded an irrevocable inter vivos trust with 3,000 shares of stock worth $571,000. The income was payable to his wife for life, and upon her death, the stock was to be returned to him, if alive, otherwise as his wife might direct by her will, and in default of such appointment, to her heirs. The taxpayer conceded the life estate was subject to the gift tax. The government conceded that the reversion was immune from gift tax. The court held that the contingent remainder was subject to the gift tax in that the essence of a gift is abandonment of control over the property, and here the settlor had neither the form nor the substance of control of the remainder.

  **c. Disclaimers:** A disclaimer has the effect of transferring a property interest. The party disclaiming is not treated as having made a gift as long as the disclaimer complies with the IRS requirements for a valid disclaimer: (1) the disclaimer is in writing; (2) the disclaimer is executed within nine months of the party receiving the property interest (or within nine months of the disclaimant reaching age 21); (3) the disclaimant accepted no interest in the disclaimed property prior to disclaiming it; and (4) the disclaimant does not designate to whom the disclaimed property is to go, but rather the property passes to the next eligible takers under the applicable law. IRC §2518.

**B. Gift tax annual exclusion:** Not all gifts trigger a gift tax. The tax code provides that each donor can give up to $10,000 a year to each donee before a gift is considered a taxable gift (with the requisite duty to file a gift tax return). IRC §2503 (b). The annual amount that can be gifted to a donee tax-free is commonly referred to as the annual gift tax exclusion. In 1997, Congress legislated that the size of the exclusion will increase in $1,000 increments to keep pace with inflation. The amount increased to $11,000 in 2002.

  **1. Future interests:** Where a donor makes a gift of a future interest, no part of the gift qualifies for the annual gift exclusion. The whole present value of the future interest is subject to the gift tax analysis.

  **Gift to a minor:** Because a minor lacks legal capacity to manage property until he or she reaches the age of majority, the issue arises whether a gift of property to a minor is, in substance, a gift of a future interest (the minor is to receive the property when the minor reaches the age of majority). The gift of property to a minor does not constitute a gift of a future interest, and therefore qualifies for the annual gift exclusion, as long as (1) the property is given to the minor despite his or her age; (2) the property is given to the guardian for the minor; or (3) if the property (and all interest generated by the property) can be used for the minor's benefit, and any unexpended property will either pass to the donee upon reaching age 21 or to the donee's estate if he or she dies before reaching age 21 (or by exercise of a general power of appointment held by the donee). IRC §2503(c).

  **2. Right or power to receive trust property:** As a general rule, when a trust beneficiary is not receiving at least trust income presently, there is no present interest and, therefore, no annual exclusion. If, however, the trust contains a provision that allows the beneficiary to immediately demand, at time of contribution to the trust, a certain dollar amount (usually equal to the amount of the annual exclusion), then for gift tax purposes, this is deemed to be a present interest, qualifying for the annual exclusion (to the donor). This is commonly known as a Crummey withdrawal right, named after the case *Crummey v. Commissioner*, T.C. Memo 1966-144, aff'd in part and rev'd in part, 397 F.2d 82 (9th Cir. 1968). These withdrawal rights usually are designed to last for only a limited period of time and then expire. It does not matter that the beneficiary actually exercises his or her right of withdrawal but, rather, that he or she has the right to do so—thus facilitating the availability of the annual exclusion(s) to the donor.

**a. Sham power:** Where the parties have an agreement or understanding that the person having this withdrawal right (Crummey power) will not exercise it, the power is a sham, is not considered a gift of a present interest, and the annual exclusion will not be available to the donor.

**b. Holder's interest a contingent future interest:** Crummey withdrawal rights are usually given, pursuant to the trust instrument, to primary beneficiaries. The trust instrument can, however, give such powers to remote contingent beneficiaries, thereby increasing the number of annual exclusions available.

**c. Example:** In *Estate of Kohlsaat*, T.C. Memo 1997–212 (1997), the decedent formed the Kohlsaat Family Trust, an irrevocable trust, to which she transferred a commercial building. Her two adult children, Peter and Beatrice, were designated as cotrustees and primary beneficiaries. Each received a one-half interest in the corpus and interest. In addition, the trust designated 16 contingent remainder beneficiaries (Beatrice's spouse, three children, eight grandchildren, and Peter's four sons). All 18 beneficiaries were each given the right to demand from the trust the immediate distribution to them of property in an amount not to exceed the $10,000 annual gift tax exclusion. The beneficiaries received notice of the right, but none requested any distribution. Respondent claimed that an understanding existed between the settlor and the beneficiaries to the effect that the beneficiaries would not exercise their right to demand distribution and that substance should triumph over form. The court ruled there was no evidence of such an understanding and ruled that the right to demand the distribution qualified for 16 annual gift tax exclusions.

**d. Failure to exercise:** Where a donee holds a Crummey withdrawal right, or general power of appointment, failure to exercise the right or power may constitute a gift of the property subject to the power by the donee to the remainderman. IRC §2041(b)(2). This is referred to as a "lapsing" right of withdrawal, or general power of appointment, and the specific rules regarding taxability are very complex.

**C. Other gift tax exclusions:** In addition to the annual gift tax exclusion, certain amounts paid by an individual on behalf of another individual for education and medical items will not be considered a taxable gift. IRC §2503(e). This exclusion is in addition to the annual exclusion.

**1. Educational tuition payments exclusion:** In addition to the annual gift tax exclusion, any and all payments one person makes directly to an educational institution to cover tuition and fees for another person are excluded from gift tax considerations, regardless of the size of the payments. IRC §2503(e).

**Tuition and fees only:** The exclusion applies only to tuition payments and not to other types of payments (e.g., books, supplies, room and board, etc.).

2. **Medical expenses exclusion:** In addition to the annual gift tax exclusion, most payments one person makes for another person's medical care are excluded from gift tax considerations, regardless of the size of the gift payments. IRC §2503(e).

3. **Must be paid directly to provider:** The exclusion for education and medical payments apply only to amounts paid directly to the provider of the education or qualifying medical services (e.g., the school, college, university or the hospital, doctor, etc.). Amounts paid to an individual who then uses the money for tuition and fees or for qualifying medical care will not qualify for this exclusion (but the payment to the individual will qualify for the annual exclusion)

D. **Deductions in computing taxable gifts:** Generally, gifts made to charity and to a spouse are deducted (in effect, not counted) in computing taxable gifts.

1. **Gifts to charity:** As a general rule, gifts to qualified charities will not result in taxable gifts and will thereby not result in the imposition of gift taxes.

2. **Marital deduction:** As a general rule, spouses are permitted to make an unlimited number of gifts to each other, inter vivos or testamentary, regardless of the amount, without incurring gift tax or estate tax consequences. (The details of the marital deduction are set forth later in this chapter in section V., The Marital Deduction.)

# III. THE FEDERAL ESTATE TAX: AN OVERVIEW

A. **Overview:** The federal estate tax system is a rather complicated system that imposes a graduated tax on an estate calculated by adding and subtracting a number of different categories of property interests and deductions.

**First step—calculate taxable estate:** At the macro level, the first step in determining a decedent's federal estate tax is to calculate the decedent's taxable estate. The decedent's taxable estate is (1) the decedent's gross estate (basically the value of all property that the decedent owned, had a beneficial interest in, or retained dominion and control over at time of death, and certain transfers made and gift taxes paid within three years of death); (2) minus various deductions (for death-related expenses, charitable deductions, and the marital deduction).

**Second step—calculate the estate tax:** The estate tax is based on applying the tax rate schedule to the decedent's taxable estate. (It is a bit more complex than that, however, because of the unified nature of the estate and gift tax schemes. Actually, the estate tax is cumulative in nature and takes into consideration, for purposes of applying the graduated estate tax rates, the decedent's inter vivos taxable gifts made after 1976. Through a somewhat complex mechanism, taxable gifts are not taxed twice, i.e., again as part of the estate tax, but are used in determining the decedent's rate of estate tax.)

**Third step—apply credits to determine estate tax liability:** Once the estate tax "before credits" is calculated, this amount is reduced by various credits including, most notably, the unified estate tax credit.

# IV. CALCULATING THE DECEDENT'S GROSS ESTATE

**A. Decedent's gross estate—an overview:** The decedent's gross estate includes the value of property that the decedent owned, had a beneficial interest in, or retained dominion and control over at the time of his or her death.

**B. Property includible in decedent's gross estate:** The Internal Revenue Code expressly identifies the different types of property interest that are includible in the decedent's gross estate for federal estate tax purposes.

**1. Decedent's probate property:** All property that passes into the decedent's probate estate (transmissible property) is part of the decedent's gross estate for federal estate tax purposes. IRC §2033.

**Nontransmissible property generally excluded:** If the decedent owned a terminable interest (i.e., a life estate) *created by someone else*, the interest will not pass into the decedent's probate estate and is not included in the decedent's gross estate. The terminable interest can even be coupled with a limited power to invade the principal and a special power of appointment, and the property is still not included in the decedent's gross estate.

**a. Nontransmissible property included if coupled with power of appointment:** If, however, the terminable interest, created by someone else, is coupled with a general power of appointment over the property vested in the decedent, the property constitutes part of the decedent's gross estate for federal estate tax purposes. IRC §2041.

**b. Decedent-created life estate included:** If inter vivos the decedent transferred the property but retained a life estate, the property is included in the decedent's gross estate. IRC §2036.

**2. Payable-on-death property included:** Property that the decedent had control over via a contract with a payable-on-death clause is included in the decedent's gross estate for federal estate tax purposes. IRC §2033.

**a. Employee death benefits:** If the decedent had the right to receive a benefit from an employment-related benefits program that also included a payment-on-death component, the property interest is includible in the decedent's gross estate for federal estate tax purposes even if the decedent never actually received any direct benefit from the program. IRC §2039.

**b. Life insurance:** Where a life insurance policy (term or whole life) was taken out on the decedent's life, the value of the proceeds of the policy is included in the decedent's gross estate for federal estate tax purposes if the decedent had any of the usual incidents of ownership over the policy at the time of death or if the proceeds were payable to the insured's executor or probate estate. The usual incidents of ownership include the right to cancel the policy, the right to change the beneficiary, the right to transfer the policy, the right to borrow against the policy, etc. The insured need not make the payments on the policy for it to be included in his or her gross estate. IRC §2042.

**3. Concurrently owned property:** There are four possible ways a spouse can own property concurrently with another person: joint tenancy, tenancy in common, tenancy by the entirety, and community property. The decedent's interest in tenancy in common and community property are probate assets, and as such, are includible in the decedent's gross estate for that reason. The decedent's interest in joint tenancy and tenancy by the entirety raise both gift tax and estate tax considerations, depending on who the other cotenant is—a spouse or nonspouse.

a. **Joint tenancy with nonspouse—gift tax:** Where a spouse enters into a joint tenancy with a nonspouse, the first issue is whether both parties contributed valuable consideration. If not, if one party puts up all the consideration for the joint tenancy property, that party is generally treated as having made a gift of the appropriate share of the property owned by the other joint tenant or tenants (because each tenant has the power to unilaterally sever his or her share). A common example of this is a parent placing a child's name on property as a joint tenant with the parent. If the value of the share exceeds the annual gift tax exclusion, there are inter vivos gift tax consequences (the same would hold true if the parties purchased the property as tenants in common).

**Exception:** Because each joint tenancy bank account or government bond has the right to withdraw all the funds or cash the bond, no gift occurs until the noncontributing party withdraws some of the money or cashes the bond.

b. **Joint tenancy with nonspouse—estate tax:** At time of death, the entire value of the joint tenancy property, as of the date of death, is included in the decedent's gross estate, minus a number calculated by multiplying the date of death value times the percentage of the original purchase price contributed by the surviving joint tenant. The burden of proof is on the decedent's personal representative to prove what percentage of the original purchase price the surviving joint tenant(s) contributed. IRC §2040(a).

**No double taxation:** If the other cotenant made no contribution either in kind to the property (joint tenancy bank account) or no contribution to the original purchase, and a gift tax resulted when the other cotenant was placed on title (e.g., a parent placing a child's name on title as a joint tenant), this gift tax will effectively be credited against the estate tax (when computing the estate tax) to make sure there is no double taxation.

c. **Joint tenancy/tenancy by the entirety with spouse:** A joint tenancy or tenancy by entirety created between spouses qualifies for the marital deduction even if one spouse puts up all the consideration or property. There is no inter vivos gift tax, and there is no estate tax upon the death of the first spouse if the spouses are the only parties to the cotenancy. One half of the joint tenancy/tenancy by the entirety date of death value is included in the deceased spouse's gross estate, but it qualifies for the marital deduction, so there are no estate tax consequences.

4. **Beneficial interest or control:** Where the decedent transferred legal title interest, but retained sufficient beneficial interest in or retained dominion and control over the property, the property will be includible in the decedent's gross estate for federal estate tax purposes. IRC §2036.

a. **Possession, enjoyment, or right to income:** Where the decedent transfers legal title to property inter vivos, but retains (1) the right to possess the property, (2) the enjoyment of the property, (3) the right to the income generated by the property, or (4) the right to control, either alone or in conjunction with others, who shall possess, enjoy, or receive the income from the property, the decedent has retained sufficient interest in or control over the property that his or her interest in the property is includible in his or her gross estate for federal estate tax purposes. IRC §2036(a)(1), (2).

**b. Astrustee:** If the transferor creates an irrevocable trust, but appoints him- or herself trustee (sole or cotrustee), and the trust is a discretionary trust, the transferor retains control over who receives the enjoyment of the property over which the transferor has discretion. Such property is includible in the transferor's gross estate for federal estate tax purposes.

**c. Right to possession:** Where the transferor retains actual possession or the right to possession for life, a presumption arises that the property is includible in the transferor's gross estate unless the transfer was a bona fide transfer for full consideration. In determining whether the transfer was a bona fide transfer for full consideration, the intent of the parties as to whether the consideration will ever be paid is a legitimate inquiry in determining whether the transaction is bona fide.

**Example:** In *Estate of Rapelje v. Commissioner,* 73 T.C. 82 (1979), in August 1969, the decedent purported to convey his home in New York to his two daughters. Nevertheless, he remained in possession until November when he went to Florida on vacation and looked at one house for sale, only to return to his New York home in May 1970. In July 1970, he suffered a stroke that partially paralyzed him. He remained in the home until his death in 1973. The Commissioner included the full value of the property in the decedent's gross estate. The Code requires property to be included in the decedent's estate where the decedent retains actual possession or enjoyment of the property—even in the absence of a right to do so. Although there was no express agreement to allow the decedent to retain possession, the court found there was an implied agreement between the parties, arising *contemporaneously* with the transfer, to allow the decedent to remain in possession. The decedent remained in exclusive possession for almost the entire time, the decedent paid the real estate taxes, and the decedent did not pay rent. The full value of the property was includible in the decedent's gross estate.

**d. Reciprocal trust doctrine:** Where two parties (typically husband and wife) set up trusts that give each other a life estate interest in the other's trust, the value of the trust in which each holds the life estate interest is includible in each party's gross estate for federal estate tax purposes.

**Example:** In *United States v. Estate of Grace,* 395 U.S. 316 (1969), Joseph Grace was a very wealthy man in 1908 when he married Janet Grace, who had no wealth or property. Joseph transferred substantial assets to her over the course of the next 23 years, but Joseph retained control over the property. In 1931, Joseph created a trust for the benefit of his wife, mandatory as to the income and discretionary as to principal. Joseph, his nephew, and a third party were trustees. Janet was given a special testamentary power to appoint any remaining corpus among the decedent and their children. Thereafter Janet executed a similar trust that had "mirror" provisions. Upon Janet's death, the Commissioner determined that the trusts were "reciprocal" trusts and included the amount of Janet's trust in Joseph's gross estate. The court ruled that the taxability of the trust corpus turns not on the settlor's motives but on the nature and operative effect of the trust transfer. The Commissioner need not prove that each trust was created as a *quid pro quo* for the other, nor does there have to be a tax avoidance motive. All that is necessary is that the trusts be interrelated, and that the arrangement, to the extent of mutual value, leaves the settlors in approximately the same economic position as they would have been in had they created trusts naming themselves as life beneficiaries. The court found these elements present with respect to Janet's trust, and thus the court included it in Joseph's gross estate.

**e. Control over trustee:** Where the settlor creates a discretionary trust and does not appoint him- or herself trustee, if the settlor retains control over the trustee through the power to remove and appoint a friendly or subordinate trustee, the settlor will be deemed to have retained dominion and control over the trust property for federal estate tax purposes. In some instances, the property will be included in the settlor's estate when there is a mere possibility that the settlor could have appointed him- or herself as trustee even though such power could only occur if the trustee resigned, died, stepped down as trustee, etc., and such contingency did not occur before the settlor's death.

5. **Power to revoke, appoint, or modify:** If at the time of his or her death, the transferor retained the power to revoke, appoint, or modify who has the right to enjoy the property, or when a party has the right to enjoy the property, the property is includible in the transferor's gross estate for federal estate tax purposes. If the transferor retained such power but released it within three years of the transferor's death, the property is still includible in the transferor's gross estate. The rule applies whether the transferor retains the power alone or in conjunction with others (friendly or adverse). If the power to revoke or modify the right to enjoy is given to a third party, friendly or adverse, the property is not includible in the transferor's gross estate unless the transferor retains control over that party. IRC §2038.

6. **Reversion:** If a transferor transfers a finite estate (life estate typically), retains a reversionary interest, and transfers an alternative future interest to a third party whose possession or enjoyment is conditioned on surviving the transferor, and the value of the reversionary interest immediately before the transferor's death exceeds 5 percent of the value of the property, the value of the property (less the possessory estate) is included in the transferor's gross estate. IRC §2037.

   **Reversionary interest:** If a transferor transfers a finite estate (life estate typically) and reserves a reversionary interest, with no express alternative gift over in the event the transferor predeceases the holder of the finite estate, only the reversionary interest is included in the transferor's gross estate. IRC §2033.

7. **Powers relinquished and transfers made within three years of death:** Discussed above are certain powers that, if held by the decedent at the time of his or her death, will cause inclusion of property in his or her estate. Typically these are powers retained with respect to trusts and include the power to revoke, alter, and amend (IRC §2038), the power retained for life to enjoy trust income or determine who gets the trust property or income (IRC §2038), or certain retained reversionary interests (IRC §2037). When an individual who retained such powers relinquishes them and dies within three years, IRC §2035 generally requires treating the decedent as if he or she still retained such powers, implicating the requisite inclusion of property in the gross estate. In addition, transfers of ownership of life insurance within three years of death will, nonetheless, require inclusion of the full proceeds in the insured's/transferor's estate. Finally, gift taxes paid on any gifts within three years of death are artificially "brought back" into the decedent's gross estate. IRC §2035(b).

8. **General power of appointment:** If the decedent held a general power of appointment when he or she died, testamentary or inter vivos, that was created by another, the property subject to the power is included in the decedent's gross estate for federal estate tax purposes (whether the power is exercised or not). IRC §2041. If, however, the power is a special power of appointment, the property is not included in the donee's gross estate, even if the donee exercises the power.

**a. Given to beneficiary/trustee:** A power to invade held by a beneficiary/trustee for the benefit of the beneficiary/trustee constitutes a general power of appointment even if there are other cotrustees who must consent to the exercise of the power, unless the other cotrustees have an interest that is adverse to the exercise of the power. IRC §2041.

**Exception:** A power vested in a trustee to invade for his or her own benefit is not included in the trustee's gross estate if the power is limited by an ascertainable standard relating to health, education, support, or maintenance.

**b. Example:** In *Best v. United States,* 902 F. Supp. 1023 (D. Neb. 1995), Alfred Anderson created a testamentary trust, naming his wife, Alma, and his son, John, trustees. The trust gave the trustees the discretion to use as much of the principal as they, in their sole and absolute discretion, deemed reasonably necessary for Alma's comfort, support, and maintenance. Upon Alma's death, the IRS asserted that she held a general power of appointment over the corpus rather than a power of appointment limited by an ascertainable standard. The IRS focused on the use of the word *comfort* as grounds for using the principal because that word is not a part of the ascertainable standard test established by the code. The court found that the word *comfort,* in the context of the other words, stated a standard no different from the examples in the Treasury regulation where the word *comfort* is used as part of an ascertainable standard. Alma did not hold a general power of appointment and the property was not includible in her gross estate.

# V. THE MARITAL DEDUCTION

**A. Introduction:** As a general rule, spouses are permitted to make an unlimited number of gifts to each other, inter vivos or testamentary, regardless of the amount, without incurring gift tax or estate tax consequences. IRC §2056.

**B. Requirements:** Property qualifies for the marital deduction as long as (1) the transferor is either a citizen or resident of the United States at the time of his or her death, (2) the property "passes" from the transferor to his or her spouse—inter vivos or at time of death, (3) the donee spouse survives the transferor, (4) the value of the property otherwise would have been includible in the transferor's gross estate for federal estate tax purposes, and (5) the property is not a nondeductible terminable interest. IRC §2056(b).

**1. Passing requirement:** The requirement that the property must "pass" from the transferor to the transferor's surviving spouse has been broadly construed to cover virtually all forms of passing a property interest—inter vivos or testamentary (probate testate, probate intestate, and nonprobate transfers).

**2. Not a nondeductible terminal interest requirement:** To qualify as a deductible interest, the property interest must be one that (1) will end up in the surviving spouse's estate (and thus subject to taxation at the time), or (2) the surviving spouse can transfer to third parties (and thus be subject to taxation at that time). If the property interest is a terminable interest, an interest that may fail or be extinguished during the donee's spouse's lifetime or that will be extinguished upon the donee spouse's death (a life estate to surviving spouse with remainder to others), the property transfer to the donee spouse does not qualify for the marital deduction.

**3. Exceptions:** There are a handful of exceptions to the requirement that the property being passed to the surviving spouse cannot be a life estate or other terminable interest.

  **a. Limited survival requirement:** If the gift to the surviving spouse is conditioned upon the surviving spouse surviving the decedent by a specific period of time not to exceed six months, the interest being transferred will qualify for the marital deduction as long as the surviving spouse meets the survival requirement. IRC §2056(b)(3).

  **b. Marital deduction power of appointment trust:** If the donee spouse is given a life estate interest in a trust, but the donee spouse is also given the power to appoint to him- or herself, or his or her estate, it will be considered a general power of appointment, causing inclusion of the property in the donee spouse's gross estate for estate tax purposes. Because the property will be taxable upon the death of the donee spouse, the transfer to the donee spouse qualifies for the marital deduction as long as the additional statutory requirements are satisfied: (1) the donee spouse has a mandatory interest in the income, payable annually, if not more frequently; (2) the power of appointment can be exercised, at a minimum, in favor of the surviving spouse or his or her estate; (3) the power is exercisable alone and in all events (i.e., the exercise of the power does not require anyone else's consent and is not contingent on anything such as not remarrying; and (4) no other party can have a power to appoint the property unless it is in favor of the surviving spouse. IRC §2056(b)(5).

  **c. Estate trust exception:** An interest does not qualify as a nondeductible terminable interest only if upon the termination of the spouse's interest the property passes to someone other than the surviving spouse or his or her probate estate. If the conveyance expressly provides that upon the death of the party, the property is to pass to his or her estate, the property will qualify for the marital deduction. (This exception is typically used only if the trust holds unproductive property that would make it difficult to qualify under the other exceptions.)

  **d. QTIP trust exception:** The qualified terminable interest property (QTIP) trust exception provides that if the surviving spouse is given a life estate interest in a trust, with a mandatory interest in the income, payable annually, if not more frequently, and no one (including the surviving spouse) has the power to appoint the property during the surviving spouse's lifetime to anyone other than the spouse, the property qualifies for the marital deduction (even if the surviving spouse is given a special testamentary power of appointment over the property—though it is not required that the surviving spouse be given this power). In addition, a qualified election (on the estate tax return of the first spouse to die) must be made in a timely manner (on a timely filed estate tax return). IRC §2056(b)(7). If the transfer qualifies as a QTIP trust, the property is included in the surviving spouse's gross estate for estate tax purposes, but the tax is paid by the persons receiving the property upon the surviving spouse's death (or if the interest is in trust, as is the norm, the tax is paid out of the trust corpus before the next interest is given effect). IRC §§2044, 2207A.

  **e. Judicially reformed trusts:** Increasingly courts are reforming trusts to achieve tax benefits, including to qualify as marital deduction power of appointment trusts, estate trusts, or QTIP trusts. Where a trust qualifies for the marital deduction as the result of judicial reformation, however, the state court proceedings are not binding for purposes of determining federal estate taxes owed unless the judicial proceedings are approved by the state's highest court. *See Commissioner of Internal Revenue v. Estate of Bosch,* 387 U.S. 456 (1967).

4. **Unlimited charitable tax deduction:** In calculating a decedent's taxable estate, the Code permits unlimited deductions for qualifying charitable transfers. IRC §2055. Twice a year the IRS publishes a list of corporations that have qualified as charitable organizations. Outright transfers to such organizations qualify for the charitable tax deduction as a matter of course. Transfers of remainder interests are more complicated.

# VI.  THE GENERATION-SKIPPING TRANSFER TAX

A. **Historical background:** Prior to adoption of the generation-skipping transfer tax in 1986, it was possible to transfer equitable property interests in trusts, from one generation to another, tax-free until the trust had to terminate pursuant to the jurisdiction's Rule against Perpetuities.

B. **Generation-skipping transfer tax:** The Tax Reform Act of 1986 attempted to close the generation-skipping transfer loophole by requiring a transfer tax on any generation-skipping transfer. IRC §2611(a). A generation-skipping transfer is one that skips a generation—a transfer where the transferee is two or more generations below the transferor's generation. Such transferees are known as "skip persons" under the Internal Revenue Code. Transfers to one's spouse or children do not skip a generation and are not subject to the generation-skipping transfer tax. Transfers from a grandparent to a grandchild or more remote descendent are subject to the generation-skipping transfer tax.

1. **Applies post-1986:** The generation-skipping transfer tax does not apply to irrevocable trusts created prior to adoption of the Tax Reform Act of 1986.

2. **Abolished 2010:** Pursuant to the Tax Act of 2001, the generation-skipping transfer tax does not apply to transfers made after December 31, 2009. The 2001 Tax Act contains a sunset clause that, unless affirmatively changed by future legislation, will make all these changes, including the repeal of the generation-skipping transfer tax, evaporate after 2010 (returning the tax laws back to the way they were prior to the 2001 Tax Act).

# VII.  STATE DEATH TAXES

A. **Overview:** All states, except Nevada, have one form or another of a death tax (though only a few have a gift tax on inter vivos transfers). The different types of state death taxes can loosely be grouped into three categories.

1. **Pick-up death tax:** The federal estate tax allows a credit against the federal estate tax for death taxes paid to a state, up to a certain amount. Many states have enacted "pick-up" death taxes that seek to take advantage of this statutory credit without increasing the death taxes imposed upon an estate. The effect of the pick-up death tax is to shift the amount of money subject to the credit from the federal government to the state. Pursuant to the 2001 Tax Act, however, the credit for state estate taxes is scheduled to phase out after 2004.

2. **Inheritance tax:** An inheritance tax is a tax imposed on a gift being transferred at death to a taker—whether the transfer is an intestate, probate testate, or nonprobate transfer. The tax

depends on the size of the gift the taker is receiving and the taker's relationship to the decedent. Those takers who are more closely related to the decedent pay a lower rate compared to those who are remotely related or not related at all. The tax is paid out of the gift typically.

3. **Miscellaneous other state death taxes:** The remaining state death tax schemes do not follow any particular pattern, though they often borrow heavily from the federal estate tax approach.

---

## Quiz Yourself on
## ESTATE AND GIFT TAXES

**101.** Liz creates an inter vivos trust that provides that the trustee is to distribute the income to Michael, and upon his death, the principal is to be distributed to her foundation for the cure of AIDS. The trust grants Liz a special testamentary power to appoint the property among her ex-spouses. Liz's did not exercise the power upon her death. Should the property in the trust be included in her gross estate for federal estate tax purposes? _____

**102.** Will purchases securities worth $20,000, taking title in the name of Will and Grace, his friend, as joint tenants with right of survivorship. Ten years later, when Will dies, the securities are worth $50,000.

**a.** Were there any gift taxes due upon Will's purchase of the securities; and how much, if any, of the value of the securities should be included in Will's gross estate for federal estate tax purposes? _____

**b.** What difference would it make, if any, if Will and Grace were married at all times during the hypothetical? _____

**103.** Frank creates an irrevocable inter vivos trust. The pertinent provisions of the trust provide that all the income is to be paid to his sister Sally for her lifetime, and upon her death, the principal is to be paid to Frank's son, Raymond.

**a.** What are the gift tax consequences of the transfer that creates the trust? _____

**b.** What are the estate tax consequences, if any, when Frank dies? _____

**c.** What are the estate tax consequences, if any, when Sally dies? _____

**104.** Donald creates an irrevocable inter vivos trust. The pertinent provisions of the trust provide that all the income is to be paid to Daisy, and upon her death, the principal is to be paid to her children, if any. Donald retains a special inter vivos power of appointment to appoint the property among his nephews.

**a.** What are the gift tax consequences of the transfer that creates the trust? _____

**b.** What are the estate tax consequences, if any, when Donald dies? _____

**105.** Godfather creates an irrevocable inter vivos trust. He gives his son Michael a life estate interest, remainder to Michael's children who survive Michael, if any, if not, to Godfather's issue per stirpes.

The trust also gives Michael a testamentary power to appoint any portion or all of the trust to anyone, including Michael's estate and the creditors of his estate. Michael dies intestate, survived by two children. Is any part of the trust included in Michael's gross estate for federal estate tax purposes? _____

106. Bill creates a testamentary trust that provides in pertinent part as follows: "All the income to his wife, Camille, and upon her death, the property is to be distributed equally to their children." The trustee is given the power to invade the principal, if necessary, during Camille's lifetime for her health. Camille was also given a testamentary power of appointment to vary the shares to the children if she deemed appropriate.

a. What are the estate tax consequences, if any, upon Bill's death? _____

b. What are the estate tax consequences, if any, upon Camille's death? _____

107. Homer's will creates a testamentary trust that provides in part as follows: "All to my son Bart for life, and upon his death, to Bart's children equally." The trust also gives Bart a special power to appoint the property among Homer's heirs. What are the tax consequences upon Bart's death assuming a son, Homer II, survives him and Bart does not exercise the power of appointment?

_____

---

## Answers

101. First, the facts fail to indicate whether the trust is revocable or irrevocable. If the trust is revocable, Liz has not relinquished dominion and control over the property inter vivos and it would be included in her estate. If the trust is irrevocable, there is still the issue of Liz's testamentary special power of appointment. The power gives her the power to change the beneficiaries. Even if she does not exercise the power, the mere retention of the power is enough dominion and control over the property that it will not constitute a gift. The property should be included in her gross estate for estate tax purposes.

102. a. When Will purchased the securities and took title in both parties' names as joint tenants, he made an inter vivos gift to Grace of one-half of the value of the securities. The $10,000 gift, however, comes within the annual gift tax exclusion amount, so no gift tax would be due. Upon death, because Grace is not Will's spouse, the percentage of the value of the property that is included in his estate is the percentage of the money he put toward the purchase price. Because Will contributed 100 percent of the purchase price, 100 percent of the value of the securities at the time of his death is included in his gross estate—here, the full $50,000 value at Will's death.

b. If Will and Grace were married, Will made a gift to his wife in the amount of $10,000, but the gift qualifies for the marital deduction and would not be taxable even if it had exceeded the annual gift tax exclusion. Upon death, one-half of the value of the property at Will's death would be included in his gross estate, but the transfer to his wife (through the right of survivorship) would give rise to a marital deduction of the same amount. Thus, no federal estate tax would result from including it in Will's gross estate.

103. a. When Frank creates the trust, he has made an inter vivos gift of the life estate interest to Sally and of the remainder to Raymond. The value of these interests is determined by government-provided life

expectancy tables—the aggregate of the two equal the value of the gift when made. The gift to Sally is considered a "present interest" and will qualify for the annual exclusion. The gift of the remainder to Raymond is not a present interest and will not entitle Frank to an annual exclusion with respect to this gift. Gift taxes will be computed on Frank's total taxable gifts for the year and he may or may not have to pay any taxes depending on how much of his unified credit he has used in prior years.

**b.** Because Frank did not retain any interest in the trust, no part of it is included in his gross estate for federal estate tax purposes when he dies.

**c.** When Sally dies, because she held only a life estate interest created by Frank and she did not hold a general power of appointment, the property is not included in her gross estate for federal estate tax purposes. There is no generation-skipping transfer tax either because Raymond does not qualify as a skip person.

**104. a.** There is no gift if the transferor retains the power to revoke or the power to appoint over the property (i.e., change beneficiaries without an ascertainable standard)—the donor has not relinquished sufficient dominion and control to make the gift complete. Here, although the trust is irrevocable, because Donald retained the power to appoint the property inter vivos among his nephews, no gifts, for gift tax purposes, result.

**b.** Because Donald retained control over who has the right to enjoy the property, the property (full amount of the trust) is included in his gross estate for federal estate tax purposes (valued as of Donald's death) even if the power to appoint is not exercised.

**105.** The general rule is that if a party holds only a life estate interest created by another party, the property is not included in the life tenant's gross estate. If, however, the party also holds a general power of appointment, a party holding a general power of appointment is treated as owner of the property for estate tax purposes, even if the party does not exercise the power. Here, Michael held a general power of appointment over the property. The property will be included in Michael's gross estate upon his death. Because the property is included in Michael's gross estate upon his death, there is no generation-skipping transfer tax issue upon his death.

**106. a.** Because the trust is a testamentary trust, all the property used to fund the trust is included in Bill's gross estate for federal estate tax purposes. The issue is whether the property qualifies for a marital deduction for the full amount of the property in trust. The general rule is that testamentary transfers to spouses qualify as long as the interest is a nonterminable interest. Life estates are a terminable interest unless coupled with a general power of appointment or unless the interest qualifies as a QTIP (qualified terminable interest property) life estate. Camille's interest is limited to a life estate. She is given a power of appointment, but only to vary the shares among the children, so the power is a special power. The interest, however, qualifies as a QTIP interest because she is given all the income during her lifetime and no one has the power to appoint any of the property during her lifetime to anyone other than the spouse. The fact that she is given the testamentary special power of appointment does not affect the analysis. Upon Bill's death, the property is included in his gross estate, but it also qualifies for the marital deduction (assuming a valid QTIP election is made on his timely filed estate tax return), thereby resulting in no net estate tax.

**b.** When Camille dies, the full value of the trust property is included in her gross estate because Bill's estate was entitled to a full marital deduction. The extra estate tax associated with this inclusion is paid out of this trust before the property is distributed to the trust beneficiaries, here, the children.

**107.** Bart holds a life estate interest in Homer's trust that is not enough to constitute a property interest for purposes of his gross estate. If the life estate is coupled with a general power of appointment, the property is included in the life tenant's gross estate. Here, Bart has the power to appoint the property among Homer's heirs only, making it a special power. The property is not included in Bart's gross estate. Because Bart did not exercise the power of appointment, however, the property will pass to his son, Homer II—Homer's grandson. Homer II is two generations removed from Homer. Bart's death and the transfer to Homer II constitute a taxable termination triggering a generation-skipping transfer tax if the amount put in the trust exceeded Homer's exemption.

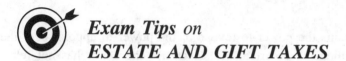

# *Exam Tips on*
# *ESTATE AND GIFT TAXES*

## The federal estate and gift tax scheme

This chapter is but a short introduction to the law of estate and gift taxes. The material has become more difficult to teach in the basic wills and trusts course because of all the recent changes in the tax code.

## The federal gift tax

If this area is tested, the issue is usually whether a valid inter vivos gift has been made. Watch for gifts of future interests—they do not qualify for the annual gift tax exclusion. If, however, the future interest is coupled with a present right to demand the property (a Crummey power or general power of appointment or right to withdraw), that right constitutes a present interest that does qualify for the annual exclusion.

## The federal estate tax

There are four steps to determining a decedent's federal estate tax: (1) compute his or her gross estate, (2) subtract various deductions, (3) apply the estate tax rate schedule to determine the tentative estate tax, and (4) apply the credits (principally the unified credit).

☛ In calculating the decedent's gross estate, the issues that arise concern nonprobate property. All probate property, whether testate or intestate, is included.

    ☞ If the decedent owned property in joint tenancy or tenancy in common, there usually are both gift tax and estate tax issues. In particular, watch for when the other joint tenant is *not* the decedent's spouse. Ask who provided the consideration to see if there are gift tax issues (for both tenancy in common and joint tenancy). Upon death of one joint tenant, distinguish between tenants in common (where the value of the decedent's share of the property at time of death is included in the decedent's gross estate) and joint tenants (where the percentage of the time of death value of the property included in decedent's gross estate is based on the percentage of the purchase price the decedent contributed when the property was purchased).

    ☞ If the fact pattern includes employee death benefits, they are included in the decedent's gross estate if the decedent had the right to receive the benefits had he or she lived long enough (i.e., retirement benefits—an annuity or pension). If, however, the statute requires that the death benefits be paid to the decedent's surviving spouse or children, the benefits are not included in the decedent's gross estate.

☞ If you see a life insurance policy, the issue typically will be whether the value of insurance proceeds on the life of the decedent are included in the decedent's gross estate. Analyze whether the decedent possessed even one of the usual incidents of ownership (control over the policy or who were the beneficiaries) or the policy is payable to the decedent's executor or estate. It does not matter who pays the premiums. If the beneficiary is the decedent's surviving spouse, include the proceeds in the gross estate but deduct the proceeds under the marital deduction.

☛ Lifetime transfers pose the most challenging issues with respect to a decedent's gross estate because on the face of the transfer including the property in the decedent's gross estate appears inconsistent with the inter vivos transfer. Be on the watch for those lifetime transfers that still qualify for inclusion in the decedent's gross estate.

☞ If the decedent retains a life estate, the property is included in the decedent's gross estate. If the decedent transfers title but retains possession, the decedent retained a life estate unless there is a bona fide transfer of the property for full consideration.

☞ If the decedent retains control over who gets to enjoy the property, the property is included in the decedent's gross estate. The most common ways of retaining control over who gets to enjoy the property are (1) to retain a power over the property, or (2) to create a discretionary trust and appoint the decedent trustee (or cotrustee)—though if there is an ascertainable standard controlling the trustee's discretion, the settlor does not retain control over who gets to enjoy the property.

☞ If the decedent retains the power to revoke or amend, the property is included in the decedent's gross estate.

☛ Watch for fact patterns involving powers of appointment. If the decedent holds a general power of appointment over property, the property is included in the decedent's gross estate, regardless of whether the decedent ever exercised the power. If, however, the decedent has a power to invade for his or her own benefit that is limited by an ascertainable standard relating to health, education, support, or maintenance, the power is not a general power of appointment.

☞ If the power is a special power, the general rule is that it is not included in the decedent's estate (even if the decedent held a limited power to appoint some of the property to him- or herself during his or her lifetime).

## The marital deduction

Although there are a number of requirements for a transfer from one spouse to the other to qualify for the marital deduction, the most important requirement is that the interest transferred must be a nonterminable interest—an interest that will last longer than the spouse's lifetime and hence be taxed upon the spouse's death.

☛ Although life estates generally do not qualify for the marital deduction, there are two exceptions to this rule that you should watch for. First, a life estate coupled with a general power of appointment is taxable upon the spouse's death and thus qualifies for the marital deduction.

Second, a qualified terminable interest property (QTIP) qualifies for the marital deduction if (1) the surviving spouse was entitled to all the income for life, and (2) no one had the power to appoint or apply the property inter vivos (a special testamentary power over the property can be given to anyone without affecting the QTIP status). The donor or the donor's spouse's executor must elect to have the property taxed in the surviving spouse's gross estate, though the tax is paid by those who receive the property.

☛ In either case, if the life estate ends upon remarriage, the property will not qualify for the marital deduction.

# Table Of Cases

# Subject Matter Index